GUMSHOES

A Dictionary of
Fictional Detectives

Mitzi M. Brunsdale

GREENWOOD PRESS
Westport, Connecticut • London

Library of Congress Cataloging-in-Publication Data

Brunsdale, Mitzi.
 Gumshoes : a dictionary of fictional detectives / Mitzi M. Brunsdale.
   p.   cm.
 Includes bibliographical references (p.   ) and index.
 ISBN 0–313–33331–9 (alk. paper)
 1. Detective and mystery stories—Bio-bibliography.   2. Detective and mystery
stories—Stories, plots, etc.   I. Title.
 PN3377.5.D4B78   2006
 809.3'7209—dc22   2005034853

British Library Cataloguing in Publication Data is available.

Library of Congress Catalog Card Number: 2005034853
ISBN: 0–313–33331–9

First published in 2006

Greenwood Press, 88 Post Road West, Westport, CT 06881
An imprint of Greenwood Publishing Group, Inc.
www.greenwood.com

Printed in the United States of America

∞™

The paper used in this book complies with the
Permanent Paper Standard issued by the National
Information Standards Organization (Z39.48–1984).

10 9 8 7 6 5 4 3 2 1

For Anne Jones
with love and thanks:

You made this one possible.

CONTENTS

LIST OF ENTRIES

PREFACE

Detective fiction could only flourish once public sympathy had veered round to the side of law and order.

—*Dorothy L. Sayers*

If Dorothy L. Sayers was right, an enormous sympathy—or longing—must exist today for law and order. "There are more people actively writing crime fiction today than there ever has been," claimed mystery historian Mike Ashley in 2002 (xi), so there must be more people reading about more and more detectives—sleuths, snoops, cops, or hard-boiled PIs—who track criminals throughout a rapidly shrinking world. Proper, genteel spinsters and eccentric aristocrats still haunt British villages and manors, beleaguered cops man squad cars and computers, and tough private eyes roam America's literary mean streets, but new crime fighters are rapidly joining them in brand-new ways. Contemporary police procedurals, still a major type of detective novel, are becoming *noir* indeed. Unexpected lead detectives, even a traditional-sized lady in Botswana, are making a go of private investigation; forensic scientists spare enraptured readers no grisly detail of scalpel, forceps, or bone saw; historical figures, real and fictional, from the Stone Age through the Age of Aquarius serve up new insights into eternal crimes; ethnic detectives open doors to faraway places and exotic cultures from the Navajo Reservation to mysterious Tibet; amateur sleuths rely on dogs, cats, birds, even a detecting computer and an incognito velociraptor; and ordinary folk become caught up in extraordinarily outrageous murder investigations. No matter how exotic the detectives, today's audiences can't seem to get enough of them.

Beneath the escapist appeal of detective stories, though, lie profound human desires: to replace chaos with order, to see that evil is punished, and to probe the mystery of wickedness in the hope of understanding it, and—just maybe—overcoming it. Like Dorothy L. Sayers many years earlier, mystery historian Bruce F. Murphy believes that contemporary detective fiction has grown so dramatically because "people like to read about what's bothering them," hence the current staggering proliferation in crime around the world, invading homes by television and the Internet. Murphy attributes "the emotional center of good mysteries" to "weakness of character and such failures of courage or surrender to temptation as can turn reasonably good men or women into criminals and at worst, murderers ... [and] the well-wrought crime story makes us aware of our intimate knowledge of the archetypal tempter and our horrified fascination with the figure of the fallen" (x–xi). These primal responses underlie the burgeoning popularity of today's detective series fiction.

Skyrocketing sales in all facets of the detective series subgenre—books, films, videos, DVDs—testify that series detection both whets and gratifies its readers' appetites. Popular lead detectives usually evolve through highly complex "back stories," divesting themselves of psychological veil after veil in novel after novel, attracting devoted readerships and producing reliable sales for authors and publishers. Today's "incredibly selective" publishers are looking for "hooks" that make new authors promotable: off-the-beaten-path occupations and avocations, untapped territories, and cultic potential (Dahlin 27), and they're getting them.

Faced with shelves and catalogs full of the excellence and variety and sheer numbers of contemporary detective series, how can a reader spend his or her reading hours—more precious than dollars—wisely? Intended for general readers, this biographical dictionary of 150 contemporary fictional detectives concentrates on helping readers, especially high school and college students, locate additional stimulating works by familiar contemporary favorites and discover exciting new authors. It also attempts to balance groundbreaking series, some with only a few books so far, against more traditional longer series, and relatively obscure but worthwhile series against widely advertised best sellers. "Contemporary" here indicates series mainly produced after 1970.

The Introduction provides a brief history of the detective series genre, including both well-known and less familiar series detectives from the early 1800s to World War I; in the Golden Age between World Wars I and II; and the hard-boiled and procedural periods from the 1940s through the 1960s. At the end of the volume, four appendices arrange the 150 entries into authors and their sleuths (Appendix A); geographical areas (Appendix B); time periods (Appendix C); and detective's field of employment (Appendix D). Appendix E lists the major literary awards in detective fiction. A Selected Bibliography of general critical and/or historical sources and a list of helpful online resources also appear at the end of the volume.

Each biographical entry begins with a heading providing basic data about its detective or a collective sleuth: the character's name(s); the detective's profession (because many are crime-solving amateurs); his or her living situation, geographic locale, time period, associate(s), and where relevant, nemesis(-es); significant relationship(s); and societal and/or personal concern(s). The expository material that follows includes the author's aim(s) for the series; a mini-psychological profile of the detective with reference to his or her literary antecedents; and indications of this series' significance to the genre. Where relevant, it also includes the detective's ethnic or cultural background, relevant family circumstances, crime-solving procedure, his or her development during the series, and attitudes toward justice and the criminal quarry. A few entries treat detectives as teams (for example, Tony Hillerman's Joe Leaphorn and Jim Chee), and several authors are represented by more than one series.

Each entry next presents a chronological list of novels in that series; the author's other series and/or important stand-alone works; the author's autobiographical works, if any; and several bibliographical sources of additional material. These sources include books if possible, but usually only short articles and/or reviews are available for contemporary authors. These have been chosen from easily accessible print and online sources. Each entry includes mention of the author's major awards, the author's Web site when available, and a "See also" list with brief descriptions of similar series by other authors (bibliographical references for these are easily located through Internet sources). In some cases, the "See also" list is followed by a listing of one or more "debut novels," recent works initiating new series in this vein. In each entry, the first mention of a detective appearing in another entry appears in **bold** type.

Mystery readers tend to be intensely devoted to their favorite detectives, and no system of selection can satisfy everyone. Since a simple listing of all series detectives in recent novels would reach staggering proportions, detectives included here must appear in at least two books in a basically non-formulaic series by an author whose major work occurs after 1970. Most of these series have received major awards. Regretfully excluded are "stand-alone" novels like Dick Francis's racing mysteries, "thrillers" like Tom Clancy's Cold War sagas, "horror" fiction/ "ghost stories" like Stephen King's page-turners, and series with criminals as central figures like Patricia Highsmith's distinguished Thomas Ripley series. Each detective here displays some important distinguishing characteristic(s), a special historical or geographic or cultural appeal, or a significant moral focus. In general, American figures tend to dominate the private eye category and British characters the cozies and police procedurals, but I have included a broad spectrum of detectives: black, brown, yellow, and red-skinned detectives as well as their WASPish British and American counterparts; gay and lesbian detectives as well as straight females and males; and historical detectives from a wide range of times and places in addition to modern-day detectives operating in Europe, Asia, Australia, and Africa. I believe all those here illustrate Ellis Peters's contention that "crime-fiction writers [have] produced as much fine literature as the literati" because they explore "the moral-psychological territory . . . largely abandoned by serious fiction" (quoted in Ashley 391).

Today as crime is pervading every human culture and genies of technology are daily erupting from their bottles with unforeseen social and psychological disasters, the swelling popularity of series detective fiction does seem to indicate that the sympathy of the reading public, at least, is increasingly veering toward law and order. The fictional men and women who try to bring justice to their societies earn their popularity in many ways: those detectives who accompany us to the beach or mountain cabin offer welcome respite from the nightly news; those we reach for on sleepless nights often share comforting insights into perplexing human behavior; and the ones we would gladly take to desert islands hold out hope that right can and will prevail, however exquisitely long the journey and however painfully high the cost. I thank all their creators, and I hope that I have done them justice.

WORKS CITED

Ashley, Mike. *The Mammoth Encyclopedia of Modern Crime Fiction*. New York: Carroll and Graf, 2002.

Dahlin, Robert. "A Massive Crime Wave." *Publishers Weekly*, April 21, 2003: 27–32.

Murphy, Bruce F. *The Encyclopedia of Murder and Mystery*. New York: St. Martin's Press, 1999.

HOW TO USE THIS BOOK

Browse!

Open to any of these entries to meet detectives in dangerous, exciting work and whole new worlds to visit. Use the "See also" references in each entry to find that detective's literary "relatives," and look in the Introduction to read about his or her literary ancestors. Check this book's appendices to find these 150 detectives listed by authors and their sleuths (Appendix A), geographical area (Appendix B), time period (Appendix C), and the detective's other line of work (Appendix D).

Research!

Due to space limitations, complete bibliographical information is not given in the "See also" references, so use library resources like *Contemporary Authors*, *Something about the Author*, and others listed in the appendix to this book to locate other appealing novels and series. Also check Internet sources like Web sites for individual authors, for the big booksellers (Barnes and Noble, Borders, Amazon, etc.), *Contemporary Authors Online*, and for other libraries' holdings, and never hesitate to ask librarians for help.

Enjoy!

Spend time with modern knights-errant, explore exotic times and places, make fruitful comparisons between characters, backgrounds, and techniques. Join others in book club discussions, revel in classic series and delve into the new ones that constantly keep appearing. Most of all, marvel at the enormous spectrum between good and evil these detectives spread out before us. From the most lighthearted to the most serious-minded, mystery novels all offer unusual insights and perceptions into people's motivations and behavior in the context of puzzles that often stretch the mind and tug at the heart.

INTRODUCTION: THE ANCESTRY OF THE CONTEMPORARY SERIES DETECTIVE

Because conflict and suspense are essential to good storytelling, crime is the basic element of many early literary productions, from the story of Cain and Abel through the archetypal story of Oedipus and the romances of the Middle Ages, so fraught with betrayals, murders, and every other surreptitiously appealing infringement of the Ten Commandments. Not until the nineteenth century, though, a time of enormous political, cultural, socioeconomic, religious, and scientific shifts, did authors and their audiences discover one of the most enduringly popular sub-subgenres of literature, the detective series.

British mystery historian Bruce F. Murphy notes that the detective descends from the dragon-slaying, maiden-rescuing knight errant, whose adversary resembles Milton's fascinating Satan in *Paradise Lost*, so that "crime and mystery fiction responded to contemporary social developments but merged with the ancient patterns of Western literature. Sin became Crime" (x). Murphy also sees the rise of the detective novel paralleling the Industrial Revolution: "heightened anonymity, social insecurity, and urban poverty are like fertilizer for criminals," and as soon as people demanded the police to protect them from urban crime, writers began exploring the detectives' methods for doing so (x).

THE FIRST DETECTIVES

The initial period of Western detective writing, its "classic age," established many patterns for later detective fiction. It extends from the early 1800s to 1914, the outbreak of World War I, which forever altered life in Europe and America. The first novel with a police detective as hero was *Richmond, or Scenes from the Life of a Bow*

Street Runner, by Thomas Gaspey, published anonymously in 1827. Richmond is a knight-errant figure who nabs thieves and protects the innocent and weak, pities victims and feels satisfied at righting wrongs.

From Paris, one of Europe's most glamorous and crime-infested capitals, came the enigmatic ancestor of all Western detectives, François Eugène Vidocq, the first paid detective in the Sûreté, France's national police. Born in Arras in 1775 and dead of poverty in Brussels in 1857, Vidocq left memoirs that inspired mainstream "greats" like Victor Hugo, Balzac, and Dickens and a host of their followers and helped germinate the detective fiction of Edgar Allan Poe and Arthur Conan Doyle. Considerable controversy surrounds Vidocq's *Memoirs*, because some commentators feel that so many bizarre incidents as he records could not possibly have happened (even in Paris) to one man, and that therefore he or someone else must have collected and fictionalized them from many sources. E.G.R. Burford's 1934 foreword to the *Memoirs* insists, however, that whoever the author was, he was an honest man determined to alleviate the horrifying lot of early nineteenth-century prisoners and help them successfully return to society.

Vidocq's *Memoirs* (1828–1829), a still-readable picaresque narrative, reveals elements discernible in the modern series detective, beginning with a boisterous petty-criminal poverty-stricken youth where he made a first-hand acquaintance with crime and its motivations. It includes wry self-portraiture, enormous attention to detail, and overwhelming sympathy for individuals caught in an often sadistic prison system. After his humorously drawn stint in the army, Vidocq fell into criminal company and was sentenced to eight years of punishment, eventually winding up in the notorious La Force prison. In 1809, he talked his way into the police system by offering his services as an informer, and rose thereafter to become a master of disguise and eventually supervisor of the Sûreté's four unsalaried agents—paid per arrest—all, like himself, former criminals on speaking terms with members of the underworld. After Vidocq resigned from the police in 1827, he attempted to rehabilitate criminals by hiring them to work in a paper mill he had purchased, but the plan backfired and he lost his entire savings. He then started the first European private investigation agency, but when he tried to reenter the Sûreté, most believe he was framed for a crime he didn't commit, and he died in disgrace. Vidocq never repudiated any of the episodes or views recounted in the *Memoirs*. Besides sympathy for the downtrodden, they reveal a keen mind alive to the vast range from evil to good in human nature and a saving grace of humor, elements adopted by many of his literary descendents.

Vidocq's near-contemporary, American poet and author Edgar Allan Poe (1809–1849) is widely considered the creator of detective fiction, although in 1949 Robert Van Gulik published his translation of *Dee Goong An: Celebrated Cases of Judge Dee*, a seventeenth-century Chinese novel about an eighth-century magistrate, proving that the Far Eastern detective genre preceded its Western counterparts. In 1841, Poe's *Murders in the Rue Morgue*, with an old woman and her daughter found dead in a sealed room, introduced Chevalier C. August Dupin, the first amateur "genius detective" who became the model for Sherlock Holmes. Dorothy L. Sayers called Poe's novel "almost a complete manual of detective theory and practice" (Introduction 81). After "The Mystery of Marie Roget" (1842), a short story that initiated the mystery based on a real event, and "The Purloined Letter" (1844), which used the device of a detective trying to replicate in his own mind the mental processes of the criminal, Poe left off writing about Dupin, an eccentric who lived behind closed shutters and came out only at night. Dupin's literary legacy includes the "locked room" stratagem, the use of a less intellectually gifted associate as chronicler, obvious though overlooked clues, a basis in true crime, and a Hegelian dialectic in which the murderer, representing the force of evil and chaos, is opposed by the detective, representing order and rationality, culminating in the solution-as-synthesis and a "triumph of understanding" (Murphy 395).

Charles Dickens (1812–1870) incorporated the Bow Street Runners, Scotland Yard's predecessor, into *Oliver Twist* and created both the first fictional English official detective, stolid and apparently unremarkable Inspector Bucket of *Bleak House*, treating him both realistically and sympathetically in the hope of building public admiration for the police. Dickens also created the first fictional private eye, Mr. Nadgett, and other fictional detectives who may be found in *Hunted Down: The Detective Stories of Charles Dickens* (1996). At his death, Dickens was working on *The Mystery of Edwin Drood* (1870), never completed.

Other early writers had become interested in police detectives as heroes. Nineteenth-century mystery scholar Everett Bleiler felt that an enigmatic writer known only as "Waters" followed in Poe's footsteps as "the originator of the British detective short story" by publishing "Recollections of a Police Officer" in 1849, the year Poe died. Like Dickens, "Waters" was also creating fictional memoirs by policemen that laid the groundwork for the twentieth-century police procedural novel, but whether "Waters" knew of Vidocq's *Memoirs* is unknown. Tom Taylor's Hawkshaw, the Great Detective, appeared in *The Ticket of Leave Man* (1863) as a philanthropist who defended the innocent.

Victorian novelist William Wilkie Collins (1824–1889), a close friend of Charles Dickens and fellow devotee of real-life and literary detection, serialized *The Woman in White* (1860) and *The Moonstone* (1868), two of the world's most influential mystery novels, in Dickens's popular journal *Household Words*, bringing Collins's work to a vast number of English-speaking readers accustomed to the conventions of comedies and novels of manners usually involving marriage. *The Woman in White*, based, like most of Collins's stories, on an actual old French case Collins discovered in some dilapidated volumes he had found while roaming Paris bookshops with Dickens, holds its secret until the very end, with a heroine who overcomes an arch-villain to claim her inheritance and preserve her life. *The Moonstone*, which T.S. Eliot lauded as "the first, the longest, and the best of modern English detective novels," was also praised by Dorothy L. Sayers for its scrupulous "fair play" in gradually revealing its secret "with the collaboration of the reader," a technique, according to Rosemary Herbert, that distinguishes the detective novel from the "sensation" novel (37). Although Collins did not create a mystery series, *The Moonstone* also presents the only appearance of rational, eccentric, rose-cultivating Sergeant Cuff, who takes over the case when a local official cannot cope, and the intuitive outcast artist/scientist Ezra Jennings, who with Cuff breaks the case as "the Bi-Part Soul" of detection (Herbert 37), forerunner of many fictional sleuths. Collins based Cuff on real policeman

Inspector Jonathan Whicher, known as "the Prince of Detectives." Cuff is underpaid, treated badly, competent in his work, and readily admits his failings: "I own that I made a mess of it.... It's only in books that the officers of the detective force are superior to the weakness of making a mistake."

Monsieur Lecoq, based on Vidocq by French mystery author Émile Gaboriau (1832–1873), considered the father of the French *roman policier* (police novel) and described by Julian Symons as "an interesting and underrated writer," appeared in several French stories first collected as *romans judiciares* (judicial novels), which incorporate police procedure into the wildly popular sensational fiction of the time. Gaboriau was well aware of the difficulty in making his hero a policeman and at first he used an amateur detective to keep Lecoq company (Symons 52). The amateur soon faded into the background, allowing the touchily eccentric Lecoq (whose name may have inspired the twentieth-century Dutch writer Baantjer's Inspector DeKok's name) to use brilliant deduction and superb intuition to solve his cases, a foreshadowing of Sherlock Holmes's renowned methods. Lecoq's trying relationship with Sûreté Chief Gévrol foreshadows the tense relation between Georges Simenon's Inspector Jules Maigret and his nemesis, the magistrate Coméliau (Murphy 294).

An American woman, Metta Victoria Fuller Victor, who wrote as "Seeley Register," created the first detective story in English and the first American detective novel, *The Dead Letter* (1866). Register extended the puzzle seen in short crime fiction to novel length and enhanced the detective's personality and methods, rejecting the misanthropy of Poe's Dupin and making her investigator, Mr. Burton, "an attractive, well-adjusted, and sociable person" with Holmesian powers of deduction. Register also established the "happy ending" precedent by eschewing capital punishment for the guilty (B.J. Rahn in Herbert 166). Register's work strongly influenced her contemporaries, especially Anna Katharine Green (see below).

Protestant-born Irishman Joseph Sheridan LeFanu (1814–1873), often compared to Poe because of his interest in horror and the supernatural, has been underrated, though he was another early mystery writer Sayers and other Golden Age writers greatly admired. Sayers included LeFanu's 1869 story "Green Tea," featuring detective Martin Hesselius, in her groundbreaking *Great Short Stories of Detection, Mystery, and Horror* (1928; retitled *The Omnibus of Crime* in the United States) and in her Introduction praised the "sheer grimness and horror" of LeFanu's *The House by the Churchyard*, one precursor of the shuddery atmospherics favored by many modern crime novelists.

Bursting on the Victorian literary scene in 1887 with *A Study in Scarlet*, Arthur Conan Doyle's Sherlock Holmes became the world's most famous literary detective. As a debt-ridden young doctor with a sick wife and failed attempts at writing behind him, Doyle struck pay dirt when he modulated Poe's formula by omitting the long psychological introductions Poe used and incorporated expository information into brisk dialogue. Doyle also endowed Holmes with "staggering conclusions from trifling indications" as Gaboriau had done with Lecoq (Introduction 93).

Holmes's relationship with Dr. Watson, according to Dorothy L. Sayers, also inspired many "admiring and thickheaded" friends of Great Detectives. Holmes meets Dr. Watson when each is seeking a roommate and astonishes him with the deduction that Watson has just returned from Afghanistan. Doyle adopted Holmes's trademark eccentric but brilliant deduction from the diagnostic talents of his medical mentor, Dr. Joseph Bell of Edinburgh. Watson soon learns that Holmes is untidy at home to the point of shooting holes in the walls, not at all versed in literature (Doyle later made up for this shortcoming in his hero), plays a Stradivarius, and is addicted to cocaine, with consequent periods of disinclination to work. As Sayers remarked, "the concrete details of daily life in Baker Street" provide the stories "a solid reality" and Watson's "sturdy independence...adds salt and savor to the eccentricities of Holmes" (Introduction 94).

Sherlock Holmes inspired many qualities of later "genius detectives": their deductive powers, their personal peculiarities, their tendency to place themselves above the law when they deem it necessary, their mastery of disguise, and their determination in tracking their vicious nemeses, like Holmes's foe Professor Moriarty, to earth—a determination so grim that it frequently causes Holmes to jeopardize his friends. Doyle's Sherlock Holmes stories sparked such "an avalanche of mystery fiction" (Introduction 95) that Holmes pastiches and parodies show no signs of abating. Whole new mystery series are currently appearing, like Laurie King's Mary Russell series featuring Holmes's young apprentice and later wife, and Carole Nelson Douglas's Irene Adler series, featuring the only woman to have bested the great detective at his own game. *Encyclopedia Sherlockiana* (reprint 1997) provides a comprehensive guide to Sherlock Holmes and his world.

Before 1920, many notable but far less known fictional detectives appeared, using unconventional or scientific means of detection. Anna Katharine Green (1846–1935), often recognized as the first woman to have published a detective novel until Seeley Register's work was discovered, published *The Leavenworth Case* eight years prior to *Study in Scarlet*, with obese and opinionated Ebenezer Gryce as her quirky New York policeman hero. Gryce, beset by feelings of inferiority, was assisted in subsequent melodramatic novels by spinster Amelia Butterworth, predecessor of Miss Marple, Dorothy L. Sayers's Miss Katharine Climpson, and a host of snoopy elderly spinsters or widows (see below). M. McDonald Bodkin's (1850–1933) novels about Paul Beck and his son pioneered the "plain man" detective, muddling through as best he can, in *Paul Beck, the Rule of Thumb Detective* (1898). Bodkin later produced *Dora Myrl, the Lady Detective* (1900), "no less absurd than other stories of the time about women detectives" and married her off to Beck Senior after they had worked on opposite sides of a case (Symons 90).

A little known but influential detective, Professor Augustus S.F.X. Van Dusen, one of the first "scientific detectives," was the creation of Jacques Futrelle (1875–1912), an American author who went down with the *Titanic* after writing such works as *The Chase of the Golden Plate* (1906). Van Dusen, known as the "Thinking Machine," reasons his way out of seemingly impossible situations like a nineteenth-century version of *Star Trek*'s Mr. Spock, but he carries his peculiar work off with humor and originality. English surgeon Richard Austin Freeman (1862–1943) pioneered the medical detective with handsome Dr. John Thorndyke, first appearing in *The Red Thumb Mark* (1907). Freeman himself is said to have performed all the experiments Thorndyke carries out. Though reading Freeman today is "like chewing dry straw"

(Symons 88), some of the experimental medical-forensic technology Thorndyke uses, like radiography, later became part of standard police procedure, and certain of his cases were actually cited in British legal texts (Murphy 189).

Other detectives disguised themselves to deceive the ungodly. Beginning with *At the Villa Rose* (1910), A.E.W. Mason's (1865–1948) rumpled and bearlike Inspector Hanaud of the Sûreté carried out Mason's requirements for a series detective: being a professional; physically resembling Sherlock Holmes as little as possible; being friendly; and being willing to act on his intuition. Hanaud uses his appearance to disarm his suspects, and he insists that the facts be viewed with "imagination on a leash," so he descends directly from Auguste Dupin's Bi-Part Soul (Herbert 91). E.W. Hornung's (1866–1921) engaging A.J. Raffles established the literary tradition of the classy gentleman thief. As a sociable and appealing Australian-born rascal, Raffles can mix with the finest at country-house parties and cricket games eschewing violence because "violence is a confession of terrible incompetence." Raffles, "a person one can believe in" because he is a gentleman who didn't inherit the money to keep up his gentlemanly show, carries out adventures that many still find delightful. He stars in the novel *Mr. Justice Raffles* (1909) and the short fiction collections *The Amateur Cracksman* (1899) and *A Thief in the Night* (1905).

One of the most unusual early detectives is Baroness Emmuska Orczy's (1865–1947) elderly, pale, thin, and balding Bill Owen, the first "armchair detective," who sits in a corner of the North Branch of the A.B.C. Teashops, tieing and untieing complicated knots as he unravels supposedly insoluble crimes. Owen never suggests "that there were no mysteries to the *police*; I merely suggested that there were none where intelligence was brought to bear upon the investigation of a crime" (quoted in Nichols and Thompson 262; italics in original). Subsequently the "armchair detective" device was used by Agatha Christie with *The Tuesday Club Murders'* collective protagonist of elderly ladies, and by Ernest Bramah with his blind detective Max Carrados, also a "superman detective" who employs his heightened senses to compensate for his lack of sight. As well as writing *The Scarlet Pimpernel* (1905) Baroness Orczy was one of the first to portray a capable female detective. Her Lady Molly de Mazareen "breaks cases by wit and daring rather than intuition" (Herbert 144). Baroness Orczy's principal contribution to detective fiction, though, is considered detection based entirely on reported information, a technique seen earlier in Poe's "The Mystery of Marie Roget."

Roman Catholic apologist G.K. Chesterton's (1874–1936) Father Brown, the first and one of the most enduringly popular clerical sleuths, appears in fifty short stories collected in five volumes beginning with *The Innocence of Father Brown* (1911) and closing with *The Scandal of Father Brown* (1935). Based on Chesterton's friend Father John O'Connor, unprepossessing in appearance and demeanor, Father Brown is "a little man" representing the commonplace (Mann 76)—short, round-faced, near-sighted, dowdy in his rusty black clerical garb and apparently absent-minded, but in the traditional Roman Catholic sense, he "hates the sin but loves the sinner" and works "on a mixture of faith, shrewdness and intuition" with methods all depending heavily on paradox (*Ibid.*). Father Brown is unfailingly unflustered by even the most horrifying crimes he encounters. He even reforms one villain, the jewel thief

Flambeau, who becomes a private investigator. Father Brown, however, cannot do much with Vidocq's literary descendent Aristide Valentin, the Sûreté's most brilliant detective, who remains rabidly anti-Catholic. Chesterton, a lifelong political and religious arch-conservative, converted from Anglicanism to Catholicism in 1932 after a long period of intense study, so Father Brown voices his creator's exceptional knowledge of theology and moral teaching in polemics ranging from his rightful and righteous denunciation of the prideful rich to his less-than-tolerant diatribes against the "evil" of Eastern art and against other religions, notably Hinduism, which he attacks for its supposed yearning for "annihilation." He also denounces pagan irrationality and compares Satanism to Puritan theology. "Chesterton makes Father Brown appear humble but meek he is not" (Murphy 64). Overall, Father Brown embodies the moral-literary principle of detective writing that Chesterton formalized much later: "the only thrill, even of a common thriller, is concerned somehow with the conscience and the will" (quoted in Symons 82), and Father Brown is unequivocal in condemning Evil. Sayers noted that one of the detective writer's most difficult tasks is bringing a villain who has been made a real person to the gallows. She noted that "Mr. G.K. Chesterton deals with this problem by merely refusing to face it," and the sordid conclusion takes place offstage, allowing the good Father to maintain his deceptively frivolous façade and his stern moral stance free of inward twinges of "tenderer human feeling" (Introduction 103). Because the powers that commonplace-appearing little Father Brown exerts in his battles against Evil come from God, Symons categorizes him as a "superman detective."

Later, American author John Dickson Carr (who also wrote under the name Carter Dickson) patterned Dr. Gideon Fell after Chesterton himself, a heavyweight, gray-haired, eccentric-appearing amateur detective who, starting with *Hag's Nook* (1933) waddled through Carr's trademark locked-room murder mystery scenarios with grotesque characters and highly colored atmospheres. Fell discusses seven types of locked-room cases and their solutions in *The Hollow Man* (1935). Carr openly acknowledged that he drew heavily on Chesterton, whom he never met, for inventing murder cases that seemed to hinge on intrusions of witchcraft and the supernatural but which had entirely rational solutions (John C. Tibbetts in Herbert 28).

Englishman E.C. Bentley (1875–1956), dedicated his first novel, *Trent's Last Case* (1913), to Chesterton, his childhood friend. On both sides of the Atlantic it was immediately greeted with enormous success as a landmark work. Agatha Christie called *Trent's Last Case* "one of the three best detective stories ever written," and many critics agreed that it was "the first modern detective story with characters who are like real human beings," though others have faulted its characters as unconvincing. It was followed by the less successful *Trent's Own Case* (1936; coauthored with Herbert Warner Allen) and the short story collection *Trent Intervenes* (1938). Philip Trent became the prototype for the gifted amateur detective heroes of the soon-to-come Golden Age of detective fiction; he is a successful painter like his father, possessed of an ample private income, at a gorgeous thirty-two, tall, blond, elegantly handsome with a "high-boned quixotic face," and famous throughout England for his skill at detection. In 1934, Dorothy L. Sayers praised Trent for establishing "the detective's right of a liberal education, and a sincere personal emotion. His conversation and his love affair for the first time in detective history, breathed the air of poetry."

Despite all his impressive qualities, however, Trent is also the first of the "fallible sleuths," created, Bentley claimed, in reaction against what he considered the artificial eccentricities and dead-seriousness of Sherlock Holmes. Dorothy L. Sayers also commented on the contra-Holmes revolution in detective writing produced by its evolution toward "fair play." "Fair play," the concept that the reader should be able to solve the mystery, calls for "a story which puts them [readers] on an equal footing with the detective himself, as regards all clues and discoveries," as well as the converse, that once the detective has begun his or her investigation, "no episode must ever be described which does not come within their cognizance." Bentley's delicately shifting points of view in *Trent's Last Case* demonstrate these principles, leading the reader from the "Watson viewpoint" where the reader sees only amateur detective Trent's external actions through what Trent sees but not what he observes; then through seeing everything that Trent sees as well as his conclusions; and finally complete mental identification with the detective. This technique is crucial to the "fair play" doctrine to which writers of the Golden Age for the most part adhered, as codified in 1929 by Father Ronald Knox (see below), but subsequently these rules have been violated in the interest of suspense and readability.

THE GOLDEN AGE SLEUTHS

The "fair play" doctrine meshed with Holmesian methods of detection and a startling new view of women in detective fiction's "Golden Age," generally coinciding with the unsettled period between the two world wars. The First World War took a ghastly toll on England and the world: Britain alone lost 750,000 soldiers, more than a tenth of those it called to serve King and country, and two million others were too grievously damaged to function normally—wounded, amputated, blinded, paralyzed, gassed, shell-shocked. Sweeping social changes rocked Britain's traditional certainties, as Prime Minister Lloyd George declared: "The nation is now in a molten state....We cannot return to the old ways, the old abuses, the old stupidities" (quoted in Briggs 258). The old race of faithful servants virtually disappeared; women won the vote, sought employment outside the home, and began to drink in pubs, and by 1919 every village chemist was selling contraceptives. The twenties were about to roar.

Although London's *Evening Standard* had thundered in 1891, "Many are the crimes brought about by the disordered imagination of a reader of sensational and often immoral rubbish, while many a home is neglected and uncared for owing to the all-absorbed, novel-reading wife" (quoted in Mann 27), more people—not just wives—were reading detective novels than ever before, finding not only escape from daily griefs and hardships but also the moral comfort that good could triumph over evil. In this atmosphere, British authors dominated the Golden Age. Dorothy L. Sayers commented, "Death in particular seems to provide the mind of the Anglo-Saxon race with a greater fund of innocent amusement than any other single subject, and when it is occasioned or accompanied by Sin in its more repugnant shapes, the fun grows faster and more furious" (Introduction 101).

Both the major detective authors of the Golden Age—Agatha Christie, Marjorie Allingham, Dorothy L. Sayers, and Ngaio Marsh—and a host of lesser writers humanized their sleuths in response to the sea changes in British society. They also upheld firm standards of mystery construction as well as a solid set of moral values. Christie, Allingham, Sayers, and Marsh all became members of The Detection Club, founded in 1928 by Anthony Berkeley. Its first two presidents were G.K. Chesterton and E.C. Bentley respectively, and Sayers devised the fearsome oath initiates were required to swear on a skull called "Eric," abjuring the use of "Divine Revelation, Feminine Intuition, Mumbo-Jumbo, Jiggery-Pokery, Coincidence, or the Act of God" (quoted in Dale 86–87). The Detection Club for the most part held fast to Msgr. Ronald Knox's 1928 "Ten Commandments of Detection" fair play standards: the criminal had to be mentioned early in the story; the supernatural was ruled out; and the detective could not commit the crime, rely on intuition, or receive help accidentally.

Perhaps the most earth-shaking upset in detective fiction the Golden Age produced, one that Sayers claimed had revolutionized the world of the mystery novel and foreshadowed the work of many detective writers of her day, her own included (Gaillard 73), derived from what Sherlock Holmes would have considered Philip Trent's chief failing: he fell in love, and the mystery story began to merge its "pure puzzle" with the sparkling comedy of manners.

Holmes's eccentricities and brilliant deductive methods abetted by Watson's common sense; Father Brown's self-effacing demeanor; and the "fair play" doctrine's demands that all clues the detective unearths must be available to the reader and that except for Divine Guidance no supernatural resources can be allowed all merged in Agatha Christie's (1890–1976) conceited and retired Belgian private detective Hercule Poirot, an unlikely-appearing but genuine latter-day knight in shining armor first seen in *The Mysterious Affair at Styles* (1920). Christie's wartime hospital work had provided her a knowledge of poisons that she put to use in writing *The Mysterious Affair at Styles*, which earned her about twenty-five pounds in its first British edition and was not published in the United States until 1930. She used the Conan Doyle techniques of "the pattern of the clue" and "the idiot friend" (quoted in Symons 102) and made Poirot short, impeccably tailored, bald, somewhat like "Humpty Dumpty with a [waxed] moustache," and his associate Captain Arthur Hastings "a Watson of incredible stupidity" (Symons 102), whom Christie later married off and banished to Argentina. Poirot then moves to a more luxurious London flat, acquires a super-efficient secretary, Miss Felicity Lemon, a freelance operator, Miss Ariadne Oliver, and George, a manservant he calls "Georges." Poirot's skill at crime-solving rests mainly on his ability to strike at the heart of a mystery, his supposed difficulty with English, really an asset that makes suspects mistakenly assume he's their intellectual inferior, and his "little gray cells," which produce those trademark leaps of deduction that consistently make a fool of Chief Inspector Japp and bring the guilty to justice. Poirot claims, "The employment of the little gray cells is a mental pleasure. They, and only they, can be trusted to lead on through fog to the truth" (*Lord Edgware Dies*, 251).

In 1926, shortly before Agatha Christie's famous case of amnesia, she published *The Murder of Roger Ackroyd*, a big departure from her successful mystery pattern. Golden Age conventions demanded that mystery authors subordinate character development to the central puzzle, that "red herrings" attempt to lead readers and detectives alike astray, and that plot should reign supreme over all other considerations, even, Murphy observes, believability (207). In *The Murder of Roger Ackroyd*, Christie explored character to a greater degree than she had earlier, and she violated Knox's rule that insists that the Watson character's thought must not be concealed. Despite these infringements of Golden Age norms, *The Murder of Roger Ackroyd* helped Christie became the most widely read of all mystery authors, and when she finally killed Poirot off in *Curtain* (1975), the little Belgian detective received the stellar accolade of a front-page obituary in the *New York Times*. Dame Agatha Christie published her *Autobiography* in 1977. *The Agatha Christie Companion* (1984) offers a wealth of material on this enormously popular author.

Growing tired of Poirot in the early 1920s, Christie invented Tommy and Tuppence Beresford, engaging young marrieds first appearing as youthful friends in *The Secret Adversary* (1922). They run a detective agency briefly in *Partners in Crime* (1929), fight Nazis spies in *N or M* (1941), and in *Pattern of Fate* (1974), now elderly, they probe a murder in their quiet retirement village. Their joint detective prowess preceded later married-couple cozies and may have influenced American author Dashiell Hammett (1894–1961), who produced the genre's most famous sleuthing couple, Nick and Nora Charles. They first appeared with their wirehaired fox terrier Asta in *The Thin Man* (1934), later made into a popular film starring William Powell and Myrna Loy. The Charleses were followed by Mr. and Mrs. North, young Manhattanites sketched first in *The New Yorker* by Richard and Frances Lockridge in 1936. Their first adventure was *The Norths Meet Murder* (1941). The Norths operate out of their cat-filled Gotham apartment, solving a variety of crimes in exotic settings through generally improbable leaps of intuition while leaving the mechanics of criminal-catching to the police. Frances Crane introduced her San Francisco private detective duo Pat and Jean Crane in 1941; Jean narrates the cases, each titled with a color, a technique later used by John D. Macdonald and Walter Mosely.

Christie presented her second most famous character, elderly Miss Jane Marple, in short stories prior to *A Murder at the Vicarage* (1930). To this point, successful detectives had usually been male, and female ones "were oddities, invented for effect, like the detectives who were blind, or crippled, or eccentric" (Mann 92). Forever knitting, uncompromisingly Victorian, indefatigably nosy, Miss Marple somewhat unconvincingly devotes herself to charming, if "a bit treacly" (Murphy 331) detection in St. Mary Meade, a little English village with an unnaturally high crime rate. Throughout the several novels and many short stories in which she appears until 1976, Miss Marple unravels some of Christie's most ingenious plot devices and sets the pattern for what Lord Peter Wimsey would have called a "cattery" of imitative cozies to come. Michele B. Slung's 1976 anthology *Crime on Her Mind* lists thirty-four women detectives appearing in fiction since 1918, and twenty of these were prior to 1900. Most, according to Slung, were "abandon[ed] in mid-career and finish[ed] off...at the matrimonial altar, in order to reassure the Victorian public of [their] ultimate femaleness." As sleuths, those who remained spinsters were spiritual descendents of Anna Katharine Green's Miss Amelia Butterworth, often functioning in the "Had-I-But-Known" school of detection (see below) and refraining from imparting essential information for fear of being ridiculed by men.

Patricia Wentworth's (1878–1961) Miss Maud Silver mysteries illustrate the "Had-I-But-Known" method, featuring a mousy former governess turned private investigator, and they are still in print, testifying to the cozy appeal of the nosy Victorian Miss Marpleish spinster. "Assisting" her former student Sergeant Frank Abbott, now an aristocratic Scotland Yard detective, Maud knits her way through heinous crimes and often acts as a matchmaker in romantic subplots. American Mary Roberts Rinehart (1876–1958) followed the predictable forehead-smiting "Had-I-But-Known" pattern often involving spinster aunts, plucky young widows or marriageable girls hearing things go bump in the night (Symons 100) in superficial neo-gothic romantic mystery novels with "the air of being written specifically for maiden aunts." Rinehart's one series sleuth was plain, middle-aged Nurse Hilda Adams—"Miss Pinkerton." Her lineal literary descendent Mignon G. Eberhardt (1899–1996) created nurse-sleuth Susan Dare, who looks like "a chill and aloof little owl," with tidy methods of detection and unconvincing secondary characters described pungently as "witless idiots" by Jessica Mann (101).

Diametrically opposed to Miss Pinkerton's prosaic character is Gladys Mitchell's (1901–1983) Dame Beatrice Adela Lestrange Bradley, the "Old Trout," a famous elderly psychiatrist and a "little, thin, black-eyed witch-like being" (K.D. Prince, quoted in Herbert 22) rumored to have descended from a long line of spell-casters, with a penchant for wearing the wild colors of a macaw. People "shrink from her as from a reptile" (Murphy 58). Seen first in *Speedy Death* (1929) and continuing for more than fifty years, Dame Bradley serves as a psychiatric adviser to the Home Office, the basis for her cases involving paranormal elements like occult rituals, ancient Greek mysticism, and even the Loch Ness Monster. As an early member of the Detection Club, Mitchell played fair by laying her clues out openly, but Dame Bradley exercises eerie insights and she relishes meting out her own retribution, even admitting she has committed three murders (Nichols and Thompson 122).

Britain's Marjorie Allingham (1904–1966) considered the mystery story a four-sided box: "A Killing, a Mystery, an Enquiry and a Conclusion with an Element of Satisfaction in it" (quoted in Herbert 7). Her sleuth Albert Campion is an aristocratic "silly-ass sleuth," a type derived from Bertie Wooster, a comic character popularized during the 1920s by humorist P.G. Wodehouse. Early in his career, Campion uses a deceptively foolish appearance as a cover to encourage people to underestimate him, but he gradually acquires more gravitas (and girlfriends) as he moves through the series. Allingham doubted that there was a more lethal hazard to the fictional detective than matrimony. Hers was an "aristocratic sleuth" with royal connections ("Campion" is his assumed name, and Allingham once confessed that his destiny was to inherit the British throne). Attended by his grotesque manservant Magersfontein Lugg, Campion carries on a protracted engagement to long-suffering Miss Amanda

Fitton, who eventually marries him, even though in *Traitor's Purse* (1941) amnesia forced him temporarily to forget who she was. Since in her later Campion novels Allingham integrated adventurous romance tinged by horror into the series, Campion seems to be downplayed as a holdover "from an earlier time and a different tradition" (Symons 165). In the witty *More Work for the Undertaker* (1948), he encounters Charlie Luke, a young copper with "a pile-driver personality" (B.A. Pike in Herbert 7) who handles most of the investigation in *The Tiger in the Smoke* (1952). Despite Campion's back-seat role, this is considered Allingham's most powerful novel. Campion's final adventure, *Cargo of Eagles* (1970), known as *Mr. Campion's Quarry* in the United States, involved Campion in a dashing treasure hunt. Allingham's husband, Youngman Carter, completed it after her death.

Lord Peter Wimsey, younger son of the Duke of Denver, first occurred to mystery author and critic, medievalist, translator, and High Anglican amateur theologian Dorothy L. Sayers (1893–1957) around 1920, when she was desperate for money and suffering from being dumped in the first of three traumatic love affairs that paralleled the development of her renowned sleuth. In a fictional *Who's Who* sketch, Sayers announced many of Wimsey's distinguishing characteristics: the aristocratic lineage, a big nose, a Piccadilly flat, the yen for pricey first editions, and shoulders "tailored to swooning point." By the summer of 1921, she was incubating her first Wimsey novel, *Whose Body?* (1923) while she was involved in a doomed relationship with "an artist with a capital A." After it failed, she told her mother at Christmas of 1922 she was coming home "with a [different] man and a motorcycle," another failed affair that culminated in her second Wimsey novel, *Clouds of Witness* (1926), and an illegitimate son whose identity Sayers kept a well-guarded secret for the rest of her life.

Lord Peter Wimsey is both the man Sayers wished she could have married and the fictionalization of many of her own dreams. In his earliest appearances he favors an upper-class drawl and inane Bertie Woosterisms masking bursts of insight that solve frustrating cases his stolid friend Inspector Charles Parker cannot fathom. Sayers, working hard at an advertising agency to support herself and (secretly) her son, craved luxuries of mind and body she could not possibly afford, so she gave them to Lord Peter. His Piccadilly flat glows in primrose and gold and flame-color, contrasting with a black concert grand piano on which he sublimely plays Mozart and Scarlatti; he speaks fluent French, proficiently manages European mistresses, and revels in rare medieval books, fine vintages, and elegant cuisine. The delights of Wimsey's palate helped give rise to the subgenre of culinary mysteries and helped inspire such diverse gourmet detectives as Nero Wolfe and Monsieur Pamplemousse (see below). Wimsey's valet, "confidential man" and assistant sleuth Mervyn Bunter, his sergeant during World War I, keeps Wimsey impeccably turned out and assists his crime-solving with camera equipment and legwork.

Sayers never doubted that the detective was "the protector of the weak...the true successor of Roland and Lancelot." She endowed Lord Peter with English gentlemanly qualities straight from the age of chivalry she loved: courtesy toward women, scrupulosity at keeping his word, and fair play, even with the criminals he tracks like big game in his early novels. After the Wimsey novels had brought Sayers fame and fortune, though, she began to be bored with his "silly-ass" persona and began to reshape him. His giddy chatter was already phasing out in *Clouds of Witness* in favor of growing emotional stability and practicality, and in *Unnatural Death* (1927), he begins to ponder the unpleasant side effects that apprehending criminals were causing him—guilt at capital punishment and painful recrimination over the deaths of the innocent.

In 1926 Sayers married "Mac" Fleming, an army veteran with a drinking problem, and their union went downhill fast. Intending by that time to kill off Lord Peter, Sayers suffered a midlife crisis that first resulted in two abortive attempts at autobiography, then in the decision to marry Peter off instead. In four novels that parallel Dante's Hell-Purgatory-Paradise journey of *The Divine Comedy*, Sayers had Lord Peter meet, pursue, and finally wed her fictional alter ego, mystery author Harriet Vane, first glimpsed by Wimsey on trial for murdering her "artist with a capital A" lover.

Sayers's brilliant introduction to *The Omnibus of Crime* (1928) is widely considered "the finest single piece of analytical writing about the detective story" (Hone 56). In it, Sayers roundly condemned "heroes who insist on fooling about after young women when they ought to be putting their minds on the job of detection" and she claimed that "the really brilliant woman detective has yet to be created" (Introduction 103, 70). Her own solution to the problem of romance, wedding the comedy of manners to the novel of detection, came in *Gaudy Night* (1935), the book that she said she had always wanted to write. Sayers brought Lord Peter and Harriet Vane together finally, he as the performing artist in detection, she as the creative one; they join their minds and hearts as equals. "Peter makes a huge settlement of inalienable wealth upon her, and she is married in cloth of gold and sables. It was every girl's dream" (Mann 113). For Harriet—and Sayers—this was "All the kingdoms of the world and the glory of them" (*Gaudy Night* 381). In their rapturous *Busman's Honeymoon*, Sayers brings Peter fully to life—and thereby, says Sayers's longtime friend Barbara Reynolds, she at last killed him off, though recently he and Harriet have been lukewarmly resurrected by Jill Paton Walsh (see below).

An American, S.S. Van Dine (1889–1939), broke "all modern publishing records for detective fiction" in 1927 with his second novel, *The Canary Murder Case*, featuring Philo Vance, now considered "a similar [to Lord Peter Wimsey] monster of snobbish affectation" (Symons 114) "among the most despised creatures of the detective genre" (Murphy 506), who according to Ogden Nash needed a swift kick in the pants (Keating 47). Nonetheless, Vance produced prodigious sales and film spin-offs for his author.

An aristocratic sleuth with genuine literary talent is Nigel Strangeways, a figure based on the poet W.H. Auden. Strangeways debuted in 1935 with *A Question of Proof* as a creation of "Nicholas Blake" because the author, future British Poet Laureate C. Day-Lewis (1904–1972), needed money to fix his roof. In his bubbly early appearances, Strangeways reflects Blake's literary expertise, his left-wing politics (in contrast to many of his conservative contemporary mystery authors like Sayers, Day-Lewis was briefly a member of the British Communist Party), and "the ingenuity and insouciance" that marked the best Golden Age mysteries (Patricia Craig, in Herbert 19). Like the early Albert Campion and Lord Peter Wimsey, Strangeways is tall, sandy-haired, handsome, off-handedly elegant, and myopic. He also frequently quotes from literary works and "bellows poetry at the top of his lungs during a car chase" (Murphy 471). As the series progresses, Strangeways becomes less radical in politics and more conventional in approach. He moves through many different settings, maintains solid relationships with Scotland Yard Inspectors Blount and Wright, and, refusing to condemn murderers as monsters, often traces their motivations to psychological damage they sustained as children. H.R.F. Keating observes that under the guise of a straightforward detective story in *The Beast Must Die* (1938), Blake presents a serious moral exploration of "that compulsion to make atonement— a sense of guilt, the traitor within the gates" (quoted from Blake in Keating 61). In this novel, narrated by a man contemplating murder, Keating concludes, "Here . . . is no play-acting but what seem entirely to be real thoughts, real mourning" (62).

Jessica Mann has observed that "At the height of the careers of Poirot, Campion, Wimsey, and the other amateur detectives, fewer than one hundred murders and major crimes took place in Britain each year" (73), and very few of these were solved by amateur detectives. As a result, authors increasingly turned to policemen as heroes. As the son of a baronet and Alsatian-breeding Lady Alleyn, New Zealander Ngaio Marsh's (1895–1982) Inspector (later Superintendent) Roderick Alleyn of Scotland Yard belongs to Britain's privileged elite, but he also chose to be a policeman. He displays a strong sense of justice and a fundamental decency toward his fellow human beings without a shred of "silly-ass" camouflage. Marsh claimed that she invariably started her novels with people, and she earned high praise, especially in the United States, for the psychological depth of her characters. From his first case, *A Man Lay Dead* (1934), throughout its thirty-one successors, Alleyn functions with equal comfort among the aristocracy and among the practitioners of art and drama. Marsh produced Shakespearean plays with young theatre groups from New Zealand's Canterbury University, and her particular love for Shakespeare's works is clearly evident in Alleyn's ease at quoting Bardic passages. His wife, the independently successful portrait artist Agatha Troy, often serves as the muse of his detecting, but never as his Watson, a role left to Inspector Fox—"Foxkin" or "Br'er Fox" as the mood strikes Alleyn (Murphy 7). Alleyn sometimes appears late at the murder site after initial investigations have been carried on by another character, but his handsome looks, natural grace, good manners, and keen intelligence ensure that he dominates each scene he enters. Marsh claimed she thought he had "developed third dimensionally in her company," and she "never got tired of the old boy" (Margaret Lewis, in Herbert 126). Neither did her fans. For her achievements Marsh was named Dame Commander of the Order of the British Empire in 1966, and Grand Master by the Mystery Writers of America in 1977. Her autobiography *Black Beech and Honeydew* (1965; revised edition 1981) chiefly discusses her family and early life, her development, and her passion for the theatre.

Like Inspector Alleyn, Scotsman Michael Innes's (1906–1994) decidedly upper-class Sir John Appleby enjoyed a long career with Scotland Yard, beginning in 1935 with *Death at the President's Lodging* (titled *Seven Suspects* in the United States). Appleby even solved cases like 1968's *Death by Water* after he had retired as head of the Yard. Appleby's wife Judith Raven is a sculptor who, with their son Bobby, sometimes assists Appleby's investigations. As "a magician with words, a relishing magician," Innes made Appleby much given to quoting vivaciously from literary "greats." Appleby also displays a light comic touch that saves the series from preciousness or pretentiousness. Symons calls Innes one of the finest of the "farceurs," who make the detective story "an oversized joke" with a dash of detection thrown in almost as an afterthought (133); one of his literary descendents is Michael Bond's inimitable Monsieur Pamplemousse (see below).

Echoes of the early Lord Peter Wimsey appear in Englishwoman Georgette Heyer's (1902–1974) Superintendent Hemingway, recalling the early Lord Peter in a late 1930s–1940s series distinguished by cleverness and farcical comedy. Margaret Erskine's (1938–1977) Inspector Septimus Finch, one of Scotland Yard's "Bright Boys," tackles gothic cases with legerdemain and extrasensory perception. On the other hand, American Dorothy Hughes (1904–1993), hailed as a Grand Master by the Mystery Writers of America, downplayed her Inspector Tobin in favor of strong women protagonists like Harriet Vane and shaped her mysteries into socioreligious commentaries.

One of few Americans elected to Britain's elite Detection Club, John Dickson Carr lived in England for fifteen years and built successful mysteries under both his own name and the pen name Carter Dickson. Symons has remarked that "what one remembers about them [Carr's stories] is never the people, only the puzzle," generally some variant of the not just "locked" but hermetically sealed room mystery where the crime committed appears impossible. Strongly influenced by G.K. Chesterton (see above), Carr himself noted that "the miracle problem" was crime fiction's toughest problem (Murphy 82), and to carry off his plots he often exceeded the bounds of "fair play." Carr's principal detective is Dr. Gideon Fell; appearing first in *Hag's Nook* (1935), Fell is an amateur detective who, like Father Brown, tackles atmospherically gothic murders that seem to have been accomplished through supernatural means but really have rational solutions. In appearance, Fell resembles Chesterton, too, being 280 pounds, wheezy, cloaked and hatted, using two canes and sporting a "bandit-like" moustache. In the most respected of Fell's detective novels, like *The Three Coffins* (1935) and *The Crooked Hinge* (1938), Fell displays what historian S.T. Joshi calls an "atmosphere of half-controlled lunacy" (quoted by John C. Tibbetts in Herbert 29) and "a Chestertonian love of fair play, chivalry, and respect for the past" (*Ibid.*). Dr. Fell insists that the chief glory of the detective story is improbability, which a good reader desires most (Keating 55), especially in his country-house mystery outings like *In Spite of Thunder* (1960).

Josephine Bell, a British practicing physician, featured young Dr. David Wintringham primarily to set the scenes of fourteen detective novels between 1937 and 1958. Often partnering with his contemporary Inspector Steven Mitchell of Scotland Yard, Dr. Wintringham was also assisted by his wife and sounding board Jill. Bell also created retired physician Dr. Henry Frost, solving murders in his South-of-England village in two novels dated 1964 and 1968.

Oxford don Gervase Fen, created by Edmund Crispin (1921–1978), the pseudonym of Robert Bruce Montgomery, a respected English composer, carried on the Golden Age tradition in the comic vein of Wimsey and Appleby well into the 1970s, combining intricate plots with effervescent comedy, paying homage to John Dickson Carr not only with Fen's name, a deliberate echo of Dr. Gideon Fell's, but by mentioning Fell in Fen's first investigation, *The Case of the Gilded Fly* (1944), which was set in a theatrical milieu. Fen usually appears disheveled, eccentric, and absent-mindedly professorial, with a Fell-like tendency to avoid discussing clues, while insisting that he understands the case fully, leaving the reader oblivious until the end of the story (Murphy 175). In *The Moving Toyshop* (1946), Fen exercises an "ebullient charm" that Keating finds best described as "rococo," because its "sheer fancy" and "truly farcical exaggeration" overwhelms readers with pleasure (82).

Other writers of the Golden Age developed many variations for the genre. Freeman Wills Crofts (1879–1957), an Irish train engineer, created highly realistic Inspector Joseph ("Soapy Joe") French, a charmingly unpretentious convivial Irish detective "remarkable for his ordinariness" (Symons 105) who likes his drink and good company and plods through his cases, often indulging his author's passion for travel by train. Another realistically pedestrian sleuth is Henry Wade's (1887–1969) Chief Inspector Poole, competent enough at his work but stolidly unimaginative and classified by Symons as one of the "Humdrums" (282). Britisher John Rhode's (1884–1965) mathematician sleuth Dr. Lancelot Priestley resembles Dr. John Thorndyke in meticulously using scientific evidence, as does J.J. Connington's (1880–1947) Sir Clinton Driffield, who combines his aristocratic background with his profession as Chief Constable, solving complex puzzle-crimes in a fictitious English county.

Two British authors with legal backgrounds carried the upper-class Golden Age sleuth into the 1940s and 1950s. Cyril Hare (1900–1958) put his Oxford training as a barrister to use in his Francis Pettigrew novels, enlivening the fine points of English law with dry humor, as in his respected *The Wind Blows Death* (1949). Hare's friend, London solicitor Michael Gilbert (1912–   ), another founding member of the Detection Club, staunchly maintained the Golden Age tradition for five decades, often with his Inspector Hazelrigg, a realistic figure resembling Crofts's Inspector French. Hazelrigg first appeared in the locked-room mystery *Close Quarters* (1947). In the 1950s, Gilbert introduced Scotland Yard's Patrick Patrella, a half-Spanish ethnic detective whom Murphy calls "one of the least known great detectives in the genre" (205).

One notable Golden Age detective was not Anglo-Saxon at all. Rotund and appealing Charlie Chan, American Earl Derr Bigger's (1884–1933) fictional Hawaiian detective who combines his "Oriental intuition" with the "Scotland Yard method" of pursuing the "one essential clue." Chan helped correct the "evil Asian" stereotype popularized by Sax Rohmer (1883–1959) in Chinese master criminal Fu Manchu, pursued by Sir Denis Nayland Smith. American novelist John P. Marquand (1893–1960) dismissed Mr. Moto, his aristocratic, polished, gold-toothed Japanese detective, as his "literary disgrace" and said he wrote these mysteries only to provide shoes for his child, but they have outlasted most of Marquand's mainstream work. Beginning with *No Hero* (1935), Moto, a highly educated secret agent, linguist, and judo master, solved six cases all based on the same pattern, in which young American or European couples become entangled in international crimes.

Exquisite literary style puts Josephine Tey (1897–1952) in a class by herself. Tey's Scotland Yard Inspector Alan Grant debuted in *The Man in the Queue* (1929) and continued to solve intricate crimes for twenty-five years. Grant may have partially inspired Ngaio Marsh's Inspector Roderick Alleyn, but Grant appears more philosophical and reflective, especially in Tey's pièce de résistance, *The Daughter of Time* (1951), where Grant, hospitalized for a broken leg and bored to distraction, "solves" the sixteenth-century murder of the Princes in the Tower, absolving Richard III and pinning the crime on Henry VII. This novel, sometimes decried for "belonging to the past," achieved considerable popularity and received high praise from H.R.F. Keating, who lauded its ability to make readers think about truth (the "daughter of Time") "and how truth can be twisted...and will tend to stay twisted, whatever truth-tellers may do" (99–100).

America evolved its own share of notable truth-tellers using the detective mode. The name recognition generated by Brooklyn cousins Manfred Lee (1905–1971) and Frederic Dannay (1905–1982) in choosing "Ellery Queen" as both their joint pseudonym and the name of their fictional detective made that sleuth the best-known American detective in the 1930s and 1940s (Marvin Lachman, in Herbert 161). The name not only generated an enormous literary empire but also spawned prizes, radio shows, and the long-running *Ellery Queen's Mystery Magazine*.

Ellery Queen the detective first appears in *The Roman Hat Mystery* (1929), composed by the cousins as an entry in a writing contest. After they won the contest but lost the $7,500 prize when the sponsoring magazine was sold, they managed to sell the story elsewhere, and both "Ellery Queens" took off. In Queen's initial appearances, he resembles then-popular (and now decried) Philo Vance as an outwardly silly and inwardly bookish famous mystery writer and amateur sleuth; like Lord Peter Wimsey, he indulges his powerful intelligence with rare books and cases that present tough puzzles, and like Sherlock Holmes, Queen utilizes both relentless logic and dazzling intuition. Early in his fictional career, Queen also acts as an occasionally condescending consultant to his father, NYPD Inspector Richard Queen. They live together in an Upper East Side Manhattan brownstone, waited on by their young servant Djuna, a formerly homeless orphan boy. Languid and self-consciously artsy in his debut, by his second, *The French Powder Mystery* (1930), Queen the detective has muscled up and now employs terse, enigmatic utterances, a symptom of the authors' often praised ability to change and adapt their character over the long series. Queen the detective underwent another dramatic change with *The Egyptian Cross Mystery* (1932), and in *Halfway House* (1936), he became a three-dimensional character.

When Queen the authors shifted to Hollywood to work as "idea men," Queen the detective did, too. Bruce Murphy finds *The Devil to Pay* and *Four of Hearts* (both 1938) "funnier and snappier," with rapid-fire 1930s film dialogue and leaner writing (412), indications of Queen the character's further growth. Queen the authors took their leading man a step further yet in the last phase of his development, the New England "Wrightsville" novels that began with *Calamity Town* (1942), chosen by H.R.F. Keating for his *Crime and Mystery: The 100 Best Books*. The mature Queen the detective has given up his show-off habits, becoming more practical, more involved with others' welfare, and less concerned with physical clues as he applies his broad knowledge of psychology and religion (Lachman, in Herbert 161). Keating praises Queen's "fresh phrases," "truth-telling observations," and "felicities" that distinguish a book as "a true novel" (67).

Early in the 1930s, American authors Rex Stout (1886–1975) and Erle Stanley Gardner (1889–1970) pursued truth in detection through variations on the Great Detective theme epitomized by Sherlock Holmes. H.R.F. Keating claims that Stout produced the last of the Great Detectives, while Gardner jammed "the final nail into the coffin of the brilliant amateur sleuth in American crime writing" (57, 47), paving the way for "hard-boiled" detectives, America's first major contribution to the genre since Poe.

Rex Stout's detectives Nero Wolfe and his sidekick Archie Goodwin have been called "the most successful detective team in American mystery fiction" (Edward D. Hoch in Herbert 187). "Born" in October 1933, the same month as Stout's daughter, 270-pound gourmandizing recluse Nero Wolfe physically resembles Sherlock Holmes's shadowy and lazy spook-running brother Mycroft. Wolfe has been described as "the most eccentric fictional sleuth to stay this side of being human" (Keating 57). Wolfe fancies rare orchids and beer, rarely leaves his New York brownstone on West 35th Street, and employs wisecracking Archie Goodwin for legwork and comic relief. Stout expanded Goodwin's Watsonian sounding-board duties to include "the sorts of things a California private eye does" (Keating 58), providing a valuable contrast to Wolfe's eccentricities. Goodwin is later joined by operatives Saul Panzer, Fred Durkin, and Orrie Cather, but Wolfe does all the heavy thinking behind their investigations.

Wolfe's first case, *Fer-de-Lance* (1935), established his *modus operandi*: between tending the 10,000 orchids in his fourth-floor conservatory and devouring luscious gourmet meals produced by his private chef, Wolfe directs Goodwin's investigations, interviews clients, strategizes the capture of villains, and summons the parties involved to his office for a culminating performance highlighting his brilliant methods. Wolfe's grouchiness, his highly intellectual reading, his irrational refusal to ride in a mechanized vehicle, and his physical laziness add up to extreme eccentricity, but his deductive talent places him firmly in the ranks of "genius detectives." Though Wolfe likes to keep his antecedents murky, one theory suggests that his father was Sherlock Holmes and his mother was Irene Adler, the only woman, according to Conan Doyle, to have outwitted the Great Detective. During World War I, Wolfe served in an intelligence unit of the Montenegrin Army, later walked 600 miles to join the American Expeditionary Force, and in 1930 bought his New York home and hired Goodwin as his right-hand man.

In *Too Many Crooks* (1938), Wolfe announced, "I entrap criminals, and find evidence to imprison them or kill them, for hire," revealing the tough core beneath the mounds of well-nourished flesh he's put on since his Nazi-slaying days. From the start Wolfe relishes his ability to make the guilty do themselves in, and he also embodies some of Stout's own strident political views, as in *The Second Confession* (1949), where Wolfe's pursuit of a suspected communist turns into a duel with Arnold Zeck, Wolfe's analogue to Holmes's nemesis Professor Moriarty.

As H.R.F. Keating has pointed out, Wolfe differs in one major respect from the British Great Detectives: they pursue criminals primarily for the love of the chase or because of a chivalric ogre-hunting obsession. Wolfe works for money, and this gives "just a thin lining of steel" to his otherwise beer-inflated flesh (Keating 58), an authentically American profit motive that presages the hard-boiled native-born American detectives to come.

Erle Stanley Gardner's lawyer-sleuth Perry Mason, by some claimed to be the most famous mystery series character since Sherlock Holmes (Murphy 334), appears in eighty-six breathlessly-paced novels, numerous short stories, eight 1930s films, a 1940s radio program, nine seasons (1957–1966) of a perennially rerun television series starring Raymond Burr, and twenty-six made-for-television movies that continued from 1985 until Burr died in 1993. Drawn from Gardner's own twenty-plus years as a practicing attorney in California and his meticulous research into forensics, Mason is "big, not the bigness of fat, but the bigness of strength . . . broad-shouldered and rugged-faced, and his eyes were steady and patient" (quoted in Keating 48). Mason is assisted by his loyal and efficient secretary Della Street and his sidekick Paul Drake, who operates a Los Angeles private detective agency. Beginning with *The Case of the Sulky Girl* (1933), they solve murder cases according to one single formula: Della Street ushers in a prospective client. Mason questions the client and a murder emerges, with the client under grave suspicion. To protect the client and unmask the real killer, Mason uses evidence nosed out by Drake, maneuvering on the brink of legality to preserve the client from the teeth-clenching clutches of Lieutenant Tragg. The novels typically end with Mason proving his client innocent in the courtroom, "after a display of legal pyrotechnics" that halts District Attorney Hamilton Burger dead in his tracks and forces the killer to convict himself/herself on the witness stand (Henry Kratz, in Herbert 127).

Most commentators agree that Gardner's early Perry Mason novels are his best. Gardner had come to the Mason novels from the pulp pages of *Black Mask* magazine, whose 1926–1936 editor Captain Joseph T. Shaw insisted that in contrast to the work of the Golden Age British writers, "action is meaningless unless it involves recognizable human characters in three-dimensional form" (quoted in Symons 144). Gardner's millions of fans found his formulaic novels satisfying because in each one Perry and Della and Drake, all recognizable three-dimensional characters, deliver honest, satisfyingly secure entertainment with a closing moral and a happy ending.

Two other notable American authors used "legal eagles" as detective heroes, combining humorous elements with tough-guy tactics that presage tougher crime novels to come. Anthony Gilbert (1899–1973) (pen name of Lucy B. Malleson) wrote fifty novels featuring energetic and rumpled redheaded lawyer Arthur Crook, who uses his wiles to defend distressed maidens of any age; in fact, his favorite age for a lady is fifty: "they don't get their sense much younger, and sense is what I'm lookin' for now" (quoted in Nichols and Thomson 147). Craig Rice (1908–1957) (pen name of Georgiana Craig) first ghostwrote *The G-String Murders* (1941) and *Mother Finds a Body* (1942) for stripper Gypsy Rose Lee, then invented the Chicago attorney John J. Malone, who boasted he'd never lost a case while solving crimes and keeping his clients out of jail. His associates Jake and Helene Justus "add the comic dash which keeps these from being hard-boiled crime tales" (Nichols and Thompson 148). As A.A. Fair, Gardner created another successful series, running from 1939 to 1970 and featuring suave law school reject Donald Lam as an elegant foil to brassy and grasping Bertha Cool, who runs her own detective agency "like a hard-boiled steamroller," one of the first of her case-hardened kind in the genre.

THE HARD-BOILED DICKS

In the United States during the 1920s, overproduction of goods, high tariffs, and war-debt government policies curtailed foreign markets, and too-liberal credit expansion led to unrealistic stock market speculation. After the market crashed in 1929, the United States experienced the Great Depression, a decade of falling prices, restricted credit, lowered production, and widespread bankruptcies and unemployment that led to emotional and social pain, an upsurge in crime and corruption, and even widespread panic. In the depth of the Great Depression, 1933, sixteen million people—a third of the U.S. labor force—were out of work. The American economic disaster affected Europe, where it contributed to the rise of Adolf Hitler, and England, where Dorothy L. Sayers saw the mystery field changing rapidly in response to the distressed economy, with new "popularity and respectability" that she said came close to alarming its friends. In 1931, she observed that mystery novels were becoming larger to provide more escape from miserable economic hardships, and she was certain that someone—she was working on it herself—would invent a new mystery formula to merge detection with psychological analysis. Thus she accurately predicted coming developments in the genre by P.D. James, Minette Walters, Ruth Rendell, and many other British women writers.

Psychological emphasis in the detective novel was growing in America as well. In 1930, an American, Helen Reilly (1891–1962), daughter of the president of Columbia University, invented Inspector McKee, a New York City policeman who resembles a British detective in manner and method. Reilly combined romantic suspense with elements of what later would be termed the police procedural novel. Another American, Helen McCloy (1904–1994), made her tall, handsome, and intellectual psychiatrist Dr. Basil Willing an adviser to the New York district attorney's office and pioneered the exploration of psychology, superstitions, and the paranormal in the classic mystery mold. Like Willing, Canadian author Margaret Millar (1915–   ) made her first sleuth, Dr. Paul Prye, a psychiatrist working in Golden Age–type novels of manners. Prye's specialty was child psychology, which allowed Millar to probe young mentalities where fiction and fantasy merge, and her subsequent work, where Millar experimented with the police procedural, the suspense novel, the historical mystery, and the horror novel among others, focused on the mysteries of the mind. Symons claims that Millar—the wife of Kenneth Millar, who wrote under the name "Ross Macdonald,"—had "few peers, and no superior, in the art of bamboozlement" (206).

While female mystery authors, mostly British but including some Americans and Canadians, were sensitively and generally tastefully writing their way out of the Golden Age detection-cum-comedy of manners by means of psychological investigations and police procedurals, a new breed of American male writers was slamming out flimsy and cheap wood-pulp paper magazines that had sprung up during World War I, initially using mostly British detective material. By the mid-twenties, the "pulps" had begun to target America's large working-class audience by featuring the "hard-boiled" U.S. "private eye," whose popularity "reflected the rise of the gangster in American society with the coming of Prohibition in 1920 and its accompanying civic and police corruption" (Symons 144).

Black Mask magazine, founded by the literary critic H.L. Mencken and theatre critic George Jean Nathan and published from 1920 to 1951, was especially instrumental in developing the quintessentially American hard-boiled detective story. The acerbic Mencken had gotten into this project only to make money, and he sold the magazine after only six months, calling it "a louse." The magazine had debuted Carroll John Daly's (1889–1958) Race Williams, tough, cynical, and psychologically grungy, considered the first "hardboiled dick." Williams carried two .44's, reveled in violence, claiming "You can't make hamburger without grinding up a little meat," and expressed himself in language "pungent as cigar smoke or garlic" (Symons 144). Williams was sure his victims deserved what he gave them, and his lurid dealings with his female nemesis, a lethal redhead, prefigure Mike Hammer's sadistic treatment of women.

Joseph T. Shaw, *Black Mask*'s editor from 1926 to 1936, helped his authors perfect the hard-boiled type of detective. As well as cultivating Erle Stanley Gardner (under a pen name) who went on to Perry Mason's more civilized cases, Shaw fostered Dashiell Hammett and Raymond Chandler, the first "greats" of hard-boiled detective fiction, as well as many lesser but then highly popular writers. Shaw demanded stripped-down prose, the rougher physical action the better, and convincing three-dimensional characters (Symons 144).

As the hero of (arguably) the archetypal private-eye novel, *The Maltese Falcon* (1930), Dashiell Hammett's (1894–1961) cold and cunning Sam Spade, whom Somerset Maugham called "a nasty bit of goods," became an American folk hero, a self-described "blond satan" with a hooked nose and cruel V-shaped face. In Spade, Hammett developed a harsh "code of honor" subsequently built into most fictional hard-boiled private eyes. H.R.F. Keating has remarked that Spade is oblivious to any kind of sentiment or softness, unafraid of death, unfettered by the desire for wealth, and unaffected by "the lure of sex," even strip-searching lissome Brigid O'Shaughnessy without a twinge of desire (41). Spade demonstrates his own kind of frontier morality by "doing something" about the death of his partner, a man he didn't even like, but he doesn't bother to look at the body before police remove it. Spade's inflexible code insists he take revenge even if he has to betray a woman he loves, a "two-edged sword, one side of which is always cutting" (Murphy 462).

While he was writing for *Black Mask*, Hammett also created The Continental Op, a nameless detective employed by the Continental Detective Agency, modeled on the Pinkerton Agency where Hammett had worked for eight years. The Op is short, obese, ruthless, and like Spade, unaffected by feminine wiles, telling one hopeful seductress, "You think I'm a man and you're a woman. That's wrong. I'm a man-hunter and you're something that's been running in front of me. There's nothing human about it" (quoted in George Kelly, Herbert 39). He gives his loyalty, totally devoid of sentiment, to his agency and colleagues. His method is to "stir things up," so that crooks can destroy each other. If they don't, he will—ruthlessly.

Other *Black Mask* writers reinforced Hammett's view of the American detective as a violent, often remorseless figure. George Harmon Coxe (1901–1984) initiated the photographer-journalist sleuth with his sloppy tough guy Flashgun Casey, who works for a Boston newspaper, and followed him with a tamer photographer, Kent Murdock, and later Jack Fenner, a Boston PI. Raoul Whitfield (1898–1945) emulated Hammett's use of violence in his early ethnic detective Jo Gar and featured former Sing Sing inmate (wrongly convicted) Mal Ourney, who poses as a newspaperman in Whitfield's first novel, *Green Ice* (1930). Lester Dent (1904?–1959) created Doc Savage, who merged elements of mystery, science fiction, and suspense in his adventures, and Paul Cain, also a Hollywood writer, favored bloody shootouts and stomach-wrenching assaults.

Not a *Black Mask* contributor but a contemporary author also noted for fictional sex and violence, journalist James M. Cain (1892–1977), no relation to Paul Cain, produced the sensational *The Postman Always Rings Twice* (1934), which Nobel Prize winner Albert Camus claimed influenced his novel *The Stranger*. Praised by Edmund Wilson as the best of "the poets of the tabloid murder," Cain also wrote *Double Indemnity* (1943), a "perfect murder" case later adapted for the screen by Raymond Chandler, who nonetheless called Cain "a Proust in greasy overalls." W.R. Burnett (1899–1982) created the first gangster novel, *Little Caesar* (1929), capturing the essence of the Prohibition-era crook. He also wrote *The Asphalt Jungle* (1949), a "caper story," with a gang of criminals working together to accomplish a complex, near-impossible crime. Both novels became highly successful films and influenced later popular literature, cinema, and television. Another popular author, reclusive and alcoholic Cornell Woolrich, produced a series of crime novels including the work "black" in each title. Though he did not feature a series detective, Woolrich's work involved themes of vengeance, terror, guilt, and obsession common to the hard-boiled subgenre. His novel *Rear Window* was superbly filmed by Alfred Hitchcock. Women authors did not trespass on the testosterone-fueled world of the fictional private eye until Gale Gallagher, pen name of Margaret Scott and Will Oursler as well as the name of the principal character, appeared as female head of the Acme Investigation Bureau in two novels written in 1947 and 1949.

Mickey Spillane (b. 1918), whose Mike Hammer is reputedly the toughest tough guy in fiction, carried the violent PI initiated by Hammett to a sadistic and simplistic extreme. In his debut novel *I, the Jury* (1947), Hammer casually gut-shoots a woman, then as she is dying tells her, "It was easy." Spillane carried the formula of equal parts vengeance, violence, and sex through an enormously lucrative series; *Kiss Me Deadly* (1952) became the first mystery novel to achieve the *New York Times* bestseller list. James L. Traylor and Max Allan Collins somewhat idealistically believe that in Mike Hammer Spillane "captured the psyche of America, from its loss of innocence after World War II to the late 1980s loss of purpose and directions. His books offer a savagely lyrical depiction of the wounded American soul" (in Herbert 185). Other commentators feel that such violence, even if it appears horrifyingly commonplace in popular literature, films, videos, and computer games, "says more about the values of today than it does about Hammer" (Murphy 229). A *Publishers Weekly* review (October 6, 2003) of Spillane's most recent stand-alone effort, *Something's Down There*, praises "this enjoyable flashback to an earlier age," citing the Spillanean hero's familiar bloody grudge: "he wished he had been packing his .45 . . . so he could turn and shoot her guts right out of her beautiful belly." Ugh.

Jonathan Latimer's (1906–1983) hard-drinking Bill Crane bridges Hammett's Continental Op and Raymond Chandler's Philip Marlowe. Latimer's interest in the offbeat and the macabre inspired his first Crane novel, *Murder in the Madhouse* (1934), where Crane, an operative for a New York detective agency, inveigles himself into a mental institution as a patient. In this boozy series, even the bulldog Champion who assists in the investigations keeps up with his human comrades in imbibing whisky, but Crane's drinking doesn't seem to stop him from amassing clues and practicing classical deduction, even when faced with a locked-room case in *Headed for a Hearse* (1935). Brett Halliday's (1904–1977) Mike Shayne (also spelled Shane) has appeared in over seventy novels and hundreds of short stories, continuing, ghostwritten, after Halliday's death. On the "wrong side of thirty," Shayne is a big raw-boned red-headed "semi-hard boiled" loner, hard on Martell's cognac, easily tempted by the ladies, and displaying many personality traits familiar from characters in both Hammett's work and Raymond Chandler's.

Chandler (1988–1959), who sold his first story, "Blackmailers Don't Shoot," to *Black Mask* in 1933, had much higher aims for the mystery genre and his series hero Philip Marlowe. Referring to Rex Stout, Ngaio Marsh, and Agatha Christie as "smooth and shallow operators," he insisted in his 1944 *Atlantic Monthly* essay "The Simple Art of Murder" that the Golden Age mystery, which he found unrealistic and false in action and character, made real people "do unreal things in order to form the artificial pattern required by the plot." He felt that Hammett's hard-boiled detective stories genuinely reflect real life: "Hammett gave murder back to the kind of people that commit it for reasons, not just to provide a corpse; and with the means at hand, not hand-wrought dueling pistols, curare and tropical fish" (quoted in Murphy 93, 455). Starting with *The Big Sleep* (1939), Marlowe, whom Chandler envisioned as resembling Cary Grant more than Humphrey Bogart, the unforgettable screen version of Marlowe, is thirty-three, attractive, and single, not marrying Linda Loring until *Poodle Springs*, finished by Robert B. Parker and published in 1989, thirty years after Chandler's death. Fired for insubordination from his job as a D.A.'s investigator in Los Angeles County, Marlowe, a classical music–loving loner, winds up working and living by himself in minimal scruffy surroundings, a tough-talking, wisecracking PI addicted to Camels and any kind of booze available.

Chandler's credo stated simply that down the mean streets a man must go who is not mean himself. He also gave Philip Marlowe a conscience: "If I wasn't hard, I wouldn't be alive. If I couldn't ever be gentle, I wouldn't deserve to be alive." Marlowe's method of detection is basically pragmatic; he listens and observes and often is beaten up for doing so. Chandler called him "a good enough man for any world." As David Rife has observed, Marlowe's name alludes to quintessential Renaissance man Sir Philip Sidney, Elizabethan playwright Christopher Marlowe, and

Joseph Conrad's shadowy narrator Marlowe. Chandler had originally intended to name his hero "Mallory," a reference to the chivalric tradition seen in Sir Thomas Malory's fifteenth-century *Morte d'Arthur*, because for Chandler Philip Marlowe is the genuine knightly hero, serving others at his own risk and pursuing justice and truth (David Rife, in Herbert 124).

First appearing in Canadian Ross Macdonald's (1915–1983) short fiction, Southern California PI Lew Archer, who often works divorce cases, made his novel debut in *The Moving Target* (1948), a novel using Marlowesque fast-paced hard-boiled action and crackling dialogue. Archer and Marlowe intrinsically differ, however. Marlowe solves his cases as a romantic hero fighting external dragons, while Archer proves his own moral courage by struggling to remain true to his values in a world that seeks to smother the individual. Larry Landrum sees Archer springing from the hard-boiled *Black Mask* school of mystery fiction, but then evolving into "the prototypical figure of the Vietnam and Watergate years" (Herbert 10). Though Archer can take a punch with the toughest private dicks, he gradually comes to rely more on talk than on his fists, interrogating less by physical intimidation than through subtly encouraging witnesses and suspects to reveal hidden matters crucial to the crime's solution. Archer believes that "every witness has his own way of creeping up on the truth" and that it's his job to ease it out of them.

In using the detective form to uncover psychological truths, Macdonald also employed a circular Nietzschean view of character and time. Lew Archer describes it in *The Doomsters* (1958): "an alternating current of guilt ran between her and all of us involved with her . . . in a closed circuit," and "it isn't possible to brush people off, let alone yourself. They wait for you in time, which is also a closed circuit." Hence Archer shares Everyman's guilt and Everyman's mortality, and his later stories "are all variations on the theme of the discovered past" controlled by Archer's presence (Symons 205). Though many believe that the pure hard-boiled detective novel ended with Hammett, Chandler, and Ross Macdonald, Julian Symons sees both Roger L. Simon's (1943–   ) Jewish detective Moses Wine, functioning in the turbulent 1960s, and Robert B. Parker's (1932–   ) long-lived Spenser (see below) as "lineal descendants" of the hard-boiled greats, especially Chandler (206). Other private investigators like Lawrence Block's Matt Scudder (see below) might be described as "atoning" for "some of the things the dicks of the hard-boiled era didn't know they were supposed to feel bad about" (Murphy 444).

PROCEDURAL POLICE

While much British mystery fiction was still moving from comedy of manners and social satire toward psychological analysis, and hard-hitting U.S. lawyers and PIs were tackling criminals head-on, the police procedural emerged in 1952 with American Hillary Waugh's (1920–   ) *Last Seen Wearing*. (In *Bloody Murder*, Julian Symons offers a helpful extended comparison of the crime novel and the detective novel [191–93]). Writing about what they know best, former police detectives frequently become authors of procedural novels, using police—male or female—as leading characters and basing stand-alone novels and detective series on their own experiences. Realistic police work, "procedure," forms the major action, so converging plot lines become the paramount feature of procedural fiction (Murphy 404). In *Sleep Long, My Love* (1969) Waugh introduced his first series protagonist, Fred Fellows, a rural police chief in a fictional Connecticut town, founding the "rural policeman/woman" form later pursued by several mystery authors. While most perform deadly serious work, others, like British M.C. Beaton's Hamish Macbeth and American Joan Hess's Arly Hanks (see below), produce riotously funny results. Waugh subsequently developed the Manhattan Homicide North series using a group of police colleagues as a collective protagonist, foreshadowing Ed McBain's 87th Precinct novels and popular television series like *Hill Street Blues* and *NYPD Blue*.

Since the early 1950s, procedural novels have become highly popular in both Britain and the United States, including both metropolitan and provincial (British) and regional (American) police work. After Waugh, British procedural authors include Maurice Procter, (1906–1973), a former policeman who in 1953 introduced Inspector Martineau of fictional Granchester, a gritty manufacturing North of England city where he battles underworld boss Dixie Costello. Edgar winner John Creasey (1908–1973) debuted George Gideon, head of Scotland Yard's Criminal Investigation Division, in *Gideon's Day* (1955), and later Yorkshire West Riding policeman John Wainwright (1921–), who also writes classic British mysteries, used a collective police protagonist, featuring diverse characters in various novels of his procedural series, such as Chief Superintendent Robert Blayde in *Landscape with Violence*, 1975.

Some female British authors, too, like Margaret Erskine and Georgette Heyer (see above) had already begun to veer toward the procedural. E.C.R. Lorac's forty-seven novels between 1931 and 1959 starred "Macdonald," a Scotland Yard detective and "a humane man ... [who has] never forgotten that a criminal may suffer, and the sight of intense suffering is ill for any human man to witness" (quoted from Lorac in Nichols and Thompson 1, 37). Christianna Brand's Inspector Cockrill (known as "Cockie") of the Kent Constabulary, appearing in eight books between 1941 and 1968, uses his native-son knowledge of his area to solve "pure puzzle" cases. "He was widely advertised as having a heart of gold beneath his irascible exterior," but some said one had to dig so deeply to find that tiny heart it wasn't worth the trouble (quoted from Brand in Nichols and Thompson 52). Yet another red-haired detective, Mary Fitt's Superintendent Mallett, uses a variety of methods to solve his cases from 1938 to 1959. " 'He's a good man—a dangerous customer, because he's unorthodox in his approach, and yet he looks so much like a policeman that people are apt to underrate him' " (quoted in Nichols and Thompson 53).

American women also began to write effective procedurals in the early 1940s. Lange Lewis (Jane Baynon) featured Los Angeles Homicide Squad detective Richard Tuck in five novels between 1942 and 1952. Some of his jealous colleagues called six-five Tuck "The Moose," or "a queer duck," because he refused to arrest without substantial evidence (Nichols and Thompson 1, 24). Considerably later, Dell Shannon (Elizabeth Linington, 1921–1988) became known as "The Queen of Police Procedurals," producing four long-running procedural series under various pen names. As "Dell Shannon," she created the LAPD's instinctive and painstaking

Lieutenant Luis Mendoza, beginning the vogue for ethnic detectives with a hero "passionately concerned to bring some order and reason, some ultimate shape to the chaos" (quoted from Shannon in Nichols and Thompson 1, 28). As "Lesley Egan," Shannon produced two series respectively starring Detective Vic Varello of suburban Los Angeles and Jesse Falkenstein, a lawyer; and under her own name, she created Hollywood detective Sergeant Ivor Maddox. Dorothy Uhnak (1933–), herself a former decorated member of the New York City Transit Police, created detective Christie Opara, appearing first in *The Bait* (1968), hailed by Anthony Boucher as the first policewoman procedural. Opara's British counterpart is Charmian Daniels, heroine of Jennie Melville's eight procedural novels written between 1962 and 1981, "one of the few fictional female police officers (in this period) . . . who is both English and provincial" (Nichols and Thompson 1, 54).

Police procedurals were also appearing in Europe and the Orient, but the attitudes of these police figures differed considerably from those of British policemen, who usually maintained their traditional stiff upper lips and dedication to "England, my England," and from American cops who, initially at least, delivered justice and sometimes vengeance with the relish of Old West lawmen. Europe's post–World War I suffering affected the development of police procedurals there, primarily because the punitive reparations inflicted on Germany by France and Britain and the Great Depression in the United States created economic conditions virtually assuring the rise of dictators Hitler and Mussolini and the eventual outbreak of World War II in 1939. Out of the Roaring Twenties and the Threatening Thirties came European Existentialism, an angst-ridden philosophical system full of debilitation and despair, in which everything depends on the individual's relation to the universe or to God. Whereas the Danish philosopher Søren Kierkegaard took the Christian stance that the individual must make a subjective commitment each time he or she faces an ethical or religious demand, French philosopher and author Jean-Paul Sartre believed that existence precedes essence; and that since there is no God and no fixed human nature, the individual is completely free and completely responsible for the choices he or she makes, a condition that fills him or her with dread and anguish. Often European authors use the police procedural—where police methods are uppermost and realistic action sometimes joins with unrealistic characters—as their vehicle for detectives who work within a framework of social pressures causing them to sympathize or even identify with the criminals they hunt.

Georges Simenon (1903–1989), a contemporary of the European existentialists, probed the plight of the individual alienated from society and found societal pressures responsible for the crimes that he portrays in his fiction. Incredibly prolific, Simenon wrote several hundred books selling a half-billion copies in his lifetime. His series featuring Inspector Jules Maigret of the Paris Sûreté opened with *M. Gallet decédé* (*The Death of Monsieur Gallet*) (1931) and ended with *Maigret et Monsieur Charles* (*Maigret and Monsieur Charles*) (1972). Maigret, appearing in over seventy novels and two dozen short stories, became famous worldwide, the best known of detectives created by post–World War I European authors.

At first Simenon heavily seasoned his quickly churned out Maigret novels with sensationalism in the pulp *Black Mask* tradition, but he also made the persistent and unpredictable Maigret, sometimes called the Sherlock Holmes of European detectives, rely heavily on intuition. Maigret, a "provincial" born in central France and a former medical student in Nantes, rose from patrolling the Paris streets on a bicycle to eventually becoming the Sûreté's equivalent of a divisional chief inspector. He lives with his wife in the Boulevard Richard-Lenoir and has a chilly office in the Quai des Orfevres; like Holmes, Maigret smokes a famous pipe, wears a famous hat and overcoat, and has an "official family," in Maigret's case comprised of his colleague Coméliau, the examining magistrate, and three assistants, Lucas, Janvier, and Lapointe. In the first group of stories, which Simenon wrote during the dismal years 1931–1934, Maigret sympathizes with criminals often forced into their crimes by economic disasters beyond their control. Maigret works through psychological explorations of character in a Parisian atmosphere that strangely both repels and attracts, livened occasionally by a flash of self-deprecating humor. After an eight-year hiatus, Simenon resurrected Maigret, but some commentators feel the 1948–1972 novels tend to ramble, with a more sinister and complex vision of the world that causes Maigret finally to turn down the post of head of the *Police Judiciare* and retire again.

Julian Symons sees Maigret's gifts as a sleuth most clearly in 1949's *My Friend Maigret*. These include the talent for "absorbing like a sponge" people's natures and an ability to conceal behind his enjoyment of local gourmet delights a "capacity for interpreting behavior, Maigret's greatest asset as a detective (157–58). In *Maigret's Memoirs* (1950), Simenon traces Maigret's mature professional successes to charming details of Maigret's biography and reveals the relationship between himself as author and Maigret as his creation.

Simenon's Maigret strongly influenced Nicholas Freeling (1927–), an English author and culinary expert whose long residence on the Continent might almost qualify him as a spiritual European. Freeling's Inspector Piet Van der Valk of the Amsterdam police appeared first in *Death in Amsterdam* (1962) before Freeling killed him off several novels later, only to make his widow and crime-solving partner Arlette Van der Valk the heroine of a whole new series. Piet Van der Valk resembles Maigret in his sympathy for those forced into criminal activity by societal pressures, but as a product of the postwar world, Van der Valk rejects idealism as "a drug that wears off quickly" and describes himself as "a poor sod of a policeman" who has to have an audience to help him think through his conclusions. These attitudes reflect social concerns of Freeling's that often seem to make his fiction veer toward polemics. More recent detectives also make Amsterdam their beat, notably Dutch authors Jan Willem Van de Wetering's Adjutant Grijpstra and Sergeant de Gier series and Baantjer's Inspector Jurrian DeKok (see below).

Dutchman Robert Van Gulik (1910–1967) grew up in Java, served in the Dutch diplomatic corps, mastered many Oriental languages, and developed a Chinese detective, Judge Dee, based on an eighth-century Chinese district magistrate who appears in a seventeenth-century Chinese work that Van Gulik, an antiquarian book collector, translated in 1949 (see above). Van Gulik went on to create popular Judge Dee novels of his own, beginning with *The Chinese Bell Murders* (1951). Van Gulik wanted to reinvigorate contemporary mystery literature by reviving the ancient

Chinese detective story, which dealt with middle- and lower-class characters rather than the aristocrats so dear to many Golden Age writers. These Chinese stories, however, were not whodunits but moral fables with strong supernatural elements (Murphy 507). The powerful and influential Judge Dee acts as a police detective with judicial authority and he is backed up not only by the Emperor, but by the judge's coterie of admirers, all reformed criminals. As opposed to metaphysical Buddhists, Dee is a pragmatic follower of Confucius who acts paternally toward others. Those foreigners, including non-Chinese Orientals, who appear in his stories are usually villains.

Japan boasts authors who have explored the detective genre from a perspective on crime and punishment that usually strikes Westerners as exotic, chilling, and sometimes enthralling. Seicho Matsumoto (1909–1992) began writing crime novels at forty and twice won Japan's highest literary honor, the Akutagama Literary Prize, as well as the Japanese Mystery Writers' Prize. His Inspector Imanishi, a fatigued middle-aged classic loner detective, follows Japanese cultural norms in refusing to announce leads because if they prove wrong, he will "lose face." For the same reason, he also claims that his investigational travels are "vacations" because he doesn't want to be paid for this work if it doesn't produce results. Imanishi's cases present several idiosyncratic themes: the effects of World War II on Japan, the traditional subjugation of women, oriental sexual customs, and variations among Japanese dialects (Murphy 263). Ellery Queen's *Japanese Golden Dozen* (1978) includes stories by Matsumoto and Shizuko Natsuki (1938–), often called Japan's Agatha Christie. Masako Togawa (1933–), formerly a night club singer, has similarly been recognized as the P.D. James of Japan. Critics have praised both Natsuki and Togawa for their literary realism, but as Symons points out, Japanese and Western concepts of reality differ widely. Later authors with Oriental backgrounds, like Rei Shimura and Sujata Massey (see below), often use the tension between East and West as a principal theme in their work.

Tensions between black and white cultures in the United States became apparent in detective fiction as early as 1932's *The Conjure-Man* by African American author Rudolph Fisher, whose hero was Harlem detective Perry Dart. Black detectives as minor figures appeared through the 1930s to the late 1940s, but a significant shift occurred when Hughes Allison made his Detective Joe Hill the protagonist of the short story "Corollary," which appeared in *Ellery Queen's Mystery Magazine* for July 1948. About a decade later, while imprisoned for robbing a white home, black author Chester Himes (1909–1984) started to write novels based on his experience of the American judicial and prison systems, combining hard-boiled detective elements with social protest. Himes's *A Rage in Harlem* (1957) initiated a series starring black detectives Coffin Ed Johnson and Grave Digger Jones, decent men trying to do a tough job in an inimical world. Johnson and Jones do have a sympathetic white lieutenant, but mostly they, like the black criminals they pursue, are treated harshly and unfairly by whites, both in the police force and outside it—Himes's means of voicing his outrage against prejudice and injustice. Jerome Bader has remarked that with their dark suits, identical .38s, and their beat-up Plymouth sedan, Johnson, badly scarred by an acid attack, and his partner Jones give a new meaning to "black humor." They also "inspire fear, respect, and awe as do the 'bad men' of African American folklore. Like Chandler's 'lonely knight,' they are the best men in their world" (Herbert 108). Another of "the best men," black Pasadena homicide detective Virgil Tibbs, appears in John Dudley Ball's (1911–1988) widely praised novel *In the Heat of the Night* (1965). Tibbs, very conservative in dress and behavior, is the antithesis of George Baxt's (1923–) "flamboyant [black] homosexual detective Pharoah Love" (see below), who debuted in *A Queer Kind of Death* (1966), the first crime novel to feature a homosexual detective, and "his hip successor Satan Stagg," appearing first in 1968's *Topsy and Evil* (Frankie Y. Bailey in Herbert 5).

Novels and series dealing with the tensions experienced by gay and lesbian detectives only begin to appear after Greenwich Village's Stonewall Riots in 1969. Until then, gay and lesbian figures were often used as particularly nasty villains like Vera Findlater in Sayers's *Unnatural Death* (1927), weak victims, or, in the case of Mickey Spillane, objects of offensive derogatory comments and taunts (David C. Wallace, in Herbert 81). Joseph Hansen's (1923–) Dave Brandstetter series, first to center on a gay detective character, began in 1970 (see below).

Humor springing from silly social customs was integral to the Golden Age mysteries and their Bertie Woosterish detectives, but with time different kinds of humor began to appear in detective novels, like the "black humor" noted above. Julian Symons aptly notes that Golden Age writers involved themselves emotionally in their work, while the crime writers he classes as "entertainers" do not, leaving them free to treat new subjects "lightly and amusingly" (223). As the pen name of Mary Jane Latsis (1917?–) and Martha Henissart (1927–1997), who worked in economics and banking respectively and like Carolyn Heilbrun (Amanda Cross) had to keep their identities secret for a long time because of possible job reprisals, "Emma Lathan" wielded a sharp satiric scalpel in the 1960s, with a setting unusual for detective fiction at the time. Lathan's classy sleuth, John Putnam Thatcher, is a vice president of Sloan Guaranty Trust, a large investment banking concern, giving Lathan ample opportunity to skewer Wall Street bigwigs and their wheeler-dealer backstabbing with "shrewd and often funny descriptions" (Symons 223). Writers incorporating comic elements into detective fiction often develop self-deprecating central characters, like Peter Lovesey's Sergeant Cribb and H.R.F. Keating's Inspector Ghote, both of whom made well-accepted leaps into television (see below for both). Joyce Porter's (1924–1992) Chief Inspector Wilfred Dover, introduced in *Dover One* (1964), is "too fat, too shabby, and too surly looking...he had a paunch, chronic dyspepsia and acute dandruff...[and a] lowering heavy-jowled mug" (*Dover Goes to Pott*, 14–15). Dover also shoves most of his work off on his assistant Sergeant Macgregor. Two other convincing comic detective series feature Chief Constable Harcourt Chubb, the bumptious creation of Colin Watson (1920–1982), and James Hazell, an unflaggingly optimistic private detective set in the 1970s by P.B. Yuill (1939–) in the dismal depths of London's slums.

Yet another kind of humor, one brought to life in E.W. Hornung's gentleman thief Raffles (see above), delights readers looking for witty Robin Hoods who romantically squeak through the clutches of the law with their ideals intact, often rescuing maidens or avenging the innocent. Leslie Charteris (1907–1993) presented the charming rogue known as The Saint in the adventures of the Saint's alter ego, Simon Templar, taken to the heart of British mystery fans in the 1930s and continuing his dashing picaresque career well into the 1970s. Whereas Simon Templar is a two-dimensional crime-solving criminal, masterful author Patricia Highsmith's (1921–1995) murderous Tom Ripley can in no sense be called a detective. As an amoral killer lurking beneath a mild-mannered exterior, he is one of the most chilling creations in crime literature.

By the mid-1960s, that era of flower children, protest movements, and societal uproar, the once-spurned detective novel began to spread its wings. From its beginnings in the "pure puzzle" mode, through its American hard-boiled permutations and their procedural descendents, the detective novel has exploded worldwide, evolving into bold new permutations and combinations. A half-century later, "Crime fiction [has] produced as much fine literature as the literati," claimed Diamond Dagger winner Ellis Peters (quoted in Ashley 390). Some are "traditional" mysteries modeled on the classic British Golden Age form, pure puzzles with an intellectual and/or aristocratic sleuth and homicides often occurring in elegant country houses populated by suspects who never referred to a "Saturday to Monday" as a "weekend" because that would have implied they had to work for a living. Newer police procedurals and private eye novels are introducing women as canny, tough, and usually more intuitive than men, roaming America's mean streets and tartan *noir* back alleys as effectively as their male counterparts. Psychological mysteries are perceptively exploring strange areas of the unconscious; legal mysteries, academic mysteries, medical mysteries, forensic mysteries relentlessly uncover the talents and failings of their practitioners. Historical mysteries, many written by female scholars with impeccable academic credentials, pose eternal duels of good and evil in altogether fascinating past cultures, and ethnic and ecological detective stories insist that problems of diversity and the environment be faced squarely and call for redress of old grievances. Techno-thrillers look into an increasingly befuddling future; humorous crime stories make readers laugh so they won't cry over human frailties; romantic mysteries merge with "cozies," exploring areas like the culinary arts; and detectives are probing nonhuman psychology (canine, feline, equine, avian, even a detecting computer and a velociraptor disguised as a human sleuth); antiquarianism; Old Masters, classical music, drama; the stock market, journalism, geriatrics, and the religious life of every persuasion; while mystery settings leap from nearly every state in the union to all the continents of earth, inner psychological depths, and the far reaches of outer space. While civility lingers in quiet fictional villages, violence pervades gang mentalities and the warped personalities of serial killers; detective writers are revealing both extremes of human wickedness and every shade of vicissitude in between.

As they always have, readers today are searching the mystery racks for "a good book" to help make sense of a world that seems daily to become more chaotic. Despairing over "popularizing Philistines" can be all too easy, as Julian Symons put it in 1992: "Strip cartoons [are] becom[ing] more prevalent and be[ing] praised for gritty realism, more unsilenced lambs...raising their sado-masochistic cry" (325).

Better to recall the predictions laid down by Dorothy L. Sayers, that redoubtable old sibyl of the detective novel: "No really good writing can ever be permanently discredited.... The touch-stone [*sic*] is in the word mystery itself. Does the book, or does it not, strike that interior note of essential mysteriousness which is a part of the nature of things?" ("Present Status" 51–52). Today's writers of detective fiction are producing more and more "good books" that provide convincing glimpses of that "essential mysteriousness," at their best rivaling the mainstream in ingenuity, verisimilitude, perceptiveness, and downright good writing. Mysteries and the fictional detectives who solve them continue to unsettle us, intrigue us, impress us, amaze us, as they grapple with that eternal human problem: the mystery of wickedness.

WORKS CITED

Ashley, Mike. *The Mammoth Encyclopedia of Modern Crime Fiction*. New York: Carroll and Graf, 2002.

Briggs, Asa. *A Social History of England*. New York: Viking, 1983.

Dale, Alzina Stone. *Maker and Craftsman: The Story of Dorothy L. Sayers*. Grand Rapids, MI: William Eerdmans, 1978.

Gaillard, Dawson. *Dorothy L. Sayers*. New York: Ungar, 1981.

Herbert, Rosemary. *Whodunit? A Who's Who in Crime and Mystery Writing*. Oxford: Oxford University Press, 2003.

Hone, Ralph. *Dorothy L. Sayers: A Literary Biography*. Kent, OH: Kent State University Press, 1979.

Keating, H.R.F. *Crime and Mystery: The 100 Best Books*. New York: Carroll and Graf, 1987.

Mann, Jessica. *Deadlier Than the Male: Why Are Respectable English Women So Good at Murder?* New York: Macmillan, 1981.

Murphy, Bruce F. *The Encyclopedia of Murder and Mystery*. New York: St. Martin's Minotaur, 1999.

Sayers, Dorothy L. Introduction to *Great Short Stories of Detection, Mystery, and Horror*. London: Gollancz, 1928 (retitled *The Omnibus of Crime* in the United States).

———. "The Present Status of the Mystery Story." *London Mercury* 23 (November 1930): 47–52.

Symons, Julian. *Bloody Murder: From the Detective Story to the Crime Novel*. New York: Mysterious Press, 1972; 3rd rev. ed. 1992.

The Adept (Sir Adam Sinclair)

Profession:	Psychiatrist
Living situation:	Eligible bachelor
Geographic locale:	Scotland; the astral plane
Time period:	1991–1996
Associates:	Detective Chief Inspector Noel McLeod; Peregrine Lovat
Nemesis:	The occult Lodge of the Lynx
Significant relationship:	Dr. Ximena Lockhart
Concerns:	Eternal supernatural battle of the Light against Evil

The five-novel crossover Adept series blends the mystery genre with fantasy, the major field of both Kathleen Kurtz and Deborah Harris. The "Adept," Sir Adam Sinclair, a practicing Scots psychiatrist, also consults with the Lothian and Borders Police in Edinburgh in crimes involving occult forces. Sinclair is a powerful agent of the Light, the ruling principle of Divine Order, "enforced by groups of dedicated individuals formed into Hunting Lodges on the Inner Planes" (*Death of an Adept* 6). As Chief Master of Scotland's paranormal Hunting Lodge, Sinclair has dedicated himself to protecting the Light and exterminating agents of the dark forces, primarily the occult Lodge of the Lynx, that eternally threaten the Light. His closest allies are his Second in the Hunt, Detective Chief Inspector Noel McLeod, twenty-year veteran of the Lothian and Borders Police, craggy and solid like a block of Highland granite, and the youthfully slight and candidly observant portrait artist Peregrine Lovat (*Death of an Adept* 14), whose Gift of extrasensory Sight enables him to act as the Hunt's occult medium.

Introduced in *The Adept* (1991), Sinclair is an eligible aristocratic bachelor in his vigorous forties, a charismatic former fencer and dressage rider, elegant and severe, at once brilliantly intense and compassionate, with dark eyes capable of both "comforting warmth" and "sudden, formidable anger" (*The Adept* 17). He is also a reincarnated Knight Templar, the powerful medieval protectors of Solomon's Temple at Jerusalem, sworn in his modern form to uphold cosmic law ("The Light"). Both McLeod and Lovat are similarly reincarnated and sworn members of the brotherhood. Sinclair's base of operations is Strathmourne House, the Sinclair family seat, where he recognizes the Gift that troubles Peregrine and initiates him into its use to help the Hunt track its evil adversaries. Sinclair's long-time butler Humphrey and his medical colleague Dr. Matthew Fraser and his wife Lady Janet Fraser also appear throughout the series.

In *The Adept*, Sinclair, who has ancestral ties to the Knights Templar, draws on his "previous selves" to protect the Light from criminals who have stolen the Hepburn Sword of an alleged seventeenth-century wizard, the Earl of Bothwell, intending to use it in black arts. Adam's heart never doubts that "the Templars had pursued a course of single-minded devotion to the defense of hallowed ground and the guardianship of secret truths"; their real treasure is not gold but arcane knowledge (*The Adept* 50). After reclaiming the Hepburn Sword, Sinclair and his associates battle evil again in *The Lodge of the Lynx*, that malignant coven seeking to capture ancient Druidical relics with immense destructive powers. Sinclair and the Hunt save the Crown, Scepter, and Seal of Solomon in *The Templar Treasure*, and in *Dagger Magic* (1995) they overcome the *Plurba*, an unspeakable Dagger Cult from Tibet attempting to resurrect a new and demonic Third Reich with black magical texts found in the hulk of a sunken Nazi U-boat.

In each adventure, Sir Adam Sinclair experiences trances in which "the Master," an entity so perfected as to no longer need corporality, probes Sinclair's vocation. Sinclair's answers confirm his unflagging dedication to the Light. He consistently pursues "the trail of a troubled spirit" not to destroy, but to "give it peace." Having suffered burning martyrdom in a former Templar life when Philip IV of France attempted to suppress the Order, Sinclair reaffirms his acceptance of self-sacrifice in his present incarnation: "I will do whatever must be done. But knowledge must come first" (*Dagger Magic* 74–75). In *Death of an Adept* (1996), Sinclair on the eve of his wedding to surgeon Ximena Lockhart again faces the Nazi-bred black magician known in Tibetan legend as the Man with Green Gloves and his hench-creatures. Captured and drugged, Sinclair lies as a human sacrifice at a Black Mass when he senses the psychic presences of Noel McLeod and Peregrine Lovat, and sends up "a psychic shout through the blanketing miasma of evil" (*Death of an Adept* 408). After being rescued by the SAS, Sinclair offers himself to destroy the essence of evil that the Hunt and their Masonic supporters trap on the astral plane.

Following in the paranormal footsteps of detectives like Dame Beatrice Bradley, a consulting psychiatrist experienced in the "netherworld of folklore and mysticism" who appears in sixty-eight novels by Gladys Mitchell (1929–1984) and clairvoyant Edwina Charles in Mignon Wagner's seven books (1976–1985) (*Silk Stalkings* 2: 23), Sir Adam Sinclair combines the appeal of the sexily intellectual modern man of medicine with the time-transcending allure of the Templar knight in shining supernatural armor.

Novels: *The Adept* (1991); *The Lodge of the Lynx* (1992); *The Templar Treasure* (1993); *Dagger Magic* (1995); *Death of an Adept* (1996).

Stand-alone novel: *Lammas Night* (1983).

Other works: Kurtz is most famous for her Deryni novels, a fantasy dynastic-historical romance series, 1970–2000, featuring the created world of Gwynedd in the Eleven Kingdoms (roughly based on medieval Wales) in four trilogies plus other novels and short story collections. With Turner Harris, Kurtz also authored two other novels based on the Knights Templar, *The Temple and the Stone* (1998) and *The Temple and the Crown* (2001).

Selected sources: Clarke, Boden, and Mary A. Burgess. *The Work of Katherine Kurtz: An Annotated Bibliography and Guide.* San Bernardino, CA: Borgo Press, 1993; Gottschall, Faye H. Rev. of *The Templar Treasure. Voice of Youth Advocates*, October 1993: 230; Green, Roland. Rev. of *Death of an Adept. Booklist*, February 1, 2001: 643; Hoebeke, Mary Anne. Rev. of *Dagger Magic. Voice of Youth Advocates*, October 1995: 234; *Publishers Weekly*. Rev. of *The Templar Treasure*, June 21, 1993: 102.

Major awards (Kurtz): Edmund Hamilton Memorial Award, 1977; Balrog Award, 1982; named Dame Grand Officer of the Supreme Military Order of the Temple of Jerusalem; Dame of the Military and Hospitaller Order of St. Lazarus of Jerusalem; Dame of Honour of the Hospitaller Order of St. John of Jerusalem.

See also: Nancy Atherton's series featuring the ghost of Aunt Dimity; John Connolly's ventures into the world of the undead featuring Charlie Parker; Catherine Dain's New Age mysteries featuring psychic healer Mariana Morgan; Charlaine Harris's vampire series featuring telepathic waitress Sookie Stackhouse; Dan James's humorous series featuring gay vampire Simon Kirby-Jones; Martha Laurence's series featuring psychic San Francisco PI Elizabeth Chase; Karen Novak's series featuring psychic New York City police detective Leslie Stone; Derek Wilson's series featuring paranormal investigator Nathaniel Gye; Sean Stewart's series featuring exorcist D.K. "Dead" Kennedy.

Debut novels: Kay Hooper's *Chill of Fear*, featuring psychic FBI agent Quentin Hayes; Wendy Roberts's *Dating Can Be Deadly*, featuring psychically gifted secretary Tabitha Emery; David Skibbens's series debut novel featuring Tarot reader Warren Ritter; Pari Taichert's *The Clovis Incident*, featuring UFOs and Sasha Solomon; Cecilia Tishy's *Now You See Her*, featuring psychic Regina Cutter; Colson Whitehead's *The Intuitionist*, featuring black elevator inspector Lila Mae Watson, who "intuits" equipment defects.

Irene Adler

Profession: Operatic diva and private inquiry agent

Living situation: Married

Geographic locale:	Europe, England, America
Time period:	Late Victorian (1880s–1890s)
Associates:	Penelope "Nell" Huxleigh; Nelly Bly (Elizabeth Jane Cochrane, aka "Pink"), Godfrey Norton, Quentin Stanhope, Sherlock Holmes, John H. Watson, M.D.
Historical figures as lesser associates:	Bram Stoker, Oscar Wilde, Sarah Bernhardt, Lillie Langtry, Louis Comfort Tiffany, Charles Frederick Worth, Baron Alphonse Rothschild, and others
Nemesis:	The Unholy Trinity (in Ripper duology)
Significant relationship:	Godfrey Norton, husband
Concerns:	Feminism; motherhood; colonialism; religion and morality; anti-Semitism

Sherlock Holmes outwitted? Yes, once—and by a woman. Appearing first in Arthur Conan Doyle's story "A Scandal in Bohemia," American Irene Adler is "perhaps the most famous woman in detective fiction" (Herbert 4), once an astonishing contralto *prima donna* of the Imperial Opera in Warsaw and former paramour of the King of Bohemia. Commissioned to repossess a photograph from Irene that compromises His Majesty, Holmes tails her in ingenious disguises, but she and the pernicious photograph elude The Great Detective—his only professional defeat.

As reworked, enlarged, and told from the point of view of Penelope "Nell" Huxleigh, Irene's English spinster companion and biographer, Carole Nelson Douglas's version of Holmes's trouncing, *Good Night, Mr. Holmes* (1990), initiates a series starring a remarkably modern woman. Her "face of the most beautiful of women" entranced Wilhelm of Bohemia, but he added ruefully, she has "the mind of the most resolute of men" (*Femme Fatale* 29). Fashioned from something "resembling iron brocade," Irene appears "decorative, but, in truth, [is] nigh impossible to ruffle or bend" (*Femme Fatale* 27). Irene eventually marries barrister Godfrey Norton and they move to Neuilly-sur-Seine near Paris, headquarters for their ensuing adventures.

In the closing days of Victoria's reign, velvet-swathed piano legs and rigorous bowdlerization dominated polite society. Victorian sensibilities outwardly deplored behavior like Irene's as "unsuitable, even immoral or promiscuous" (*Silk Stalkings* 2: 17)—Working as an American Pinkerton agent in the 1880s! Appearing on The Stage! Cavorting with the King of Bohemia!—while men secretly salivated and women envied her independence and flair. For his part, Holmes, admiring Irene's intelligence, wit, and panache, cherishes their keen professional rivalry.

Just as Holmes preferred to let the world think he had perished in his confrontation with Moriarty at Reichenbach Falls, Irene and Godfrey pretend to be killed in a Swiss train crash at the end of *Good Morning, Irene* (1991), a case that allows her to don disguises and take up with sailors off Monaco. "Independence," she insists, "does wonders for a woman." Irene, "a tigress with a sunshade" (*Good Morning, Irene* 199), also relishes her self-described role as "Itinerant adventuress, actress and stage manager of other lives, independent and unconventional" (*Good Morning, Irene* 205). On one such outing, she survives the battle of Maiwand in an Afghanistan crawling with sinister spies, in *Irene at Large* (1992), an indictment of British imperialism set nine years earlier than *Good Morning, Irene*.

The juicy Jack the Ripper duology *Chapel Noir* (2001) and *Castle Rouge* (2002) takes place six months after the abominable Whitechapel murders that Britain wanted to believe "no Englishman could have done" (*Castle Rouge* 462). Irene captains an astonishing confederation of fictional and fictionalized personages against an Unholy Trinity celebrating unspeakable rites beneath Paris streets. Initially shaken when both Godfrey and Nell mysteriously vanish, steel-grey-gowned Irene draws on her diverse connections like "fat, self-indulgent and British" Bertie, Prince of Wales, and her sometime employer, the powerful Baron Alphonse de Rothschild, who knows Jews are always blamed. Each member of this "new and uneasy detecting alliance" has a hidden agenda, but Irene arranges the scene "like a playwright," assembling the dramatis personae, letting them "speak among each other and thus speak the truth to her, all unknowing." She plays them like the virtuoso she is, dividing and conquering, "avoiding plainspeaking when irony will do" (*Castle Rouge* 7, 461, 14). With Buffalo Bill Cody and Red Tomahawk, Irene tracks Godfrey and Nell through Bohemia, Prague, and darkest Transylvania, a bravura redemptive performance for Irene, who in *Irene's Last Waltz* (1994) might have brought the kidnappings upon herself (*Castle Rouge* 463).

According to Conan Doyle, Irene Adler was born in New Jersey, but Douglas offers nothing else about her background until *Femme Fatale* (2003). Because "Douglas wants . . . women fully informed about and capable of action on the mean streets of their world" (quoted in endnote to *Femme Fatale* 481), Irene believes that "what women don't know will hurt them" (*Femme Fatale* 34), so she dauntlessly explores Krafft-Ebing's shocking theories of abnormal sexuality and the eerie realms of spiritualism and mesmerism so popular at the turn of the century while searching for her own mother, emerging from psychological and physical morasses "dingy but triumphant" (*Femme Fatale* 425). In *Spider Dance* (2004), as Douglas declared, Holmes and Irene appear as flip sides of the same brilliant coin, as Irene dares the unthinkable: founding a New Magdalen Society to rescue Fallen Women while seeking the enigmatic Woman in Black who may be Irene's parent. Throughout all her adventures, Irene Adler not only outrages male-dominant conventionality herself; she also draws other women like Nell Huxleigh and Nelly Bly into independent action with her. To "today's perspective on women, Adler is in the vanguard of the truly liberated woman" (*Silk Stalkings* 2:17).

Novels: *Good Night, Mr. Holmes* (1990); *Good Morning, Irene* (1991); *Irene at Large* (1992); *Irene's Last Waltz* (1994, revision of *Another Scandal in Bohemia*); *Chapel Noir* (2001); *Castle Rouge* (2002); *Femme Fatale* (2003).

Other series: The Midnight Louie mystery series, featuring a black feline Las Vegas detective well acquainted with the seamy side of life (he relates the darker portions of what Douglas calls her "cozy-*noir*" series and Louie's assistant publicist Temple Barr relates the rest); the Sword and Circlet fantasy series.

Selected sources: Flanagan, Margaret. Rev. of *Spider Dance*. *Booklist*, December 15, 2004: 710; *Publishers Weekly*. Rev. of *Femme Fatale*, August 22, 2003: 260; *Publishers Weekly*. Rev. of *Good Night, Mr. Holmes*, January 20, 1992: 49–50; Stasio, Marilyn. Rev. of *Good Night, Mr. Holmes*. *New York Times Book Review*, December 16, 1990: 33; Stasio, Marilyn. Rev. of *Irene at Large*. *New York Times Book Review*, August 11, 2001: 20.

Major award: American Mystery Award, 1990.

Web sites: www.fastlane.net/cdouglas; www.catwriter.com/cdouglas.

See also: Laurie R. King's feminist **Mary Russell** series; other recent Holmes-related works include Caleb Carr's *The Italian Secretary* (2002) and *Sherlock Holmes* (2005); Martin Davies's *Mrs. Hudson and the Spirits' Curse* (2004); Brian Freemantle's *The Holmes Inheritance* (2004) and *The Holmes Factor* (2005), featuring Holmes's daring son Sebastian; Barrie Roberts's various Sherlock Holmes pastiches, including *Sherlock Holmes and the King's Governess* (2005), set in 1897 during Queen Victoria's Diamond Jubilee.

Rachel Alexander

Profession:	Private investigator
Living situation:	Divorced
Geographic locale:	New York City, especially Greenwich Village
Time period:	1996–present
Associate:	Dashiell ("Dash"), a pit bull terrier
Significant relationship:	Dash
Concerns:	Dogs and their relationship to people; social issues (homelessness, AIDS, homosexuality, etc.); aging

Carol Lea Benjamin based her Rachel Kaminsky Alexander and Dash series on her personal experiences as a private detective and as a successfully published dog obedience trainer, creating a street-smart nearing-forty heroine who reserves the hard-boiled right to be as vulgar as any man, yet quivers at a baby's touch, the sight of any canine, and the right kind of bedroomy baritone. To the consternation of her "perfect" Jewish mother and her older sister Lillian (who doesn't think Rachel belongs in their family), Rachel started the Kaminsky and Son Dog Academy (her Golden Retriever Bernie was the son), gave it up to marry, then divorce, Jack Alexander, a cool outside, uptight inside Westchester dentist. Rachel finally moved to Greenwich Village and took up detective work, partly because in the throes of financial disclosure Jack had called her "the nosiest bitch" he'd ever met. Furthermore, Rachel noted, as a detective she wouldn't have to wear pantyhose (*Hire* 38).

Rachel's tough-talking chutzpah covers suspiciousness, competitiveness, and too much independence for most men's taste. It also hides a personality much too frightened to suit her own taste—and a multitude of insecurities, a "rabid counterphobia" her shrink works doggedly to neutralize. Just as Rachel's constantly kvetching mama'd told her, Rachel can't leave a scab alone even if she knows picking at it will leave a scar, and her divorce and its fallout are never far from her mind (*Hire* 36, 6, 59). Dead broke at the start of Shamus Award–winning *This Dog for Hire* and working out of the downtown brick cottage she earns in part as a caretaker for wealthy landlords, the same compassion that made Rachel forcibly rescue Dashiell from punks who wanted to torture him into a fighting dog now has her training him as a therapy dog for indigent nursing home patients and AIDS victims. Rachel feels compelled to investigate the murder of a gay artist and the dognapping of his barkless Basenji, Magritte, a strong contender for Best in Show at the famous Westminster show coming up in a week.

Rachel evolves her detecting rules as she goes along. Doing all the obvious things is high on her list, like checking mail, listening to answering machines, and never assuming anyone is innocent. She never accepts a story, however piteous, at face value, either, and that means she never forgets to keep her first rule first: follow the money. Nosing out human greed and its consequences takes Rachel, herself cheap out of nature as well as necessity, a long way in solving a string of cases that almost always involve dogs, either missing ones like Magritte and *Lady Vanishes* (1999), dogs who witness crimes, like *The Dog Who Knew Too Much* (1997), or dogs who need help and security, like *A Hell of a Dog* (1998).

Like Dashiell himself, these stories are far from cozy cutesy canine tales. Dash is a large implacable pit bull, white except for a black spot circling one eye and a Charlie Chaplin moustache, and he's Rachel's devoted partner and best friend. Nothing excites Rachel more than glimpses inside a dog's mind, and as she and Dash work together, the talents each one has complements the other's. Their relationship is more symbiosis than "animal training"; Dash's ultrasensitive nose, his primary means of investigation, means that Rachel never knows what he's going to come up with, but she always knows that it will be different from what she can "see" (*Hire* 44), providing another vital dimension to their detective work.

The case Rachel and Dash tackle in *Fall Guy* (2004) is unusual for them because Dash is the only dog involved. He assists Rachel in probing the death of NYPD detective Timothy O'Fallon, a taciturn member of Rachel's 9/11 support group whose service revolver is supposed to have discharged "accidentally." Inexplicably named as executor of O'Fallon's will—she has no idea why—Rachel knows only that O'Fallon felt a strong bond with Dash, who despite his powerful protective instincts and his constantly inquiring nose also has an uncanny canine ability to help heal psychological wounds and bring comfort to the lonely and the dying.

In the course of *Fall Guy*, Rachel falls, too. Badly hurt in a romantic relationship a year earlier, she's haunted by some persistent ghosts—her mother, whose affairs she and her sister Lili had had to settle not long ago; her failed marriage to Jack; the dead of 9/11 whom she, like so many New Yorkers, can't escape as they look daily at what's not there, breathe the debris, and walk on the ashes of the dead (*Fall Guy* 17). Rachel feels that she's living half in, half out of the gutter, not knowing what it means to be wanted except for Dash, her lifeline to stability. Rachel loves "hanging out with animals" because "fat or thin, rich or poor, it's all the same to them," and she can't help wondering if she will end up like the Alzheimer's patients she and Dash visit, "someone visiting me on Tuesdays with a friendly dog, making ten minutes in my endless week bearable" (*Fall Guy* 25). Then she meets O'Fallon's partner, sad, brooding Detective Michael Brody, and after a year of sharing her bed "with a dog and only with my dog, feeling wounded and unready to risk getting hurt again...desire changed all that" (*Fall Guy* 249). With Dash and Brody and "the city, tall and strong against the bright summer sky" (*Fall Guy* 257), Rachel Alexander finally feels wanted again.

Novels: *This Dog for Hire* (1996); *The Dog Who Knew Too Much* (1997); *A Hell of a Dog* (1998); *Lady Vanishes* (1999); *The Wrong Dog* (2000); *The Long Good Boy* (2001); *Fall Guy* (2004); *Without a Word* (2005).

Other works: *Dog Training for Kids* (1976); *Dog Problems: A Professional Trainer's Guide to Preventing and Correcting Aggression* (1981); *Mother Knows Best: The Natural Way to Train Your Dog* (1985); *Surviving Your Dog's Adolescence* (1993).

Selected sources: *Publishers Weekly*. Rev. of *Lady Vanishes*, August 9, 1999: 34; *Publishers Weekly*. Rev. of *The Long Good Boy*, August 6, 2001: 64; *Publishers Weekly*. Rev. of *This Dog for Hire*, October 7, 1996: 64; Rowen, John. Rev. of *The Dog Who Knew Too Much*. *Booklist*, September 1, 1997: 62; Rowen, John. Rev. of *A Hell of a Dog*. *Booklist*, October 1, 1998: 310.

Major award: Shamus Award, Private Eye Writers of America, 1996.

Web site: www.carolleabenjamin.com.

See also: For canine-related series, Susan Conant's Holly Winter series, featuring Alaskan malamutes; Laurien Berenson's **Melanie Travis** series, featuring poodles; Michael Bond's **Monsieur Pamplemousse** series, featuring the incomparable bloodhound Pommes Frites; for a more general animal-related series, Cynthia Baxter's series featuring veterinarian Jessica Popper, set in New York.

Roy Angel

Profession:	Trumpet player; unofficial taxi driver
Living situation:	Live-in relationship (in *Angel Underground*)
Geographic locale:	England
Time period:	Late 1980s
Associates:	Armstrongs I and II; PI Veronica Blugden
Significant relationship:	Amy May (in *Angel Underground*)

Crime takes third place to comedy and caricature in Mike Ripley's mystery novels, high-spirited junkets through London's seedy streets and a few provincial milieus. Being funny pays off for Ripley. He sold *Just Another Angel* (1988) to his first-choice publisher, the prestigious Collins Crime Club, in ten days; and his editor there, who was also Agatha Christie's last editor, asked him how many more he could write (Ashley 416). He's been at it ever since.

Ripley told *Contemporary Authors*, "[Fitzroy Maclean] Angel is not a detective, indeed he's not much of a hero at all. He is youngish, streetwise, self-contained. He has not dropped out of the rat race; he never joined it. The books are not whodunits but 'how-does-he-get-out-of-this?' adventures. Angel looks on England (and especially London) in the late 1980s as a contemporary, but an outsider by choice. "Each book involves him in a different world. . . . If a friend is in trouble, Angel will go to the wall for them—or find someone else to" (quoted in *CA Online*).

Publishers Weekly (Dec. 12, 1994) declared, "with Angel as a guide, lowlife London has never been a more seductive proposition." Angel's alluring free-spirit lifestyle includes playing jazz trumpet in sleazy joints and making a little undeclared income with Armstrong (for Satchmo), the unofficial black London taxi he owns. From experience, he's formulated practical rules to live by, like No. 23: "Never give your address after just one date," and No. 477: "When a woman admits it's difficult to ask for something, leave immediately," but he often wails to his readers, "Why don't I listen to myself?" (*Just Another Angel* 31, 37), as he slides into one irresistible scrape after another.

In *Just Another Angel*, Angel ruefully portrays himself as a poor guy who just can't say no. He's got a Galahad complex for helping quirky damsels in distress like Jo, a girlfriend who needs to get back an emerald pendant her husband gave her, or his lesbian neighbor Lisabeth who has to abandon her late-hippie timewarp and hide out in his apartment with his ferocious cat Springsteen while her partner's parents come visiting, or elderly Mrs. Scamp, who named her dog Nigger so she "could shout down the street after him and those bastards in the Race Relations office can't touch me for it" (*Just Another Angel* 39, 42, 138). By the time Angel extricates himself from such muddles of misguided chivalry and small-time villains, he's shown a side of 1980s England where histories and guidebooks fear to tread.

The same goes for all of Angel's adventures, which include financial wheeling and dealing in *Angel Touch* (1989); the animal-rights lobbyists in *Angel Hunt* (1990); and the cold world of London's homeless" in *Angel City* (1994), where according to *Publishers Weekly* "he talks to lost souls and encounters an occasional genuine angel of mercy." *Angel Confidential* (1995) brings him Veronica Blugden, a haplessly blundering PI who appears in several of his later adventures, which involve drug smuggling, counterfeiting, the high fashion "rag trade" in *That Angel Look* (1997), illicitly imported booze in *Bootlegged Angel* (1999), the movie industry in *Lights, Camera, Angel* (2001), and even archaeology and anti-genetically modified crops in *Angel Underground* (2002), showcasing Angel's fiendish family and his infuriating fashion designer live-in, Amy May.

After ten previous scandalous frolics, *Angel Underground* finds Angel floundering in a broth of hitherto uncharted hot water brewed up by the women in his life. His flaming red-haired mother Bethany, aka Mommy Dearest and The Mother from Hell, lures him to a barbecue at her home in Suffolk featuring Elvis, her deceased Vietnamese pot-bellied pig, so that she can loan Angel out to investigate the strange "closed and gossipy" archaeological goings-on threatening the godfather of her current toy-boy, SAS Captain Rupert Tyrell, whose "arse of steel" intrigues Amy more than Angel likes (*Angel Underground* 72, 58). Amy inexplicably insists on joining the dig for the purported mint of Celtic Queen Boudica (aka Boadicea), a down-and-dirty pursuit far removed from her workroom and runways but one Angel knows intimately from his public schooling and his university degree in archaeology. After a few days fraught with the dotty godfather, Mobile Thrones (aka glorified Portaloos), and the local farming mafia, Angel's flamboyant sister Finnoula turns up as leader of a crop-circling anti-gen mod crew and Angel has to rescue Amy from the ex-husband who's stalking her.

The howling unpredictability of Angel's predicaments and the unusual measures he takes to escape them irreverently combines humor and crime, leavened with enough sensibility to produce well-rounded convincing characterization. At the close of *Angel Underground*, Roy Angel finally realizes that the subterfuge and double-dealing and violence "was all because Amy hadn't been open and honest about things. . . . I was the only one who had been straight arrow all the way" (*Angel Underground* 292), one man trying to hang onto principle as the world around him goes barking mad.

Novels: *Just Another Angel* (1988); *Angel Touch* (1989); *Angel Hunt* (1990); *Angel in Arms* (1991); *Angel City* (1994); *Angel Confidential* (1995); *Family of Angels* (1996); *That Angel Look* (1997); *Bootlegged Angel* (1999); *Lights, Camera, Angel* (2001); *Angel Underground* (2002); *Angel in the House* (2005).

Nonseries novel: *Boudica and the Lost Roman* (2005).

Other works: With Maxim Jakubowski, Ripley coedits the British *Fresh Blood* anthologies featuring work by cutting-edge new authors.

Selected sources: *Booklist.* Rev. of *That Angel Look*, March 15, 1998: 1206; *Publishers Weekly.* Rev. of *Angel City*, December 12, 1994: 53; *Publishers Weekly.* Rev. of *That Angel Look*, February 16, 1998: 207; Stasio, Marilyn. Rev. of *That Angel Look. New York Times Book Review*, March 30, 1997.

Major award: Last Laugh Award (most humorous crime novel), Crime Writers' Association, 1989 and 1991.

See also: For British mystery-cum-humor, see Peter Gutteridge's comic series featuring Nick Madrid, a journalist and yoga expert assisted by Bridget Frost, "the Bitch of the Broadsheets"; Dorothy Cannell's wickedly amusing series featuring depressed and overweight interior designer Ellie Haskell; Judith Cook's series featuring former policeman turned literary tour guide John Latymer.

Carlo Arbati

Profession:	Detective Inspector, Carabinieri (Florence)
Living situation:	Single
Geographic locale:	Tuscany
Time period:	1990s
Associate:	Detective Giorgio Bruni
Significant relationship:	Cordelia Sinclair
Concerns:	The arts

A fatal heart attack at fifty-four ended John Spencer Hill's promising Carlo Arbati series, centered in contemporary Florence and resonating with the glorious art of the

Renaissance. Hill's two detective novels combine startling realism with neoplatonic Romanticism, because his magnetic hero is an "idealistic realist" (*Castrato* 24), both an insightful policeman and an award-winning poet.

At thirty-five, tall, slim, curly-haired, and immaculately tailored Detective Inspector Carlo Arbati is, as Edith Hamilton wrote of Lord Peter Wimsey, one of "the dreams that visit women's pillows" (Hamilton 6). He is also as maddeningly elusive. For Arbati, his two vocations, policeman and poet, are not contradictory but complementary. Raised in Prato near Florence by his frail maiden Aunt Angela after the death of his parents in a car crash, Arbati as a boy dreamed of becoming an astronaut but slid into the Police Academy almost by chance, because he thought the university would be "too sedentary" (*Castrato* 207). After fifteen years in the Carabinieri, the Italian national police, Arbati prizes his work there. He believes that keeping the streets safe turns the *quattrocento* fortresses of wealthy Florentine aristocrats into art museums and restaurants for everyone; "it helps ensure that Justice is served . . . that good in the end actually *does* win out over evil." Realizing fully that his position is "old-fashioned," Arbati insists that he is no impractical idealist: "My dreams are realizable because truth and justice aren't just abstractions. They're real and they're worth fighting for" (*Castrato* 207).

While as a detective Arbati's attention necessarily focuses outward, as a poet, "a recorder and remembrancer of times past" (*Castrato* 97), he looks inward, taking sanctuary in his elegantly masculine apartment to balance his policeman's necessary contacts, "the seamier side of human character," with poetry, "its finer tone." "I ask myself what makes me tick, why I think and feel they way I do about life . . . and then I try to find words to recreate these experiences" (*Castrato* 24, 213). For Arbati, his poetry is something found, not something made. He wrote his first poems looking for answers after his parents' deaths, and since then his poetry has become a consuming passion. Once intuition strikes and he has a draft, he works like a jeweler with his good-luck Parker fountain pen, striving sometimes for weeks to cut, polish, embellish, a single poem.

Arbati's introspection is not without its price. He sometimes wonders whether "there is something missing in himself, some lust for flesh and blood" that keeps him from marrying, as Aunt Angela claims, "because he fear[s] giving himself fully to another human being" (*Castrato* 99), and because his poetic Muse may be too jealous to allow him a human lover. Both of Arbati's cases strongly convey this inner conflict.

The Last Castrato (1995) offers an intricate tale of revenge and greed stemming from a shocking 1960s plot to gain fame and fortune by re-creating early operatic music—including deliberately castrating a boy to preserve his stunning soprano voice. Investigating a horrifying sequence of 1990s throat-slashings, Arbati meets Cordelia* Sinclair—in Florence to research an obscure Renaissance musical broth-

---

*Hill pays homage to great British mystery classics in the name "Cordelia," recalling Cordelia Gray's fondness for P.D. James's poet-detective Adam Dalgliesh in *An Unsuitable Job for a Woman*. In *Ghirlandaio's Daughter*, Hill also named a formidable brindled bull terrier "Bunter" after Lord Peter Wimsey's impeccable butler in Dorothy L. Sayers's Golden Age novels. Hill's Bunter ("Aarrgh!") accompanies a doughty Miss Marplesque spinster addicted to Agatha Christie's novels as bedside reading.

erhood and forget five years of abusive marriage. A modern American woman in search of herself, Cordelia's charm, intelligence, and Botticelli appearance remain on Arbati's mind for days before he unties his tongue sufficiently to ask her to dinner. They date discreetly, they exchange hopes and fears and dreams, and they also agree to part when her essential Aristotelian desire for the security of cold hard facts, like Arbati's odd-couple partner Columbo-sloppy Giorgio Bruni's inability to see the forest for the trees, clashes with Arbati's Platonic idealism that accepts all knowledge as remembering.

Although they do love each other, Arbati's relationship with Cordelia founders on "the rocky demands of separate careers...the great twentieth-century disease—the drive to fulfil oneself, to carve a career and a reputation out of the flinty rockface of self-imposed expectation." Cordelia wants to make her place in the world without depending on a man, while Carlo Arbati, "wedded to his job at the Questura and to the Muse who inspired his poetry, was unwilling—or perhaps just unable—to make room in his life for yet another mistress" (*Daughter* 18). He proves that in *Ghirlandaio's Daughter* (1996), a disturbing case in neighboring Lucca that demands an artist to catch a devious art crook. There, though attracted to a woman who reminds him of Cordelia, Arbati lets her leave his life with only a kiss on the cheek for "one of life's little ironies" (*Daughter* 239). Choosing art over love, Arbati follows the path he once described as "the journey of a corruptible pilgrim, exiled but undaunted, descending through the dark valley of self toward the light. He still thought that image said it all" (*Castrato* 24).

Novels: *The Last Castrato* (1995); *Ghirlandaio's Daughter* (1996).

Other works: Hill, an English professor at the University of Ottawa, published scholarly studies of the poets Milton, Coleridge, and Keats, as well as Euripides, the fifth-century B.C. Greek playwright and father of realism, whose tragedies were shockers that flouted traditional dramatic conventions.

Selected sources: *Booklist*. Rev. of *Ghirlandaio's Daughter*, March 15, 1997: 1229; *Booklist*. Rev. of *The Last Castrato*, May 15, 1995: 1634; Hamilton, Edith. "Gaudeamus Igitur." Rev. of *Gaudy Night*. *Saturday Review of Literature* 13, February 22, 1936: 6; *Publishers Weekly*. Rev. of *Ghirlandaio's Daughter*, January 27, 1997: 81; *Publishers Weekly*. Rev. of *The Last Castrato*, May 22, 1995.

Major awards: Arthur Ellis Award, 1996; Critics' Choice Award, San Francisco Review of Books, 1996; Harlequin Library Prize, 1996.

See also: Donna Leon's **Guido Brunetti** series, set in Venice; Michael Dibdin's **Aurelio Zen** series, set in Rome and other Italian cities; Magdalen Nabb's **Marshal Salvatore Guarnaccia** series, set in Florence.

Owen Archer

Profession: Captain of retainers, steward, and spy for John Thoresby, Archbishop of York

Living situation: Married

Geographic locale:	England, especially around York, and Wales
Time period:	1360s–1370s
Associate:	Lucie Wilton, Archer's wife
Nemesis:	Thoresby's hold on Archer
Significant relationship:	Lucie Wilton
Concerns:	His family; loyalty to his liege lord; Welsh nationalism

Medievalist Candace Robb's Owen Archer series began as a short story without Archer. When he entered the tale, it soon blossomed into a full-fledged mystery novel, *The Apothecary Rose* (1993), set in turbulent fourteenth-century York, England's second city and capital of the North. Immensely complicated political intrigues seethed in late-fourteenth-century England, with the aging king putty in the hands of his scheming mistress Alice Perrers, Edward the Black Prince an invalid, and the king's second son, John of Gaunt, maneuvering to seize the throne. Robb's fictional Owen Archer, a prize marksman and born leader of men, first swore his allegiance to the old Duke of Lancaster, whose eyes and ears Archer became after losing his own left eye defending Lancaster. Archer believes the wound resulted from his own pride and faulty judgment; it does not handicap his shooting—archers shoot with one eye closed—but being blind on one side made him vulnerable and hence endangers his fellow soldiers. Two years later, with the old duke dead, Archer becomes so deeply depressed he considers suicide. Archer distrusts the motives of York's Machiavellian Archbishop John Thoresby, patterned on an actual historical figure who was one of Edward III's Lord Chancellors, but Archer accepts Thoresby's offer of a position as his spy, and later becomes Thoresby's steward and the captain of his retainers.

In *The Apothecary Rose*, set in 1363, Thoresby sends Archer, far more morally scrupulous than the archbishop himself, as an apprentice to ailing Master Apothecary Nicholas Wilton, whose shop appears to have dispensed a herbal potion fatal to two pilgrims at St. Mary's Abbey. Soon Archer, a tall, handsome, and magnetic man, is drawn to Lucie, Wilton's young and lovely wife, trained by her elderly husband as an apothecary. After Wilton's death, Owen weds Lucie prior to the second novel in the series, *The Lady Chapel*. Whereas Archer's first case involved crimes within a York family, his second reaches from York's wool trade into the royal court itself. Archer's keen skill at interviewing witnesses and suspects, as well as his sharp (though one-eyed) observations of evidence, link with Lucie's skill as an apothecary and her inquisitive nature. In later cases, Lucie's curiosity and her bold independence often lead her into rash actions from which Archer, irked at her carelessness and fearful for her safety, must continually save her.

The murders that Archer investigates soon have national and even international repercussions. *A Spy for the Redeemer* (1999), set in 1370, finds Archer, now father of two, in his native Wales, where he had accompanied Lucie's father Sir Robert on a pilgrimage to St. David's shrine while carrying out a complex covert mission on loan from Thoresby to the new Duke of Lancaster, John of Gaunt. Delayed there by Sir Robert's death and the building of his tomb, Owen Archer finds himself the victim of a soul-searing midlife crisis.

Owen, once the dashing chief archer of old Lancaster's forces, has been helping Lucie in the apothecary, overseeing repairs at Thoresby's estate of Bishopthorpe, finding make-work for Thoresby's retainers: "Much of my time at home is dull," he realizes. In Wales he hears stirring tales of Owain Lawgoch, the "real Prince of Wales" now plotting a Welsh revolt against England. Owen reflects, "If I were free to take up arms for him, I would." But quickly, when a fellow Welshman declares that fighting for Owain, their "rightful prince" would be a proud legacy for Owen Archer's children, Owen shocks himself by replying. "If we won." "Had his love for Lucie and his children unmanned him" (*A Spy for the Redeemer* 45–46)?

Owen does return to York and Lucie, who is fractiously coping with her own troubles—not one but two charming men eager in Owen's absence to comfort her for her father's death, an attack on her inherited manor, an increasingly senile aunt, a teenaged foster son—but Thoresby, no longer Lord Chancellor, has learned of Owen's sympathy for the treasonous Welsh revolt, and Thoresby uses that knowledge as leverage against Owen in *The Cross-legged Knight* (2002). Charged by Thoresby with protecting the Bishop of Winchester, another deposed Lord Chancellor and an enemy of John of Gaunt, Owen now battles not only his own conflict between his present duties and his longing for his former soldier's life, but Lucie's post-miscarriage depression as well. He questions Lucie's judgment in a vicious murder case they are probing, and again he shakes himself badly by admitting he *was* happy in his wife—implying: Is he now? (Italics in original, *Knight* 224)

While playing his clandestine role in the shadows of powerful men and their intrigues, Owen Archer no longer wants to be bothered with the simmering troubles at home. Robb seems to be painting herself into a novelistic corner: despite Owen's love for Lucie and his children, he and Lucie are drifting asunder as she fights despair and he thinks longingly of happier days with his lost comrades. At the climax of *The Cross-legged Knight*, Owen Archer, blind with blood lust, has to be dragged away for fear he will kill the murderer with his bare hands—as a substitute, perhaps, for trying to slay those inner demons in himself and Lucie that he, up to this point in the series at least, has been unable to annihilate.

Novels: *The Apothecary Rose* (1993); *The Lady Chapel* (1994); *The Nun's Tale* (1995); *The King's Bishop* (1996); *The Riddle of St. Leonard's* (1997); *A Gift of Sanctuary* (1998); *A Spy for the Redeemer* (1999); *The Cross-legged Knight* (2002).

Other works: With *A Trust Betrayed* (2000), Robb began a new series, set in late thirteenth-century Scotland, featuring widowed Dame Margaret Kerr.

Selected sources: Flanagan, Margaret. Rev. of *The Lady Chapel*. *Booklist*, October 1, 1994: 244; *Kirkus Reviews*. Rev. of *A Gift of Sanctuary*, October 1, 1998: 1417; *Kirkus Reviews*. Rev. of *The Nun's Tale*, September 1, 1995: 1228; Pool, Gail. "Murder in Print: The Best of New Writers." *Wilson Library Bulletin*, November 1994: 104–5; Simpson, Douglas G. Rev. of *The Apothecary Rose*. *Armchair Detective*, Spring 1994: 110–11.

Online review: Harriet Klausner. *BookBrowser*: www.bookbrowser.com (December 2, 1998).

Web site: www.candacerobb.com.

See also: Paul Doherty's several medieval series featuring respectively Hugh Corbett, a late 1300s–early 1400s clerk of the King's Chancery Court; Brother Athelstan, clerk to the Coroner of London in the same period; Doherty's Canterbury Tales series, set in the late fourteenth century; and his Kathryn Swinbrooke series set in the fifteenth century; Margaret Frazer's **Dame Frevisse** series, set in fifteenth-century England; Susannah Gregory's series featuring thirteenth-century Cambridge physician and teacher Matthew Bartholomew; Michael Jenks's Knights Templar mysteries, featuring former Knight Templar **Sir Baldwin Furnshill** and set in fourteenth-century England.

Jonathan Argyll

Profession:	Art dealer
Living situation:	Single
Geographic locales:	Italy and England
Time period:	1990–present
Associate:	Flavia di Stefano
Significant relationship:	Flavia di Stefano
Concern:	Ethics in the art world

Iain Pears, art historian and Getty Fellow in the Arts and Humanities at Yale University, draws on his thoroughgoing art expertise for his Jonathan Argyll series, set mainly in Rome but pursuing far-flung art thievery across Europe and America.

Young English art historian Jonathan Argyll's witty, rarefied fictional world revolves around a Machiavellian ménage à trois: fine art, skullduggery, and bureaucracy, all intimately connected by his loose ties to Italy's National Art Theft Squad of the *Polizia*, headquartered in Rome and directed by crusty General Taddeo Bottando, who is relentlessly assisted by Flavia di Stefano, Argyll's live-in lover. Argyll, a relative babe in the thorny woods of international art dealing, has left a job with a reputable London gallery to start his own dealership in Italy, where he "just about [knows] his way around the Italian bureaucratic labyrinth" (*Judgement* 5). Each highly complex plot involves a specific artist's work with thefts and murders perpetrated by shadowy distant moneyed masterminds, and Argyll's ethical scruples keep getting in his way. Flavia, level-headed, practical, and hard-working as well as hard loving, performs much of the necessary spade- and legwork, while Argyll, a good-humored modern-day Candide, bumbles along between sporadic flashes of crucial insight.

After *The Raphael Affair* (1990), where Argyll was arrested for breaking into a church after a long-lost Raphael only to discover that the painting was missing, Argyll cheekily learns "fast about the art business. People were friendly enough, and helpful enough, but occasionally came over a bit funny when money was involved" (*Judgement* 2). In *The Last Judgement* (1993), with Argyll's "low-cost, working-from-home" dealership languishing in a bad market, he makes an exploratory trip to Paris and generously offers to carry a painting of Socrates's death back to a customer in

Rome. "OK, so it was a little bit dishonest. But not much." After all, it would make life simpler for everybody, and for goodhearted young Argyll, that's what counts (*Judgement* 5–6). The road to a struggling art dealer's hell, he soon finds, is paved with such good intentions.

According to Flavia, Argyll's trouble is his "penchant for the obscure." In the nine months they've been together, she's been trying to persuade him that to make money, he'll have to sell things people like, but instead he's covering the walls of her tiny apartment with mythological or Biblical or allegorical works with moral virtues that she finds oppressive. Furthermore, they make his prospective clients think he's deranged.

Argyll's ability to spot obscure clues is helpful, but Flavia usually wishes they'd occur to him sooner. When the customer who was supposed to receive the Socrates painting is found tortured to death and the painting is gone, General Bottando assigns Flavia to liaise on the case with her former lover Giulio Fabriano, landing Argyll, the well-meaning courier, in a particularly touchy investigation. He does come up with the crucial clue just in time for Flavia to remorselessly unmask the murderer, who then commits suicide with insect-killer. Their solution makes Bottando look so good at solving this fatal theft that he pretends Flavia takes orders from him—while they all know better.

The venality of Italian bureaucracy, the English aristocracy, and art dealers in general poses an even bigger threat to Argyll's principles and equanimity in *Giotto's Hand* (1994). The bureaucracy "believed firmly that the quality of an organization depended solely on how many jobs it provided for administrators" (*Giotto's Hand* 10), and Dottore Corrado Argan, a repulsive specimen of Total Quality Management, is slavering for the General's job. To protect his flanks and prove old age and cunning can outmaneuver youth and ambition, the General assigns Flavia to reopen an old case of a missing Uccello Madonna and Child. Argyll's dealership is still stagnant, so he heads for England to consult his former employer and avoid accepting the teaching job the practical Flavia is pushing. He carries Flavia's mandate to look into the affairs of English art dealer Geoffrey Forster, whom she suspects of hanky-panky with the missing Madonna.

Argyll literally stumbles over Forster's body in the Norfolk village of Weller. As he muddles along "helping" the Weller constabulary, Argyll befriends Mary Verney, Forster's sharp-witted landlady, who is fighting to maintain her inherited money pit of a dilapidated stately home. As Flavia careens from Rome to Florence, then to England, building a spectacular case that she hopes will save the General's bacon, the worst moral dilemma of an art dealer's life impales Argyll. For his efforts to plug leaks in her nineteenth-century plumbing, walk her Labrador Frederick, and establish the worth of her time-blackened ancestral paintings, Mary Varney presses on him an unassuming little anatomical sketch that's hung for years in her moldering bedroom. At the last split second, Argyll recognizes it for a Holy Grail of art collecting, a long-lost Leonardo da Vinci that could elevate him, his dealership, Flavia, and the General to delectably lofty heights. Now . . . should he tell Mrs. Varney? Beauty is truth and truth beauty, insisted Keats—but Keats died poor and young.

Novels: *The Raphael Affair* (1990); *The Titian Committee* (1991); *The Bernini Bust* (1992); *The Last Judgment* (1993); *Giotto's Hand* (1995); *Death and Restoration* (1996); *The Immaculate Deception* (2000).

Stand-alone novels: *An Instance of the Fingerpost* (1998); *The Dream of Scipio* (2002); *The Portrait* (2006).

Nonfiction: *The Discovery of Painting: The Growth of Interest in the Arts in England* (1988).

Selected sources: *Drood Review of Mystery.* Rev. of *The Bernini Bust*, January 2001: 22; *Los Angeles Times Book Review.* Rev. of *The Immaculate Deception*, March 19, 2001: 9; Ott, Bill. Rev. of *Giotto's Hand*. *Booklist*, June 1, 1997: 1667–68; *Publishers Weekly. Publishers Weekly.* Rev. of *The Last Judgment*, January 29, 1996: 87; Rev. of *The Raphael Affair*, August 3, 1992: 64.

Major award: Getty Fellowship, 1987–1988.

See also: Jonathan Gash's Lovejoy series focusing on antique scams; John Malcolm's series featuring honest London antique dealer Tim Simpson; Derek Wilson's series featuring Tim Lacy, a former SAS officer, now recoverer of stolen art; also Canadian author Marianne MacDonald's series featuring London antiquarian **Dido Hoare**.

Spencer Arrowood

Profession:	Sheriff of Hamelin, Tennessee
Living situation:	Single
Geographic locale:	Tennessee–North Carolina Appalachian region
Time period:	1990–present
Associates:	Joe LeDonne, Martha Ayers, Nora Bonesteel
Concerns:	The heritage and struggles of Appalachian people; the Vietnam War

Sharyn McCrumb's Ballad series celebrates the haunting and haunted hills and hollows of Appalachia and its tough hardscrabble ethnic Irish, Welsh, English, and Scottish mountaineers who have lived there since the 1700s. Appalachia's economic backbone—whiskey making, sheep raising, coal mining—has become marginal and many of its people have to leave to find work, but its "immeasurable wealth of beauty and tradition is a strong attraction from which some never escape and to which others hasten to return" (*Silk Stalkings* 2: 80).

In these novels, anchored in Smoky Mountain lore and its traditional Celtic sources, past, present, and future blend like the mists and the ghosts that linger through the Appalachians. Spencer Arrowood—pronounced "Arwood" in the mountains—like McCrumb is a great-grandchild of a Smoky Mountain circuit preacher. After his military service, Spencer's loyalty to the familiar got him elected sheriff at thirty-eight in Hamelin, Tennessee, where people still stand up "when they played 'Dixie' at football games" (*Peggy-O* 9). Arrowood has "the chiseled features and slight, sturdy build that would keep him looking thirty-eight until he was seventy" (*Walks* 301). With his Vietnam vet deputy Joe LeDonne, "a thin crust of snow over a pit of ice water" (*Peggy-O* 10), and his 1966 high school classmate secretary (later a deputy too) gaunt, tanned Martha Ayers, Arrowood settles minor local problems—speeding, burgling, drunk driving—in his low-key folksy " 'Andy Griffith rap' " manner, but their stories all involve fearful ghosts that have to be laid to rest.

Arrowood's ghosts dominate the series. In *If Ever I Return, Pretty Peggy-O* (1990), 1960s folksinger Peggy Muryon moves to Hamelin, hoping for peace and quiet to build a career comeback, awakening more of the past than Arrowood or the town would ever like: " 'Remember that I warned you,' " he tells a reporter, " 'you could go to a lot of trouble tracking down a dead man' " (*Peggy-O* 191). Arrowood knows; he lost his lover Jenny when she admitted aborting the child of Arrowood's older brother Cal, who was killed in Vietnam.

The Hangman's Beautiful Daughter (1992) roils up long-kept secrets, too. A multiple shooting at the Underhill farm—Major Paul Underhill, his wife Janet, and their eight-year-old Simon gunned to death by their adolescent son Josh—leaves two new orphans. Spencer Arrowood, exhausted and frustrated, can't escape the tormenting "Why?" Arrowood attends community events so that Wake County's people don't remember him always as a "sidekick of disaster." He understands the bad luck that dogs the poor: "Try to keep warm and your ramshackle house ignites around you" (*Daughter* 166), and he locks himself into a men's-room stall to weep for a three-year-old who's just said good bye to his dying mother, but at the Underwood funeral Arrowood, full of "pity tinged with defensiveness," relives his brother's military funeral, when "the whole world had suddenly—randomly, it seemed—needed readjusting" (*Daughter* 32).

Nora Bonesteel, Ashe Mountain's elderly wise woman gifted with the Scots "Sight," holds this series together. She had supposedly foreseen the Underhill deaths, but Arrowood wants nothing to do with her or "the supernatural business"; "such things had no place in his world of order and law and finding probable cause" (*Daughter* 32–33). Nora, like the voice of conscience, weaves the threads of the past into handcrafts revealing the present and future "for those who have the eyes to see them" (*Silk Stalkings: More* 80), but for a long time Arrowood keeps his eyes firmly closed. Not until *She Walks These Hills* (1994), does he even admit that Nora Bonesteel waits at the end of literal and symbolic mountain journeys to soothe body and spirit with her Balm of Gilead.

In *The Rosewood Casket* (1996), a tale that meshes Nora's long-lost love with unscrupulous present-day land development schemes, Nora tells Spencer Arrowood's mother Jane that he is "an angel unawares," but Nora's Sight still disturbs her son, as it does most people in the valley. His mother Jane knows "Spencer was determined not to believe in such things, and any evidence to the contrary only annoyed him" (*Casket* 14); but she suspects that Spencer chose police work, "risking his life every single day," to compete even now with Cal (*Casket* 332). Arrowood has no enemies but his badge does, and when he's shot evicting a farm family, a near-death vision puts Nora Bonesteel's old ways into perspective for him. That perspective helps him lay some of his own unquiet spirits to rest in *The Ballad of Frankie Silver* (1999), where he delves into the past to save Fate Harkryder, whom he'd helped convict, from execution. In *Ghost Riders* (2004), a multi-tiered Civil War tale links past and present when blue- and butternut-clad ghosts ominously haunt reenactors' campsites in the Smokies. Still compulsively probing his own past, Arrowood is shocked to discover that his ancestor fought for the Union, not the Confederacy, and he wonders, "What do you do when you've won the battle but lost the war?" Though he can't hear Nora's answer yet, someday, perhaps, Spencer Arrowood will: "There's been enough fighting in these mountains.... It's got to stop somewhere."

Novels: *If Ever I Return, Pretty Peggy-O* (1990); *The Hangman's Beautiful Daughter* (1992); *She Walks These Hills* (1994); *The Rosewood Casket* (1996); *The Ballad of Frankie Silver* (1999); *Ghost Riders* (2004).

Other series: The "Elizabeth McPherson" series, featuring an Appalachian-born forensic anthropologist who investigates deaths abroad, especially in Scotland; the "Jay Omega" series, humorously parodying science fiction fans in *Bimbos of the Death Sun* (1987) and *Zombies of the Gene Pool* (1992).

Nonseries novel: *St. Dale*, about stock car racing (2005).

Short fiction: *Foggy Mountain Breakdown and Other Stories* (1997).

Major awards: Edgar Award, Mystery Writers of America (1988); Macavity Award, Agatha Award, Anthony Award, Nero Award (1994); Agatha Award (1995).

Selected sources: *Armchair Detective*. Rev. of *The Hangman's Beautiful Daughter*, Spring 1992: 234; *Los Angeles Times Book Review*. Rev. of *If Ever I Return, Pretty Peggy-O*, September 9, 1990; *Publishers Weekly*. Rev. of *She Walks These Hills*, August 19, 1994: 63; *Washington Post Book World*. Rev. of *The Rosewood Casket*, April 21, 1996; *Wilson Library Bulletin*. Rev. of *If Ever I Return, Pretty Peggy-O*, September 1990: 106–7.

See also: Philip DePoy's Appalachian series featuring Fever Devlin, folklorist; Vicki Lane's Elizabeth Goodweather series, set in the North Carolina mountains; Michael Malone's Detective Justin Savil V series, set in North Carolina's Piedmont area; John A. Miller's Sheriff A.G. Farrell series, set in the rural 1950s Blue Ridge area of Virginia.

Jane Austen

Profession:	Authoress
Living situation:	Spinster
Geographic locale:	England, especially provincial towns of the South
Time period:	Early 1800s, during the Peninsular War
Associate:	Lord Harold Trowbridge, "the Gentleman Rogue"
Nemesis:	The Monster (Napoleon) and his minions
Significant relationship:	Lord Harold Trowbridge
Concerns:	England; Jane Austen's writing career; social satire

Faithful "Janeites," admirers of the Regency novelist celebrated for her polished comedies of English county manners, revel in Stephanie Barron's accomplished re-creations of Jane Austen and her world. The real Jane Austen unobtrusively wrote her own six novels at her father's Hampshire vicarage, where she spent her first twenty-five years, and, except for the posthumous (1818) *Northanger Abbey* and *Persuasion*, all were published between 1811 and 1816, toward the end of her short life. All Austen's novels display exquisite irony, firm morality, and vividly drawn characters, qualities Barron generally succeeds in emulating through the lavishly detailed milieus and fine-tuned Regency dialogue of this series.

The horizons of Barron's fictional Jane Austen expand to international proportions through Barron's backdrop, England's mortal struggle against Napoleon ("The Monster"), menacing England from both land and sea. The Peninsular War, 1808–1814, erupted when Napoleon attempted to dominate Spain and Portugal by placing his brother Joseph on the Spanish throne. When the two countries revolted, the British sent Arthur Wellesley, the future Duke of Wellington, to support the rebels. Portugal soon was rid of the French, but the costly Spanish campaign continued for years, since at considerable cost in men and wealth, the British used that conflict to tie The Monster down on the Continent, thus preventing him from destroying the Royal Navy and subjugating Britain itself.

Barron's Jane Austen, as the respectable but relatively impoverished daughter of a clergyman and his hypochondriacal upwardly-aspiring wife, wryly romps through what Edward Marston called "the England of the hackney carriage" in her first five "cases," skewering pretentious provincial "ladies who primp and faint and swoon" (*Denver Post*) and the dashing dandies, cads, and rogues who continuously provide those ladies delicious fits of the vapors.

As an indefatigable observer of minute societal foibles, Jane ironically counterpoints early-nineteenth-century frivolity—parties, theater evenings, and outings at fashionable watering places—in *Jane and the Unpleasantness at Scargrave Manor* (1996), and even, as some real Jane Austen commentators insist, carries on a "nameless and dateless" romance with an appealing clergyman in *Jane and the Man of the Cloth* (1996). Later, Jane manages to cover a good deal of southern England. *Jane and the Wandering Eye* (1997) finds her amid the elegant spas of Bath "in the discreet service of solving a murder," according to the *New York Times Book Review*'s Marilyn Stasio, but *Jane and the Prisoner of Wool House* (2001) takes her to the bustling port of Southampton, where she encounters "the naval set" through her brother Frank ("Fly"), a Royal Navy post captain waiting for a ship to command. Trying to clear the name of Frank's friend and fellow captain "Lucky Tom" Seagrave propels Jane into deliciously horrid, even pestilential, dockside stews, risking her own life and revealing the intrepid heart beneath under her circumspect whalebone and crinolines.

Though the real Jane Austen liked happy endings, *Jane and the Ghosts of Netley* (2003) offers a penetrating bittersweet view of her fictional self's heart and soul, as she stalwartly battles international espionage and intrigue with Lord Harold Trowbridge, a dangerous and well-nigh irresistible "Gentleman Rogue" Jane had encountered earlier. Trowbridge, now employed on secret missions for His Majesty's government, summons Jane to his ship moored in Southampton Water. He needs Jane to inveigle herself into the confidence of Sophia Challoner, Napoleon's "most potent weapon," into whose dainty spying ears the chagrined Lord Harold admits to

Jane, "'I have talked when I should not. I have trusted too easily. I have allowed myself to be flattered and deceived and Said Too Much.' Said Jane tartly, 'Then you have been a man'" (*Ghosts of Netley* 29).

Nonetheless unable to resist Lord Harold, Jane has a penchant for stumbling over corpses, leading her on a breakneck foray into Sophia's very boudoir to probe the murder of a shipwright and mysterious apparitions in Netley's nearby ruined abbey. Subsequently in Lord Harold's closed carriage, an unthinkably compromising situation, Jane suddenly sees into her heart and his, claiming when he asks whether he should make an offer for her hand that she aspires "to a career as an authoress, and such ladies never marry" (*Ghosts of Netley* 92) because domestic cares would leave her no time to write.

Lord Harold perishes nobly of a knife wound at the climax of *Jane and the Ghosts of Netley*, just after abandoning his pride to declare the love for her that she then reciprocates, relinquishing her prejudices about the gulf between their social stations. But his spirit dominates *Jane and His Lordship's Legacy* (2005): "'Promise me... you will write,'" he had commanded her with his dying breath (*Ghosts of Netley* 316), but his death nearly cast Jane, now in her mid-thirties, into "the black pit." Only partially recovered the next summer, just after moving into her last home, Chawton Cottage, she receives a stunning bequest: a Bengal chest crammed full of Lord Harold's personal papers, some of which the royal family would dearly love to see destroyed; but before she can pen Lord Harold's memoirs for posterity, she must solve the murder of a shiftless laborer found mutilated in the cottage's cellar, untangle rival claims to two nearby estates, and trace the legend of the stolen Chawton Emeralds. Just as she had shelved her personal worries when Sophia Challoner's threat to England had to be defused, Jane again puts duty before her sensibilities of lost love, reflecting that perhaps here at Chawton, "I might begin again" (*Lordship's Legacy*, quoted unpaginated in *Ghosts of Netley*).

Novels: *Jane and the Unpleasantness at Scargrave Manor* (1996); *Jane and the Man of the Cloth* (1996); *Jane and the Wandering Eye* (1997); *Jane and the Genius of Place* (1999); *Jane and the Stillroom Maid* (2000); *Jane and the Prisoner of Wool House* (2001); *Jane and the Ghosts of Netley* (2003); *Jane and His Lordship's Legacy* (2005).

Selected sources: *Kirkus Reviews*. Rev. of *Jane and His Lordship's Legacy*, March 1, 2005: 623; *Publishers Weekly*. Rev. of *Jane and the Ghosts of Netley*, May 12, 2003: 45; *Publishers Weekly*. Rev. of *Jane and His Lordship's Legacy*, February 14, 2005: 37; Stasio, Marilyn. Rev. of *Jane and the Wandering Eye*. *New York Times Book Review*, 1997: 26.

See also: Novels by neo-Jane Austens Pamela Aidan (*An Assembly Such as This: Fitzwilliam Darcy, Gentleman, Book I*, and *Duty and Desire: Fitzwilliam Darcy, Gentleman, Book II*, first and second of a three-volume series; other Austenite authors are Elizabeth Aston, Julia Barrett, and Emma Tennant. Laura Levine's "Jaine Austen" cozy mystery series features a sassy contemporary Austenite freelance writer in *This Pen for Hire* (2002), *Last Writes* (2003), and *Killer Blonde* (2004).

Debut novel: Carrie Bebris's *Pride and Prescience: A Mr. and Mrs. Darcy Mystery*, which starts with the wedding day of Fitzwilliam Darcy and Elizabeth Bennet.

B

Alan Banks

Profession:	Detective Chief Inspector, "Eastvale," Yorkshire C.I.D.
Living situation:	Married, then divorced
Geographic locale:	Yorkshire, England
Time period:	1987–present
Associates:	Various police subordinates
Nemesis:	Chief Constable Jimmy Riddle
Significant relationships:	Ex-wife Sandra; Detective Inspector Annie Cabbot
Concerns:	Justice; mutability of personal relationships

Peter Robinson's Detective Inspector Alan Banks thought he left violence behind when he and his family moved from London to fictional Swainsdale in the apparently peaceful "Herriot Country" of the beautiful Yorkshire Dales, but once there, like many characters who entered mystery fiction during the 1980s (Herbert 169), Banks faces both fierce domestic tensions and vicious crimes. Each case has its horde of suspects and complex motives and has to be investigated under pressure, but Banks's inner furies pursue him more savagely than his external ones throughout this award-winning police procedural series.

As a former Londoner, Banks savors the Dales's beauty and their history, both lovingly evoked in native son Robinson's atmospheric prose, but "Being more used to getting around in the city than in the countryside" (*Dedicated Man* 6), Banks sometimes scrapes a knee getting over one of those picturesque drystone walls like the one his gritty Yorkshireman superior and friend, Detective Superintendent Gristhorpe, is obsessively repairing. Banks also stumbles occasionally over the "slow, thick" Yorkshire dialect, abrupt Yorkshire manners, and obscure Yorkshire customs, many resulting from York's preponderantly Norwegian heritage, so different from the metropolitan South.

In the early novels, Banks, small, dark, somewhat Celtic Welsh in appearance, is a devoted family man, typically delighted with his son Brian, fond to distraction of his daughter Tracy, happily anticipating his wife Sandra's succulent Sunday roast beef and Yorkshire pudding. When the phone rings, though, a conscientious policeman like Banks immediately abandons roast beef and family for stomach-churning crime scenes and time-devouring trails of gruesome evidence. Sandra's plaintive "I don't suppose there's any point in keeping it warm?" (*Dedicated Man* 5) soon describes the Banks's marriage, too. Initial marital molehills—early on she attacked his Wagnerian tape of Siegfried's Funeral Music with a magnet—swell into mountainous obstacles.

At first Banks discusses his cases with Sandra, whose artist's eye and feminine intuition often help him detect nuances he might otherwise have missed: " 'They were lovers,' " she said finally, " 'I'll bet you a pound to a penny they were lovers.' . . . When he looked more closely, Banks knew that Sandra was right" (*Innocent Graves* 140). Later, to fill the space in her life left empty by Banks's devotion to his law enforcement work, Sandra devotes herself to her art gallery job, leaving Banks to "his policeman's sense of duty and his even deeper-rooted curiosity" (*Innocent Graves* 385).

Banks's job also throws him into close proximity with ambitious female officers like newly promoted Detective Constable Susan Gay in *Past Reason Hated* (1991), women determined to show their male superiors "a woman could do the job every bit as well as a man, if not better" (*Past Reason* 2). Though not at first romantically drawn to his women colleagues, Banks finds more in common with them than with Sandra, who, with their children grown and her own work stimulating, leaves him in *Blood at the Root* (1997). Deeply in denial, Banks reflects, "Maybe they both did need a little time to maneuver and regroup after all the changes of the past few years," vowing to himself "to make damn sure he kept in touch" with his children (213–14). Sensing but not acknowledging the finality of the breakup, he cranks up Mozart's *Requiem* and gets "rat-arse drunk" on Laphroaig (249), his favorite single malt Scotch, only to wake up "wifeless and hung over" and possibly jobless because of a row with hostile Chief Constable Jimmy Riddle (251). Susan, realizing "for ages it *was* Banks she fancied" and can never have because "he wouldn't look at her that way in a month of Sundays" decides to leave Eastvale (italics in original, 248).

In *Cold Is the Grave* (2000), coping with his failed marriage and his distancing children and chained to his desk in dismal career doldrums because of Riddle's animosity, Banks's days in Yorkshire seem numbered. Despite a brief fling with Detective Sergeant Annie Cabbot, Banks has just applied for transfer to the National Crime Squad, secretly hoping that moving to London might bring Sandra back. From the blue, Banks's career again interferes. Nude pictures of Jimmy Riddle's runaway teenage daughter Emily have turned up on a "Spicy Girls" Web site, and Riddle asks Banks to find her and bring her home. Sifting through the sordid details of this scandal-filled investigation with Annie Cabbot, who is facing her own problems now that their affair is over, leaves Banks stunned and numb and sick at heart through his next three cases, while Sandra remarries and bears another man's child. Police work affords Banks only a dubious solace as he tracks a serial torturer and killer of young girls in *Aftermath* (2001) while dealing with the fallout from his divorce. In *Close to Home* (2003), he abandons his long-overdue vacation on a Greek island to revisit the world of his 1960s boyhood and his own guilty fear that he might have caused the disappearance of his best friend. In *Playing with Fire* (2004), working again with Annie Cabbot, Banks loses nearly everything, including his own life. Alan Banks's tragedy is that "the loss of innocence *never* stopped happening, . . . he was still losing it . . . it was like a wound that never healed, and he would probably go on losing it, drop by drop, until the day he died" (*Cold Is the Grave* 369; italics in original).

Novels: *Gallows View* (1987); *A Dedicated Man* (1988); *A Necessary End* (1989); *The Hanging Valley* (1989); *Past Reason Hated* (1991); *Wednesday's Child* (1992); *Final Account* (1994); *Innocent Graves* (1996); *Blood at the Root* (1997); *In a Dry Season* (1999); *Cold Is the Grave* (2000); *Aftermath* (2001); *Close to Home* (2003); *Playing with Fire* (2004); *Strange Affair* (2005).

Short stories: *Not Safe after Dark* (1998).

Poetry collections: *With Equal Eye* (1979); *Nosferatu* (1981).

Selected sources: Fletcher, Connie. Rev. of *Aftermath*. *Booklist*, September 1, 2001: 57; *Kirkus Reviews*. Rev. of *Not Safe after Dark*, October 1, 1998: 1419; Mann, Caroline. Rev. of *In a Dry Season*. *Library Journal*, April 1, 1999: 131; *Publishers Weekly*. Rev. of *Cold Is the Grave*, September 4, 2000: 88; Stasio, Marilyn. Rev. of *Strange Affair*. *New York Times Book Review*, February 20, 2005: 37.

Major awards: Arthur Ellis Award, 1990 and 1991; Anthony Award, 1999.

Web site: www.inspectorbanks.com.

See also: Yorkshire police procedurals: Pauline Bell's Detective Constable Benedict Mitchell series; Patricia Hall's Detective Chief Inspector Michael Thackeray series; Reginald Hill's **Sergeant Peter Pascoe–Superintendent Andrew Dalziel** series; Peter Turnbull's Detective Inspector Hennessey series.

China Bayles

Profession:	Former attorney, now herbalist
Living situation:	Single; later married
Geographic locale:	East Texas
Time period:	1992–present
Associate:	Ruby Wilcox
Nemesis:	Pecan Springs's Chief of Police, Bubba Harris

| *Significant relationship*: | Mike McQuaid, former Houston homicide detective and divorced single parent |
| *Concern*: | Justice over law |

Both former university professor and administrator Susan Wittig Albert and her heroine, former attorney China Bayles, decided in midlife "enough was enough" (quoted in *CA Online*) and abandoned the fast track to success. Just as China Bayles found her real self raising and selling herbs in Pecan Springs, Texas, Albert opted for country life outside Austin in 1985, writing over sixty children's books and launching the China Bayles series with *Thyme of Death* (1992). At thirty-nine, after fifteen years of living on stress pills and seeing "enough of the shadow side of justice" to last the rest of her life, China Bayles escaped from her yuppie condo and a Houston law practice "protecting the constitutional rights of…big bad guys who had the wherewithal to pick up the tab for an expensive defense" with most of her sanity and some of her youth (*Thyme* 2, 1). She settled in artsy-craftsy little Pecan Springs, midway between Austin and San Antonio in flat, fertile, cedar-blanketed farmland, and made a century-old stone house both her home and her Thyme and Seasons Herb Company. China left the law for two reasons: she couldn't believe any longer that justice and the legal system operated in partnership, and she did believe that practicing law was changing her into a person she didn't like, "more arrogant, more competitive, more cutthroat than I knew myself to be" (*Thyme* 8).

The new China keeps up her Bar Association dues in case the bottom falls out of the herb business, using her legal training pro bono to solve violent crimes that disrupt Pecan Springs's peace and to rescue women victimized by greed, lust, or sheer (generally male) cussedness. In *Thyme of Death*, accompanied by her flamboyant New Age best friend Ruby Wilcox, seller of crystals, Tarot decks, and assorted earth goddess paraphernalia, China investigates the death of activist and breast cancer patient Jo Gilbert. China and Ruby refuse to believe that Jo committed suicide, and between toothsome noshes (recipes included) they uncover a gaggle of colorful suspects, including Roz Kotner, saccharine "StrawBerry Bear" TV personality and Jo's erstwhile lesbian lover.

China is also involved with dishy Mike McQuaid, a few years younger than China's forty-two, who quit his job as a Houston homicide cop because, like China, he prefers justice to the law. McQuaid, working on a criminal justice Ph.D. at the local Central Texas State University, is the divorced single father of Brian, an engaging boy China likes very much, but though she and McQuaid enjoy great sex when not interrupted by her cell phone or his, China can't open herself up to him completely because of old family ghosts—a domineering sonless father who saw to it that China followed in his legal workaholic footsteps, and a neglected alcoholic mother unable to give her any emotional support.

China's long-standing adversarial relationship with the police, especially grungy good ol' boy Chief Bubba Harris, continues through successive East Texas murders played out against the larger story of her relationship with McQuaid, which forces her to confront her childhood demons. Early books in the series feature China's female friends, like *Witches' Bane* (1993) where China has to extricate Ruby from accusations of Satanism by Rev. Billy Lee Harbuck of the Everlasting Faith Bible Church, while China copes with a visit from her mother—newly sober, but how long will it last? *Hangman's Root* (1994) freshens China's stalwart crime solving by easing up on the herb lore, and then in *Rosemary Remembered* (1995) McQuaid comes to the fore with delicious foreplay and detecting backup. China retreats to a remote convent to contemplate where their relationship should go next in *Rueful Death* (1996) and emerges bent on marriage to McQuaid, but on returning to Pecan Springs in *Love Lies Bleeding* (1997), she discovers that not only has he found another flame, he's connected to the murder of a former Texas Ranger. They reconcile in *Chile Death* (1998), where an obnoxious adulterous salesman judging a chili-cooking contest succumbs to an allergic reaction to one entry's spices, and just before their marriage in *Lavender Lies* (1998), McQuaid takes over as Pecan Springs's police chief in time to help China unmask the killer of a crooked real estate developer. Marital bliss flourishes in *Mistletoe Man* (1999), while in *Bloodroot* (2001) China returns to her Deep South roots to lay her troublesome childhood ghosts to rest. *Indigo Dying* (2002), *A Dilly of a Death* (2003), and *Dead Man's Bones* (2005) take China's insight into her friends' problems still further and allow China and McQuaid to balance their homicide solutions with their domestic relationships, fulfilling the various challenges that Albert finds in series writing. For her, this means defying expectations and showing that this familiar genre allows possibilities for growth, with the security of dependable characters and settings. Each of China Bayles's novels manages to come up fresh, like perennial herbs that flourish in arid poor-soil conditions.

Novels: *Thyme of Death* (1992); *Witches' Bane* (1993); *Hangman's Root* (1994); *Rosemary Remembered* (1995); *Rueful Death* (1996); *Love Lies Bleeding* (1997); *Chile Death* (1998); *Lavender Lies* (1999); *Mistletoe Man* (2000); *Bloodroot* (2001); *Indigo Dying* (2002); *A Dilly of a Death* (2004); *Dead Man's Bones* (2005); *Bleeding Hearts* (2006).

Short stories: *An Unthymely Death and Other Garden Mysteries* (2002; includes herbal lore sidebars).

Other series: "Kate and Charles" Victorian mysteries (with husband Bill Albert, under joint pseudonym Robin Paige); the "Cottage Tales of Beatrix Potter" series, including *The Tale of Hill Top Farm* (2004) and *The Tale of Holly How* (2005).

Other works: *Work of Her Own: How Women Create Success and Fulfillment off the Traditional Career Track* (1992); *Writing from Life: Telling Your Soul's Story* (1997); and more than sixty children's books, including several "Nancy Drew" and "Hardy Boys" mysteries.

Selected sources: *Armchair Detective.* Rev. of *Witches' Bane*, Spring 1993: 109; *Horticulture.* Rev. of *Hangman's Root*, February 1995: 72; Miller, Stuart. Rev. of *Rueful Death*. *Booklist*, October 1, 1996: 324; *Publishers Weekly.* Rev. of *Dead Man's Bones*, March 21, 2005: 76; *Publishers Weekly.* Rev. of *A Dilly of a Death*, December 15, 2003: 84.

Major awards: Danforth Graduate Fellowship; nominations, Agatha and Anthony Awards, 1992.

Web site: Partners in Crime Headquarters, Susan Wittig Albert and Bill Albert: www .mysterypartners.com.

See also: Janis Harrison's Gardening Mysteries, featuring Ozarks flower shop owner Bretta Solomon; for medieval herbal/apothecary lore; Ellis Peter's **Brother Cadfael** series; Candace Robb's **Owen Archer** series (Archer's wife Lucie is an herbalist and apothecary).

Debut novel: Anthony Eglin, *The Blue Rose: An English Garden Mystery*.

Goldy Bear (Schulz)

Profession:	Caterer
Living situation:	Originally a divorced victim of spousal abuse; later married
Geographic locale:	"Aspen Meadow" (fictional), Colorado
Time period:	1990–present
Associate:	Marla Korman
Significant relationship:	Tom Schulz
Concerns:	Parenthood; independence; cookery; justice

From an inauspicious 1990 debut in *Catering to Nobody*, described by *Publishers Weekly*'s Sybil Steinberg as "embarrassing" (June 19, 1990: 89), Diane Mott Davidson has leavened her Goldy (short for Gertrude) Bear culinary mystery series into spicy cozy-cum-cookery soufflés garnished with original recipes that leave her audience hungering for more.

Like her porridge-sampling predecessor in snoopery, slightly plump, thirtyish, and curly-haired Goldy's unquenchable stubbornness often lands her in hot water, most of it set aboil by her ex, handsome and wealthy John Richard Korman, aka "The Jerk," a womanizing ob-gyn whose other favorite indoor sport is wife-beating. Goldy refuses to take alimony from The Jerk, who keeps her seething over erratic child support and dilatory visitations with their early-adolescent son Arch, so she revamps their Aspen Meadow, Colorado, house into Goldilocks' Catering, "Where Everything is Just Right!" High-energy murders spiked with sassy dollops of sex accompany Goldy's struggles to support herself and Arch, escape The Jerk's continuing harassment, and find happiness with hunky caterer's crumpet and sheriff's investigator Tom Schulz in this 1990s Front Range variation of the traditional British village cozy. "As a caterer, Goldy knows everybody; as a homicide inspector, Tom Schulz knows everything about everybody, and, as a gynecologist, The Jerk has the inside scoop on nearly half the population" (*Silk Stalkings* 2: 148).

In the pattern-setting *Catering to Nobody*, Tom Schulz shuts down Goldilocks' Catering after The Jerk's randy father collapses from rat-poisoned lemonade at the post-funeral reception Goldy caters following the death of Arch's favorite teacher,

Laura Smiley, who was found in her bathtub with wrists slashed. To get back in business for the pre-Christmas parties that feed herself and Arch for the rest of the year, Goldy has to solve the attempted poisoning and shake the lid off a murderer with an unsavory past. Supported by her flamboyant best friend Marla Korman, The Jerk's second ex, Goldy also copes with Arch's Dungeons and Dragons preteen angst, an alcoholic ex-mother-in-law, assorted affluent gossipy townsfolk, and her burnt-child reluctance to get romantically involved with muscular Tom Schulz, who pursues her with relish and good restaurant meals and eventually proves to be a great cook himself.

Goldy's personal and business travails continually stir up the series, because all the novels involve substantial threats to her business and/or her family and friends. In *Dying for Chocolate* (1992), she's temporarily employed as a live-in cook while having an anti-Jerk alarm system installed in her home. She even puts Tom on the back burner so she can relight an old flame, Dr. Philip Miller—who then expires before Goldy's eyes. Business and romance gather steam in *The Cereal Murders* (1993), with young catering assistant Julian Teller joining Goldilocks' Catering. After Tom Shultz extricates Goldy from accusations of strangling the valedictorian of the local upscale prep school with an extension cord at the spiffy graduation do she's catering, Tom proposes to her, but at the start of *The Last Suppers* (1994) he stumbles on the body of their officiating minister and disappears. Two months after Tom and Goldy finally marry, *Killer Pancake* (1995) flattens poor Julian with the hit-and-run murder of his girlfriend in a parking lot, forcing Goldy and Tom to sniff out rancid secrets in Mignon Cosmetics when that firm launches their new makeup with Goldy's primo low-fat luncheon. *The Main Corpse* (1996) finds Goldy's business declining and Marla, on a diet-and-exercise regime after a near-fatal heart attack, suspected of murder.

The next installments in the series range from medium well to near-leathery crimes. In *The Grilling Season* (1997), Goldy yields to Arch's pleas to help The Jerk, accused of killing his current squeeze. Goldy's business takes yet another hit in *Prime Cut* (1998) when her remodeling contractor absconds, leaving her kitchen a shambles, and in *Tough Cookie* (2000), a new nemesis, health inspector Roger Mannis, closes her business down after Goldy's live spot on a local PBS cooking show goes disastrously haywire. The Jerk, sprung from prison on a technicality, returns to haunt Goldy in *Sticks and Scones* (2001), as she's feverishly preparing an Elizabethan feast for a castle dismantled in England and newly reconstructed in Colorado, and *Chopping Spree* (2002) catches her exonerating Julian, who is arrested for murdering an old school friend of Goldy's. *Double Shot* (2004) dumps Goldy from the frying pan into the fire when she discovers her new investment, The Roundhouse, a catering and event center, trashed on the eve of another post–memorial service gig and she becomes the prime suspect in The Jerk's ensuing murder.

While her colorful supporting characters spice up Goldy's scrapes, the main course of this series remains her feisty, piquant-tongued refusal to give in to the stresses of single momhood, The Jerk's machinations, the small-town pressure cooker, and an antagonistic health inspector. Soothed by her cooking whether she's caught up in a

Mixmaster of murder or shredding the unsavory types who infest her kitchen and her events, intuitive Goldy Bear, fueled by espresso and whipped cream, improvises solutions just as she cooks—with butter and love. And her recipes are simply to die for.

Novels: *Catering to Nobody* (1990); *Dying for Chocolate* (1992); *The Cereal Murders* (1993); *The Last Suppers* (1994); *Killer Pancake* (1995); *The Main Corpse* (1996); *The Grilling Season* (1997); *Prime Cut* (1998); *Tough Cookie* (2000); *Sticks and Scones* (2001); *Chopping Spree* (2002); *Double Shot* (2004); *Dark Tort* (2006).

Other series: Toni Underwood police procedural series.

Selected sources: Carrigan, Maureen. Rev. of *Tough Cookie*. *Washington Post Book World*, March 26, 2000: 13; Clark, Juleigh Muirhead. Rev. of *The Grilling Season*. *Library Journal*, May 15, 1998: 968; Klausner, Harriet. Rev. of *Chopping Spree*. *BookBrowser*, www.book browser.com, January 1, 2000; Miller, Stuart. Rev. of *Catering to Nobody*. *Booklist*, August 1990: 2158; Weiner, Debbie Ann. Rev. of *Sticks and Scones*. *Bookreporter.com*, www.book reporter.com.

Major award: Anthony Award, 1992.

Web site: www.dianemottdavidson.com.

See also: Michael Bond's **Monsieur Pamplemousse** restaurant critic series; JoAnna Carl's Chocolate Mysteries featuring Lee McKinney; Laura Child's Theodosia Browning's Charleston, South Carolina tea shop cozies; Isis Crawford's series featuring Langely, New York caterer Libby Simmons; Ellen Hart's Jane Lawless gay restaurant owner series and Hart's Minneapolis restaurant critic Sophie Greenway series; Peter King's Gourmet Detective Mysteries, visiting world-famous haute cuisine venues; Janet Laurence's Cordon Bleu chef Darina Lisle series; Amy Myers's Victorian Anglo-French master chef August Didier series; Tamar Myers's Pennsylvania Dutch Mysteries with recipes; Katherine Hall Page's series featuring Vermont caterer Faith Fairchild. Many of these culinary mysteries include bonus recipes.

Debut novels: Sandra Balzo's *Uncommon Grounds*, featuring Wisconsin coffee house proprietor Maggie Thorsen; Susan Conant and Jessica Conant-Park's *Burned*; Deborah Donnelly's *Veiled Threats*, featuring Seattle wedding planner Carnegie Kincaid; Joanne Fluke's *Sugar Cookie Murder*, featuring Minnesota cookie baker Hannah Swensen. Mystery related cookbooks include *The Cat Who Cookbook*, by Sally Stempinski and Julie Murphy; and *Food to Die For*, by Patricia Cornwell and Marlene Brown.

Martin Beck

Profession:	Homicide detective
Living situation:	Unhappily married, then separated
Geographic locale:	Sweden
Time period:	1965–1975

Associates:	Lennart Kollberg; to a lesser extent, others on the Homicide Bureau
Nemesis:	Capitalism
Significant relationship:	None
Concerns:	Political damage to police work and society

Avowed Marxists Per Wahlöö and Maj Sjöwall set out "to use the crime novel as a scalpel cutting open the belly of the ideologically pauperized and morally debatable so-called welfare state" (quoted in Murphy 33), so they envisioned their Martin Beck series as "ten parts of a single novel three hundred chapters long" (*CA Online*), a "Novel of a Crime" forming a crescendoing political polemic against Sweden's democratic socialism, which they saw as veering toward bourgeois capitalism. Commentators differ on whether their political aims for this collaborative series, halted by Wahlöö's death in 1975, succeeded, but most agree that it is "one of the best of all police procedural series" (Ashley 482).

Like Ed McBain's Detective **Steve Carella** of the 87th Precinct novels, Martin Beck focuses but does not dominate the work of Stockholm's Homicide Bureau, which he heads as Chief Inspector. Beck expects a great deal of his team, each of whom complements his brooding, often self-tormenting personality and his essentially psychological approach to crime-solving. Beck, the son of an impoverished truck driver, began his police career in 1944 as a Stockholm patrolman, attended the police academy, and joined Stockholm's C.I.D. in 1951, when he married cold, practical Inga, with whom he had two children. By the time Beck is in his mid-40s, his long-time right-hand man and closest friend Lennart Kollberg has run to physical flab, but Beck relies on Kollberg to play "the best shots," ask "the right questions," and "give the proper cues" (*Abominable Man* 30). Kollberg's uncomplicated happy marriage to lusty twenty-years-younger Gun contrasts dramatically with the chilly marital downward slide that finally causes Beck, constantly troubled with gastric distress, to move from his wife Inga's living room sofa to a two-room apartment where he can quietly smoke his Floridas, work on his clipper ship models, and listen to Bach's Brandenburg Concertos as fleeting respite from the horrors he faces in his work. He eventually finds a new romantic interest, Rhea Nielson.

As "a version of the modern antihero" (Symons 248), Beck never lets himself be taken aback, except by his own emotional coolness (*Abominable Man* 27). Besides Kollberg, who by the time of *The Abominable Man* (1972)—a fictionalized savage denunciation of brutality in Sweden's police system—is contemplating leaving the force, Beck believes his only friends are his college-age daughter Ingrid, who has also moved out of the family home, a policewoman named Åsa Torell, and maybe fellow detective Per Månsson, who works in the smaller city of Malmö. Beck maintains conscientiously correct relations with all of his team. He is sensitive to and able to pull together their various talents, like Fredrik Melander's eidetic memory, but he finds establishing personal contact with most of them, especially Einar Rönn, a dependable but plodding detective, virtually impossible. Beck is equally ill at ease with handsome young giant Gunvald Larsson, independently well-to-do and self-assured, whose savage temperament personifies the militaristic approach to police work that Beck deplores.

Beck also is ambivalent about his own capabilities. His reason and training insist that intuition has no place in police work, yet a certain irrational sense of danger he can't shake often alerts him to dicey situations and potential solutions that seem to follow no logical pattern until the pieces of complicated puzzles suddenly fall into place. As Beck is thinking through a given crime, he needs his subordinates, especially Kollberg, to provide hypotheses that Beck can then refute or pursue (*Abominable Man* 30), but failing such stimuli, as when he has to work with the capable but unimaginative Rönn, Beck feels irritated, frustrated, and impatient. He buries all those negative feelings under an imperturbable façade, beneath which his gastric juices constantly churn and recurrent colds plague his chest and nasal passages.

Beck's dedication to his job costs him his wife, who like many police wives wondered for too long why he had to do all the jobs on the force. By *The Fire Engine that Disappeared* (1971), he no longer cares whether he takes a vacation or not and at the prospect of two or three loathsome days with her and his tippling brother-in-law, Beck lies, telling Inga he has to work over a summer holiday. This small displacement of Beck's stern moral code makes him feel like a criminal for the first time since at fifteen he forged his mother's name on a school excuse. It also marks a significant moment of belated life-change for Beck. Even though he had good reasons for the lie, "it was entirely a question of personal ethics; he was taking a stand and justifying it to himself, and thus he had upset certain fundamental personal values" (*Fire Engine* 181).

Until that crisis in Beck's life, he had gloomily but patiently gone about his work, solving the murder of a young woman in *Roseanna* (1967), tracking a vanished young reporter and uncovering a drug-smuggling operation in *The Man Who Went Up in Smoke* (1968), and landing a mass murderer in *The Laughing Policeman* (1970). In *The Fire Engine that Disappeared*, though, Beck stands aside, like a Greek chorus (Murphy 32), from the disasters that novel depicts. Thereafter, Beck investigates the slaughter of an aging police officer in *The Abominable Man*, solves a classically constructed plot in *The Locked Room* (1973), untangles yet another murder and copes with a police shootout in *Cop Killer* (1975), and protects a visiting American senator from assassination in *The Terrorists* (1976), but he feels more and more uncomfortable with the hypocrisies of life in Sweden.

Through Martin Beck, his creators level political criticism in these novels at Sweden's "Crime," the betrayal of socialist ideals by the Swedish Social Democrat government, criticism that becomes more and more strident. Beck, a good cop in an evil world, watches the system he serves self-destruct, its lack of effective social programs abandoning sixteen-year-olds to prostitution and its reform schools mere preludes to drug dealing and worse. Beck internalizes his dismay into physical distress and spiritual despair, while Kollberg and Larsson strike out against the capitalist mindset that Marxists cannot tolerate, Kollberg by abandoning his police career, Larsson by using Orwellian police tactics. Finally all Beck can do is almost lose "his life in a Christ-like attempt to atone for his colleagues' sins" (Nils Nordberg in Herbert 17).

Novels: * *Roseanna* (1967); *The Man Who Went Up in Smoke* (1968); *The Man on the Balcony* (1968); *The Laughing Policeman* (1970); *The Fire Engine that Disappeared* (1971); *Murder at the Savoy* (1971); *The Abominable Man* (1972); *The Locked Room* (1973); *Cop Killer* (1975); *The Terrorists* (1976).

Other series (by Wahlöö alone): the Chief Inspector Peter Jensen series.

Other works (by Wahlöö alone): Stand-alone novels, including *A Necessary Action* (1969); *The Assignment* (1965); *The Generals* (1974).

Selected sources: Adams, Phoebe. Rev. of *Cop Killer*. *Atlantic Monthly*, June 1975; Bailey, O.L. Rev. of *The Abominable Man*. *Saturday Review*, October 28, 1972; Binyon, T.J. Rev. of *The Terrorists*. *Times Literary Supplement*, May 17, 1977; Hubin, A.J. Rev. of *The Laughing Policeman*. *New York Times Book Review*, January 31, 1971; Van Dover, Kenneth. *Polemical Pulps*. San Bernardina, CA: Brownstone Books, 1993.

Major awards: Sherlock Award (Sweden), 1968; Edgar Award, Mystery Writers of America, 1971.

See also: For collective police protagonists, Ed McBain's 87th Precinct series, centering on Detective **Steve Carella**.

Ursula Blanchard

Profession:	Lady of the Queen's Presence Chamber; spy for Sir William Cecil
Living situation:	Widowed twice, then remarried
Geographic locale:	England, France, and the Low Countries
Time period:	Early Elizabethan Period (1560s)
Associates:	Fran Dale, Ursula's tirewoman; Roger Brockley, Dale's husband and Ursula's manservant
Nemesis:	Mary Queen of Scots
Significant relationships:	Gerald Blanchard and Matthew de la Roche, Ursula's first and second husbands respectively; Hugh Stannard, her third husband
Concerns:	The Protestant cause; loyalty to Queen Elizabeth

Valerie Anand writes historical mysteries under the pen name Fiona Buckley, primarily intending her novels, she claims, to "take someone's mind off his income tax or his influenza," but she also insists that fiction "can be a means of exploring human dilemmas," allowing the author to examine important issues "without being clouded by the reader's (or the author's) own personal loyalties" (quoted in *CA Online*).

Buckley makes her fictional milieu the turbulent 1560s. Elizabeth I, daughter of Henry VIII and the ill-fated Anne Boleyn, battled to uphold Protestantism after the five-year reign of terror instituted by Henry's older daughter "Bloody" Mary Tudor,

---

*English titles and dates given for U.S. publication.

who married Philip of Spain and attempted to force England back into the Roman Catholic fold. After Elizabeth became queen following Mary Tudor's death, English Catholics rallied around the romantic Mary Stuart, Queen of Scots, descended like Elizabeth from Henry VII and scheming to seize Elizabeth's throne, generating the religious and political international intrigues central to Buckley's novels.

To Shield the Queen (1997) introduces Buckley's intrepid heroine Ursula Blanchard; daughter of one of Anne Boleyn's ladies-in-waiting, Ursula serves Queen Elizabeth in the same capacity. Both women are in their mid-twenties; both have sharp wits, dangerously hot tempers, and "something magical,...a spirit full of incantation" (*Queen's Ransom* 274). Not surprisingly, later installments in the series reveal that the women are half-sisters, fathered by Henry VIII and endowed with his formidable courage and shrewdness.

Eighteen months after Elizabeth took the throne, Ursula came to court as a poverty-stricken widow with Meg, her small daughter, to raise. Ursula and merchant Gerald Blanchard had married for love, alienating his wealthy relatives, who detested her for ruining Gerald's chances to wed her rich cousin and increase the family fortunes. After Gerald's death from smallpox, the Blanchards continue to shun Ursula, so to support herself and Meg, Ursula takes secret employment as a spy for Sir William Cecil, Elizabeth's wily secretary of state, who craftily plays Elizabeth's royal suitors from France and Spain against one another while thwarting Mary Stuart's schemes to foment a Catholic rebellion against Elizabeth. Ursula also keeps Cecil informed about the Queen's risky affection for her favorite, the dashing Sir Robin Dudley, Master of the Queen's Horse, member of a ferociously ambitious family and a courtier who had once come close to plotting against Elizabeth himself.

Most of Ursula Blanchard's murder investigations, supported by her faithful servant Dale and Dale's husband Brockley, involve historical mysteries that have spawned heated debate over the years, like the murder of Lord Darnley, Mary Stuart's English husband, and are interwoven with Ursula's own romantic attachments. Ursula's Protestant principles and patriotism force her to abandon her own second husband, magnetic Frenchman Matthew de la Roche, who had come clandestinely to England to advance Mary Stuart's cause. In *The Doublet Affair* (1998), Ursula works undercover at a country estate to spy on Mary's sympathizers, eventually saving Matthew from a grisly traitor's death by helping him escape to France. In *Queen's Ransom* (2000), Elizabeth sends Ursula herself to France, ostensibly to boost Elizabeth's efforts to win the support of the French Protestant Huguenots, but in reality, the queen and Cecil are using Ursula as bait to trap Matthew while France trembles on the brink of civil war. At the close of that novel, Ursula elects to join Matthew at Blanchepierre, his Loire chateau, but after their son is stillborn, she rushes back to England upon hearing that Meg has been kidnapped. Ursula regains Meg, but she loses Matthew to the bubonic plague after *Queen of Ambition* (2001), and in *A Pawn for a Queen* (2002), still grief-stricken, she must ride north to Scotland to rescue a cousin and trap a killer at the very court of the seductive Queen of Scots. *The Fugitive Queen* (2003) opens with Ursula's 1565 marriage to Hugh Stannard, older by twenty years, because she "had had enough of passion" (*Fugitive Queen* 3), but soon she's back at court, "teas[ing] out the important threads in the complex tapestry of political life" (*Fugitive Queen* 12). Later, in *The Siren Queen* (2005), Ursula departs from historically established mysteries and confronts less well-known political infighting as she concurrently copes with the Duke of Norfolk, who's trying to match Meg with his secretary Edmund Dean, while plots and counterplots involving the insidious Queen of Scots swirl around them and a banking conspiracy involving Italian Roberto Ridolfi threatens England's economy.

Ursula Blanchard possesses the cool-headed capacity to overcome her personal problems in the service of her sometimes exasperating, occasionally invidious, but always brilliant half-sister and queen. In case after dangerous case, Ursula Blanchard proves that she shares qualities her royal sister Elizabeth declared on the approach of the Spanish Armada in 1588: "I have the body of a weak and feeble woman, but I have the heart and stomach of a king, and of a king of England too." In her humbler but still impressive way, Ursula Blanchard proves she has plenty of heart and stomach of her own.

Novels: *The Robsart Mystery* (1997); *To Shield the Queen* (1997); *The Doublet Affair* (1998); *Queen's Ransom* (2000); *To Ruin a Queen* (2000); *Queen of Ambition* (2001); *A Pawn for a Queen* (2002); *The Fugitive Queen* (2003); *The Siren Queen* (2004).

Other works: Under "Valerie Anand," historical novels and the contemporary novel *To a Native Shore: a Novel of India* (1984).

Selected sources: Cooper, Ilene. Rev. of *The Doublet Affair*. *Booklist*, December 15, 1998: 728; DeCandido, GraceAnne A. Rev. of *To Ruin a Queen*. *Booklist*, December 1, 2000: 695; *Kirkus Reviews*. Rev. of *To Ruin a Queen*, November 15, 2000: 1575; Klett, Rex E. Rev. of *Queen's Ransom*. *Library Journal*, December 1999: 191; *Publishers Weekly*. Rev. of *Queen of Ambition*, November 12, 2001: 38.

See also: Kathy Lynn Einerson's Elizabethan period series featuring herbalist Lady Susannah Appleton; Karen Harper's series featuring Elizabeth I as sleuth; Edward Marston's **Nicholas Bracewell** series; John Pilkington's Thomas the Falconer series, set in sixteenth-century Berkshire; C.J. Sansom's Matthew Shardlake series, set in the reign of Henry VIII.

Myron Bolitar

Profession:	Sports agent; former basketball player
Living situation:	Single
Geographic locale:	New York City and environs
Time period:	1990s–present
Associates:	Windsor "Win" Horne Lockwood III; Esperanza Diaz
Significant relationship:	"Jessica"
Concerns:	Parents; fatherhood, TV trivia

As he told a Barnes and Noble interviewer in 2003, Harlan Coben likes to create surprises in his sports-oriented detective fiction: "I want every book . . . to really twist and turn. I love a book that sneaks up behind you at the end and slaps you in the back of the head" ("Meet the Writers"). Plenty of breezy head-whacks—headlong rushes, frat-house humor, protracted growing-up Jewish angst, and TV trivia addiction—energize Coben's seven novels featuring Myron Bolitar, a one-time hot pro basketball prospect from Duke who went on to Harvard law and later MB SportsReps on New York's Park Avenue, a career that Bolitar ruefully admits "makes you feel dirty sometimes" (*Back Spin* 7).

In his less than squeaky-clean profession, Bolitar enjoys a symbiotic relationship with his former college roommate, old WASP-monied preppy Windsor "Win" Horne Lockwood III, now a respected broker with his family's Lock-Horne Securities. Win handles investments and finances for MB SportsReps, Myron handles the negotiations, and Esperanza Diaz, a lissome bisexual former wrestler ("Little Pocahontas") runs everything else (*Back Spin* 7). In the messy kidnappings and murders Myron seems incapable of avoiding, Win plays a classy Doberman-style Hawk to Myron's mildly neurotic Jewish-son **Spenser**, while Esperanza, who started as their lewd and shrewd Girl Friday, becomes an attorney and a full partner in MB SportsReps. If Win's lethal midnight Batman-like vigilante excursions and Myron's 6'4", now 200-pound muscle prove insufficient to subdue a motley assortment of baddies, they can also call on another ring veteran, Big Cyndi, a female bouncer at Leather n' Lust who wears "more makeup than the cast of *Cats*," and sundry other endearingly grungy acquaintances like Zorra, a chatty transvestite, for backup.

Introduced in *Deal Breaker* (1995) as a thirty-something former "Hebrew hoopster" still living in the basement of his parents' suburban Livingston, New Jersey, home, Bolitar's an unconditionally loving son. He deals genially with his lawyer mother's malapropisms and cherishes his retired father, who'd labored all his life at a dead-end job to give Myron everything he thought a son should have. Comfortable as he is at home, Myron isn't pursuing casual affairs. A college fling that led to on- and off-court rivalry got his knee deliberately smashed on the brink of a brilliant pro basketball career and sets up full court-pressing tension that builds through the series.

Drop Shot (1996) jolts Myron and Win out of their cozy junk-food and old TV evenings fueled by Yoo-Hoos for Myron and cognac for Win, when their client Valerie Simpson, once a teenage tennis phenom now trying for a comeback at the U.S. Open, is shot dead in the food court just as Dennis Lockwood, another of MB SportsReps's stable, a street kid turned tennis prodigy, is serving for a match point. As dizzying as these cases become, Myron keeps his self-deprecation appealingly intact and unleashes a martini-dry wit toward the seedy side of big-business sports.

In *Back Spin* (1997), Myron's finally moved out of the basement and into Jessica's Soho loft, a "change [that] rivaled puberty," but though the relationship seems to be sailing smoothly, Myron feels as if "they were standing on the cusp of some deep abyss" (*Back Spin* 50). He also has to overcome his "naked aversion" to golf (*Back Spin* 7), when he's drawn into the kidnapping of golf superstar Linda Coldren's son Chad during the U.S. Open, where her husband is desperately trying to win the title he'd blown years earlier. Myron descends into biker bars and the even scarier realm of mall-crawling teenyboppers to birdie this freaky case of parent and child relations.

1999's *The Final Detail* opens with Myron recuperating on "St. Bacchanals," sprawled next to "a knee-knockingly gorgeous brunette clad only in a Class-B-felony bikini" (263), Terese being an intermittent interlude in Myron's thirteen-year on-again-off-again affair with Jessica, which eventually peters out in *Darkest Fear* (2000). Some months before that tear-jerker opens (Ashley 98), Myron had "wigged out" over a previous case and clients fled the firm. Trying to get the business back together, he's promised Esperanza he'll quit the dangerous private-eye stuff, but a youthful indiscretion rises up and deals him a one-two punch where it hurts the most—in his strong sense of family. Just as he's starting to cope with his father's heart attack and the sale of the family home, a traumatic enough combination, Myron learns that that a one-night stand with Emily, his old college flame, the night before her wedding to his archrival Greg Downing not only derailed Myron's basketball career but also produced Jeremy, a son he never suspected he'd fathered. Then comes an uppercut: the boy will die from a rare cancer unless the right bone marrow donor can be found. When Jeremy vanishes, Myron hurls himself into a panicked hunt that eventually forces him to break his own rules "just once," laying on some atrocious tough-guy tactics he hates himself for using. "It would have been better," Win tells him, "if you let me hurt him." Win would even have enjoyed that, but for Myron, "It would have been the same" disgrace (*Darkest Fear* 714).

Even Jeremy's safe return and a near-knockout blow of a closing revelation to this noir-ish chapter in Myron's unexpected role reversal from son to fatherhood can't heal Myron's guilt and self-loathing. Since Myron Bolitar has not reappeared since *Darkest Fear*, perhaps these dismal emotions prevent Myron's return to the engagingly wise-cracking self that made his earlier books so popular. For this devoted Jewish son, not just the price in self-respect he had to pay for Jeremy's life, but the realization that he lost those precious years of fatherhood forever make "what remained of his heart burst into flames" (*Darkest Fear* 776).

Novels: *Deal Breaker* (1995); *Drop Shot* (1996); *Fade Away* (1996); *Back Spin* (1997); *One False Move* (1998); *The Final Detail* (1999); *Darkest Fear* (2000). *Bolitar's Game* contains *BackSpin*, *The Final Detail*, and *Darkest Fear*; page references above are from this reprint edition.

Stand-alone novels: *Play Dead* (1990); *Miracle Cure* (1991); *Tell No One* (2001); *Gone for Good* (2002); *No Second Chance* (2003); *Just One Look* (2004); *The Innocent* (2005).

Selected sources: *Armchair Detective*. Rev. of *Deal Breaker*, Spring 1996: 242; *Los Angeles Times Book Review*. Rev. of *Drop Shot*, March 10, 1996: 11; "Meet the Writers." www .barnesandnoble.com/writerdetails, 2001; *Publishers Weekly*. Rev. of *Drop Shot*, February 5, 1996: 82.

Major awards: World Mystery Conference, Anthony Award, 1996; Mystery Writers of America Edgar Award, Private Eye Writers of America Shamus Award, and OLMA Award, all 1997.

Web site: www.harlancoben.com.

See also: Jon L. Breen's series featuring major league umpire Ed Gordon; Bill Granger's series featuring forcibly retired sports journalist Jimmy Drover; Keith Miles's Alan Saxon golf mysteries.

Harry Bosch

Profession:	Los Angeles homicide detective
Living situation:	Single; later married and divorced
Geographic locale:	Los Angeles, California
Time period:	1992–present
Associates:	First Detective Jerry Edgar; later Detective Kizmin ("Kiz") Rider
Nemeses:	Deputy Chief Irving S. Irving; "The Poet"
Significant relationship:	In later books, his young daughter
Concern:	Bosch's personal code of honor

As an undergraduate in journalism, Michael Connelly experienced his writer's epiphany: he fell in love with Raymond Chandler's novels about Philip Marlowe, a hard-boiled hard-drinking private eye loner who "follows his nose, often bruising it and other parts of his anatomy" while pursuing truth and justice according to his personal code of honor (David Rife, in Herbert 124). In one week, Connelly read them all (*Talking Murder* 42), and, inspired, spent ten years as a police beat reporter "as research for the time I would be ready to write fiction." When he did, Connelly became the only crime fiction author to win so many awards in so short a time (Ashley 105).

Connelly's success is largely due to his first protagonist, Hieronymous "Harry" Bosch, hailed by Lorenzo Carcaterra of *People* as "the best new protagonist in crime fiction since ... the late 70s" (February 10, 1992: 23). Connelly made Bosch "totally different from me" and drew on James Ellroy's method of coping with his mother's murder by writing fiction, making Bosch a homicide detective whose work helps him deal with his own mother's murder, "the motivating factor," Connelly claims, in Harry's life (*Talking Murder* 47).

Harry Bosch's cases are invariably intricate and violent. He solves a fellow Marine Vietnam vet's murder in *The Black Echo* (1992), and even before it came out, Connelly's editor told him to start his second book "with this Harry Bosch guy." Connelly made *The Black Ice* (1993) "a nod to Raymond Chandler" with "corollaries between the plot and *The Long Goodbye* ... the betrayal of friendship and so forth" (*Talking Murder* 47). For that novel, Connelly deliberately chose an ambiguous title, "*The Black Ice*," referring both to the drug that Bosch, like Marlowe, follows into Mexico, and to the road ice hazard that's invisible until it kills the unwary motorist— just what almost happens to Bosch. For his third Bosch novel, *The Concrete Blonde* (1994), Connelly rejected editorial urging to continue with "black" titles. There Bosch is on trial for killing a suspected serial killer reaching for a toupee instead of a suspected pistol, and he repeatedly refers to "the black heart," Connelly's title for the novel if the editor had insisted (*Talking Murder* 49).

"Black"—dark, mysterious, wicked, deadly—sums up both the background and the personality of Harry Bosch, a "black knight" crusading against all Connelly's social dragons. Harry's mother, a prostitute, named him "Hieronymous" after the only painting she liked, a work by the Flemish sixteenth-century painter with a passion for the grotesque and macabre. Harry never knew his father, and because his mother was murdered when he was eleven, he lived in orphanages and foster homes until he joined the Marines and went to Vietnam. After a traumatic tour of duty there, he joined the Los Angeles Police Department. Though Connelly wanted Harry to be a really good detective, he also wanted to write about Hollywood, so in his back story, drawn from an actual case Connelly had reported, Harry shot an unarmed man (later proven to be a serial killer) and was assigned to the Hollywood station rather than the LAPD's elite downtown robbery/homicide division (*Talking Murder* 49).

Like Colin Dexter's **Inspector Morse**, Harry's a lone drinker who finds solace in music; like Philip Marlowe and other hard-boiled private eyes, Harry often rights wrongs with a vengeance, and he's generally hostile toward authority (Ashley 106). Shortly before Harry tackles his mother's unsolved murder in *The Last Coyote* (1995), the book Connelly originally intended to close the series, Bosch's been suspended for shoving a superior through a window. After a confrontation with a real coyote near his earthquake-damaged cliffside house, he sees himself as that cannily feral beast, tracking his mother's killer into the higher echelons of corrupt local politics.

Connelly then left Bosch on an "involuntary stress leave" while writing about a different character, but he had Bosch return to duty in *Trunk Music* (1997), arguably his best novel, where Bosch heads to Las Vegas after a killer who stuffed the body of a Hollywood hopeful into the trunk of his Rolls-Royce. There Bosch also meets his future wife Eleanor Wish, a former FBI agent now a poker addict, but with Eleanor reverting to gambling and Bosch trying to quit smoking, the marriage quickly begins to disintegrate; some critics believe that Connelly's next works did, too.

In *Angels Flight* (1999), Bosch works a highly sensitive case with departmental hassles from antipathetic Internal Affairs investigator Irving S. Irving, almost a caricature of a rotten cop. Bosch, his old partner Jerry Edgar, and their new partner, "Kiz" Rider, a black female officer, expose powerful Internet pedophiles, but Harry deliberately strays so far from the rules that his "brutal, anti-establishment" justice shows him "evolving from the true character of early books into a sort of icon, a Dirty Harry for our times" (*Publishers Weekly*, November 2, 1998: 73), and Bosch pays a heavy price for the few graces he receives. He retires from the LAPD and flirts equivocally with the FBI, settling old scores in *The Narrows* (2004). He even lapses into gloomy stereotype while nailing "The Poet," a comic-bookish villain Bosch and another Connelly hero, FBI profiler Terry McCaleb, had encountered in *A Darkness More Than Night* (2001). Bosch then returns to the basics of police investigation in *The Closers* (2005). Kiz Rider intercedes with the new straight-arrow police chief to get Bosch right back "where he belongs—on the fifth floor of Parker Center, working cold cases for the Los Angeles Police Department" (Stasio 2005).

With Kiz's help, Bosch seems at last to find himself in his element. Though he is desperately hurting over Eleanor's departure to Hong Kong with their six-year-old daughter, Harry Bosch is still pushing judges, still riling superiors, still defying corruption and still hating computers, but he's also proving that a man can dig himself out of a black hole—if he cares enough and works hard enough, and learns to follow just a few of the rules.

Novels: *The Black Echo* (1992); *The Black Ice* (1993); *The Concrete Blonde* (1994); *The Last Coyote* (1995); *Trunk Music* (1997); *Angels Flight* (1999); *A Darkness More than Night* (2001); *City of Bones* (2002); *Lost Light* (2003); *The Narrows* (2004); *The Closers* (2005).

Other series: The Terry McCaleb series: *Blood Work* (1997); former FBI Special Agent McCaleb, retired due to a heart ailment, also appears as a profiler in *A Darkness More than Night*, clashing with Bosch when their cases intersect. McCaleb turned into Clint Eastwood in the film version of *Blood Work*.

Stand-alone novels: *The Poet* (1996); *Void Moon* (1999).

Short fiction: *Murder in Vegas: New Game Tales of Gambling and Desperation* (2005).

Selected sources: Ames, Katrine. Rev. of *Angels Flight*. *Newsweek*, February 1, 1999: 66; Maslin, Janet. "Taking Care of Business That's Never Finished." *New York Times*, May 16, 2005: E6; Nolan, Tom. "Trouble and Tenacity." *Wall Street Journal*, May 18, 2005: D14; Silet, Charles L.P. "*Angels Flight*." Interview with Michael Connelly. *Talking Murder*. Princeton, NJ: Ontario Review Press, 1999: 39–57; Stankowski, Rebecca. Rev. of *Angels Flight*. *Library Journal*, November 15, 1998: 95; Stasio, Marilyn. Rev. of *The Closers*. *New York Times Book Review*, May 8, 2005.

Major awards: Edgar Allan Poe Award, Mystery Writers of America, 1993; .38 Calibre Award (France), 1993; Maltese Falcon Award (Japan), 1995; Dilys Awards, 1996, 1997; Anthony Awards, 1997, 1999, 2003; Nero Wolfe Award, 1997; Marlowe Award (Germany), 1997; Barry Award, 1998; *Grand Prix de Littérature Policière* (France), 1999; Macavity, 1999; Sherlock, 2001; Edgar Allan Poe Award nomination, 2003.

Web site: www.michaelconnelly.com.

See also: James Ellroy's ferocious L.A. Quartet: *The Black Dahlia* (1987); *The Big Nowhere* (1998); *L.A. Confidential* (1990); *White Jazz* (1992); for a hard-boiled big-city police detective, see James Patterson's **Alex Cross** series, set in Washington, D.C.

Nicholas Bracewell

Profession:	Book holder (manager) of Lord Westfield's Men (an Elizabethan theatre company)
Living situation:	Single
Geographic locale:	London
Time period:	Elizabethan era (late sixteenth century)
Associate:	Owen Elias, Welsh actor
Nemesis:	The Puritans
Significant relationship:	Anne Hendrik, hatmaker and widow
Concern:	Security of Lord Westfield's Men

British author Keith Miles claims his fascination with history runs through everything he writes. After an enormously prolific writing career in children's books, drama, BBC radio and television, and a contemporary mystery series featuring professional golfer Alan Saxon, Miles adopted the pen name "Edward Marston" and successfully merged his lifelong passions for theatre and history in his Nicholas Bracewell series, starting with *The Queen's Head* (1988), which centers on Lord Westfield's Men, an acting troupe set in tumultuous Elizabethan England.

Marston also feels that only "boundless enthusiasm for the subject and the characters" can sustain an author through the immense expenditures of time and effort a book requires (quoted in *CA*: NRS, vol. 102: 240). That burning enthusiasm invigorates Marston's staunch and classy protagonist, English Renaissance man Nicholas Bracewell, who as "book holder" manages the roistering productions Westfield's Men stage usually in the outdoor courtyard of their spiritual home, the inn called The Queen's Head, and in the occasional aristocratic great hall. Bracewell copes manfully with logistic nightmares like primitive stage construction and equipment, hand-copied scripts distributed at the last minute, horse-and-cart transportation, and the infamous English weather—but his greatest challenges arise from the personality clashes between members of the company and the larger-scale antagonisms rife in Elizabethan society, whose play lovers included the Queen herself and whose play haters, especially the fiery-eyed Puritan fundamentalists, wanted nothing more than to burn the theatre and all its denizens in hellfire's flames and bring Elizabeth, whom they detested, down with the actors she supported.

Westfield's Men seem a microcosm of their larger Elizabethan world. Bracewell himself, son of a merchant, had sailed three years around the world with Sir Francis Drake, acquiring a sturdy arm with sword and dagger, a canny nose for intrigue and treachery, and a knowing eye for the ladies. Despite a short-lived separation, he and his lover, widowed businesswoman Anne Hendrik, share her comfortable home, Bracewell's refuge from the slings and arrows his adventures hurl at him. Outrageous fortune placed both leading actor and chief shareholder Laurence Firethorn and starring comedian and consummate grouch Barnaby Gill in Westfield's Men—dynamite together onstage and at each other's throats when off. Edmund Hoode, company playwright, constantly suffers over unrequited love; Welsh actor Owen Elias, with dramatic powers nearly equal to Firethorn's, covets Firethorn's roles; as general dogsbody, miserable little George Dart pines to act and always messes up. Bracewell must meld them all plus a gaggle of temperamental musicians, fractious extras, and mischief-making apprentices into performances that will satisfy the demanding Elizabethan audience, whose members range from boisterous sailors fresh off the queen's privateers to lusty courtiers bent on furthering their own often shady ambitions—as well as the Virgin Queen herself.

In each of the company's adventures, Bracewell unselfishly defends his squabbling colleagues from dire threats, using sword and wits to equal effect. Players walked "a tightrope between fame and oblivion" (*Trip to Jerusalem* 1), faced with the Lord Mayor's official disapproval, the Puritans' hostility, criminals infesting their audiences, the fickleness of the public, throat-slicing competition between acting troupes, and not least the savage bubonic plague, and Bracewell must surmount them all. In

The Trip to Jerusalem (1990) Bracewell leads Westfield's Men out into the dangerous high roads to escape the pestilence ravaging London, and in an ancient inn near York called The Trip to Jerusalem he uncovers a seditious plot spawned by the ferocious Catholic-Protestant discord of the times. In *The Nine Giants* (1991), Bracewell learns that the company may be evicted from The Queen's Head, while he and Anne work logically to solve a vicious assault on one of Anne's apprentices.

In more recent adventures, especially *The Devil's Apprentice* (2001), Nicholas Bracewell's personality becomes more complex. Here his logic and common sense defeat the morbid Elizabethan fascination with deviltry and witchcraft, and when he traps a malignant Puritan arsonist, he modestly shows none of his actors' prima donna thirst for the spotlight. *The Bawdy Basket* (2002) finds him torn between his loyalty to Westfield's Men and his friendship with young actor Frank Quilter, whose father was hanged for a murder he did not commit. Hurling himself once more into the breach in the cause of the falsely accused, Nicholas escapes an assassin's blade only to confront a lying moneylender who has the troupe's profligate patron Lord Westfield in his clutches. 2004's *The Counterfeit Crank* again plunges Bracewell into danger when a cardshark preys on his actors, their arrangement with The Queen's Head is jeopardized, and the company's costumes and profits mysteriously vanish; and in *The Malevolent Comedy* (2005), audiences have thinned out because the troupe has been staging slim dramatic fare.

Always kind and compassionate (sometimes to his own peril), Nicholas Bracewell opposes superstition with reason, greed with unselfishness, envy with modesty, and murder with justice. Convincingly human himself, a sensitive lover as well as a loyal friend, he brings Elizabeth's swashbuckling, bawdy, turbulent world to riotous and impassioned life.

Novels: *The Queen's Head* (1988); *The Merry Devils* (1989); *The Trip to Jerusalem* (1990); *The Nine Giants* (1991); *The Mad Courtesan* (1992); *The Silent Woman* (1992); *The Roaring Boy* (1995); *The Laughing Hangman* (1996); *The Fair Maid of Bohemia* (1997); *The Wanton Angel* (1999); *The Devil's Apprentice* (2001); *The Bawdy Basket* (2002); *The Vagabond Clown* (2003); *The Counterfeit Crank* (2004); *The Malevolent Comedy* (2005).

Other series: Alan Saxon series (contemporary sports-oriented, under the name Keith Miles); Don Hawker series (contemporary sports-oriented novels, under the name Martin Inigo); the Domesday series, featuring Norman soldier Ralph Delchard and Breton-Saxon lawyer Gervase Bret (set just after Norman Conquest; under the name Edward Marston); the Merlin Richards series (architectural; set in 1920s United States, under the name Keith Miles); the Restoration series (set in seventeenth-century England, under the name Edward Marston); the Dillman series (set on great ocean liners in Edwardian 1920s, under the name Conrad Allen); the Robert Colbeck series, featuring an inspector in the early years (1850s) of Scotland Yard.

Selected sources: Interview with Keith Miles. *January Magazine*, www.januarymagazine .com/profiles/ (October 18, 2001); *Publishers Weekly*. Rev. of *The Bawdy Basket*, September 19, 2004: 46; *Publishers Weekly*. Rev. of *The Malevolent Comedy*, June 20, 2005: 60; Stasio, Marilyn. Rev. of *Saint's Rest* and *The Wanton Angel*. *New York Times Book Review*, August 22, 1999: 25.

See also: Fiona Buckley's **Ursula Blanchard** series; Patricia Finney's two-book Simon Ames series, *Firedrake's Eye* (1992) and *Unicorn's Blood* (1998); Philip Gooden's Elizabethan-era series featuring Nick Revill, actor; Simon Hawke's late 1500s series featuring ostler Tuck Smythe and young Will Shakespeare; C.J. Sansom's *Dissolution* (2004) and *Dark Fire* (2005), set during the reign of Elizabeth I's father Henry VIII; Leonard Tourney's early 1600s series featuring Will Shakespeare.

Dave Brandstetter

Profession:	Insurance claims investigator
Living situation:	Single
Geographic locale:	Southern California
Time period:	1970–present
Significant relationships:	Rod Fleming; Cecil Harris
Concerns:	Gay-related social and political issues, especially mortality and loss; AIDS; environmental pollution; pornography; right-wing militia movements; religious fraud; destruction of stereotypes and prejudices

His publisher initially hesitated for three years, but with *Fadeout* (1970), Joseph Hansen finally made his appealing insurance death claims investigator Dave Brandstetter the first openly gay protagonist to reach a large mainstream audience (Landon Burns in Herbert 23). Hansen subsequently allowed Brandstetter to age at about the same rate as the twelve novels in the series appeared. Between *Fadeout*, where forty-four-year-old Brandstetter contemplates suicide after Rod Fleming, his lover of twenty years, died from cancer, and *A Country of Old Men* (1991), where Brandstetter, nearly seventy and failing physically, still manages to investigate a murder and help save an abused child, Hansen's major themes emerged. Brandstetter, though cultured, sensitive, and unabashedly gay, functions comfortably as a man's man in a hard-boiled profession; after losing Fleming, he builds a new lasting relationship from *Gravedigger* (1982) onward; and most importantly, as Marilyn Stasio observed in reviewing *A Country of Old Men*, beneath the "cool, reserved, rational personality" keeping lean, blond, blue-eyed Brandstetter mostly silent with "people who are hurting . . . he cares. . . . He has always cared a lot. And that's why we'll miss him" (Stasio, June 16, 1991: 21).

As the son of Medallion Insurance's wealthy much-married president, Brandstetter received creature comforts, a good education (he even served as a less-than-angelic boy chorister at St. Matthew's), and constant fatherly nagging to get married and settle down. Instead, he went into Army Intelligence, and as a kid lieutenant in Germany he both confirmed his sexual orientation and learned to look for people's goodness beneath unattractive appearances. Setting up his own house after his discharge in 1945, he fell in love with Rod Fleming, whose agonizing death nearly killed Brandstetter, too. Through the early cases Brandstetter investigates for Medallion, he gradually comes to terms with that grief, never allowing his personal pain to diminish his stubborn passion for the truth.

Brandstetter indulges his classy tastes. Some, like his classic Jaguar, offer sheer pleasure. Some are uplifting, like the Mozart and Haydn sonatas he tried unsuccessfully to share first with Fleming and later with his new lover, young black television reporter (later producer) Cecil Harris—both men preferred rock. Brandstetter also loves the fine Italian cuisine at Max Romano's restaurant, which Brandstetter eventually bought to keep a thousand happy memories alive. Brandstetter knows that some of his other habits may be destructive, but he won't stop indulging in them. He smokes far too much, he likes Dos Equis, Glenlivet, and double martinis, and he won't give up on a friend or a case or a victim who needs him.

Given Hansen's overall aim to portray homosexuals realistically without sensationalism or condescension, all of Brandstetter's cases involve contact with the gay community or gay individuals, with his later investigations expanding to a wide range of other social issues close to his and his creator's heart. In *Fadeout*, probing the staged disappearance of a country singer draws Brandstetter out of being the "morose bastard" Fleming had liked to call him (*Fadeout* 116). In *Troublemaker* (1975), Brandstetter's quiet empathy helps him deal directly with the murder of the co-owner of a gay bar, while in *The Man Everybody Was Afraid Of* (1978) he clears a gay activist accused of the murder of a notoriously anti-gay police chief and meets Harris, with whom he shares the rest of his life. *Skinflick* (1979), praised by H.R.F. Keating in *Crime and Mystery: The 100 Best Books* because Brandstetter is "a homosexual without hysteria," shows Brandstetter "putting himself in the thick of things" in the best Marlowe-Spade tradition (191), to solve the homicide of a religious zealot. He continues to rescue the weak and bring bullies to justice, especially painful when he has to face down racial prejudice and hatred in *Nightwork* (1984). After Brandstetter leaves the insurance industry for private work, he exposes a murderer whose victims are young AIDS-stricken homosexuals in *Early Graves* (1987), critically acclaimed as the best of the later Brandstetter novels.

Dave Brandstetter, haunted since Rod Fleming's death by intimations of mortality no successful case closing can exorcise, in *The Little Dog Laughed* (1986) takes on the inflammatory issue of right-wing extremists who support "democracy at home" by training guerrilla fighters to commit genocide abroad, as Margaret Cannon has remarked (*Globe and Mail*, February 18, 1987). Exhausted physically and emotionally, Brandstetter considers retirement in *Obedience* (1988), but shrugs back into harness to investigate a murder allegedly committed by a Vietnam vet who lives in a Vietnamese community. In *The Boy Who Was Buried This Morning* Brandstetter again takes on paramilitary crypto-fascists attempting to purge minority residents from a small California town, a case that nearly costs Dave and Cecil their lives because Dave's age dangerously slows him down. He quits smoking but hangs onto old values some might call prejudices, like refusing to buy a German or Japanese car, and after risking his life one more time in the cause of right, succumbing at last to the heart disease that killed his father, Dave Brandstetter dies as privately and as gracefully as he lived, determined, gallant, decent, and caring to the end.

Novels: *Fadeout* (1970); *Death Claims* (1973); *Troublemaker* (1975); *The Man Everybody Was Afraid Of* (1978); *Skinflick* (1979); *Gravedigger* (1982); *Nightwork* (1984); *The Little Dog Laughed*

(1986); *Early Graves* (1987); *Obedience* (1988); *The Boy Who Was Buried This Morning* (1990); *A Country of Old Men* (1991).

Short fiction: *Brandstetter and Others* (1984).

Other works: Hack Bohannon (a straight detective) short fiction: *Bohannon's Book* (1988); *Bohannon's Country* (1993); *Bohannon's Women* (2002). Stand-alone novels under pseudonym "James Colton."

Selected sources: *National Review.* Rev. of *Gravedigger*, May 28, 1982; Stasio, Marilyn. Rev. of *The Boy Who Was Buried This Morning. New York Times Book Review*, June 3, 1990: 32; Stasio, Marilyn. Rev. of *A Country of Old Men. New York Times Book Review*, June 16, 1991: 21; Stasio, Marilyn. Rev. of *The Little Dog Laughed. New York Times Book Review*, January 19, 1986: 17.

Major awards: Lambda Literary Awards, 1992 and 1994; Shamus Lifetime Award, 1992.

See also: Rick Copp's humorous Hollywood series featuring gay former child star Jarrod Jarvis; Michael Craft's series featuring Wisconsin gay amateur detective Mark Manning; Greg Herren's aspiring gay New Orleans PI Scotty Bradley; Michael Nava's gay Latino criminal defense attorney Henry Rios series; John Morgan Wilson's series featuring **Benjamin Justice**, disgraced gay California journalist and unofficial private investigator; Gary Zebran's Providence, Rhode Island, series featuring Daniel Caruso, a gay columnist and amateur sleuth; Mark Zubro's gay high school teacher Tom Mason series and Zubro's series featuring gay but formerly heterosexually married Chicago policeman Paul Turner.

Sarah Decker Brandt

Profession:	Nurse-midwife
Living situation:	Widowed
Geographic locale:	New York City
Time period:	Late nineteenth century
Associate:	Frank Malloy
Significant relationship:	Frank Malloy
Concerns:	Poverty; women's issues; political corruption; economic exploitation

The glittering Old New York of the fabulously wealthy "Four Hundred"—the Astors, the Roosevelts, the Vanderbilts and their peers—had its dark side, too. Political corruption and economic oppression kept the city's lower class, like recent immigrants, shop girls, factory workers, impoverished widows, poor and hopeless, often living on the streets and sidewalks of New York. By the 1880s, reform movements were slowly starting to take shape in the city, and in 1886, after overcoming his grief over the simultaneous losses of his mother and his wife two years earlier, Teddy Roosevelt returned to head the New York City police board, dedicating himself to cleaning up the massive corruption fostered by Tammany Hall bosses. Out of principle, Victoria Thompson's gutsy heroine Sarah Decker Brandt left her privileged world for the wrong side of the tracks, defying her financier father Felix Decker to marry Dr. Thomas Brandt, a devoted physician who served the East Side's needy. After Brandt is killed, Sarah, a trained nurse and midwife, remains in Greenwich Village, do-gooding with the help of Detective Sergeant Frank Malloy, himself a widowed father of a handicapped son, Brian, cared for by Malloy's domineering Irish mother.

Sarah's developing relationship with Malloy personifies the tension that existed in American cities between the classes at the turn of the century. Sarah, like every woman of her social class, had been reared from the time she could talk to trick men who wanted to marry pretty heiresses they could flaunt and cheat on (*St. Mark's Place* 216), and she knows how to manipulate men of her own class. Coming to terms with handsome but underprivileged Sergeant Frank Malloy, son of Irish Catholic immigrants, is a different matter. While working in a Lower East Side boarding house in *Murder on Astor Place* (1999), Sarah meets a pregnant sixteen-year-old girl who strongly reminds Sarah of a member of the uppercrust Van Damm family. A little later the girl's body is discovered and identified as indeed a Van Damm, and Sarah, impelled by her stubborn sense of justice for the downtrodden, returns to the Fifth Avenue mansions she frequented as a girl to find the killer with the help of Malloy, who despite his inherent honesty must pay bribes to his superiors in order to advance in rank. Both Sarah and Malloy feel the class tension that inevitably holds them apart just as much as their different detection methods do. Sarah relies on conversational probes to establish motives and opportunity, while Malloy resorts to police brutality that Sarah deplores—violent interrogation common at that time that required strong arms and quick fists.

Murder in St. Mark's Place (2000) finds Sarah and Malloy beginning to reach out gingerly to one another despite a mutual antagonism that covers a burgeoning mutual attraction, physical as well as emotional. Armed only with a hefty hatpin, Sarah braves the fleshpots of Coney Island to investigate the murder of a recently arrived German immigrant girl, determined to trap the serial killer who's been preying on "Charity Girls," poor young women one step above prostitution, who exchange sexual favors for the pretty hats, cheap baubles, or fancy shoes they can't otherwise afford. Malloy grudgingly backs her up, constantly irritated by her intrepid risk-taking and her refusal to accept the traditional place for women. At that time, women were barred not only from voting but from owning property or going into business, and a single woman like Sarah who supported herself shocked the lower classes almost as much as it did the rich and famous. By identifying Brian Malloy's handicap as deafness rather than mental retardation and finding avenues of help for the child, however, Sarah defuses much of Frank Malloy's antagonism, and as she begins to take his opinions more seriously and he in turn accepts her help, they eventually reach a new level of understanding (*St. Mark's Place* 220).

Sarah and Frank work together with increasing trust in their succeeding salacious homicide cases, which in the best romance tradition offer brief, tantalizing scenes where they contemplate the possibility of drawing closer together (Griffin 25). *Murder on Gramercy Park* (2001) involves the suicide of a shady physician; *Murder on Washington Square* (2002), revolves around another murder of a pregnant girl; and

Murder on Mulberry Bend deals with a homicide at the Prodigal Son Mission, a "home for wayward girls." Malloy is featured more vividly in *Murder on Marble Row* (2003), where Sarah's old friend Teddy Roosevelt asks Malloy and Sarah to discover the bomber who killed Gregory Van Dyke, a wealthy businessman, by blowing up his office. Here, "the Irish-American cop is allowed into [the] drawing room though nobody offers him a seat," while Sarah exerts her social connections to pry into Van Dyke's circle of friends and business associates. *Murder on Lenox Hill* (2005) brings Sarah and Malloy into a religious scandal, the murder of popular Reverend Oliver Upchurch during a Communion service by cyanide in his chalice. Upchurch possibly impregnated a beautiful but mentally retarded fifteen-year-old daughter of the wealthy Linton family, and Malloy is hesitant to become involved, but he finally yields to Sarah's prodding.

In Hamilton's well-researched world of gaslit hypocrisy and exploitation, fiercely principled Sarah Brandt and honest Frank Malloy bring together the opposing poles of turn-of-the-century urban American society. Malloy continues throughout the series to work himself up from the despised position of an Irish immigrant's son by being a "discreet and trustworthy and even kind" policeman (*Lenox Hill* 270). Sarah, who originally turned her back on the charm and wiles bred into her class, learns to use them to serve the less fortunate, and she even discovers sympathetic dimensions to the characters of her mother and father that she can reluctantly admire, as well as gratitude that she can share old and new pain and grief and joy with Malloy. Will love finally triumph over the social inequities of Old New York? Stay tuned.

Novels ("Gaslight Mysteries"): *Murder on Astor Place* (1999); *Murder on St. Mark's Place* (2000); *Murder on Gramercy Park* (2001); *Murder on Washington Square* (2002); *Murder on Mulberry Bend* (2003); *Murder on Marble Row* (2004); *Murder on Lenox Hill* (2005).

Other series: "Tates of Texas" series (historical romances).

Other fiction: Thompson has written numerous stand-alone historical romance novels.

Selected sources: Bibel, Barbara. Rev. of *Murder on Lenox Hill*. *Booklist*, June 1, 2005: 1762; Bromberg, Toby. Rev. of *Murder on St. Mark's Place*. *RomanticTimes.com*, www.romantictimes .com; Griffin, Maureen. Rev. of *Murder on Washington Square*. *Kliatt*, July 2002: 25; *Kirkus Reviews*. Rev. of *Murder on Marble Row*, April 15, 2004: 367; Klausner, Harriet. Rev. of *Murder on Washington Square*. *AllReaders.com*, www.allreaders.com; Klett, Rex E. Rev. of *Murder on Marble Row*. *Library Journal*, May 1, 2004: 143; McKee, Barbara Jo. Rev. of *Murder on Mulberry Road*. *Kliatt*, July 2002: 27.

Major award: Nomination, Edgar Allan Poe Award, 2001.

Web site: www.victoriathompson.com.

See also: For mysteries with American historical settings, in chronological order: Karen Swee's Revolutionary War mysteries, debuting with *Life, Liberty and the Pursuit of Murder* (2003), featuring widow Abigail Lawrence; Barbara Hambly's pre–Civil War **Benjamin January** series; Miriam Manfredo's Civil War series; Ann McMillan's Civil War series; Jeanne M. Dams's cozy series set in early-twentieth-century Indiana and featuring chief housemaid Hilda Johansson.

Debut novels: Donis Casey's *The Old Bastard Had It Coming* (2003), set in 1912, featuring Oklahoma frontier farm wife Alafair Tucker; Joe R. Lansdale's Sunset James debut East Texas barnburner, *Sunset and Sawdust*, set in the Great Depression of the 1930s; Larry Karp's *First, Do No Harm* (2004), featuring medical student Martin Firestone, with flashbacks to 1940s New Jersey; Milton T. Burton's *The Rogues' Game* (2005), featuring an unnamed narrator and set in post–World War II Texas; Rosemary Martin's *It's a Mod, Mod, Mod, Mod Murder: A Murder a Go-Go Mystery*, featuring secretary Bebe Bennett and set in 1960s New York City.

Guido Brunetti

Profession:	Commissario of Police
Living situation:	Married
Geographic locale:	Venice, Italy
Time period:	1990–present
Associates:	Signorina Elettra; Ispettore Vianello
Nemeses:	Vice-Questore Patta; Lieutenant Scarpa
Significant relationship:	Paola Falier Brunetti, his wife
Concerns:	Devotion to his family and to traditions of Venice; ethics of his profession; governmental corruption

Inspired to begin a crime series when she and a friend facetiously plotted to slay an obnoxious La Fenice opera conductor (Ashley 287), Donna Leon based her award-winning Guido Brunetti series on her twenty-plus years of residence in Venice. Brunetti, a principled man devoted to his wife, their children, and his faded, fascinating city, treads lightly through each of his cases, well aware that his ambitious and unethical superior Vice-Questore Giuseppe Patta and Patta's creature Lieutenant Scarpa, whom Brunetti both hates and fears, lurk hyena-like for quick solutions that will further their own careers at the expense of Brunetti's. Brunetti's allies, the relentlessly efficient computer guru Signorina Elettra and ferocious-looking but compassionate Lieutenant Vianello, counterpoint and deepen Brunetti's complex personality.

Guido Brunetti debuted in *Death at La Fenice* (1992), investigating the murder of a famous maestro found dead of cyanide poisoning during the second intermission of *La Traviata*. As Brunetti sifts through the tangled motives of colorful suspects, his deeper personal concerns surface—the sanctity of his marriage and the well-being of his children. Brunetti's wife Paola, like Donna Leon herself, teaches English literature at a nearby university. Her leftist political sympathies often clash with Brunetti's more conservative views, but her practicality and brilliant intuition often complement his cool rationality. Their daughter Chiara excels at mathematics, while their teenage son Raffaele continually tests their parental wits and patience against his stated antipathies toward getting either an education or a job. Guido loves them all so desperately that in his cases he easily and often empathizes with spouses and parents who have lost their own loved ones.

Guido is also determined never to become obligated to or dependent on Paola's parents, the enormously wealthy and powerful Venetian Count and Countess Falier. Guido does not even know how many rooms the 300-year-old Falier palazzo on the Grand Canal contains—but he occasionally must gingerly approach his father-in-law for insights into high finance and Venetian politics. Their relationship becomes less strained as the series proceeds, but it never is truly comfortable.

Guido Brunetti doesn't know what the English term "loony bin" means, but he feels that it precisely describes modern Italy (*Doctored Evidence* 66). His whole career, he feels, has been spent in useless work because of Italy's corrupt courts and their endless appeal system (*Doctored Evidence* 103). Each of his cases also pits him more precariously against Vice-Questore Patta and the Sicilian Lieutenant Scarpa. In *Death in a Strange Country* (1993), where a dead American from the Vincenza military post washes up on the Canal at San Giovanni e Paolo, Patta wants to pin the murder on an outsider, while Brunetti uncovers amoral Italian governmental intrigue and the fine Sicilian hand of the Mafia. Silver Dagger winner *Friends in High Places* (2000) also exposes political corruption, while *A Noble Radiance* (1998) moves out of Venice to a deserted farmhouse at the foot of the Italian Dolomites. A family signet ring found near a badly decomposed corpse leads Brunetti to call on his patrician father-in-law for information regarding an aristocratic family in mourning for their abducted son. Brunetti identifies with the grieving father while revealing his own horror of radio-active weaponry, just as in *Uniform Justice* (1998) the peculiar death of a different son, this one a student at the elite San Martino military academy, and the heartrending grief of the boy's unusually ethical politician father, cause Brunetti's own fears for his children to shake his faith in his profession: "How much longer can you do this, Guido?" Paola asks. "The face he saw looking back at him had the weary dullness of every grief-stricken parent he had ever had to speak to" (*Uniform Justice* 91). Such fears, coupled with the political disillusion that Paola bolsters, reinforce Brunetti's ambivalence about twisted loyalties—toward the Italian military establishment, the Mafia, and even the Vatican—so that he experiences joy "always through the filter of his unhappiness" (*Uniform Justice* 158).

And yet what initially drew Paola to Guido Brunetti was his incapability "to desire anything but happiness" (*Uniform Justice* 204), and like the glints of sunlight off Venice's fetid canals, Guido's typically Venetian love of beauty and fine food restore his spirit and bring him peace. Guido Brunetti knows that his sense of wonder will return with his awareness of the great art of Venice that surrounds him and that Paola's fine Venetian cuisine, like her sublime "*orecchiette* with cubes of *mozzarella di bufala* and *pomororini*" preceding a perfect salt-encrusted *bronzino*" (*Doctored Evidence* 195), never fails to give him "fresh heart... feeling restored and eager to resume the hunt" (*Uniform Justice* 127). He takes up his work again, restored, in *Blood from a Stone* (2005), dealing with Italy's "Senegali" immigrants, some of them illegal, and others involved with a smuggling ring that Brunetti eventually connects to the Angolan civil war, high-ranking Italian secret service officials, and a powerful industrialist with tentacles reaching into the Italian government.

For Italians, *sprezzatura* is the mark of the professional, the ability to make the difficult seem effortless and full of grace. In the near-impossible task of uncovering Italian secrecy and corruption, Guido Brunetti possesses it in abundance: *Bravissimo.*

Novels: *Death at La Fenice* (1992); *Death in a Strange Country* (1993); *Dressed for Death* (in U.K. *The Anonymous Venetian*) (1993); *Death and Judgment* (1995); *Acqua Alta* (1996); *Quietly in Their Sleep* (1997); *A Noble Radiance* (1998); *Fatal Remedies* (1999); *Friends in High Places* (2000); *A Sea of Troubles* (2001); *Uniform Justice* (2003); *Doctored Evidence* (2004); *Blood from a Stone* (2005).

Selected sources: Amador, Victoria. Rev. of *Death in a Strange Country. Bloomsbury Review*, January–February 1994: 23; Anable, Stephen. "Deaths in Venice." Interview with Donna Leon. *Publishers Weekly*, August 4, 2003: 58; *Kirkus Reviews.* Rev. of *Death and Judgment*, April 15, 1995: 511; *Publishers Weekly.* Rev. of *Acqua Alta*, September 2, 1996: 24; Symons, Julian. Rev. of *Dressed for Death. Times Literary Supplement*, June 24, 1994: 24; Waugh, Harriet. Rev. of *Death in a Strange Country. Spectator*, November 3, 1993: 37.

Major awards: Suntory Prize (Japan), 1993; CWA Silver Dagger, 2000.

Web sites: www.phys.uni-paderborn.dc/~stern/lean/books and www.twbooks.co.uk/authors/donnaleon.html.

See also: Michael Dibdin's **Aurelio Zen** series, set in various Italian cities; John Spencer Hill's **Carlo Arbati** series, set in Florence; Magdalen Nabb's series featuring **Marshal Salvatore Guarnaccia**, set in Florence; Edward Sklepowich's series set in Venice and featuring writer Urbino Macintyre; for historical Italian perspectives, Sicilian author Leonardo Sciascia's (1921–1989) stand-alone novels dealing with the Mafia in tenth-century Sicily.

Arthur Bryant and John May

Profession:	Detectives, Peculiar Crimes Unit, London
Living situation:	Bryant: never married; May: widowed
Geographic locale:	London
Time period:	Contemporary, with flashbacks to the beginning of their careers in the 1940s
Associate:	Janice Longbright
Nemesis:	Age
Significant relationships:	Nathalie, the lost love of Bryant's life; April, May's mentally disturbed granddaughter
Concerns:	Unsolved crimes; aging; devotion to The Job

According to Pauline Morgan in *The St. James Guide to Horror, Ghost and Gothic Writers*, Christopher Fowler specializes in the "Urban Nightmare." Describing his novels and short stories that preceded his Bryant-May detective novels, Fowler himself told *Contemporary Authors*, "I am a hybrid writer, mixing horror, fantasy, and science fiction with realistic settings in modern-day cities. My work is urban, violent, slightly paranoid, usually sprinkled with black humor.... London figures largely as a backdrop for the action of [my] forty or so short stories...and it frequently acts as a catalyst for supernatural events." Fowler also indicated that he planned to "continue exploring the past, present, and future lives of this fascinating city, populating it with characters real enough to exist yet sufficiently steeped in the fantastic to be able to reveal new shadows within its ancient buildings" (*CA Online*). He has accomplished exactly those aims in his detective novels featuring octogenarian detectives Arthur Bryant and John May, who have chosen to spend their entire working lives together in the Peculiar Crimes Unit (PCU) loosely connected to the London Police.

Bryant and May complement each another as perfectly as an old and happily bickering married couple often have learned to do. Bryant, unkempt in person and packrattish in office habits, is a latter-day Sherlockian eccentric genius who wallows in the joys of the past; he also mourns the loss of Nathalie, his only love, so much that he's never married. Bryant sports a keen mind stuffed with esoteric knowledge, highly abnormal methodology, a manner that could make a nun bristle (*Water Room* 10), and a superhuman ability to render electronic marvels useless. His superiors refuse to let him near the PITO, the Police Information Technology Organization, for fear of a national meltdown (*Water Room* 9). But Bryant's body is giving out; a heart attack eight years earlier slowed him down, and the explosion that he caused at the start of *Full Dark House* (2004) lost him not only his false teeth but his dignity. Each day less remains to Arthur Bryant of the London of his childhood memories, and he has no life beyond his police work. He intends to stay in harness until he dies.

John May, three years younger than Bryant, is almost exactly his partner's opposite. Still handsome, well-dressed, apparently in excellent health and spirits, he likes people, especially ladies, despite Bryant's acerbic advice, "I find it rather grotesque that you still have a sex drive at your age....You should pack it in, a man of your age, you're liable to pull something in the pelvic region" (*Full Dark House* 10). May also relishes following police procedure to the letter and excels with technology, while Bryant wanders off into peculiar tangents and hunches, doing the heavy thinking and leaving the heavy lifting to May. May's family, though, has been so unlucky that he finds it hard not to believe that "some dark star trailed them, bringing harm and hardship in its wake" (*Water Room* 52). Twenty years earlier in pursuing the Leicester Square Vampire, a villain still at large, Bryant had persuaded May to use May's daughter Elizabeth as a decoy; something went wrong, and Elizabeth died, leaving their granddaughter April mentally damaged and May inexplicably closer to Bryant than ever before.

Bryant holds the PCU team together in a "lopsided camaraderie" reassuring to the civilians they serve—"perhaps this was how all police once were" (*Water Room* 215)—even though it terrorizes their police superiors. All of the PCU team members have some kind of flaw that prevents them from functioning normally with their fellow officers. Ava Gardner lookalike Janice Longbright is the closest subordinate to Bryant and May. She will never marry because her long-time partner Ian Hargreave is already married—to the force. Janice, like her mother before her, retired from the PCU, but she returns to the unit part time, knowing that the new generation of technology-minded policemen resent its very existence, and that they will turn the

PCU into "a Disney police store" as soon as Bryant and May are gone (*Water Room* 75). In the meantime, though, Janice, old friends like Oswald Finch, the ancient pathologist sporting "the suicidal expression of a Norwegian painter" (*Full Dark House* 74), and newbies like Kershaw and Bimsley (the latter barely tolerated by Bryant as a "slack-jawed drooling neanderthal" [*Water Room* 153]) are bound together in the PCU, now separated from the Metropolitan Police and loosely supervised by MI7.

Full Dark House, the first Bryant and May novel, requires a grief-stricken May simultaneously to investigate the apparent murder of his old partner in the contemporary explosion that destroys the PCU offices while May follows Bryant's notes for reopening their first case together—eerie serial killings during the 1940 Blitz in the spooky old London Palace Theatre where a borderline-obscene production of *Orpheus in Hell* is being rehearsed. *The Water Room*, their second outing, with the PCU's very future depending on their ability to solve the case, occurs in and around the little Victorian London enclave of Balaclava Street, with torrents of history about London's underground rivers and darksome Egyptian mystery cults accompanying the classic locked-room murder of an old lady by "dry drowning."

Bryant and May hark back in many respects to the Golden Age of British mystery writing. Dean James, manager of Murder by the Book, Inc. of Houston, Texas, favorably compares their adventures to the work of Agatha Christie and Dorothy L. Sayers and praises Fowler's richness of detail and character as resembling a P.D. James mystery "but with a very modern twist," likely due to Fowler's dry-witty characterizations of today's technocrats. Bryant and May are also reviving the subgenre of the "Impossible Crime" so well accomplished by John Sladek in his Thackeray Phin novels, *Invisible Green* and *Black Aura*. In these fascinating investigations, the ultra-colorful Arthur Bryant convinces his commonsensical comrade John May and the rest of their idiosyncratic little team—and their readers, for a little while at least—that "murders are tests, and solving them's the only way to stay alive" (*Water Room* 190).

Novels: *Full Dark House* (2004); *The Water Room* (2005).

Stand-alone novels: *Roofworld* (1988); *Red Bride* (1993); *Darkest Day* (1993); *Spunky* (1994); *Psychoville* (1995); *Disturbia* (1997).

Short fiction: Several short story collections, including *Flesh Wounds* (1995) and *Personal Demons* (1998).

Nonfiction: *How to Impersonate Famous People* (humor; 1986) and *The Ultimate Party Book: The Illustrated Guide to Social Intercourse* (1987).

Other works: Fowler has also authored screenplays and BBC productions.

Selected sources: Pitt, David. Rev. of *The Water Room*. *Booklist*, May 1, 2005: 1522; *Publishers Weekly*. Rev. of *The Water Room*, May 23, 2005: 62; Stasio, Marilyn. "Mean Girls." *New York Times Book Review*, April 26, 2005: 23; Wins, Wilda. Rev. of *Full Dark House*. *Library Journal*, June 1, 2004: 175; Woodcock, Susan. Rev. of *Full Dark House*. *School Library Journal*, October 2004: 198.

See also: For mysteries with supernatural, psychic, or horror components: Catherine Dain's series featuring Mariana Morgan, psychic healer; Charlaine Harris's fantasy-mysteries featuring telepathic cocktail waitress Sookie Stackhouse, with vampires; Dean James's humorous series featuring gay vampire Simon Kirby; Katherine Kurtz and Deborah Turner Harris's **Adept** series, set in Scotland and the astral plane; Martha Lawrence's series featuring psychic San Diego PI Elizabeth Chase; Karen Novak's series featuring New York City psychic police detective Leslie Stone; David Skibbens's debut novel featuring Tarot reader Warren Ritter; Derek Wilson's series featuring paranormal investigator Nathaniel Gye.

C

Brother Cadfael

Profession:	Benedictine monk (herbalist, gardener, translator)
Geographic locale:	Environs of the Abbey of St. Peter and St. Paul, near Shrewsbury, England, close to the Welsh border
Time period:	Late twelfth century
Associate:	Deputy Sheriff Hugh Beringar
Concerns:	The Benedictine Rule: *Ora et labora* (Pray and work); justice for the downtrodden

Prolific mainstream and mystery author (ninety books in her fifty-year career) and Diamond Dagger awardee Ellis Peters claimed that she did not invent the popular Brother Cadfael (Cadfael ap Meilyr ap Dafydd) as a series character; "he simply came into being to enable her to write about Shrewsbury Abbey in the twelfth century, and only later did she decide to take up his story again" (Murphy 75) during the last ten years of her life. The various roles of a medieval abbey—land and property ownership, pilgrimage site, repository for holy relics, hospital and leprosarium, guest hostel (Katherine Alexander in Herbert 27)—provided Peters ample room to develop her twenty "Chronicles of Brother Cadfael," rich historical novels featuring attractive young lovers threatened by violence and murder.

As recounted in *Monk's Hood* (1980), fourteen-year-old Cadfael left his home at Trefriew, Wales, to serve in the Shrewsbury household of an English wool merchant. He fought as both soldier and sailor in the First Crusade (1095–1099) and later, after his conversion, took his perpetual vows of poverty, chastity, and obedience as a contemplative Benedictine monk of the Abbey of St. Peter and St. Paul near Shrewsbury. There he tends one of the finest monastic herb gardens in England, brews potions for the sick, and occasionally serves the Abbey as translator. Since Cadfael is a healer conversant with medicines and poisons, a legacy of Peters's seven years as a pharmacist's assistant, his abbots allow him to travel outside the Abbey. Cadfael's innate curiosity bolsters his already wide experience of people inside and outside his cloister walls.

Brother Cadfael works and prays in intensely troubled times when King Stephen of the House of Normandy, who ruled from 1135 to 1154, is battling Empress Maud of the House of Plantagenet for England's throne. Shrewsbury lies in the West Midlands near England's border with Wales, where in 1143 Welsh leader Owain Gwynedd was inciting rebellion against English rule. Religious heresy is mounting, and unsettling new ideas and virulent new sicknesses are returning with the Crusaders from faraway lands. Stout sixtyish Cadfael needs all of his pre-monastic experience, his scientific expertise, his highly logical mind, his clerical anonymity, and his easygoing Welsh charm and proclivity for gossip to untangle the crimes involved in the constant flow of people in and out of the Abbey's neighborhood.

In *A Morbid Taste for Bones* (1977), the first of his chronicles, Brother Cadfael travels back to Wales as translator to help obtain the bones of St. Winifred as revenue-producing relics for the Abbey. During this mission a villager opposing the transfer of the bones is found murdered, and Cadfael, "past trembling at the arrogance of man" (*Morbid Taste* 211), using the wealth of worldly experience his ecclesiastical brothers can only wonder at, not only solves the crime but brings together star-crossed lovers, a recurrent motif throughout the series. In *One Corpse Too Many* (1979), Cadfael meets Deputy Sheriff Hugh Beringar, at first his adversary. To save Hugh, though, Cadfael stakes "his own life and those of others upon his judgment of men" (*One Corpse* 111). It proves sound, for Beringar becomes Cadfael's fast friend and his staunch crime-solving ally.

Under the spiritual guidance of his superiors, first the gently lenient Abbot Heribert and then Heribert's successor, the magisterial and aristocratic Abbot Radulfus, Brother Cadfael constantly acknowledges his own very human nature: "The trouble with me . . . is that I have been about the world long enough to know that God's plans for us, however infallibly good, may not take the form that we expect and demand. And I find an immense potential for rebellion in this old heart" (*One Corpse* 178). *Monk's Hood* uncovers personality clashes inevitable for men living within an enclosed community, where Cadfael has to cope with haughty Prior Robert, "imperially tall and papally austere" (*Monk's Hood* 38), who casts covetous eyes on the abbot's chair, and the sanctimonious Brother Jerome, exuding "pious sympathy and pain" (*Monk's Hood* 13) at the possibility of Heribert's departure while envisioning himself risen to great monastic heights. Knowing that for his soul's sake he must smother his resentment and turn a Christian cheek, Cadfael nevertheless grinds his teeth, admitting to himself, "God forgive me, if I could wring your [Brother Jerome's] scrawny neck now, I would do it and rejoice" (*Monk's Hood* 116). In all his cases, Cadfael cannily finds ways to deflate those afflicted with flights of pride.

His last chronicle, *The Penance of Brother Cadfael* (1994), opening on a golden November day in 1145, reveals an astonishing episode from Brother Cadfael's past when an exceptional young knight, Olivier de Bretagne, a hostage taken by a noble defector from Empress Maud's camp, turns out to be Cadfael's son by an Eastern woman Cadfael met during the Crusade. Cadfael breaks his vows, leaves the Abbey, and rescues Olivier from a darksome dungeon in this happiest ending of all his adventures. Having upheld honor and saved his son, Cadfael returns to his cloister, to "this order and tranquility... where the battle of heaven and hell was fought without bloodshed, with the weapons of the mind and the soul" (*Penance* 196).

With her *Chronicles of Brother Cadfael*, each a thoroughly researched and deftly characterized historical romance built around an unusual hero and a precipitating incident of murder, Ellis Peters created a whole new publishing niche, the historical detective story (Ashley 389). She also argued that mystery authors produced as much fine literature as do the literati, and Brother Cadfael goes far in his humble, colorful way to prove her right.

Novels: *A Morbid Taste for Bones* (1977); *One Corpse Too Many* (1979); *Monk's Hood* (1980); *Saint Peter's Fair* (1981); *The Leper of St. Giles* (1981); *The Virgin in the Ice* (1982); *The Sanctuary Sparrow* (1983); *The Devil's Novice* (1983); *Dead Man's Ransom* (1984); *The Pilgrim of Hate* (1984); *An Excellent Mystery* (1985); *The Raven in the Foregate* (1986); *The Rose Rent* (1986); *The Hermit of Eyton Forest* (1987); *The Confession of Brother Haluin* (1988); *The Heretic's Apprentice* (1989); *The Potter's Field* (1989); *The Summer of the Danes* (1991); *The Holy Thief* (1992); *Brother Cadfael's Penance* (1994).

Short stories: *A Rare Benedictine* (1988).

Other works: The "Felse Family" detective novels, written under "Ellis Peters" from 1951 to 1979 and set in fictional "Midshire"; historical stand-alone novels and trilogies, under "Edith Pargeter"; stand-alone novels under "Ellis Peters"; and with Roy Morgan, *Shropshire* (1992) and *Strongholds and Sanctuaries: The Borderland of England and Wales* (1993). Pargeter also translated fifteen novels from the Czech between 1958 and 1977.

Selected sources: Greeley, Andrew M. Rev. of *An Excellent Mystery. Armchair Detective*, Summer 1985: 238–45; Kaler, Anne K. *Cordially Yours, Brother Cadfael*. Bowling Green, OH: Bowling Green State University Press, 1998; Lewis, Margaret. *Edith Pargeter: Ellis Peters*. Chester Springs, PA: Seren, 1994; *Library Journal*. Rev. of *The Holy Thief*, October 1, 1993: 128; Peters, Ellis. *The Benediction of Brother Cadfael*. New York: Mysterious Press, 1993; Peters, Ellis. *A Rare Benedictine*. New York: Mysterious Press, 1989; Whitman, Robin. *The Cadfael Companion*. New York: Mysterious Press, 1995.

Major awards: Edgar Award, 1963; Silver Dagger Award, 1980; Diamond Dagger Award for Lifetime Achievement, 1993; Order of the British Empire, 1994.

See also: Margaret Frazer's medieval **Dame Frevisse** series; Roberta Gillis's Magdalene la Bâtarde series, set in twelfth-century England; Susannah Gregory's Matthew Bartholomew series, set in mid-fourteenth-century Cambridge; Candace Robb's **Owen Archer** series, set in fourteenth-century York; Peter Tremayne's **Sister Fidelma** series, set in fifth-century Ireland.

Debut novel: Paul Harding's *The Nightingale Gallery: Being the First of the Sorrowful Mysteries of Brother Athelstan*, set in fourteenth-century London.

Jenny Cain

Profession:	Foundation Director
Living situation:	Married
Geographic locale:	Massachusetts
Time period:	1984–present
Associate:	Geof Bushfield
Significant relationship:	Geof Bushfield, husband
Concerns:	Social issues, especially feminism, homelessness, and domestic violence; family relationships; issues involving the law and business

The funeral of a parent often marks a traumatic turning point in human life, shifting responsibility from one generation to another. Nancy Pickard's award-winning novel *I.O.U.* (1991) opens with the funeral of heroine Jenny Lynn Cain's mother, an event that turns conventional behavior upside down. "The tightly-linked connection between Cain's family and the small town . . . makes this series work" (Herbert 151), but the linkage is ambivalent at best. Jenny admires most of the "really distinguished people" in her "little old hometown," especially the four trustees of the Port Frederick Civic Foundation, where she is the executive director (*I.O.U.* 21), but she openly rages at most of her problematic relatives. Pickard combines a "light-hearted traditional cozy with a small cast of local characters and eccentrics" and "the more poignant and at times depressing world of Cain's dysfunctional family" (Ashley 393), sparking the necessary tension for the series.

Each of Cain's cases emerges from one of the Civic Foundation grants that Jenny either assesses or awards. Her first amateur investigations are relatively light, even comic, like *Generous Death*, where "the more you give, the more likely you are to be murdered" (Herbert 151), and *No Body* (1986), where Jenny contends with a cemetery without corpses. Later, Jenny espouses social issues, like domestic violence in *Marriage Is Murder* (1987) and homelessness in *Dead Crazy* (1988). Her most revealing case is *I.O.U.*, in which Jenny probes the mysteries of her mother's past and nearly becomes a victim herself.

Jenny's mother, Margaret Mary Cain, lingered for years in a vegetative state at the Hampshire Psychiatric Hospital. Jenny's years of hopeless visits, of blaming the medical establishment for not miraculously curing Margaret's illness or even identifying its cause, explode the night her mother died of pneumonia: "Did I sleepwalk through my mother's illness? Was my mother's death awakening me?" (*I.O.U.* 7). Before the funeral, Jenny never got along with her stiffly conventional sister Sherry. Jenny also blames her father Jimmy Cain's insouciant mismanagement for pulling "the plug on our little boat of a business," ruining much of the town (*I.O.U.* 10), and leaving Jenny's incapacitated mother for trophy wife Miranda and the good Palm Springs life with trust funds untouched by the bankruptcy. At the graveside, Jenny, overcome by grief and guilt, hears a hoarse voice whisper, "*It was an accident. Forgive me*" as she stumbles—or is pushed?—toward her mother's coffin, losing her composure completely at the post-funeral open house.

As director of the Port Frederick Civic Foundation, Cain tries to help people who take risks, "the sickest, the neediest, the experimenters and the inventors, the geniuses who looked first like fools," making her board, "five elderly [male] powerhouses," nervous about "Jenny's weird projects" (*I.O.U.* 37–38). Not long before her mother's death, Jenny had promoted a controversial exhibit, copies of famous paintings with gender roles reversed—for one, an imitation of Manet's *Luncheon on the Grass* with a nude Paul Newman looking seductively over his shoulder while around him recline lascivious business-suited women executives. The resulting nasty phone calls and hate mail intensify Jenny's post-funeral "Alzheimer's of grief" (*I.O.U.* 42), forcing her to take leave from her job and realize the depth of animosity that exists toward women who break society's rules. Jenny's best friend Marsha, a psychiatrist, counsels Jenny to solve the mysteries of her own life.

Jenny's painful healing process requires two parallel investigations, her quest for the truth about her mother and her inquiry into the "Fall of the House of Cain." As facts emerge from her interviews with her mother's acquaintances, Jenny gradually fills in the blanks in her own life as she summons up a portrait of women's traditional lives in the 1970s bound by "rules, rules, rules" (*I.O.U.* 65). Both pursuits crescendo from unsettling to disturbing to near-fatal when someone locks Jenny into her garage with her car's engine running.

By the time Jenny recovers from the attempted murder and reconstructs the constellation of pressures that caused her mother's collapse into a living death, she herself has become a different woman: "everything had changed in my family and nothing had changed. . . . Maybe it was me" (*I.O.U.* 198). Pickard, "one of the leaders of the 1980s trend to portray women as individuals who gain strength through experience" (Herbert 151), here comforts both Jenny and her readers for the loss of a parent, one of the harshest blows human beings have to face, because it marks the end of childhood as well as the necessity of accepting our own mortality.

Novels: *Generous Death* (1984); *Say No to Murder* (1985); *No Body* (1986); *Marriage Is Murder* (1987); *Dead Crazy* (1988); *Bum Steer* (1990); *I.O.U.* (1991); *But I Wouldn't Want to Die There* (1993); *Confession* (1994); *Twilight* (1995).

Other series: Culinary mysteries based on Mrs. Eugenia Potter's fictional exploits in three novels written by Virginia Rich between 1982 and 1985; Cain has continued the series since 1992. Maria Lightfoot series: *The Whole Truth* (2000); *Ring of Truth* (2001), featuring an investigative crime writer.

Short fiction: *Storm Warnings* (1999).

Selected sources: *Publishers Weekly.* Rev. of *But I Wouldn't Want to Die There*, July 5, 1993: 65; *Publishers Weekly.* Rev. of *Dead Crazy*, July 29, 1988: 223; *Publishers Weekly.* Rev. of *Twilight*, September 4, 1995: 53; Stasio, Marilyn. Rev. of *But I Wouldn't Want to Die There*.

New York Times Book Review, January 3, 1993: 15; Stasio, Marilyn. Rev. of *I.O.U. New York Times Book Review*, May 5, 1991: 24.

Major awards: Anthony Award, 1985; Macavity Award, 1987; Agatha Awards, 1990 and 1991; Shamus Award, 1991.

See also: Carolyn G. Hart's Death on Demand series, featuring South Carolina bookseller **Annie Laurance Darling** and Max Darling; and Hart's journalist Henrietta ("Henrie O") O'Dwyer series; Jane Langton's **Homer Kelly** series, set in New England.

Steve Carella

Profession:	Homicide detective
Living situation:	Married
Geographic locale:	87th Street Precinct, fictionalized New York City
Time period:	1956–present
Associates:	The precinct works as a team: Lt. Peter Byrnes, in charge; Detectives Meyer Meyer, a Jewish joker; Cotton Hawes, a pastor's son transferred from an upscale precinct; tank-like racist Oliver Wendell Weeks (Fat Ollie).
Nemesis:	"The Deaf Man" in several novels, starting with *The Heckler* (1960)
Significant relationship:	Teddy Carella
Concerns:	All facets of violent big-city crime; interagency rivalries

Keeping "Evan Hunter" for his serious mainstream novels like *Blackboard Jungle* (1964), native New Yorker Salvatore Lombino uses "Ed McBain" for his fifty-plus "less sophisticated" police procedurals, "possibly the most successful procedural series ever written," set in the 87th Street Precinct of a mythical city he claims is not New York (Murphy 161). Bruce F. Murphy notes, "an overlooked aspect of the series: it is not realistic. Events within books, the mutations that occur between books, and the treatment of time, are all dealt with 'imaginatively'" (161), with dizzying shifts in perspective and multiple story lines that long after McBain pioneered them became popular in highly praised television police dramas like *Hill Street Blues*. McBain also stretches the limits of convincing collective protagonists, especially in *Hail, Hail, the Gang's All Here* (1971), which contains no less than fourteen separate story lines.

Given the limitation of character development in ensemble fiction, Detective Steve Carella, hero of McBain's first 87th Street Precinct novel *Cop Hater* (1956, filmed in 1958), remains a constant and frequently central character throughout the series, maturing though many of his associates do not. In *Cop Hater*, Carella, capable and laconic, captures a serial killer of policemen, and in *Killer's Choice* (1957), where a woman victim displays multiple personalities, the brutal crooked cop Roger Havilland redeems himself shortly before being murdered and Cotton Hawes, freshly arrived from his ritzy previous posting and unfamiliar with the Eight-Seven's violent crimes, nearly gets Carella, a little older and more ironic, killed. Chosen in 1987 as one of H.R.F. Keating's 100 best crime and mystery novels of all time, *Sadie When She Died* (1972) features Carella's suspicions about the stabbing of wealthy attorney Gerald Fletcher's beautiful wife. An intruder confessed to the killing, but Carella's disbelief erupts when Fletcher declares in the very first words of the novel, "he is *very* glad she's dead" (quoted in Keating 156, italics in quotation).

McBain calls "the Deaf Man," the arch criminal of his series-within-the 87th Precinct series, "my Moriarty or really more than Moriarty...more the Joker or the Riddler [from Batman comics]." McBain thought it would be interesting to have the bane of Steve Carella's existence be deaf, just as is Teddy, the love of his life (*Talking Murder* 193). Carella and his colleagues thwart their nemesis's plots, but he pops up again and again, more malignant than ever, intensifying Carella's cynicism about modern justice. The Deaf Man has haunted several McBain novels, from *Heckler* (1960), through *Eight Black Horses* (1985) to *Mischief* (1993) and *Hark!* (2004). In *Hark!* the Deaf Man, still out to humiliate Carella and his cohorts, shows more refined skullduggery than theretofore, while Carella is still so grief-stricken over his father's death that he's unable to attend the double wedding of his mother and his sister.

During the three decades after *Sadie When She Died*, Carella has married and had children with his lovely Teddy, who is deaf and unable to speak. Some of his colleagues, like Haviland, have come and been dispatched, while others, like Fat Ollie, seem to be perpetually thirtyish and on the make or the take while Carella remains straight, aging through increasingly bizarre criminal cases. In the second chapter of the hurtling *The Frumious Bandersnatch* (2004), Carella, "tall and lean and with the easy stride of an athlete—which he most certainly wasn't," picks up his telephone at the start of the graveyard shift and hears of the kidnapping of Tamar Valparaiso, an up-and-coming rock star, being launched in a televised live performance aboard the cruise yacht *River Princess* (*Bandersnatch* 53). Juddering from scene to scene as *NYPD Blue*'s hand-held cameras do allows few lengthy speeches for Carella, here partnered with Cotton Hawes, to reveal his growing worldly wisdom and distrust of bureaucrats. Terse choppy lines offer telling glimpses of the opinions Carella can't utter aloud: " 'It's our case, yes,' Carella said, and thought, 'So far' " (*Bandersnatch* 58).

The sleazy record mogul sponsoring Tamar's debut asks specifically for Carella to investigate her disappearance, propelling the low-income, minimum-budget big-city detective into the crack six-man FBI Joint Task Force occupying two floors of technological wizardry at One Federal Square. Sitting on his hands and wondering "what the hell he was doing here" in a room full of WASPs, Carella "suddenly felt like a little Wop mutt who had no right pissing with the big pedigreed dogs" (*Bandersnatch* 173–74). Gathering up his self-respect, his native shrewdness, and his mounting conviction that he's being set up, Carella plows doggedly through distractions, subterfuge, and a mess of smelly red herrings to a typical McBain shocker solution. In *Fiddlers* (2005), the 87th precinct must follow the "first man up" rule, where all subsequent murders belong to the precinct where the first, in this case a blind violinist shot in the face with a 9 mm Glock, was committed. Fat Ollie's romance with Patricia Gomez and Bert Kling's with Sharon Cooke heat up, and Carella and his colleagues are stretched thin tracking the killer.

In all their tough, generally thankless work, Carella and the 87th Precinct prove over and over that despite the occasional inconsistencies of these breathlessly paced novels, McBain leaves "an impression of detective life that is hard to forget" (Keating 156).

87th Precinct series novels: *Cop Hater*; *The Mugger*; *The Pusher* (1956); *The Con Man*; *Killer's Choice* (1957); *Killer's Payoff*; *Lady Killer* (1958); *Killer's Wedge*; *'Til Death*; *King's Ransom* (1959); *Give the Boys a Great Big Hand*; *The Heckler*; *See Them Die* (1960); *Lady, Lady, I Did It!* (1961); *The Empty Hours*; *Like Love* (1962); *Ten Plus One* (1963); *Ax* (1964); *He Who Hesitates*; *Doll* (1965); *Eighty Million Eyes* (1966); *Fuzz* (1968); *Shotgun* (1969); *Jigsaw* (1970); *Hail, Hail, the Gang's All Here* (1971); *Sadie When She Died* (1972); *Let's Hear it for the Deaf Man*; *Hail to the Chief* (1973); *Bread* (1974); *Blood Relatives* (1975); *So Long As You Both Shall Live* (1976); *Long Time No See* (1977); *Calypso* (1979); *Ghosts* (1980); *Heat* (1981); *Ice* (1983); *Lightning* (1984); *Eight Black Horses* (1985); *Poison* (1987); *Tricks* (1987); *Lullaby* (1989); *Vespers* (1990); *Widows* (1991); *Kiss* (1992); *Mischief* (1993); *And All Through the House* (1994); *Romance* (1995); *Nocturne* (1997); *The Big Bad City* (1999); *The Last Dance* (2000); *Money, Money, Money* (2001); *Far Ollie's Book* (2003); *The Frumious Bandersnatch* (2004); *Hark!* (2004); *Fiddlers* (2005).

87th Precinct short fiction: *The Empty Hours* (1962); *And All Through the House* (single story, 1986); *McBain's Ladies* (1988); *McBain's Ladies Too* (1989).

Other series: The Matthew Hope series.

Stand-alone novels: As "Ed McBain" and other pseudonyms, various stand-alone detective novels; as "Evan Hunter," he has produced numerous mainstream novels, notably *The Blackboard Jungle* (1954), his first major success. The "Hunter" and "McBain" authorships melded in *Candyland*, starting as a Hunter novel and switching to a McBain police procedural. McBain departs from his usual territory in *Alice in Jeopardy* (2004), tracing Floridian Alice Glendenning through a nasty kidnapping case. He also edited a volume of short fiction by superstar mystery authors, *Transgressions* (2004).

Selected sources: Hamill, Pete. "The Poet of Pulp." *New Yorker*, January 10, 2000: 62; Lukowski, Wes. Rev. of *The Big, Bad City*. *Booklist*, November 15, 1998: 548; Newquist, Roy. *Conversations*. New York: Rand McNally, 1967; Silet, Charles L. "Beyond the 87th Precinct," in *Talking Murder*. Princeton, NJ: Ontario Review Press, 1999; Stasio, Marilyn. "Cop Story." *New York Times Book Review*, January 30, 2000: 13.

Major awards: Grand Master, Swedish Academy of Detection, 1976; MWA Grand Master, 1986; CWA Diamond Dagger, 1998; American Mystery Award, 1988, 1991, 1992, 1993.

See also: Thomas Adcock's NYPD Detective Neil "Hock" Hockaday series, featuring the Manhattan Street Crimes Unit (S.C.U.M.); William Bayer's NYPD Detective Frank Janek series; Reggie Nadelson's NYPD detective Artie Cohen series; Charlie Stella's series featuring New York–New Jersey homicide detective Alex Pavlak.

Ella Clah

Profession:	Formerly Special Agent, FBI; later head Special Investigator of the Special Investigation Unit, Navajo Tribal Police
Living situation:	Single
Geographic locale:	Navajo Reservation, southwestern United States
Time period:	1995–present
Associate:	Justine Goodluck
Nemeses:	Racism; Anglo economic exploitation; Navajo skinwalkers (witches)
Significant relationship:	Harry Ute
Concerns:	Environmentalism; welfare of the Navajo people

Aimee and David Thurlo's Special Investigator Ella Clah chooses to work in "Hillerman Country," the West Virginia–sized Navajo Reservation, where 300-odd tribal police fight crime, mounting paperwork, and chronic shortages of funds, personnel, equipment, and routine maintenance. Ella's cases involve ecological and sociological issues arising from the exploitation of Navajo land. In the traditional Navajo Way, the *Dineh* (Navajo people) once lived in harmony with nature: "As long as our sheep flourished, we were never poor," but with the introduction of coal and uranium mining, power plants, and casinos, "the circle of life has become the circle of death." The *Dineh* find it harder and harder to "walk in beauty" with their land; young people ignore the old sacred ways, crime flourishes, and "The animals eat contaminated plants, then the people eat the animals, and eventually we become one with the poison" (*Tracking Bear* 104).

For the Navajo, all things are interconnected, so when evil surfaces, balance needs to be restored. "And that was [Ella Clah's] job, and her contribution to the tribe . . . [her] addiction to the incredible highs and lows of the work; the need to restore order to a world that resisted at every turn" (*Death Walker* 23, 16). After graduating from the FBI Academy with marksmanship trophies, tall, attractive Ella Clah resigned from the Bureau to return to the Rez and stay with her widowed mother Rose Destea. Created just for her, her new job as Special Investigator for the Navajo Police, answerable only to Chief Big Ed Atcitty, gives her the autonomy she's always wanted, along with a "pretty incredible" load of paperwork (*Death Walker* 17).

Ella has to balance the Navajo Way and the constantly intruding Anglo world. Neither side, however, here appears completely good or evil. In *Blackening Song* (1995), Ella faces racism and religious fanaticism from both Navajos and Anglos in the murder of her own father, a Christian minister. In *Death Walker* (1996) she tracks the serial killer of Navajo "living treasures," people who retain and teach the Navajo Way, a killer who might be either a dreaded "skinwalker" (Navajo witch) making a tribal power play, or an outsider attempting to destroy the Navajo soul. With *Enemy Way* (1998) and *Shooting Chant* (2000), family pressures on Ella mount. Rose is seriously hurt in a car accident and Ella faces single motherhood and the dark side of Rez life, the eerie skinwalkers and the Fierce Ones, a vigilante group that includes her brother Clifford, a Navajo *hataali* (shaman).

In *Tracking Bear* (2004), Navajo New Traditionalists violently advocate NEED, a new type of nuclear power plant promising immense financial benefits, while the real traditionalists like Rose, who'd seen the cancer deaths and the environmental devastation from previous uranium mining, caution against it. Caught between tradition and modernity when a member of her Special Investigation Unit is murdered, Ella stubbornly pursues the case despite threats to her own family.

As a police officer, Ella has to overcome male chauvinism, because "The presence of women...sorta smashes the tough-guy image they cherish in their little hearts" (*Death Walker* 26). She also has to liaise with resident FBI Special Agent Dwayne Blalock, who's initially "more trouble than help" (*Death Walker* 30–31), but her professionalism eventually wins his respect, and Blalock mellows "from the dogmatic Anglo she'd first met...to a laid-back, pragmatic man who'd learned to work effectively with the tribal police" (*Tracking Bear* 98).

Ella's personal conflicts also counterpoint her professional dilemmas and threaten her career. She keeps an amicable relationship with her daughter Dawn's father Kevin Tolino, a handsome Navajo attorney and member of the Tribal Council, but Dawn's simple three-year-old desire to have both a father and a mother at home together tears at Ella's heart. Ella wants to spend more time with Dawn and can't, because Ella's job, as Rose continually reminds her, takes her away from home far too much. Ella also knows "being single works best" for her (*Tracking Bear* 80), as it does for her young partner and second cousin Justine Goodluck. Rose wants Ella to marry Harry Ute, formerly with Ella's police team but now with the U.S. Marshals Service, but Harry refuses to consider returning to the Rez and Ella refuses to leave it (*Tracking Bear* 25).

Ella Clah's singular challenge is to find harmony in herself, in her work, and in her culture. The old Navajo Way that calls her to "walk in beauty" has its evil skinwalkers to defeat. The Anglos' technology promises the tribe financial security at the cost of accursed bureaucracy, stifling workshops full of "doublespeak and BS games" (*Tracking Bear* 111). All Ella can do is maintain the integrity that Blalock reminds her she must: "The day you stop doing what's right and giving one hundred percent, you will lose the part of yourself you respect the most" (*Tracking Bear* 300).

Novels: *Blackening Song* (1995); *Death Walker* (1996); *Bad Medicine* (1997); *Enemy Way* (1998); *Shooting Chant* (2000); *Red Mesa* (2001); *Changing Woman* (2002); *Tracking Bear* (2004); *Wind Spirit* (2004); *White Thunder* (2005); *Mourning Dove* (2006).

Other series: The Thurlos have produced two other Southwestern series: their Sister Agatha series, set in fictional New Mexico religious institutions like "Our Lady of Hope Monastery" and their Lee Nez series, featuring a vampire Navajo lawman.

Stand-alone novels: The Thurlos have also authored various stand-alone romance novels, most published by Harlequin, and the stand-alone mainstream novel *Second Shadow* (1993).

Selected sources: *Drood Review of Mystery*. Rev. of *Red Mesa* and *Shooting Chant*, January 2001: 23; Fletcher, Connie. Rev. of *Red Mesa*. *Booklist*, December 15, 2000: 792; *Publishers Weekly*. Rev. of *Changing Woman*, February 5, 2002: 15; *School Library Journal*. Rev. of *Enemy Way*, January 1999: 160; Zappia, Susan A. Rev. of *Shooting Chant*. *Library Journal*, April 1, 2000: 135.

See also: Philip Doss's Ute tribal investigator Charlie Moon series, set in Colorado; Brian Garfield's *Relentless* (1972) and *The Threepersons Hunt* (1974), featuring part Navajo state trooper Sam Watchman; Kathleen O'Neal Gear and W. Michael Gear's Anasazi mysteries, set in prehistoric New Mexico; Alanna Knight's stand-alone *Angel Eyes* (1997), featuring a Navajo private investigator and Anasazi legends; Jean Hager's series featuring Oklahoma half-Cherokee police chief Mitch Bushyhead and Hager's series featuring Molly Bearpaw, a full-blooded Cherokee investigator for the Native American Advocacy League; Tony Hillerman's **Joe Leaphorn** and **Jim Chee** series; J.A. Jance's Joanna Brady series, set in Cochise County, Arizona.

Elvis Cole

Profession: Private Investigator

Living situation: Single

Geographic locale: Los Angeles

Time period: 1987–present

Associate: Joe Pike

Nemesis: Scars from childhood and his Vietnam experiences

Significant relationship: Lucy Chenier

Concerns: Coming to terms with inner demons; dysfunctional families

According to Carol Starkey, the fictional ex–bomb squad operative who secretly falls for Robert Crais's complicated Los Angeles PI Elvis Cole, the press's "World's Greatest Detective," Cole keeps himself buried, hiding behind "flashy shirts and funny banter not unlike how his friend Pike hid behind dark glasses and a stone face" (*Forgotten Man* 281). Both Cole and Joe Pike, the borderline sociopathic gun shop owner who's been his closest friend for twenty years, have hurts to hide in what *Booklist* critic Bill Ott calls "A first-rate example of the double-tough-guy series" (1460). Crais gradually reveals small pieces of their harrowing pasts and emotional torments in each of their brawly and unpredictable cases.

Specializing mostly in missing person investigations, Elvis Cole starts where he continues, seemingly driven to help women in distress, the way Crais supported his own mother by laying out his first Cole novel after his own father died. A woman whose husband and son have been kidnapped calls on Cole in *The Monkey's Raincoat* (1987), a case that involves a ferocious drug lord and the murder of a Hollywood agent, necessitating excursions into the sleazy underbelly of Tinseltown. *Stalking the Angel* (1989) sends Cole in hot pursuit of a stolen Japanese manuscript into

Los Angeles's Little Tokyo and a lethal nest of Japanese gangsters. Cole relates the first investigations he and his hair-raising backup and closest friend, laconic and ominous Joe Pike, carry out in a slangy rapid-fire style resembling Chandler's, but after *Indigo Slam* (1997) reached the *L.A. Times* best seller lists, Crais seems to have realized that the traditional first-person PI format was limiting his development of the series and its people. With *L.A. Requiem* (1998), he switched to "a multi-perspective viewpoint and a deeper exploration of characters" (Ashley 117).

Each of the major supporting characters who thus reshaped the Elvis Cole series, Joe Pike, Lucy Chenier, and Carol Starkey, opens up a new facet of Cole's personality. Pike, a 6'1", 200-pound vegetarian bundle of ropy muscles and intimidation, wears his Marine Corps sunglasses 24/7, "inside and out, daytime or night" (*Forgotten Man* 68), secreting much of himself even from Cole—and it's mutual. In twenty years, they've never shared "the facts of their childhoods ... it had never seemed necessary [Cole muses]. ... Maybe it was enough that we were who we were, and were good with that; or maybe we each felt our baggage was lighter without the weight of someone else's concern" (*Forgotten Man* 69). In *L.A. Requiem* (1999), as Cole and Pike track the murderer of a wealthy Hispanic businessman's daughter, Crais's revelations about Pike become "so potent it even sobers up Elvis the eternal boy wonder," according to Marilyn Stasio.

Cole has loved Southern belle lawyer Lucy Chenier for a long time, but there's heavy baggage there, too. In *Sunset Express* (1996), Cole's detecting hampers his long-distance relationship with Lucy, and the major subplot of *Indigo Slam* (1997) hinges on her efforts to move to the West Coast to be near him, an expansion of the classic hard-boiled form to satisfy the demand today's readers crave for personal involvement, according to *Los Angeles Times Book Review* critic Dick Lochte (9). The violence integral to Elvis's life and work and even his personality, though, drives Lucy away, and by *The Forgotten Man* (2005), not long after he rescued Lucy's son from kidnapping, Lucy and Ben have moved 2000 miles away to build a new life. Cole's left with chronic pain in his hand, a leftover from rescuing Ben, and a far worse one in his heart. Cole desperately misses Lucy, longing just "to hear her voice" and wanting "to say something funny and be rewarded with her laugh" (*Forgotten Man* 90). When Lucy does visit him briefly two months after leaving, suddenly "the world was at peace" for Cole (*Forgotten Man* 199). He puts his gun above the refrigerator, takes great care on the thin ice beneath their feet, and, like the fine cooks both he and Crais are, starts a memorable spaghetti putanesca—completely forgetting he's invited Carol Starkey for dinner.

Losing her own lover in an explosion left Carol Starkey on the brink of alcoholism and in desperate emotional need, too, and by *The Forgotten Man* (2005) the mostly oblivious object of her affection has become Elvis Cole. She'd liked him ever since they met the night Lucy's son went missing; she liked Cole's "dopey sense of humor and the fierce way he had given every part of himself to find that boy, and the loyalty she saw in his friends ... and it didn't hurt he had a hot ass, either" (*Forgotten Man* 93). Carol tries hard, asking Cole out, flirting shamelessly with him, and had "pretty much done everything short of putting a gun to his head" (*Forgotten Man* 92), all to no avail, just as Elvis as a boy constantly ran away to one tawdry carnival after another, looking fruitlessly for the human cannonball his delusionally disordered mother had told him was the father he'd never known. That yearning for a parent's love still wracks Elvis Cole, so that when he's awakened at 3:58 one morning to learn a man dying in an L.A. alley has told a police officer he's looking for his son Elvis Cole, Cole can't ignore a case that pulls him closer to Carol and eventually comes close to killing him.

Poignant ironies, parallel painful pasts, and frustrated desires elevate all three characters from the conventional to the deeply perceptive. Carol loves Elvis for what he apparently can't give her, just as Elvis himself loved his deranged mother for the equally futile hope that she'd bring his father home. Joe Pike loves, too, maybe most of all. Refusing to leave the bedside where Cole lies wounded at the close of *The Forgotten Man*, the bitter battle-scarred Pike takes off his sunglasses to comfort Carol, distraught and blowing gin, and tells her, "Be stronger than this" (*Forgotten Man* 334). Trying to be stronger in spite of all the decks stacked against them is what Elvis Cole and his friends are all about.

Novels: *The Monkey's Raincoat* (1987); *Stalking the Angel* (1989); *Lullaby Town* (1992); *Free Fall* (1993); *Voodoo River* (1995); *Sunset Express* (1996); *Indigo Slam* (1997); *L.A. Requiem* (1999); *The Last Detective* (2003); *The Forgotten Man* (2005).

Other series: The Carol Starkey series, featuring a former bomb-squad member whose lover was killed in an explosion: *Demolition Angel* (2000); *Hostage* (2001). Starkey harbors a secret but growing infatuation for Cole, with whom she appears in *The Forgotten Man*; the Mad Max novels, including *The Two-Minute Rule* (2006).

Short fiction: Cole has written numerous science fiction and mystery short stories.

Television: Crais used the pseudonyms "Elvis Cole" and "Jerry Gret Samouche" for his television writing, which included scripts for (among others) *JAG*, *The Equalizer*, *L.A. Law*, *Hill Street Blues*, *The Twilight Zone*, *Quincy, M.E.*, *Miami Vice*, *Baretta*, and Crais's favorite, *Cagney and Lacey*, which he helped develop.

Selected sources: Alesi, Stacy. Rev. of *The Forgotten Man*. *Library Journal*, February 15, 2005: 114; Lochte, Dick. Rev. of *Indigo Slam*. *Los Angeles Times Book Review*, August 17, 1997: 9; Lukowski, Wes. Rev. of *Sunset Express*. *Booklist*, March 1, 1996: 1124; Nicholson, William F. "A Pair of Sleuths Worth the Travel." *USA Today*, March 3, 2005; Nolan, Tom. Rev. of *The Last Detective*. *Wall Street Journal*, April 4, 2003: W9; Ott, Bill. Rev. of *Indigo Slam*. *Booklist*, May 1, 1997: 1460; Stasio, Marilyn. Rev. of *L.A. Requiem*. *New York Times Book Review*, July 11, 1999.

Major awards: Anthony Award, 1988; Macavity Award, 1988; Shamus Award, 1997; Dilys Award, 2000.

Web site: www.robertcrais.com.

See also: Harlan Coben's wise-cracking **Myron Bolitar** series, set in and around New York; Michael Connelly's **Harry Bosch** series; Dennis Lehane's Kenzie and Gennaro series, set in Boston; Robert B. Parker's **Spenser** series, also set in Boston; Andrew Vachss's series hero Burke shares Cole's isolation, though Burke's stories are far more harrowing and noir.

Lily Connor

Profession:	Episcopalian priest
Living situation:	Single
Geographic locale:	Boston
Time period:	1999–present
Associate:	Charlie Cooper, Episcopal monk
Nemeses:	Alcohol; internal and familial conflicts
Significant relationship:	Tom Casey
Concerns:	Religious, political, and social liberalism

A landscape of battered hearts is the special province of Lily Connor, a dedicated social liberal and "tentmaker," an Episcopalian priest serving interim positions in Boston parishes. While trying to heal others, Lily battles her own demons—her recent grief at her father's death, her bitter twenty-year estrangement from her alcoholic mother, and her own alcoholism. Despite Michelle Blake's intricate plots, Lily Connor and those whose lives she touches, from her closest friend Episcopal monk Charlie Cooper and her lover Tom Casey, a police photographer, to urban Boston's drunks and addicts and psychotic street people, testify in all their maddening human frailty that no man or woman is ever an island, "entire of itself."

In *The Tentmaker* (1999), Lily accepts a temporary position at St. Mary of the Garden, an affluent downtown Boston parish whose pastor Father Frederick Barnes has just died of an insulin overdose. Still emotionally wracked by her father's death in Texas, tall, thirtyish, and ultra-liberal Lily, sporting habitual cowboy boots, parka, backpack, and clerical collar, soon finds herself ostracized by the parish's conservative vestry members and stonewalled in her efforts to discover why. After the suspicions of Father Barnes's housekeeper cause Lily to probe the pastor's death and the alcoholic church handyman suffers a near-fatal assault, Lily learns that Barnes had recently changed his conservative stance and supported the ordination of homosexual clergy, causing violent rifts within the parish and even accusations that Barnes had molested a parishioner's young son. When Lily's bishop and friend Lamont Spencer, who, being black, is well acquainted with prejudice and the grief it causes, reveals that he had used Lily to ferret out the reasons for the parish's turmoil, the dark night of Lily's soul nearly drives her to drinking again, but two men pull her back. Charlie Cooper, Lily's close friend from seminary days, himself furious at his church's equivocation over ordaining "people like us," and Mike Casey, a Roman Catholic police photographer, offer Lily nonjudgmental ears and broad shoulders when she needs them most.

After *Earth Has No Sorrow* (2001), where Lily Connor faces a crisis in her faith brought on by officiating at a Holocaust memorial service disrupted by neo-Nazi vandalism, she accepts a job in *The Book of Light* (2003) as interim chaplain at fictional Tate University, where Samantha Henderson, another seminary acquaintance, has recently been appointed chair of the Religion Department. While Lily has "plodded along battling the church's conservatism and her own skepticism and everybody's biases," Samantha's achieved everything Lily has not, becoming "a big star in the small field of Biblical studies" (*Book of Light* 4). Photographs of an ancient manuscript purportedly containing Jesus's own words and possibly revealing the original source of Luke's Gospel have mysteriously arrived in Samantha's mail, and she calls on Lily to investigate them. Struggling with her own personal and pastoral problems, Lily reluctantly agrees to help, and in doing so, she, like the Apostle Paul, experiences a shattering conversion of heart on her road to Damascus.

The key to Lily's unconventional faith and ministry lies in the Gospel writer Luke's vision of Jesus as "the man who sought out the lost" (*Book of Light* 39). Lily feels especially close to Luke's story of Zacchaeus the tax collector, to whom Jesus gave a special blessing, the chance to be generous, a story not found in the other Gospels. In pondering its source, Lily falls under the spell of the enigmatic manuscript, which gives her hope, after ten grudging years of trying to remold herself into a New Englander, that she will find who she is and what she wants and even what is possible for her. Despite the spiritual succor that Charlie offers her and her love for Tom, a haven of security in a world that Lily fears is disintegrating, Lily feels she "has no one to talk to and nowhere to go" (*Book of Light* 82), a state close to spiritual desolation.

Lily has never liked painstaking research. She prefers "stuff about people, about herself, about faith and God and Jesus" (*Book of Light* 124), and so as she laboriously translates the old text, it smites her with an excruciating revelation. Knowing in her bones that the strange pages are sacred text, when Lily grapples with the one of Christ's admonitions that pains her—*Don't judge and you won't be judged* (*Book of Light* 179)—she suddenly realizes that judgment comes from fear; that in rejecting her alcoholic mother's plea for forgiveness twenty years earlier, she had brought on herself the years of "intractable resentment" (*Book of Light* 211) driving her perilously close to drunken oblivion.

The Western church, Lily knows, has never accepted the Orthodox view of Jesus as mystic, and to protect its teachings, its hierarchy, and its power over its faithful, its servants, "the Order," tries to destroy this manuscript. Just as mysteriously as it appeared, the manuscript is spirited back to the obscurity from which it came, having revealed Lily's fears and lessened them, comforting her as priest and as a woman newly awakened from self-inflicted nightmares to the powerful paradoxical view of humanity's relation to the divine that another Anglican priest, John Donne, had glimpsed:

> For I
> Except You enthrall me, never shall be free,
> Nor ever chaste, except You ravish me.

Novels: *The Tentmaker* (1999); *Earth Has No Sorrow* (2001); *The Book of Light* (2003). Blake has also contributed poetry to various publications.

Selected sources: Fletcher, Connie. Rev. of *Earth Has No Sorrow*. *Booklist*, May 15, 2001: 1735; Klausner, Harriet. Rev. of *Earth Has No Sorrow*. *BookBrowser*, http://bookbrowser.com (April 24, 2001); Klett, Rex. Rev. of *Earth Has No Sorrow*. *Library Journal*, June 1, 2001: 224;

McLarin, Jenny. Rev. of *The Tentmaker*. *Booklist*, September 1, 1999: 70; *Publishers Weekly*. Rev. of *The Tentmaker*, August 23, 1999: 51.

See also: Cristina Sumners's Divine Mysteries featuring Reverend Kathryn Koerney, an Episcopal priest; and Julia Spencer-Fleming's upstate New York series featuring Reverend **Clare Fergusson**, an Episcopal priest and former Army helicopter pilot in forbidden love with married police chief Russ Van Alstyne.

Debut novel: Clare Mannings's *Overnight Float*, a humorous novel featuring New England college chaplain Rosemary Stubbs.

Ben Cooper

Profession:	Detective Constable, Edendale Police Division ("E Division")
Living situation:	Single
Geographic locale:	England's Peak District
Time period:	2000–present
Associate:	Detective Constable (later Sergeant) Diane Fry
Nemesis:	Mental illness
Significant relationship:	Diane Fry
Concerns:	Mental illness; ambition; conflicting loyalties

The heathered moors and stony hills of northern England's Derbyshire Peak District, "where civilization seem[s] like a dim memory" (*Dancing* 22), hold darksome secrets: ancient stone circles still used for cultic worship and hidden twisted lives that erupt into sordid murders—the gloomy backdrop for former reporter Stephen Booth's police procedural series featuring detectives Ben Cooper and Diane Fry of Edendale C.I.D. Their ambivalent relationship ensures ongoing tension that animates the series while they probe placid-seeming Edendale's murky undercurrents.

Cooper and Fry keep their own dark secrets, too. Detective Constable Ben Cooper, born and raised on the small Peak farm his brother Matt still struggles to keep going, constantly fights his own "black dog," the schizophrenia that destroyed his mother. In *Black Dog* (2000), Cooper has his heart set on promotion to detective sergeant, but his newly assigned partner Constable Diane Fry, just transferred from Birmingham, Britain's Detroit, is after the same job. Cooper senses the turmoil beneath her icy control-freak exterior as they edgily adjust to working together. Starting with the sweltering August evening when Harry Dickinson and his black Labrador discover a Reebok, and then the body of missing Laura Vernon, the swelling sexual tension between them unsettles both Cooper and Fry. Then, when Cooper has to choose between Fry's implacable ambition and his invariable sympathy for his home-turf underdogs, he engages in unprofessional conduct—and costs Fry her promotion.

Later, Fry deplores "the crazy distractions and misjudgments that had plagued her...and...the biggest misjudgment was Ben Cooper." In *Dancing with the Virgins*

(2001), a "surge of anger, churning thick and corrosive" pours from Fry's stomach into her intestines at the very mention of his name (*Dancing* 22). Troubled by her rage and feeling eased out of the farm by Matt's growing family, Cooper chats up suspects on his own although he knows he shouldn't, exacerbating the discord with Fry. "There were things he couldn't concentrate on properly with Diane Fry" (*Dancing* 230), and, being a Peak man himself, he can draw out the surly, defensive, unlettered villagers better than she can. Cooper, whose personal loyalties get him passed over for promotion for six years, is alternately attracted to and repelled by Fry, unable to open up to her as she'd like him to do, while she continually draws away from him "as if she had seen something she could not bring herself to touch" (*Dancing* 493).

Cooper, still an overworked Detective Constable, assists Fry, now a Detective Sergeant, in their third case, *Blood on the Tongue* (2002). A frozen body on Irontongue Hill, a baby's corpse in a burned-out World War II bomber wreck, and a unidentified man crushed by a snowplow give them a perplexing enough case, but Cooper again goes his own way; to Fry's exasperation he gets burned romantically when a Canadian girl comes to clear the name of her grandfather, pilot of that RAF Lancaster. As he breathes in the warm smells of a lambing shed, Ben intuitively grasps the gulf between himself and the tightly wound Fry, who, he knows, sees nothing but "mutton chops and several nice Sunday roasts milling around" (*Blood* 236). Against Fry's advice, Ben has moved into a small flat on his own patch. She mocks him as "everyone's favorite bobby," but then she amazingly insists that he's making himself a target for hoodlums, "living in the past.... The days when a bit of friendly advice or a clip round the ear would solve most things." Ben Cooper replies, "Friendly advice still doesn't go amiss now and then" (*Blood* 233).

Carrying heavy emotional baggage into *Blind to the Bones* (2003), Cooper takes a temporary rural assignment, "lateral development" that may or may not help his career, working burglaries around the dreary village of Withens, eventually infuriated to learn that he's only a pawn in a big undercover operation, "just some bumpkin copper" (*Blind* 418). Fry tackles a cold case, the old possible murder of Emma Renshaw and the recent bludgeoning death of Emma's roommate Neil Granger. Cooper's sure Fry would be glad to be rid of him, but Fry, tormented by private nightmares and suppressing screams of frustration with her present assistant, bacon-and-sausage chomping Gavin Murfin, astonishes herself by missing Cooper: "Cooper would be sympathetic.... He would understand. He would be willing to listen. And he wouldn't think any worse of her if she...even broke down and cried.... He might even encourage her." Sadly for them both, those are "All the things she didn't want" (*Blind* 120).

Cooper's sensitivity, his vulnerability, his empathy for the unfortunate, and his own needs all could help allay the repressed childhood memories whose ghastly fragments arise as Fry searches for the sister she hasn't seen for fifteen years. Fry, however, so driven by the demon ambition that she cannot cope with her own emotional problems, turns him off easily with "a little sliver of ice behind her words" (*Blind* 371), fearing to lose her independence. Ben Cooper's personal predicament embodies the twenty-first-century version of Freud's eternal question, "What do women want?"

Novels: *Black Dog* (2000); *Dancing with the Virgins* (2001); *Blood on the Tongue* (2002); *Blind to the Bones* (2003).

Other works: Unpublished stand-alone novel *The Only Dead Thing*; coauthored *The Toggenburg*, a study of Britain's oldest goat breed.

Selected sources: Fletcher, Connie. Rev. of *Black Dog*. *Booklist*, September 15, 2000: 221; Johnston, Paul. Rev. of *Black Dog*. *Tangled Web UK*, www.twbooks.co.uk (May 14, 2000); *Kirkus Reviews*. Rev. of *Black Dog*, August 1, 2000: 1073; *Publishers Weekly*. Rev. of *Black Dog*, September 11, 2000: 66; *Publishers Weekly*. Rev. of *Blood on the Tongue*, October 22, 2002: 47.

Award: Barry Award for Best British Crime Novel, 2001.

Web site: www.stephen-booth.com.

See also: Caroline Graham's Inspector Tom Barnaby series, set in a remote Engish village; Reginald Hill's **Peter Pascoe-Andrew Dalziel** series, set in Yorkshire; Peter Robinson's **Alan Banks** series, also set in Yorkshire; Peter Turnbull's Inspector Hennessey series.

Lord Edward Corinth

Profession:	Amateur detective
Living situation:	Single
Geographic locale:	England and Europe
Time period:	Late 1930s
Associate:	Verity Browne
Nemesis:	David Griffiths-Jones
Significant relationship:	Verity Browne
Concerns:	Traditional British values

As introduced by veteran British editorial director David Roberts in *Sweet Poison* (2000), Lord Edward Corinth, younger brother of the fictional Duke of Mersham, strides along in the aristocratic sleuthing footsteps of Dorothy L. Sayers's Lord Peter Wimsey in the ominous last half of the 1930s, which W.H. Auden called "a low, dishonest decade" darkened by the "gathering storm" that would soon engulf the world. Corinth is even smitten by just as unsuitable a paramour as Harriet Vane, whom Wimsey first glimpsed on trial for murdering her lover in Sayers's *Strong Poison*, for Corinth, another swooningly tailored quintessential English milord, becomes enamored of fervent young card-carrying Communist journalist Verity Browne. In the pedestrian *Sweet Poison*, set in 1935, predictably diverse guests at the Duke of Mersham's lavish dinner party—a pacifist cleric, a womanizing politician, a powerful press lord, a Nazi sympathizer, attractive Verity Browne—clash over Adolf Hitler's sudden rise to power. Lord Edward, delayed by crashing his Lagonda, arrives just before General Sir Alistair Craig VC collapses into the after-dinner port: suicide or cyanide poisoning? To the dismay of his Bunteresque valet Fenton, sparks of unacknowledged irresistible attraction fly between beaky-nosed Lord Edward, thirty-five, and chic twentyish Verity, whose outspoken Communist idealism doesn't preclude generous support from her wealthy daddy, before the murder is tidily sorted out amid plenty of period flavor.

Bones of the Buried (2001) takes Edward, bored with lotus-eating in New York, to Spain, teetering in 1936 on the brink of civil war between the new Spanish Republic, supported by the Soviets and many Westerners, and the Fascists, armed by Hitler and Mussolini. Verity, now a correspondent for the Communist *Daily Worker*, begged Edward to rescue her rabidly Stalinist lover David Griffiths-Jones from an imminent Spanish firing squad for murdering a fellow Party worker. Edward, now gloomier but more three-dimensional, believes passionately in personal liberty and also believes that Verity is genuinely dedicated to her cause, but he loathes Griffiths-Jones as a cold, calculating ideologue and shudders inwardly at Verity's other lover, a thinly-disguised wicked caricature of "Papa" Hemingway. Much as Edward yearns to see his cherished prewar England survive the coming catastrophe, he knows it cannot, so he salvages what he can: an equivocal justice and a delivery of arms to the Republicans defending Madrid, while he half-heartedly attempts to forget Verity in two other sets of willing arms.

World-weariness and disillusion seem to overtake Lord Edward after his experiences in Spain, a pale reflection of the violent and largely ignored denunciation of Soviet Communism that George Orwell, here glimpsed under his real name, Eric Blair, produced after narrowly escaping death at Communist hands in Madrid. (Orwell later passionately attacked Communism and Communist sympathizers in *Homage to Catalonia*, his least-well-received book during his lifetime.) *Hollow Crown* (2002) begins with Lord Edward discreetly answering his government's call to investigate the theft of incriminating letters from King Edward VIII to his intimate friend Mrs. Simpson. Verity and political machinations soon propel Lord Edward into a locked-room puzzle with farcical overtones that modulate, in the next installment of the series, *Dangerous Sea* (2003), into international intrigue when he accompanies British economist Lord Benyon on the Queen Mary to Washington, seeking to persuade President Roosevelt to fund Britain's preparations for the war that Edward now feels certain is inevitable. Verity is also aboard, traveling first class despite her sympathies for the proletariat; she can't help Edward much in solving a chain of shipboard murders because she is in hot pursuit of American union organizer Sam Forrest, but in spite of his game leg, Lord Edward manages to nab the killer and consummate his love for her one night before the liner docks.

Deeper, darker, and the best written of the series, *The More Deceived* (2004) finds Lord Edward called upon in April 1937 to nose out leaks in the Foreign Office that are supplying top secret information to Winston Churchill, a member of the opposition party deeply resented for his mishandling of the disastrous Gallipoli venture in World War I. When a government official who may have been one of Churchill's sources is murdered, Edward tracks the killer back to Spain, where Verity's old lover and Edward's antagonist Griffiths-Jones has sent her to Guernica, soon to be bombed by the Nazi Condor Legion. As Edward falls under Churchill's spell—the only man, he feels, who should lead England now—Edward, like Lord Peter Wimsey at the close of *Busman's Honeymoon*, continues to feel overwhelmed with the futility of his life, disgusted with its absence of meaning and purpose, its absence of religion, and even, in Edward's case, with its absence of love (*Bones* 102). Unable to propose marriage to Verity because of his devotion to democracy and her belief in revolution, Edward summons confidence in his detective ability, badly shaken by surly Chief Inspector Pride, and willingness to love Verity on the only terms he can. When Edward rescues Verity from the horrors of Guernica they reach an accommodation—Verity with eyes blasted open by Griffiths-Jones's Stalinist sadism, Edward standing up for King and country, to serve as Churchill's man in England's finest hour.

Novels: *Sweet Poison* (2000); *Bones of the Buried* (2001); *Hollow Crown* (2002); *Dangerous Sea* (2003); *The More Deceived* (2004).

Selected sources: Flanagan, Margaret. Rev. of *The More Deceived*. *Booklist*, November 15, 2004: 566; *Kirkus Reviews*. Rev. of *The Dangerous Sea*, October 15, 2003: 1255; Klett, Rex E. Rev. of *The More Deceived*. *Library Journal*, November 1, 2004: 62; O'Grady, Megan. *"Bombay or Bust." New York Times Book Review*, December 26, 2004: 17; *Publishers Weekly*. Rev. of *The Dangerous Sea*, November 24, 2003: 45; *Publishers Weekly*. Rev. of *The More Deceived*, October 11, 2004: 69.

See also: Conrad Allen's George Porter Dillman series, set on pre–World War I luxury liners; Leo Bruce's Carolus Dean series, set on Mediterranean cruise ships; Carola Dunn's Daisy Dalrymple series, full of Jazz Age ambiance; Dorothy L. Sayers's Lord Peter Wimsey and **Harriet Vane** series; Dorothy L. Sayers and Jill Paton Walsh, *Thrones, Dominations* (1998); Jill Paton Walsh and Dorothy L. Sayers, *Presumption of Death* (2002); Jacqueline Winspear's series featuring 1930s psychologist-investigator **Maisie Dobbs**. For mysteries set during the Spanish Civil War, see Edgar winner Rebecca Pawel's mournful mysteries *Death of a Nationalist*, *Law of Return*, and *The Watcher in the Pine*, featuring Spanish *Guardia Civil* Lt. Carlos Tejada.

Frank Corso

Profession:	True crime author
Living situation:	Single
Geographic locale:	United States, chiefly Seattle
Time period:	2001–present
Associate:	Meg Dougherty

"This is like something out of science fiction," declares a cop in G.M. Ford's 2004 fun-and-gun romp *A Blind Eye*. That goes for all of Ford's Frank Corso novels: it's hard to believe that this honorable loner can break all the rules and survive all the terrors he does, but once that author-reader deal is made, Corso's hard-edged investigative talent convincingly carries the fast-as-light-paced suspense tradition of hard-boiled detectives like Travis McGee where few other wannabes have gone before. Ford claims that he has been influenced most by Rex Stout, John D. MacDonald, Ross Macdonald, and Robert B. Parker, and says that he includes "little homages" to each in his books (quoted in *CA Online*).

First met in *Fury* (2001), journalist Frank Corso had once had it all: a big New York reputation and a gorgeous fiancée named Cynthia, wedding invitations all ready for the mail. Then came the fiasco, a front-page exposé of his disgrace and firing for making up facts on a major story, and now he's eating cornflakes out of a margarine tub and "wondering what in hell he was going to do with the rest of his life," with the invitations adrift on the mantel of the apartment he can't afford to keep (*Fury* 17).

Then comes Corso's chance at salvation, an offer from Mrs. V., a Seattle publisher as desperate as he is, one big leap of newspaper faith that rescues them both. Three years after she gets Corso back his press credentials to write weekly grand-apiece columns in return for all the syndicated income her paper needs to stay afloat, Corso's numbers are nearly where they were before he got fired, the *Seattle Sun*'s finally in the black again, and Corso's got bimonthly columns at two grand a pop and a true-crime book at the top of best-seller lists. Go figure.

Corso's also "rebuilt some measure of confidence in his own sanity" (*Fury* 19). To keep it, he's become a recluse, living on the *Saltheart* in the Seattle harbor with an Astroturf-covered dockside web of pressure-sensitive alarm wires so he can repel unwanted company. Trouble has no trouble finding black-clad, pony-tailed John Corso, though; that's the way he likes it. In *Fury*, convicted serial killer Walter Leroy "Trashman" Hines is six days from execution for eight brutal serial killings of Seattle women when intellectually challenged child-woman Leanne Samples, slow and sheltered, decides that no one but Frank Corso can tell the world she'd lied to put Hines on death row. Freelance photographer Meg Dougherty, herself made a freakily-embellished outcast by her rejected tattoo artist boyfriend, accompanies Corso on his trek through murky political intrigue and psychiatric terror, spectacularly rocking Corso's *Saltheart* when she becomes his lover.

Their affair ends seven months later. Corso, once bitterly wounded and now at least thrice skittish, keeps his psychological distance even from Meg. For her, that's "too much…like beating my head against a brick wall.…I always felt like I was on the outside looking in" (*Black River* 19), but they remain closest friends. During the hyped-up media circus surrounding the trial of vicious West Coast crime boss Nicholas Balagula in *Black River* (2003), a pair of cold-blooded hit men put Meg in an I.C.U. near death while Corso, shocked out of his self-preservative mode, vows vengeance. Corso under pressure is Corso on the loose from his self-imposed physical and psychological exile, and the moral indignation his mama said he had enough of for a dozen preachers erupts. He'd like the world to believe him when he claims that journalism's "not about clout…not about the quality of your work or the love of words. It's about money," and that "he used to think truth and justice would just naturally prevail" (*Black River* 41). Deep down, though, Frank Corso believes in more old ideals than he cares to admit.

Interviewing his leads, Corso deplores the societal despair that engenders crime and devastates lives. "The emerald city had become so glitzy that a little two-bedroom fixer-upper was the better part of three hundred grand.…It had gotten so the people who made the city work could no longer afford to live there" (*Black River* 95). Crying women also melt him: "He felt compelled to *do* something. To right whatever wrong had brought forth the sorrow," not just for the sufferer but "for himself, because, for reasons he'd never understood, it was the suffering of others that connected him most readily to the well of sorrow he carried around in his own heart and forced him to wonder, once again, why his own pain was so much easier to ignore than that of others" (*Black River* 247).

Corso's compulsion to right wrongs no matter what it costs him personally lands him in the middle of a high-society Texas murder case in *A Blind Eye* (2004). Stuck at snowed-in O'Hare with a Texas warrant issued for his arrest and Rangers hot on his tail, Corso—and Meg, whom he's brought along for camouflage—rent a car to outrun the storm, only to run off an icy Wisconsin road. Sheltering in an abandoned farmhouse, they discover corpses from a thirty-year killing binge under flooring ripped up to keep warm. The ensuing investigation involves hard-case comic moments, like "a guy who looked like he had been captured by vampires and was being kept as a pet," but the atmosphere turns deadly for Corso when he becomes the object of a torturer's attentions.

Far out and increasingly far-fetched—2005's *Red Tide* has Corso saving Seattle from annihilation—John Corso's attempts to protect the innocent and bring the guilty to his own kind of judgment resemble the exploits of 1960s hard-boiled detectives like Travis McGee and Philip Marlowe, because Corso, too, harbors the "passion for doing good as though it were a vice" (Murphy 316). But Corso has a near-mystical love of writing—an art form—as a means of achieving justice that he'd like to hide but can't. That contradiction makes John Corso a Third Millennium suffering healer.

Novels: *Fury* (2001); *Black River* (2002); *A Blind Eye* (2004); *Red Tide* (2005); *No Man's Land* (2005).

Other series: The Leo Waterman series, set in Seattle, starting with *Who in Hell is Wanda Fuca?* (1995).

Selected sources: Dodge, Dennis. Rev. of *Black River*. *Booklist*, July 1, 2002: 1825; Kim, Ann. Rev. of *Red Tide*. *Library Journal*, April 2, 2004: 40; *Publishers Weekly*. Rev. of *A Blind Eye*, June 23, 2003: 50; *Publishers Weekly*. Rev. of *Fury*, April 9, 2001: 53.

Award nominations: Anthony, Shamus, and Lefty Dilys Award nominations.

See also: Linwood Barclay's series featuring Zack Walker, a Canadian science fiction writer and reporter; Edna Buchanan's series featuring Miami police reporter **Britt Montero**; Jan Burke's series featuring investigative reporter **Irene Kelly**; Bill Kent's series featuring Shep Ladderback, a Philadelphia obituary columnist; Beth Saulnier's series featuring Alex Bernier, an upstate New York reporter; Kate White's series featuring Bailey Weggins, a Greenwich, Connecticut, true crime reporter; John Morgan Wilson's series featuring disgraced gay reporter **Benjamin Justice**.

Nic Costa

Profession:	Detective, Rome Police
Living situation:	Single

Geographic locale:	Rome
Time period:	2004–present
Associates:	Luca Rossi (*A Season for the Dead*); Gianni Peroni (*The Villa of Mysteries*); Teresa Lupo; Leo Falcone
Significant relationship:	Sara Farnese
Concerns:	Justice; art; societal issues

The splendor and squalor of contemporary Rome pervades Sunday *Times* columnist David Hewson's Nic Costa series, presenting a new breed of European detective, sensitive to art, idealistic despite himself, and surrounded by unusually well-delineated Roman police colleagues. As a young (and even younger-appearing) marathon-running vegetarian detective with a keen mind and a passion for Caravaggio's paintings, Costa debuts in *A Season for the Dead* (2002), a relentless exposé of human frailty and Vatican corruptibility.

In the fierce heat of Roman August, a crazed professor rushes into the sacrosanct Reading Room of the Vatican Library and just before being shot dead by a Vatican guard spreads the gruesome contents of a plastic grocery bag before medievalist Sara Farnese—the flayed skin of her English lover Hugh Fairchild. Although Roman police have no jurisdiction in the secretive Vatican, a tiny independent nation, Costa and his world-weary colleague Luca Rossi, detailed as a kind of punishment to surveillance duty in St. Peter's Square, appear first at the scene. Costa is smitten simultaneously by the crime's resemblance to one of Caravaggio's late-sixteenth-century chiaroscuro paintings, long despised by the Church for their relentless realism, and by the enigmatic Sara Farese, a woman with gradually revealed depraved secrets of her own, who makes Costa feel "small and stupid."

An unholy succession of serial homicides ensues, each related to one of Caravaggio's paintings and entwined with worldwide money laundering by a Prince of the Church, apparently with tacit acceptance by the hierarchy. The crimes also parallel Costa's ambivalent relationship with his father, "Red" Marco Costa, once a charismatic Communist leader who had hoped to pull Italy out of its postwar corruption through Marxist dogma. He and his wife had home-schooled their children accordingly, "refusing to tolerate the public schools, because, at the time, they insisted Catholicism was the state religion, to be taught to every child." Each child, though, had learned and "quietly rejected their parents' own intense brand of politics" (*Season* 134).

Bereft of both religious consolations and Marxist faith, Nic Costa nevertheless follows his father's custom of giving money every day to a refugee or street person. Sara's catalytic presence ironically brings father and son closer together during Marco's final days. She also leads Nic toward heartbreak, the loss of his partner Luca Rossi, and a near-fatal wound that sends him into alcoholic depression after his father's death.

In *The Villa of the Mysteries* (2003), Nic Costa emerges painfully from his despair over a passionate woman he'd known too little, the death of a partner he wishes he'd known better, and the father he knew too late that he loved. Nic gets a new partner, surpassingly ugly Gianni Peroni, a once-influential and successful vice cop recently caught with a prostitute and busted and, as a reprimand, saddled with Costa, who's riddled with self-doubt. Their superior, Inspector Leo Falcone, one supervisor in the corrupt Roman police system his men can trust, assigns them to investigate the disappearance of pretty young American Suzi Julius, whose photograph strangely resembles a corpse accidentally unearthed by bumptious American tourists pursuing illegal archaeological souvenirs. Falcone, disturbed by echoes in this case of an earlier investigation he'd rather forget, himself probes into the sleazy Roman criminal underworld, while pathologist Teresa Lupo, herself just returning to the force after the death of Luca Rossi, to whom she'd been strongly attracted, glimpses horrifying correspondences between these cases and ancient Dionysian orgiastic rituals suspected of being continued in Rome's shadowy netherworld.

At twenty-seven, Nic Costa has lost much of his innocence and nearly all of his idealism about police work. Gripped by a profound sense of failure but still dangerously letting other people's troubles become his own, Nic battles his attraction to Suzi Julius's mother Miranda, a peripatetic photographer taking a holiday in Rome ironically supposed to bring her closer to her daughter. After his disastrous encounter with Sara Farnese, Nic's struggles to master the emotional urges that his reason deeply fears play a modern variation on the theme of Euripides' *Bacchae*, which insists that humanity ignores or attempts to sublimate its unconscious drives at its own risk. Peroni, whose personal demons have equipped him to understand human frailty as Costa as yet cannot, sums up the curse of irrationality: "One day when you're least expecting it, the crazy gene wakes up and you know it's pointless trying to fight" (*Villa* 245). For his part, at the close of this disturbing case, the first one in which he's had to shoot a man, Nic is chiefly troubled by finding himself "not that bothered. . . . I wanted that man dead. He was a monster" (*Villa* 330).

The ancients personified humanity's "crazy gene" as Dionysus or Bacchus, god of wine and ecstasy, victor over ethics, morals, even reason itself. Dealing as a contemporary policeman with that force, young Nic Costa, always his father's son, daily has to walk that dicey tightrope between yielding to combustible rage and irrationally wiping the monsters from the face of the earth, and trying to insulate himself intellectually from that understandable but uncivilized desire.

Novels: *A Season for the Dead* (2004); *The Villa of Mysteries* (2005); *The Sacred Cut* (2005).

Other works: Stand-alone novels, among them: *Semana Santa* (1996), made into a feature film in 2002; *Native Rites* (2000); *Lucifer's Shadow* (2001). Hewson also has written travel books and desktop publishing texts.

Selected sources: Anderson, Patrick. Rev. of *A Season for the Dead. Washington Post Book World*, April 12, 2004: 2; Cifelli, Laura A.B. Rev. of *A Season for the Dead. Library Journal*, February 15, 2004: 161; *Kirkus Reviews*. Rev. of *A Season for the Dead*, February 1, 2004: 111; Lazarus, Mark. Rev. of *A Season for the Dead. San Francisco Chronicle*, April 4, 2004: M4; *Publishers Weekly*. Rev. of *The Villa of Mysteries*, December 20, 2004.

Major award: W.H. Smith Fresh Talent Award, 1996, for *Semana Santa*.

Web site: www.davidhewson.com.

See also: Southern European police procedurals: Marshall Browne's series featuring one-legged Inspector Anders of the Rome police; John Spencer Hill's **Carlo Arbati** series, set in Tuscany; Donna Leon's **Guido Brunetti** series, located in Venice and environs; Roderic Jeffries's Inspector Alvarez series, set on Mallorca; Magdalen Nabb's **Marshal Guarnaccia** series, located in Florence and environs.

Dr. Alex Cross

Profession:	Homicide detective; Ph.D. in psychology
Living situation:	Widowed
Geographic locale:	Primarily Washington, D.C.
Time period:	1991–present
Associate:	John Sampson
Nemeses:	Gary Soneji; "The Mastermind" Kyle Craig; "The Wolf"
Significant relationship:	Inspector Jamilla Hughes
Concerns:	Family; serial killings; the criminal mind

Former advertising executive James Patterson's first novel garnered thirty-one rejections before it was accepted; then *The Thomas Berryman Number* (1976) won an Edgar Allan Poe Award, and Patterson has since gone on to achieve "great fame and fortune through violence-splashed, suspense-pumped crime thrillers" (*Publishers Weekly*, March 18, 2002: 19). Patterson's Nursery Rhyme series stars Alex Cross, a Washington, D.C., homicide detective with a Ph.D. in psychology. Cross wears Harris tweeds, plays Gershwin tunes on his baby grand, and looks like Mohammed Ali in his prime, tall, black, and physically fit "for a washed up cop in his early 40s" (*Four Blind Mice* 276), pursuing cases involving serial killers and powerful psychopaths. Patterson, a white author, chose a black man as his series protagonist because he feels that "a black male who does the things that Alex does—who succeeds in a couple of ways, tries to bring up his kids in a good way, who tries to continue to live in his neighborhood and who has enormous problems with evil in the world—he's a hero" (quoted in *CA Online*).

Alex Cross is known for "obsessive investigations and his ability to get inside the minds of the most deranged killers" (Sanz 38). In Patterson's trademark stripped-down, rapid-fire novels, Cross, working with a friend or colleague, typically unravels one grisly murder after another, interviewing devious and twisted suspects across the country, relentlessly risking his own life as well as his friends', and finally reaching gory conclusions directly promoting the next installment. As his best friend John Sampson tells him in *Four Blind Mice* (2002), Cross is part lone-wolf hunter and part wannabe Cliff Huxtable, an inner conflict maintained throughout the series.

Cross's nemeses nearly always are tracking him even as he pursues them. Gary Soneji, on the surface a milquetoast mathematics professor his students call

"Mr. Chips," appears first in *Along Came a Spider* (1993), secretly kidnaps famous youngsters from under the noses of their Secret Service bodyguards; Cross's own children are Cross's Achilles' heel. Cross and his lover, Secret Service supervisor Jezzie Flanagan, unmask Soneji, but he's not finished by any means, rising up again to taunt Cross in *Cat and Mouse* (1997). "The Mastermind," first wreaking havoc in *Roses Are Red* (2000), reappears in *Violets Are Blue* (2001), where Cross is looking for a pattern in a string of vampirish murders across the United States at the same time that The Mastermind is stalking him and his family. With the best punch of Cross's life, he nails The Mastermind, exposing him sans two front teeth in *Violets Are Blue* (391) as "Kyle Craig," a bent FBI agent responsible for Cross's worst betrayal; he'll surface again in *Four Blind Mice* (2002). The "Wolf," Cross's sociopathic former boss, turns terrorist in *The Big Bad Wolf*, kidnapping men and women in broad daylight and selling them into twenty-first-century white slavery. The Wolf blasts back in Technicolor wide-angle horror in *London Bridges* (2004), threatening millions of lives and global security, and forcing Cross, who has left Metro D.C. Homicide to join the FBI, to put all of his psychological acumen and computer savvy to diabolical tests. Even though Cross impresses his new colleagues at the Bureau as "close to psychic," Patterson seems to be insisting that evil is never quite vanquished, no matter how hard a good man works to conquer it.

In spite of his thirst for dangerous work, Alex Cross is a good man, a considerate lover, a devoted family man. Despite the drug dealers hanging around, he won't leave the revitalizing Washington neighborhood where he grew up under the wing of Nana Mama, his formidable grandmother and role model, a former fearsome English teacher (is there a more frightening professional woman?). After Cross's wife dies, Nana Mama becomes surrogate parent to his children and when in *Four Blind Mice*, eighty-two-year-old Nana's health begins to fail with Damon at twelve, Jannie ten, and Little Alex thirteen months, for the first time that he can remember, Cross feels that his cherished home is about to fall apart. Concerned herself for Cross and the children, Nana actively promotes Cross's new love interest, Inspector Jamilla Hughes, who became Cross's good friend on an earlier bizarre murder case in California.

While keeping his home life secure and his love life smoldering, Cross still tracks those fiendishly warped criminals that make his cases so gruesomely fascinating. Alex Cross doesn't know why horrifying crimes like these happen in the civilized United States, but he's trying his colorful best to find out—and "to make things right, if only occasionally" (*Four Blind Mice* 355).

Novels: *Along Came a Spider* (1993); *Kiss the Girls* (1995); *Jack and Jill* (1996); *Cat and Mouse* (1997); *Pop Goes the Weasel* (1999); *Roses Are Red* (2000); *Violets Are Blue* (2001); *Four Blind Mice* (2002); *The Big Bad Wolf* (2003); *London Bridges* (2004).

Other series: The **Women's Murder Club** series.

Other works: Patterson has written numerous stand-alone novels, notably *The Thomas Berryman Number* (1976); *The Midnight Club* (1989); *When the Wind Blows* (1998); *Suzanne's Diary for Nicholas* (2001); *The Lake House* (2003); *Jester* (with Andrew Gross; 2003); *Sam's Letters* *to Jennifer* (2004); *Lifeguard* (2005); *Mary, Mary* (2005). Six of Patterson's novels have been adapted for film and/or television.

Selected sources: Huntley, Kristine. Rev. of *Violets Are Blue. Booklist*, May 15, 2001: 1708; Maryles, Daisy, and Dick Donahue. "Don't Get Mad, Get Even." *Publishers Weekly*, March 18, 2002: 19; Maslin, Janel. "Bodies Hang in California, and Bullets Fly in Florida." *New York Times*, November 29, 2001: 7; *Publishers Weekly*. Rev. of *The Big Bad Wolf*, October 6, 2003; Sanz, Cynthia. Rev. of *Jack and Jill. People*, October 7, 1996: 38; Stankowski, Rebecca House. Rev. of *Roses Are Red. Library Journal*, October 1, 2000: 148; Womak, Steven. "Stretching the Boundaries of the Thriller." Interview with James Patterson. *BookPage*, www.bookpage.com (April 2, 2002).

Major award: Edgar Allan Poe Award, 1977.

Web site: www.twbookmark.com/features/jamespatterson/index.html.

See also: Keith Ablow's series featuring Dr. Frank Clevenger, an FBI forensic psychiatrist; G.H. Ephron's series featuring Dr. Peter Zak, a Boston forensic psychologist; Jonathan Kellerman's series featuring Dr. Alex Delaware, a Los Angeles child psychologist who works as a profiler and psychological analyst; Joseph Telushin and Allen Estrin's series featuring Cambridge psychologist Dr. Jordan Geller.

Debut novel: Ian Smith's *The Blackbird Papers*, featuring elite FBI agent Sterling Bledsoe.

D

Adam Dalgliesh

Profession:	Initially Detective Chief Inspector with seven years' experience; in most later novels, Superintendent; finally Commander, Special Investigation Squad, all Scotland Yard
Living situation:	Widower
Geographic locale:	England
Time period:	1962–present
Nemesis:	Conflicts between his professional and private lives
Significant relationships:	Affair with Deborah Riscoe begun in *Cover Her Face* (1962) ended without commitment in *Unnatural Causes* (1967); mutual attraction with Emma Lavenham begun in *Death in Holy Orders* (2001) seems to climax happily in *The Murder Room* (2003)
Concerns:	His religious, ethical, and psychological doubts, fears, and hopes all feed Dalgliesh's avocation of poetry

In thirteen masterful novels written over forty-odd years, P.D. James has fleshed out a remarkably compelling portrait of Scotland Yard detective Adam Dalgliesh as "the idealized person she might have been had she been a man" (Ashley 249). A widower suffering since his mid-twenties over the death in childbirth of his wife and infant son, Dalgliesh illustrates James's adherence "to the view enshrined in English law that what consenting adults do in private is their own concern" (quoted in Murphy 123), carrying through adulthood the austere habits learned in his isolated, introspective upbringing as the only son of a Church of England canon. Sensitive, remote, enigmatic, and occasionally ruthless in his pursuit of criminals who prey on the innocent, Dalgliesh is "never endearing but always intellectually compelling" (Robin Winks, in Herbert 49).

Tall, dark, and less handsome than arresting, his face perhaps modeled after Dürer's "Portrait of an Unknown Man" (*Cover Her Face* 72), Dalgliesh exercises from the start an idiosyncratic approach to crime solving, fixing the sight of the murdered body, especially the face, firmly in his mind, a habit he began in his first big case, when he looked down at a Soho prostitute's battered corpse and said to himself, " 'This is it. This is my job' " (*Cover Her Face* 61). Though Dalgliesh never reveals this "quasi-mystical act of empathy" to others (Murphy 123), it anchors his intuitive grasp of the murderer's motives. Over and over, "Suddenly, inexplicably, he knew how it could have been done" (*Unnatural Death* 187), which he then relentlessly proves through logic in his investigation.

From the start, too, Dalgliesh suffers from guilt at the demands his profession forces on him. Facing Deborah Riscoe at the close of *Cover Her Face*, he feels "morbidly sensitive" to every word, longing to say "something of comfort or reassurance," but unable to offer a conventional "I'm sorry": "He had never yet apologized for his job and wouldn't insult her by doing so now" (*Cover Her Face* 254). Dalgliesh's devotion to his work, which time after time causes him to take Deborah for granted (*Unnatural Death* 161), inevitably ends his affair with her. Deborah brutally declares she can no longer bear "to loiter about on the periphery of his life, waiting for him to make up his mind" (*Unnatural Death* 256).

One of James's own favorite Dalgliesh novels, *The Black Tower* (1975), reveals Dalgliesh's unorthodox "combination of provocation and patience" (*Silk Stalkings* 1: 43). Faced with the murders of a blameless priest, a monstrous villain, a well-loved spinster, and a seductive temptress, Dalgliesh must amass a staggering amount of information, digest it until vital clues appear, and at last distill them into "the very essence of truth," the pattern that reveals the criminal's unique signature (*Silk Stalkings* 1: 43). *The Black Tower* also ends with a near-fatal attack on Dalgliesh, weakened as much from losing Deborah as from an atypical mononucleosis that he had feared might be leukemia, ending in a simulation of death and rebirth (*Black Tower* 284).

A Taste for Death, James's most acclaimed Dalgliesh novel, won the Silver Dagger and Macavity Awards and was named one of H.R.F. Keating's 100 Best Crime and Mystery Books. It furthers James's highly unusual technique of shifting narrative points of view among her chief characters, Dalgliesh included, opening their minds to her readers and thus allowing aspects of Dalgliesh's character otherwise impossible to reveal convincingly to emerge through others' eyes. Seen in *Cover Her Face* as "ruthless, unorthodox, working always against time" (72), Dalgliesh now displays a complexity of character that widens *A Taste for Death* into impressive mainstream proportions—the first crime novel, according to Keating, to explore "feelings, doubts, fears, and hopes concerning faith in God" (209). Now assisted by plain-clothes detective Kate Miskin, Dalgliesh continually suppresses the attraction he feels toward her because of his absolute ethical opposition to involvement with a fellow police officer (*Murder Room* 136). Dalgliesh's poetic inner self also dramatically clashes with his deductive professional self over the thorny question of faith. Eighty-year-old Lady Ursula puts his conflict to him bluntly: "'Aren't you sometimes in danger of believing that everything important in life can be put down in words? . . . I suppose that's the attraction of the job. . . . But you're a poet—or were once. You can't possibly believe that what you deal in is the truth'" (*Taste for Death* 416–17). Soaring from Dalgliesh's inner turmoil to universal significance, too, Lady Ursula suggests "'The world is full of people who have lost faith . . . policemen who have lost faith in policing and poets who have lost faith in poetry'" (quoted in Keating 210).

Most of Dalgliesh's cases call to mind the Golden Age convention of taking place in restricted settings, in Dalgliesh's case the hospitals, clinics, law courts, and government offices familiar to James through her career as a civil servant. *The Murder Room* (2003) centers on the Dupayne, a small private London museum dedicated to the frenetic years between world wars. At a crucial juncture in his relationship with Cambridge scholar Emma Lavenham, Dalgliesh is seen more often here through others' eyes, especially Kate Miskin's respectfully adoring ones, than previously—distancing him, perhaps, from the involvement with his work that had doomed his love for Deborah. Kate sees clearly the danger Dalgliesh has always faced as a detective: "the too easy fixing on a prime suspect . . . to the neglect of other lines of inquiry," coupled with "the need to avoid a premature arrest and the need to protect a third person" (*Murder Room* 357), always a mark of the constant drive to protect the innocent that occasionally led Dalgliesh to make the mistakes that so humanize him.

Precisely that human capacity to err, that necessity of learning through pain, make Adam Dalgliesh one of the most intricately and effectively realized figures in detective fiction. The poetry that once had come so "simply and easily," like his metaphysical declaration to Deborah in *Unnatural Causes*:

> Remember me, you said at Blytheburgh,
> As if you were not always in my mind (214) . . .

has become at the close of *The Murder Room* "a more cerebral, a more calculated, choice and arrangement of words" (286). But when he now considers his profession, "a job which preserved your own privacy while providing you with the excuse—indeed, the duty—to invade the privacy of others" he suddenly realizes its spiritual risks: "If you stood apart long enough, weren't you in danger of stifling, perhaps even losing, that quickening spirit which the priests here would call the soul?" (*Murder Room* 285–86). James once commented that if she met Adam Dalgliesh, she would say, "'I did enjoy your last book of verse,' and I wonder if he would then look at me very coolly" (quoted in *CA Online* from Kate Kellaway's interview). Approaching eighty, James also wondered why those who rely "on the support and comfort of their religious faith should be denied its solace at the end" (*Time to Be in Earnest* 231), but to doubting Adam Dalgliesh, she finally offers earthly consolation—happiness as Emma's lover and husband (*Murder Room* 415).

Novels: *Cover Her Face* (1962); *A Mind to Murder* (1963); *Unnatural Causes* (1967); *Shroud for a Nightingale* (1971); *The Black Tower* (1975); *Death of an Expert Witness* (1977); *A Taste for Death* (1986); *Devices and Desires* (1989); *Original Sin* (1994); *A Certain Justice* (1998); *Death in Holy Orders* (2001); *The Murder Room* (2003); *The Lighthouse* (2005).

Other series: Cordelia Gray series, featuring the first modern female private investigator: *An Unsuitable Job for a Woman* (1972), in which Adam Dalgliesh has a cameo role; *The Skull Beneath the Skin* (1982).

Stand-alone novels: *Innocent Blood* (1980); *The Children of Men* (1992).

Autobiography: *Time to Be in Earnest: A Fragment of an Autobiography*. New York: Knopf, 2000.

Selected sources: Bush, Trudy. Rev. of *Death in Holy Orders*. *Christian Century*, July 4, 2001: 32; Reese, Jennifer. Interview with P.D. James. *Salon.com:* www.salon.com (June 3, 2001); Siebenheller, Norma. *P.D. James*. New York: Ungar, 1981; Wynn, Dilys. *Murder Ink*. New York: Workman Publishing, 1977; Wynn, Dilys. *Murderess Ink*. New York: Workman Publishing, 1977.

Major awards: CWA Silver Dagger, 1971, 1975, 1986; Macavity, 1987; Grand Prix de Littérature Policière, 1988; CWA Diamond Dagger, 1987; Grand Master, Swedish Academy of Detection, 1996; MWA Grand Master, 1999; Fellow of the Royal Society of Arts, 1985; Fellow of the Royal Society of Literature, 1987; created Life Peer of United Kingdom, Baroness James of Holland Park in 1991; Litt.D., University of Buckingham, 1992; Doctor of Literature, University of London, 1993.

See also: Scotland Yard procedurals: Elizabeth George's **Inspector Lynley** series; Martha Grimes's **Inspector Richard Jury** series; Ruth Rendell's **Inspector Wexford** series; for psychological depth acuity, Minette Walters's various stand-alone novels.

Isabel Dalhousie

Profession:	Editor, the (fictional) *Review of Applied Ethics*
Living situation:	Divorced
Geographic locale:	Edinburgh, Scotland
Time period:	2004–present
Associate:	Grace, her housekeeper
Significant relationship:	John Liamor, ex-husband
Concerns:	Ethics and morality

As most successful mystery authors do, Alexander McCall Smith "uses murder only as a pretext to explore character" (Jones 61). Smith's new amateur detective, Edinburgh heiress and philosopher Isabel Dalhousie, debuting in *The Sunday Philosophy Club* (2004), couldn't be farther geographically, culturally, or professionally from his endearingly commonsensical traditional-sized **Mma Precious Ramotswe** of the Number One Ladies' Detective Agency in Botswana. Yet Isabel shares Precious Ramotswe's womanly griefs: the loss of traditions she knows are slipping away; brutal rejection by a man she'd married too young and reluctance to risk loving again; "the old moral certainties" rapidly disappearing and being replaced by "ruthlessness and self-interest" (*Club* 183).

To balance these pains, Isabel has devoted her life to the pursuit of truth. She edits the *Review of Applied Ethics* in Edinburgh, home to the Scottish Enlightenment and "a city of dark nights and candlelight, and intellect" (*Club* 87). She also responds to situations she feels make moral claims upon her by inveterate meddling. In *The Sunday Philosophy Club* she directs considerable attention to the personal affairs of her beloved niece Cat, who means everything to Isabel. Cat threw over Jamie, a sensitive young bassoonist Isabel's half in love with herself (though she righteously quashes the notion), for Toby, a bumptious specimen of "thoughtless masculinity" (*Club* 40) probably after Cat's money. After Isabel discovers that he has another girlfriend on the side, she has to tell Cat the truth about him and then pick up the pieces. Meanwhile Isabel is most unofficially probing the death of handsome young Mark Fraser, who fell almost at Isabel's feet from the gods, the steeply raked uppermost reaches of Usher Hall, after a performance by the Reykjavik Symphony.

Isabel had had her own share of losses. She had lost her "sainted American mother" (*Club* 16) at sixteen, and later she lost her father, a successful lawyer who regarded his profession as a kind of life sentence, to despondency and depression (*Club* 28). As a young woman, she fell in love so finally with charismatic hypocritical Irishman John Liamor—who lost his head in America and abandoned her for another woman—that now no other man will do. Now in her forties, Isabel feels herself too old to change much, so she has sublimated many of her regrets and most of her energy into the study of philosophy, that most abstract branch of learning; but her natural curiosity and her knack for accurate recollection of detail lead her into very concrete dicey situations in her pursuit of truth. Before she solves the mystery of Mark Fraser's death, Isabel must endure and overcome not just the loathsome Toby but other intrusions of amorality, like predatory reporters who make her feel "dirty" (*Club* 36). Isabel's vast preference for dealing with well-mannered people who pay moral attention to others makes her an anomaly in today's vicious world. Finding it difficult to go off-duty from her chosen work as the editor of a learned journal, she reflects accurately on her lot: "She was tuned to a different station from most people and the tuning dial was broken" (*Club* 141). Isabel's interests range from the poetry of W.H. Auden, whose obsession with fiendish crossword puzzles she shares, to modern Scottish paintings to classical music, which tempts her to pick up her flute and join the local Really Terrible Orchestra (whose real-life original Smith himself favors with his talents as a bassoonist), but she leaves her comfortable ivory tower enough to acknowledge that the Edinburgh she cherishes as an synonym for respectability also brought forth the inspiration for the story of Dr. Jekyll and Mr. Hyde, prototype for the dual nature of man that every detective—and every author of mystery fiction—ponders.

In both her personal and professional worlds Isabel Dalhousie wrestles with those pernicious contradictions in human nature. In academic circles that should devote themselves to truth and beauty and goodness, she sees narrow specialists, "devoid of any broad culture," elbowing out those, like herself, who still possess a sense of courtesy (*Club* 222); but she can't help reflecting that Aleksandr Solzhenitsyn, another of her spiritual mentors, insisted that "One word of truth will conquer the whole world." She momentarily wonders, "Was this wishful thinking on the part of one who had lived in an entanglement of Orwellian state-sponsored lies, or was it a justifiable faith in the ability of truth to shine through the darkness?" But the same dedication to truth that impels Isabel Dalhousie into sleuthing sustains her, and she decides, "It had to be the latter; if it was the former, then life would be too bleak to continue" (*Club* 164).

Novels: *The Sunday Philosophy Club* (2004); *Friends, Lovers, Chocolate* (2005).

Other series: The **Mma Precious Ramotswe** series, set in Botswana; the *44 Scotland Street* series, set in Edinburgh and debuting in 2005; the short fiction series featuring Professor Dr. Moritz-Maria von Igelfeld, *Portuguese Irregular Verbs*; *The Finer Points of Sausage Dogs*; and *At the Villa of Reduced Circumstances*. McCall Smith has coauthored and coedited several medical-legal texts. He has also written several children's books. (See entry for Mma Precious Ramotswe.)

Short fiction: *Children of Wax: African Folk Tales* (1991); *Heavenly Date and Other Stories* (1995).

Selected sources: Dahlin, Robert. "From Botswana to Edinburgh." *Publishers Weekly*, November 22, 2004: 23; Donoghue, Deirdre. Rev. of *The Sunday Philosophy Club*. *USA Today*, October 14, 2004; Jones, Malcolm. "Delectable Detective." *Newsweek*, October 4, 2004: 61; Smith, Candace. Rev. of *The Sunday Philosophy Club*. *Booklist*, January 1, 2005: 886.

See also: Jim Kelly's series featuring Philip Dryden, Cambridgeshire reporter; Jeanne M. Danes's series featuring Dorothy Martin, an expatriate American in a medieval English town.

Annie Laurance Darling

Profession:	Bookseller
Living situation:	Single, later married
Geographic locale:	Broward's Rock (fictional), South Carolina
Time period:	1987–present
Associate:	Max (Maxwell) Darling
Significant relationship:	Max Darling
Concerns:	Honesty and goodness; successful marriage

Popular cozy author Carolyn Hart calls the traditional puzzle-type mystery "a parable of life" far more realistic than the private detective novel centered on the "white knight on a quest." In meticulous and intricate plotting, convincingly quirky characterizations, and cozy atmosphere, both of Hart's mystery series (see below) exhibit the strong influence of Agatha Christie, whom Hart calls "the greatest writer of traditional mysteries." Hart also believes in the genre's "contribution to goodness": "The world is beset by evil and injustice but the traditional mystery will always offer a good, just and decent world to readers" (*CA online*).

Death on Demand (1987) debuts Annie Laurance in the mystery Hart says she always wanted to write. Hart's spunky, round-faced, sandy-haired incarnation of Nancy Drew operates the eponymous Death on Demand, a spiffy mystery-specialty bookstore on Broward's Rock. This touristy island off the South Carolina coast teems with mystery-mad locals and a bevy of authors with ominously first-hand criminal knowledge. Born in Amarillo, feisty and independent—at three she lost her father to divorce and as an SMU drama freshman she lost her mother to cancer—Annie spent her happiest summers with her Uncle Ambrose, a former Texas prosecuting attorney who'd retired to run Death on Demand on Broward's Rock. Later Annie abandons her failed stab at New York theatre and Max Darling (the perfect man her hormones surge for but her scruples won't let her marry) and returns to her uncle shortly before his death, when she inherits the bookstore she loves.

Annie cleverly reshapes the shop into the island's hub for gossip, literary and otherwise, setting up special bookselling flurries of mystery minutiae; but at a meeting of Annie's Sunday Night Regulars supervised by Edgar, her stuffed raven, and Agatha, her cantankerous black cat, a poisoned dart strikes down an obnoxious author bent on "Telling All" about Annie's mystery-writing guests. Since Annie becomes the prime suspect not only in this homicide but in the recent demises of a local vet and Uncle Ambrose, she can't resist investigating on her own, pedaling around furiously over swampy back roads and diving headlong into murky motivations.

Annie's aided and abetted by irresistibly charming, impossibly rich (and he bakes cinnamon rolls, too) Max Darling, a Porsche-driving insult to Annie's puritanical work ethic. Eventually their mutual attraction overcomes their differences—she says tomayto on her pizza and tacos, he says tomahto with his pesto and Perrier—and as latter-day Tommy and Tuppence, they complement and compliment one another over papaya he thoughtfully slices for her and enormous fried-fish po'boys that enviably never seem to make her gain an ounce. The connubial bliss Max and Annie achieve in their long series of adventures may seem too good to be realistic, but Hart insists that "happy marriages are quite possible...and that's what I wanted to celebrate with Max and Annie" (quoted in *CA Online*).

Spicing their bibliophiliac pursuit of murderers with tasteful passages of *l'amour*, Annie and Max draw up suspect lists, lay out timetables, and sketch maps of murder scenes in the best Golden Age tradition. Max had passed the New York bar, but he prefers not to do so in South Carolina or get a PI's license: However, he eventually yields to Annie's pressure for him to find gainful employment and sets up "Confidential Commissions," an advice agency heavily dependent on his research skills: Those skills come in handy for his Bunteresque support of Annie, who on the other hand manages to pull nearly all their cases out of the fire with last minute "tingles in her mind" (*Plank* 143)—bursts of intuition that rival Miss Alexandra Climpson's or Miss Marple's. Inseparable in their genteel Southern setting, Annie and Max deftly sidestep potentially divisive forces like Annie's reappearing father Pudge and Max's adored and dotty mother Laurel, who frequently makes Annie grind her molars. Their partnership of vastly different personalities works only because they're so much in love, so they make a vivid contrast with the messily failed relationships that regularly disrupt quiet Broward's Rock with foulest murder.

Like most parables, Annie Darling's stories are simple. Since the point of a mystery novel, Hart feels, "is to figure out who committed a crime...you're really exploring.... How did these relationships become so tortured that violence resulted?" (*CA Online*). Because their own marriage continues so happily, Annie and Max seem ideally suited to explore the mysteries of wickedness that erupt around them. In *Murder Walks the Plank* (2004), Max has updated his computer skills and acquired Dorothy L., a friendly white feline—adjuncts that accompany Annie's expansion of her book marketing skills into a mystery cruise interrupted by an attempted homicide. But he and Annie succeed mainly because they're still "so different... He came from a background of privilege. She'd known months when macaroni and cheese was all she could afford.... He was a dilettante; she was a taskmaster. He coasted; she struggled." Carolyn Hart's key to the eternal puzzle of a successful marriage is that "Together they loved" (*Plank* 148–49).

Novels: *Death on Demand* (1987); *Design for Murder* (1988); *Something Wicked* (1988); *Honeymoon with Murder* (1989); *A Little Class on Murder* (1989); *Deadly Valentine* (1990); *The Christie Caper* (1991); *Southern Ghost* (1992); *Mint Julep Murder* (1995); *Yankee Doodle Dead* (1998); *White Elephant Dead* (1999); *Sugarplum Dead* (2000); *April Fool Dead* (2002); *Engaged to Die* (2003); *Murder Walks the Plank* (2004); *Death of the Party* (2005); *Dead Days of Summer* (2006).

Hart's other amateur detective series features widowed Oklahoma journalist "Henrie O" (Henrietta O'Dwyer Collins), who Hart claims is a "braver, idealized projection of herself" (*CA Online*), solving cases "darker and deeper" emotionally (*Publishers Weekly*, January 26, 1998: 72) than Annie and Max Darling's.

Hart has also written numerous children's books and romances.

Stand-alone novel: *Letter from Home* (2003), Hart's own favorite, set in Oklahoma in 1944 and featuring a twelve-year-old girl whose mother is killed.

Selected sources: Brundage, Kay. "Death on Demand for Fun," Interview with Carolyn G. Hart. *Publishers Weekly*, January 12, 2004: 41; Clark, Juleigh Muirhead. Rev. of *Deadly Valentine*. *Library Journal*, December 1996: 169; Klett, Rex E. Rev. of *Mint Julep Murder*. *Library Journal*, August 1995: 123; Rowan, John. Rev. of *April Fool Dead*. *Booklist*, April 1, 2002: 1309.

Major awards: Agatha Award 1989, 1993, 2004; Anthony Award: 1989, 1990; Macavity Award: 1990.

Web site: www.carolynhart.com. Interview with Carolyn Hart, February 14, 2002.

See also: Deborah Adams's witty Jesus Creek series, set in a small Tennessee town; Jill Churchill's series featuring Jane Jeffry, a youthful version of Miss Marple; Joan Hess's series featuring Claire Malloy, Southern bookstore owner; Robert J. Randisi and Christine Matthews's cozy Gil and Claire Hunt Mysteries, featuring a husband and wife detecting team who met at an Omaha mystery writers' convention.

Debut novel: Caroline Cousins's cozy *Fiddle Dee Death*, featuring Margaret Ann Matthews ("Mam") and set in South Carolina's Low Country.

Lucas Davenport

Profession:	Detective, Office of Special Intelligence, Minneapolis P.D.; later runs Office of Regional Research, Minnesota Bureau of Criminal Apprehension; computer games and software designer
Living situation:	Single, later married
Geographic locale:	United States, mainly Minnesota
Time period:	1989–present
Associates:	Various
Significant relationship:	Weather Karkinnen Davenport, M.D.
Concerns:	Serial killers

On his official Web site John Sandford says that Lucas Davenport is "an amalgam of cops I've known, a couple of movie stars, and the characters in any number of thrillers I've read in the past" but there aren't any real cops like him, because "he's a little over the top."

Since 1989, Minneapolis maverick cop Lucas Davenport—tall, slender, dark-complected, Indian-looking except for warm, forgiving blue eyes and a wolverine smile—has been tracking serial criminals. Sandford drew these humanized monsters from his interviews with intelligent convicted murderers, lending Davenport's cases their own special eeriness. Introduced in *Rules of Prey* (1989) as a poetry-reading, independently wealthy, computer games-designing detective irresistible to the ladies, Davenport, number one gunslinger on the Minneapolis P.D., is called in when something his chief says "doesn't happen in the Twin Cities" (*Rules* 39) does—a series of "maddog" throat slashings.

Davenport's work both stimulates him and drags him down. He fights off depression in *Shadow Prey* (1990) and survives a serious murder attempt in *Chosen Prey* (2001). Over the years he mellows into a happily married early-middle-aged workaholic casting around for new challenges while he solves increasingly far-fetched serial homicides.

Lucas Davenport's a brilliant lawman because he makes things happen (*Hidden Prey* 169), like the clever sheriff who always outmaneuvers the bad guys. As the brainchild of author John Sandford's alter ego, Pulitzer-Prize winning journalist John Camp, Davenport plays the media like the consummate gamesmaster he is, at the same time playing his criminal quarry like a seasoned fisherman landing wily muskies on one of Minnesota's 10,000 lakes. News anchors invariably go for his "street-cop routine" (*Rules* 39), not just because he drives a Porsche to work and has five Wyatt Earp–style notches on his gun, as his envious fellow policemen claim. By judiciously leaking items, sometimes misinformation, sometimes not, to susceptible news chicks, Davenport plays mind games with mad dog killers to corner them into fatal mistakes.

Davenport's just as deadly at romance. "Lucas loved women, new women, different women. Loved to talk to them, send them flowers, roll around in the night"—but he doesn't get involved with those that are "dumb as a stump" (*Rules* 173). For a long time, Davenport doesn't get permanently involved at all, because the work he's addicted to tears up his relationships with women. In *Rules of Prey*, he's living a GQ dream, with luscious dark-haired artist Carla Ruiz stashed in his lake cabin, TV3's anchorwoman Jennifer Carey, pregnant with his child, in his shower whenever mutual consent strikes them, fond platonic childhood friend Elle Kruger, now Sister Mary Joseph, role playing with him weekly—and none of them interested in marriage. Davenport's flames never chill to bitter clinkers, either. Even though he eventually marries Weather, a gorgeous and brilliant reconstructive surgeon with exotic Finnish slanted eyes, Lucas manages to stay on amicable terms with his former girlfriends, like Jennifer Carey and his protégé Homicide Lt. Marcy Sherrill, who often ask—and take—his advice on their new love lives (*Hidden Prey* 108).

Davenport's killer police instinct is on target almost all of the time, but he can make mistakes. He was once fired for beating up a pimp ("Maybe I was too enthusiastic" [*Hidden Prey* 225]), and he's continually infuriated at procedural foul-ups, like police dispatchers who operate by the book when he's in hot pursuit of a criminal and provincial cops who cuff him while they lose the real villain. With his old-time Catholic conscience, he also can get taken in by apparent vulnerability. Major Nadya Kalin of the Russian SVR's Counterintelligence Division, in northern Minnesota to investigate the murder of a Russian seaman in *Hidden Prey*, sees what Davenport can't: that he had assumed a crafty ninety-year-old suspect on the politically radical Iron Range was merely senile, "because you [Davenport]'re afraid to look at old people who are, *mmm*, mentally dying" (*Hidden Prey* 174).

At forty-six, after twenty-five years as a cop, Davenport's cynicism is rising, with special contempt for the politics that impede his lone-wolf pursuit of justice. After six months of leading the Minnesota Office of Regional Research, a political appointment, he tells Weather, "After a while [working for the governor] feels like prostitution.... This is the first time I've felt sleazy. Chasing people down for political reasons" (*Hidden Prey* 26).

Lucas Davenport always gets his man or woman crook, but he also feels he's getting stale and frustrated about the dramatic changes in police work. Davenport harbors an ambivalent Midwest populist attitude toward the feds; he knows the FBI is the elite, but "when Lucas was a kid, cops were part of his neighborhood." Now, "the FBI's attitudes, their separateness, their secrecy, their military ethic, had filtered down to state and local cops, and...cops began to develop FBI-like attitudes...he didn't like it. It was bad for the country and it was bad for cops" (*Hidden Prey* 28).

Like the cowboy heroes in the white hat–black hat Westerns of his youth, Daneport's starting to feel obsolete. In *Hidden Prey*, realizing "If he wanted neat endings, he was in the wrong business" (341), Lucas Davenport rides off into the sunset, home to his wife and son—at least for the time being.

Novels: *Rules of Prey* (1989); *Shadow Prey* (1990); *Eyes of Prey* (1991); *Silent Prey* (1992); *Winter Prey* (1993); *Night Prey* (1994); *Mind Prey* (1995); *Sudden Prey* (1996); *Certain Prey* (1999); *Easy Prey* (2000); *Chosen Prey* (2001); *Mortal Prey* (2002); *Naked Prey* (2003); *Hidden Prey* (2004); *Broken Prey* (2005); *Shadow Prey* (2006).

Other works: Sandford has also written stand-alone novels; see *The Night Crew* (1997) and *The Devil's Code* (2000).

Selected sources: Adams, Michael. Rev. of *Certain Prey*. *Library Journal*, April 15, 2000: 141; Dunn, Adam. "Writing Prey." Interview with John Sandford. *Publishers Weekly*, April 14, 2003: 48; Frumkes, Lewis Burke. "A Conversation with . . . John Sandford." *Writer*, September 2000: 26; John Sandford Interview, www.goldengate.net (October 9, 2000); Lukowsky, Wes. Rev. of *Sudden Prey*. *Booklist*, March 15, 1996: 1220; Stasio, Marilyn. Rev. of *Secret Prey*. *New York Times Book Review*, June 7, 1998: 47.

Major awards: Pulitzer Prize (for feature writing), 1986; Distinguished Writing Award, American Society of Newspaper Editors, 1986.

Web site: *The Official John Sandford Web Site*, www.johnsandford.org.

See also: Elizabeth Gunn's series featuring Rutherford, Minnesota, Chief of Detectives Jake Hines; David Housewright's series featuring former St. Paul cop now PI Rushmore McKenzie; J.A. Jance's series featuring J.P. Beaumont of the Washington Special Homicide Investigation Team; Mary Logue's series featuring Wisconsin Deputy Sheriff Claire Watson; Robert J. Randisi's series featuring Joe Keogh of the Federal Serial Killer Task Force.

Debut novels: For Minnesota settings: Jodi Compton's *The 37th Hour*, featuring Detective Sarah Pribek of the Hennepin County, Minnesota, Sheriff's Department; K.J. Erickson's *Third Person Singular*, featuring Minneapolis detective Marshall "Mars" Bahr; Quinton Skinner's *14 Degrees Below Zero*.

Inspector Jurrian DeKok

Profession:	Detective Inspector, Amsterdam Municipal Police
Living situation:	Single
Geographic locale:	The Netherlands
Time period:	1964–present
Associate:	Inspector Dick Vledder
Nemeses:	Commissaris (Captain) Buitendam; "fat cats" of society
Significant relationship:	DeKok's boxer
Concerns:	Personal abhorrence of murder; sympathy for the underdog; societal changes

According to information he supplied to *Contemporary Authors Online*, prolific Dutch author Baantjer (he writes under the surname alone) began to write as a hobby in 1953, frustrated with "just-the-facts, ma'am" police reports he wrote for nine years as a beat cop and twenty-eight more as a municipal detective in Amsterdam. Since then he has produced about two novels a year. With about four million copies of his almost fifty DeKok novels sold in the Netherlands alone (population less than fifteen million) by 2002, Baantjer claims that his success "still amazes me because I do not feel that my writing is exceptional.... DeKok is just a 'normal' man, not a man with extraordinary brains, gifts, or habits, and certainly not a hero."

Baantjer also says that when he starts a new book, he has no idea of the murderer or the motives or the ensuing events. All his stories begin the same way: "I let somebody find a corpse. And after that I make my main characters act in the same way as I would have done while on active duty." Then, "The story develops while I am walking my dog. After our walk I put it down in writing," producing each novel in about three months.

Short, gray, grouchy, and middle-aged, 200-pound DeKok is less idiosyncratic and eccentric than Sherlock Holmes and "much warmer and more humanistic than Maigret" (Ray B. Browne, in Herbert 15), but as grumpy with his colleagues, especially his chief assistant, the long-suffering young Dick Vledder, as Colin Dexter's Inspector Morse. "A strange unrest" increasingly plagues DeKok at the outset of each case, as though he's waiting for some challenge to all his knowledge and ingenuity. He's irascible, often cursing Amsterdam's wet, cold, humid weather, his tall, distinguished, politically correct boss the Commissaris, and even hapless Vledder when only dregs remain in the office coffee pot (*Sorrowing Tomcat* 10). DeKok works out of the renowned old real-life police station at 48 Warmoes Street, the Dutch "Hill Street" and the busiest police station in Europe, abutting Amsterdam's famous Red Light District. Vledder often reflects on the similarity between "his partner, mentor and friend" DeKok and the Captain DeCocq who headed the local constabulary when Rembrandt painted "The Night Watch" in 1642, possibly modeling that great work on DeCocq's Warmoes Street headquarters (*Sorrowing Tomcat* 11).

The corpses whose discovery leads off each DeKok novel are generally society's downtrodden for whom DeKok has a special sympathy—petty criminals, prostitutes, thieves, con men, even an "innocent blackmailer" like Cunning Pete Geffel, found stabbed in the back in the lonely dunes near Seadike, Holland's bulwark against the sea, in *DeKok and the Sorrowing Tomcat* (1993; orig. 1969).

Commissaris Buitendam finds something "Keystone-Cop-like about DeKok," a brilliant detective who can't be promoted because he refuses to wear "the rigid harness of official hierarchy" but Dick Vledder knows that DeKok has a way "to get involved in the most bizarre and impossible situations, almost in the blinking of an eye" (*Sorrowing Tomcat* 19, 11). Like his boxer's lugubrious expression that hides a playful personality, DeKok's silly little felt hat, rippling eyebrows, and irresistibly mischievous schoolboy grin, his most appealing feature, mask a powerful intuition that police rules and regulations cannot contain. To gain insights into their characters, DeKok prefers to meet potential opponents on their own ground, cultivating a bumbling appearance to disarm his wealthy and powerful targets, generally big-business fat cats who fatally underestimate him. DeKok's stern Calvinistic upbringing and his puritanical civil servant's soul revolt against unctuous condescension and elegant interiors designed to impress; he brilliantly brings them to justice.

DeKok disapproves of guns and prefers tracking villains on foot, the easiest way around Amsterdam, to touch phones and walkie-talkies. For DeKok, the detective's most important weapons are persistence and self-confidence, though even those crucial qualities occasionally waver when he has to deal with women, "factors he always looked at with a certain amount of suspicion" (*Sorrowing Tomcat* 103), making him yearn for the cigars he's long since given up. In his long career women deal him worrisome surprises, "And DeKok did not really like surprises" (*Sorrowing Tomcat* 104). While occasionally a well-rounded bosom or a shapely thigh may transfix him, they never stop him from uncovering the truth. Invariably pitying prostitutes, many of whom, like Far Sonja in *DeKok and the Sunday Strangler* (2003, orig. 1993), spark his cases by being found gruesomely slain, DeKok has even been known to tamper with evidence to trap their killers, as in *DeKok and the Corpse on Christmas Eve* (2003, orig. 1993).

As bizarre as DeKok's cases become, this old "gray sleuth," remains unflappable, persistent, and intuitive, an old-fashioned hands-on cop respected by his colleagues and his bosses and adored by his readers. In a culture increasingly losing its sympathy for underdogs so often struck by misfortune, DeKok remains one of the dying breed of maverick lawmen, those who invariably sympathize with the attempts by society's outcasts to survive in a world that's no less, and perhaps more, corrupt than they are.

Novels: Baantjer began publishing his DeKok mysteries in Dutch in 1964 on an average of two a year, but they did not begin appearing in English translation until 1992. Many have not yet been published in English. All titles start with *DeKok and...*: *DeKok and the Somber Nude* (1992; orig. 1964);...*the Sunday Strangler* (1992; orig. 1965);...*Murder on the Menu* (1992; orig. 1990);...*the Corpse on Christmas Eve* (1993; orig. 1965);...*the Dead Harlequin* (1993; orig. 1968);...*the Sorrowing Tomcat* (1993; orig. 1969);...*the Disillusioned Corpse* (1993; orig. 1969);...*the Careful Killer* (1993; orig. 1971);...*the Romantic Murder* (1993; orig. 1972);...*the Dying Stroller* (1993; orig. 1972);...*the Corpse at the Church Wall* (1993; orig. 1973);...*the Dancing Death* (1994; orig. 1974);...*the Naked Lady* (1978; orig. 1993);...*the Brothers of Easy Death* (1995, orig. 1979);...*the Deadly Accord* (1997, orig. 1980);...*Murder in Séance* (1997, orig. 1981);...*Murder in Ecstasy* (1998, orig. 1982);...*the Begging Death* (1999, orig. 1982);...*the Deadly Warning* (1999, orig. 1988);...*the Murder First Class* (1999, orig. 1989);...*the Murder in Bronze* (1999, orig. 1988);...*Disfiguring Death* (2000, orig. 1991);...*the Devil's Conspiracy* (2000, orig. 1992);...*Murder on Blood Mountain* (2000, orig. 1985);...*the Mask of Death* (2000, orig. 1987);...*Murder by Installments* (2000, orig. 1985);...*Murder Depicted* (2000, orig. 1990);...*Murder in Amsterdam* (2003; orig. 1993; contains...*the Sunday Strangler* and...*the Corpse on Christmas Eve*);...*the Geese of Death* (2004, orig. 1983);...*Murder by Melody* (2005, orig. 1983).

Other works: Baantjer has authored eleven other detective novels, several volumes of short fiction, and *Leerboekje recherché* (1977), "Plain Clothes Police Manual," a teaching text. None of these have been translated into English.

Selected sources: Kim, Ann. Rev. of *DeKok and the Murder by Melody*. *Library Journal*, January 2005: 86; *Publishers Weekly*. Rev. of *DeKok and the Corpse at the Church Wall*, November 15, 1993: 75; *Publishers Weekly*. Rev. of *DeKok and the Sorrowing Tomcat*, February 1, 1993: 88; *Publishers Weekly*. Rev. of *DeKok and Murder in Ecstasy*, December 15, 1997: 51; Shaw, Gene. Rev. of *DeKok and the Corpse at the Church Wall*. *Library Journal*, November 15, 1993: 99.

Awards: Silver Medal of Royal Order of Oranje Nassau, 1979, for police work; *Televisier* award for most popular writer, 1985. Baantjer was recently knighted by the Dutch monarchy.

See also: Jan Willem van de Wetering's Grijpstra and de Gier Amsterdam Cop series; Nicholas Freeling's Piet Van der Valk series, also set in Amsterdam; somewhat farther afield, Olen Steinhauer's Emil Brod series, set in 1950s Eastern Europe.

Gregor Demarkian

Profession:	Fictional founder of the FBI Department of Behavioral Sciences
Living situation:	Widowed
Geographic locale:	Pennsylvania
Time period:	1990–present
Associates:	Fantasy author Bennis Hannaford; Father Tibor Kasparian
Nemesis:	The reality of evil
Significant relationship:	Bennis Hannaford
Concerns:	Social/political issues such as AIDS, religious activism, child abuse

Abandoning her earlier humorous mystery series starring romance author Patience McKenna, former academic Orania Papazoglou adopted the pen name "Jane Haddam" for her darker, issue-driven Gregor Demarkian series, featuring "the Armenian-American Hercule Poirot," an honorific that Demarkian loathes. Demarkian had started with the FBI as an investigator and later founded and administered the bureau's Department of Behavioral Sciences. Starting with *Not a Creature Was Stirring* (1990), a secular or Judeo-Christian holiday precipitates each of Demarkian's first fourteen cases as an informal consultant to the Philadelphia police. The more recent *True Believers* (2001), *Somebody Else's Music* (2002), *Conspiracy Theory* (2003), and *The Headmaster's Wife* (2005) involve serious contemporary societal issues and display especially penetrating psychological analyses of suspects, victims, and even Demarkian himself.

After two decades with the FBI, where he founded the Bureau's Behaviorial Sciences Unit, Demarkian retired, lost his beloved wife Elizabeth to cancer, then moved back to Philadelphia's Cavanaugh Street, the small Armenian-American enclave of his boyhood, where he finds that he thinks better. Cavanaugh Street endows this series with its own delightful collective ethnic character, and it also powerfully reminds Demarkian of a peculiarly Armenian concept of evil, human failings that a detective constantly battles and that the general public often refuses to acknowledge. Nearly two million Armenians went "to the funeral of God" (*The Crossing Place* 47), slain in the systematic 1915–1916 massacres that the Turks still refuse to admit they committed (Marsden 62)—the first modern genocide and Hitler's model for the Nazi Holocaust. Many Armenian immigrants settled in Boston, Detroit, and

Philadelphia, where their traditional intellectual gifts, their stubborn cultural and religious identity, and their proclivity for hard work provided them and their upwardly mobile children the American Good Life. Armenian ethnicity and cultural patterns are as essential to Demarkian's crime solving as they are to understanding his personality.

Once "full of tenements and ambition" (*Skeleton Key* 50), Demarkian's Cavanaugh Street now enjoys an upscale renaissance. Ohanian's Middle Eastern Food Store and the Ararat Restaurant provide rich local-color gathering spots and even richer exotic delicacies like halvah, lahvosh, paklava, and lamb-stuffed grape leaves. Cavanaugh Street's colorful residents include Old George Tekemanian, bemused by the expensive gadgets his wealthy children keep showering upon him; Donna Moradanyan, who compulsively swathes their buildings in holiday gift wrap; Lida Arkmanian, who cooks constantly in her palatial townhouse; and scholar-priest Father Tibor Kasparian, who gently guides his congregation at Holy Trinity Armenian Church. All Cavanaugh Street's residents provide a stable and comforting community from which Demarkian sallies to solve increasingly complex and spiritually troubling cases as favors to his friends.

Demarkian's earlier cases leaven homicide with humor. In *Not a Creature Was Stirring*, he encounters the hilariously-skewed old-moneyed Hannaford clan, Philadelphia Main Line patricians bent on devouring one another. Bennis Hannaford is Haddam's fictional alter ego, a thin, chain-smoking, highly successful author of sword-and-sorcery novels; fortunately so, because her rapacious father has just disinherited her. Though Demarkian never loses his memories of Elizabeth, and though Bennis, twenty years younger, frequently perplexes him, they're attracted to one another, and she often provides the intuitive leap that complements Gregor's painstakingly deductive crime-solving mental processes. Bennis soon moves into a posh floor-through duplex in Demarkian's building, and eventually, in *Conspiracy Theory*, they are living together, to the pragmatic delight of Cavanaugh Street's real arbiters of faith and morals, its formidable little old Armenian matriarchs.

Many of Demarkian's cases feature inflammatory combinations of religion and sex. *Dear Old Dead* (1994) centers on a Father's Day killing in a Harlem AIDS clinic run by gay physician Dr. Michael Pride, whose lover is a priest. When police nab Pride in a gay porn shop, the local Roman Catholic Archbishop wants the clinic closed and engages Demarkian to investigate. 1996's *Baptism in Blood* takes Demarkian to a Southern revival camp awash in redneck zealotry interspersed with a gaggle of lesbians, satanic rituals, and an atheistic bookstore owner. *True Believers* (2001) opens on a gloomier shocker: a young husband surreptitiously places the body of his wife in front of the communion rail of St. Anselm's Roman Catholic Church in Philadelphia, blows out his own brains with a .357 Magnum, and provides Demarkian and Bennis, now themselves lovers facing the possibility that Bennis may have lung cancer, one of their most troubling excursions into the tensions that flare between clashing denominations of the followers of the Prince of Peace. In *The Headmaster's Wife* (2005), Demarkian, strangely bored with his investigations and proposing so perfunctorily that he enrages Bennis, reluctantly confronts the sleazy underbelly of academia at an exclusive hypocritical Boston prep school, at the same time salvaging the self-confidence of a troubled teenager.

In all of these novels, late-fiftyish, hawk-nosed, and appealingly fit (though somewhat portly), Gregor Demarkian personifies the "continuous quest for order, a struggle against unimaginable chaos" that is Armenian history (Marsden 143). He also observes, observes, observes incessantly, as the necessary still center for Haddam's wealth of kaleidoscopically shifting flaming-individual characters and intricate subplots. Near the middle of each book, Demarkian sits down alone to the part of the case that he likes best: "the part where you could put the pieces on the table and make order out of chaos" (*Skeleton Key* 104), typically Armenian in digging deeper, "deeper into business, deeper into the mysteries, deeper into knowledge, in the hope that somewhere there is solid rock" (Marsden 91).

Demarkian's professional experience in unmasking serial killers and his considerable technical knowledge of poisons equip him for crime solving, but his patience in unraveling complicated problems, his tact in dealing with distraught VIPs, and his discreet sensitivity toward contentious situations all suit him ideally to defuse potential public relations disasters. Despite his capabilities, though, Gregor Demarkian increasingly finds himself baffled at the moral degradation of today's society. When he goes to his friend Father Tibor, who was tortured in the Soviet Gulag for refusing to give up his faith, Tibor reminds him of the reality of evil, something Armenians never forget: "Decades of indulgence in repression, torture, and summary execution.... To some people, it made no difference. They would not see, or they would explain it away. Maybe we all do this with what we believe" (*Conspiracy Theory* 215). Then Gregor Demarkian sighs over poor humanity and brings those wicked he can to justice—a justice the Armenian nation as a whole has seldom received.

Novels: *Not a Creature Was Stirring* (1990); *Precious Blood* (1991); *Act of Darkness* (1991); *Quoth the Raven* (1991); *A Great Day for the Deadly* (1992); *Feast of Murder* (1992); *A Stillness in Bethlehem* (1992); *Murder Superior* (1993); *Bleeding Hearts* (1994); *Dear Old Dead* (1994); *Festival of Deaths* (1994); *Fountain of Death* (1995); *And One to Die On* (1996); *Baptism in Blood* (1996); *Deadly Beloved* (1997); *Skeleton Key* (2000); *True Believers* (2001); *Somebody Else's Music* (2002); *Conspiracy Theory* (2003); *The Headmaster's Wife* (2005).

Other works: Patience ("Pay") Campbell McKenna's five-novel detective series (as Orania Papazoglou), featuring McKenna as a skinny, dieting, chain-smoking journalist and author of romance fiction. Haddam also wrote several "Second Chance at Love" Romance series novels under the pseudonym "Nicola Andrews"; and other stand-alone novels as "Ann Paris." Stand-alone novels *Sanctity* (1986) and *Charisma* (1992) appeared under her own name.

Selected sources: "Jane Haddam," in *Great Women Mystery Writers*, ed. Kathleen Klein. Westport, CT: Greenwood Publishing, 1994; Pitt, David. Rev. of *Skeleton Key*. *Booklist*, January 1, 2000: 883; Pitt, David. Rev. of *True Believers*. *Booklist*, April 1, 2001: 1449; *Publishers Weekly*. Rev. of *The Headmaster's Wife*, February 28, 2005: 42; *Publishers Weekly*. Rev. of *True Believers*, April 2, 2001: 42.

See also: Gillian Roberts's Amanda Pepper series, for Philadelphia setting; Les Roberts's series set in Cleveland and featuring Slovenian PI Milan Jacovich.

Justin de Quincy

Profession:	"Queen's man," undercover agent for Eleanor of Aquitaine
Living situation:	Single
Geographic locale:	London and environs
Time period:	1190s
Associates:	Luke de Marston; Serjeant Jonas
Nemesis:	Durand de Curzon
Significant relationship:	Claudine de Loudun
Concerns:	Power struggles; father-son relationship

For the twin keynotes of her writing career, tax and corporate attorney Sharon Kay Penman turned to historical fiction, because, she believes, "human nature has not changed much over the centuries.... The trappings of civilization vary ... as do beliefs and superstitions. But the core of human emotions and needs remains constant, and I attempt to convey that in my novels. Since I usually am writing of kings and queens and those who wielded power, the abuse and corruption of power also figures prominently in my writing" (Interview with Sharon Kay Penman, *Authors and Artists For Young Adults*, quoted in *CA Online*).

The intense power struggles of medieval England often set royal family members at one another's throats, offering Penman a rich lode of historical material. Several of her stand-alone historical novels deal with the turbulent fifteenth-century Wars of the Roses, but for her "Medieval Mysteries," Penman looked to the late twelfth–early thirteenth centuries, the time of Richard the Lionhearted, his formidable mother Eleanor of Aquitaine, and her youngest son John, "the Prince of Darkness," so despised a ruler that the English have never named a king "John" since.

King Richard's departure for the Third Crusade in 1189 ignited a fierce power struggle for the English throne. John was often called "Lackland" because his father Henry II had favored his oldest son and heir Henry, who died young, while Eleanor's mind and heart were fixed on Richard, who named not John but five-year-old Arthur of Brittany as his heir. With Richard out of England and Eleanor in her seventies acting as regent, John immediately began conniving with Philip II of France to supplant Richard as king. When Richard, on returning to England in 1192, was captured and held for ransom by Holy Roman Emperor Henry VI, John fomented rebellion against Queen Eleanor, who mustered all her political acumen and force to hold the throne for Richard. Against this intricate tapestry of plots and counterplots, Penman's hero Justin de Quincy, an unrecognized illegitimate son, fights his own colorful battles to win a place in a highly stratified society. He does so by becoming Eleanor's secret agent, advancing Richard's cause, helping to thwart John's machinations, and concurrently solving murders involving high and low alike.

The Queen's Man (1996), set in 1193, opens with shocking news. Richard is thought to be lost at sea, and Justin, a foundling raised as a young squire in the Winchester household of Aubrey de Quincy, the haughty and powerful Bishop of Chester, discovers that the bishop is his biological father. After a confrontation, Justin rushes away from Winchester and comes upon a dying goldsmith who asks him to carry a bloodied letter to Eleanor of Aquitaine containing information that Richard is alive but imprisoned. Eleanor astutely recognizes that the goldsmith's death means that a conspiracy against Richard is brewing, and she knows that John is already conspiring for the throne. She entrusts Justin with solving the goldsmith's murder, which he undertakes with the help of his friend undersheriff Luke de Marston and doughty Serjeant Jonas of the Tower of London. Justin also becomes entangled with two other secret agents. Durand de Curzon, supposedly working for John, is actually employed by Eleanor, but he becomes Justin's bitter enemy. Sensuous Claudine de Curzon, Eleanor's young kinswoman, beds and betrays Justin because she is a spy, too—for John.

Justin's compassion, as well as his passion for Claudine, continually complicate his life. Earlier, Justin's soft heart had driven him to rescue a puppy tossed into an icy river, and now, as a favor to his good friend Nell, a tavern keeping widow, Justin is also investigating the murder of pretty Melangell, a peddler's daughter. Justin discovers the murderer, helps the peddler and his remaining child back to Wales, and keeps himself in Nell's good graces. In *Cruel as the Grave* (1998), Eleanor, struggling to raise an enormous ransom to free Richard from an Austrian prison, sends Justin to quell John's threatened revolt; Justin risks his life at the hands of the unscrupulous Durand, who hates him. Still inflamed by Claudine even though he cannot trust her, Justin learns she is pregnant—by himself? by John?—and does the honorable thing, seeking Eleanor's help to send Claudine to a secluded nunnery and vowing to help support the child. Justin also savagely confronts his own father again, this time over the name the Bishop feels Justin has no right to take—the name whimsically suggested to Justin by none other than the queen.

For her mysteries, Penman says she thinks of a crime, then takes it from there (*CA Online*). The crime in *Dragon's Lair* (2003)—the theft of part of Richard's ransom being conveyed from Wales to Chester as bales of wool, "as valuable as gold"—propels Justin de Quincy into northern Wales, hotbed of anti-English resentment and intrigue. Despite their mutual animosity, Justin is forced to take his father, the Bishop of Chester, into his confidence as he matches wits with Davydd ab Owain, the wily prince of north Wales, who, Justin learns, had sent the ransom shipment almost entirely unguarded into an ambush, possibly with a connection to an unnamed "English lord."

Prince of Darkness (2005) opens with an even more ominous danger to Justin when his summons to Paris from Lady Claudine, now mother of his child, turns out to be a ploy engineered by John. John is now the victim of a forgery commissioned by the mother of Richard's heir Arthur of Brittany, implicating both John and Eleanor in a plot to murder Richard. Justin reluctantly agrees to help John only because of the threat to Eleanor, who is in Germany negotiating Richard's release. In devotion to Eleanor, Justin even consents to join his old enemy Durand de Curzon to foil the plot, which leads them into chambers of horrors on Mont-Saint-Michel in Brittany and an eerie Paris cemetery.

Penman, whose work appeals to young readers, hopes that she's "opening a window to the past [by recreating]...a time in which...people believed that demons lurked in the dark, that destiny was determined by blood, that change was to be feared and man was born to sin. But it was also a time in which people loved and hated and grieved as they do today....Ideally, a reader...will experience a sense of wonderment on one page, a chill on another, and a jolt of familiar recognition upon the next one!" (quoted in *CA Online*). By clinging to his values of decency and compassion in a violent machiavellian world, Justin de Quincy nobly embodies that hope.

Novels: *The Queen's Man* (1996); *Cruel as the Grave* (1998); *Dragon's Lair* (2003); *Prince of Darkness* (2005).

Other novels: Penman has written several stand-alone historical thrillers set in medieval England, notably *The Sunne in Splendor* (1982); *Here Be Dragons* (1985); *Falls the Shadow* (1988); *The Reckoning* (1991); *When Christ and His Saints Slept* (1995); *Time and Chance* (2002).

Selected sources: Connally, Molly. Rev. of *Cruel as the Grave*. *School Library Journal*, March 1999: 231; Flanagan, Margaret. Rev. of *Prince of Darkness*. *Booklist*, April 15, 2005: 1436; Jones, Trevelyan. Rev. of *Dragon's Lair*. *School Library Journal*, February 2004: 172; Melton, Emily. Rev. of *The Queen's Man*. *Booklist*, November 1, 1996: 483; *Publishers Weekly*. Rev. of *Dragon's Lair*, September 15, 2003: 48.

Major award: Edgar Award finalist, Mystery Writers of America, 1997.

Web site: www.sharonkaypenman.com.

See also: Paul Doherty's Hugh Corbett series, set in thirteenth-century England; Margaret Frazer's **Dame Frevisse** series, set in fifteenth-century England; Susannah Gregory's Matthew Bartholomew series, set in mid-fourteenth-century England; Edward Marston's Domesday series, set in eleventh-century England; Ellis Peters's **Brother Cadfael** series, set in twelfth-century England and Wales; Candace Robb's **Owen Archer** series, set in fourteenth-century England.

Peter Diamond

Profession:	Detective Superintendent, Avon and Somerset C.I.D.; temporarily (*Diamond Solitaire*), private detective
Living situation:	Married; then widowed (*Diamond Dust*)
Geographic locale:	Bath, England
Time period:	1991–present
Associates:	Various; Henrietta "Hen" Mallin, Keith Halliwell (*The House Sitter*)
Nemeses:	Computer technology; Assistant Chief Constable Tott
Significant relationship:	Stephanie Diamond
Concerns:	Dangers of technology; traditional detective work

Introduced in *The Last Detective* (1991) many years after two well-received Victorian series respectively featuring Sergeant Cribb and Bertie, Prince of Wales, gruff Bath Detective Superintendent Peter Diamond is perhaps the most appealing of prolific Diamond Dagger awardee Peter Lovesey's fictional sleuths (Ashley 301). Lovesey observes that when his writing is successful, "it can be subversive, suggest ironies, spring surprises, and now and then, chill the blood" (quoted in *Talking Murder* 173). His Peter Diamond stories do all that—boldly. Recalling 1940s and 1950s trilbied and raincoated detectives who relied on solid police plod and brilliant and/or brutal questioning, former rugby player Diamond can't identify with Shakespeare-quoting and poetry-writing television detectives. Although Lovesey's literary favorites like Jane Austen, Mary Shelley, and Coleridge play significant cameo roles in almost all Diamond's cases, the blunt fortyish detective's never read their work. He prefers biographies, especially those with "of the Yard" somewhere in the title (*Last Detective* 40), and he's convinced that Britain's decline began in 1964 with the abolition of the death penalty (*Last Detective* 118).

Since Lovesey feels that his major problem in creating contemporary mystery fiction is keeping pace with technological advancements in police work (quoted in *Talking Murder* 184), he made Diamond appealingly uncomfortable with white-coated experts and geeky computer nerds, subversively deploring the computer and all the bureaucrats who blindly worship it as a cure-all (*Last Detective* 29). Not even a very good driver, Diamond considers computer terminals "Trojan horses," and when computers and four civilian operators materialize in the Manvers Street Police Station with the promise, "We'll soon have them up and running, sir," Diamond's response says it all: "Up where? Up yours, as far as I'm concerned" (*Last Detective* 111).

In *The Last Detective* Diamond's headed the Avon and Somerset murder squad for three years when a young woman's nude body washes up in a Mendip Hills lake south of Bristol. With his wife Stephanie resigned to Diamond's regarding their bedroom as an extension of the police station, Diamond employs his sharp ear for evasion, his intimidating physical presence, his tenacious common sense, and what his SOCOs call his "cat-and-mouse" method: "Playful for a bit. Then he pounces. If he doesn't bite their heads off, he breaks their backbones" (*Last Detective* 56), but accusations of improper interrogation techniques in an earlier case cause Assistant Chief Constable Tott to saddle Diamond with ambitious computer-literate Inspector John Wigfull, eventually giving Wigfull the Lady of the Lake case as Acting Chief Inspector. Diamond has integrity. He resigns.

Comic and touching ironies abound in Diamond's post-police situation. Fearing "Steph" will be shocked by his resignation (she isn't), he buys her the most complicated microwave he can find, then to make ends meet, he takes a bartending job and another as a department store Santa, revealing his compassion for youngsters that climaxes this puzzling case and belies the intimidating Diamond exterior that inspired outlandish survival tactics in his former subordinates.

Unable to hold down other jobs, Diamond stays in Bath, a touristy town famous for its literary connections, and becomes a private investigator in *Diamond Solitaire* (1992), then makes his way back to police work in *The Summons* (1995), a case full of twists and surprises when a man he'd earlier collared for murder escapes and takes a hostage—and then Diamond discovers the man's innocent. He rejoins the Bath and Somerset C.I.D. with a classic locked-room mystery in *Bloodhounds* (1996), and copes wittily in *The Vault* (2000) with a skeleton blood-chillingly discovered beneath the house where Mary Shelley wrote *Frankenstein*. When Stephanie is murdered in *Diamond Dust* (2002), Diamond is not only removed from the investigation but becomes its prime suspect. He buries his anguish and unofficially carries on his own probe of the crime.

For a year surviving lonely nights chiefly on pizza in the company of his tough tomcat Raffles, Diamond meets his professional and personal match in feisty cigar-smoking Henrietta "Hen" Mallin, his opposite number at the Bognor Regis C.I.D. Approaching from different geographic and procedural angles, in *The House Sitter* (2004) they solve two intricately intersecting murders involving a psychological profiler and a killer who quotes Coleridge's "Rime of the Ancient Mariner." In this case, fascinating new facets of Diamond's personality appear. Still bottling up his personal grief and raging at "need to know" "Big White Chief" malpractice and corruption, Diamond finally finds assistants he can trust, especially Inspector Keith Holliwell. Diamond cannily works the system and his superiors, gradually relaxes with Hen in convenient pubs, and even handles a mouse with aplomb, if not affection, letting his fifty-year-old subconscious solve the crimes. In *The Circle* (2005), Hen Mallin becomes the lead detective on a serial murder case involved with the Chichester Writers' Circle, while its members compete with her to solve the crime. As Lovesey noted in a *Publishers Weekly* interview, he's waiting to see whether a romantic relationship will develop; Hen can hold her own with Diamond, but "he isn't ready yet, and she has seen what a pain he can be." Rough as this Diamond is, "embattled against forensic scientists and computer operators" (quoted in *CA Online*), he always comes out a clearcut brilliant winner.

Novels: *The Last Detective* (1991); *Diamond Solitaire* (1992); *The Summons* (1995); *Bloodhounds* (1996); *Upon a Dark Night* (1997); *The Vault* (2000); *Diamond Dust* (2002); *The House Sitter* (2004); *The Circle* (2005).

Other series: Sergeant Cribb Victorian historical series, pitting the stolid London sergeant against Victorian eccentricities; the "Bertie" Victorian historical series, featuring Albert Edward, Prince of Wales and the future Edward VII.

Other works: Lovesey has also written nine stand-alone crime novels, four short-story collections, and three nonfiction books on athletics.

Selected sources: Cooper-Clarke, Diana. *Designs of Darkness: Interviews with Detective Novelists.* Bowling Green, OH: Bowling Green State University Press, 1983; Keating, H.R.F. *Crime and Mystery: The 100 Best Books.* New York: Carroll and Graf, 1987; Picker, Leonard. "An Up-to-Date Victorian." *Publishers Weekly*, March 28, 2005: 60; *Publishers Weekly.* Rev. of *The Circle*, March 28, 2005: 59; Silet, Charles L.P. "Sergeant Cribb, the Prince of Wales, and Peter Diamond: Peter Lovesey," in *Talking Murder.* Princeton, NJ: Ontario Review Press, 1999: 172–85.

Major awards: Silver Dagger Awards, 1977, 1995, 1996; Gold Dagger Award, 1993; Diamond Dagger Award for Lifetime Achievement, 2000; Anthony Award, 1991.

See also: Paul Charles's Inspector Christy Kennedy series, featuring a combination similar to Diamond's typical cases involving seemingly impossible crimes in the context of police procedural novels; Bill James's contemporary **Colin Harpur** series, set in the Midlands; for the Bath setting, Morag Joss's **Sara Selkirk** series; for Victorian settings analogous to Lovesey's Sergeant Cribb series, see Anne Perry's **William Monk** series and Perry's Charlotte and **Thomas Pitt** series, set in London; Donald Thomas's Sergeant William Verity series and Thomas's Inspector Alfred Swain series.

Maisie Dobbs

Profession:	Psychologist and private investigator
Living situation:	Single
Geographic locale:	England
Time period:	1929–early 1930s
Associate:	Billy Beale
Significant relationship:	Dr. Simon Lynch
Concerns:	Peace; emotional stability; reconciliations

The shattering aftermath that World War I wreaked upon British women dominates Jacqueline Winspear's Maisie Dobbs mystery series, created, Winspear says, "from the fruits of my own curiosity" and from stories handed down by family members who had come of age during the Great War (Conversation 1:8*). Like Maisie's father, Winspear's grandfather "Jack" Winspear, who was seriously wounded during the Battle of the Somme in 1916, was a London costermonger (vegetable peddler). Winspear's grandmother Clara Atterbury Clark, like Maisie's friend Enid, worked in the Woolwich Arsenal during the war; Clara was partially blinded in an explosion there that killed several young women in her section.

Winspear also indicates that Maisie Dobbs's challenges in breaking through class barriers and the "glass ceiling" that prevented women from rising to managerial positions, as well as her wartime service as a nurse and her postwar work as a private investigator, provided experiences that allowed her "greater insights into what it means to be human." In addition, Maisie's experiences brought her a heightened understanding of the role of change in human life, "that even good changes can be challenging, and that her interactions with a person might change the outcome of events, or their thinking or attitude" (Introduction 1:9).

---

*Penguin paperback editions of *Maisie Dobbs* and *Birds of a Feather* each contain a separately paginated "Conversation with Jacqueline Winspear" regarding the novel to which each is attached, as well as discussion questions and Winspear's Introduction to each novel. These are referred to as Conversation 1 or 2 and Introduction 1 or 2 respectively.

Winspear reveals Maisie's early life through extensive flashbacks in *Maisie Dobbs* (2003). Maisie's mother died when she was eleven, and her father Frank Dobbs, a poor London working man, wanted to do the best for his bright and bookish daughter. He obtained a domestic service position for Maisie in the Ebury Street mansion of Lord Julian and Lady Rowan Compton, where Maisie worked as a "tweeny" maid, voraciously reading books on philosophy in the Compton library before and after her tough household duties. Lady Rowan, an impassioned suffragette, and her friend Dr. Maurice Blanche, a pioneering physician and psychologist profoundly concerned for London's needy, soon took an interest in a girl with such determination to learn. Blanche tutored her privately and introduced her to his friend Khan, a practitioner of yoga, and Lady Rowan engineered a scholarship for Maisie to Girton, a women's college at Cambridge, where Maisie enrolled just before the war erupted.

Driven by her sense of duty, Maisie left Cambridge, falsified her age to enter nurse's training, and left for the battlefields of France on July 20, 1916, to be plunged into the hell of a casualty station not far from the front line trenches. She had met an idealistic young doctor, Simon Lynch, shortly before she left England, and after she encounters him again in the war zone, they fall in love, only to both be badly wounded when their field hospital is shelled. Maisie recovers and nurses severely shell-shocked soldiers back in England, but Simon's mind has been permanently destroyed.

Maisie returns to Cambridge and finishes her studies, then becomes Blanche's assistant in his highly innovative and honored investigational practice, which involves psychological counseling to reestablish his clients' emotional stability. *Maisie Dobbs* the novel begins just after Blanche's retirement, as Maisie is setting up her own practice. Her first client, a husband who wants to know whether his wife is cheating during her frequent absences from their home, revives Maisie's painful memories of the war, but it also achieves a measure of healing for all concerned.

The unusual investigational methods Maisie learned at Maurice Blanche's side include her near-psychic ability to sense the significance of atmospherics in human interactions as well as physical locales, her talent for getting people to share confidences by using subtle body language and intuitive pauses in conversation, and her scrupulous attention to observational detail, meticulously noted in the file cards she constantly uses and the careful mental and physical preparation she brings to each encounter with a victim or a suspect. Successful as Maisie becomes in her profession, though, she still feels torn between two worlds, the lower-class milieu of the father she so dearly loves and the upper-class environment her talents and her hard work have achieved. In more than one way, the cold of the French winters seeped into Maisie's very bones. She maintains a cool reserve toward others, a chosen distancing that eventually disturbs and even frightens her in her subsequent cases.

Coincidence plays a significant role in Maisie's investigations, but she has adopted Maurice Blanche's position that "Coincidence is a messenger sent by truth" (*Maisie Dobbs* 205). In her morning meditations and in the quiet solitary moments she always requests when she visits a murder scene, Maisie sets aside her personal concerns to absorb, in a near-psychic, yet rational, technique Maurice and Khan had taught her, the physical details that speak the truth. The unconventionality of this method puts her at odds with appealing widower Detective Inspector Stratton, with whom she becomes acquainted in *Birds of a Feather*, but Maisie not only employs it herself, she successfully teaches it to her Cockney assistant Billy Beale, a former soldier whose leg Simon and Maisie had managed to save in France. As an example of England's "wakin' dead," unemployable handicapped veterans nightly walking London's streets, Billy becomes Maisie's right-hand man, accompanying her to crime scenes in her newly acquired red MG roadster. He is also one of her primary concerns: she cannot save all of those wounded men, but she can and does save Billy from morphine addiction in *Birds of a Feather* (2004). In Maisie's third case, *Pardonable Lies* (2005), she probes the plane-crash death of aviator Ralph Lawton during the war, reconnecting with her old friend Priscilla, who had introduced Maisie to Simon, and beginning to build a friendship with Dr. Andrew Dene, another young disciple of Maurice Blanche.

By struggling to succeed in a world where women must learn to support themselves because the men they would have married were swept away by war, Maisie Dobbs is also caught, like many people today, between "the need for uniqueness and the need to belong...and without the communities that provided some sort of support to previous generations" (Conversation 2:5). Like many today, too, Maisie wonders "when had she truly felt at home?" (*Birds* 100). Her search is universal: "When we are injured in any way," Winspear notes, "we want to go home. And if our own home is not available to us from the heart, then we will seek another that feels as if it is" (Conversation 2:9).

Novels: *Maisie Dobbs* (2003); *Birds of a Feather* (2004); *Pardonable Lies* (2005).

Selected sources: Bliss, Laurel. Rev. of *Pardonable Lies*. *Library Journal*, July 1, 2005: 59; Gropman, Jackie, and Susan Woodcock. Rev. of *Birds of a Feather*. *School Library Journal*, September 2004: 235; Klausner, Harriet. Rev. of *Maisie Dobbs*. *Books 'n' Bytes*. www.booksnbytes.com; Pearl, Nancy. "Get a Clue: Book Club Mysteries." *Library Journal*, October 15, 2004: 100; *Publishers Weekly*. Rev. of *Maisie Dobbs*, June 16, 2003: 55; Williams, Wilda. Rev. of *Birds of a Feather*. *Library Journal*, July 15, 2005: 65.

Web site: Soho Press Web site: www.sohopress.com (Winspear's publisher).

See also: Rennie Airth's **John Madden** novels, set between world wars; Kerry Greenwood's humorous **Phryne Fisher** series, set in Australia after World War I; Gillian Linscott's series featuring British suffragette detective Nell Bray; Charles Todd's series featuring World War I veteran and Scotland Yard Inspector **Ian Rutledge**; continuations of Dorothy L. Sayers's Lord Peter Wimsey and **Harriet Vane** novels by Jill Paton Walsh, *Thrones, Dominations* and *A Presumption of Death*.

Debut novel: Catriona McPherson's *After the Armistice Ball*, featuring wealthy amateur detective Dandy Gilver in Scotland just after World War I.

Inspector Espinosa

Profession:	Homicide detective
Living situation:	Divorced
Geographic locale:	Rio de Janeiro
Time period:	1995–present
Associate:	None

Brazilian author Luiz Garcia-Roza, formerly a professor of psychology and philosophy at the Federal University of Rio de Janeiro, began writing detective novels at sixty, retiring later in 1998, after thirty-five years of teaching. According to his recent interview with Mehroo Siddiqui (see below), he believes that "mystery novels, like mythological thought or ancient Greek poetry, bring to the center of a fictional narrative the most intense and fundamental questions of the human being, death and sexuality," which "are also the main questions of psychoanalysis (the parricide and the incest)" summed up in Sophocles' *Oedipus Rex*. For Garcia-Roza, a murder is "not only a problem to be solved, it is also an enigma, something that holds the truth but also holds the shadow side of the sentence, the ambiguity and the silence," so each of his detective novels leaves his readers with an "open story," a text through which they can derive other perspectives of human behavior. Garcia-Roza has quickly become internationally famous as the progenitor of "Rio *noir*," dramatic police procedural fiction with a Brazilian spice all its own.

As a novelist, Garcia-Roza's favorite American mystery writers are Dashiell Hammett, Raymond Chandler, Cornell Woolrich, and Patricia Highsmith, and his favorite novel is Dostoevsky's *Crime and Punishment*; these classics provided Garcia-Roza examples of the dark exterior and interior landscapes that dominate noir detective fiction. As a professor of philosophy, his familiarity with the work of the seventeenth-century Dutch philosopher Baruch Spinoza gave Garcia-Roza both the name and the ethical foundation for his protagonist, Inspector Espinosa, whom Garcia-Roza describes in his Web site as "on the surface an ordinary man... but at the same time, he has a critical mind and a romantic heart, he feels eccentric among his professional peers and out of place in the world." Above all, the existential Espinosa is an ethical man. Like Spinoza, Espinosa believes a powerful, or virtuous, human being acts out of understanding, and so freedom consists in being guided by the law of one's own nature. Evil, therefore, is the result of inadequate understanding.

Inspector Espinosa works in the First Precinct of Rio de Janeiro, Garcia-Roza's native city and the beautiful muse that he claims inspires his fiction, "seductive and sweet like a woman, but... as threatening as the moment that precedes a revolt" (interview on Web site). When Espinosa was born, Brazil had only lived under full democracy for about twenty years, and both corruption and what Garcia-Roza describes as "social-economic conflicts" still shake Rio. In *The Silence of the Rain*, the book that Garcia-Roza insists contains the seeds of the four Espinosa novels that have followed it, Espinosa begins as he does in them all with "a singular, isolated, and unimportant event," here the apparent murder of a mineral-exploration executive, Dr. Ricardo Carvalho, which Espinosa struggles to understand.

Espinosa's method is to examine patiently all possibilities and scenarios of a crime. He believes that all humans, criminals and saints alike, have the capacity for killing, but that powerful inner forces usually prevent that capacity from materializing into action (*Rain* 61). In his interrogations, Espinosa, a tall, thin, middle-aged man with a tired voice who lives by himself on beer, Big Macs, milk shakes, and pizza, points out coincidences and imagines possible scenes, offering up "not even hypotheses, just fantasies" that unnerve his subjects, sometimes into confession, sometimes into further crimes.

Espinosa prefers his personal life to stay that way (*Rain* 122). Though he's attractive to women—in *Silence of the Rain* he quickly beds Alma, a lissome young Ipanema gym instructor—and takes other opportunities where he may, his marriage lasted only four years, until his wife finished law school, and his own son now seems like someone else's (*Rain* 122). He doesn't trust his fellow officers, though he tries to help the younger ones; his efficiency amazes people, but he's different, so they isolate him. He has never been corrupted.

December Heat (2003), the second Espinosa novel, brings the inspector to the aid of an old friend, retired officer Vieira, who's accused of murdering a prostitute. In the course of the investigation, Espinosa meets Kika, a beautiful young artist, and agonizes over the difference in their ages. This novel also reveals important aspects of Espinosa's early life. Orphaned in his adolescence, he studied law, but when he needed money to marry, he joined the Rio police, where he's now been for fifteen years. Outside his detective work, *December Heat* uncovers Espinosa's sensuality, as he revels in sultry Rio nights and "the exquisiteness of Kika's navel."

Southwesterly Wind (2004) exposes even more of Espinosa's life when a fortune-teller's prediction causes him to probe the abstract nature of crime and the injuries it brings to all it touches, here seen against the backdrop of repressive, middle-class Rio, where the weather becomes a representative of implacable fate. *A Window in Copacabana* (2005) confronts Espinosa with three separate murders for which he soon discovers a common denominator when someone systematically kills the secret mistress of each victim. Espinosa's talent for intuitive fantasizing of potential solutions that then prove correct cause his police colleagues to distrust each other, soon becoming fear-ridden rumor-mongers themselves. *Pursuit*, the last book before Garcia-Roza allows Espinosa a well-earned vacation, starts from the problem of paranoia tacitly introduced in *A Window in Copacabana*. In *Pursuit*, a University hospital psychiatrist feels that he is being stalked by a patient who later disappears and is presumed dead. After other deaths ensue, and because Garcia-Roza indicates that no one can determine who pursues and who is being pursued, Espinosa must try intuitively to separate reality from fantasy.

Not for readers who insist on tidy final solutions to crimes or to the squeamish who shrink from near-clinical descriptions of death and sexuality, Inspector Espinosa's beautiful, brutal Brazilian atmosphere accompanies powerful psychological explorations of those most primal human urges, "the most intense and fundamental questions of the human being."

Novels:* *The Silence of the Rain* (2002); *December Heat* (2003); *Southwesterly Wind* (2004); *A Window in Copacabana* (2005); *Pursuit* (2006).

Other works: Eight theoretical works in philosophy, psychology, and psychoanalysis, written between 1972 and 1995; and a sixth novel, which Garcia-Roza calls "a parenthesis in the Espinosa series" (Siddiqui interview).

Selected sources: Bickerton, Emilie. "Down the Mean Streets of Rio." *Times Literary Supplement*, November 28, 2003: 22; Hooper, Brad. Rev. of *A Window in Copacabana*. *Booklist*, November 1, 2004: 468; Klett, Rex E. Rev. of *The Silence of the Rain*. *Library Journal*, July 15, 2002: 125; Mujica, Barbara. "Victories and Crimes of Romance." *Americas*, May/June 2004; Siddiqui, Mehroo. Interview with Luiz Alfredo Garcia-Roza. www.absolutewrite.com/novels/luiz alfredo garciaroza.htm; Stasio, Marilyn. Rev. of *December Heat*. *New York Times Book Review*, July 6, 2003: 17; Stasio, Marilyn. Rev. of *Southwesterly Wind*. *New York Times Book Review*, March 14, 2004: 16.

Major awards: Two important literary prizes in Brazil for *The Silence of the Rain*, 1997.

Web site: www.garcia-roza.com.

See also: Cuban author Arnoldo Correa's noir series featuring retired policeman Alvaro Antonio Molinet: *Spy's Fate* (2002); and *Cold Havana Ground* (2003), dealing with Afro-Cuban religion and folklore; Chilean author Antonio Skármeta's *El Baile de la Victoria*, a combination thriller and romance that has won the Premio Planeta, one of Spain's most prestigious literary awards.

---

*All titles and dates given are for English translations from the Portuguese by Benjamin Moser.

Debut novel: Cuban author Leonardo Padura's *Havana Red*, featuring a macho cop known only as "the Count," "whose investigation into the murder of a transvestite leads him to ruminate on his own metaphysical attraction to this philosophy of mimetics and erasure" (Marilyn Stasio, *New York Times Book Review*, August 14, 2005: 23).

F

Marcus Didius Falco

Profession:	Informer and imperial agent; later also Procurator of the Sacred Geese at the Temple of Juno
Living situation:	Single; later married
Geographic locale:	Rome, Roman Britain, and points between
Time period:	A.D. 70s
Associates:	Helena Justina; Lucius Petronius Longus
Nemesis:	Organized crime
Significant relationships:	Chloris; Helena Justina (later his wife)
Concerns:	His family and friends

During the first century A.D., in spite of the deranged successors of Augustus Caesar, the Roman Empire was relentlessly expanding, its highly disciplined legions bringing the *Pax Romana*—Roman sport, Roman roads, Roman taxes, Roman law—to far-flung outposts like Britain, whether the natives liked it or not. By the A.D. 70s, when soldiers' general Vespasian, a "jovial old cove," jumped up from nowhere and made himself Emperor of Rome (*Silver Pigs* viii), a complicated and occasionally corrupt legal system administered Roman justice and enforced it through the legions and the *vigiles*, an imperial police force employing street-smart informers like Lindsey Davis's Marcus Didius Falco, an irreverent private investigator with decidedly republican (as opposed to imperial) views.

Falco's literary ancestor is Raymond Chandler's Philip Marlowe, who believed, "If I wasn't hard, I wouldn't be alive. If I couldn't ever be gentle, I wouldn't deserve to be alive: (*Playback*, quoted in Murphy 329). Like Marlowe, too, handsome thirtyish plebian Falco, "more intelligent than he lets on" (*Jupiter Myth* 63) and perennially strapped for funds because he has to support his mother and his dead brother's family, knows he's a rogue—and a well-nigh irresistible one, at that. As he tells his stories, Falco's self-effacing and glib of wit, on the surface "a clown with a hint of danger" (*Jupiter Myth* 66), but after service in the legions (like every adult Roman male citizen), he knows how to kill—and he does.

Unlike Marlowe, though, Falco's no loner. His old legion tent mate and closest friend Lucius Petronius "Petro" Longus, Captain of the Aventine Watch of the *vigiles*, is an old-school cop, loyal, tough, and like Falco true to an ethical code that often nearly gets them both killed. Both men also become entangled with formidable women. After a messy divorce, Petro carries a major torch for Falco's razor-tongued sister Maia, and after a love 'em and leave 'em amatory career, Falco meets his own match in his first case, *Silver Pigs* (1989). In Britain by order of the emperor's son Titus to investigate a conspiracy to defraud the Empire, Falco encounters Helena Justina, the shockingly self-divorced daughter of the enormously wealthy and aristocratic Senator Decimus Camillus Verus. Falco sees her as a dismaying amalgam of patrician Roman matron and Liberated Woman: "domineering eyebrows," "air of tight-lipped distaste"—overall, "a spiteful virago" (*Pigs* 76). Tension immediately crackles between them, gradually modulates into helpless mutual infatuation, and eventually (after Falco's interlude with the devastating Chloris) climaxes in an unorthodox marriage and two daughters Falco adores, making Falco a family man in spite of himself. Helena Justina often accompanies him into mean Roman or provincial streets, her courage and sense of honor more than equal to his.

Falco's cases fluctuate between imperial commissions and private investigations. His connection with Helena's powerful parents, who like him very much, advances him willy-nilly into the next higher class of Roman society, the equestrians, and his service to Vespasian, an emperor notoriously tight with a coin, gives Falco the resounding title of Procurator of the Sacred Geese at the Temple of Juno, a ghastly no-salary sinecure. Falco cheekily makes the best of it: "it nicely gave the impression that . . . I was a feeble man of money who lived off his wife's income" (*Jupiter Myth* 80). As a native of Rome, a city "crammed with the world's worst con men," Falco shares his family's reputation as "a special brand of sweet-faced liars," and he deliberately cultivates his "frank and trustworthy gaze . . . a look I had once reserved for women and still employed with creditors" (*Jupiter Myth* 65, 26).

Ten years after serving in the Second Augusta Legion, Falco has matured considerably. Back as an imperial auditor in Britain for *The Body in the Bath House* (2001) and *The Jupiter Myth* (2002), he takes on a pro bono job in the latter case for Helena's uncle, the Procurator of Finance, out of "the old Didius affliction"—he feels responsible (*Jupiter Myth* 112). Falco's become expert, too, at knowing when to break the rules and when to keep them. He reluctantly fends off ear-nibbling Chloris, now a female gladiator ruthlessly bent on establishing their old relationship: "I had moved on—way, way into another life. . . . I had loyalties nowadays; I had new standards" (*Jupiter Myth* 134).

Returning to Rome in A.D. 75 for *The Accusers* (2004), all of Falco's principles are severely tested in a distasteful case he takes for a pair of weasely lawyers because he's short on cash. Involving blackmail, Roman law, scandal, corruption, and intrigue, it turns into a dicey probe of a senator's suspicious death. Falco emerges with principles intact, even delivering an amusing public speech with rhetorical flourishes in the classical tradition of Demosthenes and Cicero. Like Chloris, who though an outcast, died on her own terms, the engaging Marcus Didius Falco ultimately stands for "skill, talent, comradeship, and good faith" (*Jupiter Myth* 320).

Novels: *The Silver Pigs* (1989); *Shadows in Bronze* (1990); *Venus in Copper* (1991); *The Iron Hand of Mars* (1992); *Poseidon's Gold* (1993); *Last Act in Palmyra* (1994); *Time to Depart* (1995); *A Dying Light in Corduba* (1996); *Three Hands in the Fountain* (1997); *Two for the Lions* (1998); *One Virgin Too Many* (1999); *Ode to a Banker* (2000); *A Body in the Bath House* (2001); *The Jupiter Myth* (2002); *The Accusers* (2004); *Scandal Takes a Holiday* (2004).

Selected sources: Haffert, Barbara. Rev. of *One Virgin Too Many*. *Library Journal*, September 1, 2000: 356; Lustig, Jodi. Rev. of *Poseidon's Gold*. *Armchair Detective*, Fall 1993: 112; Rosenfeld, Shelle. Rev. of *Silver Pigs*. *Booklist*, May 1, 2000: 1608; Salpini, Susan. Rev. of *Three Hands in the Fountain*. *School Library Journal*, September 1999: 242; Warshaw, Justin. Rev. of *A Body in the Bath House*. *Times Literary Supplement*, June 23, 1995: 25.

Major award: Ellis Peters Award, 1999.

See also: John Maddox Roberts's Decius Caecilius Metellus series, set in first-century B.C. Rome; Steven Saylor's **Gordianus the Finder** series, also set in the turbulent time of Cicero, Catiline, and Julius Caesar; for contrast between depictions of the West and East Empires, Mary Reed and Eric Mayer's John the Eunuch series, set in sixth-century Constantinople.

Debut novel: Jane Finnis's *Get Out or Die*, set in Northern Britain in A.D. 91 and featuring two Nancy Drew look-alike Roman maidens, Aurelia Marcella and her sister Albia, innkeepers of the Oak Tree Mansio that caters to the elite of this newly conquered Roman province.

Erast Fandorin

Profession:	At first a Moscow Police clerk and civil servant fourteenth class; later promoted to an espionage agent
Living situation:	Single; later married and widowed
Geographic locale:	Imperial Russia, with Continental and English sidetrips
Time period:	Late 1870s
Nemesis:	Amalia Kazimirovna Bezhatskaya ("Cleopatra")
Significant relationship:	Elizaveta Alexandrovna von Evert-Koloskoltsev ("Lizanka")

Under the pen name Boris Akunin (the surname comes from the Japanese word for "evil"), Republic of Georgia–born author Grigory Chkhartishvili has produced eleven internationally popular mystery novels, selling over ten million copies in Russia alone, but only a few have been translated into English. Akunin's hero is young Erast

Petrovich Fandorin, left orphaned and destitute at nineteen by the death of his wastrel bankrupt father in the late 1870s, when Czarist Russia's aristocracy flaunted their glittering decadence, its intellectuals seethed with dreams of violent revolution, and little of Russia's strangling bureaucracy escaped corruption. In Andrew Bromfield's sensitive and witty translation, the Erast Fandorin novels hark back to Nikolai Gogol's 1836 *Inspector General,* a wicked satire of petty officialdom, with Fandorin himself, an aspiring police detective, often resembling one of Russia's "holy fools," naïve bumblers who keep rising from blows of fate to accidentally achieve spectacular success.

As Richard Lourie remarked in his *New York Times* review, Erast Fandorin's debut in *The Winter Queen* (1998, tr. 2003), combines "impulsive passion and cool ratiocination, with touches...of the demonic," suggesting the tumultuous early years of the nineteenth century in Russia as much as the late 1870s, when Mikhail Lermontov's Byronic *Hero of Our Time* (1840) personified the spirit of rebellion, nihilism, reckless adventure, and frustration then sweeping many of Russia's privileged young men toward oblivion. Fandorin's superior, Detective Superintendent Grushin of the Moscow Police, sends police clerk fourteenth grade Fandorin, twenty-one, to investigate the suicide via "American roulette" of wealthy university student Pyotr Kokorin in Moscow's Alexander Gardens, before the horrified eyes of luscious society debutante Lizanka and her German chaperone. Enduring "exquisite suffering in the name of beauty" in a "Lord Byron" corset on which he'd splurged a third of his first month's salary (*Queen* 10), Fandorin settles into his detective vocation as he trails the mysterious "Cleopatra," rich temptress Amalia Bezhatskaya, into a sequence of murders performed under Fandorin's very nose. Their victims have mysteriously willed enormous assets to Englishwoman Lady Astair's international orphanage organization.

With his nose quivering on the trail of international consipiracy, Fandorin stubbornly survives stupefying beginner's luck in a high-rolling gamblers' den, a narrow escape from an aristocratic dead-eye duelist, and the lethal wiles of Cleopatra. He squirms out of a watery grave and even eludes the brain-frying electrical experiments of a renegade German physicist. Naïve though he is, Fandorin draws on his instinct, intuition, and the English, French, and German learned in his affluent childhood, as well as the dandyish gambler's wardrobe he inherited from his father, and relentlessly pursues the Azazel criminals across Europe.

Often in these serpentine plot twists, Fandorin proves just too good a detective. The villains he's tracking fear him as unpredictable, thus unstoppable, "one of the lucky breed" (*Queen* 124). Nonetheless, after a strenuous month encased in the unyielding Lord Byron, Fandorin is no longer as "fresh as a Yaroslavl cucumber," the kind of uninvited guest snooty butlers automatically deny admittance. Promoted five steps in the arcane hierarchy of the tsarist civil service, he's made himself into "Fandorin, officer of the third section, on urgent business" (*Queen* 208), the pebble the arch-conspirator "was fated to stumble on" (*Queen* 229). Eventually Fandorin becomes the ecstatic bridegroom of the lovely and wealthy Lizanka—just before one of those typically Russian tragic swoops of fate strikes him down again.

Murder on the Leviathan (1999, tr. 2004) follows the now white-haired young Fandorin into an homage to Agatha Christie set on the gigantic *Leviathan* bound for

Calcutta. Akunin surrounds his hero with a cast of ten suspicious characters, any one of whom may have killed eccentric antiquarian Lord Littleby and ten of his servants. Fandorin slyly takes over the investigation from Police Commissioner Gauche and unmasks a poignant arch-villain while exposing the moral turpitude of the upper classes, again proving that Slavs laugh and cry in the same minor key.

The Turkish Gambit (2000, tr. 2005) finds the now-elegant young Fandorin disguising himself as a peasant in Bulgaria in the 1877–1878 clash between Russia and Turkey. Fandorin remains in the background for much of this novel, but he rescues brave little heroine Varvara, an "emancipated" young woman, from various jams and helps her dispel accusations that her fiancé is a spy. Able to surmount ghastly plots, outwit ingenious murderers, and rescue damsels in distress while quoting Russian literary greats like Nekrasov, Dostoevsky, and Pushkin, Erast Fandorin lives up to his noble (if spendthrift) ancestry, and equipped with "Lord Byron" proves himself a superb tragicomic hero of his time.

Novels: *The Winter Queen* (1998, tr. 2003); *Murder on the Leviathan* (1999, tr. 2004); *The Turkish Gambit* (2000, tr. 2005); eight more novels not as yet published in translation.

Akunin has also published several Russian translations of Japanese works, including a work by Yukio Mishima and three novels by Seiichi Mishima.

Selected sources: Chazan, Guy. "Roll Over, Dostoevsky: Serious Russian Writers Reinvent the Thriller—Grigory Chkhartishvili Writes Popular, Classy Whodunits; At Peace in the Cemetery." *Wall Street Journal*, February 25, 2002: A1; Gannon, Sean. Rev. of *Murder on the Leviathan*. *People*, May 31, 2004: 56; Ott, Bill. Rev. of *The Winter Queen*. *Booklist*, May 15, 2003: 1637; Schwarzbaum, Lisa. "Czar Struck: Russian Author Boris Akunin Imports His Best-Selling Mystery-Thriller Series Set in 19th-Century Moscow." *Entertainment Weekly*, May 23, 2003: 79; Vishevski, Anatoly. "Answers to Eternal Questions in Soft Covers: Post-Soviet Detective Stories." *Slavic and East European Journal*, Winter 2001: 733–39.

Major awards: Russian Writer of the Year, 2000; Antibooker Prize, 2000; Gold and Silver Daggers Award shortlist, 2003.

See also: Stuart Kaminsky's Soviet and post-Soviet Russian Inspector Porfiry Rostnikov series; Michael Pearce's *Dmitri and the Milk Drinkers* (1997) and *Dmitri and the One-Legged Lady* (1999), featuring Scottish-Russian lawyer Dmitri Kameron in the 1890s, a brief hopeful period when Russia's tsarist government might have turned to democracy. Reggie Nadelson's Russian-born New York policeman and later PI Artie Cohen anti–Russian Mafia series and Martin Cruz Smith's **Arkady Renko** series both deal with contemporary Russian police procedure.

Kate Fansler

Profession:	University professor
Living situation:	Married after first novel
Geographic locale:	New York City and suburbs
Time period:	1964–2003
Associate:	Husband Reed Amhearst

Nemesis:	The male academic establishment
Significant relationship:	Reed Amhearst, former Assistant District Attorney
Concerns:	Feminism; decline of higher education

Amanda Cross's thirteen Kate Fansler mysteries span four decades of the academic career of Cross's alter ego, outspoken feminist Carolyn Heilbrun, Columbia University's Avalon Professor of English and Humanities. Forced to use the pseudonym until she received tenure, Heilbrun decided in the 1960s that the mystery genre had deteriorated from its 1920s–1930s Golden Age heyday of Christie, Tey, Allingham, and Sayers, and that "it was being tailored to its readership." She resolved to produce "fiction that was erudite, intelligent and literary and which featured strong, independent women" (Ashley 120).

Like Heilbrun, Kate Fansler is a committed feminist professor of English Literature at a Manhattan university. Some commentators feel "The problem with the series has always been Kate Fansler herself" (Murphy 120), often accused of being "snobbish and elitist" (Ashley 120). Fansler takes her investigations of academic tensions that often drive its scholars to violence dead seriously, with only a trickle of comic relief.

Kate Fansler's earliest murder cases seem to show Kate and her creator at their best. *In the Last Analysis* (1964), her first case and an Edgar nominee, allows Fansler to trap the killer with her intimate knowledge of Freud's theories; in *The James Joyce Murder* (1967), she works within chapters each named for one of the stories of Joyce's *Dubliners*; in *The Theban Mysteries* (1971), she saves a Vietnam draft dodger from prosecution by tracing parallels to Greek tragedy; and as a visiting lecturer at Harvard in the award-winning *Death in a Tenured Position* (1981), she solves the poisoning of that august male bastion's first tenured woman English professor.

Kate's formidable erudition, though, cuts at least two ways, and it makes her relationship with husband Reed Amhearst near-intolerably artificial. Since in the best feminist fashion, Kate and Reed must function as intellectual equals, their conversation often is stilted, "a parody of nineteenth-century novelistic discourse. Reed declares to Kate, 'I wait, eagerly attuned. . . . I have never fathomed the mystery of your familial connections.' This from a boy who grew up in Baltimore" (Murphy 170). Rather than the glorious marriage of true and brilliant minds celebrated in Dorothy L. Sayers's *Gaudy Night* and *Busman's Honeymoon*, the relationship of Kate Fansler and Reed Amhearst too often sacrifices verisimilitude to incongruous political correctness: they "mature without growing up . . . continu[ing] to speak as if they had written down the dialogue while proctoring a final exam, and their cases become more bizarrely contrived" (Murphy 170).

Those cases also show that Kate Fansler knows all too well the price women pay for careers in higher education. *In the Last Analysis* has Kate observing that most of her urban college students are living near their homes, and their lives outside of Academia go on. "Sometimes they are women torn between mind and family," she muses, but she cares "to know little" about any of their troubles (*Last Analysis* 11). The headmistress of the girls' prep school Kate herself attended, the scene of *The*

Theban Mysteries, gently satirizes traditional teaching: "Have we perhaps for too long supposed teaching to be a ritual in which I, the elder and supposedly wiser, hand on to you, the younger and more innocent, the fruits of my learning and experience? Perhaps teaching is really a mutual experience between the younger and the older, perhaps all there is to be learned is what they can discover between them" (*Mysteries* 24). Kate notes wryly that plain girls long for "the accepted destiny of a feminine place in a male world" (*Mysteries* 130), a world often wracked by war because men need an excuse to get away from their wives" (*Mysteries* 134).

Death in a Tenured Position (1981) flung Kate's and Cross's now tenured gauntlet square in the face of the male Ivy League establishment. The fictitious Harvard English Department, forced to find "a dame, well established and, if possible, not given to hysterical scenes" (*Position* 3), hires Professor Janet Applebaum, who is shortly found dead in their men's room. Kate Fansler, "tired to death of male pomposities and longwindedness" as the token woman on too many university committees, sets wearily about solving the murder.

In her ensuing appearances, the flames seem to have passed out of Kate's belly, leaving sour intellectually dyspeptic ashes. In *Honest Doubt* (2000), her last adventure, a new female sleuth, Estelle "Woody" Woodville takes center stage and Kate Fansler is downgraded to a peripheral kibitzing role between five p.m. drinkies sessions. Despite a law degree, Woody knows little about professors, less about English literature, and next to nothing about Tennyson, the specialty of victim Professor Charles Haycock, chairman of elite Clifton College's English Department, whose entire staff has good reason to want dead.

Kate serves as Woody's consultant and shoulder-to-cry-on, revealing in the process her own bitter regrets, especially the decline of the teaching profession: "When my generation of professors was getting tenure, the academic picture was a lot rosier than it is today . . . there is too little money for faculty, too few positions for the generation of new Ph.D.'s coming along, hiring them part-time and as adjuncts, where they make too little money with no benefits and no real part to play in the department (*Honest Doubt* 54). For Kate, now burned out, teaching has become "tiresome. The students have read less and less, often can't write worth a damn, even in graduate school" (*Honest Doubt* 55). This bleak view of today's Academe proved Cross's bitter final comment on the profession to which she and Kate Fansler had devoted their lives.

Novels: *In the Last Analysis* (1964); *The James Joyce Murder* (1967); *Poetic Justice* (1970); *The Theban Mysteries* (1971); *The Question of Max* (1976); *Death in a Tenured Position* (1981); *Sweet Death, Kind Death* (1984); *No Word from Winifred* (1986); *A Trap for Fools* (1989); *The Players Come Again* (1990); *An Imperfect Spy* (1995); *The Puzzled Heart* (1998); *Honest Doubt* (2000).

Short fiction: *The Collected Stories* (1997).

Scholarly nonfiction: Heilbrun wrote many scholarly books, many on feminist themes, notably *Reinventing Womanhood* (1979) and *Writing a Woman's Life* (1988).

Autobiographies: *The Last Gift of Time: Life Beyond Sixty* (1997); *When Men Were the Only Models We Had: My Teachers Barzun, Fadiman, Trilling* (2001); *But Enough About Me: Why We Read Other People's Lives* (2002).

Selected sources: Bargannier, Earl F. *Ten Women of Mystery*. Bowling Green, OH: Bowling Green State University Press, 1981; Boden, Julia B. *Carolyn G. Heilbrun*. New York: Twayne, 1996; Cooper-Clark, Diana. *Design of Darkness: Interviews with Detective Novelists*. Bowling Green, OH: Bowling Green State University Press, 1983; *Feminist Writers*. Detroit: St. James Press, 1996; Kress, Susan. *Carolyn G. Heilbrun: A Feminist in a Tenured Position*. Charlottesville, VA: University Press of Virginia, 1997.

Major awards: Nero Wolfe, 1981; several honorary degrees, notably from Smith College, Brown University, and Duke University.

See also: J.S. Borthwick's series featuring English professor Sarah Deane, set in Maine; Canadian Gail Bowen's Professor Joanne Kilburn series, set in Regina, Saskatchewan; Anna Clarke's series featuring English professor Paula Glenning and set in England; Bill Crider's series featuring English professor Sally Good; Jane Langton's series featuring Massachusetts American literature professor **Homer Kelly**; Joan Smith's series featuring feminist English lecturer **Loretta Lawson**, set in London and Oxford; Veronica Stallwood's series featuring Oxford resident and novelist Kate Ivory; Virginia Swift's series featuring Professor "Mustang" Sally Alder, set in Wyoming; Sarah Stewart Taylor's series featuring Massachusetts art history professor Sweeney St. George; Pamela Thomas-Graham's series featuring African American Professor Nikki Chase of Howard University; Lea Watt's series featuring Maggie Summer, an antique-print dealer and history professor.

Debut novels: Mark Cohen's *The Fractal Murders*, featuring University of Colorado mathematics professor Jayne Smyers; Alicia Casper de Alba's *Desert Blood*, featuring California academic Ivon Villa in pursuit of a serial killer; Janice Law's *The Lost Diaries of Iris Weed*, featuring Connecticut Romance and Victorian poetry professor Jason "Lars" Larson.

Clare Fergusson

Profession:	Episcopalian priest
Living situation:	Single
Geographic locale:	Upstate New York
Time period:	2002–present
Associate:	Russ Van Alstyne
Significant relationship:	Russ Van Alstyne
Concerns:	Priestly vocation; teenage pregnancy; gay rights; environmentalism; social justice

"A woman priest. If that didn't beat all" (*Bleak Midwinter* 3). When newly ordained mid-thirtyish Rev. Clare Fergusson arrives in fictional Millers Kill, New York, no one knows quite what to make of her. St. Alban's Episcopalian congregation "didn't exactly embrace novelty and innovation," and hiring her "may have exhausted their reserves of daring for the next ten years" (*Bleak Midwinter* 21). Julia Spencer-Fleming makes Clare's bluntness, honed by her years as an Army helicopter pilot, and her fierce dedication to "do-gooding" as necessary to her priesthood continually raise the hackles of her conservative male-dominated vestry (church council). Clare comes face to face with entrenched attitudes, desperate societal wrongs, and romantic temptation in the attractive person of Vietnam vet and Millers Kill police chief Russ Van Alstyne, nearly fifty, traditional—and married.

Not just the zero-degree wind chill of icy upstate New York but glacial human hearts dominate Malice Domestic winner *In the Bleak Midwinter* (2002), opening with Clare's discovery of a newborn baby on St. Alban's steps. Not long after, a young mother is found murdered. Against this frigid backdrop, sparks immediately fly when Clare meets Van Alstyne in the hospital where she takes the baby, and embers start to smolder when they discover they have similar backgrounds—Clare's service in the Eighteenth Airborne Corps and Van Alstyne's career army experience, first in the infantry, then the MPs. At first Clare underestimates both Millers Kill weather and the obstacles she faces there, like the recalcitrant old vestry bulls who dig in against her plan for a mentoring program to help young unwed mothers. She also tries to scuttle the mutual attraction she and Van Alstyne feel, which surfaces when he rescues Clare, as usual underdressed for the cold and refusing to trade her low-slung classic roadster for a four-wheel drive, after she knocks a bad guy down with a tree and coshes him unconscious with a rock (*Bleak Midwinter* 259). After a Christmas Eve embrace that shocks them both, Clare sends Russ home to the strains of a wintry Christmas hymn, and to the good-looking but usually absent wife who'd really wanted him to take that private security job in Phoenix four years ago.

Troubled by her feelings for Van Alstyne, which threaten her vocation, Clare keeps her distance from him for over a year, until three scathing gay-bashings occur in *A Fountain Filled With Blood* (2003). One victim, Bill Ingraham, had headed a development company planning to build a ritzy resort on a PCB-contaminated site near Millers Kill, and Van Alstyne has already had to arrest his own mother for illegal environmental protesting. When Clare defies his direct order and leaks the gay connection between the killings to the press, she drives the beleaguered police chief to outbursts repeatedly requiring a rueful "'Scuse my French." Incurable do-gooding impels Clare first to offer Van Alstyne a private sermon on chastity, then to get drunk and flirt, and finally scare hell out of him on a harrowing climactic life-saving helicopter ride.

After coping with the fallout from these unclerical actions in *A Fountain Filled With Blood*, by the next Ash Wednesday Clare has muted her frontal-assault approach to parish problems. During the ensuing Lent, with the warnings of her grandmother and her Army instructor ringing stereophonically in her ears, she maintains a gritted-toothed tact in dealing with recalcitrant parishioners while making her peace with Van Alstyne over Wednesday noon lunches at the Kreemy Kakes Diner. Spanning some eighty years, *Out of the Deep I Cry* (2004) brings Clare's stubborn puzzle-solving bent to the fore as she and Van Alstyne untangle a complex web of decades-old deaths. In this installment of their forbidden relationship, Russ's tiny, curvy "pocket goddess" wife Linda, whose drapery business frequently takes her away from home, is vacationing in Florida with her divorced sister. Clare again uses her Army training to haul herself and Van Alstyne out of nasty physical predicaments, but she can't escape their surging emotions. Clare, the kind of priest who dons vestments for services even when no one else is present, does her best to keep faith with her heavenly Boss by sending Van Alstyne a Dear Russ letter, but she gives herself away after the Easter

Vigil service when he confesses to her, "The parts of me that always felt alone, the parts of me that I always kept hidden away...I could see that you had them, too" (*Out of the Deep* 324). Clare simply answers, "Yes."

In the one scathing day covered in *To Darkness and to Death* (2005), Van Alstyne would like to spend his fiftieth birthday hunting in the mountains while Linda is preparing for the gala opening of a new luxury resort nearby and Clare Fergusson is making St. Alban's ready for her bishop's annual visit; but a combination of kidnapping, assault, blackmail, and murder shocks Van Alstyne into a fateful decision—to leave Linda, who's loved him for twenty-five years. The solemn language of old and new Common Prayer continually calls Clare Fergusson to her priestly duty, but her human need, crying for a partner of the soul, just as insistently draws her to Russ Van Alstyne. A woman priest. Is that going to beat all the difficulties that lie ahead for them?

Novels: *In the Bleak Midwinter* (2002); *A Fountain Filled with Blood* (2003); *Out of the Deep I Cry* (2004); *To Darkness and to Death* (2005).

Selected sources: Brundage, Kay. "From Helicopters to Holy Orders: *PW* Talks with Julia Spencer-Fleming." *Publishers Weekly*, March 8, 2004: 54; Klett, Rex E. Rev. of *In the Bleak Midwinter*. *Library Journal*, February 1, 2002: 136; O'Brien, Sue. Rev. of *A Fountain Filled with Blood*. *Booklist*, February 15, 2003: 1055; *Publishers Weekly*. Rev. of *Out of the Deep I Cry*, March 8, 2004: 53; *Publishers Weekly*. Rev. of *To Darkness and to Death*, May 30, 2005: 43.

Awards: St. Martin's Press Malice Domestic Award, 2002; Anthony Award, 2003; Edgar Allan Poe Award nomination, 2005.

Web site: www.juliaspencerfleming.com.

See also: Michelle Blake's series featuring Texas-born Episcopal priest **Lily Connor**, set in Boston; Dianne Greenwood's series featuring Church of England Deaconess Theodora Braithwaite; Lee Harris's series featuring Christine Bennett, a former Franciscan nun who left the convent after fifteen years to care for her mentally challenged cousin; Kate Gallison's series featuring Mother Lavinia Grey, Episcopal vicar of St. Bede's Church in New Jersey; Veronica Black's Sister Joan series, featuring life in an English Roman Catholic convent; Cristina Sumners's Divine Mystery series, featuring Episcopal priest Kathryn Koerney in a fictional Harton, New Jersey, setting.

Sister Fidelma

Profession:	*Religieuse* (nun); *dálaigh* (advocate) of Brehon (ancient Irish) law courts
Living situation:	Single
Geographic locale:	Ireland; Northumberland; Rome; Wales
Time period:	Mid-seventh-century A.D.
Associate:	Brother Eadulf
Significant relationship:	Brother Eadulf
Concern:	Truth

In the early twentieth century Irish poet William Butler Yeats announced, "Romantic Ireland's dead and gone," but in Sister Fidelma's "Mysteries of Ancient Ireland," Celtic scholar Peter Tremayne has dramatically revived the country's seventh-century-A.D. "Golden Enlightenment" with romance in both its senses—exotic adventure and heart's deep longing. While the rest of Europe floundered through its violent, plague- and superstition-ridden Dark Ages, Irish universities educated students from all corners of the Continent. Male and female Irish missionaries established churches and universities as far as the Ukraine, the Faroe Islands, and southern Italy, and as Margaret Flanagan has observed, Irish women played a "unique, often coequal, role during this surprisingly enlightened time."

Sister Fidelma, daughter of one Irish king and sister to another and a brilliant legal scholar as well as a beautiful young woman, represents Irish Christianity, very different from Rome's. Converted in the fifth century by St. Patrick, Ireland's Celtic (Columban) Church disagreed with the Roman Church's liturgical and ritualistic reforms of the previous century. One fundamental dispute involved the role of women and the issue of celibacy. Claiming authority from Saints Peter and Paul, the Roman Church demanded obedience from all Christendom in barring women from the priesthood. The Celtic Church believed that its authority derived from St. John the Divine, to whom Christ confided the care of his mother Mary, who symbolized in that situation His Church (*Absolution* 230–32). The Celtic Church also upheld the Irish pagan druidic laws that gave women far more rights and protection than any other country at that time and considered women coequal with men in all offices and professions. In the early Christian era, Irishwomen celebrated Mass as priests and Brigid, founder of Fidelma's religious community at Kildare, was ordained a bishop by St. Patrick's nephew Mel. Although the Council of Nicea in 325 condemned clerical marriage, it was not banned in the Roman Church until the reforming papacy of Leo IX (1049–1054), and in Ireland, *conhospidae* or "mixed" religious houses long flourished, "where men and women lived raising their children in Christ's service" (*Absolution* ix).

Like many other Irish girls at that time, Fidelma studied at a bardic school. Her teacher was the Brehon Morann of Tara, one of the great judges of Ireland, and by her twenties she achieved the second highest degree in the complicated Irish educational system: as an *anruth*, she could speak as an equal to kings. Her field, Irish law, included both criminal and civil codes, and in her capacity as a *dálaigh* (advocate of the courts), she gathers and assesses evidence independently of other law enforcement agencies. The motto of Fidelma's profession is "The truth against the world" (*Absolution* 82), and despite her youth, she upholds it unequivocally with the kind of brilliance Yeats called "a mind/That nobleness made simple as a fire."

With flashing green eyes and red hair rebelliously escaping her headdress, Fidelma also has what Yeats called "beauty like a tightened bow, a kind . . . not natural in an age like this, being high and solitary and most stern." Faced in *Absolution by Murder* (1994) with the murder of her Irish friend Abbess Étain at the great Council of Whitby in 663, where Northumbrian King Oswy must choose between Roman and Irish Christianity, Fidelma also collides with Eadulf, a tall, dark, brown-eyed Saxon monk built like a warrior, in a "moment of pure chemistry" (*Absolution* 50). Eadulf had studied in Ireland and Rome, and had he not become a Roman *religieux* he would have been a hereditary *gerefa*, or officer of Saxon law. In contrast to Fidelma's legal specialization, Eadulf is experienced in many fields like medicine, herbalism, Saxon law, and puzzle-solving, so Oswy chooses him to assist Fidelma in investigating Étain's murder.

Eadulf remains close to Fidelma through most of her ensuing cases. His skills and quiet charm, his knowledge of human nature, and his deference to Fidelma's knowledge of Irish law complement her passionate pursuit of the truth in Rome in *Shroud for the Archbishop* (1995), at sea (in spite of Eadulf's tendency to seasickness) in *Act of Mercy* (1999), in Wales in *Smoke in the Wind* (2001), and back at Ireland's Abbey of Imleach, where a priceless group of holy relics of its founder St. Ailbe mysteriously disappears in *The Monk Who Vanished* (1999).

Fidelma leaves Eadulf in Rome for almost a year at the start of *The Subtle Serpent* (1996), a year filled for her with "memories and longing." She misses "their arguments, their conflicting opinions and philosophies.... Their arguments would rage but there was no enmity between them" (*Serpent* 26). Instead, a deep bond, much more profound than simple companionship, develops between them. Even though in Ireland nuns and monks could and did marry and live together, their mutual attraction is constantly thwarted when each hopes the other will speak what they most want to hear—and each holds back for fear of being misunderstood. On the verge of leaving Eadulf for a pilgrimage to the tomb of St. James in Spain, Fidelma still yearns for him as the only man of her age with whom she can be herself "without hiding behind her rank and role in life" (*Monk* 315). Romantic Ireland is dead and gone? Not for Fidelma and Eadulf—or their readers.

Novels: *Absolution by Murder* (1994); *Shroud for the Archbishop* (1995); *Suffer Little Children* (1995); *The Subtle Serpent* (1996); *The Spider's Web* (1997); *Valley of the Shadow* (1998); *The Monk Who Vanished* (1999); *Act of Mercy* (1999); *Our Lady of Darkness* (2000); *Smoke in the Wind* (2001); *The Haunted Abbot* (2004); *The Leper's Bell* (2005); *Badger's Moon* (2005).

Short fiction: *Hemlock at Vespers: Fifteen Sister Fidelma Mysteries* (2000): *Whispers of the Dead: Fifteen Sister Fidelma Mysteries* (2004); *Ensuring Evil and Other Stories* (2005).

Other fiction: Tremayne, one of Britain's foremost experts on the ancient Celts, has also written several Dracula novels and many other stand-alone novels.

Nonfiction: Tremayne has published many scholarly historical studies, notably *A Dictionary of Celtic Mythology* (1992); *The Druids* (1995); *The Chronicles of the Celts* (1999); *Erin's Blood Royal: The Gaelic Noble Dynasties of Ireland* (1999).

Selected sources: Flanagan, Margaret. Rev. of *Hemlock at Vespers. Booklist*, March 15, 2000: 1333; Flanagan, Margaret. Rev. of *The Spider's Web. Booklist*, July 1998: 1866; James, Dean. Rev. of *The Subtle Serpent. Library Journal*, May 1, 1999: 140; *Publishers Weekly*. Rev. of *Murder by Absolution*, November 17, 1995: 55; *Publishers Weekly*. Rev. of *Valley of the Shadow*, February 28, 2000: 65.

Awards: Inaugurated Bard of the Cornish Gorsedd, 1987; *Irish Post* Award, 1988.

Web site: www.sisterfidelma.hypermart.net.

See also: For contrast between Irish and English monasticism, Margaret Frazer's **Dame Frevisse** series, set in fifteenth-century England; Ellis Peters's **Brother Cadfael** series; Priscilla Royal's Eleanor, Abbess of Tyndal series, set in thirteenth-century England.

Sir John Fielding

Profession:	Magistrate, Bow Street Court
Living situation:	Married
Geographic locale:	Principally London
Time period:	Late eighteenth century
Associate:	Jeremy Proctor
Nemesis:	Fielding is blind
Significant relationship:	Lady Fielding
Concerns:	Concepts of criminal justice and police force

Bruce Alexander began work on this Georgian-era mystery series around 1979, but he set the project aside for ten years (Ashley 109). Beginning in 1994 with *Blind Justice*, the ten Sir John Fielding novels to date offer historical portraiture as keen-witted as Hogarth's sketches—didactic, realistic, and often uproariously satiric. In the late 1700s, England's Parliament was beginning to enact new laws that initiated the concept of criminal justice. Sir John Fielding, "The Blind Beak of Bow Street," was an actual historical figure, magistrate of London's Bow Street Court, and half-brother to Henry Fielding, considered the father of the English novel. Sir John Fielding also founded the Bow Street Runners, the first police force. "More human and less irascible than his historical counterpart" (Ashley 109), in *Blind Justice* Alexander's fictional Fielding saves a London orphan, Jeremy Proctor, from hanging for a crime the boy did not commit. Jeremy, who narrates the novels, becomes Fielding's eyes and his legal assistant.

As Bow Street Court's magistrate, Sir John settles disputes, judges lesser crimes and misdemeanors, and binds persons charged with high crimes and felonies over for trial in the higher court. His superior is Lord Chief Justice William Murray, Lord Mansfield, and because "Sir John's abilities and his reputation did exceed his office," Lord Mansfield often seeks him out for "advice and counsel and to undertake special missions for the Court." (*Experiment in Treason* 31). Accordingly Jeremy often travels throughout England to bring back special reports of the famous and infamous for Sir John's consideration, and, as Jeremy says, Sir John ties "together the bits we had learned and seen along the way so that they [tell] a continuous story" (*Smuggler's Moon* 219).

Like many blind people, Sir John Fielding relies effectively on his other senses and his sharp intuitive powers. According to the adoring Jeremy, Sir John is "the most able interrogator in all of Britain," who "seems to sniff an untruth and hear the lie in the liar's voice...[and] he seems to see better with his blind eyes than the rest of us can with our own" (*Smuggler's Moon* 206). Sir John enjoys a wide acquaintance with diverse elements of London's stratified society, including dubious individuals like Black Jack Bilbo, proprietor of a notorious gambling establishment. "I like the man, and there's an end to it," is Sir John's gruff reply to criticism of his relationship with Bilbo, who "could never be accepted as a respectable gentleman in London society" (*Color of Death* 29). In Fielding's courtroom, "notorious for its rowdiness and disorder," Fielding also relishes his "shouting matches with the riffraff of Covent Garden," and, packing one batch of miscreants off to Newgate for three months, he metes out firm justice designed, he says, as an experiment in reducing the number of robberies in London (*Experiment in Treason* 209).

Fielding is also fearless when assigned by Lord Mansfield to deal with the rich and famous, like the haughty Lord Hillsborough, secretary of state for the American colonies, who has experienced a "rather extraordinary burglary" with international implications. Lord Hillsborough first stonewalls Fielding, and on their second meeting is hardly more forthcoming. Fielding coolly declares, "in spite of what I was led to expect from you by the Lord Chief Justice, I have gotten very little more from you than I did at my first visit here.... Come, Jeremy, let's away from here" (*Experiment in Treason* 41). Sir John delights in puncturing fatuous egotists, like the "serpentine" Mrs. Trezavant and her "elephantine" husband, who superciliously tries to put Sir John down: "We have no need for your investigative powers." Sir John then pulls London's biggest literary lion out of his hat: "'May I present Dr. Samuel Johnson?'" and elicits from Mrs. Trezavant "an entire vocabulary of cooing and twittering sounds interspersed with phrases of abject idolatry" (*Color of Death* 239).

At home with his wife, family, and assorted individuals whom, like Jeremy, they "adopt," Sir John acts as a tactful, considerate, and kindly paterfamilias, ready with praise and material assistance in educating Jeremy; Lady Fielding's pretty teenage secretary Clarissa Roundtree, "writer of romances yet to be written" and Jeremy's inamorata; for young cook Molly Sarton; and for Annie Oakum, their former cook, who becomes the toast of London as Juliet after Fielding places her in David Garrick's renowned Drury Lane Theater company.

As "delightful Georgian versions of Nero Wolfe and Archie Goodwin," Sir John Fielding and his young protégé Jeremy Proctor serve up a pungent stew of history, boldly drawn characters, and sparkling dialogue from England's Augustan Age, demonstrating yet again, as Alexander Pope put it, "The proper study of mankind is man."

Novels: *Blind Justice* (1994); *Murder in Grub Street* (1995); *Watery Grave* (1996); *Person or Persons Unknown* (1997); *Jack, Knave and Fool* (1997); *Death of a Colonial* (1999); *The Color of Death* (2000); *Smuggler's Moon* (2001); *An Experiment in Treason* (2002); *The Price of Murder* (2003); *Rules of Engagement* (completed by Alexander's wife Judith Aller and mystery author John Shannon, and published posthumously in 2005).

Selected sources: Flanagan, Margaret. Rev. of *Watery Grave*. *Booklist*, September 15, 1996: 223; *Publishers Weekly*. Rev. of *Rules of Engagement*, January 10, 2005: 43; Rockicki, Melissa Kuzma. Rev. of *Person or Persons Unknown*. *Library Journal*, August 1997: 140; Stasio, Marilyn. Rev. of *Blind Justice*. *New York Times Book Review*, October 23, 1994: 24; Stasio, Marilyn. Rev. of *Watery Grave*. *New York Times Book Review*, November 10, 1996: 62; *Wall Street Journal*. Rev. of *Murder in Grub Street*, November 1, 1995: A12.

See also: Deryn Lake's series featuring eighteenth-century London apothecary John Rawlings, a real-life associate of Sir John Fielding; Janet Gleeson's series featuring Nathaniel Hopson, an assistant cabinetmaker in eighteenth-century England.

Phryne Fisher

Profession:	Private investigator and philanthropist
Living situation:	Blissfully single
Geographic locale:	Mostly St. Kilda, near Melbourne, Australia
Time period:	1920s
Associate:	Detective Inspector Jack Robinson
Nemesis:	Former lover René Dubois
Significant relationship:	Lin Chung, lover
Concerns:	Adventure; women's issues; haute cuisine and haute mode

Kerry Greenwood claims that she gets her ideas from "everything I have ever seen, dreamed, imagined, read, eaten, touched, smelled, or heard" (*Crime Factory* Web site)—and what a splendid torrent of arcane knowledge, bubbly imagination, and throbbing sense appeal she unleashes via her 1920s Australian amateur detective the Hon. Phryne Fisher.

Just as Dorothy L. Sayers endowed her fabulously wealthy sleuth Lord Peter Wimsey with gourmet delights conjured up by the imperturbable Bunter, allowed him to drive "Mrs. Merdle," a mighty purring Daimler, and equipped him with a dashing libido fixated on the autobiographical **Harriet Vane**, Greenwood has given Phryne formidable inheritances, cannily invested; an unquenchable thirst for speed she pursues in both her red Hispano-Suiza and her very own Gypsy Moth; Mr. and Mrs. Butler, her unflappable cocktail-concocting butler and her genius-level cook; and a ravenous sexual appetite ("that's what stable boys are for," Phryne muses [*Castlemaine* 64]) now satisfied—mostly—by her exotic green-eyed Chinese lover, Lin Chung, "of surpassing amatory skill and extensive education" (*Montparnasse* 29). Phryne, "the adventurous and ravishingly beautiful darling of the Jazz Age in Melbourne, a study in gorgeous silks...triumphant in love and in crime," becomes Australia's "High Class Girl Dick" (*Montparnasse* 15) with a vengeance, shocking everyone whenever possible and ingeniously punishing the ungodly. When she returns to Melbourne after a sojourn in France, Phryne quickly acquires a colorful entourage: her wharfie friends Cec and Bert for heavy artillery; her faithful Calvinistic terracotta-sweatered maid Dot Bryant; her often bemused policeman matey Jack Robinson, and her adopted daughters Jane and Ruth, rescued by Phryne from a life of poverty and potential white slavery.

Phryne's first case, *Death by Misadventure* (1991), undertaken for some of her posh acquaintances, seems a relatively simple backdrop for her own flamboyant hijinks. Soon, though, in *Flying Too High* (1992), after she's established herself as a private investigator and settled in an exquisite home in Melbourne's St. Kilda suburb, her cases acquire sobering social significance. However frothy their surfaces, the secondary plots of Phryne's delicious detections are almost always desperately serious, involving Australia's "Illegal abortion and some of its unsavory practitioners, cocaine traffic and use, and white slavery" (*Silk Stalkings* 2:20) as well as practices and attitudes established in the country's early days, when poor women, orphaned children, and Chinese laborers were exploited horrifically.

Murder in Montparnasse (2002) explains the major source of Phryne's social consciousness and deepens insight into her character: she herself has been starved, frightened nearly out of her wits, and even debased. While the rest of her family gobbled up their unexpected inheritance and rapturously sank into their luxurious English estate at the outbreak of World War I, Phryne rushed "over there" and became a volunteer ambulance driver, dragging dying soldiers out of filthy verminous trenches. "Bathed in blood, collecting amputated limbs for burial," Phyrne soon discover[ed] she was not proof against shock. But she persisted" (*Montparnasse* 17). France awarded her the *Medaille d'Honneur* after the 1918 Armistice.

Phryne's pride, however, received a near-mortal blow in Paris. Refusing to return to her taurine baronet Daddy and the life of an English debutante, she stayed in Paris, supporting herself by nude modeling and living with René Dubois, a Frenchman who leeched off her earnings and treated her shamefully—just as her friends in Gertrude Stein's Sapphic coterie had warned her he would. In *Murder in Montparnasse*, Phryne has to come to terms with René's betrayal while simultaneously solving the serial murders of Aussie veterans of Gallipoli, friends of her friends Bert and Cec. This dampens even Phryne's high spirits for a while, though with therapeutic clothes purchases, remedial cocktails, and a convenient arrangement with Lin Chung's new bride Camellia, Phryne makes a rapid recovery.

The capers that follow usually intertwine Phryne's familial problems with her investigations. In *The Castlemaine Murders* (2003), for example, Phryne's "acidulated bitch of a sister" (17), the Hon. Miss Eliza Fisher, thrown out by their father for her rampant socialist views, arrives concurrently with the discovery of a mummified corpse complete with bullet wound in the forehead and Lin Chung's own investigation into the 1857 theft of gold bullion rightfully belonging to his ancestors. By this time Phryne is beginning to wish she'd never acquired her whole entourage and "could just ravish her beautiful lover on the floor of the parlour" (*Castlemaine* 86), but she rises to the occasion, girds her delectably slender loins in "Opalescence," a shamefully expensive creation by Madame Fleuri, High Priestess of the Mode, and unforgettably proves herself in novel after novel to be "a woman of uncanny powers" (*Castlemaine* 232) in love and detection as well as war.

Novels (dates of U.S. publication unless otherwise specified): *Flying Too High* (Melbourne, 1990); *Death by Misadventure* (1991); *Murder on the Ballarat Train* (1992); *Death at Victoria Dock* (Melbourne, 1992); *The Green Mill Murder* (Melbourne, 1993); *Blood and Circuses* (Melbourne, 1994); *Ruddy Gore* (Melbourne, 1995); *Urn Burial* (Victoria, 1996); *Raisins and Almonds* (St. Leonards, 1997); *Death Before Wicket* (St. Leonards, 1998); *Away with the Fairies* (Crows Nest, N.S.W., 2001); *Murder in Montparnasse* (2002); *The Castlemaine Murders* (Crows Nest, N.S.W., 2003); *Queen of the Flowers* (Crows Nest, N.S.W., 2004); *Alien Invasions* (2006).

Other novels: Greenwood has written numerous stand-alone novels, among them *Cassandra*, *Electra*, and *Medea*, reworkings of classical myths. She has also written young adult science fiction, including *Whale Road*, *Cave Rats*, and *Feral*. *Feral* (1998) was described by *Magpies* reviewer Helen Purdie as "an interesting study of a future society whose good intentions have been subverted by evil men" (September 1998: 37–38).

Short fiction: Greenwood has contributed short stories to several anthologies, including *Shadow Alley*, edited by Lucy Sussex; and *A Dick for a Day*, edited by Fiona Giles.

Nonfiction: Greenwood has written nonfiction about the commission of crimes, including *The Thing She Loves: Why Women Kill* (1996), a study of women's motivations for murder; *On Murder: True Crime Writing in Australia* (2000) and *On Murder 2: True Crime Writing in Australia* (2002); *A Different Sort of Real: The Diary of Charlotte McKenzie, 1918–1919* (2001).

Selected sources: *Age*. "On the Couch with Kerry Greenwood." www.theage.com.au; Carroll, John. Rev. of *Death at Victoria Dock*. *Australian Book Review*, July 1992: 57–58; Carroll, John. Rev. of *Montparnasse*. *Australian Book Review*, June 1994: 63; Klett, Rex E. "Crime in the Commonwealth." *Library Journal*, June 1, 2005: 104; Margitts, Jayne. "An Interview with Kerry Greenwood." *Between the Lines*, www.thei.aust.com/isits/btl; McLarin, Jenny. Rev. of *The Castlemaine Murders*. *Booklist*, September 15, 2004: 212; Turnbull, Sue. "Phryne in Sydney." *Australian Book Review*, July 1999: 32.

Major Awards: Aurealis Award, 1996; Children's Book of the Year Award, 2002; Davitt Award (Sisters in Crime), 2002; Ned Kelly Lifetime Achievement Award, 2003.

See also: For contemporary Australian settings, Peter Corris's Chanlderesque PI Cliff Hardy series, set in Sydney; Marele Day's series featuring Australian's first female PI, Claudia Valentine; Garry Disher's new police procedural series *The Dragon Man* (2004) and *Kittyhawk Down* (2005), featuring Melbourne detective Hal Challis; and *Blood Junction* (2004). For historical Australian settings, see Peter Corris's lighter and more humorous series featuring Richard Browning, who goes to Hollywood in the 1940s to divide his time between acting and private investigation; and for a late 1950s Australian setting, Peter Doyle's series about petty criminal Billy Glasheen. For post–World War I settings and modern-minded heroines, see Carola Dunn's Daisy Dalrymple series, set in England; Jill Paton Walsh's **Harriet Vane** extensions of Dorothy L. Sayers's Lord Peter Wimsey novels; Jacqueline Winspear's **Maisie Dobbs** series, set in London.

Debut novel: Caroline Carver's Debut Dagger novel featuring journalist India Kane, set in the Australian bush village of Cooinda.

Dame Frevisse*

Profession:	Benedictine nun
Living situation:	Single
Geographic locale:	Oxfordshire, England

---

*In medieval English usage, "Dame" is the title of vowed "choir nuns" whose primary religious duty is to chant the Holy Office at specified times daily, while "Sister" is reserved for "lay sisters" who do much of the manual labor of the nunnery.

Time period: Mid-1400s

Concern: Justice

"As for it being easy to be wed to him [Christ]," declares Margaret Frazer's Dame Frevisse, Benedictine nun of St. Frideswide's priory in mid-fifteenth-century Oxfordshire, "it was and it wasn't, and there were days when 'wasn't' was very strong" (*Clerk's Tale* 152). Frevisse, genuinely pious, is "as pragmatic as devout." Traveling with her footloose parents, she "had spent all her childhood managing other people being difficult" (*Novice's Tale* 168, 159), a singular qualification for the demands of constant enclosed life with ten other women, as well as with the visitors she as her nunnery's hosteler must accommodate. After her parents' deaths, Frevisse had lived in the wealthy household of her uncle Thomas Chaucer, the politically powerful son of the *Canterbury Tales*' author in the Plantagenets' zenith, when Henry V, Shakespeare's "star of England," astoundingly vanquished the French at Agincourt. Thomas Chaucer, a trusted advisor to royalty, also fostered Frevisse's love of learning, her quick wit, and the quiet confidence that enables her to unravel the medieval legalities complicating the homicides she investigates.

In 1431, the date of the *The Novice's Tale* (1992), the Benedictine rule of silence at St. Frideswide's nunnery shatters when boisterous Lady Ermentrude, drunk as a lord, comes to remove her ultra-devout niece Thomasine two weeks from the girl's profession of vows. Shortly after her dramatic arrival, Ermentrude loudly collapses and dies gruesomely of poison. Tall, dark-browed Frevisse, with her strong face and eyes "seeing much and remarking on everything with subtle mockery" (*Novice's Tale* 4) mistrusts unscrupulous Master Montfort, the "crowner" (coroner) investigating the death. Insisting that ignorance breeds fear, Frevisse asks permission from her canny elderly prioress Domina Edith to question the priory's guests, exactly the sort of intellectual challenge that her inquisitive mind needs. Frevisse's unwavering pursuit of justice complements her vocation, making this aspect of her marriage to Christ an easy one.

Holy charity is difficult for Frevisse. She has to endure her sisters' foolishness, especially their superstitions about demonic possession, and she has to tolerate Thomasine's "utter earnestness" and "shrinking humility" (*Novice's Tale* 87, 126). Frevisse also suffers from an excessive sense of responsibility, earned very young because her parents had none, scruples that her conscience will not let her abandon. Frevisse's irrepressible dry wit sometimes intimidates others, and even less charitably, when faced with Montfort's corrupt bureaucracy, Frevisse has to fight down "the double urge to smack the self-pleased condescension off his face and to verbally rip his illogic to shreds" (*Novice's Tale* 128).

After *The Novice's Tale*, a case conducted within St. Frideswide's, Frevisse moves outside the convent on religious errands, seeking a serial killer in *The Servant's Tale* (1993) and in *The Bishop's Tale* (1994) establishing whether the death of a man who dares God to smite him was human or divine retribution. Years later, at the start of *The Clerk's Tale* (2002), though, Frevisse feels herself slipping into the sin of accidie, "weakness of spirit" that can lead to the ultimate sin of despair (*Clerk's Tale* 5). After many years, the unchanging routine of nunnery life has become a "grey weight" on her spirit, obstructing rather than assisting her search for God, "the only thing she had ever found worth her whole heart's longing" (*Clerk's Tale* 92). She gladly accompanies her new prioress on an errand of mercy to neighboring St. Mary's convent, only to discover that Master Montfort himself lies murdered there. Because the murder, the ensuing inquest, and Montfort's funeral are inundating St. Mary's with guests, Frevisse and Domina Elisabeth must stay with a respectable widow nearby. Montfort's son Christopher, the new crowner, requests Frevisse's help solving the homicide, plunging her into some of her most trying days as a bride of Christ.

Frevisse is starting to feel old, continually distracted from soul-satisfying prayer by "the lately learned tangle of other people's lives" (*Clerk's Tale* 69). Angry as she is, too, at the troubles people make for themselves, especially such a grievous sin as murder, she finds she cannot pray for Montfort's soul as her obligation to follow Christ's example of forgiveness demands. In coming to St. Mary's, Frevisse gets what she seemed to want, a change in her daily routine, only to discover that the tumult of ordinary life has exhausted her, body, mind, and spirit. To regain her spiritual equilibrium, she must not only solve Montfort's murder but at last pray sincerely for his soul because his death was unjust.

In the Middle Ages, young well-bred women had to accept either arranged marriage, sometimes as early as thirteen or fourteen, with the accompanying acute dangers of childbirth, or take the veil, removing themselves from the world. Frevisse traded freedom of the body for the freedom of the soul, knowing that more reasons than one led women to the cloister, "and for some of us the love of God is maybe the least of them" (*Novice's Tale* 105). Frevisse's divine Bridegroom allowed her to use her questing mind, her courage, her passion for truth, her conviction that once justice is bypassed, "the unjustness grows...the law fails, and where will any of us be then except in chaos and danger?" (*Clerk's Tale* 306). "She could command armies," declared her uncle Thomas Chaucer. "A pity she's a woman" (*Novice's Tale* 15).

Authorship: Mary Monica Pulver had originally planned a novel set in fifteenth-century England and Gail Frazer, at first her historical research assistant, became her collaborator for the first six books in the Dame Frevisse series. Beginning with the *The Prioress' Tale* (1997), the series is being written by Gail Frazer alone, under the pseudonym "Margaret Frazer."

Novels: *The Novice's Tale* (1992); *The Servant's Tale* (1993); *The Outlaw's Tale* (1994); *The Bishop's Tale* (1994); *The Boy's Tale* (1995); *The Murderer's Tale* (1996); *The Prioress' Tale* (1997), series written from this novel on by Gail Frazer alone; *The Maiden's Tale* (1998); *The Reeve's Tale* (1999); *The Squire's Tale* (2000); *The Clerk's Tale* (2002); *The Bastard's Tale* (2003); *The Hunter's Tale* (2004); *The Widow's Tale* (2005); *The Sempster's Tale* (2006).

Stand-alone novel: *A Play of Dux Morand* (2004).

Selected sources: Bibel, Barbara. Rev. of *The Hunter's Tale*. *Booklist*, December 15, 2003: 731; Cleary, Maryell. Rev. of *The Boy's Tale*. *Armchair Detective*, Winter 1996: 109–110; Klett, Rex E. Rev. of *The Reeve's Tale*. *Library Journal*, January 2000: 166; Lamb, Sister Avila. Rev. of *The Outlaw's Tale*. *Kliatt*, May 1994: 9; *Publishers Weekly*. Rev. of *The Bastard's Tale*, December 23, 2002: 49.

Award nominations: Edgar Allan Poe Award nominations, Mystery Writers of America, 1994, 1998.

See also: Paul Doherty's various medieval series: his Hugh Corbett series, set in thirteenth-century England; his Canterbury Tales series, set in Chaucer's late fourteenth century; his Brother Athelstan series, set in late-fourteenth-century London; his Kathryn Swinbrook series, set in the fifteenth century; Ellis Peters's **Brother Cadfael** series, set in twelfth-century Shrewsbury, England; Priscilla Royal's Eleanor, Abbess of Tyndal, series, set in thirteenth-century England; for contrast between medieval English and Irish religious traditions, see Peter Tremayne's **Sister Fidelma** series, set in mid-seventh-century Ireland.

Sir Baldwin Furnshill

Profession:	Former Knight Templar; now Keeper of the King's Peace (magistrate)
Living situation:	Single through first six books of the series; then marries Lady Jeanne de Liddinstone
Geographic locale:	England's West Country, especially Dartmoor and the Stannaries, Devon's ancient tin-mining area
Time period:	Early fourteenth century, the reign of Edward II
Associate:	Simon Puttock, Bailiff of Lydford Castle
Nemeses:	King Philip of France and Pope Clement V
Significant relationship:	Lady Jeanne de Liddinstone
Concerns:	Maintaining law and order in a turbulent historical period

An amateur historian who lives in the very area once owned by the family of the main character of his books (Ashley 255), Michael Jecks described the period when Sir Baldwin Furnshill and Simon Puttock labored together to keep the King's Peace in Devon as "a dreadful time...[after] two years of appalling famine," with worsening Anglo-French relations leading "to the Hundred Years' War; the king was weak and rumored to be a homosexual, not a desirable label in a warrior culture; and there was soon to be a civil war" (quoted from the *Tangled Web UK* Web site). Jecks's hero Sir Baldwin Furnshill had been a Knight Templar, one of the warrior-monks whose "most noble Order of Knights" had arisen in the twelfth-century Crusades to protect pilgrims to the Holy Land. By 1307, the Templars had become the bankers of Europe, and "two implacably avaricious men," Pope Clement V and Philip IV of France, joined forces to accuse the Templars of heresy, pillage the Order's wealth, and destroy them. In 1314, Philip ordered the Templars' last Grand Master, Jacques de Molay, and almost all of its knights tortured and burned at the stake, and Sir Baldwin Furnshill, who had witnessed de Molay's denunciation of Pope and King before his execution, became "a cynical and caustic man" (*Mad Monk* 62) bent on a terrible vengeance.

In *The Last Templar* (1995), Jecks's first Medieval West Country tapestry of savage fourteenth-century life, Sir Baldwin Furnshill meets Simon Puttock, Bailiff of Lydford Castle. The men become fast friends, encountering realistic and well-developed eccentrics, criminals, lowlifes, and high-born miscreants of every stripe and themselves convincingly growing and developing through the series.

Tall, dark-haired Sir Baldwin Furnshill looks about a decade younger than his forty-three years, late middle age by fourteenth-century standards. He bears an old-fashioned black beard, scars of great suffering, and melancholy, grief-stricken eyes. He conveys "the arrogance that came from...battle and testing his prowess, but there was also a humility, and a kindness, and an almost tangible yearning for peace and rest, as though he had...seen almost too much" (*Last Templar* 29). As a landless second son, he had left England in 1290 at seventeen, returning twenty-six years later to take possession of Furnshill Manor after the death of his older brother. Sturdy Simon Puttock has just become bailiff of the castle of Lydford, a constable-like position awarded for the generations-long service the Puttocks have provided to the noble de Courtenays. As bailiff, Simon can become wealthy and powerful—if he successfully maintains Lydford's productivity and tax revenues and the King's Peace in the area, which includes the Stannaries, ancient tin mines still a major source of Devon's income.

Simon Puttock immediately senses Furnshill's worth and pain, but as an honest burgher, Simon also knows "what [a knight] wanted, he would take" (*Last Templar* 68), and so Simon experiences twinges of doubt about Furnshill's motives when they begin to investigate a series of suspicious deaths by fire. Furnshill, though, refuses to consider using torture, an accepted medieval interrogation, and while he exacts his own grisly retribution for the deaths of de Molay and his fellow Templars, Furnshill eventually overcomes his distrust of strangers and befriends Simon, acknowledging the bailiff's "obvious honesty and honor" (*Last Templar* 211). For his part, Simon searches his own heart and finds Furnshill justified when Furnshill places himself in Simon's hands for justice. To the knight's shock and horror, Simon nominates him as the next magistrate of Crediton, the official Keeper of the King's Peace.

Solving crimes together throughout Devon, knight and commoner Furnshill and Puttock share decency, honor, and common purpose, consistently putting duty above their personal commitments. In *The Leper's Return* (1998), they deal humanely with the prejudices that the disease, like AIDS today, inspired. In *Squire Throwleigh's Heir* (1999), Sir Baldwin, softened by love, is preparing for his marriage to Lady Jeanne de Liddinstone when he and Simon have to unravel a suspicious death, and later, in *Belladonna at Belstone* (1999), Furnshill leaves his new bride and Simon his adored wife Margaret to investigate the mysterious death of an over-scrupulous young nun. Lady Jeanne joins Sir Baldwin and Simon Puttock on a trip to a winter festival at the cathedral town of Exeter in *The Boy-Bishop's Glovemaker* (2000), involving another agonizing death, and Sir Baldwin probes assassinations in *The Mad Monk of Gidleigh* (2002). His knight's code finds such murders cowardly and repellant, but they cause him to doubt the faith in himself that his cross-hilted two-handed sword represents. Having killed an innocent man and feeling that "I carry the weight of too many men's sins and grief on my shoulders" (*Mad Monk* 433), Furnshill, Simon at his side, undertakes a grueling penitential pilgrimage to Spain in *The Templar's Penance* (2003), enduring shipwreck on the return trip in *Outlaws of Ennor* (2004) and solving more murders in the English countryside before finally reaching home in *The Tolls of Death* (2004). Even after his Order's destruction, the stern values Sir Baldwin Furnshill lives by bear out the Templar motto, "Not to us, Lord, not to us, but to Thee be the glory."

Novels: *The Last Templar* (1995); *The Merchant's Partner* (1995); *A Moorland Hanging* (1996); *The Crediton Killings* (1997); *The Abbot's Gibbet* (1998); *The Leper's Return* (1998); *Squire Throwleigh's Heir* (1999); *Belladonna at Belstone* (1999); *The Traitor of St. Giles* (2000); *The Boy Bishop's Glovemaker* (2000); *The Tournament of Blood* (2001); *The Sticklepath Strangler* (2001); *The Devil's Acolyte* (2002); *The Mad Monk of Gidleigh* (2002); *The Templar's Penance* (2003); *Outlaws of Ennor* (2004); *The Tolls of Death* (2004); *The Chapel of Bones* (2004); *The Butcher of St. Peter's* (2005); *a Friar's Bloodfeud* (2005).

Autobiographical sketch: *Tangled Web UK*, www.twbooks.uk.

Selected sources: Butler, Gwendoline. Rev. of *The Leper's Return*. *Crime Time On-Line* (www.crimetime.co.uk), September 5, 2001; *Kirkus Reviews*. Rev. of *Belladonna at Belstone*, March 15, 2000: 340; *Kirkus Reviews*. Rev. of *Squire Throwleigh's Heir*, April 15, 2000: 515; Klett, Rex E. Rev. of *The Traitor of St. Giles*. *Library Journal*, October 1, 2000: 152; *Publishers Weekly*. Rev. of *The Boy-Bishop's Glovemaker*, March 19, 2001: 79.

Web sites: www.michaeljecks.co.uk and www.twbooks.co.uk/authors/mjecks.html.

See also: Simon Beaufort's series featuring English Crusader Sir Geoffrey de Mappestone, set in twelfth-century Jerusalem; Alys Clare's Josse D'Acquin series, set in medieval France; P.C. Doherty's Brother Athelstan series, set in the 1370s–1380s; Susanna Gregory's mid-fourteenth-century Matthew Bartholomew series; Bernard Knight's Crowner John series, featuring returned crusader Sir John de Wolfe and set in twelfth-century Devon, England; Edward Marston's Domesday series, set just after the Norman Conquest in 1066.

G

Inspector Ghote

Profession:	Inspector, Bombay Crime Branch (C.I.D.)
Living situation:	Married
Geographic locale:	Bombay (now Mumbai), India
Time period:	1964–present
Associate:	In *Breaking and Entering*, Axel Svensson
Nemesis:	Corrupt business and officialdom
Significant relationship:	Protima, his wife
Concerns:	Justice; morality

The twenty-two novels and two short-story collections featuring little Inspector Ganesh Vinayak Ghote (pronounced "Go-tay") of the Bombay Crime Branch represent about half the fiction output of magisterial British mystery author and *Times* (London) critic H.R.F. Keating, who did not visit India until he was ten years into the series. Keating's actress wife initially urged him to begin writing mysteries because he enjoyed them so much, and according to the *Dictionary of Literary Biography* each of his early novels was "an experiment of a different sort," together "showing Keating feeling his way toward his own idiom and . . . discover[ing] that the mystery form need not be empty of thematic content." Keating expanded his audience dramatically with Inspector Ghote, an inept native detective in an exotic locale who debuted in the Edgar and Gold Dagger winning *A Perfect Murder* (1964) by "solving" a murder that never happened, with the ostensible victim a man *named* "Perfect." Ghote has since become "one of the most successful series sleuths in modern letters.... [He] has grown, but the directions of the growth have always seemed implicit in the earlier characterizations" (*CA Online*).

Creating Ghote, Keating maintains that he chiefly put "a recognizable human being into broad general situations likely to happen to any one of us" (*St. James Guide to Crime and Mystery Writers*). The undersized henpecked husband of formidable Protima and beleaguered father of young Western-smitten Ved, poor bumbling Ghote is also at the mercy of his corrupt and/or Brahmin police superiors as well as victimized by the strictures of his caste-ridden society, whose dictates force him into outwardly humble and even servile behavior all the while conjecturing, theorizing, plotting, and seething within. Ghote is a brown-skinned Everyman in a colorful, violent land still coping with the aftermath of white imperialism, pitting his shrewdness and intimate knowledge of Bombay, its dizzying diversity, and its intricate customs against criminals who flout the dictates of human decency. Keating also told an interviewer that Ghote "is me ... inside him is a lot of me" (quoted in *CA Online*).

The element of conscience is the common denominator to Ghote's cases. Though Ghote prides himself on strictly adhering to the rules, he abandons them for a higher good in *Inspector Ghote Trusts the Heart* (1972), disobeying his superior by attempting to rescue a kidnapped child. *Under a Monsoon Cloud* (1986) hinges upon an even more brutal moral dilemma: in a case with no crime to solve, no suspects, not even any clues, Ghote confronts the mystery of human rage and it almost destroys him. Just before the monsoon breaks, young Ghote, posted to a remote village, witnesses his long-time police officer idol "Tiger" Kelkar fling a brass inkstand at an irritating subordinate, killing him. So as not to wreck Kelkar's brilliant reputation, Ghote participates in a coverup, only to learn a year later during the ensuing investigation that Kelkar has committed suicide, leaving a note accepting all blame but exposing Ghote to questions that could scuttle his own hard-won police career. Protima urges him to lie and he lies as well to his counsel Mrs. Ahmed, a civil libertarian who also represents his conscience, but eventually he muddles through this painful ethical paradox with his principles only a little shaken.

When Ghote travels to London in *Inspector Ghote Hunts the Peacock* (1968) and to Los Angeles in *Go West, Inspector Ghote* (1981), ethical questions yield to the comedic effects of Ghote's "embarrassment and wonder" (Murphy 203) at the two huge cities of Western civilization, but in *Doing Wrong* (1993), called by Julian Symons "the finest and most serious Ghote novel," Ghote's duties and moral sensibilities again clash when he must track a killer, an upwardly mobile local politician snarled in his own self-made ethical trap, on a jam-packed pilgrim train journey to the holy city of Benares.

In *Breaking and Entering* (2000), which Keating claims to be the last case of his old friend and alter ego (quoted in *TW Books* Web site), Ghote deals with several levels of ethics at once. As a mere inspector relegated to the relatively minor investigation of a series of cat burglaries while his superiors grab the sensational locked-room murder of prominent air-conditioning mogul Ajil Ajmani, Ghote has to circumvent the deceptions endemic to Bombay's largely on-the-take police while he endures the condescension and subterfuge of wealthy Bombay matrons whose "jewelries" have been cunningly lifted by the elusive "Yeshwant" (nicknamed for a famous folkloric climbing lizard). When shockingly hailed from a tourist bus by Swedish detective Axel Svensson with "red-red face and blue-blue [Swedish] eyes" (*Breaking and Entering* 6), whom Ghote had last worked with at the start of his career, Ghote's compassion for the lonely widowed Swede clashes with his utter horror at Svensson's Western "boring-in demands" (*Breaking and Entering* 16), devastatingly impolite by Indian standards of etiquette. Ghote yields to pity only to find Svensson is just as horrified when the little Indian Inspector, having determined to "thrust his way" into a reluctant witness's heart (*Breaking and Entering* 235) unexpectedly thrusts a whetted fish-knife into the same man's throat, drawing blood and the answers he needs. Svensson's recoil from India's casual acceptance of violence and death counterpoints the comic linguistic interplay between the Swede's inability to manage Indian names and Inspector Ghote's charmingly fractured Indian English. This last of Inspector Ghote's cases sums up one of Keating's and Kipling's major themes: East is East and West is West, and though they encounter one another in Keating's amusing and thoughtful explorations of universal human nature under the stress of serious moral dilemmas, they never, ever, truly meet.

Novels: *The Perfect Murder* (1964; filmed in 1990); *Inspector Ghote's Good Crusade* (1966); *Inspector Ghote Caught in Meshes* (1967); *Inspector Ghote Hunts the Peacock* (1968); *Inspector Ghote Plays a Joke* (1969); *Inspector Ghote Breaks an Egg* (1970); *Inspector Ghote Goes by Train* (1971); *Inspector Ghote Trusts the Heart* (1972); *Bats Fly up for Inspector Ghote* (1974); *Films, Films, Inspector Ghote* (1976); *Inspector Ghote Draws a Line* (1979); *Go West, Inspector Ghote* (1981); *The Sheriff of Bombay* (1984); *Under a Monsoon Cloud* (1986); *The Body in the Billiard Room* (1987); *Dead on Time* (1988); *The Iciest Sin* (1990); *Cheating Death* (1991); *Doing Wrong* (1993); *Asking Questions* (1996); *Bribery, Corruption Also* (1999); *Breaking and Entering* (2000).

Short stories: *Inspector Ghote: His Life and Crimes* (1989); *Inspector Ghote and Some Others* (1991).

Other series: The Jack Stallworthy series and the Harriet Martens series, both set in contemporary Britain; as Evelyn Hervey, the Harriet Unwin series.

Nonseries: Various stand-alone detective novels, notably *The Dog It Was That Died* (1962); *The Murder of the Maharajah* (1980); *Jack the Lady Killer* (novel in verse) (1999).

Nonfiction: *Murder Must Appetize* (1975); *Sherlock Holmes: The Man and His World* (1979); *Great Crimes* (1982); *Writing Crime Fiction* (1986); *Crime and Mystery: The 100 Best Books* (1987); *The Bedside Companion to Crime* (1989); *Crime Waves* (1991). Keating has also edited and/or contributed to several detective-related works, notably *Agatha Christie: First Lady of Crime* (1976); *Crime Writers: Reflections on Crime Fiction* (1978); *Whodunit?* (1982); *The Best of Father Brown* (1991); *The Man Who: Stories in Honour of Julian Symons' Eightieth Birthday* (1992).

Selected sources: Bargannier, Earl F. *Twelve Englishmen of Mystery.* New York: Popular Press, 1984; H.R.F. Keating, www.twbooks.co.uk, September 9, 2002 (list of titles and plots, with Keating's commentary; *Publishers Weekly.* Rev. of *Bribery, Corruption Also,* June 21, 1999: 59; Symons, Julian. *Bloody Murder,* 2nd ed. New York: Viking, 1982; Tamaya, Meera. *H.R.F.*

Keating, Post-Colonial Detection: A Critical Study. Bowling Green, OH: Bowling Green State University, 1993.

Major awards: Gold Dagger Award, 1964, 1980; Edgar Allan Poe Award, 1965, 1980; named Royal Society of Literature Fellow, 1991; Diamond Dagger Award for lifetime achievement, 1996.

See also: Paul Mann's Bombay police detective **George Sansi** series. For Southeast Asia–related contemporary series, see John Burdett's Detective Sonchai Jitpleecheep series, set in Thailand; Colin Cotterill's coroner Dr. Siri Paiboum series, set in Laos.

Debut novel: Nury Vittaghi's *The Feng Shui Detective*, featuring C.F. Wong, a "geomancer" (feng shui master), set in Singapore.

Gordianus the Finder

Profession:	Private investigator
Living situation:	Married
Geographic locale:	Ancient Rome
Time period:	80–48 B.C.
Significant relationships:	Bethesda (slave lover, later his wife); Cassandra (in *A Mist of Prophecies*)
Concerns:	Ethics and morality

Civil strife dominated Roman history in the first century B.C. The Roman Republic began to break down around 100 B.C. from class dissention and slave uprisings. Reform attempts failed, and the feud between consuls (two concurrent chief executives) Marius and Sulla erupted into civil war in 82–79 B.C. Originally sharing leadership with Crassus in the First Triumvirate that followed, the generals Pompey and Julius Caesar fell out; Caesar defeated Pompey in 48 B.C. and before his assassination in 44 B.C. laid the foundation for the Roman Empire. Marcus Tullius Cicero (105–141 B.C.), Rome's greatest orator and anti-Caesar party leader in the Senate, prosecuted the conspirator Catiline and defended the Republic. The complicated decades-long relationship between Cicero and Gordianus forms the backstory of Steven Saylor's *Roma Sub Rosa* series.

Each of Gordianus's cases involves an important historical event, and as the world around him dramatically changes, so does Gordianus the Finder. As an investigator, Gordianus knows his place in Rome, "multiple cities in one" (*Roman Blood* 19), where patrician wealth and superficial decorum cover a multitude of sordid atrocities. When someone seeks his services, "[that person] keeps a certain distance and restraint...as if I were a leper. I take no offense—so long as my accounts are paid on time and in full" (*Roman Blood* 3). Cicero's first important case as a young advocate and orator in 80 B.C., the time of the savage dictator Sulla, involves an unspeakable crime in patristic Rome: an Umbrian landowner is accused of murdering his father, and Cicero engages Gordianus to investigate. From the outset, Gordianus holds his own with the famous orator; Cicero has high political ideals, but Gordianus knows the brutal reality: the poverty-stricken Rome that Sulla is leaving to posterity breeds gangs of young criminals with no politics or loyalty "except the loyalty that money buys" (*Roman Blood* 44). The successful outcome of this case, as Gordianus comments thirty years later in *A Mist of Prophecy* (2002), makes both their reputations.

Working for Cicero and other powerful Romans, Gordianus learns to guard his own flanks. Nearly murdered himself in *Arms of Nemesis* (1992), he learns to use a bodyguard, at first Eco, the mute adopted son Gordianus saved from the streets, and later his brawny son-in-law Davus. Risking his life probing the murky Roman underworld during Spartacus's doomed slave rebellion in *Arms of Nemesis*, Cataline's conspiracy in *Cataline's Riddle* (1993), and the war between Caesar and Pompey that starts in *Rubicon* (1999) and continues through *A Mist of Prophecies* (2002), the "awfully impertinent" Gordianus exercises his special gifts, skill in deduction, flashes of intuition, and his ability to make people confide in him, to tell him secrets "even when they shouldn't." Above all, Gordianus has integrity; finding truth is his passion. Those gifts gain Gordianus a fortune, a fine family, and "the respect of powerful men" (*Mist* 118)—until the Roman economy, plagued by runaway inflation and enormous food shortages, almost collapses in 48 B.C.

With Roman leadership in shambles and Cicero fled to join Pompey, a weary semiretired Gordianus finds himself in debt for the first time, his fortune "swallowed up by a certain greedy banker. My family has been torn apart. As for the respect of powerful men, . . . If you can show me a way to eat it, I'll prepare it for dinner and invite you to take the first portion" (*Mist* 118). In *A Mist of Prophecies*, Gordianus also bitterly acknowledges that he has made much of his own misery. By trying to stay neutral in the clash between Caesar and Pompey, Gordianus, now in his sixties, has disinherited Meto, the other adopted son he loves dearly but who is now an aide to Caesar. "Cassandra," a beautiful exotic seeress, falls into his arms and his life at the forum one day, bringing him a second youth before, dying of poison, she again embraces him in public. At home, his beloved Bethesda, the half-Jewish slave from Egypt he loved, freed, and married, is wasting away from a mysterious illness. Worry, guilt, grief, and fear for his loved ones drive Gordianus, as torn asunder as Rome itself, to investigate Cassandra's murder so that he can find some peace.

Bethesda insists that only bathing in the waters of the Nile can cure her, so Gordianus takes her back to Alexandria in *The Judgment of Caesar* (2004). At this dangerous time "no place is safer than any other." Pompey, who swore to kill Gordianus in *A Mist of Prophecies*, is planning a last-ditch naval attack on Egypt, where Julius Caesar has encountered its goddess-queen Cleopatra. Gordianus becomes the crux of the complex power struggle between Caesar and Pompey and Cleopatra and her brother-husband Ptolemy, themselves vying for Egypt's throne, when Meto is charged with attempting to poison Caesar and Cleopatra. Gordianus, wracked by enormous personal loss when Bethesda vanishes near a Nile shrine to Osiris, embarks on a dangerous investigation to try to save Meto. As the decency of old republican Rome that Gordianus has struggled so long to preserve crumbles around him, Gordianus pays a heavy price for being what Cicero called him: "the last honest man in Rome" (*Mist* 46).

Novels: *Roman Blood* (1991); *Arms of Nemesis* (1992); *Catalina's Riddle* (1993); *The Venus Throw* (1995); *A Murder on the Appian Way* (1996); *Rubicon* (1999); *Last Seen in Massilia* (2000); *A Mist of Prophecies* (2002); *The Judgment of Caesar* (2004).

Short fiction: *The House of the Vestals* (1997); *A Gladiator Dies Only Once* (2005).

Under pseudonym Aaron Travis: Several gay-related novels and many short stories.

Stand-alone historical novel: *A Twist at the End: A Novel of O. Henry* (2000), based on the life of American writer.

Selected sources: Fletcher, Connie. Rev. of *Last Seen in Massilia*. *Booklist*, April 15, 1999: 1484; Picker, Leonard. "Murder and Cleopatra: *PW* Talks to Steven Saylor." *Publishers Weekly*, May 10, 2004: 40; *Publishers Weekly*. Rev. of *A Mist of Prophecies*. April 15, 2002: 45; *Publishers Weekly*. Rev. of *Rubicon*, April 12, 1999: 57; Smith, Clay. "Author Literatus." *Austin Chronicle*, www.auschron.com/issues/vol18/issue44, November 3, 2000. Interview with Steven Saylor.

Major awards: Lambda Literary Award for gay men's mystery, 1994; Critics' Choice Award, 1995.

See also: John Maddox Robert's Decius Caecilius Metellus series, also set in the first century B.C.; Lindsey Davis's **Marcus Didius Falco** series, set in the A.D. 70s; Rosemary Rowe's series featuring manumitted slave Libertus in the reign of Emperor Commodus (A.D. 180–192); Marilyn Todd's Claudia Seferius series, set in ancient Rome.

Liz Graham

Profession:	Police detective, Castlemere C.I.D.
Living situation:	Married to Brian Graham, art teacher, Castle High
Geographic locale:	"Castlemere" in England's Fen Country
Time period:	1993–present
Associates:	Frank Shapiro, Liz Graham's superior, and Caolan "Cal" Donovan, her subordinate
Concerns:	Integrity of police; justice

Award-winning journalist Jo Bannister at first wrote science fiction novels, then traditional British cozy mysteries in a short series starring former physician turned mystery author Clio Rees and Chief Inspector Harry Marsh and international thrillers that led to her Mickey Flynn series, full of international intrigue and violence. Bannister's third series, set in fictional Castlemere in Britain's brooding Fen Country near Cambridge, features an unlikely trinity of beleaguered police detectives: young, fey, and temperamental Ulsterman Sergeant Cal Donovan; fiftyish avuncular Jewish-but-not-kosher Detective Chief Inspector Frank Shapiro; and bright, stable, upwardly-aiming Inspector Elizabeth "Liz" Ward Graham, who stands between Shapiro and Donovan in rank, age, personality, and other telling respects.

Praised by a *Publishers Weekly* reviewer for the "depth and intensity" of her major characters and for their ability to cope simultaneously with several major crimes, Bannister firmly maintains that "entertainment is the writer's side of the contract"

(*CA Online*). The Castlemere procedural series entertains chiefly through the intricate development of the relationship between Graham, Shapiro, and Donovan as the cases they work twist around each other in bleak urban desolation. As introduced in *A Bleeding of Innocents* (1993), Inspector Liz Graham is transferred to Castlemere to help D.C.I. Shapiro after another detective has been killed. Tall, square-faced, fair-haired and ruddy-cheeked, a horsewoman since childhood, fit and handsome rather than beautiful (*Changelings* 174), Liz is the daughter of county gentleman Edgar Ward, a former Hunt Secretary, who tacitly disapproves of Brian Graham, Liz's sensitive, perceptive, and endearing art-teacher husband. On her way up faster than most women in the British police system, Liz has to work hard, bite her lips often, and use plenty of tact to win over the men of Castlemere C.I.D. As her superior, Shapiro enjoys her respect and everyone else's for his practical, self-effacing leadership, while sullen and intuitive Cal Donovan constantly challenges Liz's patience and diplomacy.

By *A Taste for Burning* (1995), the three have securely bonded. With Shapiro accused of sabotaging the investigation of an eight-year-old arson case and suspended, Liz takes over the case just when a pyromaniac who has already struck three times threatens a newly opened shopping mall with hundreds of potential victims. Shapiro is nearing retirement; his marriage has failed from work-related tensions and he's alienated from his "average shiftless twenty-three-year-old son" (*Taste* 15). Shapiro's relationship with Liz and Donovan now is nearly familial, yielding dividends most of their associates can't see: caring more about his work than most cops do, Donovan seems frustrated and intolerant to them, while Shapiro after thirty years can effortlessly think more effectively than any other detective can. Shapiro gets Donovan to do masterful leg-work and in return, Donovan gets to work with an "unacknowledged master"—Shapiro—of their profession (*Taste* 16). Others often call Liz Graham "a nice woman," but her green eyes conceal a core of adamant. She works well with both Shapiro and Donovan, effectively holding a rank that makes her rare as a woman in a tough man's world: "Nice women don't do that" (*Taste* 50). She supports Donovan's freewheeling hunches even when they seem to scuttle her own favorite theories, and she forthrightly admits to Shapiro that she doesn't have his experience and consistently asks and follows his advice. In solving *A Taste for Burning*, which involves intense racial prejudice, all three realize that they've fought it all their own lives: Liz as a woman, Donovan as an Irishman, and Shapiro as a Jew in England.

In *Changelings* (2000), the strengths of the team have become their weaknesses. A diabolical blackmailer is terrorizing Castlemere and local merchants are wavering in their resolve not to give in to threats. Shapiro, fifty-six, overweight, and recovering from a bullet wound in the back, is ready to take the public's heat to protect his Queen Street force—especially Liz, whom all three of them want to get his job when he retires, and Donovan, who's psychologically shaky from too many injuries in too short a time. Until Shapiro gently chides her, Liz can't see that by singlemindedly pursuing criminals she's been doing to her own marriage what Shapiro now regrets doing to his. Donovan, also recuperating from a four-month-old line-of-duty gunshot, goes missing on his canal boat *Tara* with his pit bull Brian Boru and incipient pneumonia, sending matter-of-fact Liz into near panic. After inheriting Donovan from her predecessor, Liz has endured his moods, his temper, his cavalier disregard for police procedure because she knows he fights as hard with his heart as Shapiro does with his head (*Changelings* 67), and when circumstances indicate that Donovan has drowned, Liz's stability vanishes, and she breaks down while interrogating a suspect.

When this case explosively closes, Shapiro reestablishes a relationship with his ex-wife Angela, confirmed loner Cal Donovan takes a forlorn handicapped child into his life, and Liz Graham, shaken by shooting a killer to defend a children's hospital, relaxes her grip on her career and follows Shapiro's advice—"Put your head up, and get your head straight"—and she goes home to Brian (*Changelings* 374). By confronting their own weaknesses in the line of their duty, Shapiro, Donovan, and Liz have all become "changelings."

Novels (Castlemere series): *A Bleeding of Innocents* (1993); *Charisma* (1994; in U.K. *Sins of the Heart*); *A Taste for Burning* (1995; in U.K. *Desires*); *No Birds Sing* (1996); *Broken Lines* (1998); *The Hireling's Tale* (1999); *Changelings* (2000).

Other series: Clio Rees, ex-doctor—now mystery writer—and Chief Inspector Harry Marsh series; Mickey Flynn series (hard-hitting action); former pathologist, now newspaper advice columnist Rosie Holland series (1998, 2000); the Brodie Farrell series, including *Breaking Faith* (2005).

Other works: Early in her career, Bannister published three science fiction novels. She has also written several stand-alone crime/detection novels, notably *Gilgamesh* (1989), *The Lazarus Hotel* (1997), and *The Fifth Cataract* (2006).

Selected sources: Klett, Rex E. Rev. of *The Hireling's Tale*. *Library Journal*, December 1999: 191; Klett, Rex E. Rev. of *The Depths of Solitude*. *Library Journal*, December 1, 2004: 95; Miller, Stuart. Rev. of *Changelings*. *Booklist*, February 15, 2000: 1087; *Publishers Weekly*. Rev. of *Broken Lines*, February 22, 1999: 70; *Publishers Weekly*. Rev. of *Changelings*, October 16, 2000: 52; *Publishers Weekly*. Rev. of *The Hireling's Tale*, November 29, 1999: 56; *Publishers Weekly*. Rev. of *No Birds Sing*, July 15, 1996: 63.

Major awards: Northern Ireland Press Award, 1981; Edgar Allan Poe Award nomination, 1993.

See also: David Lawrence's Detective Stella Mooney series, set in London; Lynda LaPlante's DCI Jane Tennant series; Jill McGown's Chief Inspector Lloyd and Sergeant (later Inspector) Judy Hill series.

Cordelia Gray

Profession:	Amateur detective
Living situation:	Single
Geographic locale:	Cambridge and Dorset, England
Time period:	1972–1982
Nemesis:	Prejudice against women as detectives

Significant relationship: Adoration of Adam Dalgliesh from afar

Concern: Proving detection is a suitable job for a woman

Her creator P.D. James has noted that she identifies with Cordelia Gray and enjoyed working with "a youngish woman, vulnerable, but I think courageous in setting out regardless" (quoted in Herbert 87). By far less complex and intriguing a sleuth than. James's illustrious Scotland Yard Commander Adam Dalgliesh, young Cordelia Gray brings "no qualifications or relevant past experience . . . and indeed no capital except her slight but tough twenty-two-year-old body, [and] a considerable intelligence" as well as a little shorthand and typing (*Unsuitable Job* 9, 31) to running Pryde's Detective Agency when her mentor and business partner Bernie Pryde unexpectedly commits suicide, but she seems to thrive on it.

Cordelia endured an uncomfortably Spartan upbringing, since her mother died when she was only a hour old, and her father, "an itinerant Marxist poet and amateur revolutionary" had to choose between toting her from grim lodging to lodging with his Marxist comrades and setting her out into a succession of foster homes. Cordelia's schooling at the Convent of the Immaculate Conception, short on science but long on literature, stood her in good stead in her first case, aptly titled *An Unsuitable Job for a Woman* (Herbert 87). She is hired to investigate the death of young, well-to-do Mark Callender, found hanging by his neck with a picture of a nude woman nearby. Able to identify literary references at the drop of a quotation, Cordelia perseveres in untangling a plot full of twisted motivations and desires.

She also possesses a thoroughly modern sensibility about sex, which allows her perhaps a more objective view of the victim's romantic associations than a older—or male—detective might have had. Recalling her own two lovers, Cordelia "had never thought of virginity as other than a temporary and inconvenient state" (*Unsuitable Job* 112)—the nuns had clearly not made much impression on her in this regard—and concluded that "Lovemaking . . . was overrated, not painful but surprising" (*Unsuitable Job* 112).

Cordelia can also draw on her mentor Bernie's recollections of Adam Dalgliesh, with whom Bernie had worked when Dalgliesh was a Detective Inspector. According to Bernie, Dalgliesh's minute knowledge of gun handling had trapped more than one murderer who had tried to pass the crime off as suicide. When Cordelia, who had earlier sent a hand-picked bouquet of flowers to Dalgliesh when he was in hospital in *The Black Tower*, tests out that gun-handling theory, she discovers the truth about Callender's death.

Cordelia Gray's only other case, *The Skull Beneath the Skin* (1982), occurs in an island castle with a violent history off the Dorset coast amid a private performance of the blood-curdling Jacobean revenge tragedy *The Duchess of Malfi*. Engaged as a bodyguard to aging actress Clarissa Lisle, who is staging the show as a means of regenerating her career, Cordelia manages to unmask a wily killer through cool deduction, meticulous research, and physical courage in a moldering crypt, using "her sanity, her honesty, her memory, her nerve" (*Skull* 327). Dalgliesh does not appear even as a reminiscence here.

James may have briefly considered Cordelia Gray as a possible match for complex, brooding detective-poet Adam Dalgliesh, but since she chose not to continue Cordelia's detective career, James seems to have abandoned that notion. "I suppose I *approve* of Cordelia very much," James once commented (Herbert 87), but approval, in the end, was not enough to sustain Cordelia Gray—for either James or Dalgliesh.

Novels: *An Unsuitable Job for a Woman* (1972); *The Skull Beneath the Skin* (1982). See also **Adam Dalgliesh**.

Autobiography: *A Time to be in Earnest: A Fragment of an Autobiography*. New York: Knopf, 2000.

Selected sources: *Newsweek*. Rev. of *The Skull Beneath the Skin*, September 13, 1982; *New York Times Book Review*. Rev. of *The Skull Beneath the Skin*, September 12, 1982; *New York Times Book Review*. Rev. of *An Unsuitable Job for a Woman*, January 16, 1972; *Times Literary Supplement*. Rev. of *The Skull Beneath the Skin*, October 29, 1982; *Washington Post Book World*. Rev. of *The Skull Beneath the Skin*, September 19, 1982.

Awards: See **Adam Dalgliesh**.

See also: Women private investigators, especially the intrepid British variety, starting with Zelda Popkin's five-novel Mary Carney series (1938–1942); Gale Gallegher's two novels (1947 and 1949) featuring a woman PI of the same name; Jo Bannister's Brodie Farrell series; Liza Cody's contemporary **Anna Lee** series, with Lee taking a minor role in Cody's Eva "Bucket Nut" Wylie series as well; Mick Herron's Zoë Boehm series, set in Oxford; for a European woman PI, Cara Black's Aimée Leduc series, set in Paris.

Marshal Salvatore Guarnaccia

Profession:	Marshal of the Carabinieri
Living situation:	Married
Geographic locale:	Florence, Tuscany, Italy
Time period:	1981–present
Associates:	Various Carabinieri subordinates
Nemesis:	Substitute Prosecutor Virgilio Fusarri
Significant relationship:	Teresa Guarnaccia, his wife
Concerns:	Morality; sympathy for the underdog

As an English expatriate in Florence since 1975, Magdalen Nabb effectively uses a dual perspective in her Marshal Guarnaccia detective novels. The first novels highlight Tuscany's "expat" community seen through Guarnaccia's personal and professional eyes as an NCO of the Carabinieri, Italy's spiffy black-uniformed national police, while the later ones focus on the essential and sometimes fatal secrecy of Florentine life, both native and expatriate, as Guarnaccia, a transplanted Sicilian, sees them, although both perspectives function significantly in all of Guarnaccia's cases.

Like Conan Doyle's portrayal of London and George Simenon's of Paris, Nabb's depiction of the sinister effect beautiful Tuscany exerts on her characters is vital to her stories. The pipe-smoking Marshal's literary ancestry, however, is not English but European. Featuring "the most Maigret-like of contemporary policemen" (Ashley 357), the Marshal's first case, *Death of an Englishman* (1981), won high praise from Nabb's mentor Simenon. Nabb may also have drawn on Leonardo Sciascia's detective novels illustrating the differences between Sicilians and other Italians (Murphy 361).

Guarnaccia's young Carabinieri-in-training Bacci in *Death of an Englishman* does "not like the Marshal because he was Sicilian and he suspected him of being, if not actually Mafia, at least *Mafioso*, and he knew that the Marshal knew of his suspicion and even encouraged it" (*Englishman* 9). The Marshal himself reminds Bacci that some "things are beyond you... because you're a Florentine. These are things that any Sicilian over the age of five knows by experience" (*Englishman* 53).

The Marshal also physically offends Bacci, being fat and fortyish like Maigret, another "transplanted provincial" (Murphy 321), and afflicted with eyes that stream uncontrollably in sunlight, perhaps a not-so-subtle clue to his enormous sympathy for humanity. Being young, vigorous, and full of himself, Bacci spends most of *Death of an Englishman* learning from the Marshal how to begin to be a detective—one who relies on understanding the psychology of daily life, especially among the lower classes often trapped into crime by circumstances or "simple human folly" (*Silk Stalkings* 71), to solve his cases. Just as tenacious as Sherlock Holmes but far more compassionate toward the criminals he tracks, the Marshal fights off a nasty case of flu to unmask the murderer, even as he reminds Bacci to "give up chasing buses and generally looking for excitement and... keep your eyes firmly fixed on the ordinary details of life" (*Englishman* 168).

After *Death of a Dutchman* (1982), *Death in Springtime* (1983), and *Death in Autumn* (1985), cases involving dead or missing foreigners, Marshal Guarnaccia probes bitter World War II memories in *The Marshal and the Murderer* (1987) and the misery of Florence's 1966 flood in *The Marshal and the Madwoman* (1988). He returns to the relationships between Italians and foreigners in later novels, especially *The Marshal at the Villa Torrini* (1993), where an Englishman is believed to have drowned his wife in the bathtub.

2001's *Property of Blood*, arguably the Marshal's darkest case, treats not physical homicide but the destruction of a woman's personality through kidnapping, a crime often masterminded by Tuscan criminals for ransom and implemented by Sardinian shepherds in the gloomy hills above Florence. The victim, up-and-coming fashion designer Olivia Birkett, widow of Conte Ugo Brunamonti, tells her story to the Marshal, while in parallel flashbacks "he conducts the silence... his strongest professional weapon" to rescue her (*Property* 37). While he interviews Olivia's son and daughter and her associates, servants, and friends, the Marshal's brain is "filming every fleeting expression, his ears recording every word but listening for the ones she didn't say" (*Property* 38). As the NCO assigned to steer Olivia's family through the ordeal, the Marshal has to let his superiors, ambitious Captain Maestrangelo and the strangely ominous Substitute Prosecutor Virgilio Fusarri, manage the case, but when Marshal Guarnaccia settles down "like a bulldog" the Captain sensibly allows him to develop the solution.

The Marshal's success depends on discovering what troubles his own soul about the case, something staring him in the face that he cannot see (*Property* 110) until his wife Teresa's *spaghetti alla mollica*, hefty red wine, and calm support restore the Marshal's soul. Like Maigret, he enjoys a happy marriage, especially after his wife and the two children he adores join him in Florence, and after a good night's rest at Teresa's comforting side, he wakes refreshed, the mists cleared from his mind, and he sees suddenly "what was in front of his nose": a "barking mad" daughter obsessed with hatred for the mother who sacrifices everything for her (*Property* 157, 175). Though Marshal Guarnaccia cannot change the outcome of this sad case, he has the satisfaction of solving it; he realizes, "You couldn't work up a television documentary about a dull NCO in a country village ... [and] an equally unimportant marshal from a small station in Florence who had listened to him" (*Property* 235). In *The Innocent* (2005), when a woman's body is discovered in Florence's Boboli Gardens, Guarnaccia uncovers the killer but wishes this time he had not, feeling not quite a native, not quite an outsider in his native Italy. By appearing to do nothing important, like Inspector Maigret, Marshal Guarnaccia really does everything—and of course his superiors get the glory.

Novels: *Death of an Englishman* (1981); *Death of a Dutchman* (1982); *Death in Springtime* (1983); *Death in Autumn* (1985); *The Marshal and the Murderer* (1987); *The Marshal and the Madwoman* (1988); *The Marshal's Own Case* (1990); *The Marshal Makes his Report* (1991); *The Marshal at the Villa Torrini* (1993); *The Marshal and the Forgery* (1995); *The Monster of Florence* (1996); *Property of Blood* (2001); *Some Bitter Taste* (2002); *The Innocent* (2005).

Stand-alone novel coauthored with Paolo Vagheggi: *The Prosecutor* (1986).

Selected sources: *Bookseller*. "Solving the Bloody Crimes of Florence," October 18, 2002: 30; Fraser, Antonia. "Skulduggery in Florence." *Spectator*, April 12, 2003: 37; Kim, Ann. Rev. of *The Innocent*. *Library Journal*, June 1, 2005: 106; Klett, Rex E. Rev. of *Property of Blood*. *Library Journal*, September 1, 2001: 238; Ott, Bill. Rev. of *Some Bitter Taste*. *Booklist*, September 15, 2002: 210; Pearl, Nancy. "Mysterious Europe: Crime in the Old World." *Library Journal*, April 3, 2003: 156.

Major award: British Crime Writers' Association award for best first novel, 1981.

See also: Andrea Camilleri's Sicilian Inspector Salvo Montalbano series; Michael Dibdin's Commissario **Aurelio Zen** series, in various Italian settings; John Spencer Hill's **Carlo Arbati** series; David Hewson's **Nic Costa** series; Donna Leon's Commisario **Guido Brunetti** series, set in Venice; Timothy Williams's Commissario Trotti series.

Arly Hanks

Profession:	Police Chief
Living situation:	Divorced
Geographic locale:	Rural Arkansas
Time period:	1987–present
Associate:	None
Nemeses:	Ruby Bee Hanks and Estelle Oppers
Significant relationship:	Jack Wallace (in later books)
Concern:	Social issues in rural America

Welcome to rural Maggody, Arkansas, population 755, struggling despondently for a half mile along both sides of a state highway in the Ozarks (*Malice in Maggody* 18). Here almost all the inhabitants are eccentric and most of the visitors from outside are venal, corrupt, or just plain "tetched"—home base for Joan Hess's award-winning cozy series that often shifts convincingly to genuine pathos. Native daughter Ariel "Arly" Hanks, Maggody's first woman police chief, escaped from Maggody to college, then briefly married a Manhattan advertising hotshot who left her for a "blond and mindless" model specializing in foot commercials (*Muletrain to Maggody* 1). Arly "wished them happiness, herpes, and bunions" (*Malice in Maggody* 18), got a quick and ugly divorce, and returned to lick her wounds in Maggody, where her mother Ruby Bee (Rubella Belinda) runs the town's only bar and grill as well as the six-unit Flamingo Inn, referred to by locals as the Maggody Stork Club (*Malice in Maggody* 20).

Throughout the series, Ruby Bee and her best friend, fire-engine-red-haired Estelle Oppers, proprietor and sole operator of Estelle's Hair Fantasies, conspire with the rest of Maggody "to prevent law and order from ever settling in permanently in their fair burg" (*Silk Stalkings: More* 77). Constantly engineering ploys to get Arly married off and producing grandbabies, Ruby Bee and Estelle launch their own black projects in every novel, obstructing Arly's attempts to solve the hilarious crimes that Maggody citizens and "furriners" keep perpetrating.

From *Murder in Maggody* (1987) through *Malpractice in Maggody* (2006), Chief Arly Hanks stands dead center in the clash between outside cultures and Maggody's stubborn backwoodsy rural traditions. In most of her cases, some exterior force—a Hollywood film crew in *Mortal Remains in Maggody*, a raunchy evangelical religious sect in *Miracles in Maggody*, the pornographic lure of the Internet in *murder@maggody.com*, burning-eyed fanatic Civil War reenactors in *Muletrain to Maggody*, even *Martians in Maggody*—invades Maggody's space, the locals retaliate, and Arly has to deal with the body or bodies that result.

Because she grew up in Maggody, Arly is virtually unshockable. She manages Technicolor inbred hill and holler dwellers, named and described with gleeful hyperbole and aplomb, like Brother Verber, the mail-order diploma'd pastor of the Voice of the Almighty Lord Assembly Hall whose sermons cover lust, adultery, perversion, and fornication, all frontally featured in his closetful of well-thumbed magazines (*Muletrain to Maggody* 36). Arly can face down even Raz Buchanon, "ornery, foul-mouthed, and most likely a soldier in Satan's army" (*Muletrain to Maggody* 35) and moonshiner extraordinaire, leading the pack of barbaric Buchanons, so interrelated Arly has long since quit trying to untangle them.

Despite all the obstacles these wild characters drop into her path, Arly Hanks couldn't be better suited for her job of sifting through the subterfuge and separating the meager wheat from the clouds of pernicious chaff (*Silk Stalkings: More* 78). Under all the humor, though, the real miseries of America's rural needy stand out clearly through Arly's perceptive eyes. She reflects that a depressed rural area offers little or no future to its young people: "everybody remotely my age [mid-thirties] had been married for more than fifteen years and had grubby children, leaky washing machines, unpaid bills, and lifetime subscriptions to *TV Guide* and the *National Enquirer*" (*Muletrain to Maggody* 17–18). Senile old Hospiss Buchanon represents the failure of social programs to help the elderly poor: "She steals the plastic flowers from the [cemetery] plots and tries to sell them to tourists driving through town," Ruby Bee tells Arly. "Just last fall Estelle and me took her some sweaters and a few blankets we bought at a flea market. It ain't like any of the high-minded members of the Missionary Society would see fit to help her out" (*Muletrain to Maggody* 180). Arly does manage to place young Hammet, a feral illegitimate Buchanon, in a foster home, because with his single mother, he and his siblings subsisted mainly on corn meal and rice "Her" bought by selling "'seng and hooch" and assorted favors, and a couple of times a year they'd even have "fatback and black-eyed peas" (*Muletrain to Maggody* 219).

Arly Hanks so tirelessly treads the thin line between Maggody's human comedies and its savage social injustices that she deserves some fun and frolic of her own. Toothsome Jack Wallace appears first in *Maggody and the Moonbeams* and later, during *Muletrain to Maggody*, Arly spirits him off for beer, Scrabble, and skinny-dipping dalliance in her private sanctuary at Boone Creek. Though she's not ready to abandon Maggody just yet, she's looking forward to vacation time with Jack. Maggody, Arkansas, its broadly gut-busting surface covering a multitude of all-too-real sins, surely has its moments. Arly Hanks would say, "Yeah, right."

Novels: *Malice in Maggody* (1987); *Mischief in Maggody* (1988); *Much Ado in Maggody* (1989); *Madness in Maggody* (1990); *Mortal Remains in Maggody* (1991); *Maggody in Manhattan* (1992); *O Little Town of Maggody* (1993); *Martians in Maggody* (1994); *Miracles in Maggody* (1995); *The Maggody Militia* (1997); *Misery Loves Maggody* (1998); *murder@maggody.com* (2000); *Maggody and the Moonbeams* (2001); *Muletrain to Maggody* (2004); *Malpractice in Maggody* (2006).

Other series: bookseller Claire Malloy series, set in fictional Farberville, Arkansas; Theo Bloomer series (as Joan Hadley), botanical mysteries.

Short stories: *Death of a Romance Writer* (2002).

Other works: Hess also wrote young adult mysteries for Silhouette.

Selected sources: *Armchair Detective*. Rev. of *Miracles in Maggody*, Fall 1995: 457; *Booklist*. Rev. of *Miracles in Maggody*, September 1, 1995: 46; *Publishers Weekly*. Rev. of *The Maggody Militia*, September 1, 1997: 36; *Publishers Weekly*. Rev. of *Muletrain to Maggody*, January 26, 2004: 234; Stasio, Marilyn. Rev. of *Maggody in Manhattan*. *New York Times Book Review*, October 18, 1992: 40.

Awards: American Mystery Award, 1990, for *A Diet to Die For*; Agatha and Macavity Awards, 1991.

See also: Jeff Abbott's Jordan Poteet series, featuring Poteet as a small-town librarian in Mirabeau, Texas; Deborah Adams's Jesus Creek series, set in rural Tennessee; K.C. Constantine's police chief Mario Balzic series, set in Rocksburg, Pennsylvania; Carolyn G. Hart's **Annie Laurance Darling** in the Death on Demand series featuring Annie's eponymous mystery bookstore in Broward's Rock, South Carolina, and Hart's "Henrie O" series featuring retired reporter Henrietta O'Dwyer Collins; Frederick Ramsay's series set in Picketsville, Virginia, featuring Sheriff Ike Schwartz; Charlotte Weir's series featuring Kansas police chief Susan Wren.

Debut novel: Judy Clemens's *Till the Cows Come Home*, featuring motorcycle-riding Stella Crown and set in Pennsylvania dairy country.

Colin Harpur

Profession:	Chief Superintendent, C.I.D.
Living situation:	Married, then widowed
Geographic location:	Unnamed Midlands city north of London
Time period:	1985–present

Associate:	Assistant Chief Constable Desmond Iles
Significant relationship:	In early novels, Ruth Avery
Concerns:	Crime-fighting; amorality

Like other writers who explore the drab grey no-man's-land of crime fighting in contemporary northern Britain, prolific Welsh author Bill James concerns himself in his Harpur and Iles series primarily with the disturbing moral issue of how far to use evil to fight evil (Ashley 248). James also explores the equally murky relationships between police and criminals, using what fellow crime author Peter Gutteridge calls "achingly funny" situations to point up the dark ironies of a British policeman's lot today.

Detective Chief Superintendent Colin Harpur and Assistant Chief Constable Desmond Iles are numbers three and two respectively in their unnamed north-of-England police force. They serve in a Masonic Lodge–run force (though Harpur is not a Mason) with a reputation for violent interrogations almost as powerful as its rivalry with a neighboring Irish-Catholic constabulary that the machiavellian Iles detests and the essentially decent Harpur respects. Harpur, a "fair-haired Rocky Marciano," likes to think of himself as a "kid-glove cop," but in introspective moments, he ruefully acknowledges that he often looks like a "thuggish-looking, threatening snoop" (*Lolita Man* 90, 152). Through their long and complicated association, Harpur has learned what makes the elegant, erratic, intuitive Iles tick: "[Iles] yearned to be responsible and good, and to sound responsible and good.... The trouble was that a kind of ravening selfishness would now and then slink up on its belly and rip the throat out of this intention... like a Miracle Play version of the fallibility of Man" (*Lolita Man* 99–100). Through the series, Iles's foul-mouthed flights of fancy mount into frothy-muzzled near-paranoia, while Harpur's responses become more and more laconic, eventually reducing to "Thank you, sir's" that only partially camouflage Harpur's bedeviled feelings of uselessness as he fights not only the villains around them but his own inner weaknesses—like his affair with Iles's wife.

In the earlier novels, Harpur and his own wife Megan, whose fling with Harpur's former superior had earlier landed Harpur his present high rank, tacitly agreed not to pry into one another's lives, but little affection, though some genuine respect, remains between them. Harpur often relied on Megan's sharp mind and her sense of balance for significant clues to solving a crime, as in *The Lolita Man* (1986), where Harpur, full of anger, loathing, and fright for the city's children, tracks the serial killer of five teenage girls, mousy wallflowers with fevered romantic imaginations. When the killer's next target becomes his friend's daughter Cheryl-Anne, Harpur himself, who can't face looking at more murdered children, leaves his nicely typed documents and supervisory duties for old-fashioned basic shoe-leather detection (*Lolita Man* 38), haunting Cheryl-Anne's expensive girls' school close to the home of Harpur's current lover, Ruth Avery. While lying in wait for his quarry, Harpur realizes that he may wants this case over so badly because he may understand the killer too well. One afternoon after he studies a bikini-clad Cheryl-Anne sunning with his daughters, Harpur goes inside to Megan's literary discussion group where, sensing and loathing within himself the instinct of the predator—"A cop could come to resemble his quarry, the resemblance was so close" (*Lolita Man* 54)—Harpur, because of his own attraction to young girls, begins to deduce the identity of the killer.

While Harpur obsesses over protecting Cheryl-Anne Day, Iles's perfervid hatred for the neighboring Irish Catholic police and his career-enhancing dirty tricks swell into blackmail of Harpur and nasty skullduggery toward his opposite numbers. Against Iles's vocal opposition and ultimately without Iles's knowledge, Harpur lends a hand to Mark Lane, his opposite number on the Catholic force, in return getting his help in nabbing the killer. Lane later becomes Chief Constable, the principal target for Iles's brutal underhanded conniving and the object of Harpur's sympathy when the job eventually drives Lane into a nervous breakdown.

After Megan's death, Harpur takes up with Debbie, a pretty young college student who in *Gospel* (1992) becomes involved with associates of one of Harpur's informers, a wealthy, powerful, and exceptionally dangerous man (Stilwell 275). Debbie also becomes the pawn in a gangland vendetta. Harpur's attempts to infiltrate the local criminal overlords' organization dominate the rest of his cases, counterpointed by Chief Constable Lane's mental-emotional deterioration and Desmond Iles's incessant scheming for Lane's position. In *Kill Me* (2000), Harpur's complex undercover operation against local drug dealers collapses into a bloody shootout. Harpur's agent Naomi Anstruther loses both her former lover and a young man with whom she'd shared a rebound affair. Harpur, whose proclivity for keeping things to himself has intensified over the years, hovers mostly in the background, refusing to rise to Iles's increasingly hysterical bait of "wife-fits," and trying to protect both Naomi and the Chief from Iles while attempting to stop local villains and encroaching London crime bosses in their slimy tracks. In *The Girl with the Long Back* (2004), Iles is in trouble, with a contract out on his life and the prospect of a new, tough Chief Constable to replace Lane, but "It dismayed Harpur to think of [Iles] crushed and humbled, though God knew such a malevolent, pirouetting, egomaniac vandal half deserved it.... Diminish Iles and you could undermine life's whole fragile structure" (*Girl* 287). Gangster leader Mansel Shale once related a bleak, black irony of today's law enforcement to Harpur: both Shale and Chief Lane live in former church rectories, "a worthwhile link with each other and organized religion" (*Kill Me* 257). Turf conflicts between homegrown villains like Shale and Panicking Ralph Ember and encroaching big-city hoodlums continues in *Easy Streets*, where Harpur not only has to solve a fatal fire bombing on his patch but deal with the pretentiousness and venality of his immediate superior Desmond Iles. Such parallels between the motivations and methods of the crooks and the cops who pursue them make Colin Harpur the man in the middle, flawed but decent, doing his best in a world that forgives him even less than he does himself.

Novels: *You'd Better Believe It* (1985); *The Lolita Man* (1986); *Halo Parade* (1987); *Protection* (1988); *Come Clean* (1989); *Take* (1990); *Club* (1991); *Astride a Grave* (1991); *Gospel* (1992); *Roses, Roses* (1993); *In Good Hands* (1994); *The Detective Is Dead* (1995); *Top Banana* (1996); *Panicking Ralph* (1997); *Lovely Mover* (1998); *Eton Crop* (1999); *Kill Me* (2000); *Pay Days* (2001); *The Girl with the Long Back* (2004); *Easy Streets* (2005).

Other series: Under "David Craig": the Roy Rickman trilogy, featuring a Home Office Agent in a near-future Britain close to becoming a Soviet satellite state; the Bellecroix and Roath series; the David Brade series, set in James's native Cardiff and teaming detectives Brade and Clyndwr Jenkins; the DC Sally Bithron series, set in Cardiff.

Stand-alone novels: James has written several stand-alone novels, including *Whose Little Girl Are You?* (1974), appearing under the name "David Craig." James used "James Tucker" for *Blaze of Rust* (1979), but changed that short series' authorship to "Bill James" and in 1998 began a series about female detective Kerry Lake, authoring its first two novels as " Judith Jones," and for the third resuming "Bill James."

Selected sources: Baker, John F. "Hot Deals." *Publishers Weekly*, November 8, 2004: 11; Colmes, Alan. Interview with Bill James. *Hannity and Colmes (Fox News)*, January 11, 2005; Plagens, Peter. Rev. of *The Girl With the Long Back*. *Newsweek*, April 5, 2004: 58; *Publishers Weekly*. Rev. of *The Girl With the Long Back*, February 2, 2004: 42; Stasio, Marilyn. Rev. of *The Girl With the Long Back*. *New York Times Book Review*, March 28, 2004: 12.

See also: John Harvey's series featuring Nottingham police detective Charlie Resnick; William McIlvanney's award-winning Inspector Jack Laidlaw series, set in Glasgow; Ian Rankin's "tartan *noir*" series featuring Edinburgh Inspector **John Rebus**; Roy Lewis's police procedural Inspector John Crow series, set in the north of England; and for black humor, Peter Gutteridge's Nick Madrid series.

Dr. Tony Hill

Profession:	Clinical psychologist and profiler
Living situation:	Single
Geographic locale:	Principally northern England; in *The Last Temptation*, northern Europe
Time period:	1995–present
Associate:	Detective Carol Jordan
Nemeses:	Sexual inadequacies; self-doubt
Concern:	Serial killings

After her two earlier series featuring lesbian Scottish journalist Lindsay Gordon and private detective Kate Brannigan, Scottish journalist, playwright, and author Val McDermid opened her new contemporary thriller series—since adapted for television—with *The Mermaids Singing* (1995). The series features tormented clinical psychologist Dr. Tony Hill, who is just beginning his career in criminal profiling, and homicide Detective Inspector Carol Jordan, who is fighting her way upward in a hostile male-dominated profession.

Carol finds Tony Hill a "suffering healer" outwardly attractive to women: "Around five-eight, slim, good shoulders...short dark hair, side parting, dark eyes, probably blue...wide mouth, lower lip fuller than upper. Shame about the dress sense, though....Probably he wasn't married or in a permanent relationship" (*Mermaids* 21). Carol overlooks Hill's struggles with personal inadequacies only he can see in himself.

A domineering mother's constant dismissal of him as "contemptible" rendered him impotent, a psychological disorder he compulsively hides, though his training insists that he should reveal it in order to face and conquer it. Chameleon-like, each day he selects a different persona to show the outside world, choices he makes out of knowledge, skill, and necessity, façades behind which he struggles through his daily crises, like the stage fright that prevented him from pursuing an academic career and still nearly incapacitates him when he has to address an audience.

After three grisly gay-related homicides fictional frozen-North "Bradfield's" press has labeled "Queer Killings," Assistant Chief Constable (Crime) John Brandon calls on Hill, presently engaged in setting up the National Criminal Profiling Task Force, to convince Bradfield's weary, wary police that they should support, even join, this vanguard of a revolution in crime fighting. To the disgust of old-fashioned cat-o'-nine-tails-preferring coppers like Superintendent Tom Cross, Brandon also assigns Carol Jordan as Hill's liaison. While Carol finds herself immediately drawn to Hill, she cannot understand why he constantly repels her subtle unspoken advances.

Both Tony Hill and Carol Jordan are edgy outsiders in Bradfield. Originally from Warwick, Carol took the fast track into the Met after university at Manchester; Hill, from Halifax, studied at London University, then at Oxford for a D.Phil., and spent eight years in special hospitals. Carol appreciates that Tony treats her as an equal, and she enjoys sharing with him their primary mission of discovering the serial murderer, far more satisfactory than fielding ego-boosting pitches tossed her way by many of her male colleagues (*Mermaids* 53). Hill's stomach lurches, though, every time Carol attempts a playful personal remark. He first puzzles her, then annoys her as a woman, while he remains convinced that the "damaged man" inside him is an incurable emotional and sexual cripple (*Mermaids* 72).

Unable to achieve a physical relationship with any woman, Hill discovered earlier during research into the British telephone sex industry that the best physical release he can hope for is a frustratingly nonclimactic degree of sexual stimulation via the husky contralto of "Angelica," who frequently initiates suggestive calls to him. This practice fills him with bitter self-disgust and throws his personal and professional lives out of balance. As the search for Bradfield's cunning serial murderer heats up and more bodies appear with ever more diabolical evidences of torture, Hill seeks within himself insight into the murderer's psyche, but in a shattering self-realization he sees that because he himself is the killer's mirror image, only hunting the killer can keep Tony Hill from being like him.

In reading the killer's diary, Hill realizes that "These were the footsteps of his own personal nemesis that he was tracing, and it was an uncomfortable journey.... [H]e had spent his working life worming his way into the heads of those who kill, only to end up one of them" (*Mermaids* 275–76). In the horrifying climax of *The Mermaids Singing*, Tony Hill has to put on his most demanding actor's façade to save himself, only removing that mask and revealing his impotence to Carol, in a momentary catharsis that hurts them both more than it heals.

Tony Hill continues to fight against himself through increasingly darksome psychological landscapes. In *The Wire in the Blood* (1998) he tracks a new serial murderer targeting the National Criminal Profiling Task Force itself. For Hill and the police officers he's training in offender profiling techniques, this is an excursion into hell that ends with indelible blood on Hill's own hands. Two years later, in *The Last Temptation*, Hill pursues a wider-ranging quarry, a psychopath who, after seeking psychologist-victims across northern Europe, now has Carol Jordan squarely in his lethal sights. Through the murk of the Nazi atrocity–ridden past and the criminal post–Cold War world, Hill becomes so burned out by the psychological demands of profiling that he decides to return to academia after this one last case he takes on to save Carol. By the time each of them walks this high wire without a net (*Temptation* 427), "each fear[s] that what had been broken inside the other might never be fixed" (*Temptation* 431)—the price of empathizing that one step too close to the abyss.

Novels: *The Mermaids Singing* (1995); *The Wire in the Blood* (1998); *The Last Temptation* (2001); *The Torment of Others* (2005).

Other series: The Lindsay Gordon series, featuring a hard-drinking lesbian socialist Scottish feminist and journalist; the Kate Brannigan series, featuring a red-haired private investigator based in Manchester and equal to anything the criminal world throws at her.

Stand-alone novels: McDermid has also written several stand-alone crime/detection novels.

Nonfiction: *A Suitable Job for a Woman: Inside the World of Women Private Eyes*. Scottsdale, AZ: Poisoned Pen Press, 1999.

Selected sources: Jones, Louise. "*PW* Talks with Val McDermid." *Publishers Weekly*, August 12, 2002: 280; Maxwell, Lynne. "Serial Detectives at Work." *Lambda Book Report*, March 2000: 26; Phillips, Kathy. "On the Outside Edge." *Women's Review of Books*, July 1998: 32–33; Silvas, Sharon. "Val McDermid: The Mistress of Sleuth." Spinsters Ink Web site: www.spinsters-ink.com (May 2, 2003); Taylor, Gilbert. Rev. of *The Mermaids Singing*. *Booklist*, December 15, 1996: 713.

Major Awards: Gold Dagger, 1995; *Le Masque de l'année*, 1997; *Le Grand Prix des Romans d'Aventures*, 1998; Dilys Award, Anthony Award, and Macavity Award, all 2001.

Web site: www.valmcdermid.com.

See also: For forensic psychologists/psychiatrists: Keith Ablow's Dr. Frank Clevenger series; James Patterson's African American Dr. **Alex Cross** series, set in Washington, D.C.; G.H. Ephron's Dr. Peter Zak series, set in Boston; Jonathan Kellerman's Alex Delaware series, set in Los Angeles; Joseph Telushin and Allen Estrin's Dr. Jordan Geller series, set in Cambridge.

Debut novel: Jack Kerley's *The Hundredth Man*, featuring Detective Carson Ryder, in charge of the Mobile, Alabama, Police Department's new Division of Psychopathological and Sociopathological Investigative Team.

Dido Hoare

Profession: Antiquarian and bookseller
Living situation: Divorced
Geographic locale: Mostly London, England

Time period:	1996–present
Associate:	Barnabas Hoare
Concerns:	Son Ben; antique books

Marianne Macdonald, a Canadian who moved to England to study at Oxford when she was twenty, told *Contemporary Authors* that she crafts her fiction out of her own experiences and for her own satisfaction, "because I love words and constructing whole things with words." She began writing at twelve, continued as a young adult with children's books, then wrote plays and scholarly works while a lecturer at English universities, and finally began her popular mystery series with *Death's Autograph* (1996), featuring the unforgettably-named London antiquarian and book seller Dido Hoare. Macdonald describes her working method as "a slow process of developing my main characters, and then plotting a story in which I attempt to explore their motives and emotions" (*CA Online*).

Macdonald also claims that the major influence on her mysteries is American detective novelist Sara Paretsky, and Dido's uncompromising independence, unquenchable curiosity, liberal politics, and decidedly modern love 'em and leave 'em attitude toward romantic partners all do recall Paretsky's ground-breaking V.I. Warshawski, female private eye extraordinaire. Dido, named by her classics-loving parents for the tragic Carthaginian queen abandoned by Aeneas in Virgil's Roman epic *The Aeneid*, narrates her stories with plenty of razor-keen irony. She's very much her own woman, a "small, pretty" 5'3" gin-preferring spitfire of thirty-two. Just out of her British university, she'd worked for a New York publisher, then returned to England for her mother's funeral, refusing to yield when her conventional sister Pat urged her to move in with their widowed father both then and a few years later, after her bitter divorce from artsy con man Davey Winner. Dido accurately reckons that she and Barnabas "would have been at one another's throats" (*Autograph* 25).

Dido faces her worst personal nightmare, being lost in the dark, at the start of *Death's Autograph*. Returning alone late one night from a book-buying expedition, fretting over Barnabas, a retired Oxford don recuperating from a recent heart attack, and blaming herself for having been a soft book-buying touch when she's barely managing to support herself and her arrogant tomcat Mr. Spock, Dido's frighteningly tailgated on narrow twisting back roads. Soon after, her shop is burgled and Barnabas receives a threatening letter, events all connected to Davey's charming-scoundrel reappearance and a one-night flareup of old flames before Davey's car, himself inside, blows up on a London street.

Enter "dishy bloke" (*Autograph* 30) DI Paul Grant to investigate Davey's demise, and before long Dido, attributing an onset of indigestion to stress, matter-of-factly confesses that as she gets older, her behavior is less ladylike (*Autograph* 90). She abandons any pretense of maidenly surprise one afternoon in his borrowed flat when Grant proposes they go to bed, because she "decided not to be stupid. For one thing, I liked his eyes....Furthermore it seemed like the best offer I'd had in a long time. Finally, I'd never made love before on a mattress on top of scaffolding. It all made sense" (*Autograph* 133).

After Barnabas gleefully relives his old Army Intelligence days by helping solve Davey's murder, Dido emerges a million pounds richer and several weeks pregnant—by the departed Davey. Unfazed, she opts to keep the baby, sends Grant back to his on-again, off-again marriage, and upgrades her business, indefatigably joining forces again with Barnabas to bring other villains to justice in *Ghost Walk* (1997), *Smoke Screen* (1999), and *Road Kill* (2000).

In *Blood Lies* (2001), with son Ben, the seventeen-month-old love of her life, in tow, Dido takes Barnabas's advice to leave Mr. Spock and the bookshop to him and Ernie Weekes, Dido's assistant and sometime bodyguard, and go to the country for some rest from more recurrent nightmares—last February she'd had to sluice an assailant by driving over him with her car. But upon revisiting her girlhood friend Lizzy Waring, Dido soon discovers that beneath the idyllic Somerset vistas around Monksdanes, the Warings' rundown estate, sinister undercurrents and horrid family secrets threaten to drown them both. In spite of the Somerset C.I.D.'s opinion that Dido is around too often to suit them and is "therefore up to no good," Dido unleashes her "uncontrollable curiosity" and follows her "pointy nose" (*Blood Lies* 209, 200). Ably assisted by elderly Mrs. Molyneux, an intelligence-gathering dynamo, and Barnabas, who again charges to Dido's rescue and provides the sounding board she needs to make sense of this "big mess" (*Blood Lies* 166), Dido works up a drawing-room dénouement that out-Poirots Poirot.

Marianne Macdonald notes that she starts "with an idea—a mixture of theme, character, and situation and finds her subject matter as she write[s]" (*CA Online*). In each of Dido Hoare's investigations, her breezily self-described pigheaded pursuit of the truth acts as the catalyst that brings antique book–dealing, violent crime, and fascinatingly quirky characters together in effervescent convention-shattering reactions. This modern day Dido would tidily skewer pious Aeneas with his own sword before she'd ever let him make a fool of her.

Novels: *Death's Autograph* (1996); *Ghost Walk* (1997); *Smoke Screen* (1999); *Road Kill* (2000); *Blood Lies* (2001); *Die Once* (2002); *Three Monkeys* (2005).
Macdonald has also authored several children's books.

Nonfiction: *Ezra Pound: purpose/form/meaning*. London: Pembridge Press, 1983. Macdonald has also edited two scholarly books, *The State of Literary Theory Today*. London: Middlesex Press, 1982, and *Ezra Pound and History*. Orono: University of Maine Press, 1985.

Selected sources: Cooper, Natasha. Rev. of *Ghost Walk*. *Times Literary Supplement*, August 15, 1997: 21; DeCondido, GraceAnne A. Rev. of *Blood Lies*. *Booklist*, August 1, 2002: 1932; DeCondido, GraceAnne A. Rev. of *Die Once*. *Booklist*, May 1, 2003: 1548; Klett, Rex E. Rev. of *Death's Autograph*. *Library Journal*, October 1, 1997: 129–30; Melton, Emily. Rev. of *Three Monkeys*. *Booklist*, May 1, 2005: 1528; Stasio, Marilyn. Rev. of *Smoke Screen*. *New York Times Book Review*, December 26, 1999: 21.

Award: Woodrow Wilson Fellowship, 1954–1955.

See also: Kyril Bonfiglioli's Mordecai Trilogy, featuring questionable art dealer Charlie Mordecai, and *The Great Mordecai Moustache Mystery* (1996), completed from Bonfiglioli's notes by Craig Brown; Jonathan Gash's series featuring shady antiques dealer Lovejoy; Lyn

Hamilton's antique dealer Lara McClintock series, set variously in the United States, Europe, and Mexico; William Artin's antiquarian Peter Fallon series, set in Boston; Lea Wait's Maggie Summer series about a professor who is also an antique print dealer and amateur detective, set in Maine.

I

Isaac of Girona

Profession:	Physician
Living situation:	Married
Geographic locale:	Spain
Time period:	Fourteenth century
Associates:	Raquel, his daughter; Yusuf, a Moorish boy, ward of the King of Aragon; Berenguer de Cruïlles, Bishop of Girona
Significant relationship:	Judith, Isaac's wife
Concerns:	Judaism and Christianity; medical and social issues of the Middle Ages; politics

Buttressed by Caroline Roe's Ph.D. in medieval studies and her expertise in both modern and medieval French, Catalan, and Spanish, her Chronicles of Isaac of Girona feature a blind Jewish physician living near what is now Barcelona who "knows more of the world than most who can see" (*Potion* 120).

Three cultures converged in medieval Spain. Conquered by Rome in the second century B.C., Christianized three centuries later, and uneasily harboring Jewish refugees from the A.D. 70 Diaspora, nearly the whole Iberian peninsula was overrun in 711 by Moslem Moors who fostered industry and learning. For a while, the three cultures edgily coexisted, but Christian animosity toward the other two groups grew steadily. By the mid-fourteenth century, small Christian kingdoms were struggling to oust the Moors, who maintained their stronghold at Granada until Spain's unification in 1492. Well prior to the onset of the fearful Spanish Inquisition in 1478, Christian resentment in Spain was building not only against the Moors but against the Jews, widely hated for their success in financial dealings then forbidden to Christians and popularly accused of murdering Christ. Some Christians nonetheless respected the expertise of Jewish scholars and physicians, and Isaac's skill at diagnosing and healing ills of both body and spirit gained him wide respect and the patronage of the powerful Berenguer, Bishop of Girona.

Remedy for Treason (1998) begins with the Black Death, which in Isaac's time killed a third of Europe's population. It passes over Isaac's immediate family because he insists on scrupulous hygiene and keeps cats; he has observed that houses with cats "suffer less from the pestilence than do their neighbors"; but, he cannily warns his wife, "say not a word of this to anyone, or they will steal our cats" (*Remedy* 6)—a reflection not only on his neighbors' morality but on the racial tensions that make minorities keep their advantages to themselves.

Isaac knows he is growing blind and his trusted apprentice Benjamin has died from the plague: "And how do I find [another] one in the midst of death and desolation? . . . Everyone who isn't dead is doing the work of two or three." Judith, Isaac's beloved quick-tongued wife, tells him he has to make do with daughters "until his son Nathan is old enough" (*Remedy* 5–6). Briefly Rebecca, then Raquel, with her sharp eyes and deft, steady hands, serve Isaac well. In kindness and gratitude Isaac also takes in another apprentice, Yusuf, a twelve-year-old Moorish lad from Valencia, for saving Isaac from being stoned to death by a mob "in the middle of a riot . . . on the eve of a Christian holiday," an act as dangerous for Yusuf as it is for Isaac (*Remedy* 30).

Isaac uses all of the senses his blindness has heightened and every ounce of his healer's instinct to untangle the plots swirling around his patron Bishop Berenguer. Caught up in royal intrigue and trapped by a Christian fanatic in *Remedy for Treason*, Isaac gently calms the man's madness until help arrives to save the life of the child-heir to Aragon's throne. After Yusuf provides the key to the treasonous plot threatening the King's son, Yusuf becomes a ward of the King to be trained as a knight, but he also chooses to live with Isaac and learn medicine from him as well.

Isaac also needs every bit of tact and compassion he possesses to heal Judith's bitterness when Rebecca marries outside the Jewish faith. When Judith declares, "Rebecca is dead," Isaac replies, "There is no harm in forgiveness," then supplies exactly the right dose of husbandly persuasion: "You are a . . . very beautiful woman. . . . Passion is a clever physician—he gives sight even to the blind man" (*Remedy* 258–59).

As a healer, Isaac has access to all levels of his society, making him an ideal detective despite his blindness, for he probes not only the physical but the psychological reasons for his patients' illnesses, especially in *Consolation for an Exile* (2004). As the interests of the King of Aragon spiral outward, so do the investigations Isaac undertakes for Bishop Berenguer. Isaac is aided in his medical work by Raquel and Yusuf and in his political adventures by Oliver de Centelles, a king's officer charged with security on the border between Aragon and Castile. The smoldering mix of

Christians, Moslems, and Jews allows Isaac to participate in several plot lines at once, where, constantly aware of the pitfalls of ethnicity and prejudice, he manages to skirt them skillfully, a good man, as Bruce Alexander put it, in a bad time. Less is seen of Isaac in *A Potion for a Widow* than in the earlier novels, but he still deduces the solution to another murder that threatens King Pedro the Ceremonious and his redoubtable queen, Eleanora of Sicily. Having experienced persecution himself, Isaac analyzes the roots of hatred and revenge as products of greed, a predominant source of conflict in the turbulent Middle Ages: "So many have died and unwittingly enriched distant heirs with their lands and goods that our times have bred an army of liars and thieves...it has become a part of ordinary life" (*Potion* 266). For Isaac of Girona, though, this is a life whose sunset hardships and sunrise joys, like Reb Tevye's, he gladly accepts and celebrates. *L'chaim.*

Novels: *Remedy for Treason* (1998); *Cure for a Charlatan* (1999); *Antidote for Avarice* (1999); *Solace for a Sinner* (2000); *A Potion for a Widow* (2001); *A Draught for a Dead Man* (2002); *A Poultice for a Healer* (2003); *Consolation for an Exile* (2004).

Selected sources: Hesing, Willetta L. *Detecting Women 2.* Dearborn, MI: Purple Moon Press, 1996; *Kirkus Reviews.* Rev. of *A Draught for a Dead Man*, October 1, 2002: 1431; *Kirkus Reviews.* Rev. of *A Poultice for a Healer*, October 1, 2003: 1203; *Publishers Weekly.* Rev. of *A Draught for a Dead Man*, October 21, 2002: 58; *Publishers Weekly.* Rev. of *Consolation for an Exile*, October 4, 2004: 73.

Awards: Arthur Ellis Award, 1987; Barry Award, 2000.

See also: Paul Doherty's series featuring Kathryn Swinbrooke, a physician in fifteenth-century England during the reign of Edward IV; Susanna Gregory's series featuring physician and teacher Matthew Bartholomew of fourteenth-century Cambridge University; Sharan Newman's series, set in twelfth-century France and featuring part-Jewish **Catherine LeVendeur**; Ellis Peters's **Brother Cadfael** series set in the twelfth-century Shrewsbury border area between England and Wales and featuring a detecting monk-herbalist; Candace Robb's series, set in fourteenth-century York and featuring **Owen Archer** and his apothecary wife Lucie Wilton; Kate Sedley's series featuring lapsed monk and now peddler Roger the Chapman during England's fifteenth-century Wars of the Roses.

J

Cliff Janeway

Profession:	Former police detective, now antiquarian bookseller
Living situation:	Single
Geographic locale:	United States, mainly Denver, Colorado
Time period:	1980s
Significant relationship:	No one permanent
Concerns:	Book collecting; personal honor; justice

The used and rare book business, says former Denver bookseller John Dunning, is "the greatest business that you could imagine." Some of his customers were area policemen, so when Dunning started *Booked to Die*, he knew he was going "to do a cop who collected books, quits the force and becomes a book dealer." Hence Cliff Janeway, a fierce-looking, dark-haired, thirty-something bruiser (*Promise* 32), what Dunning would like to be, he says, if he "had that kind of nerve, that kind of physical stamina" (*Talking Murder* 103).

Janeway tells his own stories in the classic hard-boiled tradition: a seemingly impossible problem appears involving a violent crime, usually murder in a sordid big-city setting, and the detective is cynical about power, bureaucracy, and wealth. Each of Janeway's biblio-mystery cases is different. Although the first, *Booked to Die*, recalls *The Maltese Falcon*, Dunning didn't want book dealer Janeway trapped in a formula, pursuing one rare book per novel. Instead, he wants each book to illuminate a facet of the book world that the average reader doesn't know, "a tragedy that transcends the hunt for one book" (*Talking Murder* 106). The tragedies are mostly Janeway's.

Dunning gestated his hero Cliff Janeway, at first "distant and cold, almost aloof," for a long time. After deciding that Janeway "needed a kick in the pants," Dunning gave him "some fire" (*Talking Murder* 106) and finished *Booked to Die* (1992) in four months, featuring Janeway as a crackerjack Denver homicide cop whose apartment looks like the Denver Public Library. Janeway operates both his police work and his book collecting on hunches—and he's usually dead right. He's not a conventional believer, because he thinks "some kind of religion" will always "persecute and shred, burn and destroy...keeping us in the Dark Ages" (*Promise* 22). Books, Janeway believes, bring humanity light.

In the precomputer 1980s, the "real bookscout... [was] an outcast, a fighter, or a man who's been driven out of every other line of work.... [T]he eye for books [is] almost spooky—the nearest thing you can think of to prove the existence of God" (*Booked* xi–xii). One night in 1986 Janeway's called from a warm bed beside fellow cop Carol, "pretty and bright, and maybe this is what love is" (*Booked* 8), to a seedy downtown Denver homicide scene, the latest in a two-year string of derelict murders. Janeway knows the killer: Jackie Newman, a sociopath sadist who'd gotten off before because he has friends in slimy places. This time Jackie's killed a book scout Janeway also knows, and Janeway becomes obsessed: he wants Jackie dead or locked away forever.

After Newman goads him into a vicious assault, Janeway's disgraced, losing Carol and quitting the force under suspension. The murdered book scout had taken an old man—who'd inherited a lot of books he didn't think were valuable—for a big-time ride, and Janeway's still too much of a cop to let anything, including Rita McKinley, who sends him up "like an ember doused with gasoline" (*Booked* 176), get in the way of solving the case. Although he opens the rare book business he's always wanted, a world of hurt lurks just underneath Janeway's flip, tough-talking exterior, and all the great finds his bookman's eye brings him never completely heals it.

The Bookman's Wake (1995) catches Janeway hired to bring in Eleanor Rigby, "Just like the song" (*Wake* 13), a bail jumper accused of stealing a priceless edition of Edgar Allan Poe's "The Raven." As enthralled with Eleanor as he is with the old book, Janeway walks "a tightrope with deep trouble on both sides" (*Wake* 301) in a plot filled with "Love and hate. Sex. Life and death. Fear. Money and politics" (*Wake* 350). Invariably a cavalier with women, Janeway makes the most of his amatory opportunities ("We slipped around like a pair of peeled avocados twisted together in Saran Wrap" [*Wake* 364]), but disillusion and loss as always set in, softened but never wiped out by the touch of a fine book or a woman's face. Janeway gets a good collar on a rotten crook, but a woman he could have loved buys him a crucial fifteen-second kill with her own life.

By 1987, Cliff Janeway of *The Bookman's Promise* (2004) is a little older, a lot wiser, and just home from the Poe affair with a career payday in his pocket and an ache in his heart, wanting "less hype and more tradition" (*Promise* 7) and looking for the big turning point in his book life. Janeway calls himself "the great cynic of my day" (*Promise* 31), but he always pulls for the underdog, this time a dying old lady swindled out of her family's valuable library. This case's catalyst is a memoir by charismatic nineteenth-century adventurer Sir Richard Burton, as handsome and violent and magnetic as Janeway himself. When Janeway can't get what he wants with charm, his old cop's hunches, and his habit of passing off compliments with a hokey comedy routine, he falls back on a debt that a mobster pal owes him. Janeway again has a bittersweet win, because to do it he must destroy a good friend who made a mistake.

The Sign of the Book (2005) finds Janeway comfortably selling books out of his East Colfax shop, partnered in love and business by stellar lady lawyer Erin D'Angelo, who asks Janeway for a little favor: would he see what he can do for her friend Laura Marshall, jailed under suspicion of murdering Laura's husband Bobby, who just happens to collect first editions? Of course, Janeway can't resist either Erin or the challenge, and Erin is drawn in, too, to represent Laura in a case that seems ironclad against her. Janeway needs all his police experience to read the sinister signs of this case, a case that nearly kills Erin and brings Janeway to the brink of despair.

Tragic irony could be Cliff Janeway's middle name. Janeway's love of books upholds the thirst for justice that sends him out to fight for the downtrodden, but he always pays a heavy price in busted ribs and broken dreams. One of his rescued souls declares, "I thought you were a bookseller. I thought you were a scholar. Then you come out here and turn into some warrior straight from the Middle Ages" (*Promise* 160). Cliff Janeway's always looking at the black sky, wondering "what books tomorrow will bring" (*Wake* 432)—and what maidens he'll have to save, what dragons he'll have to slay.

Novels: *Booked to Die* (1992); *The Bookman's Wake* (1995); *The Bookman's Promise* (2004); *The Sign of the Book* (2005).

Stand-alone novels: Dunning's stand-alone novels include *Two O'Clock, Eastern Wartime* (2001).

Nonfiction: *The Arbor House Treasury of True Crime* (1985) and *On the Air: The Encyclopedia of Old-Time Radio* (1998).

Selected sources: Klett, Rex E. Rev. of *The Bookman's Promise*. *Library Journal*, March 1, 2004: 110; Lambert, Pam. "The Thrill of the Hunt." *People Weekly*, June 12, 1995: 27; Melton, Emily. Rev. of *The Bookman's Wake*. *Booklist*, April 1, 1995: 1381; Ott, Bill. Rev. of *The Bookman's Promise*. *Booklist*, February 1, 2004: 932; Stasio, Marilyn. Rev. of *The Bookman's Wake*. *New York Times Book Review*, May 7, 1995: 27.

Major award: Edgar Paperback Award nomination, 1981.

See also: Lawrence Block's New York book dealer and part-time burglar Bernie Rhodenbarr series; John M. Daniel's series featuring Santa Barbara bookstore owner and publisher Guy Mallon.

Benjamin January

Profession: Trained surgeon and pianist

Living situation: At first widowed; then remarried

Geographic locale:	New Orleans and vicinity
Time period:	Early nineteenth century
Associates:	January's wife Rose; violinist Hannibal Sefton
Nemesis:	Slavery
Significant relationship:	Rose
Concerns:	Racial identity; freedom from slavery

Having begun her writing career with vampires, sword-and-sorcery fantasy, and science fiction, Barbara Hambly shifted to historical mysteries with *A Free Man of Color* (1997). Her protagonist Benjamin January is a free dark-skinned Creole surgeon and pianist with one white grandfather. *Booklist*'s David Pitt places January among the genre's "most unusual and interesting protagonists" in a series Pitt describes as "literary time travel."

Born a slave in New Orleans, January takes his first love, music, to France in 1817. He lives there for sixteen years, studying surgery and vowing never to return to a land where the color of his skin, not his skill as a healer, his talent as a pianist, or his changed status as a free man, "still dictated what he could and could not do" (*Dead Water* 3). January's color bars him from making a living as a surgeon even in France, and after his first wife dies in a Paris cholera epidemic, January, half-mad with grief, returns to New Orleans in 1833, where he is drawn into murder investigations that form an irresistible sinister chiaroscuro of intertwining black sorcery and white power, a fragile societal balance resting on the fulcrum of slavery.

The institution of slavery fills January with helplessness, rage, and disgust at its effects on both slaves and masters. Immediately on his return in *A Free Man of Color* (1997), virtually a contradiction in terms in the antebellum South, only a flimsy scrap of paper—his manumission—and his own wits save him, a huge African-looking man in his early forties, from being hanged for a murder he didn't commit. Poverty traps him in New Orleans, and his family cannot or will not help much. January hasn't seen his father since he was eight, and his light-skinned Creole mother lives in a home on the Rue Esplanade, an investment from her days as a white man's mistress—her ticket to freedom. She pretends she had never been a slave or mother of a slave's children— she even pretends not to know Benjamin, her own son, if she passes him on the street with someone she wants to impress. One of January's sisters becomes a white man's mistress, too, the goal of the tastefully—and erotically—educated quadroons and octoroons of the "free colored demimonde" (*Dead Water* 9), while the other, Olympia Snakebones, has become a powerful voodooienne. January grieves deeply at the humiliation the Deep South brings women of color—genteel prostitution, pagan rituals, or manual labor in other people's houses.

Time after time, January also has to hide his own training and talents or use them in a fashion insulting his intellect and jeopardizing his freedom. In *Fever Season* (1998), with New Orleans gripped by a cholera outbreak whose dangers he understands all too well, January volunteers his services at a charity hospital and learns that freed men of color are ominously vanishing. *Graveyard Dust* (1999) places January, with his rational scientific training and his profound Roman Catholic faith in the path of a voodoo curse as well as the still-lurking cholera, while he tries to help his sister, herself accused of murder, and save a young child from abuse. January temporarily lays his surgeon's skills aside for *Die Upon a Kiss* (2000), where he plays in the orchestra of a production of Verdi's *Othello* as a human killer stalks one after another of the company's members.

January's personal life takes a new direction in *Days of the Dead* (2003). At last emerging from the loss of his first wife, he marries Rose, a courageous young black woman with quixotic dreams of establishing a school where girls of color can learn science, mathematics, and Latin as well as more alluring traditional accomplishments. Rose and January cross into Mexico to help a friend accused of slaying the son of a wealthy Mexican hidalgo, and they encounter Mexico's strange mixture of Spanish and Indian culture, with its emphasis on death, its political corruption, and its omnipresent poverty made all the more dismaying because of its contrast with the opulence of its haughty ruling class and its equally arrogant Roman Catholicism.

At the beginning of *Dead Water* (2004), voodoo priestess Queen Regine curses January, and despite his rejection of superstition, he faces calamities he cannot ignore. He and Rose have bought a house where Rose has started the school of her dreams, but due to an embezzlement, their account in the bank of a white man they had trusted vanishes, and he and Rose are on the verge of losing home and school and nearly everything they possess. Worst of all, they may be forced to live with January's mother. The banker promises not to let January down, if the "free man of color" will only find the stolen gold, so January must travel up the Mississippi on a steamboat, accompanied by Rose, seething with righteous indignation, and their white friend Hannibal Sefton, a violinist and laudanum addict. As their cover, January and Rose must pretend to be what they fear most, slaves, even though masquerading as Sefton's houseboy allows January companionship with his friend and fellow musician. All the while, January is tormented by evil dreams of losing Rose and being illegally seized and sold by slave dealers; several of them are actually aboard the *Silver Moon*, a microcosm of the Southern caste-ridden society.

January surreptitiously investigates embezzling suspects, plays the piano for white shipboard soirées, and anguishes over the spiritual malaise that slavery causes, even though one of their fellow passengers, young widower Jefferson Davis, ironically displays genuine sympathy for the slaves huddled on the *Silver Moon*'s open deck, headed for a Memphis market. On this perilous journey Benjamin January and his Rose grasp as never before the complexities and perplexities of the turbulent antebellum period of racial fears and slave revolts, "punished, brutally for whites, and for blacks with the animal fury of terrors that the slave-holders would not even admit they felt" (*Dead Water* 168).

January and Rose manage to recover the gold and restore it to their banker, but they also encounter an undercover abolitionist who shows them something even more valuable. He asks them to jeopardize everything they are trying to build for themselves, even "the school . . . you're opening for girls" so that "One day, God willing, we will be able to strike down slavery root and branch, and eliminate it from this country. Until that time, we're trying to save those we can, one by one, soul by soul" (*Dead Water* 367). At first January cannot respond to that moral urgency, one that could take away the little they've fought to achieve, but Rose's gray-green eyes convince him to put all they have at the service of the Underground Railway. Benjamin January's old dream of losing Rose vanishes and a new one takes its place, a certainty that "God never gives anyone gold to use for themselves alone" (*Dead Water* 370) and Queen Regine's curse turns into a blessing that Benjamin January never expected.

Novels: *A Free Man of Color* (1997); *Fever Season* (1998); *Graveyard Dust* (1999); *Sold Down the River* (2000); *Die Upon a Kiss* (2001); *Wet Grave* (2002); *Days of the Dead* (2003); *Dead Water* (2004).

Other series (fantasy and science fiction): the Darwath Series; the Sun Wolf series; the Sun-Cross series; the Windrose series; the Star Trek series.

Stand-alone novels: Hambly's numerous works include vampire novels such as *Those Who Hunt the Night* (1988), and fictionalizations of television scripts such as *Beauty and the Beast* (1989). She also wrote *The Emancipated Wife* (2005), a life of Mary Todd Lincoln.
Hambly also edited *Women of the Night* (1994) and *Sisters of the Night* (1995).

Selected sources: Adler, Dick. Rev. of *A Free Man of Color*. *Tribune Books*, July 6, 1997: 2; Coleman, Shirley Gibson. Rev. of *Graveyard Dust*. *Library Journal*, July 1999: 131; Klett, Rex E. Rev. of *Die Upon a Kiss*. *Library Journal*, June 1, 2001: 222; Pitt, David. Rev. of *Dead Water*. *Booklist*, July 1, 2004: 1798; *Publishers Weekly*. Rev. of *Days of the Dead*, June 9, 2003: 40; Stasio, Marilyn. Rev. of *Sold Down the River*. *New York Times Book Review*, July 23, 2000: 20.

Web site: www.barbarahambly.com.

See also: For historical period: Michael Killian's series featuring Civil War spy Harrison Raines; Harold Schecter's 1840s series featuring author Edgar Allan Poe.

Debut novel: Lou Jane's *The Spice Box*, a food-themed series opener featuring Irish immigrant Bridget Heaney, an assistant cook in Civil War–era New York City.

Richard Jury

Profession:	Detective Chief Inspector (later Superintendent), Scotland Yard
Living situation:	Single
Geographic locale:	England
Time period:	1981–present
Associates:	Melrose Plant; Sergeant Wiggins
Nemesis:	Superintendent Racer
Significant relationships:	Jane Holdsworth; Lady Jenny Kennington; Vivian Rivington
Concerns:	Justice; children; animals

In 1977, Anglophile Martha Grimes suddenly knew "I wanted to . . . write books set in English pubs. . . . Now, unless I have the pub name first, I can't write the book" (quoted in *CA: NR* 102, p. 105). Grimes's popular pub-titled Richard Jury series has shaded from lighthearted to somber, initially portraying engagingly quirky British village life, then moving into serious issues requiring increasing pychological depth and empathy. Both of Grimes's major figures, Scotland Yard's Richard Jury and aristocratic professor of French Romantic poetry Melrose Plant, exhibit their Golden Age ancestry. In their first appearances, well educated and handsome, like Ngaio Marsh's magnetic Roderick Alleyn, the Latin-quoting Jury, tall, reddish-brown-haired, with eyes the color of old well-cared-for pewter, makes women reach for their mirrors when he walks into a room (*Silk Stalkings* 45). Melrose Plant, having jettisoned his titles—Lord Ardry, Earl of Caverness, etc.—out of boredom, like Dorothy L. Sayers's early silly-ass-appearing Lord Peter Wimsey, is "one of the most eligible men in the whole of the British Isles . . . [with] intelligence, looks, character, warmth"—and best of all, he's "filthy rich" (*Silk Stalkings* 80). Jury and Plant hit it off so splendidly in *The Man With a Load of Mischief* (1981)—where a victim drowns in Long Piddleton pub's ale keg—that Plant politely asks Jury to deal him in on future investigations.

Much fun in the early Jury-Plant outings involves the near-caricature eccentrics around them. Plant interacts deliciously with his pub buddies and his ultra-obnoxious American-born Aunt Agatha, while Jury copes manfully with envious Superintendent Racer, hypochondriacal Sergeant Wiggins, Cyril the Rasputin-like office cat, and Jury's picturesque fellow renters in London, like topless dancer Carole-anne Palutski, who declares Jury is her first failure (he thinks he may be her first success).

Beginning with their third case, the award-wining *The Anodyne Necklace* (1983), Grimes got her characters under more control (Ashley 202). There Jury exercises his Holmesian deduction while watching games of "Wizards and Warlocks" and in *The Jerusalem Inn* (1984), he narrowly misses romance on a holiday with unspeakable relatives in the English countryside while Plant endures an archetypical British house party with dotty artsy aristocrats. Jury also displays enormous patience and compassion for innocents caught up in ghastly crimes. Avoiding cozy sentimentality, he communicates especially effectively with children and animals, who figure largely as helpers or informants in most of his cases, building up to *The Grave Maurice* (2002), where he wittily and poignantly empathizes with both kidnapped fifteen-year-old Nell Ryder, daughter of his surgeon, and with her grandfather's racehorses that Nell loves. When Jury feeds Criminal Type a few sugar cubes, the horse almost gets Jury's hand into the bargain, "But that was the way when you were mobbed up: eat first, ask questions later" (*Grave* 418).

Jury's light touch also defuses the antagonism of surly, self-serving Superintendent Racer and helps him elicit crucial information from unruly suspects, but when his work impinges upon his relations with women, they no longer clutch for their mirrors so quickly, sensing his growing insecurity, which began in 1991's *The Old Contemptibles*. There Jury, now a Superintendent, plunges into an obsessive love affair with moody, unstable widow Jane Holdsworth. For two weeks he proves "There's certainly enough passion to go around" (*Running Footman* 283), spending every night with her and still unable to "give a clear description of anything but the bedroom" (*Contemptibles* 30)—only to become a prime suspect in her death. With research help from Plant, posing as a seedy librarian in the Lake Country, Jury is shattered to learn that Jane had used him to cover up her suicide.

Jury's scars from that wound doom his feelings for Lady Jenny Kennington, whom he met briefly in *The Old Contemptibles*. After braving the American West to probe three serial killings in *Rainbow's End* (1995), Jury glimpses Jenny and Plant together, assumes they're in love, and grieves his way back his London policeman's life, sequestering himself until he briefly appears at the end of *The Lamorna Wink* (1999).

Even sadder memories—his parents, killed during World War II, and his orphaned childhood—envelop Jury in *The Blue Last* (2001). He hates coincidence, so he thinks his way into suspects' minds, paralleling his own painful private world with theirs until he is shot at the end of the case (*Last* 244–45). While recuperating in *The Grave Maurice*, Jury to his amazement again finds himself in a precarious emotional state, this time over Vivian Rivington, one of Plant's Long Pidd cronies: "What in God's name," Jury reflects, "was he up to, always falling in love at first sight?" (*Maurice* 206). Jury then faces one of his most melancholy investigations, the death of a little girl, in *The Winds of Change* (2004), joined by Melrose Plant and Brian Macalvie of the Devon and Cornwall police. Even though Jury and Plant keep on solving their stickily colorful cases with panache, for this suave gentlemanly detective, the jury in his romantic trial remains out.

Novels: *The Man With a Load of Mischief* (1981); *The Old Fox Deceived* (1982); *The Anodyne Necklace* (1983); *The Dirty Duck* (1984); *Jerusalem Inn* (1984); *The Deer Leap* (1985); *Help the Poor Struggler* (1985); *I Am the Only Running Footman* (1986); *The Five Bells and Bladebone* (1987); *The Old Silent* (1989); *The Old Contemptibles* (1991); *The Horse You Came In On* (1993); *Rainbow's End* (1995); *The Case Has Altered* (1997); *The Stargazey* (1998); *The Lamorna Wink* (1999); *The Blue Last* (2001); *The Grave Maurice* (2002); *The Winds of Change* (2004); *Old Wines Shades* (2006).

Other series: The pre-teen Emma Graham series, including *Belle Ruin* (2005).

Poetry: *Send Bygraves* (1989).

Stand-alone novels: Several, including *Biting the Moon* (1999), *Cold Flat Junction* (2001).

Selected sources: *Book Reporter*, www.bookreporter.com (September 10, 2001), interview with Martha Grimes; Chambers, Andrea. "The Terribly English Mysteries of Martha Grimes Are a Welcome Addition to the Public Domain." *People Weekly*, February 2, 1987: 64; Lejune, Anthony. Rev. of *The Case Has Altered*. *National Review*, December 22, 1997: 68; Melton, Emily. Rev. of *The Stargazey*. *Booklist*, August 1998: 1920; Stasio, Marilyn. Rev. of *The Lamorna Wink*. *New York Times Book Review*, November 7, 1999: 36.

Award: Nero Wolfe Award, 1983.

Web site: www.marthagrimes.com.

See also: Deborah Crombie's **Duncan Kincaid**-Gemma James series; Elizabeth George's Inspector **Thomas Lynley** series; and Caroline Graham's Tom Barnaby series; Jill Paton Walsh's two continuation novels featuring Dorothy L. Sayers's **Harriet Vane** and Lord Peter Wimsey.

Benjamin Justice

Profession:	Former reporter
Living situation:	Single
Geographic locale:	West Hollywood, California
Time period:	1996–present
Associate:	Alexandra Templeton
Nemeses:	Alcohol; guilt
Significant relationship:	Jacques, Justice's lover
Concerns:	Social issues, particularly homophobia and child abuse

Pain—emotional, physical, spiritual—permeates journalist John Morgan Wilson's Benjamin Justice series, set in West Hollywood and based on Wilson's experiences in newspaper work, screenwriting, television, and celebrity profiling (Ashley 501). Justice, a gifted gay journalist, had won the Pulitzer Prize for his *Los Angeles Times* story about a gay couple struggling with the approaching death of one partner from AIDS, but Justice had to return the prize because he had fabricated the story. He and his editor Harry Brofsky both leave the *Times* in disgrace; Brofsky joins the second-rate *Los Angeles Sun* and tries to rebuild his reputation and the *Sun*'s, but Justice sinks deeper and deeper into alcoholic oblivion. Rescued from living in his 1965 Mustang by two elderly homosexual friends, Justice now stays in their West Hollywood single-room garage apartment, doing odd writing jobs for a public relations firm to keep cheap white wine in his refrigerator, and scourging himself over the death six years earlier of his lover Jacques from AIDS.

At thirty-eight, Justice believes his "one dark and reckless act of fraud" destroyed his dignity and his career; nothing matters to him any more. When Brofsky arrives one night, desperately needing his former "bleeding heart reporter" (*Simple Justice* 17) to help him restore his career by researching a breaking story about a murdered gay man in "Boy's Town," Justice first refuses, then grudgingly agrees, lured by a faint hint his reporter's instinct catches in a television clip of the accused, a Hispanic teenager who has confessed to the crime.

Always "soft about young men in trouble" (*Simple Justice* 245) because he had endured unspeakable abuse at the hands of his own policeman father, Justice returns to the newspaper world knowing that by becoming involved in other people's lives again, he's inevitably going to be hurt. He gradually learns throughout the series that the worst agony is self-inflicted guilt.

Brofsky assigns Justice to investigate for Alexandra Templeton, a beautiful and talented up-and-coming black reporter. With some difficulty, they hammer out a working relationship, and though he never wants to go to bed with her, Justice finds himself falling for her "in a crazy way" (*Simple Justice* 281). While they probe this homicide as colleagues and friends, Justice discovers that hate crimes springing from profound racial tensions are ominously rising. Gangs connected to the prison system are increasingly involved in gay-bashing, and corrupt politicians like Justice's old enemy Senator Masterman are profiting from carefully orchestrated crime-fighting crusades. Justice also finds himself disconcertingly drawn to the senator's married son Paul, whose physical attractions are reinforced for Justice by Paul's revelation of the father-son difficulties he's had to overcome. As soon as he meets Paul, Justice feels his old journalistic exhilaration returning for a story loaded with possibilities—or maybe, Justice thinks, he's kidding himself: "Maybe I was just experiencing the giddiness and confusion of a puerile crush" (*Simple Justice* 112).

Although Justice is a hard-headed reporter capable of immense dedication in uncovering facts, he is also victimized by his own dark emotions. His primary driving force is rage at his own father, whom Justice had killed after finding him raping Justice's little sister. As a youth, Justice channeled some of that anger into wrestling and later he sublimated it into relentless newspaper exposés. Now, however, that smoldering rage erupts unexpectedly in a brief fling with a Korean man he picked up in a bar, revealing to Justice ugly resemblances he himself bears to the vicious father he despised.

As Harry Brofsky tells him, too, Justice has a dangerous yen for risk-taking. He seems to thrive on excitement, and the closer he comes to the edge, the more intense he becomes. Just as he may be put on the *Sun*'s staff, Justice appears to blow his chances again by breaking too many journalistic rules, but Alexandra Templeton helps him partially redeem himself. The rest costs Justice time and pain to do for himself.

At the door of a gay bar one night, Justice glimpses a man "surrounded by men close to half his age with "a thin, false smile that looked propped up by alcohol and desperation" (*Simple Justice* 207), hoping one might want him. This epiphany of himself in a few years makes him walk on by into the night, eventually saving the Latino youth who'd wrongly confessed to that Boy's Town murder.

Benjamin Justice slowly mellows, losing more of his edgy brashness in each of his succeeding cases, all of which involve gay-related crimes. *Revision of Justice* (1997), set against Hollywood's frenetic screenwriting world, carries on Justice's painful self-realization as he investigates various guests at a party where a young screenwriter is found dead. In *Justice at Risk* (1999), he faces the possibility that he may have contracted the HIV virus, which comes shatteringly true in *Blind Eye* (2003), possibly the finest novel of the series, "an exposé fueled by anger, bewilderment, and pain" (*Kirkus Reviews*). Here Justice loses an eye and gains another fragment of wisdom by witnessing nearly unimaginable scenes of sexual abuse and murder. Now in his mid-forties, he's considerably subdued by his condition and his hard-won insights into his own behavior. Contracted by a major publisher to write his autobiography, he's attempting to find the priest who molested him when he was twelve, putting himself in a deadly confrontation with the powerful Archdiocese of Los Angeles, which stops at virtually nothing to cover up cases of priestly pedophilia. Later, *Moth and Flame* (2005) reveals Justice depending on Prozac to dampen his libido and help him face an increasingly ghost-ridden Hollywood as he tries to complete a booklet on the city's history for a murdered actor-turned-writer. In each case, Justice savors some triumphs against hefty odds, rescuing the brutalized innocent when he can and proving to himself that genetics don't necessarily determine an individual's fate.

When Harry Brofsky first pulled him out of the dark night of his soul, all Benjamin Justice wanted was to get that Latino boy out of jail: "It was the right thing to do. A matter of simple justice. . . . I wanted to be able to put things right . . . to summon up whatever was good inside me and do something with it, to carry on with strength and belief" (*Simple Justice* 153). In all of his novels, despite the pain that comes to him from being gay in a straight society, Benjamin Justice tries to do the right thing, no matter how much it hurts: simple justice indeed.

Novels: *Simple Justice* (1996); *Revision of Justice* (1997); *Justice at Risk* (1999); *The Limits of Justice* (2000); *Blind Eye* (2003); *Redeeming Justice* (2004); *Moth and Flame* (2005); *Rhapsody in Blood* (2006).

Other series: The Philip Damon series: *Blue Moon* (2002); *Good Morning, Heartache* (2003), set in the 1960s heyday of big band music and cowritten with bandleader Peter Duchin, Wilson's inspiration for Damon (Ashley 502).

Nonfiction: *The Complete Guide to Magazine Article Writing* (1993); *Inside Hollywood: A Writer's Guide to the World of Movies and TV* (1998).

Selected sources: *Booklist*. Rev. of *Revision of Justice*, April 15, 1998: 1410–11; Klett, Rex E. Rev. of *Moth and Flame*. *Library Journal*, March 1, 2005: 71; *Publishers Weekly*. Rev. of *Moth and Flame*, January 10, 2005: 42; *Publishers Weekly*. Rev. of *Simple Justice*, June 24, 1996: 48; Schimel, Lawrence. Rev. of *Redeeming Justice*. *Lambda Book Report*, March–April 2004: 24.

Major awards: Edgar Allan Poe Award, 1997; Lambda Literary Award, 2000.

See also: Joseph Hansen's **Dave Brandstetter** series, set in southern California; R.S. Zimmerman's series involving a gay news reporter; Mark Zubro's series featuring gay high school teacher Tom Mason, set in Chicago and Zubro's series featuring gay Chicago cop Paul Turner; Michael Nava's series featuring gay Latino criminal defense attorney Henry Rios, set in San Francisco.

Homer Kelly

Profession:	Lawyer; former police lieutenant; professor of American literature, Harvard
Living situation:	Married
Geographic locale:	Massachusetts
Time period:	1964–present
Associate:	Mary Morgan Kelly
Significant relationship:	Mary Morgan Kelly
Concerns:	Art; science; sense of place; American Transcendentalism, especially the works of Henry David Thoreau

For Jane Langton, who also writes award-winning children's books, "Without an inherited literary pattern, a writer could not even begin to write . . . but if he doesn't use his own life experience . . . his book will be inert, an exercise, a formula. . . . My books start with an interest in a place . . . most often Concord, Massachusetts, with its several layers of history. . . . But it is the present time, littered about with the past, that I seem to want to write about" (quoted in *CA Online*).

In creating her sleuth Homer Kelly, Langton drew upon the classic mystery patterns she found in the works of Edith Nesbit, Dorothy L. Sayers, and John D. MacDonald (Ashley 281), integrating them with her long residence near Concord and Walden Pond and her love for Thoreau's work. "I wasn't afraid that I would imitate Thoreau—how could anyone do that? But I could play with the ideas I so much loved" (quoted in *CA Online*). Both Homer Kelly and Mary, the love of his life, share Langton's devotion to Thoreau. Homer, son of an Irish traffic cop from Cambridge and a classicist mother ("hence, Homer"), "pick[ed] up a law degree at Northeastern night school and read [Ralph] Waldo [Emerson] and Henry [David Thoreau] on the side" (*Transcendental Murder* 85), and worked as a police lieutenant. After starting his "ecstatic interminable squabble" (*Escher Twist* 240) of marriage to six-foot librarian Mary Morgan, he becomes Professor of American literature at Harvard, where Mary also teaches. Homer is Lincolnesque—tall, ungainly, ugly as an ape, Mary thought at first—and given to horrific glow-in-the-dark ties and inveterate flights of poetic quotation, especially from Langton's favorites, British Romantics like Coleridge and Wordsworth, and the American nineteenth-century Transcendentalists Thoreau, Emerson, and Emily Dickinson, whose spirits permeate Kelly's first case, the exuberantly witty *Transcendental Murder* (1964).

Kelly arrives in Concord on the eve of Patriot's Day, its annual reenactment of Dr. Samuel Prescott's not-so-famous ride carrying Revolutionary news that brought a few thousand Minutemen to the "rude bridge that arch'd the flood," stone walls, and hill slopes, "ambushing the British retreat, turning it into a rout" (*Transcendental Murder* 53). Invited as a Harvard associate professor to address Concord's Alcott Association, Homer struggles unsuccessfully to contain himself when Ernest Goss, a local "expert," divulges astonishing letters revealing heavy-breathing declarations of hitherto unknown passions between Transcendentalist authors like Louisa May Alcott and Thoreau, and when Goss turns up shot with a Revolutionary "Brown Bess" musket and his son Charley is the prime suspect, Homer alternates his cranky Yankee courtship of Mary with crime solving.

Homer's detection methods resemble rigorous scholarly research, so Mary's help as a professional librarian is vital. In all their cases, Homer uses "his formidable literary knowledge to connect events and suspects and to arrive at the solution" (*Silk Stalkings: More* 36). His Concord investigations, like *Good and Dead* (1986) and *God in Concord* (1992), highlight the relevance of Thoreau's philosophy of individualism, his social criticism, and his devoted naturalism to contemporary issues, especially *God in Concord*, where a student from India visiting Walden Pond learns with horror that plans are afoot to turn the area into a shopping mall. Homer's "games of life and death" (*CA Online*) also directly involve the impact of history on current events, like Edgar Award nominee *Emily Dickinson is Dead* (1984), in which Homer investigates the ramifications of a valley flooded to create a reservoir, and *Murder at Monticello* (2001), with a plot *Publishers Weekly* found "as twisting and complex as the upper reaches of the Missouri River."

Homer's catholic and wide-ranging interests also include science, particularly astronomy (Langton's husband is a physicist), which dominates *Dark Nantucket Noon* (1975), set during an eclipse viewed on Nantucket Island, and art, encountered when the Kellys travel to Florence in *The Dante Game* (1991); Oxford, England, in *Dead as a Dodo* (1996); and world-famous canals in the intricately plotted and sophisticated *Thief of Venice* (1999). Music figures strongly in *Divine Inspiration* (1993), where Homer and organ technician Alan Starr search out the mother of a baby abandoned on the steps of Boston's Church of the Commonwealth, and art and science mesh in *The Escher Twist* (2002), one of Homer's gloomier outings, a meditation on the ravages of aging, twisted love, and revenge.

In late middle age, both Mary and Homer prefer teaching Harvard's freshmen, "blank slates," "annihilating their pitiful ignorance," Mary declares, "spreading out banquet tables of good stuff for the first time" (*Escher Twist* 48), but viewing his students' "plump young faces ... with clever bright eyes that knew him not" and their overweening computer technology, Homer feels himself becoming invisible (*Escher Twist* 96), raging inwardly at the coming dying of his light in a society that commits its aged treasures to awful institutionalization.

Novels (most illustrated by Langton): *The Transcendental Murder* (1964; as *The Minute Man Murder*, 1976); *Dark Nantucket Noon* (1975); *The Memorial Hall Murder* (1978); *Natural Enemy* (1982); *Emily Dickinson is Dead* (1984); *Good and Dead* (1986); *Murder at the Gardner* (1988); *The Dante Game* (1991); *God in Concord* (1992); *Divine Inspiration* (1993); *The Shortest Day* (1995); *Dead as a Dodo* (1996); *The Face on the Wall* (1998); *The Thief of Venice* (1999); *Murder at Monticello* (2001); *The Escher Twist* (2002); *The Deserter: Murder at Gettysburg* (2003); *Steeplechase* (2005).

Other works: Langton has also written many children's fantasy books, like *The Mysterious Circus in Hall Family* (2005).

Selected sources: Carr, John C. *The Craft of Crime*. Boston: Houghton Mifflin, 1983; Langton, Jane. "Down to the Quick: The Use of Daily Reality in Writing Fiction." *Horn Book*, February 1973: 24–30; Melton, Emily. Rev. of *The Shortest Day*. *Booklist*, November 1, 1995: 457; Pitt, David. Rev. of *Murder at Monticello*. *Booklist*, January 1, 2001: 924; *Publishers Weekly*. Rev. of *The Deserter: Murder at Gettysburg*, May 19, 2003: 56.

Major award: Nero Wolfe Award, 1984.

See also: For academic ornithological interests, J.S. Borthwick's Sarah Deane and Alex Mackenzie series, set in Maine, and Anne Cleeves's George Palmer-Jones series, set in England's rural bird-watching habitats; for academic settings: Amanda Cross's **Kate Fansler** series; Paula Gosling's homicide cop Jack Stryker and English professor Kate Trevorne series set in small-town Michigan; for New England settings, Gerry Boyle's journalist Jack McMorrow series, set in Maine; Jan Brogan's journalist Hallie Ahern series, set in Rhode Island; Philip R. Craig's J.W. Jackson series, set on Martha's Vineyard; Sarah Graves's house restorer Joshua Tiptree series, set in Maine; Cynthia Riggs's ninety-year-old Victoria Turnbull series, set on Martha's Vineyard; Nancy Means Wright's Vermont farmer Ruth Wilmarth series.

Debut novel: David Manuel's Faith Abbey mystery series debuts with *A Matter of Roses*, featuring Brother Bartholomew, a modern-day Brother Cadfael, set convincingly in eastern Massachusetts.

Irene Kelly

Profession: Journalist
Living situation: Single; later married

Geographic locale:	Fictional "Las Piernas," southern California
Time period:	1993–present
Associates:	Homicide detective Frank Harriman; Lydia Ames, Irene's best friend
Significant relationships:	Conn O'Connor; Frank Harriman
Concerns:	Women's issues; economic and political corruption

As mystery historian Mike Ashley has observed, "Jan Burke's strength is in exploring the effects of crime upon [Irene] Kelly and on the victims or their relatives" (75). Guilt, the major effect that crime exerts on Irene herself, rises from her Irish Catholic girlhood and constantly forces her to do penance for self-perceived lapses in charity or faith or love. Both a tough-talking, grittily witty investigative reporter and a self-described "failed Catholic" woman, Irene constantly rakes herself over long-smoldering coals, resurrecting old sins while trying to forgive the sinners—or at least bring them to justice.

Goodnight, Irene (1993) establishes this blue-eyed black Irish rose as outwardly gutsy as almost any male private investigator, but her lace-curtain brouhahas with her redheaded sister Barbara always fizzle in Irene's pangs of conscience, solidly instilled by the good Sisters at their Catholic grade school. As Sister Theresa of St. Anne's Hospital keeps demonstrating to Irene, those old-time nuns had unerring X-ray vision "where your guilty conscience was concerned" (60).

Conscience also affects Irene's professional relationships. Two years earlier, after a nasty confrontation with the Las Piernas *Express*'s "ass-pinching sleazeball" owner Winston Wrigley III (*Goodnight* 81), walking proof to the females on his staff that some men can be pigs, Irene hopped in her faded-blue Karmann Ghia ragtop and went to work for a local public relations firm, though her heart still yearned for the paper's roaring presses.

It throbs even more for O'Connor, a old newspaperman in the classic mold and father of Barbara's worthless ex-husband Kenny. O'Connor's been Irene's long time mentor, father-figure, and emotional refuge, insisting that PR work made her "a race horse hitched to a plow." O'Connor himself had relentlessly been probing the forty-year-old unsolved murder of "Handless Hannah," and after a mysterious explosion blows him and his home to smithereens and a drive-by shooter targets Irene and Las Piernas homicide detective Frank Harriman, Irene decides to investigate O'Connor's death on the q.t. To return to the *Express*, she endures a ghastly let's-be-friends-again dinner with Wrigley noisily flossing his teeth, grits her own, and goes after O'Connor's killers like a diminutive avenging angel.

Irene's known hunky Frank Harriman since they were both growing up in Bakersfield. Both now are closing in on forty, both have had their flings, and both have managed to hang onto their shared ideal of doing the public some good (*Goodnight* 20). Neither conscience nor the natural hostility between police and press can keep Irene and Frank apart, especially since their respective supervisors encourage their professional cooperation to solve O'Connor's murder. Their relationship steadily swells into steamy (when marital, causing no scrupulous backlash) sex. It also brings

Irene a hefty support group. Frank has his detective partner Pete Baird keep an eye out for Irene's welfare, and her best friend and sublime Italian cook Lydia Ames can always be counted on for a spare bed, terrific lasagna, and earthy advice. On the job, Irene's classically cranky news editor John Walters consistently puts her reporter's instinct ahead of bureaucratic distrust, and Wild Bill Cody, Irene's twenty-pound tomcat, fickle where food's concerned, still provides her dependable comfort, curling up with Irene and their two rescue dogs Deke and Dunk on cold Harrimanless nights.

Irene and her friends battle heavy contemporary social issues. *Sweet Dreams, Irene* (1994) involves a D.A. candidate being blackmailed with inflammatory photos of his son, allegedly involved in a Satanic cult, and Irene's sleuthing lands her in a locked closet at the villain's mercy, producing lasting claustrophobia that badly shakes her self-confidence. She recuperates enough in *Dear Irene* (1995) to probe hate mail that connects threatened serial killings with ancient mythology, but again she becomes the focus of a killer's rage and her own tormenting what-ifs.

Remember Me, Irene (1996) batters Irene with darker, more deadly, and far more personal shockwaves of political corruption, leaving her more guiltily torn by her own rejection of the poor and homeless than by society's. Old griefs—magnified by that old-time Irish Catholic sense of sin that not even confession or absolution could completely wipe out—nearly engulf Irene after the night when, out of disgust and fear, she rejects a drunken homeless black man who tries to get her attention. After he's been murdered, Irene learns his identity—Lucas Monroe, a gifted instructor whose statistics class she'd loved in college. A decades-ago love affair that lost Irene her pride rises up to haunt her, too, and though happily married now to Frank, Irene's guilt over both situations drives her into yet another dicey investigation where her claustrophobia and her self-reproach threaten to swamp her emotional equilibrium.

Irene's past surfaces even more completely in *Bloodlines* (2004), which brings together three parallel strands of journalistic experiences: veteran reporter Jack Corrigan's mentorship of Conn O'Connor in 1958; Irene's journalistic "adoption" by O'Connor in 1978; and Irene's tutelage of two green reporters in 1998, all filled with heartbreaks unmended over years of grief and guilt. In both her work and her personal life, Irene has to skirt journalism's big pitfall of cynicism. She's often inconsiderate with her coworkers and then rocked with remorse, and she even "chickens out" sometimes when the going gets tough (*Remember* 363), but she learns from her mistakes; after a slip years ago got a friend fired, she's never since revealed a source.

Learning to accept herself brings Irene some relief from recrimination, too. After Lucas Monroe's mother reminds her that she did something when many would have done nothing, Irene can "go out there and keep doing something" about all the pain she sees around and in her (*Remember* 450). *Bloodlines* also gives her a sense of "events coming full circle...it's the human relationships that stick in the mind and the heart." Through solving these crimes, Irene Kelly finally begins to forgive herself for being a fallible human being.

Novels: *Goodnight, Irene* (1993); *Sweet Dreams, Irene* (1994); *Dear Irene* (1995); *Remember Me, Irene* (1996); *Hocus* (1997); *Bones* (1999); *Flight* (2001); *Bloodlines* (2004).

Short fiction: Burke has written numerous short mystery stories, including the Agatha Award–winning "The Man in the Civil Suit" (2000), *Nine* (2003), and *Eighteen* (2004).

Selected sources: Flores, Marc. "Four Mystery Writers to Keep You on Your Toes." *USA Today*, November 20, 2002; Klett, Rex E. Rev. of *Bloodlines*. *Library Journal*, December 1, 2004: 94; Melton, Emily. Rev. of *Sweet Dreams, Irene. Booklist*, March 1, 1994: 1183; *Publishers Weekly*. Rev. of *Bloodlines*, December 20, 2004: 40; *Publishers Weekly*. Rev. of *Flight*, January 29, 2001; *Publishers Weekly*. Rev. of *Hocus*, March 3, 1997: 67.

Major awards: Macavity Award; Ellery Queen Readers Award; Edgar Allan Poe Award; Agatha Award for Best Short Story; all awarded in 2000.

Web site: www.janburke.com.

See also: For journalistic connections: Jan Brogan's series featuring reporter Hallie Ahern; Edna Buchanan's series featuring **Britt Montero**, based in Miami; Barbara D'Amato's freelance journalist Cat Marsala series, set in Chicago and emphasizing social issues; Robert Eversz's series featuring Los Angeles paparazza Nina Zero; Antonia Fraser's **Jemima Shore** series; Carolyn Hart's veteran journalist "Henrie O" series; Laurence Klavan's series featuring Roy Milano, Hollywood movie newsletter editor; Val McDermid's journalist Lindsay Gordon series, set in Scotland. For tough California female investigators: Sue Grafton's **Kinsey Millhone** series; Faye Kellerman's series featuring Rina Lazarus and LAPD Lieutenant Peter Decker; Marcia Muller's **Sharon McCone** series.

Julian Kestrel

Profession:	Regency dandy; secret agent
Living situation:	Single
Geographic locale:	England
Time period:	1820s
Associates:	Digger, his valet; Dr. MacGregor
Concern:	Honor

English chivalry rides its snow-white charger again, demolishing ogres and rescuing distressed damsels in Kate Ross's exquisitely researched four-novel Regency mystery series. Before Boston trial lawyer Ross's untimely death from cancer at forty-one, she re-created the glittery aristocratic society world of 1820s England and its darksome criminal underbelly, and placed her attractive hero, at twenty-six the "paragon of dandies" Julian Kestrel (*A Broken Vessel* 131), squarely between the two.

Julian Kestrel appears out of nowhere in *Cut to the Quick* (1993). He has a "dark, irregular face," rich mahogany hair, brown greenish-tinted eyes, immaculate linen, a slender, medium-height frame, and above all "he had *presence*, the way royalty probably did in the old days, before it was fat and fussy and came from Germany" (*Cut to the Quick* 20; italics in original). Kestrel's presence—not so much what he wears, for his finances are slim, but the way he wears it—has made him the reigning dandy of London when charm and wit and sang-froid and a clairvoyant sense of fashion meant everything to the British haute monde, who scorned business acumen as dull and political savvy as seedy.

On the surface "vain and light-minded and too clever" for his own good (*Cut to the Quick* 147), possessing consummate etiquette, musical expertise, and impeccable tailoring, Kestrel recalls Lord Peter Wimsey—not the silly-ass playboy of Dorothy L. Sayers's early mysteries, but the sensitive scholar-cum-amateur detective who chivalrously wooed and won her alter ego, author Harriet Vane, with his respect for her intellect as well as "shoulders tailored to the swooning point" (Sayers, *Have His Carcase* 286). Kestrel's interest in crime solving, like Wimsey's, arises out of boredom but soon becomes his ruling passion, like the knight's quest to conquer evil with a trusty squire—Kestrel's not-quite-reformed pickpocket valet Digger—and sympathetic friend, Dr. MacGregor, Kestrel's Watson, at his side.

Personal honor, which means everything to a latter-day chevalier like Julian Kestrel, provides the crux of each of his cases. *Cut to the Quick* exhibits Kestrel at his suave best in untangling a classic locked-room murder of an unidentified girl found stabbed to death in his bed. It includes hidden passageways, family secrets, and the de rigeuer confrontation scene to vindicate the innocent and unmask the killer at Bellegarde, Sir Robert Fontclair's country house. *A Broken Vessel* (1994) uncovers Kestrel's parentage—his father was a gentleman cut off with only a shilling by his wealthy family for marrying an actress—while Kestrel (mostly) fends off the advances of Dipper's *fille de joie* sister Sally, who has nipped a mysterious note from one of her customers. With the backing of Magistrate Samuel Digby, Kestrel, aided by Dipper, Sally, and MacGregor, solves another vicious murder, shuts up a horridly hypocritical "house of reformation" for women of the streets and puts a child prostitution ring out of business. Having thus achieved recognition as an amateur sleuth, in *Whom the Gods Love* (1995) Kestrel probes the death of gifted young Alexander Falkland, found with his head smashed in by a bloody poker. Because of his social position, Kestrel, taking the case over from the Bow Street Magistrate's Court and its famous Runners, can grasp the implications of Alexander's connections with greater acuity than they can. He ties them together with enormous panache, always maintaining his gentleman's honor in dealing with everyone from the aristocracy to their kitchen slaveys.

The last and most complicated of Julian Kestrel's cases, *The Devil in Music* (1997), winner of the Agatha Award, takes him to 1820s Italy, dominated by Imperial Austria and seething with revolutionary intrigue and murder. Four years earlier Marchese Lodovico Malvezzi of Milan, where people of his class went to La Scala six nights a week, three seasons of the year, died and his enigmatic young English tenor protégé Orfeo vanished. Fearing a political conflagration, the government covered up the death, but now Italian papers are trumpeting Malvezzi's death as murder. Having invited Dr. MacGregor to accompany him on one of his periodic trips to the Continent, Kestrel chafes at MacGregor's sober Scots sensibilities, bored to distraction by his "most chaste sojourn" in years. On hearing of Malvezzi's murder, Kestrel reacts like the bird of prey his name suggests. Soon he is knee-deep in seductive Italian ladies and the sublimities of Italian opera, stripping layer after layer of complex motives from a labyrinthine political plot and eventually revealing hitherto unsuspected aspects of his own background and talent.

After his father's death, young Kestrel had escaped from his mother's parsimonious relatives—just as she had—and he fled to Paris, where the Comte d'Aubret rescued him from starvation. Thanks to d'Aubret, Kestrel received grand operatic training and a gentleman's income for life, but he turned his back on a musical career to secretly serve his government under the guise of a foppish dandy. Now, as well as righting wrongs to society as an amateur detective, Kestrel honorably avenges slights to his late impoverished father, who had been reduced to working as a hackney writer. As with Lord Peter Wimsey, who served as a British undercover agent on the eve of World War II, Julian Kestrel could not love women or country so much, loved he not honor more.

Novels: *Cut to the Quick* (1993); *A Broken Vessel* (1994); *Whom the Gods Love* (1995); *The Devil in Music* (1997).

Selected sources: Klett, Rex E. Rev. of *The Devil in Music. Library Journal*, August 1, 1997: 140; *Publishers Weekly*. Rev. of *The Devil in Music*, July 14, 1997: 68; Stasio, Marilyn. Rev. of *A Broken Vessel. New York Times Book Review*, May 15, 1994: 25; Stasio, Marilyn. Rev. of *The Devil in Music. New York Times Book Review*, September 7, 1997: 34; Vickerel, JoAnn. "Word of Mouth." *Library Journal*, April 1, 1995: 152.

Awards: Gargoyle Award, 1994; Agatha Award, 1998.

See also: Bruce Alexander's eighteenth-century series featuring real blind magistrate **Sir John Fielding**, who founded the Bow Street Runners; Stephanie Barron's **Jane Austen** series; Carrie Bebris's Mr. and Mrs. Darcy Mysteries, featuring characters based on Jane Austen's *Pride and Prejudice*; Daryn Lake's eighteenth-century series featuring the real British apothecary John Rawlings, who was associated with Sir John Fielding.

Duncan Kincaid

Profession:	Detective Superintendent, New Scotland Yard
Living situation:	Divorced
Geographic locale:	England
Time period:	1990s–present
Associate:	Detective Sergeant Gemma James
Significant relationship:	Gemma James
Concerns:	Professional and personal integrity in relationships; parental obligations

For this contemporary New Scotland Yard procedural series, Texan Deborah Crombie has produced British settings and Scotland Yard procedures widely praised for their scrupulous authenticity. Crombie also achieves a finely-tuned portrayal of the failures of emotional attachments in today's moral climate and their personal costs to the men, women, and children involved. Detective Superintendent Duncan Kincaid and Detective Sergeant Gemma James balance mutual respect, mutual attraction, and mutual friction as their complicated working and personal relationships progress.

Appearing first in *A Share in Death* (1993), Duncan Kincaid is mid-thirtyish, intelligent, sensitive, subtly upper-class, and newly promoted to Detective Superintendent, just coming off a "particularly beastly" string of serial killings in Sussex and bedeviled by the suspicion that the mountain of paperwork he's facing for the murderer's trial will be ignored by "a bleeding-heart jury." He'd sought promotion to get out into the field again, but he's beginning to think that its greatest benefit might be the acquisition of Sergeant Gemma James, about ten years his junior, a divorced single mother raising a young son, with an easygoing demeanor that masks "a quick mind and a fierce ambition." Gemma, though, can't conceal a twinge of working-class envy about Kincaid's upcoming Yorkshire vacation: "'Too bad some of us don't have cousins with posh holiday flats,'" she wryly observes (*Share in Death* 1–2). When a body appears in the Jacuzzi of that elegant time-share and the victim for the first time turns out to be an acquaintance, Kincaid fights down "that addictive surge of heightened perception" that starts a case, determined not to get involved (*Share in Death* 29). But as soon as prickly DCI Bill Nash of the mid-Yorkshire C.I.D. nails Kincaid as "one of Scotland Yard's fancy men," Kincaid plunges into the investigation and sends Gemma to make inquiries for him in the South. Later when she joins him in Yorkshire, the unacknowledged sexual tension between them sparks their edgy trademark dialogue, Duncan's peremptory "Where the hell have you been?" countered by Gemma's "I've just busted my bum to get here" (*Share in Death* 180).

That tension intensifies through their following cases, where Kincaid's shrewd intellectual analyses of motivations and evidence finds its complement in Gemma's earthy experience of British working-class life. Kincaid, being chronologically older, also emotionally matures faster than Gemma does. They close *Leave the Grave Green* (1995) with a passionate encounter that profoundly shakes them both. Although Duncan realizes "what he'd wanted had been right under his nose," Gemma contemplates transfer or resignation, her professional ambition overruling her heart, and at the start of *Mourn Not Your Dead* (1996), she insists "It was all a dreadful mistake" (*Mourn Not* 2). Kincaid, initially frozen in his tracks, steadily maintains a new-found patience, and by the end of that case, Gemma admits her mistake in seeing their situation as "black or white. You or the job" (*Mourn Not* 288).

Now Gemma's lover as well as her detective superior, Kincaid uncovers a startling secret about his own past when in *Dreaming of the Bones* (1997) his ex-wife Victoria, twelve years after their divorce, involves him in an old case with new repercussions. She dies unexpectedly, leaving Duncan with Kit, the twelve-year-old son he didn't know he had fathered, and Gemma "a bit frightened" at this new development (*Dreaming* 188).

Duncan and Gemma, who has applied for a promotion to end their on-the-job partnership, are just settling into their new roles when Kincaid is called to Glastonbury, the mystical burial place of King Arthur and Guinevere, to probe peculiar goings-on involving New Age Druids and ancient manuscripts in *A Finer End* (2001). When Gemma discovers she's about eight weeks pregnant, Kincaid is so lost "in the wonder of it" (*Finer End* 320) that the series' focus seems to be swinging toward Gemma, who feels "alight with excitement at the prospect of the inevitable changes to come" (*Finer End* 324), family life with Kit and her son Toby in a lovely Notting Hill flat Kincaid rented for them.

In *And Justice There Is None* (2002), that happy picture shatters. Gemma, a newly promoted Detective Inspector assigned to a new patch, manages her first murder case and suffers a miscarriage. Still mourning that loss in *Now You May Weep* (2003), Gemma becomes involved in a violent death in the colorful whisky-distilling Scottish Highlands. Left back in London, Kincaid is supportive, but he is fighting an ugly custody battle with his former mother-in-law for Kit, who refuses to take a DNA test to prove Kincaid's paternity. *In a Dark House* (2005) takes Kincaid into a fearful case of parental abduction and murder while Gemma is coping with the disappearance of a young hospital administrator as well as her own personal crises; their cases intertwine ominously, forcing each to confront some threatening inner demons.

Coping with the inevitable stresses between men and women in today's murky moral and social atmosphere—unhappy first marriages and ugly divorces, in-law complications, the strains of single and step-parenthood, clashes between two career paths—forms the thematic backbone of this successful series and the key to the development of Duncan Kincaid's character. At the close of *Now May You Weep*, when he abruptly sees that "it was not Kit who needed to grow up and be sensible" (*Now May You Weep* 365), Duncan Kincaid suddenly becomes a real father.

Novels: *A Share in Death* (1993); *All Shall Be Well* (1994); *Leave the Grave Green* (1995); *Mourn not Your Dead* (1996); *Dreaming of the Bones* (1997); *Kissed a Sad Goodbye* (1999); *A Finer End* (2001); *And Justice There Is None* (2002); *Now May You Weep* (2003); *In a Dark House* (2005).

Selected sources: Dingus, Anne. "Briterature." *Texas Monthly*, November 1997: 26; Miller, Stuart. Rev. of *Mourn Not Your Dead*. *Booklist*, May 15, 1996: 1571; *Publishers Weekly*. Rev. of *Dreaming of the Bones*, August 4, 1997: 69; Stasio, Marilyn. Rev. of *A Share in Death*. *New York Times Book Review*, March 21, 1993: 2; Zvirin, Stephanie. Rev. of *Kissed a Sad Goodby*. *Booklist*, March 1, 1999: 1157.

Award: Macavity Award, 1998, for *Dreaming of the Bones*.

Web site: www.deborahcrombie.com.

See also: Gwendolyn Butler's series featuring Chief Commissioner John Coffin, set in the Second City of London, just south of the Thames; Clare Curzon's series featuring Superintendent Mike Yeadings and Sergeant Angus Mott of the Thames Valley Police; Anthea Fraser's series featuring Detective Chief Inspector David Webb and Detective Sergeant Ken Jackson of the fictional county of Broadshire; Martha Grimes's series featuring Inspector **Richard Jury** and aristocratic Melrose Plant; and Elizabeth George's series featuring aristocratic Inspector **Thomas Lynley** and sloppy working-class Detective Sergeant Barbara Havers.

Debut novels: Cassandra Chan's *The Young Widow*, featuring Scotland Yard Detective Sergeant Jack Gibbons; David Lawrence's noir *The Dead Sit Round in a Ring*, featuring Detective Sergeant Stella Mooney; Stewart MacBride's *Cold Granite*, featuring Aberdeen Detective Sergeant Logan MacRae; Graham Thomas's *Malice in the Highlands*, featuring likable New Scotland Yard's Chief Superintendent Erskine Powell.

Deborah Knott

Profession:	Lawyer; later district court judge
Living situation:	Single; eventually married
Geographic locale:	"Colleton county," rural North Carolina
Time period:	1992–present
Associate:	Sheriff's Chief Deputy Dwight Bryant
Nemesis:	Love-hate relationship with her father, Keziah "Kezzie" Knott
Significant relationship:	Dwight Bryant
Concerns:	Family ties; justice with mercy; Southern culture and tradition

Southern tradition and hospitality meet Southern gothic in Margaret Maron's Judge Deborah Knott series, set in Maron's own home territory, rural North Carolina. Maron's literary landscape, like William Faulkner's, "contains the intertwined histories of [those] who inhabit it" (Lorena Stookey, *St. James Guide to Crime and Mystery Writers*), surrounding Deborah Knott with the warm-hearted and the cold-blooded and almost every shade of human frailty in between.

Many of the major characters who complement Deborah Knott's complex personality throughout the series appear in *Bootlegger's Daughter* (1992), the series' highly praised debut. Since the 1700s, the Knotts have farmed in Colleton County, where nearly everyone is related to everyone else, and Deborah comes by her stubbornness and her "wild streak" naturally. Her father, Keziah "Kezzie" Knott, "a scoundrel but not a hypocrite" (*Bootlegger's Daughter* 54), enjoys the reputation of being North Carolina's biggest bootlegger, even though he's had to do time for selling "white lightning."

Like most Southern gentlemen, Kezzie doesn't approve of ladies messing with politics; he didn't cotton at all to his only daughter, born after a pack of boys, being a lawyer, and he didn't speak to her for five months when she announced she was going to run for a district court judgeship—as a yellow dog Democrat, of course. Deborah's often mused about how much fun it would be to be a man in a Southern town, so as a judicial candidate she takes to heart some cryptic advice from a black female judge: "I thought my big problem was going to be race. Honey, race is nothing compared to being a woman in a good ol' boy district" (*Bootlegger's Daughter* 238–39).

Deborah's mother, Kezzie's second wife, died when Deborah was eighteen, so Deborah came home on college vacations to Aunt Zell, Deborah's "mother without the wild streak" (*Bootlegger's Daughter* 69). At thirty-four in *Bootlegger's Daughter*, Deborah's still single "with dirty linen" (*Bootlegger's Daughter* 24). She'd had a crush on handsome widower Jed Whitehead but no real sparks flew, and she'd nearly married State Special Agent Terry Wilson six years earlier because it'd have been "so much damn fun," but that moment passed, too. Now she and her brothers' friend Sheriff's Chief Deputy Dwight Bryant are mutually attracted, but it takes them a long time—until *Rituals of the Season* (2005)—to finally tie the knot in spite of a couple of grisly new murders, a years-old resurrected homicide, and a fire at the country club that was supposed to host the wedding reception. Deborah's hardly the kind of shrinking Victorian violet the nineteenth-century etiquette book chapter epigraphs to *Rituals of the Season* describe. She's definitely an expert at multitasking and she rises to all these challenges with aplomb.

Professionally Deborah needs all the steel magnolia grit she can muster. As a junior partner in Lee, Stephenson, and Knott, she's always seen the practice of law as a game where she can exercise her built-in competitiveness, and she hates to lose "with a purple passion" (*Bootlegger's Daughter* 72). Good ol' boy judges who let their prejudices interfere with justice outrage her sense of fair play, too, so when Deborah runs for that district court judgeship, she vows that she'll never use the position to satisfy personal biases. She also realizes that the power of the office attracts her, even though she knows it's limited: these judgments can't exceed $10,000 and she can't send anyone to jail for more than two years.

Though Deborah's cases involve controversial issues like homosexuality, child abuse, family loyalties, and religious obsessions, she's able to view them from at least two perspectives. Interior debates spice up Deborah's first-person narration, as when her "inner pragmatist" demands, "Oh, spare me any more Sunday School sermons!" and her salty "Good Samaritan preacher" responds, "Oh, go to hell!" (*Bootlegger's Daughter* 184). The preacher usually wins; Deborah can't stand seeing anyone cry uncomforted, and her judicial philosophy always tempers justice with mercy—even for Kezzie, who throws her a big pig pickin' to celebrate their reconciliation and advance her campaign. When Deborah loses, Kezzie comes up with a new idea that takes just a mite of conscience-compromising between pragmatist and preacher for another chance at a judgeship. Tough, compassionate, charming, unfailingly fair-minded about the complicated social and political issues of the New South, Deborah Knott never fails to give the good ol' boys a run for their money.

Novels: *Bootlegger's Daughter* (1992); *Southern Discomfort* (1993); *Shooting at Loons* (1994); *Up Jumps the Devil* (1996); *Killer Market* (1997); *Home Fires* (1998); *Storm Track* (2000); *Uncommon Clay* (2001); *Slow Dollar* (2002); *High Country Fall* (2004); *Rituals of the Season* (2005).

Other series: The Sigrid Harald series, featuring a female NYPD lieutenant whose icy-calm exterior conceals inner insecurity.

Stand-alone novels: *Bloody Kin* (1985); *Last Lessons of Summer* (2003).

Short fiction collections: *Shoveling Smoke*, 1997; *Suitable for Hanging* (2004). Maron has also written numerous other short stories.

Selected sources: Klett, Rex E. Rev. of *High Country Fall. Library Journal*, July 14, 2004: 64; Marchino, Lois A. Rev. of *High Country Fall. Magill Book Reviews*, 2004; *New York Times*. Rev. of *Bootlegger's Daughter*, May 24, 1992; *Publishers Weekly*. Rev. of *Killer Market*, June 16, 1997: 38; *Publishers Weekly*. Rev. of *Rituals of the Season*, June 27, 2005: 44.

Major awards: Edgar Award, Agatha Award, Anthony Award, Macavity Award, all 1992, a hitherto unprecedented clean sweep of principal awards for a mystery novel (*Bootlegger's Daughter*); Agatha Awards, 1996, 2000, 2003.

Web site: www.margaretmaron.com.

See also: For legal sleuths with southern settings: Elliott Light's two series novels *Lonesome Song* (2002) and *Chain Thinking* (2003), featuring rural Virginia attorney Shep Harrington; Cathy Pickens's debut novel *Southern Fried* (2004), featuring female attorney Avery Andrews and set in rural South Carolina.

For mysteries involving the Appalachian area, see Sharyn McCrumb's **Spencer Arrowood** novels.

For mysteries featuring lawyers in other U.S. areas, see: William Bernhardt's series featuring defense attorney Ben Kincaid; Alafair Burke's series featuring Oregon deputy DA Samantha Kincaid; Christopher Darden and Dick Lochte's series featuring West Coast hack lawyer Mercer Early; John De Cure's series featuring California surfing lawyer J. Shepard; Linda Fairstein's series featuring sex crimes prosecutor Alexandra Cooper; Lia Matera's two San Francisco-based legal series featuring legal student Willa Jansson and corporate lawyer Laura Di Palma respectively; Perri O'Shaughnessy's series featuring Lake Tahoe attorney Nina Reilly; Barbara Parker's series featuring Gail Connor and Anthony Quintana; Twist Phelan's Pinnacle Peak series featuring attorney Hannah Dain; David Rosenfelt's series featuring Paterson, NJ, defense attorney Andy Carpenter; Lisa Scottoline's novels centered on the Philadelphia all-female law firm of Rosato & Associates; William Tapply's series featuring Boston attorney Brady Coyne; Betsy Thornton's series featuring Chloe Newcombe, a victim's advocate in Cochise County, Arizona; David J. Walker's series featuring Chicago lawyer Dugan; Kate Wilhelm's series featuring Eugene, Oregon, criminal lawyer Barbara Holloway.

Debut novels: Dick Cady's *The Executioner's Mask*, featuring Indianapolis lawyer Sonny Ritter; Michele Martinez's *Most Wanted*, featuring Federal prosecutor Melanie Vargas; Louise Ure's *Forcing Amaryllis*, featuring Arizona trial consultant Calla Gentry.

Tromp Kramer

Profession:	Lieutenant, Trekkersburg Murder and Robbery Squad, C.I.D.
Living situation:	Single
Geographic locale:	South Africa
Time period:	1962–present
Associate:	Bantu Detective Sergeant Mickey Zondi
Significant relationship:	The Widow Fourie
Concern:	Apartheid

Established as policy in South Africa by the 1948 Afrikaner Nationalist Party, apartheid separated whites from "nonwhites"—Coloureds (mulattos), Asiatics (mostly Indians) and Africans (called Bantus, about 70 percent of South Africans). The system also separated one group of Bantus from another, forcing them onto reservations too poor to support them, and outside the reservations Bantus were strictly prohibited from owning land, traveling with their families, or working without permits. Apartheid finally collapsed under internal and external economic and political pressures, aided by writers like South African–born British reporter and author James McClure, whose eight novels featuring white African police lieutenant Tromp Kramer and his assistant, Bantu detective sergeant Mickey Zondi "probably helped bring about its demise . . . [by] skillfully dramatiz[ing] scores of situations and incidents that reveal the system's inhumanity" (Donald C. Wall, *The St. James Guide to Crime and Mystery Writers*).

Kramer and Zondi met in *The Song Dog* (1991), a prequel to the chronologically first of their novels, *The Steam Pig* (1971). Detached in *The Song Dog*'s setting of 1962, the year of Nelson Mandela's imprisonment, from fictional Trekkersburg, an urban setting he prefers, young Lieutenant Tromp Kramer arrives in small-town Jafini, vulgar, edgy, often willfully brutal in speech and manner and under orders to investigate two violent deaths. Maaties Kritzinger, "one of the best" local coppers and head of Jafini's C.I.D., and "the biggest nympho Zululand has ever seen," voracious Annika Cloete, wife of a politically-connected game warden often away in the bush, had been blown to smithereens by a mysterious explosion. Kramer, a farmer's son and loner cop well known to his white police colleagues as "this lunatic from the Free State" (*Song Dog* 113) and to Bantus as "The Great Bull Elephant," goes by the book only to embarrass his rural opposite number and keeps Bantu subordinates in line by grazing their feet with an occasional well-placed shot from his Walther PPK.

When Kramer meets Mickey Zondi, missionary-educated and since sixteen a native policeman, now assigned undercover near Jafini to hunt down his cousin, the killer of missionary nuns, and personally bent on restoring honor to his tribe, the two men immediately sense a kinship neither can acknowledge. Throughout the series, Zondi, more intuitive and probably more intelligent than Kramer, lives with his wife Miriam in a hut with a dirt floor and addresses Kramer as "my boss," while Kramer, knowing that "being seen as a kaffir-loving liberal" is equivalent to the white South African lawman's greatest fear, being branded as a coward (*Song Dog* 39), in public keeps Zondi firmly in his wretched place as "the cheekiest damn kaffir" he's ever met (*Song Dog* 154), while coming to respect him as a man and colleague.

From the start of their relationship, when Zondi is alone with Kramer, Zondi sees "more to Tromp Kramer than just the big bad cop the rest of the world seemed to see—kaffirs especially" (*Song Dog* 196), a side that Kramer only shows the world when he thinks no one notices, like feeding a hungry kitten or catching the sadness in his landlady (and later lover), the buxom Widow Fourie's laughter "when [her] kids are about." When the series began with *The Steam Pig* (1971), though, "the big bad cop" who "charg[es] out and get[s] his man" and "the hell with official channels" (*Steam Pig* 6, 20, 36) at first defines Kramer's pursuit of rough justice, often via matter-of-fact interrogation room brutality. *The Steam Pig* underscores "the iniquity of apartheid" by revealing its tragic effects on a family reclassified from white to "coloured." When the mother of that family mourns her daughter's death, a loss white South Africa casually dismisses as "not quite the same as killing a white" (*Steam Pig* 189), her tears soften even Kramer, himself battling "the Brotherhood of Arse-creepers Anonymous" out after his professional hide.

Of all Kramer's cases implicitly denouncing apartheid, only *The Sunday Hangman* (1977) was banned in South Africa as showing too much of the government's brutal prison regime; otherwise the authorities felt the Kramer-Zondi novels accurately portrayed their system (Ashley 310), though many of its aspects are downright ugly. *The Caterpillar Cop* (1972) involves a youth whose racist activities bring on his murder; *The Gooseberry Fool* (1974) shows a government spy slain in his kitchen, and Zondi, tracking the man's missing houseboy, is nearly killed himself by a mob of Zulu women. *The Sunday Hangman* (1977) delves into South Africa's violent past, and *The Blood of an Englishman* (1980) uses stomach-wrenching autopsy details and nasty physical clues to help Kramer and Zondi, who likes nothing better than seeing whites kill whites, get their man. In *The Artful Egg* (1984), hailed by H.R.F. Keating as one of his 100 best crime and mystery novels, Keating finds that Kramer has convincingly progressed "from the cheerful beater-up of black suspects" to "a 1980s 'kaffir-lover,' friend as well as comrade-in-arms to Mickey Zondi," a remarkable portrayal of Kramer "as both inherently colour prejudiced and as a complex, caring human being" (Keating 207). As his last word in this provocative series, McClure closed *The Song Dog* with a striking vision seen through an ancient native witch-woman channeling her guardian spirit Song Dog's predictions: first, Kramer and Zondi should beware the wife of a prisoner—Mandela—captured the week Zondi and Kramer solved their mystery at Jafini; and then, "one far-off night," Kramer and Zondi "would stand alone together, arm in arm in a black township, wearing red necklaces...on the orders of that selfsame—" (*Song Dog* 274). That arresting final image illuminates McClure's "particular gift," the heartrending contrast of "life's delights and life's horrors" in turbulent late-twentieth-century South Africa (Keating 208).

Novels: *The Steam Pig* (1971); *The Caterpillar Cop* (1972); *The Gooseberry Fool* (1974); *Snake* (1975); *The Sunday Hangman* (1977); *The Blood of an Englishman* (1980); *The Artful Egg* (1984); *The Song Dog* (1991).

Nonseries novels set in South Africa: *Rogue Eagle* (1976); *Imago: A Modern Comedy of Manners* (1988).

Nonfiction: *Killers* (1976); *Spike Island: Portrait of a Police Division* (1980); *Cop World: Policing on the Streets of San Diego, California* (1985).

Selected sources: Altinel, S. Rev. of *The Song Dog. Times Literary Supplement*, December 13, 1991: 20; *English in Africa*, "The Mystery of McClure's Trekkersburg 'Mysteries': Test and Non-reception in South Africa," May 1995: 48; Henry, W.A., III. "Apartheid, He Wrote." *Time*, August 5, 1991: 58; Stasio, Marilyn. Rev. of *The Song Dog. New York Times Book Review*, August 25, 1991: 20; *Times Literary Supplement*. Rev. of *The Blood of an Englishman*, April 18, 1980.

Awards: Gold Dagger, 1971; Silver Dagger, 1976.

See also: Gillian Slovo's *Morbid Symptoms* (1984), confronting apartheid in her Kate Baeier series, and also her stand-alone thrillers set in South Africa, *The Betrayal* (1991) and *Red Dust* (2000).

Loretta Lawson

Profession:	University lecturer (don) and amateur detective
Living situation:	Separated, later divorced
Time period:	1987–1996
Geographic locale:	London, later Oxford
Nemesis:	The male academic establishment
Significant relationship:	John Tracey, journalist and ex-husband
Concern:	Feminism

Created by British journalist Joan Smith, who became fascinated "with the effects of male hatred upon women" by covering the Yorkshire Ripper murders (Ashley 443), feminist don Loretta Lawson yields to the tensions exerted on women who dare to invade the chauvinistic male-dominated British academic world. In the first and second of this five-novel series, *A Masculine Ending* (1987) and *Why Aren't They Screaming?* (1988), Loretta's traditional literary orientation, her free-loving lifestyle, and her intuitive crime-solving challenge male authority in and around one of London University's colleges. By the third, *Don't Leave Me This Way* (1990), Loretta's self-confidence as a sleuth has been so shattered by lack of support from London police that she moves to Oxford, demonstrating in *What Men Say* (1990) how preconceived antifemale attitudes can manipulate and mislead male detectives (Ashley 443). In *Full Stop* (1995), set ten years after *A Masculine Ending*, Loretta solves a crime while visiting in New York before taking up an Oxford lectureship. Throughout the series, Loretta sustains a succession of blows to her professional and inner selves while struggling against male prejudice, blows that seem to impair her reasoning and deflate her increasingly shaky female self-image.

Initially in *A Masculine Ending*, Loretta, relatively new to her profession, copes levelheadedly with its built-in stresses, here caused nearly as much by her sisters in Academe as by their male counterparts. Slated to give a paper at an international feminist symposium in Paris, Loretta knows the attendees are seethingly split over the U.S. delegates' ludicrous proposal, backed by the French and Italian contingents, to forbid their journal *Fem Sap* to use any masculine grammatical endings whatsoever: "Every verb ending and all nouns, they agreed, should be treated as feminine" (*Masculine Ending* 3). Loretta commonsensically feels that this would create "horrible confusion," either relegating a whole body of literature "to the dustbin" or mangling it "out of recognition" (*Masculine Ending* 4), but her colleagues shrilly disagree.

Arriving in Paris, though, Loretta is fatigued by travel delays, so enraged by a pass from a total stranger that she claims to be a lesbian (she is dramatically heterosexual), dismayed by the sleazy neighborhood of the flat a male colleague has loaned her, and appalled to find a male figure dead to the world in the next bedroom, Loretta collapses into a troubled sleep. Returning from the next day's conference session after a shriekingly stalemated *Fem Sap* meeting that degenerated into an exchange of insults, Loretta finds that the other bedroom is now occupied only by a jumble of bloodied sheets.

Loretta's practicality dwindles. She avoids contact with the Sûreté, returns to England, and pursues one ill-conceived and dubious "investigation" after another, preferring the strident advice of her feminist friend Bridget to that of her amicably-separated husband John Tracey, who finds "any manifestation of organized feminism positively terrifying" (*Masculine Ending* 29). The victim, dashing "egghead" Oxford Professor Puddephat, is not only an arrogant deconstructionist bent on dismantling the edifice of world literature but also "one of the people most opposed to the women's support group in the English faculty" (*Masculine Ending* 58). While muddling through to the solution of the crime, Loretta takes the sexual initiative in a rapturous one-night fling with a Rupert Brookesque undergraduate.

Loretta's London lectureship is later slashed to part time by an all too familiar process—"the axe was falling disproportionately on female lecturers ... [since] it just happened, regrettably, to be the women who did not have tenure" (*What Men Say* 82). A relentless administrative proponent of "modernization" demands that all faculty "justify themselves" (*What Men Say* 160), so Loretta scouts out other positions. In New York after a visiting professorial stint, she finds herself in *Full Stop* harried to near-fatal distraction by obscene phone calls, losing most of her sang-froid and all of her common sense.

Despite Loretta's early reasonable concern for women's rights, the discrimination, petty cruelties, and vaunting male ambition she faces prove more than she can easily bear. Obtaining only a part-time Oxford position, she makes ends meet by writing literary reviews and taking in boarders, not by setting herself up as a private detective.

The only consolation for Loretta in her closing *Full Stop* appearance is that her Rupert Brookesque toy-boy returns, middle-aged, bloated, furtively crooked—and murdered.

Novels: *A Masculine Ending* (1987); *Why Aren't They Screaming?* (1988); *Don't Leave Me This Way* (1990); *What Men Say* (1993); *Full Stop* (1996).

Other works: *Different for Girls*, essays on attitudes shaped by preconceived concepts of gender and female icons, such as Diana, Princess of Wales, eerily published the week of Diana's death in 1997.

Selected sources: "Fiction in Brief." *Times Literary Supplement*, April 28, 1995: 24; Johnson, Roberta. Rev. of *Full Stop*. *Booklist*, July 1996: 1510; Klett, Rex E. Rev. of *What Men Say*. *Library Journal*, May 1, 1994: 142; Melton, Emily. Rev. of *Full Stop*. *Booklist*, April 15, 1996: 1424; Scott, Mary. "Sisterly Sleuths." *New Statesman and Society*, June 23, 1995: 47.

See also: Amanda Cross's series featuring New York English professor **Kate Fansler**; for British academia, Scarlett Thomas's series featuring crime fiction lecturer Lily Pascale, set in Devon; Christine Poulson's series featuring Cassandra James, Cambridge professor and actress; Veronica Stallwood's series featuring Oxford novelist Kate Ivory.

Joe Leaphorn and Jim Chee

Profession:	Leaphorn: Lieutenant, promoted to Captain, then retired from Navajo Tribal Police; Chee: Sergeant and temporarily Acting Lieutenant, Navajo Tribal Police
Living situation:	Leaphorn: Middle-aged and married as series begins, then widowed; Chee: A generation younger than Leaphorn; single; rejects marriage twice because of conflicts with his Navajo heritage
Time period:	1970–present
Geographic locales:	Leaphorn: Four Corners region where Colorado, Utah, Arizona, and New Mexico meet; reservations of the Navajo, Hopi, Apache tribes; Chee: Four Corners region, though he works in a wider area than Leaphorn did
Associates:	Each other; Officer Bernadette Manuelito, Navajo Tribal Police, later a rookie Border Patrol Officer
Nemeses:	Leaphorn: White exploitative interests; ongoing conflicts with the FBI and the Bureau of Indian Affairs; Chee: Big American business; bureaucracy in general; the FBI and BIA
Significant relationships:	Leaphorn: after death of wife Emma, Prof. Louisa Bourbonette, a white anthropologist; Chee: Mary Landon, an American teacher; Janet Pete, a Navajo lawyer; Officer Bernadette Manuelito

Concerns:	Leaphorn: Native American anthropology; exploitation of indigenous peoples and their lands and resources; Chee: Reverence for Navajo tradition and strong desire to become a *yataalii* or Singer (shaman); conflict between respect for Leaphorn and clash with Leaphorn's skepticism about Navajo traditional values

Tony Hillerman's acclaimed series of Native American mysteries begins with *The Blessing Way* (1970), *Dance Hall of the Dead* (1973), and *Listening Woman* (1978), all featuring "legendary" Navajo Tribal Police Lieutenant Joe Leaphorn. Hillerman then wrote *People of Darkness* (1980), *The Dark Wind* (1982), and *The Ghost Way* (1984), all starring Navajo Tribal Police Sergeant Jim Chee. From *Skinwalkers* (1987) through *Skeleton Man* (2004), Leaphorn and Chee both appear in Hillerman's next eleven novels.

H.R.F. Keating observed that "Out of [Hillerman's] contrast between their [Southwestern Native American peoples'] approach to life and that of the majority of Americans all around them, there emerges a sharper, better picture of dilemmas and difficulties common to humankind everywhere" (*Crime and Mystery* 163). Seen first in *The Blessing Way*, Joe Leaphorn intimately knows and takes pride in his Navajo heritage, but he also sort facts, places them in order, and produces logical deductions, functioning effectively in the white academic world, earning a master's degree in anthropology and once considering becoming a professor. Since joining the Navajo Tribal police, Leaphorn, now middle-aged, has never relied on luck. He instead expects humans to behave the way they naturally behave. He can innately sort out "the chaos of observed facts" and discern that natural order (*Blessing Way* 151) that saves him considerable labor in his police work, but he has also come to realize that just those "meticulously logical conclusions" (*Blessing Way* 148) make his in-tuitive Navajo self—which sees any departure from human norms as unnatural and unhealthy—uneasy. This powerful inner conflict personalizes the large-scale di-lemma of the 180,000 Southwestern Native Americans living in a desolate and largely uninhabited area larger than New England, surrounded by an ocean of white people, some of whom want to plunder the region's natural resources and destroy the natural beauty the Navajo (the Dineh) so cherish.

Sergeant Jim Chee studied anthropology, too, but he returned from the University of New Mexico with two quite differing ambitions—to become a Tribal Policeman and to become a *yataalii*, a shaman who sings the various rituals of Navajo traditional belief. Chee not only accepts his heritage, he believes that it determines his work as a policeman, because the Navajo concept of *hosrah*, living in beauty and harmony with nature, considers crime a fatal disruption of universal truth.

In *The People of Darkness* (1980), Chee demonstrates intense curiosity about white culture and in *The Ghost Way* (1984), he is strongly tempted to marry white teacher Mary Landon, but looking back in *The Sinister Pig* (2003) he recognizes their cultural in-compatibility: Mary was only "looking for the proper trophy to take back to Wisconsin to sire her Wisconsin children" (94). Chee's next amour, half-Navajo lawyer Janet Pete, had only been "seeking the appropriate Navajo male willing to be taught the value system of urbane America (*Sinister Pig* 94). Both women forced Chee to choose between Navajo culture and white America's, and not until Chee finally overcomes his self-doubts can he reconcile his devotion to the Navajo Way with his desire to love and be loved by pretty Navajo Bernadette Manuelito, who accepts both her heritage and his own.

When Leaphorn and Chee come together in *Skinwalkers* (1987), they inevitably clash, just as do the cultures they represent. Leaphorn is a tough, pragmatic cop captain a generation older than Chee; Leaphorn plays hunches and gets results. Chee wants badly to impress Leaphorn, but their thought processes differ too widely for them ever to become true partners. In the widely praised *Thief of Time* (1988), involving a quest for the lost ancient Anasazi culture, Leaphorn finds Chee's traditionalism individualistic and romantic and accuses the young sergeant of denying reality, while Chee can't help being disturbed by Leaphorn's skepticism about Navajo beliefs. Ironically, after Leaphorn's beloved wife Emma, for whom he came back to the reservation, tragically dies in *Thief of Time* (1988), Leaphorn painfully reconsiders the Navajo taboos regarding the dead, and Chee, in his first performance as *yataalii*, must sing Leaphorn's traditional religious rites.

Subsequent novels show Leaphorn entering, then chafing at, retirement despite the soothing presence of Professor Louisa Bourbonette, while Chee's cases increasingly take center stage, though Leaphorn's intuitive insights are crucial to their solutions. Their investigations probe the white man's greedy pursuit of gain and glory, lamentably national as well as individual: "the FBI, the DEA, and the Customs Service [are] pushing and shoving for media credit and TV time" (*Sinister Pig* 225). *Hunting Badger* (1999), where Leaphorn settles into being "a stocky old duffer" and Chee renounces his dream of becoming a shaman, pulls their two investigations of "Federal Bureau of Ineptitude" and casino crime together. *The Sinister Pig* (2003) takes them into "the very heart of America's version of the Persian Gulf" and the depths of oil revenue fraud; and *Skeleton Man* (2004), returns them to the eerie domain of skinwalkers and shapeshifters and Native American spirituality. Leaphorn and Chee gradually accommodate each other's talents and desires, not as the strained task force of two in the Tribal Police Special Investigation Office they had uncomfortably shared in *Sacred Clowns* (1993), but as two faces of a culture portrayed with a consummate clarity that makes us see ourselves as others do. In these novels, despite their stumbles, Joe Leaphorn and Jim Chee, each in his own way and in the Navajo Way, truly "walk in beauty."

Novels: Joe Leaphorn novels: *The Blessing Way* (1970); *Dance Hall of the Dead* (1973); *Listening Woman* (1978). Jim Chee novels (published together in 1990 as *The Jim Chee Mysteries*): *People of Darkness* (1980); *The Dark Wind* (1982); *The Ghost Way* (1984). Leaphorn and Chee together: *Skinwalkers* (1987); *A Thief of Time* (1988); *Talking God* (1989); *Coyote Waits* (1990); *Sacred Clowns* (1993); *Fallen Man* (1996); *The First Eagle* (1998); *Hunting Badger* (1999); *The Wailing Wind* (2002); *The Sinister Pig* (2003); *Skeleton Man* (2004).

Stand-alone novels: *The Fly on the Wall* (1971); *Finding Moon* (1995).

Other works: Hillerman has also written one children's book and the nonfiction adult book *The Great Taos Bank Robbery and Other Indian Country Affairs* (1973). He edited *The*

Mysterious West (1994); coedited with Rosemary Herbert *The Oxford Book of American Detective Stories* (1996); coedited with Otto Panzler *The Best American Mystery Stories of the Century* (2000).

Autobiography: *Seldom Disappointed* (2001); *Talking Mysteries: A Conversation with Tony Hillerman* (1991; self-published in somewhat different form in 1989 as *Words, Weather and Wolfmen*).

Selected sources: CheckerBee Publishing Staff. *Tony Hillerman: A Reader's Checklist and Reference Guide.* Middletown, CT: CheckerBee Publishing, 1999; Dejolie, LeRoy. "Navajo Land: A Native Son Shares His Legacy." *Arizona Highways*, April 2005: 18–24; Greenberg, Martin, ed. *The Tony Hillerman Companion.* New York: HarperCollins, 1994; Linford, Laurence D. *Tony Hillerman's Navajoland.* Salt Lake City: University of Utah Press, 2001; Reilly, John M. *Tony Hillerman: A Critical Companion.* Westport, CT: Greenwood Publishing, 1996.

Major awards: Edgar, 1974; *Grand Prix de Littérature Policière*, 1987; Western Writers Silver Spur, 1987; Anthony, 1988; Macavity, 1989 and 1992; Nero Wolfe Award, 1991; MWA Grand Master, 1991; Grand Master, Swedish Academy of Detection, 1993; Anthony Lifetime Achievement, 1994, and best anthology, 1995. Hillerman's most cherished award: "Special Friend to the Dineh," from the Navajo Nation, 1987.

See also: Brian Garfield's series featuring part-Navajo State Trooper Sam Watchman; Kathleen O'Neal Gear and W. Michael Gear's Anasazi Mysteries, featuring physical anthropologist Dr. Maureen Cole; Mardi Medawar's Tay-Bodal Mysteries; Kirk Mitchell's series featuring **Anna Turnipseed**, a Modoc FBI Special Agent, and Emmett Quanah Parker, a half-Comanche lawman; Thomas Perry's series featuring Jane Whitefield, a part–Seneca Indian who helps people in difficulties establish new identities; Aimee and David Thurlo's series featuring **Ella Clah**, a Navajo Special Investigator, and their series featuring Lee Nez, a half-vampire Navajo lawman; for Albuquerque setting, Rudolfo Anaya's series featuring Chicano detective Sonny Baca; for other Southwestern and Western and/or Native American cultural backgrounds and settings: Margaret Coel's series featuring Father John O'Malley and Arapaho Vicky Holden, set on the Wyoming Wind River Reservation; Rick DeMarinis's series featuring El Paso bodybuilder Uriah Walkinghorse; Christine Gentry's series featuring half-Blackfoot paleoartist Ansel Phoenix; Steven F. Havill's series featuring Undersheriff Estella Reyes-Guzman of Posada County, Colorado; Kent Krueger's series featuring part-Ojibwa detective Cork O'Connor, set in Northern Minnesota.

Anna Lee

Profession:	Private investigator
Living situation:	Single
Geographic locale:	England (and Florida Keys in *Backhand*)
Time period:	1980–1991
Associate:	Bernie Schiller
Nemeses:	Martin Brierly; Beryl Doyle
Significant relationships:	Ian Olsen; "Quex"; Raoul "Rule" Sanchez
Concerns:	Feminism; the underdog

Liza Cody, trained at the Royal Academy School of Art as an artist and designer, packs mean visual feminist wallops into the award-winning six-novel Anna Lee series and three additional novels in which Anna, one of the first and still few convincing British female private investigators, appears in a minor role as employer of private investigator Eva "Bucket Nut" Wylie, "The London Lassassin," a disbarred pro woman wrestler. Anna Lee's *Head Case* (1985) became a television series pilot in 1993, followed by TV versions of *Dupe* (1980) and *Stalker* (1984) as well as new Anna Lee scripts written by others. The evolution of the main character made Cody feel that she had lost her original concept of Anna, so Cody turned to "hulking, foul-mouthed, and short-tempered" "Bucket Nut" Wylie (Mifflin 53), "a character of such convincing reality, it's hard to believe she doesn't exist somewhere" (*Publishers Weekly* 57).

As introduced in *Dupe*, Bucket Nut's employer, ex-police officer Anna Lee, knows all about the "restrictions and repressions" of working in a tough man's world—constant condescension from her infuriatingly stuffed-shirt boss Martin Brierly; heavy-handed chauvinistic putdowns from her all-male colleagues; and twenty-four carat bitchiness from Beryl Doyle, Brierly Security's dragonish office manager. Slightly built but wryly self-confident, Anna is accustomed to making the best of frustrating circumstances. She grew up happy though smothered by her narrow Dulwich home where "any carefree movement seem to result in a breakage," she enjoyed her police work for five years, and now she's happy with the increased freedom she's grittily made for herself as the only woman PI at Brierly's (*Dupe* 30–31).

As independent as Anna has become—she proudly does her own maintenance on her cherished Triumph, since one of her phobias is crowded London public transport—she knows Brierly downplays her ability and assigns her cases that appear routine, even boring. While Anna works them, though, they turn out to be vicious crimes with grim and unexpected twists. Although she often consults her mentor, sympathetic nonsexist Bernie Schiller, the one of her fellow detectives she'd call on first in a crisis, Anna almost always works alone, using her favorite drawing-out device, "the Narcissus ploy," making witnesses or suspects reveal more than is wise by becoming a quietly responsive mirror (*Dupe* 79). Anna gamely suffers physically in the line of duty, but Bernie and her loyal friends Bea and Selwyn Price come through with tea and sympathy and rides home from the hospital.

All of Anna's cases prove her conviction that it's what you do with your talent that counts (*Dupe* 64). Martin Brierly's constantly looking for a reason to sack her, so she has to be twice as good as the men he employs. In *Dupe* she probes the car-crash death of a wealthy young woman whose overbearing father and browbeaten mother suspect foul play. Though a few of Anna's teeth are knocked out and her ribs kicked in and her face looks like "a bleeding Turner sunset" (*Dupe* 204), she doggedly hangs onto her integrity. In *Bad Company* (1982), despite feeling vulnerable as a physically weak woman in an increasingly violent London, she survives a routine surveillance that gets her kidnapped by sadistic British hoodlums. *Stalker* (1984) involves her in a deer-poaching and murder case on a private estate in Somerset, and in *Head Case* (1985), Anna opens up a dangerous family secret while looking for a missing teenaged girl. Loaned out to a bigger security firm in *Under Contract* (1986), she has to guard a mouthy female rock star surrounded by petty and spiteful hangers-on.

In Anna's last starring role, *Backhand* (1992), her life starts spinning out of control. Brierly's has taken its "small-minded, tightfisted respectability" up-market, and Anna's job has dwindled to selling security systems to the newly rich. She's now driving and tuning a Peugeot, but she's losing her flat to the "creeping gentrification" of her comfortably shabby Holland Park neighborhood (*Backhand* 6, 11), and "Quex," her enormous Irish chemical-engineer three-or-four-times-a year lover, moves in with her, breaking one of the unspoken rules that allows her to maintain her cherished independence. He cooks—but he leaves her kitchen an ungodly mess. Accused of being "a hard woman" when she complains, Anna reflects that "it was probably because she was bored rigid" (*Backhand* 28), so she rejoices when her current banal assignment, chasing down another missing teenager, suddenly becomes "alive—like an animal she could track, tame, and maybe, eventually ride" (*Backhand* 73). This case, full of negatives, takes her to the Florida Keys, sultry with American-style gang killings, steroided pool attendants, leathery senior citizen tennis enthusiasts and Rule Sanchez, another big man who takes up a lot of Anna's space and imagination. Her resentment of enduring Beryl's unreasonable bossiness and her clenched-molar subservience toward Martin Brierly, who usurps both the credit and the money Anna earns, end at last when Brierly gleefully fires her, forcing her to follow Bernie's advice to go to work for herself. Just as achingly real as Eva Wylie, the employee she can't resist hiring, Anna Lee poignantly and convincingly sets out on the next stage of a New Woman's life.

Novels: *Dupe* (1980); *Bad Company* (1982); *Stalker* (1984); *Head Case* (1985); *Under Contract* (1986); *Backhand* (1992).

Other series: Eva "Bucket Nut" Wylie series, with Anna Lee as minor character: *Bucket Nut* (1992); *Monkey Wrench* (1994); *Musclebound* (1997); *Gimme More* (2000).

Short fiction: *Lucky Dip and Other Stories* (2003).
Cody has also coedited several crime story anthologies.

Selected sources: Berlins, Marcel. Rev. of *Head Case*. *Times Literary Supplement*, January 11, 1985; Binyon, T.J. Rev. of *Dupe*. *Times Literary Supplement*, December 26, 1980; Callendar, Newgate. Rev. of *Bad Company*. *New York Times Book Review*, February 7, 1982; Callendar, Newgate. Rev. of *Under Contract*. *New York Times Book Review*, August 2, 1987; Mifflin, Margot. Rev. of *Bucket Nut*. *Entertainment Weekly*, June 2, 1995: 53; *Publishers Weekly*. Rev. of *Musclebound*, April 10, 1995: 57; Slung, Michelle. Rev. of *Under Contract*. *Ms.*, June 1986.

Award: John Creasey Memorial Award, 1981.

See also: Sarah Dunant's three Hannah Wolfe series, set in London; Sue Grafton's "Alphabet" series, featuring California PI **Kinsey Millhone**; Marcia Muller's **Sharon McCone** series, set in San Francisco; Val McDermid's series featuring Lindsey Gordon, a hard-drinking British lesbian feminist and McDermid's forceful Kate Brannigan series, set in Manchester, England; Sara Paretsky's **V.I. Warshawski** series, set in Chicago; Jacqueline Winspear's 1930s series featuring London psychologist-detective **Maisie Dobbs**.

Debut novel: Victoria Blake's *Bloodless Shadow*, featuring London private investigator Samantha Falconer, a former world judo champion.

Catherine LeVendeur

Profession:	Former religious novice
Living situation:	Married
Geographic locale:	Medieval Europe, especially France
Time period:	Twelfth century
Associate:	Edgar, a Saxon nobleman
Significant relationship:	Edgar
Concerns:	Justice; religion; anti-Semitism

Scrupulously researched by medievalist Sharan Newman, the Catherine LeVendeur series offers a colorful tapestry of medieval Europe, "woven," Newman emphasizes, "around real events." Catherine's curiosity and passion for justice drive her to explore the diverse medieval society through women's roles both in and out of the convent, Jewish life in Europe, the poor, monastic life in general, and "many other previously neglected aspects of medieval life" (*The Devil's Door* 405). Catherine LeVendeur was born to an affluent merchant family in Paris and became a novice at the Convent of the Paraclete established by the religious scholar Peter Abelard and headed by Abbess Heloise, once tragically Abelard's lover.

During the Middle Ages, the Church monolithically ruled nearly every aspect of its believers' lives. Questioning official dogma was forbidden as heresy on pain of death or excommunication or both, but a few scholars, like Abelard, who taught at Notre Dame's cathedral school, maintained a rigorous intellectual pursuit of truth at enormous personal costs. Encouraged by Heloise, Catherine's intellectual pursuits, unusual for a woman, shake her vocation and threaten both the abbess and Abelard, whose enemies still seek to prove heresy against them. Because Catherine directs the copying of an allegedly heretical psalter in *Death Comes as an Epiphany* (1993), the abbess suspends her from the convent to investigate the matter in Paris, where Catherine faces her father's fury and her mother's mental disintegration and meets the Saxon nobleman Edgar, whom she will later marry. After they solve the murder of Edgar's stone-carver master together, Catherine returns to the Paraclete only to be drawn into another murder in *The Devil's Door*. She and Edgar plan to marry, both turning away from the monastic lives their families had decided on for them.

Their married life takes them on ever-widening adventures laced with intrigue and murder across Europe and into Scotland and Spain. At first the murders she solves focus on Catherine herself, raised as a devout Catholic but keeping secret the Jewish heritage of her father's family. She also struggles with her insatiable thirst for knowledge, fears that she may share her mother's dementia, the unquenchable love she shares with Edgar, and determination to preserve her family at all costs. Catherine juggles the traditional roles of wife and mother with scholarship and amateur sleuthing, vastly challenging pursuits for women in the restrictive Middle Ages, and she faces each obstacle with righteous anger toward injustice. When she witnesses a brutal case of wife-beating, she vows, "The proud and haughty need to be brought low" (*Devil's Door* 11)—and time after time, she does so.

Catherine is altogether modern in her attitude toward sex, which her Church approved only for procreation. On her pilgrimage to Compostela after a stillbirth, she declares, "even if I know there is no possibility of a child, I'll still long for the times Edgar's body is with mine" (*Strong as Death* 225). Their physical passion sustains them and gives Catherine the children they desire so much. Edgar turns his back on his own high position in Britain to support her, so that his sensitivity and devotion lend her the strength to carry on her stubborn crusade against injustice.

Catherine's Jewish heritage connects her to a despised segment of medieval society widely blamed for the death of Christ as well as deeply resented for their money-lending activities, forbidden at that time to Christians, and it causes her considerable anguish. In the anti-Semitic German city of Trier to save her sister Agnes from accusations of murder, Catherine begins to lose her father Hubert, who had been baptized long ago and "passed" as Christian but who now yearns more for the faith of his fathers with each atrocity incited against the Jews by the rabble-rousing monk Radulf and sanctioned by most leaders of the Church. Meanwhile, Catherine, pregnant again, finds "stability . . . only in her devotion to her children" as her mind works on Agnes's predicament, "fiercely . . . pulling together all the loose ties of information they had" (*The Difficult Saint* 321), eventually accepting her father's decision to devote himself to studies of the Torah with the Jewish community at Arles. In *The Witch in the Well* (2005), the pragmatic Catherine hears strange legends about her grandfather's family at Blois, and since she holds little faith in magic, she feels compelled to seek out entirely rational causes for the sinister events there, reliving her own painful past with a mentally ill mother, who had disappeared after being implicated in a serious crime.

Catherine's ability to grasp many-faceted moral issues rather than accepting the merciless black-and-white dictates of the Church sets her apart from the two conventional images of women in the Middle Ages: the noble-born, humble, long-suffering lady on the pedestal in emulation of the Virgin Mary and the temptress daughter of Eve, with whom, the Church insisted, all man's sins and pain began. Catherine's fine mind draws her dangerously to progressive religious thinkers like Abelard and Bernard of Clairvaux, who opposed the persecution of the Jews. It also forces her to objectively observe human conduct, both individual and collective, while her warm heart and easily aroused passions pit her solidly against injustice, especially when inflicted on the poor, who often were driven to crimes to survive, like the forlorn woman Mondete, now a prostitute, raped in her childhood with "no father to run home to on earth or in heaven. They had both abandoned me" (*Strong as Death* 227). Defending those whom her Church should defend but ignores, Catherine LeVendeur lives out Abelard's contention that "assiduous and frequent questioning is indeed the first key to wisdom . . . for by doubting we come to inquiry; through inquiring we perceive the truth."

Novels: *Death Comes as Epiphany* (1993); *The Devil's Door* (1994); *The Wandering Arm* (1995); *Strong as Death* (1996); *Cursed in the Blood* (1998); *The Difficult Saint* (1999); *To Wear the White Cloak* (2000); *Heretics* (2002); *The Outcast Dove* (2003); *The Witch in the Well* (2005).

Other fiction: Newman has written one children's book as well as a trilogy about King Arthur's Queen Guinevere: *Guinevere* (1981), *The Chessboard Queen* (1983), and *Guinevere Evermore* (1985).

Other works: Newman has also coedited the 1997, 1998, and 2000 volumes of *Crime Through Time*, the first two with Miriam Grace Monfredo.

Selected sources: Atkins, James D. "Witch a Well-Done Mystery." Rev. of *The Witch in the Well. AP Weekly Features*, May 8, 2005; *Booklist*. Rev. of *Strong as Death*, September 1, 1996: 68; *Booklist*. Rev. of *The Wandering Arm*, October 15, 1995: 388; *Publishers Weekly*. Rev. of *Cursed in the Blood*, June 29, 1998: 39; *Publishers Weekly*. Rev. of *Death Comes as Epiphany*, June 7, 1993: 54.

Award: Philadephia Children's Reading Round Table Award, 1976.

See also: Margaret Frazer's **Dame Frevisse** series, set in fifteenth-century England; Richard Jecks's Knights Templar series, featuring **Sir Baldwin Furnshill** and set in fourteenth-century England; Ellis Peters's **Brother Cadfael** series, set in twelfth-century Shrewsbury, between England and Wales; Candace Robb's **Owen Archer** series, set in fourteenth-century York; Kate Sedley's Roger the Chapman series, set in the fifteenth-century English Wars of the Roses; for medieval attitudes of and about Jews, see Caroline Roe's **Isaac of Girona** series, set in fourteenth-century Spain.

Pharoah Love

Profession:	NYPD detective
Living situation:	Single
Geographic locale:	New York City
Time period:	1960s

Probably the earliest gay black detective in crime fiction, homicide detective Pharoah (author George Baxt intended the misspelling) Love ("a hell of a name for a detective," as Love himself observes in his first case, *A Queer Kind of Death*, 8) prowls the meanest streets of New York City's gay world in the 1960s, "when harassment, violence, secrecy, and shame were more common [for gays]" (Murphy 30). After the first three Love novels, a critically lauded trilogy of crime novels of the absurd, screen and television writer Baxt abandoned his hip, edgy, handsome protagonist for other projects, bringing Love back over twenty-five years later in *A Queer Kind of Love* and *A Queer Kind of Umbrella* (1994 and 1995 respectively).

Anthony Boucher commented that *A Queer Kind of Death* "deals with a Manhattan sub-culture wholly devoid of ethics or morality . . . and you must by no means miss it" (29). In this dangerous territory, laconic Pharoah Love treads lightly and lethally as a big cat, constantly aware of multiple reasons for fearing prosecution (Murphy 30) and surrounded by characters who often descend into underground comic caricature while pursuing vicious ends that justify any maliciously selfish means.

Pharoah knows he was a good street cop and now he knows he's a good detective, so when he's assigned to find the killer of male prostitute Ben Bentley (née Bergheim), electrocuted by a portable radio hurled into his bathtub, Love takes his time, playing the murderer as tidily as if he's with a mouse—or a sewer rat: "Don't push. Let him come after you. He'll call" (*Queer Kind of Death* 68).

Shocking even himself, Pharoah falls in love with his prime suspect, Seth Piro, about Love's own age of forty and the victim's former lover. Love handles Seth with velvet-covered claws, effortlessly concocting mind games that convince Seth, who's in analysis himself, that Love could easily qualify as a psychiatrist. Bedeviled by his own recurrent whimpering, growling nightmare and his childissh fear of the dark, Pharoah lays himself on the line with Seth, admitting, "When you do the kind of work I do, it's hard to divorce yourself from it, even with people you sincerely like. And . . . I like you very much" (*Queer Kind of Death* 154), but beneath that soft velvet lurk razor-sharp claws. After telling Seth that Seth's tears at Ben's funeral had touched him soul to soul, Pharoah confesses that the last time he himself had cried was when his kid brother was knifed in a fight. " 'I found the bugger. He's dead now.' Seth was chilled by the matter-of-fact way Pharoah recited the incident. 'No one harms mine,' he said flatly" (*Queer Kind of Death* 29).

Decked out sveltely in Brooks Brothers' best and driving a new red Jaguar, soft-spoken Pharoah Love gets his man in more ways than one in *A Queer Kind of Death*, continuing successfully with most of the same criminal lunatic characters into his next two cases. After Pharoah Love's twenty-five-year hiatus, though, Baxt's original dazzling kaleidoscopic narrative cuts and his scintillating wit, heavy on wicked campy puns, seem to become watered down as he abandons the avant-garde for more conventional hard-boiled mystery writing. By the 1990s, the novelty of darkly ironic Pharoah Love as a black gay detective has somewhat worn off, too, so for shock value Baxt has him strike out into the broader reaches of New York's organized crime.

A Queer Kind of Umbrella takes Love to the seamy underworld of Chinese crime lord Kao Lee, leader of the fearsome Chi Who gang, awaiting the latest shipment of his Asian slave trade, 300 illegal aliens crammed into the hold of the *Green Empress* lying off the Far Rockaway beach. Newly updated with a trendy ponytail and a flashy earring, and sent into "uncontrollable rapture" by arias from the opera *The Pearl Fishers* (*Umbrella* 110), Pharoah's been borrowed by the FBI from his NYPD boss Christy Lombardo, Fifth Precinct Chief of Detectives, to go underground to China's Fujian Province and infiltrate the Chi Who's alien-smuggling operation. Now in deep cover aboard the reeking *Green Empress*, Love is faced with "a true Chinese puzzle. Nests within nests" (*Umbrella* 38). He's also smitten with sympathy for the aliens and hatred for their exploiters, who Pharoah says "don't want their employees starving, just poverty stricken and at their mercy." Their plight makes him reflect, "After two months on that boat I began to understand what it must have been like for my ancestors coming over here on slave ships" (*Umbrella* 70).

In his last two novels, neo-Pharoah Love has mellowed from sinuously beautiful feline menace into practical grey-whiskered pussycat, devoting himself to the classic deduction he thinks detectives are supposed to do instead of unleashing the blistering ironies that made his earlier incarnation so much fun. His antagonists are less absurd and more grungy, his actions need backups, and his wit is now blunted by politically correct social conscience. It's a shame, but inevitable; like the rest of us, Pharoah cat, you've gotten old.

Novels: *A Queer Kind of Death* (1966); *Swing Low, Sweet Harriet* (1967); *Topsy and Evil*, also introducing another black sleuth, Satan Slagg (1968); *A Queer Kind of Love* (1994); *A Queer Kind of Umbrella* (1995).

Other series: Baxt's wacky two-novel Sylvia Plotkin and NYPD detective Max Van Larsen series; and his eleven-novel Celebrity Murder series starring such twentieth-century cultural icons as Bette Davis, Clark Gable, and Tallulah Bankhead.

Baxt also wrote several stand-alone novels and a chapbook, *Scheme and Variations* (1994). Baxt also worked on five films and numerous television plays, especially *The Defenders* series.

Selected sources: Baker, James N. "Welcome back, Pharoah." *Newsweek*, July 4, 1994: 44; Boucher, Anthony. Rev. of *A Queer Kind of Death. New York Times Book Review*, May 14, 1967: 29; Callendar, Newgate. Rev. of *Swing Low, Sweet Harriet. New York Times Book Review*, May 14, 1967: 32; Herbert, Rosemary. "Process of Elimination." *Library Journal*, March 1, 1984: 510; Lakowsky, Wes. Rev. of *A Queer Kind of Umbrella. Booklist*, September 1, 1995: 44; *Times Literary Supplement*. Rev. of *Swing Low, Sweet Harriet*, June 1, 1967: 15.

Award: Best Mystery Novel Award nomination, Mystery Writers of America, 1967.

See also: Roger L. Simon's Moses Wine series chronicling American cultural history since the 1970s; Joseph Hansen's gay insurance investigator **Dave Brandstetter** series; Michael Nava's series featuring gay California lawyer Henry Rios; Richard Stevenson's series featuring modern Albany gay detective Donald Strachey; John Morgan Wilson's scathing **Benjamin Justice** series.

Thomas Lynley

Profession:	Detective Inspector, Scotland Yard
Living situation:	Single; later married
Geographic locale:	Great Britain
Time period:	1988–present
Associates:	Detective Sergeant Barbara Havers; Simon Allcourt-St. James; Deborah Cotter St. James; Lady Helen Clyde (later Lynley's wife)
Significant relationships:	Deborah St. James; Lady Helen Clyde
Concerns:	Social issues, especially incest, racial tensions, child welfare; infertility

Handsome, impeccably tailored Detective Inspector Thomas Lynley is eighth Earl of Asherton and a Bentley-driving successor to Dorothy L. Sayers's Lord Peter Wimsey. Around him clusters an elite British social group that, combined with New Scotland Yard and murder and contrasted with the gritty working-class personality of Lynley's "homely, stubby-featured" sergeant Barbara Havers, seems to guarantee perennial popular success for Elizabeth George's immensely detailed and highly successful mystery novels, less procedural than psychological investigations.

Lynley, who chooses not to use his title, is pivotal to most of these murder cases. He is usually assisted by his closest friend, forensic scientist Simon Allcourt-St. James, crippled years earlier in a drunk-driving accident with Lynley at the wheel. Simon marries photographer Deborah Cotter, Lynley's former fiancée, daughter of Lynley's long-time valet. Lynley marries Lady Helen Clyde, Simon's talented laboratory assistant. The romantic entanglements and resulting conflicts generate considerable angst for Lynley, who experiences episodes of painful introspection. Beginning with the award-winning *A Great Deliverance* (1988), a grisly atmospheric Yorkshire decapitation case, Lynley's usual partner, Sergeant Barbara Havers, seethes with inbred resentment toward the British upper-class old-boy network while she grapples with poverty and an aging Alzheimer's-stricken mother. Their working relationship is touchy at best, although Lynley's essential decency and compassion eventually win Havers's devotion. George portrays Lynley through the eyes and thoughts of the other main characters, so some commentators believe "we cannot say we know him well from any point of view—as a police officer, an earl, or a man" (*Silk Stalkings: More* 60).

As a police officer, Lynley manages to defuse the animosity most of his Yard colleagues feel toward his wealth and position. His superiors find him useful in "kid-glove handling" situations involving VIPs like the Earl of Stinhurst, a major suspect in *Payment in Blood* (1989). There, Lynley's major challenge is less the police job than it is Sergeant Havers, "chomping at the bit to be the first from her grammar school to slap handcuffs on an earl." In these early stages of their partnership, Lynley "shudder[s] at the thought that he and Sergeant Havers were about to be joined . . . in a wedlock of careers he would never be able to escape" (*Payment* 13–14). By 2001's *A Traitor to Memory*, however, their professional "marriage" has modulated from mutual suspicion to guarded cooperation—guarded because Havers has come to adore Lynley across the unapproachable gulf between their stations.

As an earl, Lynley outrages most of his family by working as a policeman, which the old butler of the family estate in Cornwall refers to as "his lordship's whimsy" (*Payment* 10). Lynley doesn't hesitate to use his position (or his Bentley) to good advantage, and his inborn air of command as well as his innate good manners gain him the confidence of provincial (even Scots) colleagues. His fine mind and elitist education equip him to deal rationally and decisively with complex problems, as even Havers admits: "she fleetingly wished that Inspector Lynley were with her. He never seemed to have any vague or unsettling feelings about anything . . . she could have done with a good Inspector-Sergeant confab" (*In the Presence of the Enemy* 395). Lynley works hard to get Havers's rank back after she runs afoul of their superior in *A Traitor to Memory*.

As a man, Lynley's emotional reactions to his convoluted relationships become increasingly stressful, especially his connection to Simon and Deborah St. James as their murder cases shift from atmospheric puzzlers to social-issue studies. In *A Traitor to Memory* (2001), Lynley, once engaged to Deborah, who desperately wants the children she can't have, has to tell her that his wife Lady Helen is pregnant. Worse, when his fiancée Deborah was eighteen and studying in Santa Barbara, Lynley had visited her several times, and now, "he didn't wish to say it, would have given anything to avoid it. But at the last moment he forced himself to admit . . . 'I knew'" (*Traitor*

699). Even though Deborah admits she lost that baby, like all her subsequent pregnancies, to a genetic defect, Lynley still has to face his guilt at leaving her alone in California, another shadow, like his guilty responsibility for Simon's paralysis, which will never leave him. He shoulders this burden alone, convinced it "had nothing to do with Helen and even less to do with the future Lynley intended to share with her" (*Traitor* 703).

Just as Dorothy L. Sayers eventually tired of Lord Peter, George may have temporarily exhausted her fictional possibilities with Thomas Lynley, and in *A Place of Hiding* (2003), she turned to Deborah as a heroine, as Sayers did with her autobiographical novelist Harriet Vane. Advanced to Acting Superintendent but reduced to a supporting role in this novel, Lynley remains mostly in the background as Deborah and St. James wrestle with Deborah's infertility as they extricate her California friend China River and China's leftover hippie brother Cherokee from a messy murder on the Channel island of Guernsey.

With No One as Witness (2005), though, returns George's focus to Lynley and Havers as they investigate the racially implicated linked murders of four young men, three of them black or racially mixed. *With No One as Witness* (2005) brings Lynley back to George's New Scotland Yard center stage, Havers again at his side, with black Detective Sergeant Winston Nkata assisting them in a hunt for a psychopathic serial killer of adolescent boys. Havers has botched up yet again and has been broken from Detective Sergeant to Constable, while Lynley, pressured to find the psychopathic serial killer, gingerly copes with touchy Assistant Commissioner David Hillier. The novel ends on a note of heartbreaking anguish, as Lynley suffers his most tragic blow yet at the close of this taut, impassioned mystery. For all his recriminations and his grace under pressure, for most of this intricately plotted series, Thomas Lynley remains, like Lord Peter Wimsey, the elegant, stiff-upper-lipped, and absolutely indispensable linchpin.

Novels: *A Great Deliverance* (1988); *Payment in Blood* (1989); *Well-Schooled in Murder* (1990); *A Sensible Vengeance* (1991); *For the Sake of Elena* (1992); *Missing Joseph* (1993); *Playing for the Ashes* (1994); *In the Presence of the Enemy* (1996); *Deception on His Mind* (1997); *In Pursuit of the Proper Sinner* (1999); *A Traitor to Memory* (2001); *A Place of Hiding* (2003); *With No One as Witness* (2005).

Short story: "The Evidence Exposed," in George's short fiction collection *I, Richard* (2001; published in 1999 in the U.K. as *The Evidence Exposed*).

Stand-alone novel: *Remember, I'll Always Love You* (2001).

Nonfiction: *Write Away: One Novelist's Approach to Fiction and the Writing Life* (2004).

Other works: George has also edited *A Moment on the Edge: 100 Years of Crime Stories by Women.*

Selected sources: Carey, Lynn. "Elizabeth George Reveals Why Britain's the Setting for Her Best-Selling Mysteries." *Knight-Ridder/Tribune News Service*, August 6, 1997; Garner, Dwight. "Out of Ohio." *New York Times Book Review*, April 10, 2005: 34; Gussow, Mel. "Golly! A Yank Wrote Those Oh-So-British Mysteries?" *New York Times*, December 14, 1999:

B1; Nolan, Tom. Rev. of *Deception on His Mind. Wall Street Journal*, July 25, 1997: A12; Stasio, Marilyn. Rev. of *Well-Schooled in Murder. New York Times Book Review*, August 12, 1990: 21.

Major awards: Agatha Award and Anthony Award, 1989; *Grand Prix de Littérature Policière*, 1990; MIMI Award (Germany), 1991.

Web site: www.elizabethgeorgeonline.com.

See also: American authors writing British-style mysteries: Deborah Crombie's **Duncan Kincaid**-Gemma James series; Martha Grimes's **Richard Jury** series; for psychological depth, P.D. James's **Adam Dalgliesh** series.

M

Marti MacAlister

Profession:	Detective, Lincoln Prairie Police Force
Living situation:	Widowed; then remarried
Geographic locale:	Lincoln Prairie (fictionalized Waukegan), Illinois
Time period:	1992–present
Associate:	Detective Matthew "Vik" Jessenovik
Significant relationship:	Ben Walker
Concerns:	Family and children's issues

Marti MacAlister, the first black woman homicide detective in mystery fiction, is tough, intelligent, intuitive—and anything but noir. For years, Eleanor Taylor Bland, whose father was black and mother white, balanced her writing with her work as a cost accountant for Abbott Laboratories, refusing to play the race card in her novels. Bland prefers to address other societal problems through MacAlister's cases, most of them taking place in a suburban Chicago community. Bland told *Contemporary Authors*, "I write about social issues, particularly those that affect women and children, and also about members of society who I do not feel have a voice unless we speak for them. . . . I write about what makes me angry or engages me emotionally."

Homicide detective Marti MacAlister engages her readers both intellectually and emotionally. After ten years' service, four commendations, and the death of her husband Johnny, a fellow Chicago cop who supposedly shot himself while working under cover, Marti MacAlister leaves the Windy City, where she's built up a reliable network running the gamut from FBI agents to mob figures, for Lincoln Prairie, Illinois, modeled on Bland's Waukegan. Though Marti's never militant about feminism, at thirty-six she quietly holds her own with the boys, both colleagues and criminals. Her vice cop office mates Cowboy and Slim dub her "Big Mac"—she's 5'10", 160 pounds, with a healthy appetite for jelly doughnuts and a rare T-bone despite her daughter Joanna's determined creation of cholesterol-lowering salads— and she doesn't make the office coffee because Cowboy does it better. She ignores their girlie-calendar office décor—she saw worse in Chicago—and relishes using her uptown connections and urban street-smarts to collar criminals preying on the helpless. Teamed up with fiftyish Polish-American detective Matthew "Vik" Jessenovic, Marti defuses his initial thinly-veiled chauvinism with competence and courage. Her colleagues come to trust her because they know she can take care of herself—and she'll take care of them.

The raw, chilling cases Marti and Vik investigate almost all involve victimized women and children in the maggoty underbelly of suburbia. Their first, *Dead Time* (1992), centers on homeless boys scrounging a living off Lincoln Prairie's streets, throwaway children who saw the killer of a mentally ill woman in a rundown hotel. *Slow Burn* (1992) explores arson at a Lincoln Prairie medical clinic, a hit and run accident, and a child porn racket; and *Gone Quiet* (1994), set in Lincoln Prairie's black community, treats the murder of a Baptist deacon who is secretly a pedophile.

The scope of "Big Mac's" crime-solving soon widens. In *Done Wrong* (1994), Marti returns to Chicago to look into Johnny's death, a harrowing experience that proves he was murdered and finally brings closure to her and her children Joanna and Theo. *Keep Still* (1996), takes Marti back to Lincoln Prairie and into the excruciating realities of child abuse. *See No Evil* (1998) again features the quiet horrors of street life, and *Tell No Tales* (1999) treats the murder of a mentally ill recluse, a character type Bland often uses to comment on today's fatal neglect of the psychologically infirm.

In *Scream in Silence* (2000) Marti and Vik pursue an arsonist and psychopathic bomber, and in *Whispers in the Dark* (2001), they face prostitution, the drug trade, and AIDS, three of "the more violent conflicts between society's 'insiders and the excluded,'" according to *Publishers Weekly*. *Fatal Remains* (2003) takes Marti into the brutal history of slavery and the exploitation of Native Americans, while *A Cold and Silent Dying* (2004) exposes Marti, Vik, and Marti's close friend Sharon to a vengeful serial killer while Marti struggles with the jealousy of her new white superior, Lt. Gail Nicholson, who thinks Marti's success is due to tokenism rather than talent and hard work.

As sensational as these cases are, constantly forcing Marti MacAlister to find new ways of implementing her powerful desire for justice for the downtrodden, it's her calm strength of character that sustains her. In her own childhood, Marti was poor but safe, but when the series begins with *Dead Time*, she's learned how viciously today's world can exploit children.

Marti brings her daughter Joanna, then fourteen, and nine-year-old Theo, all of them still mourning Johnny after his death a year and a half earlier, to Lincoln Prairie to make a new, more secure life, sharing their home with Sharon, a divorced teacher whom Marti's known since kindergarten, and Sharon's daughter Lisa. In the course of her work, Marti meets Ben Walker, a quiet, caring paramedic raising a son Theo's age alone, and over several novels their relationship grows into love and eventually marriage. That solid relationship allows Marti and Ben to shelter their extended family, including Marti's Momma, under a peaceful roof. Her oasis of well-adjusted family life sustains and refreshes Marti no matter how devastating her cases become. Ben soothes Marti's physical and psychological wounds with a hot tub, an omelet, and a full body massage, and she knows how lucky she is to have found him.

Marti successfully builds an effective working relationship with Vik, too. At first Vik, an old-fashioned middle-aged dominant-male detective, distrusts her as a woman partner, resents her big-city experience and suspects her of big-city moral turpitude. "Man's work, policing. . . . We don't let anything as unreliable as intuition interfere with common sense and sound judgment. . . . Look, kid, I know that when you were in the big city you got to draw your weapon on the least little pretext to keep a situation from getting out of hand because you're a female. . . . This isn't Chicago, MacAlister . . . we're professionals. . . . No breaches of anyone's civil rights" (*Dead Time* 14–15). Taciturn and brooding over his beloved wife Mildred's tragic decline from MS, Vik eventually comes to value Marti's feminine intuition because it often works.

Marti also tempers the corrosive disgust Vik harbors toward a judicial system that allows criminals to get off simply because they say they're sorry. She'd felt that way once, too, and she remains furious at the thought of people getting away with murder, but now she lives by Johnny's words and even helps Vik understand them: "You do your job. You do it right. You don't take shortcuts, you don't go home early, you don't leave anything undone. You build a solid case against them. You bring them in. You don't let them get away with it. And that's all you can do" (*Dead Time* 134).

In one of today's toughest jobs, Marti MacAlister succeeds not so much in spite of being a woman but because she is one. She doesn't worry about burnout because she knows what's really important. "I have time for my family. My kids don't complain that they never see me. Most of the time, I'm not too tired for my husband. Sometimes I get to do something to help somebody. And I work with a partner who is still married to his childhood sweetheart and, after twenty-five years on the force, still believes there is good in the world" (*Fatal Remains* 218). Marti MacAlister doesn't preach her faith in humanity, she lives it, and for herself and her readers, that's what counts.

Novels: *Dead Time* (1992); *Slow Burn* (1992); *Gone Quiet* (1994); *Done Wrong* (1995); *Keep Still* (1996); *See No Evil* (1998); *Tell No Tales* (1999); *Scream in Silence* (2000); *Whispers in the Dark* (2001); *Windy City Dying* (2002); *Fatal Remains* (2003); *A Cold and Silent Dying* (2004); *A Dark and Deadly Deception* (2005).

Other works: Bland also edited *Shades of Black: Crime and Mystery Stories by African-American Authors* (2004) and contributed to this volume with her grandson Anthony Arnell Bland.

Selected sources: Burns, Ann, and Emily J. Jones. Rev. of *Scream in Silence*. *Library Journal*, November 1, 1999: 103; Champlin, Charles. Rev. of *Gone Quiet*. *Los Angeles Times Book Review*,

July 10, 1994: 8; Corrigan, Maureen. Rev. of *Keep Still*. *Washington Post Book World*, August 18, 1996: 8; Miller, Stuart. Rev. of *Whispers in the Dark*. *Booklist*, September 15, 2001: 1245; *Publishers Weekly*. Rev. of *Whispers in the Dark*, October 1, 2001: 47; Skenazy, Paul. Rev. of *Done Wrong*. *Washington Post Book World*, July 16, 1995: 6.

Awards: PEN Oakland Josephine Miles Award; Chester A. Himes Mystery Fiction Award; Most Influential African American of Lake County Award.

See also: Barbara Neely's award-winning (and ironically named) Blanche White series; Terris McMahon Grimes's award-winning Theresa Galloway series; for a male analogue, see John Ball's series, featuring black Pasadena homicide detective Virgil Tibbs.

Hamish Macbeth

Profession:	Constable
Living situation:	Single
Geographic locale:	Northwest Scottish Highlands
Time period:	1985–present
Associates:	Priscilla Halburton-Smythe; later Olivia Chater, Elspeth Grant
Nemesis:	Detective Chief Inspector Blair
Significant relationships:	Priscilla Halburton-Smythe; D.I. Olivia Chater; Elspeth Grant
Concerns:	Justice; family loyalty; traditional values

Writing as M.C. Beaton, prolific romance author Marion Chesney centers this cozy series on a paradoxical protagonist who cannily makes himself appear shiftless enough to avoid being promoted from the humble constable's job he loves. Hamish Macbeth's heart is in the Highlands and he intends to stay there in Lochdubh, a village established in the eighteenth century to promote the fishing trade and dwindling ever since. Now Lochdubh hibernates during its awful seaside winters and depends economically on the summer tourist trade, mostly English visitors, attracted by the Highlands' gorgeous scenery and their salmon- and trout-filled lochs and rivers, and welcomed with "outward Highland courtesy and inner Highland hate" (*Gossip* 4).

That juicy ambivalence anchors each of Hamish Macbeth's cases. Except for occasional poaching, speeding, and domestic flare-ups, Lochdubh's locals are mostly lawbiding, but situations rapidly sour the bonny banks and braes when by long-standing English custom, "everyone goes to Scotland in August to kill things" (*Gossip* 11), as in *Death of a Gossip* (1985): a group of English fishing students from Hell arrive at the Lochdubh Hotel for a week of fly-tieing, back-biting, and murder.

Under the guise of the scrounging village constable considered too lazy even to poach, tall, gangly, flaming-red-haired Hamish has built himself a comfortable niche in Lochdubh—a new house combined with a one-cell police station and a new Morris for his rounds; some sheep, chickens, and geese and a slavering guard dog named Towser. Mooching his morning coffee and noontime sandwiches from fishing school operators John and Heather Cartwright, Hamish dons a dull-witted appearance that masks a keen wit and a talent for justifiable rudeness so well that its bumptious targets, like the awful Lady Jane, a gossip columnist for the London *Evening Star* newspaper, can never quite pin it down. Few know that Hamish scrupulously follows an old Gaelic custom: the oldest son must remain unmarried until his younger siblings are self-supporting. Hamish sends most of his salary and venison, egg money, and the prize money he regularly wins from hill-running to his parents, who are raising six young children on the family croft in Ross and Cromarty. He thus can "shoulder his responsibilities without compromising his values" (*Silk Stalkings: More* 74).

Lady Jane has enough dirt on the fishing students to make them each fervently wish her dead. When she is found floating, gruesomely garroted, in a salmon pool, Hamish initially wants to let the big brass from Strathbane, Detective Chief Inspector Blair and his assistants Jimmy Anderson and Harry MacNab, handle the case, but Blair informs Hamish that he's not up to such an important crime, putting Hamish's Scots blood to the boil. While Hamish stubbornly pursues and nabs the killer, he's also obliquely courting Priscilla Halburton-Smythe, whose snobbish father is pushing her toward wealthy Englishman John Harrington. Hamish also helps out two innocent fishing students, Charlie, a schoolboy caught up in his parents' custody wrangle, and Alice, a pretty secretary victimized as much by her own silly dreams as by a handsome English rotter with a low-slung roadster.

Hamish's subsequent "heartwarming if violence-filled adventures" always involve both professional and personal challenges, like *Death of an Addict* (1999), where he and attractive Detective Inspector Olivia Chater infiltrate the county's biggest drug ring. While Blair continues to downgrade Hamish as a provincial clod, Hamish invariably refuses the efforts Blair's superior Superintendent Peter Daviot and his wife Susan make toward his promotion. Hamish's holiday frolic *A Highland Christmas* (1999), set in neighboring Cnothan, is more lighthearted, but *Death of a Celebrity* (2002) returns him to Lochdubh and darker glimpses into human nature.

Hamish still carries a torch for Priscilla—who fruitlessly prodded and chivvied Hamish about rising in the world while helping him with his investigations and holding him at chilly arm's length—even as he hears about her engagement to Harrington. Swearing off women altogether and taken off another homicide, Hamish unofficially solves the death of Crystal French, a slept-her-way-to-the-top television personality who had produced a corrosive series of exposes of local citizens. By joining forces with Blair's temporary replacement, DCI Patrick Carson, Elspeth Grant, a half-gypsy newspaper astrologer with "the sight," and his new blue-eyed dog Lugs, Hamish traps yet another killer with "the lying ease of the true Highlander" (*Celebrity* 108) while keeping his Highland values intact. When Carson, after frequently sharing Hamish's single malt, turns ungratefully stuffy and blames Hamish "for wanting to stay a village constable," Hamish replies, "It's because I'm a village constable that I solved your murders for you. I know people better than I know police procedure." For his part, Lugs bites "the retreating detective chief inspector on the backside" (*Celebrity* 264). Scotland forever.

Novels: *Death of a Gossip* (1985); *Death of a Cad* (1987); *Death of an Outsider* (1988); *Death of a Perfect Wife* (1989); *Death of a Hussy* (1990); *Death of a Snob* (1991); *Death of a Prankster* (1992); *Death of a Glutton* (1993); *Death of a Traveling Man* (1993); *Death of a Charming Man* (1994); *Death of a Nag* (1995); *Death of a Macho Man* (1996); *Death of a Dentist* (1997); *Death of a Scriptwriter* (1998); *Death of an Addict* (1999); *A Highland Christmas* (1999); *Death of a Dustman* (2001); *Death of a Celebrity* (2002); *Death of a Village* (2003); *Death of a Poison Pen* (2004); *Death of an Outsider* (2005); *Death of a Bore* (2005); *Death of a Dreamer* (2006).

Other series: The **Agatha Raisin** mystery series, set in the Cotswolds; under "Marion Chesney," various romance series: the "Six Sisters" series; the "A House for the Season" series; the "School for Manners" series; the "Poor Relation" series; the "Daughters of Manning" series; the "Travelling Matchmaker" series; under "Helen Crampton," two romance novels; under "Ann Fairfax, four romance novels; under "Jennie Tremaine," twelve Dell Romances; under "Charlotte Ward," one romance novel.

Selected sources: DeCandido, GraceAnne A. Rev. of *A Highland Christmas. Booklist*, October 1, 1999: 345; Melton, Emily. Rev. of *Death of a Dentist. Booklist*, August 1, 1997: 1884; Melton, Emily. Rev. of *Death of an Addict. Booklist*, April 15, 1999: 1468; *Publishers Weekly*. Rev. of *Death of a Scriptwriter*, April 13, 1998: 55; *Publishers Weekly*. Rev. of *Death of a Traveling Man*, May 23, 1994: 9.

See also: The Susannah Stacey (pseudonym for Jill Staynes and Margaret Storey) intuitive Superintendent Robert Bone series; Rhys Bowen's Constable Evan Evans series, set in Wales.

John Madden

Profession:	Detective Inspector, Scotland Yard; later a farmer
Living situation:	Single; later married
Geographic locale:	Surrey, England
Time period:	1921; then 1932
Associates:	Angus Sinclair; Billy Styles
Significant relationship:	Dr. Helen Blackwell
Concern:	Savagery versus civilization

As a Reuters journalist, Rennie Airth has chronicled much of the world's pain; as a novelist, he brings it to excruciating life. Airth's output of fiction is small but distinguished: the *Times Literary Supplement* described *Snatch!* (1969) as "thriller of the year," and Harriet Waugh, also writing for *TLS*, called *Once a Spy* (1981) "subtle, ingenious, and neatly fashioned" (quoted in *CA Online*). Later Airth's family scrapbook, dedicated to his uncle who had died in World War I, inspired Airth to create a hero who personalizes the staggering aftermath of "the war to end all wars."

World War I's casualty rates, overall an estimated ten million people killed and twice that number wounded, are so vast as to have become nearly incomprehensible— and today, sadly, almost forgotten. British losses alone bankrupted an entire British generation, destroying sons, brothers, and fathers and causing a major shift in society, with women entering fields previously unheard of for them. Too many of Britain's future leaders perished, like the over 2,700 Oxford men who died in the trenches. For every three young officers who went "over there" knowing their life expectancy could be measured in weeks, one was killed, one returned so badly damaged that he could not function in society, and the third struggled for the rest of his life with emotional if not physical wounds. At the close of the war sixty thousand English soldiers were in mental hospitals (*River of Darkness* 77). World War I also sowed the seeds of catastrophes to come, for the Allies' brutal reparation demands forced Germany into chaotic inflation and paved Adolf Hitler's path to power. To many, like Irish poet William Butler Yeats, the center of Western civilization seemed no longer able to hold, and an ominous new barbarism had sprung upon them.

Scotland Yard Detective Inspector John Madden of Rennie Airth's *River of Darkness* (1999) and *The Blood-Dimmed Tide* (2005) forces readers to share his shattering realization that imperialist, territorial, and economic rivalry among the great powers, the factors that brought about World War I, caused the West's moral disintegration and loosed savagery upon the people and land he loves. Between the world wars, rough human beasts prowled England and the Continent, human beings twisted by heredity and history into predators that psychiatric science had barely begun to comprehend or even postulate, killers that law enforcement was technologically and even psychologically ill-equipped to apprehend.

Home from the Great War, John Madden, now a "tall, grim man with a scarred forehead" and "deep-set eyes that seemed to look at you from another world ... seemed more like a monk than a policeman" (*River of Darkness* 4). In 1916, Madden had grieved so deeply over the simultaneous loss of his wife and young daughter from influenza that for two years he sought oblivion in the trenches, but fate sent him home to England again and to Scotland Yard, "a hollow survivor just going through the motions of life" (Dickey 10). In *River of Darkness* he faces horrifying killings at Melling Lodge in Highfield, a small Surrey village, all but one of the Fletcher family brutally stabbed to death. Hand-to-hand experience tells Madden that the murder weapon is a bayonet wielded with military efficiency, "a short, stabbing thrust followed by a half-twist to break the friction as the weapon is withdrawn" (*River of Darkness* 24). Madden painstakingly probes the killings under the direction of his dapper friend Chief Inspector Angus Sinclair and with the help of brash young Detective Sergeant Billy Styles. Madden also falls in love with Highfield's physician Dr. Helen Blackwell, friend of one of the victims, who takes Madden to a lecture given by Viennese psychoanalyst Franz Weiss, a pioneer in the new field of abnormal psychiatry. Weiss theorizes that the sexuality flowing through human lives can, under the influence of a damaged psyche, produce a "river of darkness," a compulsion leading to serial killings.

Madden has been badly damaged, too. Since the 1918 Armistice, "a charnel house of memories" threatened to engulf him: "What he kept from his mind by day he was forced to relive in his dreams ... from which he would wake, night after night, choking on the imagined smell of sweat and cordite and the stench of half-buried corpses." Madden had finally accepted himself as permanently scarred, bereft of hope, with his solitary life "all that was left to him" (*River of Darkness* 32), when he went down to Surrey—where Helen, the first night they met, fell victim to "the demon sex" (89) and began to heal him with her love.

As Christopher Dickey has observed, Madden at the start of *River of Darkness* moves "at the unhurried pace of the walking wounded" and only comes to life as he begins to understand the murderer's ferocity. When Helen becomes the serial killer's next target, Madden's driving sense of duty to his job and "his passion to keep England as humane as he remembered it" (Dickey 10) impel him to a climactic choice between civilization and savagery. Injured and enraged as he himself is, with a blade an inch from the killer's throat, Madden chooses civilization—and places him under arrest.

In the ten years between *River of Darkness* and *A Blood-Dimmed Tide*, John Madden has yielded to Helen's wishes and retired early from Scotland Yard. They now live in Helen's family home near Melling Lodge with their children, ten-year-old Rob and irrepressible six-year-old Lucy. Madden has bought the kind of farm he grew up on, and though he employs a manager, he works there himself at the hardest physical labor he can find out of a nagging guilt for living away from his land.

Guilt, too, drives John Madden to revert to his old commanding role when a young girl is found brutally murdered not far away from their home, her face disfigured beyond recognition by hammer blows. As more children's bodies turn up across England, the Yard is called to an investigation that eventually reaches into Europe on the eve of Hitler's rise to power, and chancing Helen's fury, Angus Sinclair calls on his old friend Madden again, bringing Billy Styles, Dr. Franz Weiss, and other characters familiar from *River of Darkness* back into the peaceful life Madden has built for himself in Surrey.

Throughout this case, Madden continues "to be gnawed by anxiety, a deep-seated unease" from the moment he'd seen Alice Bridger's shattered face, an image linked with his horrifying memories of the war. He realizes his feeling is irrational, but the murder seems to have opened a door again "into the world of savagery and barbarism which bitter experience had taught him lay just outside the frail fabric that bound ordered society" (*Blood-Dimmed Tide* 166). These murders summon Madden again to his own inner battle: again Helen tries to prevent Madden from becoming involved; again Dr. Weiss insists that some murderers are born evil; again Madden's sense of guilt and duty prevails. Again he risks his life to save an innocent, and again he turns away from weapons, choosing to rely on his "copper's voice" (*Blood-Dimmed Tide* 174) to bring his quarry to bay. In this new savage environment filled with human monsters, John Madden represents decency, compassion, honor, and courage in the face of evil—all those civilization-binding ideals that seem to be flying apart as his world again prepares for war.

Novels: *River of Darkness* (1999); *The Blood-Dimmed Tide* (2005).

Stand-alone novels: *Snatch!* (1969); *Once a Spy* (1981).

Selected sources: Dickey, Christopher. "The Bad Soldier." *New York Times Book Review*, August 1, 1999: 10; Grimond, Kate. "Copses and Corpses." *Spectator*, November 13, 2004: 46; McNichol, Nancy. Rev. of *River of Darkness*. *Library Journal*, May 15, 1999: 123; Pitt, David. Rev. of *The Blood-Dimmed Tide*. *Booklist*, June 1, 2005: 1737; Stasio, Marilyn. "A World Grown Savage." *New York Times Book Review*, July 24, 2005: 15.

See also: For post–World War I Scotland Yard cases: Charles Todd's **Inspector Ian Rutledge** series; for pre–World War I and wartime homicide cases: Anne Perry's Reavley novels, *No Graves As Yet* (2003), *Shoulder the Sky* (2004) and *Angels in the Gloom* (2005); for two contrasting female responses to the war and its aftermath, see Kerry Greenwood's **Phryne Fisher** series, set in Australia with flashbacks to its heroine's ambulance-driving days; and Jacqueline Winspear's **Maisie Dobbs** series, set in England with flashbacks to Maisie's months as a casualty station nurse in France.

Kathleen Mallory

Profession:	Detective Sergeant, Special Crimes Section, NYPD
Living situation:	Single
Geographic locale:	New York City
Time period:	1994–present
Associates:	Detective Sergeant Riker; Charles Butler
Significant relationship:	None

Two pain-filled plots dominate this hardest-boiled procedural series. One develops the present career of Carol O'Connell's Detective Sergeant Kathleen Mallory, a drop-dead gorgeous, virtually sociopathic mid-twenties computer genius wielding her .357 Smith and Wesson hand cannon mercilessly to defend the good and destroy the evil of her black and white big-city world. The other gradually unveils the "back story," Mallory's harrowing childhood as a throwaway youngster on New York's meanest streets. Taken in sequence, the Mallory novels form a blistering montage of horrors within and without the human personality.

Mallory's Oracle (1994) opens with Mallory's rescuer, Louis Markowitz, first Commander of the NYPD Special Crimes Unit, found dead near the third of three elderly murdered women. Although on compassionate leave, Mallory, the youngest SCU detective and its only woman, remorselessly tracks his killer through the eerie world of stage magic and phony spiritualism, assisted by two men, her night-job employer Charles Butler and Markowitz's old partner, Columbo-sloppy Detective Sergeant Riker. Mallory icily keeps the world at arm's length, but each man adores her in his own way. Butler, a wealthy forty-year-old bibliophile and psychologist with a husky build, an eidetic memory, and a loony-looking grin, runs an elite headhunting agency where Mallory flouts the law and her superiors by off-duty hacking into any system she pleases. Butler secretly and hopelessly loves her, realizing that her deep-seated psychological problems prevent her from making emotional attachments. After a rotten divorce, Riker's drinking broke him from captain back to sergeant. Now in his declining fifties, he's a sensitive, dead-honest cop, subject to binges and episodes of depression, who risks what's left of his career for Mallory, the child of his old friend. She cares enough about Riker to see that he doesn't shoot himself.

Throughout the series, which chronicles a succession of increasingly bizarre homicide cases, out-of-sequence scraps of Mallory's early life surface like bits of discarded photographs. No one knows who her parents were or why they abandoned this ethereally lovely golden-haired child-thief with the shockingly perceptive green eyes. Her own jagged memories begin with the last four digits of a phone number her dying mother had inked on one small palm, making the child "an addict of hope" (*Crime School* 150), begging change from prostitutes to "dial three untried numbers, then the four she knew. If a woman answered, she would say, 'It's Kathy. I'm lost'" (*The Man* 5). No one ever acknowledged her.

Riker and Lou Markowitz, the best poker player in the universe, captured that homeless child, gave her a mother in Helen Markowitz, and taught her everything they knew about police work. Mallory grew up in the Special Crimes Unit and became their first technical support, getting the SCU's whole system of "crappy secondhand computers up and running when she was thirteen years old" (*Crime School* 176). But Helen dies and then Lou dies, Riker can't stay off the booze, and the lost child inside Kathy Mallory keeps fruitlessly searching for the mother who abandoned her.

Crime School (2002) assembles a few more fragments of Mallory's early life, when she "ran with whores and lived by guile, surviving on animal instinct to get through the night" (*Crime School* 375). One of Riker's snitches, a hooker known only as Sparrow, is found hanged, near death, chopped-off hair stuffed in her mouth, a fire burning—a gruesome repeat performance of a murder committed when ten-year-old Mallory was first in Markowitz's home. Working the case against the wishes of their superior Lieutenant Coffey, Riker finds a disturbing link between Sparrow and Mallory that sends Mallory, always happiest in attack mode, on an inexorable hunt for the killer. A hardened realist from childhood, Mallory's taken perfection for her trademark, from her impeccably tailored blazers to her immaculate high-tech black-and-white-decorated apartment. Interviewing witnesses and suspects, she convincingly passes off her guesswork as absolute certainties, and she has a reputation for ruthless payback that makes her "the ultimate cop . . . a perfect instrument of revenge" (*Crime School* 376).

As an adult, Mallory never reads fiction, but as a child, Riker knows, she'd been smitten by cheap predictable Westerns—for security? The shabby paperback he'd illegally filched from the scene of Sparrow's hanging floods Mallory with jumbled memories of arson and murder, horrifying rat-ridden images that break "into her conscious mind against her will" (*Crime School* 281), obsessing her with the sureties of white hats and black hats, of knowing the good guys from the bad, of the ultimate redemption of a youthful killer. Charles Butler, who loves her, believes that Kathleen Mallory's tragedy is "some malady that had no name but was akin to vampirism," for Kathy Mallory never looks in mirrors, "never expecting to find herself there" (*Crime School* 375).

Always seeking, never finding, always probing, never trusting, only rarely so much as touching another human being, Kathleen Mallory upends the conventional wisdom that insists that only remorse separates cops from their twins, the killers. The strange child Kathleen Mallory is mother to a strange, strange woman.

Novels: *Mallory's Oracle* (1994); *The Man Who Cast Two Shadows* (1995); *Killing Critics* (1996); *Flight of the Stone Angel* (1997); *Shell Game* (1999); *Crime School* (2002); *Dead Famous* (2003); *The Winter House* (2004).

Selected sources: Anderson, Karen. Rev. of *Shell Game*. *Library Journal*, June 15, 1999: 109; "Carol O'Connell: Watching Mallory Grow a Soul." *At Wanderer's Well*, www.dancingbadger .com (October 8, 2002); Melton, Emily. "*Booklist* Interview: Carol O'Connell." *Booklist*, April 15, 1998: 1370; *Publishers Weekly*. Rev. of *Dead Famous*, August 4, 2003: 55; Thomas, Devon. Rev. of *Judas Child*. *Library Journal*, April 15, 1998: 115.

See also: For psychologically troubled female detectives, Abigail Padgett's series featuring Barbara Joan "Bo" Bradley, a child abuse investigator; Nancy Pickard's **Jenny Cain** series, involving Cain's dysfunctional family.

The Mamur Zapt (Gareth Cadwallader Owen)

Profession:	Head of the secret police in British-dominated Egypt
Living situation:	Single
Geographic locale:	Egypt, especially Cairo
Time period:	Pre–World War I
Associates:	Georgiades and Nikos, Owen's subordinate detectives; Mahmoud el Zaki
Significant relationship:	Zainab, daughter of Nuri Pasha
Concerns:	Liberal social views, especially toward natives; harmful effects of British class system

The dizzying political situation of pre–World War I Egypt, keystone to the strategic and volatile Middle East, dominates this exotic series, sardonically comic on the surface but roiling beneath with deadly undertows and crocodilian villainy. Michael Pearce's first-hand knowledge of modern Egyptian history and powerful sympathy for the region's native underdogs permeates these novels. Seized by the Ottoman Turks in the sixteenth century and invaded by Napoleon in 1798, Egypt went bankrupt under its Khedive Ismail Pasha over the building of the Suez Canal, and by 1908, when *The Mamur Zapt and the Return of the Carpet* (1990) begins, the British Consul-General "advised" the puppet Khedive; the British Sirdar commanded the Egyptian Army; British officials ran the police in Cairo and Alexandria; and a British civil servant called the Mamur Zapt led Egypt's Political Branch, its secret police.

Gareth Cadwallader (his liberal mother's bow to her Welsh relations) Owen had moved from school to army and found himself excluded from senior positions by Old Boys with Oxford and Cambridge degrees that a poor Anglican clergyman's son like Owen could not have afforded. He left the army and India for Egypt, where an administrative fluke and Owen's Arabic, fluent enough to outcurse local camel drivers, got him appointed Mamur Zapt as a young man, plunging him into a welter of conniving Arabs, Europeans, Greeks, Armenians, and Copts, and four competing legal systems. Owen, sensitive to Arab culture and preferring real Egypt to the hotel version, adopted some Arab customs but maintained the strong sense of justice his mother taught him, cheekily facing down British Army arrogance, treading lightly among the baronial Pashas who dominated Egypt's feudalistic society, and sending villains up with tongue-in-cheek Welsh wit.

Owen's first case involves the attempted murder of Nuri Pasha, a rich Egyptian politician and notorious womanizer, just before "the Return of the Carpet," an annual Cairene Moslem religious observance. Owen's informants hint that the attack on Nuri may foreshadow a Nationalist assassination attempt against the current Khedive and the British Sirdar during that event. Owen, his dark Welsh coloring intensified by years of sunburn and his Celtic intuition tuned to the Arab propensity to work hot and cold, knows instinctively when to leave native matters to his assistants, the wily Greeks Georgiades and Nikos, while Owen himself, an inveterate opera-loving city person, frequents late-night haunts of Cairo's wealthy and powerful, picking up nuances and innuendoes to stir a wide assortment of administrative pots.

Owen's relationship with Mahmoud el Zaki, a young Nationalist official of the Parquet, the Prosecutor's Department of the Egyptian Ministry of Justice, also working to unravel the motives behind the attack on Nuri Pasha, individualizes the uneasy relationship between early-twentieth-century Egypt and Britain. As much as Owen admires Mahmoud's interrogation technique, which draws information from suspects by touching their emotions, and as respectful as Owen is to Mahmoud's own Arab sensibilities, cultural misunderstandings still cause occasional flare-ups. Mahmoud has to balance his distrust of British officialdom with his genuine liking and respect for Owen, while Owen learns how to wait, to watch, and to find the right words to stabilize their informal partnership.

Owen also falls under the spell of a modern Cleopatra while defusing the anti-British threat during the Return of the Carpet. Most wealthy Egyptian women were confined, bored and lonely, to the harem, but Zainab, with the volatility of a diva and the genes of Nuri Pasha and his favorite French-flavored courtesan, matches Owen's subtlety of mind and progressive political sympathies. After several relatively light-hearted cases like *The Mamur Zapt and the Donkey-Vous* (1990), an investigation of vanished French and English tourists, and *The Mamur Zapt and the Men Behind* (1991), probing the worlds of Cairene student rabble-rousers and slave- and weapons-trafficking, Owen's outlook darkens. By the time of the witty and astute award-winning *The Mamur Zapt and the Spoils of Egypt* (1993), he and the shockingly progressive Zainab have become lovers and unofficial partners in detection, for Zainab can go where no man, especially a British Mamur Zapt, dares—into the homes and hearts of sequestered Arab women.

Just when the pillaging of Egyptian antiquities by unscrupulous American and European dealers is reaching its apex, Miss Skinner arrives in Cairo, niece of a U.S. presidential candidate and "a splendid lady [in] a mighty hat" (*Spoils* 32), rigid of lip and corset. Miss Skinner's mission is to singlehandedly stop the traffic in stolen artifacts, and after she narrowly escapes being shoved under a passing tram, the Mamur Zapt, his friend Paul Trevelyan from the Consul-General's office, and Mahmoud el Zaki all are swept willy-nilly into her crusade. (Zainab compares her to a jumping camel.)

Through his cases, Gareth Owen's roots gradually shift. Even though he can never quite shake off his British origins, with his parents dead and no close relatives, he's made Egypt his home. Owen's friendship with Mahmoud, his love for Zainab's largeness of spirit that put her at odds with her society, his ease with Cairo and its multifaceted population, and his recognition that Welshman and Arab are brothers under the skin all plunge him into a dangerous quandary in *The Face in the Cemetery* (2001), set just at the August 1914 outbreak of World War I, after Zainab has moved into his flat. This case forces Owen to consider whether he and Zainab can build a lasting mixed marriage, for a man defined by his work can function in an expatriate world, but can a woman of expensive tastes live rejected by her extended family? Torn, too, between his patriotic desire to enlist again in the British Army and the duty he feels toward the Egypt he is helping to govern, Gareth Owen can't quite make East and West meet, but in him they reach a convincing, if as yet unsettled, accommodation.

Novels:* *The Mamur Zapt and the Return of the Carpet* (1988); *The Mamur Zapt and the Night of the Dog* (1989); *The Mamur Zapt and the Donkey-Vous* (1990); *The Mamur Zapt and the Men Behind* (1991); *The Mamur Zapt and the Girl in the Nile* (1992); *The Mamur Zapt and the Spoils of Egypt* (1993); *The Mamur Zapt and the Camel of Destruction* (1993); *The Snake-Catcher's Daughter* (1994); *The Mingrelian Conspiracy* (1995); *The Fig-Tree Murder* (1996); *The Last Cut* (1998); *Death of an Effendi* (1999); *A Cold Touch of Ice* (2000); *The Face in the Cemetery* (2001); *The Point in the Market* (U.S. 2005).

Other series: The Dmitri Kameron series, featuring Kameron as a half-Scottish, half-Russian lawyer in 1890s Russia: *Dmitri and the Milk Drinkers* (1997); *Dmitri and the One-Legged Lady* (1999). The Sandor Seymour series, debuting with *A Dead Man in Trieste* (2004), features Seymour as a British Special Branch agent investigating the death of the British consul knee-deep in 1911 Balkan politics.

Selected sources: Callendar, Newgate. Rev. of *The Mamur Zapt and the Night of the Dog. New York Times Book Review*, May 26, 1991: 22; Gray, Judith. Rev. of *A Cold Touch of Ice. Crime Time*, www.crimetime.co.uk (October 21, 2002); Irwin, Robert. Rev. of *The Mamur Zapt and the Camel of Destruction. Times Literary Supplement*, December 3, 1993: 20; Kahala, Keith. Rev. of *The Mamur Zapt and the Donkey-Vous. Armchair Detective*, Fall 1992: 494; *Publishers Weekly*. Rev. of *The Mamur Zapt and the Spoils of Egypt*, August 14, 1995: 74.

Award: CWA Last Laugh Award, 1993, for *The Mamur Zapt and the Spoils of Egypt*.

See also: Boris Akunin's **Erast Fandorin** series, set in tsarist Russia; Elizabeth Peters's **Amelia Peabody** series, set mostly in Egyptian archaeological digs; for international intrigue in the early 1930s, Rebecca Pawel's Carlos Tejada series, set during the Spanish Civil War; David Roberts's **Lord Edward Corinth** and Verity Browne series; for a Moroccan contemporary setting, see Carmen Posadas's *The Last Resort: A Moroccan Mystery*, "a novel of morals and murder" (*Publishers Weekly*, June 27, 2005: 45).

Debut novel: Barbara Nadel's *Belshazzar's Daughter: A Mystery of Istanbul*, featuring that Turkish city's Police Inspector Cetin Ikmen.

---

*Dates given show British publication; U.S. publication in each case is somewhat later.

Kate Martinelli

Profession:	Homicide detective
Living situation:	Single
Geographic locale:	San Francisco
Time period:	1993–present
Associate:	Inspector Alonzo Hawkin
Significant relationship:	Leonora "Lee" Cooper, Ph.D.
Concerns:	Sexual orientation; religion and morality; feminism; relationship of art to women; homelessness; child-rearing; spousal abuse

Novelist and theology scholar Laurie R. King reads "a lot of English crime fiction" (*Talking Murder* 144). Golden Age greats like Sayers made morality plays out of their crime stories, and so does King, whose lesbian homicide detective Kate Martinelli fights the good fight between good and evil in the context of contemporary social issues. This series stresses "explorations of how people find solutions to coping with whatever life throws at them—whether as villain or victim" (Ashley 271–72).

King develops her central series characters in a mega-novel while rounding off a different focal figure in each separate book. Kate Martinelli is newly promoted to San Francisco Homicide in the Edgar-winning *A Grave Talent* (1993) and paired with experienced Inspector Alonzo Hawkin, "the epitome of the one-track mind" (*A Grave Talent* 13), who is initially suspicious of a green woman partner. Since King wanted to keep Martinelli's working relationship with Hawkin free of erotic overtones, Martinelli initially remains in the closet. In their first case, Vaun Adams, perhaps the greatest living woman artist, lives out the feminist contention that "women have to be ten times as good as men to overcome their early training" (*A Grave Talent* 94). After serving a sentence for strangling a six-year-old girl, Adams becomes the prime suspect in serial murders of area girls. "How she got in that position and how good people can get her out," King says, "is what the book is about" (*Talking Murder* 146).

As one of those "good people," Kate copes with what life hands out by learning to take risks. One of her biggest is "coming out," for she is "a very tight, self-controlled, well-hidden individual . . . not just because of her sexual orientation" (*Talking Murder* 146). Kate's lover Lee, a psychotherapist, enables Kate to "let go, entirely, utterly. With Lee, she was absolutely vulnerable, freely open to crushing criticism or heart-filling communion. With Lee. Alone" (*A Grave Talent* 91).

Lee, though, is stressed by her practice and already considering a change of scene when Kate brings Vaun Adams into their home for protective custody. The climactic shootout of *A Grave Talent* partially paralyzes her and brutally changes her relationship with Kate, who becomes Lee's caregiver and "comes out" to a media "jamboree" full of "high culture, pathos, and titillation" (*To Play the Fool* 11).

Kate also faces a haunting metaphysical risk: "What is innocence? . . . Is . . . Adams . . . truly: an innocent? A mirror who has seen considerable evil, in herself as well as others, and reflects it back, along with the good, becoming ever brighter in the process?" (*A Grave Talent* 92–93). The contest between good and evil animates *To Play the Fool* (1995), where King tried to create a twentieth-century "holy fool . . . to challenge the concrete structure" of today's tightly compartmented society (*Talking Murder* 147).

King's Fool, enigmatic itinerant preacher Brother Erasmus, is the chief suspect in a Golden Gate Park homicide and Kate learns that the Fool's "essential ministry . . . is to undermine beliefs, to seed doubts, to shock people into seeing truth" (*To Play the Fool* 112). Her professional risk is that "likable people can be villains, that personality and charisma are, if anything, more likely to be found attached to the perpetrator than the victim. . . . But damn it, Erasmus was different" (*To Play the Fool* 199).

Kate also risks losing Lee from "guilt and struggle and financial problems . . . and [Lee's] agonizingly slow progress. . . . Odd pockets of cold air . . . [that] appeared without warning" and "all the minute adjustments that kept the marriage balanced" (*With Child* 68). *With Child* (1996) started as Lee's book but to King's surprise and Kate's mortal shock, Lee "walked off into the islands in Puget Sound" (*Talking Murder* 147), to rethink their relationship while Kate and Hawkin probe a case rife with dependencies involving the kidnapping of Al's stepdaughter Jules. Hawkin finally shows Kate that she has smothered Lee as surely as the shooting had stolen Lee's independence.

Night Work (1999) grapples with spousal abuse and female vengeance, at first humorously treated through the Ladies of Perpetual Disgruntlement, an area feminist vigilante group, who wreak "wickedly funny minor revenge" on abusive husbands. Soon, though, the case turns deadlier, involving worship of Kali, the Hindu goddess of destruction, "that immense power that exults in the destruction of men' loosed on the world" (*Night Work* 255).

After eight months a "stronger and more purposeful" Lee returns to Kate. Their renewed intimacy makes Kate more rested at home, more efficient at work, able to accept her next big risk, one that months earlier had almost shattered the bond between them when Kate overreacted badly. Not long after the shooting, Lee told her she wanted to try for a baby. Since Kate is stronger and more purposeful, too, she's now willing to take on the thrilling and frightening risks of parenthood. While Kate cannot see what their relationship will become, she feels certain that because "Lee still chose to be with her; the rest of it will find a way" (*Night Work* 192).

Novels: *A Grave Talent* (1993); *To Play the Fool* (1995); *With Child* (1996); *Night Work* (1999).

Other series: Mary Russell series: *The Beekeeper's Apprentice* (1994); *A Monstrous Regiment of Women* (1995); *A Letter of Mary* (1996); *The Moor* (1998); *O Jerusalem* (1999); *Justice Hall* (2002).

Other works: Laurie R. King has also written stand-alone novels, including *A Darker Place* (1999); *Folly* (2001); *Keeping Watch* (2003).

Selected sources: Adler, Dick. Rev. of *With Child*. *Tribune Books*, September 3, 1995: 4; "Andrea's Page: Interview with Laurie King." *Capitola Book Café*, www.capitolabookcafe.com; Maxwell, Lynn. "Serial Detectives at Work." *Lambda Book Report*, March 2000: 26; *Publishers Weekly*. Rev. of *Night Work*, January 17, 2000: 46; Stampe, Mia. Interview with Laurie R. King. *Kriminal Litteraere Nyheder*, www.ebfic.com/krininyt/art; Stasio, Marilyn. Rev. of *Night Work*. *New York Times Book Review*, February 20, 2000: 20.

Major awards (for Kate Martinelli series): Edgar Award, Mystery Writers of America, 1994; John Creasey Dagger, 1995 (both for *A Grave Talent*); Edgar Award nomination, 1996 (for *With Child*).

See also: For lesbian police detectives, private investigators, and amateur detectives: Katherine V. Forrest's series featuring former Marine and LAPD detective Kate Delafield; Clare McNab's Police Inspector Carol Ashton series set in Sydney, Australia; Lauren Wright Douglas's series featuring PI Caitlin Reece; Randye Lordon's series featuring New York ex-cop PI Sydney Sloane; Val McDermid's series featuring Scottish journalist Lindsay Gordon; Penny Mickelbury's two novels featuring Lieutenant Gianna Maglione of the Washington, D.C., Police Department's Hate Crimes Unit; Nikki Baker's series featuring Chicago African American financial analyst and amateur detective Virginia Kelly; Sandra Scoppettone's Greenwich Village PI Lauren Laurano; Barbara Wilson's series featuring amateur detective Pam Nilsen and Wilson's two Cassandra Reilly novels, *Gaudi Afternoon* (1990) and *Trouble in Transylvania* (1993); Penny Sumner's two Victoria Cross novels, *The End of April* (1992) and *Crosswords* (1995); Mary Wings's **Emma Victor** series; Eve Zaremba's series featuring Canadian lesbian PI Helen Karemos.

Debut novel: Ingrid Black's *The Dead*, featuring "Saxon" (no first name given), a former FBI agent turned true crime writer, who is the lover of Dublin Detective Chief Superintendent Grace Fitzgerald.

Sister Mary Helen

Profession:	Professed religious, former teacher and principal; latterly a volunteer in shelter for homeless women
Geographic locale:	San Francisco
Time period:	Contemporary
Associates:	Sister Eileen; Sister Anne; Detective Kate Murphy (later Bassetti)
Nemesis:	Detective Dennis Gallagher
Concern:	Serving God by ministering to society's victims

Being a professed Sister of St. Joseph of Carondelet almost as long as her septuagenarian heroine Sister Mary Helen has been in religious life has equipped Sister Carol Anne O'Marie to pursue two personal evangelical goals. As the only mystery author who is a Roman Catholic nun still in the convent, she can give special authenticity to her fiction dealing with convent life. As she observed in a *Chicago Tribune* profile, her writing also provides her a vehicle "for explaining my values in life and some of the gospel to a larger and more diverse audience."

O'Marie patterned Sister Mary Helen after an actual nun of the same name, O'Marie's former principal and superior, who, as O'Marie told the *Chicago Tribune*, "is a selfless lady and very supportive. She has not done any sleuthing but she would be very capable of it." Encountered initially in *A Novena for Murder* (1984), the Miss Marpleish Sister Mary Helen, seventy-five and fifty years a parish schoolteacher and sometime principal, has recently and reluctantly obeyed her Superior's "Senility

Sermon" and retired to her Order's Mount St. Francis College for Women near San Francisco. This she has avoided since her own training there since she wants to work with real people and their real problems. Down-to-earth and occasionally even earthy, Sister Mary Helen adopted Vatican II's modernizations after forty years in the religious habit, keeping her religious name but changing to a navy blue suit or an Aran cardigan and having her hair styled in a practical feather cut. Now in St. Francis College's Sisters' Residence (which she cannot call anything but a convent) whose nuns, as in real convent life, display a wide variety of attitudes toward Roman Catholic beliefs and practices, she gingerly mediates the generation gap between easily scandalized traditionalist Sister Therese (pronounced "trays") and moccasin-shod, yoga-practicing and incense-burning Sister Anne, the college's youthful guidance counselor. Faced with the brutal murder of the history professor under whom she was supposed to do research at the college, Sister Mary Helen enlists Sister Anne and Sister Eileen, Mary Helen's Irish-born friend since they entered the Order together. With the help of a former student, Detective Kate Murphy, currently living "in sin" with Vice Detective Jack Bassetti, whom Mary Helen, bothered not at all by their relationship, finds quite dishy, the old nun solves the crime despite the teeth-gnashing opposition of Kate's cigar-chomping partner, Detective Dennis Gallagher, a true believer that nuns, like all women, should stay in their conventional pre-liberated places.

Just as she took up the cause of exploited illegal Portuguese immigrants in *A Novena for Murder*, Sister Mary Helen, like Miss Marple not aging much through the series, pursues justice for the downtrodden through each of her ensuing cases. Though physically she sometimes feels "like an old model T without gas" (*Novena* 149), she's "one helluva sharp old lady," as Gallagher grudgingly admits (*Novena* 29), and her five decades in the classroom unerringly enable her to unleash a devastating "school-marm stare" (*Novena* 150) and read guilt or innocence in suspects' eyes. Describing herself as "damn mad" that miscreants terrorize her college and oppress the helpless, she often gives in to "detective fever," caught and exacerbated by the paperback mysteries she addictively reads, camouflaged in her plastic prayer book cover.

The passion for social justice that in 1990 impelled Sister Carol Anne O'Marie to cofound a daytime drop-in shelter for homeless women in downtown Oakland fuels Sister Mary Helen's volunteer work at the Refuge, the fictional setting in downtown San Francisco for her recent investigations. In *The Corporal Works of Murder* (2002), Sister Therese still flutters to the chapel to pray and Sister Anne still gulps down nausea at the sight of bashed heads and slit throats, while Sister Mary Helen sturdily pronounces the prayers for the dying now in English, not Latin, over a young street woman struck down near the Refuge—who turns out to be an undercover Vice Squad detective. While Gallagher threatens to pull Sister Mary Helen in for being a "general nuisance" because she won't "stay in the convent where she belongs" as "old nuns are supposed to do" (*Corporal Works* 75), Sister Mary Helen prays for permission to meddle (*Corporal Works* 57). She covertly uses her connections with her street women "girlfriends" to track Junior Johnson, the most powerful gang lord in the local 'hood—until Junior turns up, head shattered, near the Dutch Windmill in Golden Gate Park and another undercover officer lies dead in his own blood.

Sister Mary Helen carries out her author's conviction that mystery novels represent today's version of medieval morality plays, exemplifying the eternal battle of good against evil and the search for justice in the face of human corruptibility. With a lifetime of prayer and literary quotations packed in her clever old mind, Sister Mary Helen is sure that God's hand is guiding her to the solution of these crimes, sometimes even hearing "a deep, hearty chuckle" although He doesn't intervene directly (*Corporal Works* 38). Instead, as she meditates on the pity and love she knows "a compassionate God feel[s] toward his suffering creatures" (*Corporal Works* 142), Sister Mary Helen relies on her God's indirect revelation, where a scrap of remembered poetry leads her to a intuitive solution:

> It was good, it was kind, in the Wise One above,
> To fling Destiny's veil o'er the face of our years,
> That we dread not the blow that shall strike at our love,
> And expect not the beams that shall dry up our tears. (*Corporal Works* 140)

Novels: *A Novena for Murder* (1984); *Advent of Dying* (1986); *The Missing Madonna* (1988); *Murder in Ordinary Time* (1991); *Murder Makes a Pilgrimage* (1993); *Death Goes on Retreat* (1995); *Death of an Angel* (1997); *Death Takes Up a Collection* (1998); *Requiem at the Refuge* (2000); *The Corporal Works of Murder* (2002).

Selected sources: *Best Sellers*. Rev. of *A Novena for Murder*, July 1984: 184–85; *Chicago Tribune*. Rev. of *Advent of Dying*, October 4, 1987; *Los Angeles Times*. Rev. of *Advent of Dying*, May 19, 1984; *Publishers Weekly*. Rev. of *Advent of Dying*, March 9, 1984.

See also: D(iane). M. Greenwood's Deaconess Theodora Braithwaite (Anglican) series, set in England; Lee Harris's series featuring former Franciscan nun Christine Bennett; Monica Quill's (pen name of Ralph McInerny) Sister Mary Teresa series, set in Chicago and featuring the last three sisters of the fictional Order of Mary and Martha; Winona Sullivan's Sister Cecile series; Veronica Black's Sister Joan series; Aimee and David Thurlo's Sister Agatha series, set in New Mexico.

Sharon McCone

Profession:	Private investigator
Living situation:	Single
Geographic locale:	San Francisco
Time period:	1977–present
Associates:	All Souls Legal Cooperative members
Significant relationships:	Greg Marcus (*Edwin of the Iron Shoes*), Don Del Boccio (*Games to Keep the Dark Away*), and George Kostakos (*The Shape of Dread*); more recently Hy Ripinsky (*Listen to the Silence*, etc.)
Concerns:	Liberal social/political issues

Marcia Muller fulfilled her early intention of using "the classical puzzle form of the mystery to introduce a contemporary female sleuth" (quoted in *CA Online*) by creating small, dark-haired, part Native American, part Scots-Irish Sharon McCone, the first female hard-boiled private investigator in American crime fiction. McCone's first case, *Edwin of the Iron Shoes* (1977) did not catch on well with publishers, who felt that readers had little interest in female protagonists, but after 1982's *Ask the Cards a Question*, McCone's cases have captured increasing attention, praised for intricate and well-constructed plots, lovingly detailed West Coast settings, and richly developed characters. Muller also has collaborated with her husband, author Bill Pronzini, bringing McCone and Pronzini's Nameless Detective together in *Double* (1984) and a short story collection, *Duo* (1998) as well as non-McCone novels and many mystery anthologies.

In 2000, Muller revealed that Sharon McCone began her career as Muller's "alter ego: taller, thinner, braver, etc. But over the years, we've become a whole lot alike. We share the same political views, the same outlook on the world, the same outlook on people" (quoted in Bibel, 1596). McCone's liberal social and political views incubated in the 1960s at the University of California–Berkeley, where she majored in sociology, also studied psychology, and worked part-time in security. After she failed to find a job in her field and turned to detective work, she joined Hank Zahn's San Francisco–laid back All Souls Legal Cooperative, a low-cost legal services provider to the needy. All Souls compensates its employees with free office and living space in a shabby Victorian house on Bernal Heights. Though McCone has her own apartment complete with fat old spotted cat Watney, her colleagues become her extended family: Hank, his wife and tax attorney Anne-Marie, McCone's assistant Rae Kelleher, criminal law specialist Jack Stuart, Ted Smalley, All Souls' indispensable office manager and his gay partner Neal; and later McCone's nephew Mick Savage, who lives with her staffer Charlotte Keim. McCone's involvement in their personal problems and relationships continues even after she leaves All Souls to start her own agency, McCone Investigations, in *Wolf in the Shadows* (1991).

McCone's social conscience impels her to respect the downtrodden and victimized individuals she encounters in her work. She often reflects on the stinginess and hypocrisy society shows toward minorities, even before she learns in *Listen to the Silence* (2000) that her birth mother is Shoshone attorney Saskia Blackhawk. While McCone's initial cases broadened the scope of private eye novels, as in *Games to Keep the Dark Away* (1984), involving deaths in a hospice and a social worker gone missing, 1989's American Mystery Award-winning *The Shape of Dread* gives McCone more profound psychological depth. Investigating a years-old homicide, McCone intuitively feels that black crack addict client Bobby Foster, on Death Row, did not commit the crime. As McCone probes deep into the victim's past, she exposes her own vulnerability and faces her own needs, losses, and mistakes.

In a tender interlude during *Games to Keep the Dark Away*, Sharon McCone tells her disk jockey lover Don Del Boccio, "Somehow, I've always known the right questions to ask. And people open up to me.... They'll still tell me things they wouldn't tell their best friend." He replies, "You look like you won't judge people" (105–6), but as her cases darken and become more psychologically complex, Sharon feels her old liberal values shaken and her trademark empathy wavering. Despite her "third ear" for others' pain, she often presents a rigid, "pushy, severe, and dominant" face to the world (*Shape of Dread* 78). She abhors killing of any kind, but in *The Shape of Dread*, she acknowledges her own "primal rage" toward unrepentant criminals, exploiters of the innocent, and the have versus have not divisiveness caused by "the worst political machine west of Chicago" (*Dead Midnight* 17). Fortyish and somewhat mellowed in *Dead Midnight* (2002), she's listening as ever to what people don't say, but she's lost some of the free-wheeling MG-driving, .38-toting bravado she'd sported twenty years earlier. Her .357 Magnum stays mainly at home with her two cats now; she's finally come to terms with the computer and the cell phone and the encroaching need for glasses, and she cherishes her Cessna two-five-two-seven-Tango primarily because it can zip her up the coast to Mendocino County, where she and Hy Ripinsky, the new lover with whom she shares a mysterious spiritual bond, have built what seems a permanent home.

Commenting on her relationship with Sharon McCone, Marcia Muller admitted in 2000, "I think that I am trying to work something out through her"—probably the answers to some of life's thorniest old questions about justice and society, the individual's right to live and love, and responsibility to one's neighbor. Having years before chosen a path "that few people—particularly women, at the time—would have chosen ... [with] long hours, sleepless nights, frustration, dangers, and enough demons to cast an epic-length horror film ... too much violence, too many evil deeds done as the result of greed, cowardice, or just plain stupidity" (*Dead Midnight* 254), Sharon McCone is still willing to pay the price, the occasional "overwhelming sense of emptiness." She's a truthseeker.

Novels: *Edwin of the Iron Shoes* (1977); *Ask the Cards a Question* (1982); *The Cheshire Cat's Eye* (1983); *Games to Keep the Dark Away* (1984); *Leave a Message for Willie* (1984); *Double* (with Bill Pronzini) (1984); *There's Nothing to be Afraid Of* (1985); *Eye of the Storm* (1988); *There's Something in a Sunday* (1989); *The Shape of Dread* (1989); *Trophies and Dead Things* (1990); *Where Echoes Live* (1991); *Pennies on a Dead Woman's Eyes* (1992); *Wolf in the Shadows* (1993); *Till the Butchers Cut Him Down* (1994); *A Wild and Lonely Place* (1995); *The Broken Promise Land* (1996); *Both Ends of the Night* (1997); *While Other People Sleep* (1998); *A Walk Through the Fire* (1999); *Listen to the Silence* (2000); *Dead Midnight* (2002); *The Dangerous Hour* (2004).

Short fiction: *Deceptions* (1991); *The McCone Files* (1995); *Duo* (with Bill Pronzini) (1998); *McCone and Friends* (2000).

Other series: Elena Oliverez novels: *The Tree of Death* (1983); *The Legend of the Slain Soldiers* (1985); *Beyond the Grave* (with Bill Pronzini) (1986). Joanna Stark novels: *The Cavalier in White* (1986); *There Hangs the Knife* (1988); *Dark Star* (1989).

Nonseries novels: *The Lighthouse* (with Bill Pronzini) (1987); *Point Deception* (2001); *Cape Perdido* (2005).

Selected sources: Bibel, Barbara. "The *Booklist* Interview: Marcia Muller." *Booklist*, May 1, 2000: 1596; Melton, Emily. Rev. of *A Walk Through the Fire*. *Booklist*, April 15, 1999: 1483; *Mystery Books* www.mysterybooks.about.com (June 17, 2000) transcript of chat with Marcia Muller and Bill Pronzini; *Publishers Weekly*. Rev. of *Ask the Cards a Question*, April 30, 1982: 48;

Publishers Weekly. Rev. of *While Other People Sleep*, April 17, 1998: 48; Schecter, Andi. Rev. of *McCone and Friends*. *Specials About* www.specials.about.com/service (December 2, 2000).

Major awards: American Mystery Award, 1989; Shamus Award, 1991; Life Achievement Award, Private Eye Writers of America, 1993; Anthony Awards, 1994, 1996.

See also: For women PIs: Linda Barnes's Carlotta Carlyle series, set in Boston; Janet Evanovich's series featuring bounty hunter **Stephanie Plum**, working out of New Jersey; Sue Grafton's **Kinsey Millhone** "Alphabet" series; G.A. McKevitt's detective agency owner Savannah Reid, set in San Carmelita, California; Sara Paretsky's **V.I. Warshawski** series. Alexander McCall Smith's private detective **Mma Precious Ramotswe** is in a class by herself.

Peter McGarr

Profession:	Chief Superintendent, Special Crimes Unit, Garda Síochána
Living situation:	Widowed
Geographic locale:	Republic of Ireland
Time period:	1977–2002
Associate:	Noreen Frenche McGarr
Significant relationship:	Noreen Frenche McGarr
Concerns:	Contemporary Ireland's "troubles"; aging; gardening as therapy

There's no Celtic romance in the bleak Ireland of Chief Inspector Peter McGarr of the Irish Republic's Garda Síochána (national police), protagonist of Bartholomew Gill's seventeen down-and-dirty Dublin police procedurals. Named for one of Gill's grandfathers (the pen name "Bartholomew Gill" came from the other), Peter McGarr is in his fifties and physically nondescript; "Anonymity, he had found, was the most effective mask in police work" (*Death of an Irish Sinner* 340). Short, bald, grey-haired but still muscular, his aquiline nose bent a little to one side, he is a tough-talking, hard-nosed, flamboyant professional who left brilliant careers with Interpol on the Continent and Criminal Justice in Paris to head the Garda's Special Crimes Unit. McGarr made Noreen Frenche, a petite auburn-haired art historian twenty years his junior and daughter of an influential Irish political family, not only McGarr's wife but also his unofficial crime-solving partner through almost all of the series.

Beginning with *McGarr and the Politician's Wife* (1977), dealing with a yacht club allegedly involved in gun-running, and *McGarr and the Sienese Conspiracy* (1977), somewhat pedestrian crime novels, McGarr's character becomes increasingly complex, just as the plots of these "theme" novels appear progressively more involved against the stormy backdrop of Ireland's present-day tensions. These include the country's powerful criminal subculture, the machinations of the Irish Republican Army—which McGarr detests—the thorny centuries-long Irish land ownership question, the nationalistic ramifications of Ireland's artistic and literary treasures, even the operations of the Irish Roman Catholic hierarchy, still a dominant force in Irish politics and life—all in all, the Irish preference for fighting over eating. As the dull-appearing but bulldog-determined McGarr interacts with his police subordinates, his overtly political superiors, and a broad range of suspects ranging from shanty-Irish lowlifes to the highest echelons of Irish society and religion, new facets of McGarr's character unfold with each investigation—cases that usually culminate in brawling donnybrook endings typical of McGarr's lower-class Dublin roots as seventh of nine children of a Guinness brewery worker (*Death in Dublin* 11).

Those roots underlie a surface smoothed by the comfortable acquaintance with the arts McGarr acquired through Noreen and his Continental connections, occasionally grounds for suspicion on the part of his Garda colleagues. In most of his cases, McGarr draws on both sides of his personality as well as on his penetrating insight into the psychological processes of his opponents. Tackling with perhaps too much of Noreen's assistance (Ashley 183) the IRA's plot to assassinate the Reverend Ian Paisley in *McGarr and the Method of Descartes* (1984), literary conundrums in *The Death of a Joyce Scholar* (1989; shortlisted for an Edgar Award) and the stylish *Death of an Ardent Bibliophile* (1995), a tour de force in which a perverted bookseller acts out a bitter Swiftian view of human nature (Murphy 205), an old lover's suspicious demise while fly fishing in *Death on a Cold, Wild River* (1993), and Opus Dei, the secretive and dangerous Roman Catholic order sanctioned and supported by John Paul II in *Death of an Irish Sinner* (2001), McGarr must come to grips with Noreen's violent murder in his last case, *Death in Dublin* (2003). Some find McGarr's drinking, a commonplace of Irish culture, and his sex life, both with Noreen and after her death with enigmatic scholar Kara Kennedy and gingery *Ath Cliath* reporter Orla Bannon, "rather boring" (Murphy 205). More convincingly, after losing Noreen, McGarr becomes a genuinely tragic figure. Now "necessarily blind to [Dublin's] changes and nuances" (*Death in Dublin* 10), McGarr makes his work "the sole sustaining element in his life, the one constant activity that helped him forget" (*Death in Dublin* 11), but it gives him little pleasure. When Noreen was alive, gardening had been McGarr's "way of truly re-creating himself" (*Death in Dublin* 69), but now he pulls weeds the way he brings criminals to justice: steadily, but without passion. He is troubled by aging and loss and too much violent death, and the necessity of moving on. As Irish poet William Butler Yeats put it, "the fascination of what's difficult has dried the sap" out of Peter McGarr's bones, "and rent spontaneous joy and natural content / Out of [his] heart."

Novels: *McGarr and the Politician's Wife* (1977; reissued as *Death of an Irish Politician* 2000); *McGarr and the Sienese Conspiracy* (1977; *Death of an Irish Consul*); *McGarr on the Cliffs of Moher* (1978; *Death of an Irish Lass*); *McGarr at the Dublin Horse Show* (1980; *Death of an Irish Tradition*); *McGarr and the P.M. of Belgrave Square* (1983); *McGarr and the Method of Descartes* (1984); *McGarr and the Legacy of a Woman Scorned* (1986); *The Death of a Joyce Scholar* (1989); *The Death of Love* (1992); *Death on a Cold, Wild River* (1993); *Death of an Ardent Bibliophile* (1995); *Death of an Irish Seawolf* (1996); *Death of an Irish Tinker* (1997); *The Death of an Irish Lover* (2000); *The Death of an Irish Sinner* (2001); *Death in Dublin* (published posthumously, 2003).

Other works: Gill also wrote five stand-alone novels and contributed to Dilys Wynn's *Murderess Ink* (1980).

Selected sources: Fletcher, Connie. Rev. of *The Death of an Irish Lover*. *Booklist*, May 1, 2000: 1616; Klett, Rex E. Rev. of *The Death of an Irish Sinner*. *Library Journal*, July 2001: 130; Ott, Bill, and Brad Hooper. Rev. of *The Death of an Irish Tinker*. *Booklist*, November 15, 1999: 1459; Stasio, Marilyn. Rev. of *The Death of An Irish Sinner*. *New York Times Book Review*, May 28, 2001: 52; *Stop, You're Killing Me!* www.stopyourekillingme.com, December 18, 2001; brief biography of Gill.

Award nomination: Edgar Award nomination, 1989.

See also: Jo Bannister's Castlemere series, which includes volatile Irish police detective Cal Donovan in Bannister's group of protagonists; Ken Bruen's ferociously noir **Jack Taylor** series, set in Galway; John Brady's series featuring Sergeant (later Inspector) Matt Minogue of the Dublin C.I.D.

Debut novel: Andrew Nugent's *The Four Courts Murder*, featuring Dublin Inspector Denis Lennon and his partner Sergeant Molly Power.

Travis McGee

Profession:	Unlicensed private detective
Living situation:	Single
Geographic locale:	Florida
Time period:	1964–1985
Associate:	Meyer, an economist
Nemesis:	The forces of corruption
Significant relationship:	He loves 'em and leaves 'em
Concerns:	Knight-errantry; Florida environmentalism

Through John D. MacDonald's hard-hitting color-coded series, his latter day knight-errant hero Travis McGee survives "all bullets and all wild or wily women" (Williams 8). A handsome 6'4" former football player, McGee lives in Bahia Mar, south Florida, on a houseboat called "The Busted Flush" that he won in a poker game, and drives a pickup converted from a Rolls-Royce. He takes his retirement in chunks as he goes along and describes himself as a "salvage expert," and like many earlier wise-cracking hard-boiled heroes, he's cynical about human nature and enormously successful with women, possibly "the first modern mystery hero to pursue a consciously 'alternative lifestyle' " (Murphy 316), but he's individualized by admitting to and recognizing his own weaknesses and vulnerabilities (Ashley 314). He tries to mend his ways by sallying forth in his early novels to right wrongs, usually involving victims of con artists, assisted by his friend, an economist named Meyer. Later, he takes on larger causes, especially the exploitation of Florida's environment by big business and governmental corruption.

MacDonald initially called his hero "Dallas McGee," but changed to "Travis" following the assassination of President John F. Kennedy in 1963. McGee's first case, chronicled in *The Deep Blue Goodbye* (1964), establishes the pattern for all the rest: McGee sets out after a bad guy who's ruined a woman's life, survives brutal physical injuries, "charms and beds women (with miraculous therapeutic effect)" (Ashley 314), then inflicts even worse damage on his antagonist, smashing heads, terrorizing, and exterminating the villains, and by the end of each case he's saved "something important—a life, a reputation, a fortune, a friendship" (*CA Online*).

Critics have observed that many of McGee's cases employ dated devices, for example LSD in *Nightmare in Pink* (1964), set in New York City. As Bruce Murphy points out, too, McGee's pop psychology, often voiced in sixties jargon, today seems "frankly offensive or at least tacky" (316). Feminist critics have also found McGee's attitude toward women objectionable. Barbara Lawrence has attributed "much of the suffering endured by the women [in the series], particularly the psychological suffering" to McGee because he "has such personal magnetism and attraction that women proposition him before the introductions are completed" (*Clues*, Spring–Summer 1990). According to Lawrence, McGee dislikes successful women and in fact despises all women who are not totally submissive to him. MacDonald refuted that notion in a letter to *Contemporary Authors*, suggesting that such misinterpretations lie with "readers who believe they see proof of their pre-prejudices in whatever they come upon" (quoted in *CA Online*).

On the other hand, MacDonald's least typical McGee novel, *The Green Ripper* (1979), won him many new appreciative readers and the National Book Award. Eminent mystery critic H.R.F. Keating compares MacDonald's work, especially *The Green Ripper*, to Charles Dickens's novels in terms "of feelings, of sentiment, and of sentimentality," because MacDonald opens this novel with a warm cozy portrait of recalled sensuous pleasures from Gretel, McGee's current bed partner. Then things blow up: Meyer cries "universal woe," Gretel dies from a slow-acting poison, and after a lushly sentimental funeral, McGee goes on to social commentary on the shopping-center commercialization of Christmas. McGee's also surrounded by Dickensian characters—a "tart with a heart," "a brainwashed religious nut"—before he rushes, Sidney Carton style, to beard the evil organization in its very den (Keating 195–96).

Even in the exaggerated style at which some readers today bristle, McGee's combination of sentiment and swagger still holds a certain rose-within-a-hairy-fist appeal: "I had to be a roamer, a salvage expert, a gregarious loner, a seeker of a thousand tarnished grails, finding too many excuses for the dragons along the way" (quoted in Murphy 316). By the time Travis McGee gets to *The Lonely Silver Rain* (1985), however, he's discovered he has a bright, brainy daughter, Jean, who wants to be a veterinarian, and parenthood profoundly affects him: "Lately I have been bringing out the worst in people," he reflects, "No more" (*Rain* 231). Now with "a way to continue" (*Rain* 229), he puts almost everything he has in a trust for Jean and goes back to his salvage operations. Overall, this engaging swinger-beach-bum-pop-philosopher is no fourflusher; he always delivers what he promises, and his books still make his readers like him—a lot.

Novels: *The Deep Blue Goodbye* (1964); *Nightmare in Pink* (1964); *A Purple Place for Dying* (1964); *The Quick Red Fox* (1965); *Bright Orange for the Shroud* (1965); *Darker Than Amber* (1966); *One Fearful Yellow Eye* (1966); *Pale Gray for Guilt* (1968); *The Girl in the Plain Brown Wrapper* (1968); *Dress Her in Indigo* (1969); *The Long Lavender Look* (1970); *A Tan and Sandy Silence* (1972); *The Scarlet Ruse* (1973); *The Turquoise Lament* (1973); *The Empty Copper Sea* (1978); *The Green Ripper* (1979); *Free Fall in Crimson* (1981); *Cinnamon Skin* (1982); *The Lonely Silver Rain* (1985).

Stand-alone novels: MacDonald wrote over forty mainstream and mystery novels plus three science fiction novels; about two-thirds of his total output was first published in now highly collectible paperback editions (Ashley 314).

Short-story collections: MacDonald wrote six short-story collections, including *The Good Old Stuff* (1982) and *More Good Old Stuff* (1984) and one science fiction collection, *Other Times, Other Worlds* (1978). He wrote over 500 short stories, most early ones under various pen names.

Nonfiction: With Lewis D. Moore, MacDonald wrote *Meditations on America: John D. MacDonald's Travis McGee Series and Other Fiction* (1994) and six other nonfiction works.

Autobiographical works: *One More Sunday* (1984); *A Friendship: The Letters of Dan Rowan and John D. MacDonald 1967–1974* (1986).

Selected sources: Campbell, Frank D. *John D. MacDonald and the Colourful World of Travis McGee*. San Bernardino, CA: Borgo Press, 1988; Geherin, David. *John D. MacDonald*. New York: Unger, 1982; Landrum, Larry, Pat Browne, and Ray B. Browne, eds. *Dimensions of Detective Fiction*. New York: Popular Press, 1976, pp. 149–61; Merrill, Hugh. *The Red Hot Typewriter*. New York: St. Martin's Minotaur, 2000; Shine, Walter, and Jean Shine. *A MacDonald Potpourri*. Gainesville, FL: University of Florida Libraries, 1988; Williams, Nick B. Rev. of *The Green Ripper*. *Los Angeles Book Review*, May 4, 1980: 8.

Major awards: Benjamin Franklin Award (for best American short story), 1955; *Grand Prix de Littérature Policière* (best foreign novel, France, 1964); Grand Master, Mystery Writers of America, 1972; National Book Award, 1980.

Web site (fans): www.members.bellatlantic.net/~mwarble/slipf18.htm.

See also: Lawrence Block's **Matt Scudder** wounded-hero series; James Hall's Thorn series, which emerged from his fascination with Travis McGee; J.A. Jance's J.P. Beaumont series, in part derived from Travis McGee (Ashley 207, 252); Brett Halliday's Mike Shayne series for an earlier Florida setting; for contemporary Florida PIs, see Stuart Kaminsky's series featuring Lew Fonesca, set in Sarasota, and Kaminsky's series featuring paraplegic PI Lincoln Rhyme; for Florida environmentalism, see Carl Hiassen's stand-alone humorous mystery novels; for classic hard-boiled detecting, see Bill Pronzini's Nameless Detective series and for period detecting in the same vein, Pronzini's John Quincannon stories, set in 1890s San Francisco.

Alex McKnight

Profession: Former police detective; sometime private investigator; small resort cabin landlord

Living situation:	Divorced
Geographic locale:	Upper Peninsula, Michigan
Time period:	1998–present
Associates:	Leon Prudell, Vinnie LeBlanc, Jackie Connery
Nemesis:	Chief Roy Maven, Sault Ste. Marie P.D.
Significant relationship:	Natalie Reynaud (in *Ice Run*)
Concerns:	Personal loyalty; responsibility

On entering the Private Eye Writers of America contest for the Best First Private Eye Novel of 1997, Steve Hamilton wanted to be true to the wise-cracking tough-guy private eye "formula"—but he couldn't (*CA* 174, p. 191). Instead, he told *Amazon.com*, "I just tried to tell a good story, with a main character you can really care about, some suspense, some dark humor, and a sense of what it's like to live next to the coldest, deepest lake in the world." He did it and won with Alex McKnight's first case, *A Cold Day in Paradise* (1997), set in Michigan's rugged Upper Peninsula.

Late-fortyish McKnight's "whole rundown" hurts. He grew up in a working-class Detroit suburb and his mother died when he was eight. After high school, he had four years as a minor-league catcher with good hands who went after too many bad pitches, and eight years as a Detroit cop. In 1984 he watched his partner Franklin die in the same shootout that left a bullet one centimeter from McKnight's own heart, was invalided out at three-quarters pay, and got divorced. He came to sell his father's cabins near Paradise on the shores of Superior and stayed, renting the cabins and doing "the private eye thing" and always torn between "The absolute solitude. . . . The desolate beauty" and his "habit of taking on other people's problems" (*Ice Run* 16, 147).

McKnight tells a good story, taking "just about every cliché in the field and turn[ing] it upside down" (quoted in *CA* 174, p. 191). Readers care about him because he cares about other people. For a friend, he'd "do anything" and does (*Ice Run* 147)—but some aren't friends at all, dragging him back into a world he'd rather forget, like a gambling millionaire accused of murdering his bookie in *A Cold Day in Paradise* who asks McKnight for help. The real killer seems to be the man who shot McKnight's police partner and put the bullet next to McKnight's heart, but McKnight helped send that shooter to prison for life, where he's been incommunicado ever since. On a good ballplaying day, McKnight made the big play when it counted, even if he had to take a lot of punishment (*Paradise* 262), and that's how he solves this case and all the rest, getting bashed and slammed, hurt body by bad guys and soul by women who tell him he looks like the guy who delivers the firewood, until finally he can see how it all fits together (*Paradise* 262).

McKnight's "dark humor" helps him through the pain. He uses it on people he genuinely thinks don't like him, like Sault Ste. Marie's police chief Roy Maven, seeing in them things he hates so much in himself that they pull him down into depression: "that voice an old cop uses like a dentist uses like a drill. . . . That good old cop swagger . . . I had slipped into it myself now and then. . . . It's not the kind of thing you want to take home. Just ask my ex-wife" (*Paradise* 18, 53).

McKnight's wife walked out on him just after he was shot, but he manages to keep some real friends, even if it's hard for him to listen to them. Leon Prudell, an inept PI who thought at first that McKnight had stolen his job, becomes McKnight's even more inept partner, then solid ally when the partnership dissolves. Vinnie LeBlanc, McKnight's Indian neighbor, backs him up unquestioningly; and Jackie Connery, owner of McKnight's refuge the Glasgow Inn, supplies good Canadian beer and a roaring fireplace and tells McKnight what he doesn't want to hear: "'I'm scared to death for you, Alex. I really am'" (Ice Run 148). In spite of McKnight's involvement in the last four homicides on Maven's turf, the chief tries to spare him a brutal beating in Ice Run: "for once in your life did it occur to you that I was trying to do you a favor?" (86).

For McKnight, living next to implacable Lake Superior means confronting some of the deep, cold realities he's tried to drown in himself. In all the cases he takes on for his friends, loneliness and depression and the fear of growing old and helpless haunt him: "I imagined myself as an old man, living one traumatic day of my life over and over. . . . Then one night I'll go outside into the cold, cold air and they won't find me until the next morning" (Ice Run 249, 68). McKnight holds back the dark with loyalty to his friends, responsibility to the jobs he doesn't have to undertake, and over and over, like Don Quixote, he rides off to rescue a damsel who's far different than she appears to be, and he's hurt every time. In Ice Run (2004), set in an icy Upper Peninsula February, McKnight's unnaturally "smiling and laughing" at the Glasgow Inn, cutting down on the beer, eating salad for the first time in fifteen years, and showing signs of working out. After he dyes his hair, Jackie's sure of it: Alex is in love—and the case he take on for his tormented lover Ontario police detective Natalie Reynaud proves one of his most dangerous.

This modern knight of the woeful interior countenance can't resist tilting at the windmills life puts in his way, constantly confusing his dreams and nightmares with reality—or does Alex McKnight really glimpse Superior's best gift: "When water destroys, it makes everything look new. It can even be beautiful" (Blood Is the Sky 67)?

Novels: A Cold Day in Paradise (1998); Winter of the Wolf Moon (2000); The Hunting Wind (2001); North of Nowhere (2002); Blood Is the Sky (2003); Ice Run (2004).

Selected sources: Burns, Ann. Rev. of North of Nowhere. Library Journal, August 15, 2003: 152; Fletcher, Connie. Rev. of Blood Is the Sky. Booklist, May 1, 2003: 1545; Fletcher, Connie. Rev. of Ice Run. Booklist, May 1, 2004: 1508; Publishers Weekly. Rev. of A Cold Day in Paradise, July 6, 1998: 53; Publishers Weekly. Rev. of The Hunting Wind, May 21, 2001: 85.

See also: Doug Allyn's series featuring Michelle "Mitch" Mitchell, an underwater welder, single mother, and amateur detective working in Michigan; Joseph Heywood's series featuring Upper Peninsula conservation officer (woods cop) Grady Service; for a historical Upper Peninsula setting, Kathleen Hills's series featuring Constable John McIntire.

Debut novel: Henry Kisor's Season's Revenge, featuring Lakota Deputy Sheriff Steve Martinez, set in the Upper Peninsula's deep woods.

Bruce Medway

Profession:	"Fixer" for traders; sometime private investigator
Living situation:	Single, in long-term relationship
Geographic locale:	Benin, Togo, and Nigeria, West Africa
Time period:	1995–present
Associate:	Detective Bogado of Benin Police; temporarily Medway's partner in M & B "Investigations and Debt Collections"
Nemesis:	Mafia capo Roberto Franconelli
Significant relationship:	Heike Brooke
Concerns:	Organized crime; sympathy for black Africans

The merciless tropical sun beats down on some of the darkest human corruption in Robert Wilson's demonic chiaroscuro of "The White Man's Grave," the small coastal countries of Benin and Togo between Ghana and Nigeria, "the warm, damp hole in the armpit of Africa" (*Instruments* 1) where British expatriate Bruce Medway "fixes" noir deals between shady and shadier and downright black-hearted European, Eastern, and African traders. Introduced in *Instruments of Darkness* (1995), Medway, 6'4" and thirtyish, lost his job at a London shipping company, nearly perished crossing the Sahara, and found the laid-back life in West Africa suited him, where everyone's "mastered the art of waiting and sweating" while looking for "the fast, hard buck" (*Instruments* 2, 6). A self-titled "odd-job man" (*Instruments* 103), Medway makes a modest living collecting money, organizing and managing dicey trading operations, and finding missing persons, but he has his principles: he won't work for criminals or take on divorce cases—or so he insists until he's inveigled or blackmailed into horrifying cases that prove physically and emotionally threatening to him and his friends.

Hired by a big-time native wheeler-dealer in *Instruments of Darkness* to find vanished sheanut trader Steven Kershaw, Medway soon becomes involved in a rat's nest of sado-masochistic murder, drug-dealing, and dishonor among brutal thieves. Africa's casual violence, its stomach-wrenching cruelty toward the weak, its pervasive undercurrent of potential mob rule and anti-white riots all force Medway and his readers to slog blindly through a miasma of hate and greed, until the intricate crime at last becomes clear about midway through the novel.

Medway sometimes wonders why he stays in Africa, grubbing around "in this half-lit world of trade and commerce" (*Instruments* 36). He quit smoking, but he drinks far too much of anything alcoholic when Johnny Walker Red Label, his guzzle of choice, isn't available, winding up in monumental hangovers, his mouth full of "bad-egg saliva" and more often than not his body pummeled and his head sprouting a lump "like a horse's knee" from encounters with musclemen paid to immobilize him—or worse (*Instruments* 174).

Each of Medway's cases seems to be more sordid than the one before. After discovering the horrifying truth about Steven Kershaw's disappearance, Medway takes on the ultra-sleazy African porn industry in *The Big Killing* (1996), mafia money-laundering and toxic waste in *Blood Is Dirt* (1997), and in *A Darkening Stain* (1998) the ominous vanishing of five native schoolgirls, perhaps sold into prostitution. While trying to extricate innocent victims from the clutches of the ungodly, Medway greets each horror with humor as dry as a Martini waved once past the vermouth bottle, and he has a penetrating eye for the revelatory detail, like jeans with a "nail-tearing grip" about to disgrace a skinny visiting Englishwoman (*Instruments* 190), or the "market mamma bottom" adorning Madame Severnou, an African drug magnate with a voice Medway can feel against his carotid (*Instruments* 7).

Neither threats nor money nor sex could keep Bruce Medway in Africa if he didn't want to stay. The people hold him there—Moses, his philosophic black driver, quaint and faithful and long-suffering; Helen, Medway's native cook with motherly worries about his drinking; Mr. Bagado, educated and trained in England, a multilingual African detective so at the mercy of his corrupt superiors that he works on an empty stomach for days, without pay for months, pursuing justice even while suspended. Bagado shows Medway what he, as an Englishman, can't see: that Bagado acts not out of duty as a policeman, but as a human being. What's inside the heart, Bagado insists, makes a man extraordinary only when he shows it.

That lesson out of Africa comes home to Medway after his hottie Berliner lover Heike Brooke is kidnapped in *Instruments of Darkness*. Suddenly realizing their relationship means far more to him than riotous Scotch-fueled fumbles and tumbles, he shows Heike what's really in his heart—and eventually in *A Darkening Stain* she's pregnant with his child. After Bagado rejoins the Benin police after a sojourn with Medway's short-lived "Investigations and Debt Collection" agency, he involves Medway in a crusade to save young native girls from being sold to "fat cats" who think sex with a virgin will cure them of AIDS (*Stain* 282).

In Africa, Bruce Medway can't be indifferent any more. Africa drives him crazy, because he sees both Africa's infinitely maddening contradictions, its "limbless poverty at every street light," and "fat people in bars eating money," the Africans' habit of telling "you everything except the one thing you want to hear" and then "their innocence, the way they join their lives to ours" (*Stain* 59). But Africa saves him, too. When Bruce Medway tells Heike, "If I thought I wasn't going to see Bagado or Moses or Helen again…I'd feel impoverished" (*Stain* 20), he finally shows what's in his heart—out of Africa's darkness, a warm, compassionate light.

Novels: *Instruments of Darkness* (1995); *The Big Killing* (1996); *Blood Is Dirt* (1997); *A Darkening Stain* (1998).

Stand-alone novels: *A Small Death in Lisbon* (1999); *The Company of Strangers* (2001); *The Blind Man of Seville* (2003); *The Vanished Hands* (2004).

Selected sources: *Publishers Weekly*. Rev. of *The Big Killing*, October 6, 2003; *Publishers Weekly*. Rev. of *Blood Is Dirt*, June 7, 2004; *Publishers Weekly*. Rev. of *A Darkening Stain*, June 7, 2004.

See also: James McClure's Detective **Tromp Kramer** series, set in Trekkersburg, South Africa; Walter Satterthwaite's short story collection set in East Africa and featuring Sergeant M'butu and Constable Kobari of the Kenyan police; Alexander McCall Smith's No. 1

Ladies' Detective Agency series, featuring delightful traditionally built **Mma Precious Ramotswe**.

Lord Meren

Profession:	Eyes and Ears of Pharaoh Tutankhamun
Living situation:	Widowed
Geographic locale:	Egypt
Time period:	Mid-fourteenth century B.C.
Associate:	Kysen, Meren's adopted son
Nemesis:	Pharaoh Akhenaten
Significant relationship:	Anath (in *Slayer of Gods*)
Concerns:	Personal honor; love for family

Lynda Robinson says her Ph.D. in anthropology and archaeology gave her "the ability to understand and recognize the importance of differing cultural values and the paramount importance of culture and language in shaping individual beliefs and character" (quoted in *CA Online*). The reign of Egypt's famous boy pharaoh Tutankhamun, with its exotic values and hieroglyphic language, shaped Robinson's ancient Egyptian detective Lord Meren, a man of principle, integrity, and intellect.

Prior to Tutankhamun's reign over Upper and Lower Egypt, an enormous religio-political upheaval shook the Two Lands under the heretic pharaoh Akhenaten, son of the great Amunhotep III and in Robinson's view older brother to Tutankhamun. Seeing that the enormous power and wealth amassed by priests of the god Amun threatened even himself, Akhenaten abandoned the old Egyptian pantheon, declared himself the son of the one true god, the sun deity Aten, and built a new capital at Tel-el-Amarna (Horizon of the Aten), fanatically persecuting Amun's followers until he died. Akhenaten had executed Lord Meren's noble father for refusing to accept the new god and tortured eighteen-year-old Meren into overt submission, but Meren secretly remained opposed to the pharaoh. Meren's mentor Ay, a wily and powerful courtier, married his stunningly beautiful daughter Nefertiti to Akhenaten, and as his "great royal wife" she wielded considerable influence for twelve years, even trying to restore the pharaoh to traditional belief until she mysteriously vanished from royal monuments and correspondence. Meren believed that she was murdered and surreptitiously began investigating her death. After Akhenaten's own death and their brother Smenkhare's brief reign, the boy pharaoh Tutankhamun, advised by his chief minister Ay, moved his capital back to Thebes and reestablished the old gods, making Lord Meren "Friend of the King" and "the Eyes and Ears of Pharaoh," his chief of security and intelligence.

In Meren's first case, *Murder in the Place of Anubis* (1994), Tutankhamun charges Meren with discovering the murderer of the hated scribe Hormin, found dead in the embalming temple of Anubis. Sifting through the intrigues swirling around the king,

Meren eventually uncovers domestic plots involving Tutankhamun's scheming queen and international menaces, the encroaching Syrian and Hittite kingdoms and Nubian bandits skulking on Egypt's borders. Meren's methods include the threat of torture, but he relies more on his ability to conceal "the true face of his *ka*, his soul" under "what he likes to call his unseen mask . . . to seek out Maat, the essential truth and harmony of life by which the world existed" (*Anubis* 13). Meren perfected that mask during Akhenaten's ferocious last years, when Egypt was on the brink of civil war, but the necessity of continuing to wear it haunts him with nightmares that echo his waking moral quandary: Meren suspects that Ay plotted to kill the heretic pharaoh, but he, Meren, did nothing to prevent Akhenaten's death. Had Meren "confused the good of the country with his own need for vengeance" (*Anubis* 15)?

Meren wears many other unseen masks that his father and old Ay taught him: "facades constructed to suit his purpose of the moment" (*Anubis* 14) as he struggles to maintain truth and harmony—and survive. Meren also teaches young Tutankhamun "not to trust a brother or know a friend, and when lying down to guard his heart himself," as one of the young king's own ancestors had written (*Anubis* 14). All of Meren's cases illustrate that harsh principle of survival, but in *Slayer of Gods* (2001), Meren comes fatally close to forgetting it himself.

Charged by Tutankhamun with avenging "the incomparable Queen Nefertiti" (*Slayer* 45) whom Tutankhamun loved as his second mother, Meren sets out to untangle the intricacies of her death. Already knowing that Nefertiti was poisoned by her steward Wah, now dead, shortly after Akhenaten forced her to appear as his co-pharaoh in Egypt's double crown, Meren, recovering from an arrow wound meant to assassinate Tutankhamun in *Drinker of Blood* (1998), narrows the eleven-year-old trail to three powerful suspects. Anath, "the Eyes of Babylon," a beautiful spy trained by Ay, rescues Meren from an attack in a dark alley, and he becomes infatuated with her. Since the death of his wife Sit-Hathor, Meren has been renowned for his loyalty, integrity, and self-control in a court where the lack of privacy has always been the hazard of rank, but Anath distracts him so cleverly from his struggle for harmony and balance that his enemies can menace his cherished daughter Bener and his adopted son Kysen, his detecting assistant—until Meren unveils Anath as one of their vicious leaders.

Meren's character, his charm, his skill at intrigue, and his ruthlessness make him an ideal courtier-detective. Refusing to believe in coincidence, he waits, "Like a leopard crouched in tall grass . . . while a piece of information from one place, and a fact from another drifted together with inconsequential remarks from yet another source . . . [and] his view of certain events shifted with the suddenness of a whip stroke" (*Slayer* 209). Blinded though he'd been by Anath, Meren still counts his personal humiliation as nothing compared to the safety of his children and his king, the restoration of rightness and order.

Novels: *Murder in the Place of Anubis* (1994); *Murder at the God's Gate* (1995); *Murder at the Feast of Rejoicing* (1996); *Eater of Souls* (1997); *Drinker of Blood* (1998); *Slayer of Gods* (2001).

Other works: Historical romance novels, under "Suzanne Robinson."

Selected sources: Flanagan, Margaret. Rev. of *Murder at the Feast of Rejoicing. Booklist*, January 1, 1996: 798; Flanagan, Margaret. Rev. of *Eater of Souls. Booklist*, April 15, 1997: 1412; *Library Journal*. Rev. of *Eater of Souls*, May 1, 1997: 144; *Publishers Weekly*. Rev. of *Drinker of Blood*, September 7, 1998: 88; *Publishers Weekly*. Rev. of *Murder at the God's Gate*, January 2, 1995: 62.

See also: P.C. Doherty's Lord Amerotke series, featuring the Pharaoh's Chief Judge and set around 1479 B.C.; Lauren Haney's series featuring Lieutenant Bak of the Medjay Police, set in southern Egypt in the Eighteenth Dynasty; for archaeological mysteries, see Elizabeth Peters's **Amelia Peabody** series, set in the early twentieth century.

Kinsey Millhone

Profession:	Former police officer, now private detective
Living situation:	Twice divorced
Geographic locale:	California
Time period:	1982–present
Associate:	None
Nemeses:	Bureaucracy; chauvinism; sex discrimination
Concern:	Righting past wrongs

Sue Grafton claims that she created Kinsey Millhone to "exorcis[e] the desire to murder her own ex-husband" (*Silk Stalkings: More* 222) during a tough custody battle over their three children. This popular series strikes blunt-instrument style at bureaucracy and male chauvinism through its convincing protagonist, an independent, resourceful lone woman sticking up for the helpless and hitting persecuting males where it hurts—sometimes below the belt—before turning them over to California's judicial system. Released regularly around her "birthday," each of the alphabetically named cases Kinsey narrates starts with an introductory "report to a client" followed by a breezy account of disinterring some past crime or misdemeanor, in the style of Ross Macdonald and Raymond Chandler. Her usual epilogue closes formally, "Respectfully submitted, Kinsey Millhone."

After graduating from the police academy in the 1980s, Kinsey joined the Santa Teresa, California, Police Department; but she found its bureaucratic restrictions and chauvinism stifling. Working briefly for the California Fidelity Insurance Company, she was fired by "a hotshot efficiency expert" (*"I" Is for Innocent* 2), so she set up her own private investigation agency. As a departure from the macho hard-boiled male detective who bashes, boozes, and womanizes, Kinsey Millhone, in her thirties, adapts women's typical strengths—patience, attention to detail, perseverance—to her work: "There's no place in a P.I.'s life for impatience, faintheartedness, or sloppiness. I understand the same qualifications apply for housewives....Usually, I start in the same place, plodding along methodically, never knowing at first what might be significant. It's all detail; facts accumulated painstakingly" (*"B" Is for Burglar* 27).

While assembling those facts, though, Kinsey needs to be tough. If wisecracking her way through a confrontation doesn't work, she can bash if she has to, running and target shooting to keep her muscles and skills well tuned. Like her male counterparts, she's been shot at, roughed up, nearly killed, and kidnapped (in *"H"*), all matter-of-factly recounted as simply doing her job. She can work with men if they treat her fairly; she's the only person she knows "who doesn't express contempt for all the lawyers in the world" and she "likes cops, too; anyone who stands between me and anarchy" (*"J" Is for Judgment* 2). After two divorces she keeps her romantic encounters brief, though her two exes come back to plague her in *"E"* and *"O"* respectively. She's fond of her sexy octogenarian landlord Henry Pitts and neighborhood bar-and-grill owner Rosie, for a long time the closest she has to family, but by choice Kinsey works and lives alone.

Being fired, Kinsey learned, "is the pits, ranking right up there with infidelity in its brutalizing effect...one's self-image is punctured like a tire by a nail." After going through the same awful stages as a terminally-diagnosed patient and "a steady stream of loathsome thoughts about the man responsible," Kinsey pulls herself together and starts over, feeling "the optimism rising through [her] veins like maple syrup" (*"I" Is for Innocent* 3).

Starting with *"J" Is for Judgment* (1993), Kinsey's traumatic childhood memories deepen and broaden her characterization. At five, she spent hours in a wrecked car with her parents' corpses, and for months afterward she refused to come out of a blanket-filled cardboard box in her Aunt Gin's house. She fumbled through high school, "glum and disenfranchised," hung out with other "low sorts," was "undistinguished and unnoticed" (*"Q" Is for Quarry* 279). As an adult, she still sticks to small, enclosed places, living in a converted single-car garage and using her beige 1968 Volkswagen as a second home/office, loaded with files, books, clothes and shoes, and a case of motor oil—all reinforcing her insistence on self-sufficiency.

"J" Is for Judgment (1993) marks a watershed for Kinsey. She's been so concerned with others' past lives she's not paid much attention to her own, just accepting "what I was told, constructing my personal mythology on the flimsiest of facts." When hitherto ignored relatives pop into her life, her perspective shifts: "I'd actually managed to feel superior about my isolation....I was special. I was self-created, a loner, which suited me to perfection. Now I had to consider the possibility of this unknown family unit...whether I would claim them or they would claim me (*"J"* 127).

At thirty-seven in *"Q" Is for Quarry* (2002), Kinsey suffers a "general malaise...bored, restless, and disconnected from humanity at large" (1) when she relives that horrible car crash not far from her family's old ranch home. Boredom quickly yields to remembered pain and unsettling new discoveries, as Kinsey tentatively begins to reach out to her new-found relations, wondering why she feels threatened by their offers "of simple comfort" and asking herself, "While my mother was gone, couldn't I experience some small fragment of her love through my cousins and aunts?" (*"Q" Is for Quarry* 137). Kinsey lands on her feet again in *"R" Is for Ricochet* (2004), finding love—on her terms—with red Mercedes–driving "studly, stylish cop Cheney Phillips," proving that she's not "the perfect detective for the era of victimhood" (Murphy 214) but an optimistic and independent and, yes, loving and lovable modern woman.

Novels: *"A" Is for Alibi* (1982); *"B" Is for Burglar* (1985); *"C" Is for Corpse* (1986); *"D" Is for Deadbeat* (1987); *"E" Is for Evidence* (1988); *"F" Is for Fugitive* (1989); *"G" Is for Gumshoe* (1990); *"H" Is for Homicide* (1991); *"I" Is for Innocent* (1992); *"J" Is for Judgment* (1993); *"K" Is for Killer* (1994); *"L" Is for Lawless* (1995); *"M" Is for Malice* (1996); *"N" Is for Noose* (1998); *"O" Is for Outlaw* (1999); *"P" Is for Peril* (2001); *"Q" Is for Quarry* (2002); *"R" Is for Ricochet* (2004); *"S" Is for Silence* (2005).

Short stories: *Kinsey and Me* (1991).

Other works: Grafton has also edited several crime story anthologies and contributed to various periodicals as well as writing several screenplays and teleplays.

Selected sources: Chambers, Andrea. "Make No Bones About It, Sue Grafton's Detective Heroine is a Real Pistol." *People*, July 10, 1989: 81; Kaufman, Natalie H., and Carol M. Kay. *"G" Is for Grafton: The World of Kinsey Millhone*. New York: Henry Holt, 1997; *Publishers Weekly*. Rev. of *"R" Is for Ricochet*, June 14, 2004: 47; Stasio, Marilyn. Rev. of *"R" Is for Ricochet*. *New York Times Book Review*, August 8, 2004: 32; Williams, Wilda. Rev. of *"P" Is for Peril*. *Library Journal*, April 15, 2001: 131; "Your Conversation with Sue Grafton." McDougal Littell Web site, www.mcdougallittell.com (June 6, 2001).

Major awards: Shamus Awards, 1985, 1991, 1995; Anthony Awards, 1985, 1986, 1987, 1991; Doubleday Mystery Guild Award 1989, 1990, 1991, 1992, 1993, 1995.

Web site: www.suegrafton.com.

See also: For California women private investigators, Janet Dawson's Jerio Howard series, set in Oakland and the Bay area; Linda Grant's Catherine Sayler series, dealing with San Francisco white-collar crime; Karen Kijewski's Kat Colorado series, set in Sacramento; Marcia Muller's **Sharon McCone** series, set in San Francisco; Gloria White's Bonnie Ventana series, set in San Francisco; for women private investigators in other areas, see Linda Barnes's Carlotta Carlyle series, set in Boston; Catherine Dain's Freddie O'Neal series, set in Reno; Sara Paretsky's **V.I. Warshawski** series, set in Chicago; Sharon Short's three Patricia Delaney novels, set in Cincinnati; Sandra West Prowell's three Phoebe Siegel novels, set in Billings, Montana; Sandra Scoppetone's Lauren Laurano series, set in New York; Valerine Wesley's series featuring black private investigator Tamara Hayle; Eve Zaremba's Helen Karemos series, set in Canada.

William Monk

Profession:	Former Bow Street Police detective; now private agent of inquiry
Living situation:	At first single; then married
Geographic locale:	England, mostly London
Time period:	Mid-Victorian Period (1850s–1860s)
Associates:	Sergeant John Evan; Hester Latterly Monk; Sir Oliver Rathbone; Lady Callendra Daviot
Nemeses:	Amnesia; Superintendent Runcorn

Significant relationship:	Hester Latterly Monk
Concerns:	Social injustice; Victorian hypocrisy; moral dilemmas

Many historians characterize the Victorian Period as transitional, or in Thomas Carlyle's metaphor, with one age in its death throes, the next struggling to be born. Anne Perry individualizes that change in William Monk, a "private inquiry agent" hunting criminals in Victorian London. As Monk struggles to regain his memory, lost in an 1856 carriage accident, he destroys his old personality and makes himself a new man. Awakening in *The Face of a Stranger* (1990) from a three-week coma not even knowing his own name, Monk must deduce his whole former life "little by little, pieced together from fragments of evidence, letters, records of his police cases when he was still one of the most brilliant detectives London had seen, and from the reactions of others and their emotions toward him" (*Defend and Betray* 61).

Monk soon learns that he is a London detective in Sir Robert Peel's Metropolitan Police Force. His gentleman's clothes are elegantly tailored, and a "powerful, not easy," face looks back from his mirror, dark, saturnine, with "intense luminous" grey eyes. "If there was humor it would be harsh, of wit rather than laughter" (*Stranger* 16), hinting at a vain and ambitious personality, "ruthless, unpredictable, clever, wildly humourous and quick tongued, and yet also vindictive, fiercely emotional, honest regardless of whom it hurt, himself included, and moved by the oddest of pity" (*Defend and Betray* 62).

Superintendent Runcorn assigns Monk, recovered physically but psychically shaky, to investigate the murder of aristocratic Crimean War hero Major Joscelin Grey with sympathetic Sergeant John Evan. Mutual dislike flares between Monk and outspoken Hester Latterly, a former nurse in the Crimea and furious defender of the downtrodden, a friend of wealthy Lady Callendra Daviot, Grey's aunt and one of the governors of the Royal Free Hospital. Hester's defiance of authority soon causes her to lose her infirmary position there, while by uncovering secrets Grey's influential aristocratic family intends to keep hidden, Monk fuels Runcorn's simmering hatred of him. In *A Dangerous Mourning* (1991), where eminent barrister Sir Oliver Rathbone dominates the trial of the Grey case perpetrator, Monk explodes against Runcorn and is dismissed from the police for insubordination. Lady Callendra finds Hester private nursing cases and sets Monk up as a private inquiry agent whom Rathbone employs in subsequent sensitive cases.

"The more he remembers, the less he [Monk] likes himself" (Herbert 150), and through others' eyes, too, Monk sees that he had been "dedicated to the pursuit of justice greater than merely the law, but a man without friendships or family ties," admired and feared by insubordinates and resented by his superiors, frightened by his footsteps on their heels (*Defend and Betray* 67). Ejected from the police, Monk hurls his defiance into Runcorn's teeth: "What I do now is what I have always done, . . . tidy up the cases you can't manage and clean up behind you!" (*Sudden, Fearful Death* 201). As an independent agent, Monk lacks the support of an established police force, but in Victorian class-dominated society, Peel's detectives had to operate within rigid political and cultural strictures that Monk can to some extent ignore.

In spite of himself, too, Monk begins to respect Hester Latterly for her stalwart nonjudgmental efforts on behalf of London's helpless and hopeless, and they soon share lessons in necessary compromise. They can never achieve the impossible victories over social wrongs that Hester passionately desires, but they can engineer simple conclusions of individual tragedies, "and some measure of justice" (*Sudden, Fearful Death* 359), and in *Weighed in the Balance* (1996), their romance begins. "In order to love someone else, you must first be true to yourself," Hester tells Monk. He responds, "You are pompous, opinionated and insufferable—but you are right" (373). After a stormy courtship in *A Breach of Promise* (1998) and an unconventional marriage of true minds beginning in *The Twisted Root* (1999), he loves her beyond distraction, beyond his own life itself.

William Monk finally breaks through the veil of his amnesia in *Death of a Stranger* (2002), where he and his old adversary Runcorn achieve a startling accommodation. Monk also risks his own life to vindicate another man, the mentor who long ago "selflessly, and without limit" (336) laid the foundation for the better person Monk is becoming. In the harrowing *A Shifting Tide* (2004), when Lady Callendra has left for Vienna, Monk's work has fallen off and Hester's charity clinic for London's prostitutes faces financial ruin, Monk accepts a case in London's vicious Thames shipping docks, unknowingly plummeting Hester into mortal danger. Gray-faced with dread, the once-arrogant William Monk confronts his old prideful self and the social complacency toward injustice of Victoria's England that Hester battles daily to help bring about a better world: "How many can fall, and we all just press onward without even seeing the space they've left? . . . Are there people suffering, crippled with grief, and we don't notice that either?" (259).

Novels: *The Face of a Stranger* (1990); *A Dangerous Mourning* (1991); *Defend and Betray* (1992); *A Sudden, Fearful Death* (1993); *The Sins of the Wolf* (1994); *Cain His Brother* (1995); *Weighed in the Balance* (1996); *The Silent Cry* (1997); *A Breach of Promise* (1998); *The Twisted Root* (1999); *Slaves and Obsessions* (2000); *A Funeral in Blue* (2001); *Death of a Stranger* (2002); *The Shifting Tide* (2004); *The Dark Assassin* (2006).

Other series: Thomas and Charlotte **Pitt** series, also set in Victorian London; the Reavley novels, set on the eve of World War I: *No Graves As Yet* (2003), *Shoulder the Sky* (2004), *Angels in the Gloom* (2005).

Other works: Perry has also written two stand-alone novels and contributed to a history of Mormonism in Britain.

Selected sources: Gulli, Andrew. Interview with Anne Perry. *Strand Magazine*, 2004: 42–49; Kleeburg, Michael. Rev. of *A Breach of Promise*. *Magill Book Reviews*, May 1, 2000; *Publishers Weekly*. Rev. of *The Shifting Tide*, March 29, 2004; Stasio, Marilyn. Rev. of *Cain His Brother*. *New York Times Book Review*, March 19, 1995: 19; Stasio, Marilyn. Rev. of *The Shifting Tide*. *New York Times Book Review*, May 9, 2004: 17; Wickman, Barbara. Rev. of *The Face of a Stranger*. *Magill Book Reviews*, May 1, 1991.

See also: Carole Nelson Douglas's **Irene Adler** series; Laurie R. King's **Mary Russell** series; Alanna Knight's Inspector Jeremy Faro series, set in nineteenth-century Edinburgh and Knight's series featuring Faro's daughter Rose McQuinn; Peter Lovesey's Sergeant Cribb-Constable Thackeray series, set in 1880s England.

Britt Montero

Profession:	Crime reporter
Living situation:	Single
Geographic locale:	Miami
Time period:	1992–present
Associate:	Lottie Dane
Nemesis:	Gretchen Platt
Significant relationships:	Kendall McDonald; Dennis Fitzgerald
Concerns:	Social issues; Cuban freedom-fighter heritage

As a fifteen-year veteran crime reporter for the *Miami Herald*, Edna Buchanan displayed relentless determination in pursuing her stories, even once shoving a mugger aside and telling him there wasn't time because she had to meet a deadline (Ashley 72). Buchanan loved being a reporter because "Sometimes you could really make a difference...I loved chronicling the adventures of real-life heroes," and after she took a leave of absence from reporting in 1988, she found she also loved writing fiction because, "I get to let the good guys win and the bad guys get what they deserve, which is so unlike life as a journalist....I can expose injustice and let my characters vent the outrage that I had to suppress as a reporter" (Howell 38). Buchanan's background in crime reporting, her indefatigable drive for a story, her thirst for justice, and her outrage at abuses converge in her Cuban-American crime reporter heroine Britt Montero, everything, Buchanan has said, that she herself would like to be: fearless, tough, unstoppable.

First appearing in *Contents Under Pressure* (1992), Montero and her best friend Lottie Dane, her colleague and leading *Miami Herald* staff photographer, are soon drawn into an investigation of police brutality, corruption, and racial hatred. D. Wayne Hudson, a black former pro football star who has been coaching under-privileged youngsters, lies technically dead in a Miami hospital, fatally beaten by police when Hudson was apparently attempting to outrun them. Refusing to believe that the squeaky-clean Hudson could have been a criminal and outraged at the acquittal of the officers responsible for the beating, Britt covers the ensuing racial riot and finally establishes the truth, though two of her friends, Officers Ted Farrell and Francie Alexander, pay terrible prices for being honest cops.

Britt has to pay some heavy dues of her own in preserving the kind of integrity that had gotten her father, a Cuban freedom fighter, shot by one of Castro's death squads. Blond, green-eyed, and skinny, Britt likes her life as a single liberated woman, free to cuddle up with tomcat Billy Boots and later Francie's toy poodle Bitsy or enjoy a stunning sunrise over the bay after an invigorating solitary run, but she's also got a mom who nags her about lacking both a suitable fashion sense and a suitable hus-band. Despite wondering why everybody thinks the answer to one's problems is a man, Britt falls for big, electric-blue-eyed Kendall McDonald, an ambitious homicide detective firmly determined to advance through the police ranks. In *Contents Under*

Pressure their personal relationship soon steams up to the boiling point, but policemen and crime reporters are natural antagonists, and when he gives her a cuckoo clock as a Christmas present, Britt knows instinctively that their time is up, even though their intermittent and covert romantic interludes continue until halfway through *You Only Die Twice* (2001). Then Britt meets Dennis Fitzgerald, a handsome special agent from the State Attorney's office.

Britt never doubts that her journalistic duty comes first, either. Once committed, she's addicted to chasing a story to its conclusion, even if it means putting herself in the line of fire. Ignoring problems, she believes, simply makes them worse, and she's out to tear the lid off crime and hypocrisy whenever she can. She's a good listener—a vital trait for an investigative reporter—and even though she exasperatedly wonders why the crazies single her out, her curiosity drives her to ask criminals: how did they get that way? why do they do it? no matter how gruesome their answers and actions may be. Britt hardly ever cries—at least not where anyone can see—because she's convinced that for a woman journalist, "one small sign of weakness or lack of resolve and you are lost" (*Pressure* 115).

Grim determination carries Britt Montero through plenty of rough patches. Continually harassed by Gretchen Platt, a *Herald* assistant city editor who wants Britt to cover ten-best-dressed lists for the society page, and her mother, who'd like to see Britt selling designer duds, Britt instead becomes the target of a serial rapist who's preying on women in downtown Miami restrooms in *Miami, It's Murder* (1994). She finds her professionalism and competence seriously questioned in *Suitable for Framing* (1995), when a young reporter Britt mentors turns out to a she-wolf in a lamb's curly coat. Montero matches herself against a hurricane and her father's killer in *Act of Betrayal* (1996); in *Margin of Error* (1997), a supposedly cushy assignment turns into a romantic involvement that complicates her relationship with McDonald. She even matches wits with a female serial killer who shoots her male victims post-seduction with lipstick-coated bullets in *Garden of Evil* (1999).

Britt Montero sees print journalism as one constant in an uncertain world, even though she realizes that it, too, is becoming dismayingly "all things to all people" in *You Only Die Twice* (2001), possibly Buchanan's best novel in terms of character development, plot development, and authenticity (Weinberg F1). Britt Montero shares Buchanan's inability to leave a "cold case" alone, and by solving this missing person case, she finds her own emotional way home, accepting that her affair with McDonald is over and meeting her mother halfway in a convincing reconciliation.

Never rushing so fast through her cases that she can't appreciate the beauty of Miami's tropical scenery or stop to comfort a wailing child, Britt Montero embodies Edna Buchanan's theory of "journalism procedurals." Buchanan "shares trade secrets with her readers" in novels that could be good textbooks for cub reporters (Weinberg F1), but she never lets anyone forget that for both Britt and Buchanan, journalism has got to have a heart.

Novels: *Contents Under Pressure* (1992); *Miami, It's Murder* (1994); *Suitable for Framing* (1995); *Act of Betrayal* (1996); *Margin of Error* (1997); *Garden of Evil* (1999); *You Only Die Twice* (2001); *The Ice Maiden* (2002).

Other series: the Miami-based Cold Case Squad novels: *Cold Case Squad* (2004); *Shadows* (2005).

Stand-alone novels: *Nobody Lives Forever* (1990); *Pulse* (1998).

Nonfiction: *Carr: Five Years of Rape and Murder* (1979); *The Corpse Had a Familiar Face: Covering Miami, America's Hottest Beat* (1987); *Never Let Them See You Cry* (1992). Buchanan has contributed short fiction and articles to numerous magazines.

Selected sources: Carroll, Dennis J. Rev. of *Act of Betrayal. New York Times Book Review*, March 24, 1996: 19; Howell, Kevin. "New Technology Solves Old Cases and Writes New Books." iVillage, www.ivillage.com/books (September 10, 2001), transcript of chat session with Edna Buchanan; Lukowsky, Wes. Rev. of *Miami, It's Murder. Booklist*, December 1, 1993: 659; *Publishers Weekly*, Rev. of *Cold Case Squad*, April 19, 2004: 38; Skenazy, Paul. Rev. of *Margin of Error. Washington Post Book World*, July 20, 1997: 10; Weinberg, Steve. Rev. of *You Only Die Twice. Denver Post*, April 5, 1998: F1.

Major awards: Buchanan won the 1986 Pulitzer Prize for general reporting. Buchanan also received the Green Eye Shade Award, Society of Professional Journalists, 1982; and Edgar Award nominations, 1990, 1994.

See also: Jan Burke's **Irene Kelly** series, set in southern California; Lucille Kallan's Maggie Rome series, set in Connecticut; Susan Kelly's Liz Connors series, set in Massachusetts; Val McDermid's Lindsay Gordon series, set in Glasgow, Scotland; Jean Warmbold's three 1980s novels featuring investigative reporter Sarah Calloway, involving timely issues like AIDS, terrorism, white supremacists, and the Israeli-Palestinian conflict.

Inspector Morse

Profession:	Detective Chief Inspector, Thames Valley Constabulary, Kidlington
Living situation:	Single
Geographic locale:	Oxford, England
Time period:	1975–1999
Associate:	Sergeant Lewis
Nemesis:	Superintendent Strange
Significant relationship:	None
Concerns:	Puzzle-solving; classical music, especially Mozart and Wagner

Colin Dexter's Inspector Morse series successfully combines elements of Golden Age mystery with realistic, even dingy settings and his hero's psycho-intuitive approach, a "hybrid quality that is the author's greatest contribution to the genre" (Murphy 141). Dexter, a former national cryptic crossword solving champion and himself a crossword compiler, cleverly incorporates dead ends, red herrings, and false leads into all of Morse's cases, sometimes building up chains of assumptions that go nowhere and force intellectual reexamination or intuitive shifts in perspective. The brutal crimes Morse investigates also provide unsettling contrasts between the Oxford university milieu and the area's lower-class "estates" (housing projects), paralleling the area's inevitable town-and-gown cultural clashes.

Inspector Morse's first name—Endeavor—is not revealed until *Death Is Now My Neighbor* (1997), a symptom of his essential shyness, like his solitary drinking, that demonstrates his irascible determination to preserve his privacy and distance himself from his associates and readers. He also cannot reach out to desirable women who attract him. In nearly every book, women are intrigued by this "conceited, civilized, ruthless, gentle, boozy, sensitive man" (*The Way Through the Woods* 41) but Morse, paralyzed like J. Alfred Prufrock by "Do I dare?" allows door after appealing boudoir door to remain closed to him. This powerful irony creates sympathy that might otherwise be nipped in the bud by his intellectual snobbery. "In a town full of people with advanced degrees, Morse meets with stupidity at all levels" (Murphy 349), and he possesses almost no tolerance for fools.

In their first case, *Last Bus to Woodstock* (1975), Morse and his long-suffering associate Sergeant Lewis encounter rape and murder, particularly jarring beneath the dreaming spires of Oxford. This juxtaposition of the sordid real and the soaring ideal—Morse's workaday world and the glorious operatic visions of Parsifal and Sarastro—dominates the entire series. 1992's *The Way Through the Wood*, with Morse on a rare holiday to Dorset, typifies the cranky inspector's ability to peer within the mind of his criminal adversary. A year after a pretty Swedish student disappeared, a complex "riddle-me-ree," an anonymous five-stanza poem sent to the Thames police and published in the *Times*, suggests the location of her body, immediately igniting Morse's tenacious curiosity. Many readers respond to the *Times*, even Morse, initiating an epistolary interchange that eventually unmasks the criminal. The sheer cleverness of the device compensates for Morse's (and Dexter's) violations of one of the Golden Age's prime dictums, "playing fair" with the reader. Morse sometimes refuses to share clues or his postulates and answers even with his trusted subordinate, the pedestrian but conscientious Sergeant Lewis, whose attitude toward Morse swings regularly between awe and exasperation.

Death is Now My Neighbor reveals the wages of Morse's dietary sins, the diabetes that will kill him in *The Remorseful Day* (1999). Even his bullying superior Superintendent Strange asks, "Do you ever worry about how your liver's coping with all this booze?" Morse decides that "the long-term disintegration of his liver and his lungs was a price well worth paying, even with diabetes, for the short-term pleasures of alcohol and nicotine" (*Death Is Now My Neighbor* 147, 206). As Lewis patiently tracks witnesses and clues to the sniper killing of physiotherapist Rachel James, he too tries to tell Morse that he's ruining himself, but ignoring Lewis, his "hard-nosed dietician's homily" and his doctor's recommendations to avoid stress, Morse produces his characteristically intuitive solution to the murder.

Morse then refuses Superintendent Strange's order to officially reinvestigate the year-old death of Yvonne Harrison in *The Remorseful Day*, instead pursuing inquiries about it behind the C.I.D.'s back. Looking back over his life, Morse attributes his successes to "a curious combination of hard thinking, hard drinking [the two, for Morse, being synonymous], hard work [usually undertaken by Sergeant Lewis], and yes, a sprinkling here and there of good fortune" (*The Remorseful Day* 13). One last time "Some light-footed mouse...scuttled across his scapulae...it seemed as if someone had switched the electric current on behind his eyes." Morse's final bolt of intuition hits him only a few days before a fatal heart attack: "It all happened so quickly" (*The Remorseful Day* 323, 332). As Lewis takes his last leave of Morse, Lewis thinks "of that wonderful memory, of that sensitivity to music and literature, above all of that capacity for thinking laterally, vertically, diagonally—whicheverwhichway [*sic*] that extraordinary brain should decide to go" (*The Remorseful Day* 346), a fitting epitaph for puzzling Inspector Morse, the "Kasparov of cruciverbalists" (*Death Is Now My Neighbor* 141).

Novels: *Last Bus to Woodstock* (1975); *Last Seen Wearing* (1976); *The Silent World of Nicholas Quinn* (1977); *Service of All the Dead* (1980); *The Dead of Jericho* (1981); *The Riddle of the Third Mile* (1983); *The Secret of Annexe 3* (1986); *The Wench Is Dead* (1989); *The Jewel That Was Ours* (1991); *The Way Through the Wood* (1992); *The Daughters of Cain* (1994); *Death Is Now My Neighbor* (1997); *The Remorseful Day* (1999).

Short stories: *Morse's Greatest Mystery and Other Stories* (1993; revised 1995).

Other works: Dexter, under the name "N.C. Dexter" has also coauthored two scholarly texts with E.G. Rayner.

Selected sources: DeHaven, Tom. Rev. of *The Way Through the Wood*. *Entertainment Weekly*, December 12, 1997: 78; Gervat, Fred M. Rev. of *The Remorseful Day*. *Library Journal*, February 1, 2000: 121; Melton, Emily. Rev. of *The Daughters of Cain*. *Booklist*, March 1, 1995: 1139; Stasio, Marilyn. Rev. of *Death Is Now My Neighbor*. *New York Times Book Review*, March 2, 1997: 20; Tonkin, Boyd. "Watching the Detectives." *New Statesman*, September 20, 1996: 45.

Major awards: Silver Dagger, 1979; Gold Dagger, 1989, 1992; Diamond Dagger, 1997.

See also: W.J. Burley's Superintendent Charles Wycliffe series, set in Cornwall; Douglas Clark's Chief Inspector Masters and Chief Inspector Bill Green series; Bill James's Chief Superintendent **Colin Harpur** series, set in the Midlands; Jill McGown's Detective Inspector Lloyd series, set in the Stansfield Criminal Investigation Division; Susannah Stacey's series featuring Superintendent Robert Bone of Tunbridge Wells in Kent, England; farther afield but with an English flavor, Laurie Mantell's Detective Sergeant Steve Arrow series, set in New Zealand.

O

Maureen O'Donnell

Profession:	None
Living situation:	Single
Geographic locale:	Glasgow, Scotland
Time period:	1998–present
Associates:	Leslie, Maureen's friend; policeman Hugh McAskill
Nemesis:	Dr. Angus Farrell
Former significant relationship:	Dr. Douglas Brady
Concerns:	Mental stability; survival; social issues, especially those of disadvantaged inner-city women

A rising star in noir crime fiction, Scottish author Denise Mina draws on her own family's Catholic orientation and her searing experiences as a hospice nurse and a university tutor in criminal law to bring a "world of drug dealers, broken families, sanctimonious healthcare workers and debilitated victims to startling life" (*Publishers Weekly* 45). After taking a law degree from Glasgow University and starting a Ph.D. program concentrating on mental illness in female offenders, Mina turned to writing noir fiction that strips Glasgow's social ills to their raw and bleeding bones.

In a 2005 interview, Mina declared that the older Scottish generation is proud of her books, so they buy them "in a foreign language to show off my name on the cover, but so no one can read the sexy bits inside or the parts where people don't go to chapel." That inbred reluctance to "let the neighbors know" about family problems, especially those considered morally or religiously questionable, underlies Mina's powerful trilogy centered on young Maureen O'Donnell, raised Catholic in Glasgow, sexually abused by her father with her alcoholic mother's and spiteful sisters' knowledge. The resulting shock and horror drove Maureen to a mental breakdown. Maureen becomes that most unlikely of sleuths, the detective as victim, as she solves crimes involving helpless, disturbed, and poverty-stricken Glasgow women—including herself—while struggling to maintain her tenuous grasp of on her own sanity.

Garnethill (1999) finds Maureen "underfed and brittle" (37), eight months following her release from three years in a state mental institution. She blearily wakes one morning after a bout of heavy drinking to discover her lover, Dr. Douglas Brady, son of a prominent Scottish European Parliament Member, tied to a chair in her living room with his head nearly severed from his mutilated body. Two Glasgow detectives, hostile Joe McEwan and sympathetic Hugh McAskill, interrogate Maureen and her drug-dealing brother Liam as prime suspects, so to save herself and Liam, Maureen undertakes a search for the killer. The quest leads her to a vicious scandal involving the rapes of helpless female patients in the George I ward of Northern Hospital, where she herself had been a patient.

After unmasking Dr. Angus Farrell as the killer-cum-rapist and engineering her own kind of revenge, Maureen works in *Exile* (2001) with her motorcycle-riding feminist chum Leslie at a battered women's shelter. Farrell, now being held him in a psychiatric hospital, is intimidating her by mail, but Maureen and Leslie have another murder to solve: one of the shelter's women clients, formerly involved in drug-smuggling, has been found floating in the Thames, and Maureen's problems multiply viciously. When Farrell is finally brought to trial in *Resolution* (2002), a year after the events of *Garnethill*, Maureen, fearing for her life as well as her sanity, must testify against him. Michael, Maureen's abusive father, is back in Glasgow, too, with the support of Maureen's drunken mother and her oblivious sisters. One of them, Una, is pregnant and intends to allow their parents to help with the baby, to prove that Maureen's accusations against Michael are unfounded—and fear for the baby preys constantly on Maureen's mind. At the same time, Maureen's near-illiterate street acquaintance Ella McGee is beaten to death and Ella's murder is pursuing Maureen and Leslie as well.

Rough of tongue as any foul-mouthed navvy, raw of throat from cheap fags and rotgut, so brutalized by her father's sexual abuse and her drunken mother's verbal torment that she feels responsible for her own pain, and so undone by her sisters' self-serving willingness to throw her to the wolves, Maureen somehow finds the courage to take them all on. After she lets her mother Winnie and her hypocritical sisters have a piece of her tongue they'll never forget in *Garnethill*, Maureen lives down her constant lapsed-Catholic guilt and need for ritual, the distrust of the local police, and the cowardice of her brother Liam, the only wobbly support she has in this outrageously dysfunctional family.

Maureen O'Donnell's survival depends in part on the compassion of others. However imperfect their help is, it gives her the confidence she needs to start saving herself. In all three novels, Leslie prods Maureen to keep on trying to find her lover's murderer; in all of them, too, McAskill's sympathy—he's also a survivor of parental abuse—and even McEwan's brusque interrogation stiffen Maureen's resolve to end this painful period in her life. Maureen O'Donnell fights her way clear of her paralyzing fears—of Farrell, of her father, of facing herself in a mirror—so that she can make something of herself despite her harrowing circumstances. Although Maureen's road to sobriety is a mercilessly recounted sequence of small successes and occasional big relapses, at the close of *Resolution*, she accepts that she's done "unconscionable things that would change her life for ever" and wakes happy: "no one could reproach her for it," and she's "going to enjoy today" (*Resolution* 436). Maureen O'Donnell's pain-wracked one-day-at-a-time triumph pays a remarkably warm tribute to the resilience of the human spirit.

Novels (dates given for U.S. publication): *Garnethill* (1999); *Exile* (2001); *Resolution* (2002).

Other novels: *Sanctum* (U.K. publication 2002); *Deception* (2004); *The Field of Blood* (2005), the opening novel of a new trilogy set in Glasgow and featuring unlovely Patricia "Paddy" Meehan, who works as a "copy boy" at *The Scottish Daily News* but who has the potential to become a first-rate reporter—"a tough look," says Marilyn Stasio, "at what it means to be female and Catholic and on your own in a society that doesn't much value those qualities" (*New York Times Book Review*, July 10, 2005: 31).

Radio play: *Hurtle*, BBC Radio 4, 2003.

Short fiction: Mina has written numerous short stories, including "Helena and the Babies," published in *Fresh Blood 2*, Do Not Press, 1999.

Selected sources: Arthur, Budd. Rev. of *Garnethill*. *Booklist*, April 15, 1999: 1483; *BBC News Online*: www.news.bbc.co.uk (June 9, 2004), "Denise Mina"; *Crime Time Web site*: www.crimetime.co.uk (June 9, 2004), "Sexual Slavery in Glasgow: Denise Mina on Her work, *Resolution*"; Lunn, Bob. Rev. of *Exile*. *Library Journal*, February 15, 2001: 202; *Publishers Weekly*. Rev. of *Garnethill*, March 1, 1999: 63; Stasio, Marilyn. Rev. of *Resolution*. *New York Times Book Review*, June 23, 2002: 18; Weber, Nancy. "Tartan Noir: *PW* Talks with Denise Mina." *Publishers Weekly*, May 9, 2005: 45.

Major awards: John Creasey Memorial Dagger, 1998; Macallan Short Story Dagger, 1998; *Scotland on Sundays*/Glenfiddich Spirit of Scotland Award, 2000.

Web sites: www.denisemina.co.uk; Contemporary Writers in the UK Web site: www.contemporarywriters.com, "Denise Mina."

See also: American author Abigail Padgett's series featuring Barbara Joan "Bo" Bradley, a child abuse investigator who is bipolar herself; Andrew Vachss's unsettling series featuring "Burke" (no other names used), an ex-con on a crusade to track down and take revenge on child molesters. For the inner-city Glasgow setting and problems, see William McIlvanney's Inspector Jack Laidlaw series, which questions the meaning of life. For "dark suspense," see Ed Gorman's violently noir Jack Dwyer series; Joe Lansdale's Hap Collins (straight and white) and Leonard Pine (gay and black) noir series.

Michael Ohayon

Profession:	Chief Inspector, later Superintendent of Criminal Investigations, Jerusalem
Living situation:	Divorced
Geographic locale:	Israel
Time period:	1988–present
Associate:	Police subordinate Eli Bachar
Significant relationships:	Various women, most recently Ada Levi, an old flame
Concern:	Israel's internal tensions

Batya Gur's *The Saturday Morning Murder: A Psychoanalytic Case* (1988, tr. 1992) became the first mystery novel by an Israeli to win a substantial American audience. Formerly a literature teacher and presently a literary critic for *Ha'aretz*, Israel's most prestigious newspaper, Gur claims that the "sheer desperation" of a midlife crisis at thirty-nine drove her to write detective fiction, following novelists whose work she loved, especially Raymond Chandler (only now being translated into Hebrew) and Rex Stout. She portrayed Michael Ohayon, tall, ravishingly handsome, sad-eyed, and hurting, to some extent in her own idealized image, too: "I have a short temper and am a difficult person, but I couldn't make him a woman.... He was created from the need to tell a believable story" (*Publishers Weekly*, November 8, 2004).

While the Al Aqsa intifada rages around them, both Ohayon and his creator are often in trouble with their own government. Gur passionately believes that "There are serious social issues neglected by both the Israeli and the Palestinian leadership, who seem to use the conflict to avoid dealing with them" (*Publishers Weekly*, November 8, 2004). Against the violent backdrop of the Israeli-Palestinian conflict where his son, like all young Israelis, faced death as a soldier, Ohayon's convincing cases all involve internal Israeli tensions rarely exposed to the outside world, because Ohayon, a Jew born in Morocco and brought by his Zionist parents to Israel at three, has always felt himself an outsider in the Jewish homeland.

In Gur's novels, the Ashkenazic Jews who emigrated to Israel after World War II with their European looks, their European cultural background, and their fearful experiences of the Holocaust often oppress the Mizrahim, Jews born in the Mideast or North Africa, and disagree violently with sabras, Jews born in Israel after 1948. Within these groups violent confrontations also occur, especially intergenerational feuds and socio-philosophical clashes between the idealistic old Zionists and their increasingly materialistic offspring—smitten, their parents claim, by "the curse of affluence" (*Kibbutz* 159). In his early forties, Ohayon chain-smokes his way through similar battles, having twenty years ago forfeited a brilliant academic future as a Cambridge-trained scholar of European history to stay with his son Yuval during Ohayon's divorce from his Ashkenazi wife Nira, daughter of a wealthy diamond merchant and a classically ferocious Jewish mother. Ohayon then studied law and joined the police, finding an avuncular mentor in Emanuel Shorer, his superior, but despite Shorer's urging him to marry again and settle down, Ohayon has chosen to be homeless since he left for the gifted children's boarding school at twelve, living like a gypsy in impersonal Jerusalem flats, unable to achieve stability in any of his fleeting affairs because of his reserve in personal relationships, caring most for his son but afraid to declare his love openly for fear of rejection.

Chief Inspector Ohayon's first case, *The Saturday Morning Murder*, is set at the Israeli Psychoanalytic Institute where Gur's former husband was a candidate. Ohayon, discreet and tactful, contrasts sharply with the mostly arrogant *yekkes*, the German Jews who founded the Institute, and with the literature faculty of Jerusalem's Hebrew University in his second case, *Literary Murder: A Critical Case* (1989; tr. 1993). There he delicately probes the deaths of two literature professors slain the same weekend, applying his innate sensitivity and raising the technique of silence he'd learned from Shorer to interrogational art. "Michael almost always made the people he was talking to feel as if he lacked the knowledge, but not the ability, to understand . . . [so] They dropped their guards" (*Kibbutz* 160).

Preferring to work independently and trusting his team with equal autonomy, Ohayon, now a Superintendent working with the National Unit for the Investigation of Serious Crimes, is assigned to a secretive Israeli agricultural commune in *Murder on a Kibbutz* (1991; tr. 1994), shortlisted for an Anthony award, where two parathion poisonings explode the kibbutz's surface serenity. Ohayon risks both his own reputation and Shorer's to solve these seemingly motiveless crimes while coping with a jealous local police commander, a former kibbutznik who resents Ohayon's Moroccan background and rapid promotions, and when Ohayon's interrogation of a married Knesset member and lover of one of the kibbutz victims ends abruptly with the subject's heart attack, Ohayon acquires a not entirely unwarranted name for police severity.

In *Bethlehem Road Murder* (2001; tr. 2003), a beautiful young woman is found beaten to death near an apartment Ohayon has just bought in this racially mixed Jerusalem neighborhood where everyone knows everyone else, a mirror of the whole Middle East, seething with old hurts and eternal hatreds. One of modern Israel's worst scandals, the heartbreaking injustice wreaked by the Ashkenazim on Jewish immigrants from Arab countries, haunts this case and forces Ohayon to consider retirement just when he meets Ada Levi, his boyhood sweetheart, again, a bittersweet reunion shaken when Eli Bachar, Ohayon's best friend and most trusted assistant, reveals too much about Ohayon to an unscrupulous reporter. Though he is as ever uncertain of his ability to solve the homicide, after Michael Ohayon lays his personal griefs aside to sink completely into his work again with the patience of Job, using "his eyes . . . that look of his . . . and then he was silent and struck" (*Bethlehem* 154) in the name of justice, in Ada's arms at least he is an outsider no longer.

Novels:* *The Saturday Morning Murder: A Psychoanalytic Case* (1992; orig. 1988); *Literary Murder: A Critical Case* (1993; orig. 1989); "Next to Hunger Road" (*Mikevish hara'av 'semolah*,

---

*After their publications in Israel, most of Gur's mystery novels were translated by Dalya Balu and published in the United States. Approximate English titles and original publication dates are given for those as yet untranslated.

1990); *Murder on a Kibbutz: A Communal Case* (1994; orig. 1991); "Afterbirth" (*Lo kakh te 'artii li*, 1994); *Murder Duet: A Musical Case* (1999; orig. 1996); "Stone for a Stone" (*Even tahat even*, 1998); "Spy Within the House" (*Meragel be-tokh ha bayit*, 2000); *Bethlehem Road Murder*, tr. by Vivian Eden (2004; orig. 2001).

Selected sources: Cooper, Ilene. Rev. of *Murder on a Kibbutz. Booklist*, November 15, 1994: 581; Kenney, Susan. "Death Comes to the Professor." *New York Times Book Review*, December 23, 1993; Ott, Bill. Rev. of *Murder Duet. Booklist*, September 15, 1999: 236; Picker, Leonard. "A Product of Sheer Desperation: *PW* Talks with Batya Gur." *Publishers Weekly*, November 8, 2004; *Publishers Weekly*. Rev. of *Literary Murder*, October 11, 1993: 72; Stasio, Marilyn. Rev. of *The Saturday Morning Murder. New York Times Book Review*, June 21, 1992: 21.

See also: Rochelle Krich's series drawing on her Orthodox Jewish background and featuring LAPD detective Jessie Drake, and Krich's new series featuring Orthodox Jew and private investigator Molly Blume; S.T. Haymon's series featuring Detective Inspector Ben Jurnet, who is in love with a Jewish woman who will only marry him if he converts to Judaism; Harry Kemelman's series featuring **Rabbi David Small**, who often reflects on Jewish history and customs.

Gideon Oliver

Profession:	Physical anthropologist
Living situation:	Widowed; later remarried
Geographic locale:	Worldwide
Time period:	1982–present
Associate:	John Lau
Significant relationship:	Julie Tendler, Oliver's second wife
Concerns:	Forensic investigation; enjoying life's pleasures

Aaron Elkins returned from Europe in 1978 after two years teaching anthropology for the Overseas Division of the University of Maryland on various NATO bases and soon found his niche writing classy, meticulously plotted mystery novels. *Fellowship of Fear* (1982) introduced Dr. Gideon Oliver, an appealingly modest professor of physical anthropology (Elkins's comment: "Of all things!") employing rigorous scholarly methods in solving murders ancient and recent, all across the globe.

Bereft after his wife Nora's death in a car accident two years earlier, Oliver jumps at the chance to leave Northern California State University temporarily for a visiting fellowship with the United States Overseas College (USOC), based in atmospheric old Heidelberg. The *Gemütlichkeit* has scarcely set in, however, when an enigmatic spook supervisor propositions Gideon to do just a harmless little errand for his country. In rapid succession Oliver's room is burgled and he himself is assaulted, seduced (though not unwillingly), and inexplicably robbed of several pairs of socks.

Oliver is no milquetoast ivory-tower professor type. A six-foot former college boxer who at thirty-eight has maintained a reasonably fit physique, he's enraged at being manipulated. He likes stormy days better than sunny ones, he's capable of cold, lucid anger at injustice, and he fights his mysterious assailants back on their own turf, wounding a few and sending others to the morgue. Though he's by no means on the prowl, he also knows his soft brown eyes, his husky frame, and his broken nose make him attractive to women, and he enjoys his first romantic encounter since his wife's death when Janet Feller, languid of thigh and provocative of glance, swoops upon him in the full flush of liberated womanhood. Gideon soon discovers "Women had changed a lot in the decade since he'd been in active pursuit" (*Fellowship* 114). One change, though, isn't as palatable to Oliver: "feminists often bore and sometime irritate him with their grim, contentious rhetoric" (*Fellowship* 106), and since Janet's research turns out to be "A Study of Oppression, Sexism, and Bibliophily" even some bedroom steamatics can't keep them together for long. For now, at least, Oliver decides to steer clear of Meaningful Relationships, though he admits to himself, "A Good Lay wouldn't have been bad, either" (*Fellowship* 156).

As an amateur detective, Oliver's at most medium-boiled. He uses profanity rarely because doing so indicates that he's slipped into a "loutish tantrum" he detests. Oliver can't get out of Heidelberg's *Zum Roten Ochsen*, a venerable male-student hangout famous from *The Student Prince*, fast enough because those "lusty male voices" and clanking beer steins awaken for him "an ominous scene out of the 1930s: flushed, sweating faces, glazed and fervent eyes. . . . It wasn't for him"; and a super-efficient German secretary who loftily declares the Teutonic manifesto, "We work when we must" causes him to think sardonically, "Heil Hitler" (*Fellowship* 108, 101).

Detail oriented and wholeheartedly dedicated to scientific ratiocination, Oliver earns the informal title of "Skeleton Detective" in his first few novels, nonplussing European police detectives with his keen deductions from bony remains found in Italy, Spain, Washington State, England, France, and even Yucatan. He has company in his travels, too. He'd met a young park ranger, Julie Tendler, who became the second Mrs. Oliver. FBI agent John Lau, whom Oliver first met in *Fellowship of Fear*, also becomes his friend and partner in investigations. Oliver starts "to think like a cop" (140), too, making for exciting adventures with Lau in succeeding novels like *Old Bones* (1987), where Oliver tidily disproves a popular theory that a dismembered skeleton disinterred from the cellar of a French Resistance fighter's family chateau belonged to a hated SS officer.

"Them dry bones" prove almost as magnetic for Oliver as is Julie. *Skeleton Dance* (2000) takes him back to the dawn of civilization as he interviews scientists at France's *Institute de Préhistoire* about supposedly fossilized bones that turn out to be an elaborate hoax. While espionage plots and counterplots generally leave Oliver feeling as though he's been listening to someone read an IRS manual (*Fellowship* 143), he waxes moist-eyed poetic over a stone possibly undisturbed for three thousand centuries, the near-mystic musing that had attracted him to anthropology in the first place (*Fellowship* 176).

Gideon Oliver's cases nearly always involve good local cuisine, delectable wines, and spectacular scenery. *Good Blood* (2004), a convoluted tale of conniving Italian aristocrats, leads Oliver and Julie to a holiday near Lake Maggiore with a friend who runs budget kayak and bike tours. Oliver, now fortyish, arranges to stay in a comfortable hotel and feast at some memorable trattorias between professional sessions studying a skeleton he'd excavated for the local carabiniere colonel, who's gingerly directing a search for the local padrone's sixteen-year-old only son and heir. In *Where There's a Will* (2005), set in Hawaii, Oliver and John Lau, both twitchy after only a few days of vacation, investigate remains found in a ten-year-old plane crash, a case involving a hefty fortune and the enormous Hoaloha cattle ranch. Oliver's never at ease with emotional fireworks (*Blood* 218) and most of his post-stress reactions are lulus, but Julie and good food always bring him around. Like his fictional predecessor Dr. John Thorndyke, Dr. Gideon Oliver delightedly deduces remarkably accurate facts from the tiniest fragments of skeletal scientific evidence. Gideon revels in his highly specialized field as "a secret vice and sport" (*Blood* 127) that's understandable and even fascinating as he unravels far-flung mysteries and genially savors his way through the scenery and cuisines of some of the world's most exotic settings.

Novels: *Fellowship of Fear* (1982); *The Dark Place* (1983); *Murder in the Queen's Armes* (1985); *A Deceptive Clarity* (1987); *Old Bones* (1987); *Curses!* (1989); *Icy Clutches* (1990); *Make No Bones* (1991); *Dead Men's Hearts* (1994); *Twenty Blue Devils* (1997); *Skeleton Dance* (2000); *Good Blood* (2004); *Where There's a Will* (2005).

Other series: The Chris Norgren series, featuring an art museum curator; the Ben Revere series, featuring a Boston art expert tracing art looted by the Nazis during World War II; with Charlotte Elkins, a lighter series featuring female pro golfer Lee Ofsted and policeman Graham Sheldon.

Stand-alone novels: *Loot* (1999); *Turncoat* (2002).

Selected sources: Forister, Ann. Rev. of *Good Blood*. *Library Journal*, January 15, 2004: 166; McLarin, Jenny. Rev. of *Where There's a Will*. *Booklist*, April 1, 2005: 1348; Miller, Sharon. Rev. of *Old Bones*. *Seattle Times/Seattle Post-Intelligencer*, July 3, 1988; Needham, George. Rev. of *Skeleton Dance*. *Booklist*, March 15, 2002: 1332; Stasio, Marilyn. Rev. of *Twenty Blue Devils*. *New York Times*, January 19, 1997: 7:20.

Major awards: Edgar Allan Poe Award, 1988; Agatha Award (with Charlotte Elkins), 1992; Nero Wolfe Award, 1993.

See also: Margot Arnold's series featuring American anthropologist Dr. Penelope Spring and British Sir Toby Glendower, an archaeologist; Dana Cameron's series featuring archaeologist Emma Fielding; Beverly Connor's series featuring forensic archaeologist Lindsay Chamberlain; Roy Lewis's series featuring archaeologist Arnold Landon; Sharyn McCrumb's series featuring forensic anthropologist Elizabeth MacPherson; Kathy Reichs's series featuring forensic anthropologist Temperance Brennan and Detective Andrew Ryan. For series dealing, like Elkins's Norgren series and Ben Revere series, with art and art history, see Dorothy Dunnett's Johnson Johnson series; Marcia Muller's series featuring Elena Oliverez, a Mexican-American art museum curator in Santa Barbara, California, and Muller's series featuring Joanna Stark, an art security consultant; also Kyril Bonfiglioli's witty series featuring shady English art dealer Charlie Mordecai; Iain Pears's **Jonathan Argyll** series, set in England and Europe.

Monsieur Pamplemousse

Profession:	Food critic for *Le Guide*; former Sûreté detective
Living situation:	Happily married to Doucette Pamplemousse
Geographic locale:	France
Time period:	1983–present
Associate:	Pommes Frites, bloodhound extraordinaire
Nemesis:	Director Leclercq of *Le Guide*
Significant relationship:	Doucette Pamplemousse
Concerns:	*Haute cuisine*; fine wines; *les femmes*

Monsieur Aristide Pamplemousse and former Sniffer Dog of the Year Pommes Frites become funnier and funnier in Michael Bond's comic culinary series spoofing police procedurals. On the ladder of civilization, Mark Twain placed the French several rungs lower than the Comanches, probably because Gallic laissez-faire creativity in the pursuit of *l'amour* and *la cuisine* tends to shock *les bourgeois transatlantiques*; Monsieur Pamplemousse's exploits in boudoir and dining room, mentored by the unflappable Pommes Frites, overshadow the murder cases that they solve between dining experiences.

Forcibly retired from the Sûreté due to "The Case of the Cuckolded Chorus" of the Folies Bergère ("Some husbands have long memories") (*Monsieur Pamplemousse* 18), Monsieur Pamplemousse teams up with Pommes Frites, winner of the Pierre

Armand Golden Bone Trophy but made redundant by the Sûreté's budgetary cuts. Together they form a formidable team of incognito gastronomic inspectors for the elite *Le Guide*, whose coveted three-stockpot ranking is one of the highest culinary achievements in Bond's fictional France.

Greed and expediency drive the French criminals and bureaucrats Monsieur Pamplemousse and Pommes Frites encounter to deliciously horrifying acts. Sent out on an impossible mission by Director Leclercq, as always protecting his own coattails, their first case (*Monsieur Pamplemousse*, 1983) sets the pattern for the series: *l'amour* and *la cuisine* trump *le crime*. Evaluating Madame Sophie's Hotel-Restaurant La Langoustine in the idyllic French countryside, Pommes Frites agrees that the *sauce Madère* of an otherwise exquisite *Filet de Boeuf en Croute* is too salty, and when Pamplemousse carves the *pièce de résistance*, a whole specially-reared corn-fed truffle-stuffed chicken encased in a freshly scraped pig's bladder and stewed in chicken comsommé for two and a half hours, the black hairy head of a thirty-year-old man appears. While Pamplemousse quells his queasy fellow diners with remarkable sang-froid: "And you, *monsieur*, did you enjoy your liver? Or do you now wish you'd ordered the *truite*?" "a loud crunching sound... came from a spot somewhere near his feet" (*Monsieur Pamplemousse* 22).

Despite his role in the loss of the corpus delecti and his sufferings under his master's bed while Monsieur Pamplemousse selflessly endures the torments of Madame Sophie's frenzied passion, Pommes Frites gallantly assists in bringing the perpetrators to justice. Their subsequent cases follow similar lines, more than a soupçon of horror seasoning each adventure, with dashes of titillating innuendo and incongruities adding incomparable exotic flavors.

In *Monsieur Pamplemousse on Vacation* (2003), Pommes Frites's role expands from gustatory assistant to associate sleuth when a brutally dismembered body washes up on the beach outside the Hôtel au Soleil d'Or, disrupting the guests' appetite for grouper and other flesh-eating marine life. Pommes Frites doggedly tracks the criminals and uncovers stolen treasures while his master struggles with the Director's latest instrument of torture, the European Union's cutting-edge multinationally designed laptop equipped with voice-recognition, a miniature video camera, and *quelle horreur*! a keyboard *en anglais*! With the digital camera clasped firmly between his teeth, Pommes Frites faithfully records his master's tour de force: Monsieur Pamplemousse, rendered unconscious in the line of duty, is energetically invigorated with the kiss of life by a Russian music mistress who is vigorously straddling him, her substantial endowments, as Doucette later dryly observes, totally unhampered by a *brassière*.

Solving their cases with such panache, Monsieur Pamplemousse and Pommes Frites illuminate a culture so remote as to be mostly incomprehensible and entirely comedic to stuffier Anglo-Saxon sensibilities, but the humor they unleash—*c'est magnifique*.

Novels: *Monsieur Pamplemousse* (1983); *Monsieur Pamplemousse and the Secret Mission* (1984); *Monsieur Pamplemousse on the Spot* (1986); *Monsieur Pamplemousse Takes the Cure* (1987); *Monsieur Pamplemousse Aloft* (1989); *Monsieur Pamplemousse Investigates* (1990); *Monsieur Pamplemousse Rests His Case* (1991); *Monsieur Pamplemousse Stands Firm* (1992); *Monsieur Pamplemousse on Location* (1992); *Monsieur Pamplemousse Takes the Train* (1993); *Monsieur*

Pamplemousse Afloat (1998); *Monsieur Pamplemousse on Probation* (2000); *Monsieur Pamplemousse on Vacation* (2003); *Monsieur Pamplemousse Hits the Headlines* (2004).

Other series: Children's series: the "Paddington Bear" series; the "Thursday" series; the "Olga Da Polga" series and picture books; the "Parsley" series; two puppet series, "The Herbs" and "The Adventures of Parsley."

Other works: Bond has also written numerous stand-alone books for children, radio and television plays for both adults and children, and full-length animated Paddington films shown worldwide.

Selected sources: *Armchair Detective*. Rev. of *Monsieur Pamplemousse Rests His Case*, Summer 1991; Colta, Marialisa. "Portrait of a Happy Eater: Paperback Writer." *Gourmet*, January 1, 1999: 33; Klett, Rex E. Rev. of *Monsieur Pamplemousse Rests His Case*. *Library Journal*, September 1, 1991: 235; *Publishers Weekly*. Rev. of *Monsieur Pamplemousse Investigates*, October 12, 1990: 48; *Publishers Weekly*. Rev. of *Monsieur Pamplemousse Rests His Case*, October 12, 1990: 48.

Major awards: American Library Association Notable Book Citation (for children's books); Order of the British Empire, 1997.

See also: Culinary detectives, especially JoAnna Carl's Chocoholic Mysteries; Diane Mott Davidson's series featuring caterer **Goldy Bear**; Ellen Hart's series featuring Jane Lawless, a Minneapolis restaurant owner, and her series featuring Sophie Greenway, a Minneapolis food critic and magazine editor; Peter King's Gourmet Detective series, set in Europe's finest dining locales; Daniel Pennac's "Belleville Quintet," featuring Benjamin Malaussène and set in Paris's Arb neighborhood; Janet Laurence's series featuring Darina Lisle, a Cordon Bleu chef, caterer, and author; Amy Myers's series featuring Victorian-era Anglo-French master chef Auguste Didier.

Charles Paris

Profession:	Actor
Living situation:	Amicably separated
Geographic locale:	England, especially London's theatre milieu
Time period:	1975–present
Associate:	Gerald Venables, solicitor
Nemesis:	The Bottle
Concerns:	Alcoholism; contemporary British theatre, radio, and television

Middle-aged alcoholic actor Charles Paris springs deftly from Simon Brett's experiences producing light comedies for BBC Radio and London Weekend Television. Paris's debonair veneer covers a heart breaking from boredom and disgust at his own shortcomings, and he falls into amateur detecting while "resting," the professional actor's euphemism for unemployment. Paris had been a promising newcomer in the 1950s, but when the series opens with *Cast in Order of Disappearance*

(1975), Paris is in his forties, amicably separated, and overly fond of Bell's Scotch. He's descended to character roles, farcical portrayals of middle-aged roués that hit too close to home, and small mindless television appearances that insult his intelligence and self-respect, driving him to the arms of aspiring starlets and the bottoms of increasingly topped-up glasses. As Martha Alderson noted in *Clue: A Journal of Detection* (Fall/Winter 1983), Paris's "youthful dreams of fame were mostly just that."

Paris's adventures decant the bubbly surface of life upon the wicked London stage into depressing dregs of the day-to-day theatre slog that drives Paris to recreational sex, to Bell's, and eventually to amateur detection. Like Charles's acting career itself, all of these pursuits start out promisingly, but none satisfies him for long. In *Cast in Order of Disappearance*, after years of living boozily "from hangover to hangover, with the odd affair between drinks" another large Bell's temporarily gives Charles "a feeling of positive well-being." He knows his lack of matinee-idol looks had scuttled stardom for him in the 1950s, but at forty-seven, flush from "a ghastly television series" and "lightly silvered at the temples" he still attracts women (*Cast* 15, 8) like little blonde Jacqui, recently dumped by a wealthy lover. One glass and cuddle after another mounts from pub to her white fur-covered bedstead, but at the climactic moment Charles suffers "the dreaded Distiller's Droop."

Concluding that "Marriage is the last refuge of the impotent" (*Cast* 15), Charles ruefully heads for his estranged wife Frances, where bed and breakfast temporarily restore his self-confidence—like riding a bicycle after many years, Charles thinks—but when Jacqui's lover dies suspiciously, leaving her pregnant and penniless, Charles's amatory failure makes him feel paternally obligated to investigate the death. Bumbling through a tangle of murky motives, Charles draws on his Old Actors' Network, he stoops to toadying to bumptious ham-actor star Bernard Walton, once directed by Charles, and he even draws out suspects by passing himself off as Scotland Yard "Inspector McWhirter."

Cast in Order of Disappearance sets the pattern for all of Charles Paris's cases, each arising from his dismal pursuit of acting jobs to keep ahead of the Inland Revenue and pay the rent on his sordid little London flat. Each case also deals some blow to his masculinity or his actor's pride, tumbling him into another bottle of Bell's and the inevitable results: hungover fears of failure, loneliness, poverty, and aging. Every time Charles gets a hack part, at least one murder ensues, causing him to muddles through various theatrical settings using his skill at character portrayal and disguise and occasionally assisted by Gerald Venables, a near-caricature of the prototypical sleazy attorney.

Between drinking bouts Paris investigates the death of a performer electrocuted at a beachfront music hall in *A Comedian Dies* (1979); *The Dead Side of the Mike* (1980) finds him weltering through another BBC radio drama and looking into a young woman's apparent suicide; *Situation Tragedy* (1981) gives Paris a job in a new television program but also confronts him with a murder that occurs onstage, while in *Dead Giveaway*, revealing the workings of popular television game shows, Paris not only faces the on-set poisoning of a media celebrity but takes a heavy hit himself, since he realizes he was asked to appear on this *What's My Line* knockoff simply because so few people in the audience know who he is or what he does.

The considerable sympathy generated by Paris's Pagliacci edge probably accounts for much of this self-destructive loser's success with women—and readers. Charles Paris's outward struggles to secure meaningful employment and his inward battles over drink and womanizing increasingly outweigh the murders he solves. Between 1982's *Murder Unprompted*, which chiefly involves Paris debasing himself (and knowing it) to snag a role in a West End stage play, and *A Reconstructed Corpse* (1993), which shows him sunk to playing a missing man on a television true crime show, Paris sinks lower on the sad downward spiral of alcoholism, despising himself but unable to stop.

For all its onstage boffos and Charles's offstage philandering, *Dead Room Farce* (1998) portrays a late-fiftyish man forced at last to confront his alcoholism. Like every charming alcoholic, Charles Paris has been telling himself he can quit any time—but so far he hasn't wanted to. Reduced to living in "a shambles of old papers and grubby clothes" (*Farce* 21) and constantly debilitated by hangovers, Charles feels tortured by recriminations: he'd betrayed Frances more often than he can remember, and he'd neglected his daughter Juliet, middle-aged at twenty-one and married to a stultifying accountant. At this point, Charles also sees that he's not drinking to make life different—just to make it seem different. His sobering self-loathing may yet drive Charles Paris to a happy ending, taking sobriety one step, one day, at a time (*Farce* 182).

Novels: *Cast in Order of Disappearance* (1975); *So Much Blood* (1976); *Star Trap* (1977); *An Amateur Corpse* (1978); *A Comedian Dies* (1979); *The Dead Side of the Mike* (1980); *Situation Tragedy* (1981); *Murder Unprompted* (1982); *Murder in the Title* (1983); *Not Dead, Only Resting* (1984); *Dead Giveaway* (1985); *What Bloody Man Is That?* (1987); *A Series of Murders* (1989); *Corporate Bodies* (1991); *A Reconstructed Corpse* (1993); *Sicken and So Die* (1995); *Dead Room Farce* (1998).

Other series: Mrs. Melita Pargeter series; the Fethering series, featuring Carole Seddon.

Short fiction: *Tickled to Death* (1985).

Other works: Brett has also authored plays and radio and television scripts as well as edited several humor collections and short mystery fiction anthologies.

Selected sources: Connors, Theresa. Rev. of *Murder Unprompted*. *Library Journal*, May 15, 2000: 150; Kaufman, James. Rev. of *Situation Tragedy*. *Christian Science Monitor*, March 3, 1982; Pitt, David. Rev. of *Dead Room Farce*. *Booklist*, August 1998: 1972; Seymour, Miranda. Rev. of *Murder Unprompted*. *Times* (London), February 18, 1982; Stasio, Marilyn. Rev. of *Dead Room Farce*. *New York Times Book Review*, October 11, 1998: 28.

Major awards: Writers' Guild of Great Britain, 1973; Broadcasting Press Guild Award, 1987.

See also: Linda Barnes's Michael Spraggue series featuring an American private investigator who becomes an actor; Jane Dentinger's Jocelyn O'Rourke series, set in the New York theatre world; Ruth Dudley Edwards's witty series featuring Robert Amiss, a down-on-his-luck civil servant; Simon Shaw's Philip Fletcher series, starring a villainous actor who becomes an amateur detective; Marian Babson's humorous series featuring Trixie Dolan and Evangeline Sinclair, aging actresses trying for a comeback on the London stage.

Peter Pascoe and Andrew Dalziel

Profession:	Pascoe: Detective Sergeant (promoted gradually to Chief Detective Inspector during series); Dalziel: Detective Superintendent; both Mid-Yorkshire C.I.D.
Living situation:	Pascoe: married in *An April Shroud*; Dalziel: divorced
Geographic locale:	Yorkshire, England
Time period:	1970–present
Associates:	Detective Sergeant Edgar Wield; WDC Shirley Novello; Detective Constable "Hat" Bowler
Significant relationships:	Eleanor "Ellie" Soper Pascoe; Dalziel: Amanda "Cap" Marvel
Concerns:	Crime and justice

Reginald Hill's popular Pascoe-Dalziel Mid-Yorkshire C.I.D. series, "not detective stories but crime novels," illustrates contemporary British class conflicts with two protagonists, superficially an odd couple but in reality complementary personalities who learn the rough lessons of life from each other (Keating 189). Superintendent Dalziel ("Fat Andy," "His Fatship," or "that fat bastard," depending on Dalziel's most recent interaction with the speaker) uses his old-school tough-copper experience and his fitful flashes of intuition, usually late in a case, to flush out crooks. Whereas Dr. Watson invariably agreed with his Great Detective's positions, Peter Pascoe, sensitive and intelligent, degreed in sociology and 1970s-liberal in outlook, offers a parallel perspective to each one of Dalziel's. Readers generally identify with the bright, polite, literate Pascoe—"it is easy to prefer the aesthete to the Neanderthal" (Murphy 125)—but sometimes Pascoe gets lost in the details of a case or is paralyzed by fear for his wife and child, while the coarse groin-scratching Dalziel always delivers the goods he ferrets out between guzzles and gobbles at the pub. From mutual antipathy, their relationship gradually evolves into mutually respectful teamwork in solving crimes arising from the grimmer aspects of today's British life.

Unlike strict police procedurals, personal situations "that begin unofficially or revolve around people known to the main characters" (Murphy 125) usually spark the Pascoe-Dalziel cases. Each early case focuses on one of the two detectives with the other entering obliquely but indispensibly. *Ruling Passion* (1973) takes Pascoe and Ellie Soper, both initially put off by Dalziel's relentless vulgarity, on a reunion holiday to Oxfordshire, where they walk into a triple shotgun homicide with an old friend of Pascoe's as prime suspect. Investigating outside his own bailiwick, Pascoe's depressed, his "bright ideas seem[ing] to be leading nowhere," but back at headquarters, Dalziel decides, "Pascoe's a good lad. He has his daft moments, but who doesn't? Most of what he said was worth thinking about" (*Ruling Passion* 233–34). Over Ellie's succulent roast pheasant after the case is solved, old detective pragmatism allays young uncertainties. Pascoe muses: "it's relatively so easy to be objective and impersonal in our business. . . . X kills Y. Find him. Charge him. Forget him.... [but] Y is unique ... for someone." Dalziel urges, "Forget names. Stick to X and Y. Life's a series of wrecks. Make sure you're always washed up with the survivors" (*Ruling Passion* 319).

Glaring realism lights up all of life's wrecks that Pascoe and Dalziel encounter, like the bizarre variation on the classic country house murder Dalziel falls into while Pascoe and Ellie are honeymooning in *An April Shroud* (1975). Pascoe's dentist fills him in on a local sadomasochistic men's film club in *A Pinch of Snuff* (1978). Dalziel, at least half drunk, stumbles into a murder in the house behind his in *Bones and Silence* (1990).

Later, the focus of the series spirals outward to include new elements and vistas including the imperturbable and gay (though not uncloseted until later) Sergeant Edgar Wield, who offers "cold analysis" while Pascoe goes off emotionally "half-cocked" in 1990's *Bones and Silence* (429). *Recalled to Life* (1992) takes Dalziel to New York to probe the thirty-year-old Mickledore Hall Murder, where some of his bullheaded certainties start to erode. So does the accustomed view of this "fat, balding, boozy, middle-aged bobby" when Fat Andy, back in England, finds luscious Linda Steele on his bed, "his y-fronts taking the strain" (351). In 1996's *The Wood Beyond*, Dalziel meets his carnal match in Amanda "Cap" Marvel, the spectacularly bosomed leader of an animal rights raiding party, while Pascoe exonerates his great-grandfather, wrongly executed for cowardice in a Flanders field.

Painful personal issues, especially parental agonies, dominate the most recent Pascoe-Dalziel cases. In *On Beulah Height* (1998), a subtle shift also begins between the two men. With Pascoe's daughter Rosie dangerously ill and the unsolved disappearance of three little girls in Dalziel's young detective days haunting Fat Andy, Dalziel feels responsible for all of them. "The pain of their parents weighed so heavily that even those broad shoulders were close to bending," and he gives "Wieldy" "the nearest to a plea for help" he's ever likely to utter (*Beulah* 337, 421). In *Arms and the Women* (2000) where Ellie and Rosie are kidnapped, Dalziel lapses into unaccustomed introspection, "rare if not unique" without at least a two-gallon skinful of bitter beer.

The pains of fatherhood change Pascoe, too. So distracted by fears for Ellie and Rosie that he's relegated his job to his lowest priorities (*Beulah* 412), Pascoe falls back on old-fashioned police procedure: "his phraseology was straight out of a TV cop show" (*Beulah* 426). Under the pressure of Ellie's kidnapping in *Arms and the Women*, Pascoe even slips into Dalziel's terse four-letter vernacular and Fat Andy's strong-arm style (*Arms* 409). In the intricate duology *Dialogues of the Dead* (2001) and *Death's Jest-Book* (2002), Pascoe, still kind and professional with callow young Detective Constable "Hat" Bowler, seethes with rage at Franny Roote, the released felon Pascoe had helped convict and who is now gleefully stalking Pascoe. The sight of Franny hurls Pascoe "deep into loom and snarl" (*Dialogues* 15), an obsession with putting Roote away again for good: "by God! He'd let the bastard know what he thought of him!" (*Jest-Book* 521)—and then Roote's shot saving Rosie when Pascoe, woozy with Kung Flu, can't, inundating Pascoe in a flood of tragic irony. Dalziel extends his pretended country-bumpkin persona into 2004's *Good Morning, Midnight*, an intricate case involving the supposed suicide of antique dealer Palinurus Maciver, while Pascoe draws on his sensitivity and his intimate knowledge of literature to stimulate fresh ideas from each of them.

After decades as a team, boorish Andy Dalziel and bookish Peter Pascoe have washed up as survivors of plenty of life's wrecks, and like an old married couple, they're taking on one another's traits. Dalziel's tough common sense rubs off on gentlemanly Pascoe, Pascoe's compassion on grungy Andy Dalziel: like love and marriage, in this good police work you can't have one without the other.

Novels: *A Clubbable Woman* (1970); *An Advancement of Learning* (1971); *A Ruling Passion* (1973); *An April Shroud* (1975); *A Pinch of Snuff* (1978); *A Killing Kindness* (1980); *Deadheads* (1983); *Exit Lines* (1984); *Child's Play* (1987); *Under World* (1988); *Bones and Silence* (1990); *One Small Step* (1990); *Recalled to Life* (1992); *Pictures of Perfection* (1994); *The Wood Beyond* (1996); *On Beulah Height* (1998); *Arms and the Women* (2000); *Dialogues of the Dead* (2001); *Death's Jest-Book* (2002); *Good Morning, Midnight* (2004).

Stand-alone novel: *The Stranger House* (2005).

Short stories: *Pascoe's Ghost* (1979); *There Are No Ghosts in the Soviet Union* (1987); *Brother's Keeper* (1992); *Asking for the Moon* (four novellas; 1994).

Other series: The Joe Sixsmith series, featuring Sixsmith as a balding West Indian private investigator.

Other works: Hill has authored numerous stand-alone novels in several genres, including the spy story *Traitor's Blood* (1986), the thriller *Who Guards the Prince?* (1982), and the suspense novel *Fell of Dark* (1971). Hill has also written science fiction novels as "Dick Morland"; adventure novels as "Patrick Ruell"; and historical novels as "Charles Underhill." Under his own name, he produced the nonfiction study *Crime Writers: Reflections on Crime Fiction* (1978).

Selected sources: Callendar, Newgate. Rev. of *A Killing Kindness. New York Times Book Review*, January 18, 1981; Leber, Michele. "Fear and Trembling: Chiller Thrillers." *Library Journal*, October 1, 2004: 122; *Publishers Weekly*. Rev. of *Arms and the Women*, August 30, 1999; *Publishers Weekly*. Rev. of *Death's Jest-Book*, September 1, 2003; Stasio, Marilyn. "Blood, Thunder, and Grace." *New York Times Book Review*, October 24, 2004: 27; *Times Literary Supplement*. Rev. of *Bones and Silence*, August 17, 1990; Waugh, Harriet. "Closely Related Deaths." *Spectator*, February 21, 2004: 32.

Major awards: Gold Dagger Award, Crime Writers' Association, 1990; Diamond Dagger Award, 1995.

See also: Yorkshire police procedurals: Pauline Bell's Detective Constable Benedict "Benny" Mitchell series; Peter Robinson's **Detective Chief Inspector Alan Banks** series; Peter Turnbull's Detective Inspector Hennessey series.

Amelia Peabody

Profession:	Egyptologist and archaeologist
Living situation:	Married
Geographic locale:	Egypt; England

Time period:	1884–1920s
Associate:	Radcliffe Emerson
Nemesis:	Sethos, the Master Criminal
Significant relationships:	Husband Radcliffe Emerson; Ramses, their son; Abdullah, their long-time *reis* (overseer)
Concerns:	Archaeology; Egyptology; women's rights

Archaeologist and Egyptologist Dr. Barbara Mertz, author of two scholarly books on ancient Egypt, uses "Elizabeth Peters" as her pseudonym for the popular Amelia Peabody series, "a rather giddy, frivolous sendup of various forms of genre fiction: the detective story, the gothic novel, just about everything you could think of," and she's given her readers "a very jolly time of it" (Brainerd 39), rekindling the traditional "cozy" mystery form much as Charlotte McLeod did. Peters's characters have changed, however, and so have the themes and historical issues of the series. As Victorian certainties about the White Man's Burden shattered in the Great War and its awful aftermath, so the focus of this series shifts from "Peabody" and her adored Emerson, called "the Father of Curses" by his native diggers, to their formerly holy-terror son Ramses and his physician wife Nephret, a champion of women's rights.

Lavishly outspoken, Amelia Peabody never meant to marry. She originally believed that "a woman born in the last half of the nineteenth century of the Christian era suffered from enough disadvantages without willfully embracing another" (*The Mummy Case* 3), but she met her match, handsome, bull-headed unsponsored archaeologist Radcliffe Emerson, in *Crocodile on the Sandbank* (1975), as Amelia, a late-thirties spinster with a recently inherited fortune was setting off on a Grand Tour. Reader, she not only married him, but the adventures sparked by their tumultuous union ignited "loving pastiches of the traditional mystery" including the works of Agatha Christie, Arthur Conan Doyle, and even H. Rider Haggard (Ashley 389).

Intelligence was not admired or encouraged in proper Victorian ladies, nor was independent wealth in an era when women were supposed to meekly endure the fiscal domination of their fathers, brothers, and/or husbands. "Peabody's" (that being Emerson's affectionate usage) sparkling wit, her devastating tool belt and offensive-weapon parasol, and her formidable list-making brainpower (even when she was wrong) sustain her, Emerson, their extended family and acquaintances, and their devoted native workers through walking mummies, camels dying on treks to secret desert oases, obnoxious American tourists, the wiles of Sethos the Master Criminal, and a mysterious female known only as Bertha amid Peabody's favorite archaeological sites, bat dung–encrusted collapsing pyramids—all "historically accurate and hilariously funny" (*Silk Stalkings* 2: 36) as seen through Amelia's eyes in the earlier novels.

Peters's more recent "Eternal Quartet" (*Seeing a Large Cat*, 1997; *The Ape Who Guards the Balance*, 1998; *The Falcon at the Portal*, 1999; *He Shall Thunder in the Sky*, 2000) tidies up many plot threads and broadens and darkens the series's perspective. As Amelia's son Ramses, once described to Peters's delight as "the most awful child in mystery fiction" approaches sixteen, Peters lets Amelia share her story-telling point of view with him, because it's "fun to show what he thought of her and what he was doing on the side" (*Publishers Weekly* 43). Peters uses "the contemporary diary of Mrs. Emerson as the primary narrative," with material from "Manuscript H" (later identified as by Ramses) and "Letter Collection B" of the Emerson Papers "at appropriate points" (*He Shall* xi). Hitherto veiled facets of Amelia's character thus surface, like a certain foolhardiness that often leads to delicious near-disaster. Ramses observes, "He [the killer] may take a notion to attack one of us next, especially if Mother goes on in her customary fashion." Nephret replies, "She does have a habit of getting in the way of murderers, bless her" (*Seeing a Large Cat* 195).

Ramses often chooses not to disturb his mother—if anything could—with his own pursuits as an Egyptian-speaking, -looking, and -thinking "Brother of Demons" ready-made to become a foreign agent during a historically-based 1915 attack on the Suez Canal, a little-known sidelight to the Great War, in which the Emersons' nephew Johnnie was killed at the somber close of *He Shall Thunder in the Sky*. Perhaps to spare Amelia the grim combination of menopause and the harrowing postwar years, Peters is returning to the 1907–1914 period preceding Ramses' marriage to Nephret (*Guardian of the Horizon* xi).

In her fifties still fancying scarlet gowns and whisky-and-soda inner stiffeners, Amelia maintains her dedication to "the three things that...give meaning and purpose to my life: crime, Egyptology, and Radcliffe Emerson!" (*The Hippopotamus Pool* xi). She dons trousers, tool belt, and boots to save her son and husband (*He Shall Thunder* 457), and in clairvoyant dreams their beloved *reis* (overseer) Abdullah, who gave his life to save her, directs her to solutions of thefts, assaults, and murders. In *The Serpent on the Crown* (2005), Amelia in 1922 is looking forward to a peaceful dig in the Valley of the Kings, but first she has to defuse threats to her entire family and solve yet more gruesome murders.

One of Amelia's most charming attributes is her forthright passion, indeed lust (though couched in the requisite Victorian verbal camouflage) for her dishy cleft-chinned husband. Master Criminal Sethos, earlier unmasked as a trusted secret agent of the British War Office and Emerson's illegitimate brother, confesses that as Emerson's "dark counterpart" he had sought Amelia's affections, but her passion for Emerson has never wavered since the long-ago night when she shamelessly made him "the happiest of men.... I would not have had the courage to come to you," said Emerson. But Amelia was no shrinking Victorian violet, and now as grandparents, Emerson is still asking her, "Er, hmph. Did you lock the door?" (*He Shall Thunder* 484).

Novels: *Crocodile on the Sandbank* (1975); *The Curse of the Pharaohs* (1981); *The Mummy Case* (1985); *Lion in the Valley* (1986); *The Deeds of the Disturber* (1988); *The Last Camel Died at Noon* (1991); *The Snake, the Crocodile and the Dog* (1993); *The Hippopotamus Pool* (1996); *Seeing a Large Cat* (1997); *The Ape Who Guards the Balance* (1998); *The Falcon at the Portal* (1999); *He Shall Thunder in the Sky* (2000); *Lord of the Silent* (2001); *The Golden One* (2002); *Guardian of the Horizon* (2004); *The Serpent on the Crown* (2005); *The Tomb of the Golden Bird* (2006).

Collection: *Amelia Peabody's Egypt: A Compendium*, edited by Elizabeth Peters and Kristen Whitbread (2003): maps, old engravings and illustrations, and serious historical and archaeological information.

Other series: Jacqueline Kirby series, contemporary cozy featuring Kirby as a romance novelist; Vicky Bliss series, featuring Bliss as a historian-antiquarian seeking art treasures; Cheryl Cardoza series (as Barbara Michaels), with gothic suspense and supernatural ingredients.

Other works: Peters has also written romantic suspense novels as "Barbara Michaels" as well as numerous stand-alone novels. She edited *Elizabeth Peters Presents Malice Domestic: An Anthology of Original Traditional Mystery Stories* (1992). In addition, she has produced nonfiction studies of ancient Egypt, notably *Red Land, Black Land* (1966).

Selected sources: Brainerd, Dulcie. "Barbara Michaels—Elizabeth Peters." *Publishers Weekly*, October 23, 1987: 39; *CBS News Nightwatch*. "Interview with Barbara Mertz," 1991; Lewis, Alison. Rev. of *Amelia Peabody's Egypt. Library Journal*, February 15, 2004: 125; Marchino, Lois A. Rev. of *He Shall Thunder in the Sky. Magill Book Reviews*, May 1, 2001; *Publishers Weekly*. Rev. of *He Shall Thunder in the Sky*. May 1, 2000: 43; Rose, Mark. "Queen of the Novel." *Archaeology*, March–April 2005: 46; Sacket, Wendy. Rev. of *The Snake, the Crocodile, and the Dog. Magill Book Reviews*, February 1, 1993.

Major awards: Grand Master Award, Bouchercon, 1986; Agatha Award, 1989; Grand Master, Mystery Writers of America, 1998; Malice Domestic Lifetime Achievement Award, 2003.

Web sites: Barbara Mertz home page: www.mpmbooks.com; www.ameliapeabody.com.

See also: Michael Pearce's **Mamur Zapt** series featuring Captain Gareth Owen and set in pre–World War I Cairo; Lynda Robinson's series featuring **Lord Meren** of ancient Egypt; P.C. Doherty's series featuring Judge Amerotke of circa 1479 B.C. Egypt; Margot Arnold's series featuring archaeologist Sir Toby Glendower; Jessica Mann's two novels featuring archaeology professor Thea Crawford: *Troublecross* (1973); *Captive Audience* (1975).

Jimmy Pibble

Profession:	Detective Superintendent, New Scotland Yard
Living situation:	Married, then widowed
Geographic locale:	England
Time period:	1968–79
Associate:	Sergeant Mike Crewe
Nemesis:	The Adversary
Concerns:	Integrity; aging

Prolific award-winning author Peter Dickinson thinks of his crime writing "as science fiction with the science left out," produced by creating "whatever he needed as facts for his story and [doing] the research afterwards" (Keating 141). Dickinson's Supt. James "Jimmy" Willoughby Pibble series turns the conventional English mystery "inside out, making it as surreal and fantastic as possible and then, through the skill of his writing, takes us back through the mirror to make it all believable" (Ashley 139). Dickinson won two hitherto unprecedented consecutive Gold Daggers in the process. According to the *New York Times*' Newgate Callendar, "any book in which James Pibble appears is *ipso facto*, going to be a good book" (May 14, 1972).

In *The Glass-Sided Ants' Nest* (1968), Jimmy Pibble is "aging, unglamorous, graying toward retirement" (*Nest* 1), the self-deprecating result of Dickinson's aim to create "a detective who was not at all James Bondish, was unsexy, easily browbeaten, intelligent, fallible" (quoted in *Contemporary Authors* 88, 94), with "a reputation for having a knack with kooky cases" (*Nest* 1). The subplot in each novel is Pibble's struggle against his destined Adversary, "the creature of his waking nightmare," embodied in a handsome, dashing, amoral cad, "a lounging, contemptuous male" who "makes his [Pibble's] innards cringe" and "shrivel[s] his soul" (*Nest* 32, 1)— everything that honest Jimmy Pibble's own dark side would like to be and everything his integrity will not allow to surface.

Sent back to a beat he'd covered fifteen years earlier, Pibble finds a tiny primitive New Guinea tribe, the Kus, living in the "inherent dreadfulness" (*Nest* 2) of Flagg Terrace's attics, brought there by British anthropologist Dr. Eve Ku, their adopted member and benefactor who's preserving them as her own private research "ants' nest." When their chief's head is fatally bashed in, Pibble's prime suspect is former Group Captain (really former Flight Sergeant) Bob Caine, a cocksure avatar of the Adversary. During World War II, the Japanese had slaughtered nearly the whole Ku tribe and Eve's missionary parents for sheltering Caine, and now Eve's Christian charity houses Caine and his mousy-haired wife Sukey gratis in the Flagg Terrace basement. Pibble, adrenaline spicing his blood, thirsts to nail Caine, though Pibble recognizes this obsession as "irresponsible, inefficient, and immoral" (*Nest* 98), potentially disrupting the entire investigation.

Pibble also readily acknowledges he is "more herbivore than carnivore" (*Nest* 138). He can don a sympathetic nonthreatening facade that usually gets witnesses and suspects to say more than they intend, but he knows this is "playing dirty"—not so far removed, really, from the Adversary's Mephistophelian disguise as Faust's black poodle—or here, Caine's talent for "mak[ing] you feel happy and clever simply because he's bothering to pay attention to you" (*Nest* 74). As Pibble grazes away at tiny clues, trying to connect them into a coherent whole, willing new insights to emerge, he rightly suspects that his efforts will often end in misery. In the shocking climax of *The Glass-Sided Ants' Nest*, his failure to grasp one vital fact's significance brings down senseless tragedy, as happens to Somerset Maugham's and Graham Greene's suffering protagonists. Eventually Pibble, knowing he won't ever make a "topflight officer," is fired from the police, proving his supercilious wife's contention that he's too unassertive to gain credit for his genius. Pibble then takes up private investigations, with cases just as strange as his police work.

Despite his engaging and often self-effacing sense of comic incongruity, the same tormenting sense of responsibility for causing suffering that overcame Lord Peter Wimsey in *Busman's Honeymoon* haunts Jimmy Pibble: "the cheerful surface of his job had rotted away, leaving only the wicked skeleton" (*Nest* 170). *The Old English Peep Show* (1969) sends Pibble to a country-estate-turned-theme-park with a scaffold that really works and a pair of free-ranging lions who do in the butler. In *The Sinful Stones* (1970), a bizarre religious cult in the remote Hebrides is holding a ninety-year-old Nobel Prize–winning scientist captive. Pibble escapes with the scientist, "only lucid at four-hour intervals"; a drunken nurse; and a teenaged schizophrenic (Bargannier

65). In *Sleep and His Brother* (1971) children afflicted by a disease that turns them into "sleepily charming psychic detectives" (Keating 141) assist Pibble, and in the "everything-but-the-kitchen-sink plot" of *The Lizard in the Cup* (1972), Pibble, on another island as bodyguard to a Greek millionaire, copes with monasticism, the Mafia, theft, drugs, and political subversion (Murphy 393).

The last and blackest of Pibble's cases, *One Foot in the Grave* (1979), is set in "Flycatchers," a luxurious nursing home, where Pibble at sixty-four is slowly recovering from the ravages of old age, starvation-level poverty, and high blood pressure. While pitifully attempting suicide by hypothermia to escape the final outrage of senility, Pibble encounters a corpse, and his former Sergeant, now Chief Superintendent Mike Crewe, helps revive enough of Pibble's self-confidence and mental acuity to solve his last murder case.

The scintillating comic sparkle animating Pibble's novels, no doubt accentuated by Dickinson's seventeen years as editor of *Punch*, shines all the brighter for the Adversary's shadow. For "copper's copper" Jimmy Pibble, ultimate wickedness always lies in the corruption, especially in bent police officers, that poisons "the wells of justice" (*One Foot* 37)—and still, Jimmy Pibble never lets himself or his readers forget "the whole trouble with police work": "You come plunging in, a jagged Stone Age knife, to probe the delicate tissues of people's relationships, and of course you destroy far more than you discover…the nubbly scars of your passage will remain" (*Nest* 130).

Novels: *The Glass-Sided Ants' Nest* (1968; in UK *Skin Deep*); *The Old English Peep Show* (1969; in UK *A Pride of Heroes*); *The Sinful Stones* (1970; in UK *The Seals*); *Sleep and His Brother* (1971); *The Lizard in the Cup* (1972); *One Foot in the Grave* (1979).

Other series: Princess Louise series: *King and Joker* (1975); *Skeleton-in-Waiting* (1989).

Other works: Dickinson has written numerous stand-alone novels, notably *The Poison Oracle* (1974), *The Last Houseparty* (1982), *The Yellow Room Conspiracy* (1994), and *Some Deaths Before Dying* (1999). He has also authored many children's books, among them winners of the *Boston Globe* Horn Book Award, 1977, and the Whitbread Children's Award, 1979 and 1990.

Selected sources: Bargannier, Earl. Rev. of *One Foot in the Grave. Armchair Detective*, Summer 1980: 65; Callendar, Newgate. Rev. of *The Lizard in the Cup. New York Times Books Review*, January 29, 1978; *Chicago Tribune Book World*. Rev. of *The Sinful Stones*, July 19, 1970; Stasio, Marilyn. Rev. of *Some Deaths Before Dying. New York Times Book Review*, June 27, 1999: 26; Townsend, John Rowe. *A Sounding of Story-Tellers*. New York: Viking, 1979.

Major awards (see above for awards for children's books): Gold Daggers, 1968, 1969; *Guardian* Award, 1977, American Library Association Carnegie Medal, 1980, 1981.

See also: James Anderson's comic British murder mysteries that are parodies of class, *The Affair of the Blood-Stained Egg Cosy* (1975) and *The Affair of the Mutilated Mink Coat* (1982), featuring Inspector Wilkins; Dorothy Cannell's cozy British series featuring overweight and depressed interior decorator Ellie Simon; Australian Mark McShane's various eccentric and/or surreal series respectively featuring former Detective Sergeant Norman Pink and "Apple" Porter, who, like Dorothy Gilman's **Mrs. Pollifax**, makes an unlikely spy, but functions admirably as one.

Joe Pickett

Profession:	Game warden
Living situation:	Married
Geographic locale:	Wyoming
Time period:	2001–present
Nemeses:	Big government; big business; Sheriff Bud Barnum
Significant relationship:	Marybeth Pickett
Concerns:	Environmental issues; integrity; corruption in government agencies

Away out there C.J. Box has a name for justice: it's Saddlestring, Wyoming's Game Warden Joe Pickett, a High Noon hero who stands up all alone for his family, for friends and animals and the wilderness—everything that's at risk from human greed and corruption. One of only fifty-five Wyoming game wardens, Joe's almost always on his own. For $32,000 a year, minimal housing, and an SUV, he works 173 to 259 hours a month come sleety rain, howling blizzards where if he gets stuck he dies, or Wyoming's high country sunshine, directed to spend a third of his time on public contact, another third on harvest game collection, and the rest on law enforcement (*Winterkill* 41). Pickett gets shot at, knocked over the head, threatened with suspension, and frequently visited by his loopy mother-in-law. His supervisor is 250 miles away, Twelve Sleep County Sheriff Bud Barnum is on the take, and Joe's constantly compared unfavorably with legendary Warden Vern Dunnigan and hassled by bureaucrats from the U.S. Fish and Wildlife Service, the U.S. Forest Service, the Bureau of Alcohol, Tobacco, and Firearms, and the FBI. It's the job description from hell, and Joe's not about to give it up. It's his life.

Family comes first for Joe Pickett, and he's got a fine one. In *Open Season* (2001), he protects his pregnant wife Marybeth and their daughters, Sheridan, seven, and her younger sister Lucy—not just from crooked officials but from a hefty temptation, a big fat job offer from InterWest Resources, a pipeline company heading for a remote valley that shelters Miller's weasels, long thought extinct. If their existence gets out, the Engangered Species Act will force InterWest to scrub the enormously expensive project. When Joe, investigating a local murder, gets too close to discovering the weasels for InterWest's comfort, first Vern Dunnigan, who's slithered his way into InterWest's pay, tries to bribe Joe, and then Joe's crooked fellow warden Wacey Hedeman menaces Marybeth and Sheridan, who's secretly made pets of three of the little animals. That's enough for Joe, whose own unhappy childhood made him choose this job. He can't hit stationary targets with his official-issue pistol, but he's a crack wing shot with his personal Remington Wingmaster shotgun, and when Wacey draws on him, Joe shoots the legs from under the man who caused Marybeth to lose her baby and tried to kill his daughter.

"Joe had always considered individual words as finite units of currency, and he believed in savings.... [W]ords meant things. They should be spent wisely" (*Open*

Season 162). Joe almost always lets his actions speak for him, and even though some of them aren't entirely wise—early on, he'd arrested the governor of Wyoming for fishing without a license (*Open Season* 5)—he invariably chooses the right way, not the easy way, taking a long time to think out what he wants to say. Marybeth frets "that perhaps people would think Joe was slow," but Joe backs his words up with conviction, unlike other people who wastefully spew out words "like unaimed machine-gun bullets" (*Open Season* 162).

The convictions Joe won't abandon lead him into dicey situations, like the seriocomic twenty-first-century range war between environmentalists and industry in *Savage Run* (2002), the clash between a militant mountain-man group and government agents run amok in *Winterkill* (2003), and head-to-mutilated-head confrontations between paranormal experts and rapacious natural gas explorers in *Trophy Hunt* (2004). Joe's "a really good guy" (*Winterkill* 200) with flaws that keep him humble and convincing: in *Open Season* a suspect actually takes Joe's gun away, and in *Winterkill* he exposes himself to deadly fire trying to save their adopted daughter. Joe's a fair judge of people, too, but he often errs on the side of compassion, recognizing "a tendency in himself to assume morality and rationality in others because he aspired to those qualities himself." He knows if he committed a murder, he couldn't hide it: "Hell, he'd confess to Marybeth so fast he'd leave skid marks" (*Winterkill* 84), so he believes he can tell guilt from innocence. The one thing he can't stand is cruelty, so "Murderers and molesters of children [are] beyond Joe's comprehension" (*Winterkill* 84)—and therefore he's going to put them out of business. After his fellow game warden Will Jensen allegedly commits suicide, Pickett gets transferred from Saddlestring in *Out of Range* (2005) to the posh touristy Teton district around Jackson Hole, full of "animal-rights activists, wolf lovers, big-shot developers, politicians, movie stars, all kinds of riffraff" where he reinforces his growing reputation as a bullheadedly stubborn lawman.

Joe consistently follows his instincts when they tell him there's more to a crime or an apparent suicide than what's obvious, accounting for his bulldog tenacity in tracking suspects when practicality and even survival in deadly whiteouts counsel prudence. When his family or the animals he protects are threatened, too, Joe's capable of a consuming righteous rage, and he firmly maintains his own firm moral standards. When Joe Pickett teaches his daughter Sheridan, "It's all about accountability... there need to be consequences for thoughtless or cruel behavior" (*Winterkill* 304), Joe's restating the old code of the American West that he lives by, when strong silent good guys wreaked justice at the O.K. Corral, and one lone man could make a big difference. "There aren't many like you left," Marybeth tells Joe. "You have a good heart and your moral compass is a model of its kind. You need to do what you need to do" (*Open Season* 193).

Novels: *Open Season* (2001); *Savage Run* (2002); *Winterkill* (2003); *Trophy Hunt* (2004); *Out of Range* (2005).

Nonfiction: *Montana, Wyoming, and Idaho Travel-Smart* (Santa Fe, NM: John Muir, 1998).

Selected sources: Karam, Edward. Rev. of *Savage Run*. *People*, July 1, 2002: 41; Ott, Bill. Rev. of *Open Season*. *Booklist*, May 1, 2001; 1622; Stankowski, Rebecca House. Rev. of

Winterkill. Library Journal, April 15, 2003: 130; Stasio, Marilyn. Rev. of *Out of Range. New York Times Book Review*, May 8, 2005: 37; Tierney, Bruce. "Mystery Is at Home on the Range with Wyoming Writer C.J. Box." *BookPage.com*, www.bookpage.com (August 28, 2002).

Major awards: *New York Times* Notable Book Award, 2001; Edgar Award for Best First Novel, 2002; Gumshoe First-Novel Mystery Award, 2002.

Web site: www.cjbox.net.

See also: Nevada Barr's National Park series, featuring National Park Ranger **Anna Pigeon**, accompanied by a cat named Piedmont and a dog called Taco; Sandy Dengler's series featuring National Park Ranger Jack Prester. For amateur detectives roaming the American West's wide open spaces, see Peter Bowen's series featuring Montana cattle inspector Gabriel du Pré; Susan Slater's Bill Pecos series, set in New Mexico; Clayton McKinzie's series featuring Wyoming special investigator Antonio Bourns. For Western lawmen, see Susan Cooper's Sheriff Milt Kovak series set in Oklahoma; Bill Crider's Sheriff Dan Rhodes series set in Texas; Jamie Harrison's Sheriff Jules Clement series set in Blue Deep, Montana; Jon Talton's series featuring Phoenix Deputy Sheriff David Mapstone; J.A. Jance's series featuring former Arizona sheriff Brandon Walker. Patricia Hickman's Depression-era historical series features Jeb Nubey, a former outlaw studying to be a preacher.

Debut novels: Liz Adair's *The Lodger*, featuring Deputy Sheriff Spider Latham, a Mormon procedural mystery; Craig Johnson's *The Cold Dish*, featuring Sheriff Walt Longmire and set in Bighorn Country, Wyoming; Jim Tenuto's *Blood Atonement*, featuring fly fishing guide Dahlgren Wallace, set in Montana.

Anna Pigeon

Profession:	National Park Ranger
Living situation:	Widowed; later remarried
Geographic locale:	Various U.S. National Parks
Time period:	1993–present
Associate:	Pigeon's sister Molly, a psychiatrist
Significant relationship:	Sheriff Paul Davidson
Concerns:	Environmentalism; feminism; alcoholism; human connections

Nevada Barr claims that she began her Anna Pigeon series by putting a character like herself into a murder mystery (quoted in *CA Online*). Barr's own experience as a National Park Service ranger lends authenticity to the various cases that face Anna Pigeon, a law enforcement ranger whose work includes upholding law and order, protecting Park visitors as well as the Parks themselves and their animal inhabitants, and assisting with search and rescue operations. That's a tall order for a physically small, big-hearted woman who tragically lost the husband she loved and battles a desire for oblivion in drink. With all her offense and defense capabilities, Anna Pigeon is a dedicated loner in her first few novels, preferring fur and paws and the wide-open spaces to human contacts and stifling urban environments. Later, as Barr makes Anna begin to acknowledge the increasing physical and emotional vulnerability of aging, Anna struggles to regain the ability to reach out to others, even as she shocks herself with how violently she will defend the National Parks she loves—landscapes so effectively drawn that each becomes a vivid living character by itself.

Track of the Cat (1993), the first Anna Pigeon mystery, takes place in Texas's Guadalupe Mountains National Park, highlighting a strong "ecofeminist" theme (Wesson 22). Anna refuses to believe a mountain lion has killed a ranger, so she investigates the death while long-distance counseling with her psychiatrist sister Molly back in New York City. Although Charles Champlin, reviewing for the *Los Angeles Times Book Review* (May 23, 1993: 8), accurately observed that the physical isolation somewhat unnaturally forces Anna to make her horse her Dr. Watson–like sounding board as she unravels the secrets buried among the park's workers, the combination of outdoor grandeur and inner clashes, particularly Anna's battles against her concurrent physical and emotional claustrophobias, set the dynamic pattern for the rest of the series. Anna investigates a serious crime threatening a National Park, experiences and overcomes harsh injuries, solves the crime, occasionally loses a lover (in this case FBI agent Frederick Stanton, who later marries Molly), and almost always gains a friend (*Silk Stalkings* 2: 261).

A Superior Death (1994), located in Isle Royale National Park, surrounded by the frigid waters of the largest Great Lake, again has Anna diving for clues among Park employees and visitors and "eerie underwater landscapes of sunken ships and floating corpses" (Stasio 19). Anna works again with Stanton in *Ill Wind* (1995), counterpointing her search for the killer of a detested ranger in Mesa Verde National Park with probes of questionable local construction practices and the ancient mystery of the vanished Anasazi. In the powerful *Firestorm* (1996), a classic locked-room type of mystery, Anna must unmask a killer in the midst of a group of Northern California firefighters encircled by raging flames. *Endangered Species* (1997) takes her to Cumberland Island National Seashore, Georgia; *Blind Descent* (1998) makes her descend into the spooky depths of New Mexico's Carlsbad Caverns; and *Liberty Falling* (1999) returns Anna to New York to help Molly through a critical illness while probing mysterious accidents in Gateways Park, which includes Liberty and Ellis Islands. In *Deep South* (2000), Anna discovers more than a killer's identity in Mississippi's Natchez Trace Park, this time acquiring new insights into Civil War history and a complicated new love interest, Sheriff Paul Davidson, who is also an Episcopal priest—and married.

After *Blood Lure* (2001), which reached the *New York Times* bestseller list and again featured a victim supposedly killed by a wild animal, this time in Watertown-Glacier International Peace Park on the Montana-Canadian border, and 2002's *Hunting Season*, Barr revisited the Civil War in *Flashback* (2003), spinning two parallel mysteries for Anna Pigeon to solve while she ruminates over Davidson's proposal, made immediately upon finalization of his divorce. A mysterious fatal boat explosion off Dry Tortugas National Park, a group of tiny U.S. islands not far from Cuba, puts her back under dangerous waters, while old family letters Molly forwarded sets Anna on the trail of the enigmatic Dr. Samuel Mudd, convicted for alleged involvement in the plot to assassinate Abraham Lincoln and held a prisoner at Garden Key's squalid Fort Jefferson prison, now the Dry Tortugas Park's headquarters.

In *High Country* Anna is nearing fifty, newly engaged to Davidson, and returning as an undercover waitress to Yosemite National Park where she had waited table many years earlier. Anna dons wait staff uniform, apron, and a maternal persona as she investigates drug-peddling among the Park's employees and intruding thugs. Hunted by a grisly sociopath on a miles-long wintry High Sierra trek with a cracked ankle and frostbite, Anna discovers shockingly just how far she'll go to defend the Park and herself, and in her next adventure, *Hard Truth* (2005), now married to Davidson, Anna leaves him in Mississippi for an assignment to Rocky Mountain National Park in Colorado to find a serial killer. There she joins forces with Heath Jarrod, a woman who reminds Anna of herself. Jarrod is a former mountain climber who after a near-fatal fall has been confined to a wheelchair. Together they manage to rescue young girls who have escaped from a cultic religious camp nearby.

With each novel, Anna discovers new needs she hadn't realized she had, not just her longing for the magnificent outdoor vistas that dispel her claustrophobia, or for her three-legged dog Taco, who wards off the midnight jeebies from Anna's bedside, or for the cantankerous love of her aged tomcat Piedmont. Maybe it's her own advancing age, Anna thinks, musing over her growing lack of patience with her own stupidity, the reason she rarely drinks any more and scarcely ever gets sun-burned. In *High Country*, teetering on the brink of a midlife crisis and tempted toward a comforting one-night stand with a hunky sous-chef, Anna Pigeon opts for her home, her husband, and the comfort of a lifetime commitment. Anna Pigeon's realized that self-recriminations are hell (*High Country* 169), so she doesn't intend to go there, ever.

Novels: *Track of the Cat* (1993); *A Superior Death* (1994); *Ill Wind* (1995); *Firestorm* (1996); *Endangered Species* (1997); *Blind Descent* (1998); *Liberty Falling* (1999); *Deep South* (2000); *Blood Lure* (2001); *Hunting Season* (2002); *Flashback* (2003); *High Country* (2004); *Hard Truth* (2005).

Other work: *Bittersweet* (1984).

Nonfiction: *Seeking Enlightenment—Hat by Hat: A Skeptic's Path to Religion* (2003). Nevada Barr has also edited *Nevada Barr Presents Malice Domestic 10: An Anthology of Original Traditional Mystery Stories* (2001).

Selected sources: Barcott, Bruce. Rev. of *High Country*. *Outside Magazine*, June 2004: 34; Christensen, Susan. "Author's House Is Her Own Wild Kingdom." *USA Today*, January 23, 2004; Klett, Rex E. Rev. of *Hard Truth*. *Library Journal*, February 1, 2005: 57; Reynolds, Jean. Rev. of *Blood Lure*. *People Weekly*, February 5, 2001: 39; Shindler, Dorman T. "Taking on History's Mysteries." *Publishers Weekly*, January 27, 2003: 230; Stasio, Marilyn. Rev. of *A Superior Death*. *New York Times Book Review*, April 17, 1994: 19; Stasio, Marilyn. "Sax and Violence." *New York Times Book Review*, March 27, 2005: 21; Wesson, Mimi. *Women's Review of Books*, January 1995: 22.

Major awards: Anthony Award and Agatha Award, 1994; *Prix du Roman*, French National Crime Fiction Awards, 1995; Barry Award, 2001.

Web sites: www.nevadabarr.com; http://members.tripod.com/~MindHarp/nbarr.html.

See also: Sandy Dengler's National Parks series featuring ranger Jack Prester; for wide-open-spaces settings: Susan Cooper's series featuring Oklahoma sheriff Milt Kovak; Bill Crider's series featuring Texas sheriff Dan Rhodes; Janice Harrison's series featuring Blue Deep, Montana sheriff Jules Clement; K.C. Greenlief's series featuring search and rescue volunteer Will Buchanan, set in New Hampshire's White Mountains; Clayton McKinzie's series featuring Wyoming special investigator Antonio Burns.

Thomas Pitt

Profession:	Inspector (later Superintendent), Bow Street Police
Living situation:	Married
Geographic locale:	London
Time period:	late Victorian Period (1890s)
Associates:	Charlotte Ellison Pitt; Constable James Murdo; Detective Victor Narraway
Significant relationship:	Charlotte Ellison Pitt
Concerns:	Social-religious causes and moral dilemmas from the perspective of Perry's Mormon beliefs

In a 2004 interview with Andrew Gulli for *Strand Magazine*, Anne Perry observed, "I'm a great admirer of [Victorian mystery author and moralist] G.K. Chesterton. I'm trying to…not exactly fill his shoes, but follow in his footsteps" (44). Perry thus incorporates her passionate belief in social justice and the "desire to do something about it" into the principal characters of her longest-running mystery series, Londoners Thomas and Charlotte Pitt, voices of social conscience in a society dominated by a generally hypocritical and repressive ruling class.

Perry never allows her readers to forget that the Pitts' unlikely (and to most Victorians inappropriate) marriage unites representatives of two very different British social classes. As a Bow Street metropolitan policeman Thomas Pitt ranks much lower on the Victorian social scale than blue-blooded Charlotte Ellison, with whom he falls in love and whom he eventually marries in the series, each book of which is titled after historic London locales. Their marriage allows them to examine both the middle class and the upper class aspects of murder cases and many inflammatory societal issues, because Pitt, as a working official, cannot set a professional or, heaven forfend, a social foot in the elegant townhouses that Charlotte's ancestry entitles her to visit (*Silk Stalkings* 2: 1). Neither can he, as a man, be privy to the women's gossip that often produces vital clues, so Charlotte's help is indispensable in unraveling these sticky mysteries.

A multitude of social issues, most of them updated but still rampant in the twenty-first century, confront Thomas Pitt. In his time the elegant complacent "haves" of England shunted their children to nurseries, governesses, and boarding schools, swathed the indecency of their piano legs in velvet skirts, and forbade gentlemen from referring to a chicken's leg or breast in mixed company (hence "white meat" or "dark meat") while the "have nots" endured widespread hunger, diseases, and crime;

prostitution flourished; women and children worked eighteen-hour shifts or more in mines, factories, and workhouses; and debtors languished in unspeakable prisons. London's rising crime rate—not just theft and homicide, but white slavery, child abuse, illicit economic exploitation—not only meant long hours and desperate situations for the Metropolitan Police; it also forced them to uphold a grossly unfair double standard, dealing harshly with the lower classes "while protecting the upper classes as much from distasteful knowledge and intrusion as crime itself" (*Silk Stalkings* 1: 34).

As a loving husband and father, Thomas Pitt naturally wants to shield his family, but he soon finds that Charlotte shares his sympathy for the unfortunate and possesses a mind perhaps even quicker than his, so he can discuss his cases with her and even call on her for specialized help in investigations like *Bethlehem Road*'s (1990) case of political assassination, where a suffragette whose child and property have been lost because of England's unfair divorce laws seems to be a prime suspect and Charlotte can far more easily gain another woman's confidence than any policeman could.

Highgate Rise (1991) poses the Pitts a case of arson and possible murder in a genteel London suburb, where a doctor is suspected of setting the fire in order to inherit his wife's fortune. Pitt describes himself here as "Inspector of police, and I hope, discoverer of truth, or at least a measurable portion of it—we will never know it all, but sometimes enough to assist what serves as justice. . . . I will not stop trying, whatever I have to do to overturn to find the truth" (*Highgate Rise* 85–86). Pitt needs all that bulldog tenacity when his pursuit of truth clashes head-on with the wagon-circling of the upper classes, but he has to rely on Charlotte's experience and insight into their habits and attitudes as well. Here, as in most of his other cases, Pitt finds himself conflicted, often moved "more by pity not to intrude on a very obvious distress than the sort of impersonal curiosity his profession dictated" (*Highgate Rise* 184).

Pentecost Alley (1996), the case of a prostitute ritually murdered, possibly by a hell-raising scion of a powerful family, draws Pitt, now a superintendent of police, into one of Perry's persevering concerns—the predicament of talented women restricted by upper-class conventions from exercising their gifts. Charlotte's redoubtable Aunt Vespasia, bored to tears by embroidery and possessed of a keen eye for vicissitude, assists Pitt here; she easily recognizes "a nouveau riche bully" when she sees one and warns Pitt to handle the wealthy father of a major suspect with kid gloves, as "a man of great power and no clemency at all" (*Pentecost Alley* 211).

One of Pitt's most recent cases, *Long Spoon Lane* (2005), is eerily contemporary: an anarchist bombing aims at empowering corrupt police officials and quashing civil liberties. Pitt, as in *The Seven Dials*, is now attached to the Special Branch, and accompanied by his colleague Victor Narraway rises to the challenge of exposing a secret society, the "Inner Circle," connected to the highest parliamentary circles.

In all of Thomas Pitt's cases, Perry builds her major interest, the conflict of ethics, into the tension between Pitt's integrity and his compassion, for from the beginning he has always felt "a stab of pity" when his passion for justice steels him to peel the layers of hypocrisy from a high-born aristocrat who thought "he was untouchable by the sordid realities Pitt represented" (*Bluegate Fields* 11). That combination of pity and rock-solid integrity makes Thomas Pitt "a bridge between classes and centuries as well" (*Silk Stalkings* 1: 35).

Novels: *The Cater Street Hangman* (1979); *Callander Square* (1980); *Paragon Walk* (1981); *Resurrection Row* (1981); *Rutland Place* (1983); *Bluegate Fields* (1984); *Death in the Devil's Acre* (1985); *Cardington Crescent* (1987); *Silence in Hanover Close* (1988); *Bethlehem Road* (1990); *Highgate Rise* (1991); *Belgrave Square* (1992); *Farrier's Lane* (1993); *The Hyde Park Headsman* (1994); *Traitor's Gate* (1995); *Pentecost Alley* (1996); *Ashworth Hall* (1997); *Brunswick Gardens* (1998); *Bedford Square* (1999); *Half Moon Street* (2000); *The Whitechapel Conspiracy* (2001); *Southhampton Row* (2002); *The Seven Dials* (2003); *Long Spoon Lane* (2005); *Cardington Crescent* (2005). *A Christmas Guest* (2005) features "Grandmama" Mariah Ellison from the Pitt series.

Other series: The **William Monk** series, also set mostly in Victorian London; the World War I series, *No Graves As Yet* (2003), *Shoulder the Sky* (2003), and *Angels in the Gloom* (2005). The spiritual fantasy series begun with *Talthea* (1999) and *Come Armageddon* (2003) is a vehicle for Perry's Mormon religious views.

Stand-alone novel: *The One Thing More* (2000), a historical murder mystery set during the French Revolution.

Short fiction: Perry's numerous short stories have not been collected as yet. Many of them feature characters familiar from her novels: "An Affair of Inconvenience" (1998) features Charlotte Pitt's Great-aunt Vespasia; solicitor Oliver Rathbone's father Henry, from the William Monk series and based on Perry's own father, appears in "The Blackmailer" (1996). The Edgar-award winning short story "Heroes" features a World War I army chaplain (Ashley 386), foreshadowing Joseph Reavley in *No Graves As Yet* (2003) and *Shoulder the Sky* (2004).

Other works: Perry has also edited *Malice Domestic 6* (1997), *Death by Horoscope* (with Martin Greenberg; 2001), and *Death by Dickens* (2004).

Nonfiction: Perry has contributed to a history of Mormonism in Britain.

Selected sources: Breen, Jon L. "Murdering History." *Weekly Standard*, January 3, 2005: 31–35; Connors, Theresa. Rev. of *Cardington Crescent*. *Library Journal*, April 1, 2005: 132; Connors, Theresa. "Silence in Hanover Close." *Library Journal*, July 1, 2005: 131; Gulli, Andrew. "Interview with Anne Perry." *Strand Magazine*, 2004: 42–49; Kovash, Ronald. "An Inspirational Fiction Workshop on DVD." *Writer*, June 2005: 49; Mitgang, Herbert. Rev. of *Belgrave Square*. *New York Times*, June 12, 1992: C21.

Major awards: American Mystery Award, 1993; Herodotus lifetime achievement award, 1999; Edgar Award, 2000.

Web site: www.anneperry.net.

See also: Perry's William Monk series; Alanna Knight's Inspector Jeremy Faro series, set in Victorian Edinburgh and Knight's companion series featuring Faro's daughter Rose McQuinn; Peter Lovesey's Sergeant Cribb series, set in 1880s London.

Stephanie Plum

Profession:	Bounty hunter
Living situation:	Divorced
Geographic locale:	Trenton, New Jersey
Time period:	1994–present

Associates:	Joe Morelli; "Ranger"; Connie; Lula
Significant relationships:	Joe Morelli; "Ranger"
Concerns:	Staying solvent; having wheels; getting her man

Outrageous! Spandex-clad! Belly-laugh funny! Bounty huntress Stephanie Plum prowls the wilds of Trenton, New Jersey, seeking fame and fortune enough to keep herself and her hamster Rex housed and fed and her Hungarian pot roast–pushing mother off her shapely back. Once Stephanie loses her job haggling over the cost of full-fashion nylon underpants as a discount lingerie buyer, she gets six months behind on her apartment rent, her cherished Miata's repossessed, and she's sunk to asking relative Vinnie ("A worm. A sexual lunatic." [*One* 12]), a bail bondsman, for a job. Then the fun begins.

Until, "as she says, she 'ran out of sexual positions'" (quoted in Ashley 158), Janet Evanovich wrote romance novels. Then, looking for big success, she thought, "Give the audience something nobody else is giving it." So she did, taking everything she did well in romances—"positive characters, sexual tension, humor—and squashed them into a mystery format. Sue Grafton and Sara Paretsky were doing hard-boiled women. I did a soft-boiled woman" (Plagens 56).

It worked. Evanovich's best-selling Stephanie Plum series rollicks through madcap chases à la Lucy Ricardo tossing salad in the travel trailer, sexy shower scenes with and without one of two hunky heroes, zany relatives like pistol-packin' Grandma Mazur (Evanovich's real Aunt Lena), at least one vehicle blown up per novel, and a heroine with "Bette Midler's mouth and Cher's fashion sense" (Stasio 1994, 17).

Some critics quibble at Plum's success. Writing for *Armchair Detective*, Marvin Lachman found the plot of her debut *One for the Money* (1994) "minimal," Plum's first-person narration "unsophisticated" and "irritating," and her prior relationship with Latin lover and vice cop Joe Morelli unconvincing (287). (He "charmed the pants off [Plum at sixteen] four minutes after closing, on the floor of Tasty Pastry" [*One* 4]). Others thought Plum's dialogue "contrived" but considered Plum herself "intelligent, cheery, and genuine" (Wilson 68). Most reviewers, however, concur with Charles Champlin of the *Los Angeles Book Review* that Stephanie's moral seems to be "when the going gets tough, the tough get funny" (8).

In *One for the Money*, Plum's supposed to haul in Joe Morelli, who's skipped on a $100,000 bond after being nabbed for shooting an unarmed man. Decked out in turquoise eyeliner and black and purple Gore Tex, munching her way through fast food and evading the clutches of homicidal-maniac-rapist boxing champ Ramirez, Stephanie must call on fellow bounty hunter Ranger, a spooky neo-Batman with Armor All biceps, setting up a sexually tense triangle that lasts throughout the series.

Aided and abetted by Vinnie's chatty secretary Connie and Lula, a street-smart hooker with detective aspirations, Stephanie gets Morelli vindicated, champ Ramirez neutralized, Rex a fresh supply of hamster nuggets, and herself the $10,000 finder's fee. In Grandma Mazur's 1953 powder-blue-and-white Buick, she pursues fugitive Kenny Mancuso and a batch of coffins missing from a local funeral parlor in *Two for the Dough* (1996), while Morelli, "whose libido has been stuck on overdrive" since his first taste of Tasty Pastry (*One* 325), hotly pursues Stephanie herself. Next Plum tracks "Uncle Mo," a fugitive candy-store owner, in *Three to Get Deadly* (1997), causing Ranger to lose his black Beemer. Morelli finally kisses her—"and she's all for it" (*One* 328), but then he disappears for months. When he resurfaces in *Four To Score* (1998), Stephanie's ready and willing, but she also has to nab a car-thieving bail-jumping waitress with the help of Grandma Mazur, who's hell-bent on wearing bike shorts and packing heat herself. Ranger supplied Stephanie a modest Smith and Wesson .38, but she prefers to rely on her seventeen-gram key-chain model Sure-Guard neurospray, guaranteed to drop a 300-pound man in six seconds.

High Five (1999), where both Ranger and Morelli declare heated intentions, landed Stephanie Plum on the hardcover best-seller lists. Back in the Buick to find missing Uncle Fred (Grandma Mazur rides stun gun), Stephanie has to do something about her quandary—her "hots for Ranger" and her itch for Morelli: "Two of the men on my list of desirables actually desire me back. The problem being that they both sort of scare the hell out of me" (*One* 331, 333).

That's Evanovich's problem, too: her readers lined up between either Joe or Ranger, and it became "increasingly difficult for [Evanovich] to keep both groups happy" (Plagens 56). *Hot Six* (2000) makes matters worse, with Ranger wanted for murdering a gunrunner's son, Morelli proposing marriage, and Grandma Mazur moving in with Stephanie for the foreseeable future. *Seven Up* (2001) gets Grandma a suitor of her own, Eddie DeChooch, Ranger gets a deal that involves Stephanie's bedroom, and Morelli's got teeth-grinding frustration. *Hard Eight* (2002) brings Stephanie a bag of reptiles on her doorknob and tarantulas in her Honda (later predictably blown to bits), and the necessity of making up her mind for good about Morelli. *To the Nines* (2003) takes her to Las Vegas with Connie and Lula and a serial killer after them, while Stephanie's mother houses Stephanie's pregnant-out-of-wedlock sister Valerie. *Ten Big Ones* (2004) has Stephanie moved in, then out, of Morelli's place, testing out Ranger's swanky earth-toned Batcave and its to-die-for shower gel, while in *Eleven on Top* threatening letters make Stephanie leave the bounty-hunting business to Lula while Plum herself takes over an office job for dangerously sexy Ranger.

Like Shakespeare's Cleopatra, Evanovich's thirty-year-old Stephanie Plum doesn't age, nor do her irrepressible youthful antics decay. "When you make gravy," Evanovich says, "you take a big pot of ingredients . . . and boil it down to a little pot of stuff which is the essence" (Plagens 56). For a lot of readers, that recipe's Plum perfect.

Novels: *One for the Money* (1994); *Two for the Dough* (1996); *Three to Get Deadly* (1997); *Four to Score* (1998); *High Five* (1999); *Hot Six* (2000); *Seven Up* (2001); *Hard Eight* (2002); *To the Nines* (2003); *Ten Big Ones* (2004); *Eleven on Top* (2005).

Other series: Evanovich has begun a new comic series with *Metro Girl* (2005), featuring Alexandra "Barney" Barnaby, a former stock car racer chasing down her missing brother.

Other novels: Evanovich has written numerous romance novels, both alone and with Charlotte Hughes.

Selected sources: Champlin, Charles. Rev. of *One for the Money*. *Los Angeles Book Review*, November 20, 1994: 8; DeCandido, GraceAnne. "Story behind the Story: Stephanie Plum as Indiana Jones." *Booklist*, May 1, 2001: 1629; DeCandido, GraceAnne. Rev. of *Eleven on Top*. *Booklist*, May 15, 2005: 1612; Lachman, Marvin. Rev. of *One for the Money*. *Armchair Detective*, Summer 1995: 287; Plagens, Peter. "Standing in the Line of Fire." *Newsweek*, July 12, 2004: 56; Stasio, Marilyn. Rev. of *One for the Money*. *New York Times Book Review*, September 4, 1994: 17; Stasio, Marilyn. Rev. of *High Five*. *New York Times Book Review*, June 27, 1999: 26; Williams, Wilda. Rev. of *Seven Up*. *Library Journal*, June 1, 2001: 224; Wilson, Kate. Rev. of *One for the Money*. *Entertainment Weekly*, November 11, 1994: 68; Wyatt, Edward. "For This Author, Writing Is Only the Beginning." *New York Times*, June 22, 2005: E1.

Major awards: John Creasey Memorial Award, 1995; Dilys Award, 1995, 1998; Last Laugh Award, 1996; Silver Dagger Award, 1997; Lefty Award, 1998, 1999.

Web site: www.evanovich.com.

See also: Joan Hess's police chief **Arly Hanks** comic mystery series, set in Maggody, Arkansas; Sparkle Hayter's humorous television reporter Robin Hudson series; British author D.M. Greenwood's humorous clerical series featuring Anglican deaconess Theodora Braithwaite; Australian Kerry Greenwood's 1920s comic series featuring the **Hon. Phryne Fisher**.

Debut novel: Sheryl Anderson's *Killer Heels*, featuring advice columnist Molly Forrester, a blend of "a splash of Carrie Bradshaw, a dash of Stephanie Plum, and a wee bit of Kinsey Millhone" (*Publishers Weekly*, April 19, 2004: 44). For a list of recent chick-lit mysteries, see Marilyn Stasio, "A Girl's Guide to Killing," *New York Times Book Review*, August 21, 2005: 14–15.

Mrs. Pollifax

Profession:	CIA spy
Living situation:	Widowed; later married to Cyrus Reed
Geographic locale:	Worldwide
Time period:	1966–present
Associate:	John Sebastian Farrell
Nemesis:	Evil anti-American foreign agents
Significant relationship:	Cyrus Reed
Concerns:	Boredom; patriotism

Spanning over thirty years, Dorothy Gilman's much-reprinted Mrs. Pollifax series takes its unlikely sexagenarian heroine to exotic and dangerous faraway places, where she pits her Miss Marpleish curiosity, her most imperious Women's Club intrigue-smiting voice, and her devotion to truth, justice, and the American way against vile minions of totalitarian regimes. Widowed for eight years with her son Roger and daughter Jane grown, married, and living far from her New Jersey apartment, and bored enough to consider stepping off her rooftop geranium garden into oblivion,

Mrs. Emily Pollifax suddenly realizes she loathes charity work and has always wanted to be a spy. Accordingly, she soon arrives at the CIA's Langley, Virginia, headquarters, small, cushiony, white-haired and feminine, with a ridiculously beflowered hat and her trademark "conspiratorial and twinkling" smile (*Unexpected* 6). Her demeanor and appearance captivate the Company's Mr. Carstairs, then looking for an authentic, true-blue American tourist for a simple courier assignment to Mexico City. By a fluke, Mrs. Pollifax gets the job and it almost immediately goes haywire, landing her and dashing U.S. operative John Sebastian Farrell, too handsome for his own good, in a bleak Albanian prison, captured as pawns in a Cold War power struggle.

Mary Helen Becker has commented that Gilman's leading characters are "Naïve and innocent to begin with, apparently handicapped by age, poverty, or emotional problems, [but] they pit their courage, perseverance, and resourcefulness (fortified by inner strength discovered in time of need) against the organized powers of evil" (*Twentieth-Century Crime and Mystery Writers*, quoted in *Contemporary Authors Online*). Her innocent-abroad exterior lands Mrs. Pollifax her first job for the Company, but her inner survival skills prove far more impressive than OSS veteran Carstairs or even Mrs. Pollifax herself could have imagined. Years of suburban wife- and motherhood have equipped her to endure lice-ridden imprisonment, lack of plumbing, and ghastly food; to grit her teeth, dig a bullet out of Fleming's arm with only brandy for an anesthetic; and to charm Albanian Major Vassovic with smiles and massages before she knocks him unconscious with a rock to effect their escape.

Looking back in *Mrs. Pollifax Unveiled* (2000) over the strange detour her life had taken, Emily Pollifax concludes that it "had ... enriched and changed her" (138). From the start of her association with the Company, Mrs. Pollifax's openmindedness and innate kindness make her dangerously sympathetic to strangers. She's unfailingly compassionate and generous to the many poverty-stricken Third World denizens who often unexpectedly help her, but her warm heart frequently leads her to be too trusting, involving her in outrageous entanglements her CIA boss never expected. In the course of her many trips for Carstairs, she meets "incredible people," like the inscrutable Chinese fellow captive she rescues in Albania much to Farrell's discomfiture, and later even "a man who had been very dear to her," who had unforgettably told her, "If only you had been born in Bulgaria, *Amerikanski*, we could have changed the world!" (*Unveiled* 138).

Over her fictional thirty-year career the world changes enormously around Emily Pollifax, too, preventing her from falling victim to her old enemy, boredom, which for her is sheer Hell: "not having enough to do, and too much time to contemplate one's deficiencies" (*Unveiled* 104). In *Mrs. Pollifax Unveiled*, Carstairs reflects, "Life was so much simpler when half the world backed the Soviet Union, and the other half lived in terror of the Soviet Union. Remove the Cold War and internal conflicts multiply in countries by the week" (*Unveiled* 97–98). Those plots, coups, and civil wars provide Mrs. Pollifax a wide spectrum of boredom-preventing challenges, and she astonishes Carstairs by rising nobly to every single one with a remarkable sang-froid born of stubborn realism: she knows herself. Seemingly not aging much as the series progresses—although she marries lawyer Cyrus Reed, whom she met on an adventure in Zambia—Emily Pollifax knows her thoughts move in a straight line, with "a simplicity that often startled other people . . . one had to work with the tools available" (*Unveiled* 114).

Mrs. Pollifax's tools may be as straightforward as stampeding sheep, but her experiences mushroom after she first offers her services to the CIA. Instead of subsiding genteelly into nursing-home stagnation, she hones her practical talents. Originally a decent markswoman because as a girl she'd shot rats with her cousin John, she eventually approaches her black belt in karate. With her recently acquired smattering of Third World languages like Albanian and Arabic and her preference for people over monuments, she functions independently even when terrorists kidnap Farrell. Tortured earlier herself in Hong Kong, Emily Pollifax also has earned considerable insight into the psychological risks of intelligence gathering, which, coupled with her willingness to implement her homely experiences in a completely new sphere of activity, enables her to face even the worst consequences of spookdom with equanimity; all she fears is the loss of her dignity. Far from being the "lamb among wolves"—without a cyanide suicide pill at that—Carstairs imagines she is, Emily Pollifax represents what Victoria Nichols and Susan Thompson call "true liberated womanhood," successfully humanizing her confederates and most of her opposition (*Silk Stalkings* 1: 238–39) with good humor, mutual respect, and refreshing humility.

Novels: *The Unexpected Mrs. Pollifax* (1966); *The Amazing Mrs. Pollifax* (1970); *The Elusive Mrs. Pollifax* (1971); *A Palm for Mrs. Pollifax* (1973); *Mrs. Pollifax on Safari* (1977); *Mrs. Pollifax on the China Station* (1983); *Mrs. Pollifax and the Hong Kong Buddha* (1985); *Mrs. Pollifax and the Golden Triangle* (1988); *Mrs. Pollifax and the Whirling Dervish* (1990); *Mrs. Pollifax and the Second Thief* (1993); *Mrs. Pollifax Pursued* (1995); *Mrs. Pollifax and the Lion Killer* (1996); *Mrs. Pollifax, Innocent Tourist* (1997); *Mrs. Pollifax Unveiled* (2000).

Other series: *The Clairvoyant Countess* (1975); *Kaleidoscope: A Countess Karitska Novel* (2002), featuring psychic Madame Karitska. Gilman wrote numerous young adult novels under the name Dorothy Gilman Butters.

Nonfiction: *A New Kind of Country* (New York: Doubleday, 1978).

Selected sources: Callendar, Newgate. Rev. of *The Unexpected Mrs. Pollifax*. *New York Times Book Review*, March 20, 1966; Callendar, Newgate. Rev. of *The Amazing Mrs. Pollifax*. *New York Times Book Review*, March 8, 1970; DeCandido, GraceAnne A. Rev. of *Mrs. Pollifax Unveiled*. *Booklist*, January 1, 2000: 883; Klausner, Harriet. Rev. of *Mrs. Pollifax Unveiled* and *Thale's Folly*. *Under the Covers*, www.silcon.com; *Stop, You're Killing Me!* (murder mystery site) www .stopyourekillingme.com/Dorothy-Gilman.html.

Major award: Catholic Book Award for *A Nun in the Closet*, 1976.

Web site: www.geocities.com/jmkowalchuk (Dorothy Gilman home page)

See also: Margot Arnold's Smith and Glendower series, featuring well-traveled Penny Smith and archaeologist Toby Glendower; Donald Bain's Jessica Fletcher series, modeled on the popular *Murder, She Wrote* television series; Eleanor Boylan's Clara Gamage series, featuring the widow of Elizabeth Daly's popular Golden Age Henry Gamage series; Stephanie

Matteson's Charlotte Graham series, featuring an intrepid sixty-something four-time Oscar-winning actress.

Debut novel: Charles Benoit's humorous *Relative Danger*, featuring young Pennsylvania brewery worker Douglas Pearce, who goes on a whirlwind around-the-world chase looking for his information about his long-dead uncle amid rogues, rotters, and vamps.

Jim Qwilleran

Profession:	Journalist
Living situation:	Divorced
Geographic locale:	Midwest United States
Time period:	1966–present
Associate:	Koko (Kao K'o Kung)
Significant relationship:	Polly Duncan
Concern:	Philanthropy

Feline behavior—people hate it or love it—catalyses Lillian Jackson Braun's popular series featuring divorced journalist and recovering alcoholic Jim "Qwill" Qwilleran and his aristocratic Siamese associates, psychic-seeming Koko (Kao K'o Kung) and demure Yum Yum. Although brutally dismissed by Stephen King as "a shortcut, a kind of emotional shorthand employed by writers who can't really write for readers who can't really read" (quoted in Murphy 88), the cat mystery vogue launched by Braun with *The Cat Who Could Read Backwards* (1966) has broadened into a sizable furrier subgenre of the "cozy." Braun, originally a journalist herself, began "*The Cat Who...*" series after her own Siamese fatally fell from a tenth-floor balcony. After three moderately successful novels followed by an eighteen-year hiatus, she returned to the series, winning Edgar and Anthony nominations and an enormous audience for her many ailuromysteries.

As introduced in the 1960s, Qwilleran is tall, untidy, only ten pounds overweight, now sober, and fighting a midlife crisis. Following a dubious career curve from sports to police reporting to war correspondence to the Publishers' Trophy and a book on urban crime and then a descent into short-term jobs, unemployment, booze, and divorce, he's arrived at the little Midwestern *Daily Fluxion* aching for the chaos and camaraderie of a City Room run by old nail-spitting crusaders. Instead he finds electric pencil sharpeners and the new precision-honed breed of editor "who approached newspapering as a science" (*Read Backwards* 8). Assigned to prove himself by writing art features, Qwill meets George Bonifield Mountclemens the Third, the *Flux*'s gadfly art critic who regularly manages to make the *Flux*'s readers want him dead. Qwill also falls for Mountclemens's handsome Siamese Kao K'o Kung, familiarly known as "Koko." After Mountclemens is indeed murdered, Qwill follows Koko's radar whiskers and his own, an overgrown salt-and-pepper moustache, interviewing suspects and witnesses with his trademark brotherly approach, "two parts sympathy, two parts professional curiosity, and one part low blood pressure" that had "won confidence from old ladies, juvenile delinquents, pretty girls, college presidents and crooks" (*Read Backwards* 18). Not until he decides to treat Koko as an equal partner, though, does Qwill's dogged method pay off. Koko's innate curiosity, his fluid feline stealth, and his spitting, Far Eastern kick-boxing fighting style save Qwill from a nasty assault and provide the intuitive leap that allows Qwill to solve the case.

Returning in *The Cat Who Saw Red* (1986), Qwill, Koko, and their partner Yum Yum now enjoy great good fortune, an enormous freak inheritance that allows Qwill, still fiftyish and sober, to move them and his typewriter to a luxuriously restored apple barn full of cat balconies near Pickax, population about 3000, in Michigan's remote Upper Peninsula. Qwill quietly oversees the Klingenschoen Foundation, munificent source of the area's economic development, which allows him the frequent changes of scene he enjoys and the cats in typical feline fashion thoroughly loathe. Qwill's feature-writing assignments take him to a smorgasbord of crime venues, like the haute cuisine scene in *The Cat Who Saw Red*, the classical music world in *The Cat Who Played Brahms* (1987), and Shakespearean drama in *The Cat Who Knew Shakespeare* (1988). With time, Qwill's become increasingly cozy and decreasingly catty, though he still needs Koko to point an elegant paw at vital clues.

By the time of *The Cat Who Went Up the Creek* (2002), Qwilleran has become convinced of Koko's flair for thought transference. Local librarian Polly Duncan, also owned by two Siamese, is the only woman in courtly Qwill's life. With Polly vacationing with her sister, Qwill takes Koko and Yum Yum to solve a mysteriously depressing atmosphere and later actual murder at the neighboring Nutcracker Inn, a Klingenschoen-funded enterprise capitalizing on the area's rare black walnut trees. Qwill genially allows people to pour their troubles out to him, employing his journalistic "persuasive hyperbole and truth-telling before the fact" (*Creek* 152), but "a certain sensation in his left temple" that heralds Koko's sapphire-blue stare catapults Qwill from his chair to his typewriter and creative crime-solving. Qwill always needs time to absorb the significance of Koko's own investigations, like a pair of brown oxfords and the area behind the inn's adjoining vacation cabins, but when the supercat's behavior does sink in, Qwill finds Koko's "ability to predict events . . . unnerving" (*Creek* 90). Polly has consistently tried to squelch the notion of cats with supranormal powers (*Creek* 221), but Qwill maintains that the gruesome "death howl" Koko uses to announce wrongful death has never been wrong.

Saving this series for many readers from soggy sentimentality and cagey cuteness are Koko's convincingly observed Siamese idiosyncrasies, Qwill's willingness to trust feline instincts, and the mutual interspecies respect they display. Old journalist Qwilleran refuses to accept as dogma the contention of grizzled police detectives in Down Below Michigan who consider Koko "psychic." Instead, Qwill acknowledges only a reliable nose for news clad in silky cream seal-pointed fur: "'That cat knows when people are up to no good.'" He wonders, too, how much of Koko's involvement is extrasensory perception and how much is coincidence (*Creek* 226)—and therein hangs the success of Jim Qwilleran's tales.

Novels: (All begin with *The Cat Who...*): *...Could Read Backwards* (1966); *...Ate Danish Modern* (1967); *...Turned On and Off* (1968); *...Saw Red* (1986); *...Played Brahms* (1987); *...Played Post Office* (1987); *...Knew Shakespeare* (1988); *...Sniffed Glue* (1989); *...Went Underground* (1989); *...Talked to Ghosts* (1990); *...Lived High* (1990); *...Knew a Cardinal* (1991); *...Moved a Mountain* (1992); *...Wasn't There* (1992); *...Went into the Closet* (1993); *...Came to Breakfast* (1994); *...Blew the Whistle* (1994); *...Said Cheese* (1996); *...Tailed a Thief* (1997); *...Sang for the Birds* (1998); *...Saw Stars* (1999); *...Robbed a Bank* (2000); *...Smelled a Rat* (2001); *...Went Up the Creek* (2002); *...Brought Down the House*; *...Talked Turkey* (2003); *...Went Bananas* (2004); *...Dropped a Bombshell* (2005).

Short fiction: *The Cat Who Had 14 Tales* (1988); *Short and Tall Tales* (2004); *The Private Life of the Cat Who...* (2005).

Additional reading: *The Cat Who...Companion*, by Sharon A. Feaster (1998); *The Cat Who Cookbook*, by Sally Stempinski and Julie Murphy with foreword by Lillian Jackson Braun; includes cat-treat recipes.

Selected sources: *Kirkus Reviews.* Rev. of *The Cat Who Brought Down the House*, November 15, 2002: 1658; Leide, Kathryn. Rev. of *The Cat Who Brought Down the House*. *Booklist*, May 1, 2003: 1526; Moore, Claudia. Rev. of *The Cat Who Smelled a Rat*. *School Library Journal*, May 1, 2003: 175; Smith, Carol. Rev. of *The Cat Who Talked Turkey*. *Booklist*, May 1, 2004: 1451; Whitten, Robin. "Listen Up!" *Christian Science Monitor*, April 30, 1998: 84.

Web site: Unofficial Fan Club: www.geocities.com/Heartland/Estates/6371/lillian.html.

See also: Feline-related cozy mystery series: the Lydia Adamson (pseudonym of Frank King) million-selling cozy series featuring stray-cat adopting Alice Nestleton; Marian Babson's Douglas Perkins and his cat Pandora series and Babson's cat-related stand-alone novels, especially *Canapés for the Kitties* (1997); Rita Mae Brown and Sneaky Pie Brown's Mary Minor "Harry" Haristeen series set in Virginia's Blue Ridge Mountains, with much of the action told from the animals' points of view; Marion Babson's Dame Cecile Savoy and Trixie and Evangeline series; Carole Nelson Douglas's Midnight Louie series featuring Las Vegas publicist Temple Barr and intrepid tomcat Midnight Louie; Evan Marshall's series featuring literary agent Jane Stuart and Ninky; Shirley Rousseau Murphy's series featuring feline sleuth Joe Grey, set in Molina Point, California.

Debut novel: Clea Simon's *Mew Is for Murder*, featuring Theda Krakow, freelance feature writer, who stumbles into the murder of a Cambridge, Massachusetts, "cat lady."

R

Agatha Raisin

Profession:	Retired public relations executive
Living situation:	Divorced
Geographic locale:	"Caresly," Cotswolds, England
Time period:	1993–present
Associates:	Sir Charles Fraith; Mrs. Bloxby
Significant relationship:	James Lacey, ex-husband
Concerns:	Aging; boredom

Besides writing her gently humorous **Hamish Macbeth** series set in the Scottish Highlands, M.C. Beaton turned from her hundred-plus romance novels written under several pen names to create a trenchant portrait of female midlife crisis, the Agatha Raisin series, set in a tidy Cotswold village. Abrasive and upwardly mobile with a vengeance, Agatha hauled herself out of a Birmingham housing project slum and clawed her way to financial success heading a lucrative public relations firm, taking early retirement in her fifties and moving to "Caresly," where she snoops her way into murder cases and lands in one fizzling romantic relationship after another.

  With her good legs (the last to go), glossy brown hair (a miracle of modern chemistry), and small bear-like eyes revealing the disposition of a frustrated polecat, Agatha Raisin descends from those forlorn middle-aged women at the seaside resort in Dorothy L. Sayers's *Have His Carcase*, making fools of themselves over the waiters, but the lower-class background Agatha conceals gave her the ruthlessness to pursue what she wants (even men) while her well-invested earnings allow her considerable leverage to get it. Once she gets it, though, Agatha has to be the boss, and she suffers for it. Mrs. Bloxby, the vicar's wife and Agatha's long-suffering confidante, worries that Agatha's addiction to falling in love, unflinchingly chronicled through the entire series, will lead to disaster, but despite her nasty habit of dumping her friends, most of Agatha's one-time lovers show up when she needs them.

As a testimony to the milk of human kindness, some people seem to sense that under Agatha's porcupinish defenses lies a vulnerable human being. Mistreated friends like local Detective Sergeant Bill Wong, her first and oldest pal in Caresby, keep coming back for more, and after a brief fling with Agatha, Sir Charles Fraith, ten years her junior, still drops in and out of her life, cadging expensive restaurant meals but providing moral support and hints at resumed intimacy. Agatha alternately bullies and cajoles him into helping her establish her own private detective agency in *The Deadly Dance* (2004), but when they have to share a hotel room while working that case, Agatha can't resist dousing Charles's lingering hopes with, "And I wish you wouldn't parade around the room naked. It's disconcerting" (*Dance* 129).

In a retirement that seems anything but the rural idyll she'd expected, Agatha must develop some new survival skills. She even shows signs of de-scroogification. While she was still working, Agatha was deservedly friendless and didn't mind it, since she loves being in charge. In the Cotswolds, however, with time on her hands, bristly hairs sprouting on her upper lip, and constantly denied arthritis twinging at one hip, she gradually comes to see the value of friendships. She battles her loneliness with hypnosis that makes her cigarettes taste like burned rubber, Pilates classes that she surprisingly discovers she likes, and her cats, for whom she cooks fish, though she microwaves horrid frozen atrocities for herself. Her primary means of staving off the midnight willies over encroaching age, though, is snooping into her neighbors' affairs each time she suffers a disappointment in her own. By *Agatha Raisin and the Day the Floods Came* (2002), she remains badly bruised after her divorce from former neighbor James Lacey, who left her to enter a French monastery (Really? Or was that a convenient way of dumping her? Agatha's suspicious mind keeps asking). Charles, too, was out of her clutches; he'd dismayingly married a much younger Frenchwoman and they're expecting twins. Agatha hurls herself onto remote Robinson Crusoe Island, where inspiration for her next detecting case strikes her, her antidote for all those thwarted desires for affection and romance.

Even though she always feels that she doesn't fit in anywhere, Agatha fights back after every setback. As a detective, she blunders more than she strikes pay dirt, and Raisin Investigations Ltd. never receives much credit from either the press or from Detective Inspector Blodge, but her persistence, her courage, and her shrewd cunning often lead her into unexpected solutions. By *The Deadly Dance*, this acid-tongued "old trout" whom, according to Mrs. Bloxby, men still find sexy, starts to evolve into someone the villagers begin to relate to: hell-bent on reformation, Agatha blows up the community kitchen cooking an oversized turkey for her friends. Who hasn't had a cooking disaster? Merry Christmas, everyone.

Novels: *Agatha Raisin and the Quiche of Death* (1992); *Agatha Raisin and The Vicious Vet* (1993); *Agatha Raisin and the Potted Gardener* (1994); *Agatha Raisin and the Walkers of Dembley* (1995); *Agatha Raisin and the Murderous Marriage* (1996); *Agatha Raisin and the Terrible Tourist* (1997); *Agatha Raisin and the Wellspring of Death* (1998); *Agatha Raisin and the Witch of Wyckhadden* (1999); *Agatha Raisin and the Wizard of Evesham* (1999); *Agatha Raisin and the Fairies of Fryfam* (2000); *Agatha Raisin and the Love from Hell* (2001); *Agatha Raisin and the Day the Floods Came* (2002); *Agatha Raisin and the Case of the Curious Curate* (2003); *Agatha Raisin and the Haunted House* (2004); *The Deadly Dance: An Agatha Raisin Mystery* (2004); *The Perfect Paragon* (2005).

Other series: The Hamish Macbeth series, set in Lochdubh, Scotland. Beaton has also written many historical romances and six romance series under various pen names (see entry for Hamish Macbeth).

Selected sources: DeCandido, GraceAnne A. Rev. of *Agatha Raisin and the Wellspring of Death*. *Booklist*, June 1, 1998: 1730; Klett, Rex. Rev. of *Agatha Raisin and the Terrible Tourist*. *Library Journal*, September 1, 1997: 223; *Publishers Weekly*. Rev. of *Agatha Raisin and the Haunted House*, September 8, 2003: 43; *Publishers Weekly*. Rev. of *Agatha Raisin and the Wizard of Evesham*, March 15, 1999: 50; *Twentieth Century Romance and Historical Writers*, 3rd ed. Detroit: St. James Press, 1994.

See also: Nancy Atherton's cozy Aunt Dimity series; Marian Babson's series featuring aging actresses Trixie Dolan and Evangeline Sinclair, trying for a comeback on the British stage.

Mma Precious Ramotswe

Profession:	Professional detective
Living situation:	Divorced and eventually remarried
Geographic locale:	Botswana
Time period:	2000–present
Associate:	Mma Makutsi, Assistant Manager of the No. 1 Ladies' Detective Agency
Nemeses:	Western-style greed; Note Makoti
Significant relationship:	Mr. J.L.B. Matekoni, owner of Tlokweng Road Speedy Motors
Concerns:	Morality; traditional values

Botswana, Mma Ramotswe's beloved homeland, lies just north of South Africa, abutting the Kalahari Desert. As lovingly drawn in Alexander McCall Smith's popular series, Botswana's generally peaceful people now face social, governmental, and environmental upheavals, and new wealth from diamond mining, sweeping them from traditional ways into a future full of physical and spiritual temptations. As the adored motherless child of gentle Obed Ramotswe, Precious inherited her father's cattle herd, guaranteeing her independence and allowing her to create the "No. 1 Ladies' Detective Agency" to right some of the moral wrongs she sees about her.

Precious Ramotswe knows injustice herself. Married too infatuated and too young to Note Makoti, a slick trumpet player and incorrigible ladies' man who beat her so badly while pregnant that her only baby died soon after birth, she often reflects on the growing number of Botswanans who, because of poverty, unemployment, and AIDS are growing up fatherless, many not even knowing who their fathers are. "There must always be a great gap in their lives. Perhaps if you don't know there's a gap, you don't worry about it, If you were a millipede, a *tshongolo* . . . would you look at the birds and worry about not having wings? Probably not."

Now comfortably middle-aged and traditionally sized, Mma Ramotswe has become "the Miss Marple of Botswana," according to *New York Times* reviewer Alida Becker. Mma Ramotswe follows her philosophical speculations only up to a point, because "they tended to lead her to further questions which simply could not be answered." She cherishes the old Botswana morality just because it feels right, as she knows everybody knows, and directs her considerable energies, common sense, and ingenuity to solving her clients' problems, usually caused by their greed for Western-style fancy clothes and expensive cars; "helping people to find out things they already know" (*Cheerful Ladies* 33).

Those problems chiefly involve domestic issues—a missing child, a straying husband, a business rival (male), the plight of undertrained young people, a family's squabbles over an inheritance, the search for a worthy Botswana beauty queen, even an American mother who needs closure to her son's death. By observing millipede-sized clues to human behavior, Mma Ramotswe tactfully rights wrongs with unflagging good sense and good humor. Morality is for everyone, she believes, and making up one's own rules about it is simply selfishness, which she refuses to tolerate. She feels bound to help everyone who consults her, often donating her services: "You simply could not help everybody. But you could at least help those who came into your life. That principle allowed you to deal with the suffering you saw. That was your suffering."

Mma Ramotswe believes that for educated women like herself it is better for both spouses to have something to do. She eventually marries a paragon of decency, Mr. J.L.B. Matekoni, proprietor of Tlokweng Road Speedy Motors and physician to her tiny white van of uncertain age. He proves as upright and kind as Note Mokoti was caddish—almost too good-hearted. Without consulting Mma Ramotswe, he takes in two orphans, the girl crippled but bright, the boy desperately needing parental guidance, and Mma Ramotswe copes admirably with this family she never expected. She also discreetly heads off the potential heartbreak of her brilliant but plain assistant Mma Makutsi, who despite her 97 percent typing score at the Botswana Secretarial College runs afoul of another wolf in genteel Western clothing.

Mma Ramotswe deeply regrets that crime is growing in Botswana, due, she believes, to selfishness, "when towns became bigger and people became strangers to one another" (*Cheerful Women* 4). In *The No. 1 Ladies' Detective Agency* (2002) she singlehandedly confronts a witch doctor (it was the right thing to do). In *Tears of the Giraffe* she promises the American mother who, like Precious herself, lost a child, "I will help you, my sister." In *Morality for Beautiful Girls* (2002), Mma Ramotswe concludes that although society can cause crime, she can always pinpoint an individual evildoer: "something which women had known for a very long time—they could tell what men were like just by looking at them." She continues to spot and leisurely dispose of such criminals in both *The Kalahari Typing School for Men* (2003) and *The Full Cupboard of Life* (2003), between soothing cups of red bush tea (traditionally built ladies never hurry in Botswana's heat). Viciously blackmailed by Note Makoti in *In the Company of Cheerful Women* (2005), Mma Ramotswe still finds compassion—and a graceful way out of his clutches.

Mma Ramotswe knows that her place in creation is humble, but she also knows its value. Mma Ramotswe's compassion and sensibility, like the legendary giraffe's tears that Botswanan women weave into handsome baskets, means something—and everything—to those she helps: "A giraffe has nothing else to give—only tears." As Mma Makutsi learned from Precious Ramotswe, "that is what makes our pain and sorrow bearable—this giving of love to others, this sharing of the heart" (*Cheerful Ladies* 233).

Novels: *The No. 1 Ladies Detective Agency* (2000); *Tears of the Giraffe* (2001); *Morality for Beautiful Girls* (2001); *The Kalahari Typing School for Men* (2002); *The Full Cupboard of Life* (2004); *In the Company of Cheerful Ladies* (2005).

Other series: **Isabel Dalhousie** series, featuring Dalhousie as a contemporary Scottish philosopher and amateur detective: *The Sunday Philosophy Club* (2004); *Friends, Lovers, and Chocolate* (2005). The Portuguese Irregular Verbs series, featuring Dr. Mortiz-Maria von Igelfeld, Professor of Romance philology: *Portuguese Irregular Verbs* (2003); *The Finer Points of Sausage Dogs* (2004); *At the Villa of Reduced Circumstances* (2004).

Serialized novel: *44 Scotland Street* appeared daily in *The Scotsman*; published in 2005 as a book.

Short fiction: *Children of Wax: African Folk Tales* (1991); *Heavenly Date and Other Stories* (1995); *The Girl Who Married a Lion and Other Stories* (2004).

Nonfiction: McCall Smith has written and edited many reference volumes on medical ethics, some with collaborators.

Other works: McCall Smith has also authored several children's books.

Selected sources: Dunford, Jane. "Botswana Sells It By the Book." *Travel Weekly*, April 1, 2005: 54–56; Malcolm, Janet. "Remember the Ladies." *New York Times Book Review*, April 24, 2005: 16–17; Maslin, Janet. "A Genteel Life in Botswana." *New York Times*, March 12, 2005: E8; *Publishers Weekly*. "The No. 1 Most Prolific Author," May 28, 2005: 22; *Kirkus Reviews*. "Q and A: Alexander McCall Smith," June 1, 2005: 14; Schmidt, Heidi Jon. Rev. of *In the Company of Cheerful Ladies. People*, May 30, 2005: 48.

See also for African settings: Robert Wilson's series featuring expatriate British "fixer" **Bruce Medway** in Benin, West Africa; Walter Satterthwaite's *The Gold of Mayani* (1995) short stories set in East Africa and featuring Kenyan Police Sergeant M'butu and Constable Kobari.

Easy Rawlins

Profession:	School custodian, unlicensed investigator
Living situation:	Divorced
Geographic locales:	Houston; Los Angeles
Time period:	1940s–1960s
Associates:	Mouse (Raymond Alexander); Saul Lynx
Nemesis:	Racism
Significant relationship:	Bonnie (in *Bad Boy Brawly Brown*)
Concerns:	Racial constraints on freedom; domestic violence; police brutality

"Good fiction," Walter Mosley says, "is in the sentence and in the character and in the heart of the writer" (*Talking Murder* 203). Chester Himes's 1960s crime series addressed the world of black policemen in Harlem, but Mosley's widely praised Easy Rawlins novels are the first major crime fiction to induce "a large biracial audience to cross over the line that typically separates the black and white mainstreams of popular literature" (Herbert 136). Much of the series' success derives from Mosley's convincing ear for black language and his conviction that he's doing "something good" by opening white people's minds to "what happens next in these black lives" (*Talking Murder* 206), but mostly reluctant detective Ezekiel "Easy" Rawlins himself illuminates significant moments of history from the 1940s through the 1960s for black people, for Los Angeles, and for America (*Talking Murder* 202).

The series actually began with the pathological killer Mouse, Rawlins's only friend, who looked up on page four of a story Mosley wrote in the 1980s and says, "Hey, Easy, how you doin'?" (*Talking Murder* 202). In *Gone Fishin'*, also written in the 1980s, rejected by fifteen agents, and not published until 1997, Easy, orphaned at eight in the deep South, narrates his defining moment of truth, a shattering trip he took in 1939 at nineteen with Mouse, south from Houston into bayous, spooky sex, illness, and murder. Easy's an unwilling accomplice when Mouse executes his step-father and another black man as a cover. Wanton slaughter sickens Easy, but he's learned, don't question—"that's what life was like back then....Maybe life was so tough we were too tired to lend a hand" (*Gone Fishin'* 49). Easy loses his soul and thinks he can't believe in God or family or love anymore, carrying guilt that haunts him like a malignant voodoo charm for the rest of his life. Out of guilt and fear, he also learns to read and write to spirit the thought of death away.

Mosley's method is to "have a guy...about to open the door. He doesn't know what's on the other side and neither do I." Easy's stories, each bearing a color in its title as John D. MacDonald's do, share the same pattern: an acquaintance needs an apparently simple favor that promises a reward but instead catapults Rawlins into lethal circumstances. Easy knows "Poor men like me are no more than a pair of hands to work, if there's work to be had" (*Gone Fishin'* 239), so he takes each job. Every time, he learns too late that he's always "manipulated by the rich and powerful (and white) to infiltrate areas he knows but which are beyond their bounds" (Ashley 350). He's also "hampered, manipulated and victimized" by the primarily white LAPD (Murphy 350), starting with *Devil in a Blue Dress* (1990) set in 1948 Watts, the Los Angeles suburb infamous for racial violence and police brutality. In General "Blood and Guts" Patton's Third Army (he'd volunteered), Easy hadn't minded if the white boys hated him, but he'd made them respect him. Now, despite all the hassles he endures while chasing down a white girl who likes illegal black nightspots, Easy stands up for himself again, telling his white boss, "My name is Mr. Rawlins" (*Devil* 73). As an unpaid investigator, he feels the joy of "a poor black man who'd soaked up pain and rage for a life time" (*Devil* 188) acting on his own for the first time.

Easy gets older as the world around him changes but his mind, though aging, stays the same. In each novel, Easy deals with a topical issue like the 1950s Communist-hunting in *A Red Death* (1991), an awkward plot with Rawlins an unwilling pawn of political machinations. *White Butterfly* (1992), possibly the most powerful of the series, shows much less of the search for a serial killer than it explores Rawlins's character through male-female relationships and the issue of domestic violence. *Black Betty* (1994), like its predecessors, reveals how easily white policemen got by with killing blacks in pre-desegregation days: "There wasn't one Negro in a hundred who'd talk to police" and "the papers hardly ever even reported a colored murder" (*Devil* 165), but Easy outsmarts the LAPD at their own game. *Bad Boy Brawly Brown* (2002) picks him up in 1964 at forty-four, working as a school custodian, living at last with the right woman, Bonnie, loving his two foster children, and blaming himself for Mouse's death. Tracking the missing Brawly Brown for Brown's worried parents, Easy comes up against "the Free Men," young black revolutionaries. He decides they're trying "to create freedom out of the sow's ear called America" where there's always somebody out to get you (*Bad Boy* 44). About midway through the "obstacle course" he calls his life, Easy realizes the Free Men can't really understand "the pain and ecstasy of what it was to be Negro in this country" (*Bad Boy* 15). Mosley's powerful *Little Scarlet* (2004), taking place during the 1965 Watts race riots in California, highlights Rawlins's anger "that urged me to go out and fight after all the hangings I had seen, after all of the times I had been called nigger and all of the doors that had been slammed in my face." *Cinnamon Kiss* (2005) shows Easy's achievements, at last a decent job, his children doing well, a good woman in his house, and some respect from the white authorities, all about the disintegrate, just at the height of the Vietnam Era. Rawlins works his way out of this deadly situation again by taking a missing persons job in San Francisco arranged for him by his friend Saul Lynx. Easy gets acquainted with the counterculture there and gets the job done, but it's never easy for Easy to make his way in the difficult times Mosely paints so vividly in his novels.

Mosley's Easy Rawlins novels are related to the hard-boiled genre, but rather than making Easy a "superman" like Sam Spade or Philip Marlowe, he forces Easy to "move forward" (*Talking Murder* 202), going deeper and deeper into Rawlins's very heart and soul. If Easy Rawlins can be the everyman Mosley intends, then somewhere, sometime, color may no longer matter.

Novels: *Devil in a Blue Dress* (1990); *A Red Death* (1991); *White Butterfly* (1992); *Black Betty* (1994); *A Little Yellow Dog* (1996); *Gone Fishin'* (1997); *Bad Boy Brawly Brown* (2002); *Little Scarlet* (2004); *Cinnamon Kiss* (2005).

Other series: The Socrates Fortlow series, featuring an African American hero trying to redeem himself after a twenty-seven-year sentence for murder.

Short fiction: *Six Easy Pieces: Easy Rawlins Stories* (2003).

Nonfiction: *Workin' on the Chain Gang: Contemplating Our Chains at the End of the Millennium* (1999). Mosely provided the introduction to and coedited (with Manthia Diawara, Clyde Taylor, and Regina Austin Norton) *Black Genius: African-American Solutions to African-American Problems* (1999).

Autobiography: *Life Out of Context* (2005).

Other works: *Always Outnumbered, Always Outgunned* (1997; featuring Socrates Fortlow); *Futureland: Nine Stories of an Imminent World* (2001).

Mosley has also written several stand-alone novels, notably *Fear Itself* (2003) and *The Man in My Basement* (2004).

Selected sources: Berger, Roger A. "'The Black Dick': Race, Sexuality, and Discourse in the L.A. Novels of Walter Mosley." *African American Review*, Summer 1997: 281–95; Forbes, Steve. Rev. of *Gone Fishin'*. *Forbes*, August 11, 1997: 28; *Publishers Weekly*. Rev. of *Little Scarlet*, May 24, 2004: 47; Silet, Charles L.P. "The Other Side of Those Mean Streets." *Talking Murder* (Princeton, NJ: Ontario Press, 1999): 200–206; Stasio, Marilyn. Rev. of *Little Scarlet*. *New York Times Book Review*, July 25, 2004.

Major awards: John Creasey Memorial Award, 1991; Shamus Award, 1991; O. Henry Award, 1996; Chester Himes Award, 1999 (all Crime Writers' Association).

Web site: www.twbookmark.com/features/waltermosley/index.html.

See also: Clarence L. Cooper's stand-alone novels dealing with drug and crime problems from the perspective of young blacks; David Fulmer's series featuring New Orleans Creole PI Valentine St. Cyr; Chester Himes's Coffin Ed and Grave Digger Jones series, featuring two black New York City detectives; Ed Lacy's black PI Toussaint Moore series (Lacy was white but married to a black woman); George Pelikanos's series featuring black Washington, D.C., PI Derek Strange; Ernest Tidyman's series featuring black Greenwich Village PI John Shaft; for the New Orleans music scene, Ace Atkins's series featuring Nick Turner, a "roots music field researcher"; for a pre–Civil War perspective, Barbara Hambly's series featuring free black physician-turned-private investigator **Benjamin January**, working out of New Orleans.

Jack Reacher

Profession: Former U.S. Army military policeman; now a drifter

Living situation: Single

Geographic locale: Various U.S. sites

Time period: 1990–present
Nemesis: "The big guys"

Abruptly "made redundant" after eighteen years as a presentation director for such series as *Prime Suspect* and *Cracker* on Britain's Granada Television, tall, casually dressed, keenly intellectual Briton Lee Child moved in 1998 to New York, where he'd always wanted to be, after creating 6'5" casually dressed and sharp-witted tough American ex-M.P. Jack Reacher, "exactly what I would be," claims Child, "if I could get away with it" (Donahue 44). Reacher is the hero of a page-turner suspense/mystery/crime series—Child claims "it's a little bit Jesuitical to work out exactly which is which"—rapidly growing in popularity since *Killing Floor* (1997), which won the Anthony Best First Novel award.

Deploring the trend toward increasingly dysfunctional heroes, Child looked back through Golden Age private eyes like John D. MacDonald's Travis McGee, his special favorite, and Western loners like Shane, through medieval crusaders, straight to Homer's Ulysses, to produce "a straightforward, uncomplicated, untroubled hero—mentally and physically capable, not uptight—functional in every way" (Donahue 44). Reacher is a mutated Robin Hood; as he puts it himself at the close of *Persuader* (2003), he doesn't so much defend the "little guys" as he hates the "big guys"—powerful unscrupulous mega-bullies—wherever he finds them, from small towns to the highest levels of business, crime, government, even the military.

Arrested at the start of *Killing Floor* as the prime suspect in two violent murders that rock sleepy little Margrave, Georgia, Reacher is far more than he at first seems. On the surface a taciturn thirty-six-year-old hobo, he's a West Point graduate, a former U.S. Army major whose career in the military police, where he'd apprehended trained-to-kill lawbreakers, fell victim to the 1990s "peace dividend." This grown-up Army brat born in Berlin and shuttled from base to base now carries no identification, not even a middle name, on a "meaningless pilgrimage" (*Killing Floor* 76) across the United States he's served but never knew; and he doesn't want to think about weird killers any more, preferring solitude and invisibility and coolly extricating himself from a corrupt Southern prison system by intelligent deduction and police-procedural experience. Then the sky crashes down on Jack Reacher: one of those mutilated men he was accused of killing in Margrave, Georgia, is his brother Joe.

As an unequivocal loner, Reacher has no help, no backup, no facilities to solve these crimes, but he doesn't have to worry about laws, inhibitions, or distractions, either (*Killing Floor* 150). His cop's nose not only smells a worried man a mile away, it leads him to people he can trust, like Margrave's black chief detective Finlay and good-looking brunette Officer Roscoe, who starts Reacher thinking about a hut on a Jamaican beach and a little recreational grass. For Reacher, though, such relationships have to be transitory; a night or two of heaven—a plain old bar and a stunning woman and a decent band (*Killing Floor* 154)—and he's back on his self-imposed job, tracking killers and slaying them not out of revenge for his own humiliation but to honor his brother's memory, a self-imposed mission Roscoe can never accept or understand.

After leaving Finlay in Margrave to clean up the malignant conspiracy beneath the town's idyllic surface, Reacher drifts across America's deceptively peaceful backwaters—homeless, jobless, friendless, even dogless, because Child wanted "something much more freewheeling, much less anchored" than the comfortably anchored series his contemporaries were producing (*Publishers Weekly* May 31, 2004, 45). Kidnapped and held for ransom in *Die Trying* (1998), solving the murder of a stranger who's been searching for him in *Tripwire* (1999), Reacher becomes more complex and more intriguing with each successive novel.

In Child's first bestseller list maker *The Enemy* (2004), a prequel opening on New Year's Eve of 1989, the Cold War's been won and the U.S. Army's teetering on the verge of downsizing, the source of the criminal case that shatters twenty-nine-year-old Major Jack Reacher's trust and sets him on his lonely personal quest for justice. Going back in time for *The Enemy* allows acquaintance with Reacher's younger, bolder self, dumb enough to think he's any man's equal (*Enemy* 357), and occasionally insubordinate, six years a military investigator who doesn't mind smacking people around and who can freeze drunken Marines with one ice-blue glare. *The Enemy* also reveals Reacher's remarkable mother, a French Resistance heroine at thirteen now dying from cancer with unquenchable panache in Paris, making Reacher realize he has lost something he never knew he had (*Enemy* 305). Reacher's brother Joe, modeled on Child's own older brother (Donahue 45), also appears here, a Treasury Department operative trying to warn Jack that the world is dramatically changing, no matter how much Jack wants to hold onto the old Army values he cherishes.

The Enemy again pits Reacher against "the big ones," this time military bureaucrats who are defending their turf by setting him up as a fall guy, a pawn in a lethal game of chess with Delta Force hunter-killers hot on his heels. Better at cracking heads than cracking books (*Enemy* 351), Reacher makes a near-fatal mistake, but he sees that the convenient out the Army offers him is unethical and does the right thing, though it costs him his rank and eventually his belief in the Army itself.

Jack Reacher's next case, *One Shot*, set in Indiana, begins with another shocker: after a sniper kills five innocent victims from a parking lot garage and is arrested, he says only, "Bring Jack Reacher to me" (*PW* 45). The loner Jack Reacher, in spite of himself, is becoming indispensable to naïve, law-abiding humanity.

Novels: *Killing Floor* (1997); *Die Trying* (1998); *Tripwire* (1999); *Running Blind* (2000); *Echo Burning* (2001); *Without Fail* (2002); *Persuader* (2003); *The Enemy* (2004); *One Shot* (2005).

Selected sources: Bergin, Paul A. Rev. of *Killing Floor*. Armchair Detective, Summer 1997: 372; Donahue, Dick. "Late to the Crime Scene." *PW* Interview. Publishers Weekly, May 31, 2004: 44–45; Gervat, Fred M. Rev. of *Running Blind*. Library Journal, June 1, 2000: 194; Lukowsky, Wes. Rev. of *Tripwire*. Booklist, April 15, 1999: 1468; Winks, Robin. Rev. of *Echo Burning*. Boston Globe, June 24, 2001.

Major awards: Anthony Award and Barry Award, 1998; "Thumping Good Read" Award, England, 1999; Washington Irving Awards, 1999, 2000.

Web site: www.leechild.com.

See also: Dark American private investigator series, especially Michael Connelly's loner **Harry Bosch** series; Ed Gorman's series featuring ex-cop, now security guard and part-time actor Jack Dwyer; Joe Lansdale's series featuring straight white man Hap Collins and gay black man Leonard Pine; Andrew Vachss's blacker-than-black series featuring "Burke," an ex-con turned soldier of fortune who crusades against child abusers.

Debut novel: Somewhat softer-boiled than Jack Reacher, Michael Kronenwetter's *First Kill* features Wisconsin private investigator Hank Berlin.

John Rebus

Profession:	Detective Inspector, Lothian and Borders C.I.D.
Living situation:	Divorced
Geographic locale:	Scotland; mostly Edinburgh and environs
Time period:	1987–present

REBUS: An enigmatic representation of a word or phrase by pictures, symbols, etc. (*American College Dictionary*). JOHN: First name of the black private eye John Shaft created by white American author Ernest Tidyman and admired by Scots author Ian Rankin (Herbert 164).

With *Knots and Crosses* (1987), his first John Rebus novel, Rankin originated a type of detective fiction that American violent-crime author James Ellroy has dubbed "Tartan *noir*." Rebus is an introspective, cynical cop so deeply wounded as to be antisocial, who works in Edinburgh, called by some a "secretive, repressive and conspiratorial city" (Ashley 405) and this crime fiction explores social issues with the common denominator of violence: John Rebus's murder cases involve drug dealing, serial killings, child abduction, gun-running, war criminals, governmental and military corruption, pedophilia, refugee smuggling and trade, Satanism. "All these take Rebus to the edge" (Ashley 205).

Rebus is a puzzle—most to himself. Raised by a "good enough father" whose idolization of his younger son Michael made John Rebus feel like an intruder in their home (*Knots* 1), Rebus broke away early, spent eight years in Britain's paratroops and after qualifying for the elite SAS (Special Air Squadron) suffered a nervous breakdown before joining the Lothian and Borders police. After fifteen years on the force, *Knots and Crosses* finds him middle-aged (he ages in the series), resentful of corrupt authority, smoking and drinking far too much, believing in God but unable to worship with a congregation, divorced and failing, he fears, at fatherhood, sickened at the human depravity his job forces him to witness, and guilt-ridden by memories of his behavior during his savage SAS testing years earlier. Rebus finds beauty in the heartbreak of good jazz and in the printed word (*Knots* 112); he turns to his favorite book, Dostoevsky's *Crime and Punishment*, at least once a year: "If only, he thought, modern murderers would exhibit some show of conscience more often" (*Knots* 30).

Knots and Crosses holds the key to the puzzle of John Rebus: Rebus's own conscience. Rankin began this novel as a treatment of the Jekyll and Hyde theme, pitting

Rebus against a killer of young girls. Rebus feels he is somehow responsible for these crimes, and his conscience torments him throughout the rest of the series. Gold Dagger–winning *Black and Blue* (1997), one of the darkest of the Rebus books, is the only novel of his to have satisfied Rankin (Ashley 405). At first shunted off to Aberdeen, base for Britain's North Sea oil exploration and exploitation, because of insubordination toward a crooked superior, Rebus, now a Detective Inspector, lands in the midst of the "Johnny Bible" serial murder case that copycats unsolved 1960s serial killings. In solving it, Rebus travels "north of Hell" into a killer's mind and his own: "*Was* he obsessed? How different was Johnny Bible's shrine from the scene in his own kitchen, the table covered in cuttings?" (*Black and Blue* 377).

By nature and brutal conditioning, Rebus plays by his own rules, not anybody else's (*A Question of Blood* 17). Friends and women come and go in his life, like his early partner Jack Morton, who reappears in *Black and Blue*, letting Rebus goad him into a fistfight that affords Rebus some temporary relief: "Crying for himself and...for all the victims he couldn't help and would never ever be able to help" (*Black and Blue* 253). Although Rebus fears that the guilt from his SAS testing will haunt him sexually forever, his affair with Gill Templer, begun in *Knots and Crosses*, continues, although she is now a Detective Chief Inspector looking toward loftier positions that Rebus's troublesome inability to play the necessary games will always bar him from achieving. Eventually Gill opts for promotion, distancing herself from Rebus, and Siobhan Clarke becomes Rebus's sometime apprentice and partner.

By *Dead Souls* (1999), Jack Morton is dead, Rebus's daughter Sammy is confined to a wheelchair, and Dr. Patience Aitken is briefly in Rebus's bed while he struggles with cases of murder and pedophilia that force him to relive his own adolescence and take responsibility for its mistakes. In *Set in Darkness* (2000) Siobhan Clarke returns to everyday C.I.D. at St. Leonard's from an assignment to Sex Crimes, partnering, almost mothering, Rebus, who's tempted by suicide, feeling older by the day, living alone in a flat filled with "eau de bachelor" and ghosts—"dead colleagues, victims, expired relationships" (*Set in Darkness* 23). In *The Falls* (2000) their edgy partnership reverses, with Rebus constantly reminding her to eat and rest ("You sound like my mum," Siobhan declares) almost as often as she nags him about his cigarettes and whisky.

Rankin is said to see "a finite lifetime" to this series (Ashley 405), and *A Question of Blood* (2003) seems to bring Rebus full circle with two intertwining cases: a seemingly senseless shooting of schoolchildren ending with the gunman's suicide, and a suspicious apartment fire killing a stalker who had been tormenting Siobhan. John Rebus's hands are severely burned and his affair with Jean Burchill is cooling. Gill Templer, now Detective Chief Superintendent, tells Siobhan more than either realizes: "John likes to look out for you, doesn't he, Siobhan? ... John's got this knight-in-tarnished armor thing, hasn't he? Always has to be looking for another dragon to fight" (*A Question of Blood* 13). The dragon in *Fleshmarket Alley* (2005) is a group of conscienceless criminals who threaten Rebus and Siobhan in one of their most complex cases. For years Rebus's most dangerous dragon has been his guilty raging memories of his SAS testing, but in *A Question of Blood* he'd finally met them head-on and poured his fourth Scotch down the drain. Someone had once reminded him that "we Scots are 'creatures tamed by cruelty'" (*Black and Blue* 165), and if so, John Rebus at long last may be solving the puzzle of himself.

Novels: *Knots and Crosses* (1987); *Hide and Seek* (1991); *Tooth and Nail* (1996); *Strip Jack* (1992); *The Black Book* (1993); *Mortal Causes* (1994); *Let It Bleed* (1995); *Black and Blue* (1997); *The Hanging Garden* (1998); *Dead Souls* (1999); *Death is Not the End* (2000); *Set in Darkness* (2000); *The Falls* (2001); *Resurrection Men* (2002); *A Question of Blood* (2003); *Fleshmarket Alley* (2005; *Fleshmarket Close* in the UK).

Short fiction: *A Good Hanging and Other Stories* (1992).

Other works: Rankin has also written stand-alone novels, including *Blood Hunt* (2006), both under his own name and as "Jack Harvey," and short fiction unrelated to Rebus, *Herbert in Motion*, 1997.

Selected sources: Boztas, Senay. "It's PC Rebus as Detective Finds His Conscience." *Sunday Times* (London), March 28, 2004: 14; Peters, Tim. "The Puzzle of Inspector Rebus." Interview with Ian Rankin. *Publishers Weekly*, January 5, 2004: 45; Stasio, Marilyn. Rev. of *Black and Blue*. *New York Times Book Review*, December 14, 1997: 30; Taylor, Charles. "Paint It Noir." *New York Times Book Review*, February 22, 2004; *Times Literary Supplement*. Rev. of *Mortal Causes*, September 23, 1994: 22.

Major awards: Crime Writers' Association Dagger Award for short fiction, 1996; Gold Dagger, 1997; Sherlock Award, Best British Detective (2001).

Web site: www.ianrankin.net.

See also: "Tartan noir" series: Christopher Brookmyre's series featuring unscrupulous Scottish investigative reporter Jack Parlabane; John Harvey's series featuring Nottingham police detective Charlie Resnick; Quintin Jardine's series featuring Edinburgh Assistant (later Deputy) Chief Constable Robert Skinner and Jardine's Oz Blackstone series, set in the Scottish countryside; William McIlvanney's Detective Jack Laidlaw series, set in Glasgow; Denise Mina's **Maureen O'Donnell** novels, also set in Glasgow.

Debut novel: Simon Kernick's *The Business of Dying*, featuring Dennis Milne, a former London detective turned private hit man now pursuing his own brand of savage justice by taking out evildoers without benefit of arrests, trials, or convictions.

Arkady Renko

Profession:	Chief Homicide Investigator
Living situation:	Widowed
Geographic locales:	The former Soviet Union; the present Russia; Germany; Cuba
Time period:	1980–present
Associates:	None survive
Nemesis:	Former KGB Major Pribluda

| *Significant relationship*: | Irina Asanova |
| *Concern*: | Personal integrity in a morally bankrupt world |

Spanning the recent history of Russia and the worldwide ramifications of its decades of Soviet Communism, former reporter Martin Cruz Smith's Arkady Renko novels trace Renko's painful personal odyssey from Brezhnev's Moscow to Siberia and the Bering Sea, back to a new Russian mafia-infested Moscow, a Germany rife with Teutonic efficiency and corruption, a dying Cuba haunted by *santeria* and moral decay, and yet again Moscow, stricken with memories and grief.

Arkady Vasilevich Renko, tall lank-haired son of a famous World War II Red Army general, appears first in *Gorky Park* (1981; winner of the Crime Writers' Association Gold Dagger and filmed in 1983). His sole trusted subordinate calls him "the only honest man in Moscow" (*Gorky Park* 43). As Chief Homicide Investigator for the MVD, the Soviet militia strictly limited to internal criminal cases, Renko clashes with Major Pribluda of the KGB, the infamous Soviet secret police charged with matters of state security, because the abyss between the Soviet system and its suffering citizens revolts him: "God, Arkady thought, an apparatus accuses...innocent people, abducts them to slave camps, tortures them, rips out the heart of their adult lives, and then, when one man [Arkady himself] from the apparatus treats them with the rudiments of decency, they are fountains of joy. What right did he have to a kind word from them?" (*Gorky Park* 21–22). When three frozen and mutilated corpses appear in Moscow's Gorky Park bearing Pribluda's brutal trademark, Renko, shadowed by a KGB informer passed off as an MVD officer, pursues an investigation that jeopardizes Renko's job, his life, and his very soul, for he falls in love with Irina Asanova, a beautiful dissident working at Mosfilm, the state-run movie studio.

Arkady buys Irina's freedom with his own imprisonment and exile to Siberia. In *Polar Star* (1989), set on a Russian factory ship that services American fishing trawlers in the Bering Sea, Renko probes a shipboard murder, and when the Soviet Union collapses, he returns to Moscow in *Red Square* (1992), to find the city dominated by the Russian mafia that runs the economy of the entire country. Surrounded by greedy remnants of the Soviet *nomenklatura* plundering the nation's assets, Renko clings to the voice of Irina Asanova he hears on Radio Liberty, an émigré station based in Germany. He finds her there—and the Russian mafia as well, swilling good German beer, touring the Autobahns in BMWs, and relentlessly searching for Investigator Renko, who knows too much about them. Arkady survives, but he tragically loses Irina. In *Havana Bay* (1999), suicidal from grief, he arrives in a down-at-heels Cuba now at odds with its former Russian mentors, to investigate Pribluda's disappearance despite opposition from both Russian and Cuban police systems. After Cuban detective Ofelia Osorio thaws his suicidal resolve, Renko returns to Moscow, as healed in soul as an honest man at the mercy of his corrupt government can be.

However, like Solzhenitsyn's Ivan Denisovich, another decent man victimized by Soviet Communism, Arkady's existence is defined by the dehumanizing totalitarianism that no matter its name has not yet perished from this earth. Prevented by his moral conscience from rising in the Party, Arkady lost his first wife Zoya to an unscrupulous bureaucrat. Driven by his scruples and his intuition to solve the Gorky Park murders, he loses his friend and partner Pasha to Party betrayal; coming full circle in *Havana Bay* (1999), unable to accept Cuban temporizing in the death of Pribluda, who has come to be a strange kind of friend, Arkady risks the life he had intended to throw away.

After Renko's harrowing trip back to Russia, *Wolves Eat Dogs* (2005) takes him into the post-Soviet Age and the eerie Zone of Exclusion around the sarcophagus of the Chernobyl nuclear plant, where, with his dosimeter constantly adding up the deadly radiation he's absorbing, Renko trawls for secrets connected to government corruption and shady capitalistic fortunes. According to a *Publishers Weekly* reviewer, Renko's "vulnerable heart and dogged temerity" are his weaknesses, especially in this bleakest of spiritual netherworlds.

In the Nobel Lecture the Soviets prevented him from presenting in person, Aleksandr Solzhenitsyn asked rhetorically what could sensitize human beings to the joys and sorrows of faraway others. His answer: "It is art. It is literature." "Soul," humanity's indefinable but distinguishing characteristic, is the special province of Russia's great realist writers, who insist that the price of sustaining the soul has always been the recognition of shared human suffering. Arkady Renko is a literary paradigm for all those faraway others who lived and died under Stalin and his successors and who are living and dying the same way still, decent human beings at the mercy of political-economic forces that refuse them their basic human rights and threaten their very souls. Renko's own soul—his unquenchable search for justice, his ability to cut through doublespeak, his profound capacity for love and grief, his refusal to sacrifice his principles to expedience—everything that pits Arkady Renko against the corrupt systems he faces makes him a hero of our precarious times, his quiet voice the voice of our brother.

Novels: *Gorky Park* (1981); *Polar Star* (1989); *Red Square* (1992); *Havana Bay* (1999); *December 6* (2002); *Wolves Eat Dogs* (2004).

Other series: The Inquisitor series (written as Simon Quinn and since disowned by Smith), features Francis Xavier Killy, a lay brother Vatican investigator: *His Eminence, Death* (1974); *Nuplex Red* (1974); *The Devil in Kansas* (1974); *The Last Time I Saw Kansas* (1974); *The Midas Coffin* (1975); *Last Rites for the Vulture* (1975). Under "Simon Quinn," Smith also authored numerous "Slocum" novels and other stand-alone Western novels.

Nonfiction: Smith edited *Death by Espionage: Intriguing Stories of Betrayal and Deception* (1999).

Other works: Smith has also written stand-alone novels under his own name, notably *Stallion Gate* (1986), a novel about the Manhattan Project that developed and tested the first atomic bomb, and *Rose* (1996), a historical novel about mining conditions in Victorian England.

Selected sources: Beddow, Reid. Rev. of *Red Square. Washington Post Book World*, November 1, 1992: 3; Conaty, Barbara. Rev. of *December 6. Library Journal*, August 2002: 147; Ott, Bill. Rev. of *Havana Bay. Booklist*, May 1, 2000: 1590; *Publishers Weekly*. Rev. of *Wolves Eat Dogs*, January 3, 2005: 41; Stasio, Marilyn. Rev. of *Red Square. New York Times Book Review*, June 16, 1996: 50.

Major awards: CWA Gold Dagger, 1981, for *Gorky Park*; Hammett Prize, 1997, 2000.

Web site: www.literati.net/MCSmith.

See also: The Adam Hall (pseud. of Elleston Trevor) Quiller series, set in Boris Yeltsin's Russia; Stuart Kaminsky's series featuring Inspector Porfiry Rostnikov of the Moscow Police and later sent to the Office of Special Investigations, suspected by his organization because he is married to a Jewish woman; Reggie Nadelson's series featuring Russian-born New York police detective (later private investigator) Artie Cohen, dealing with the Russian Mafia and the problems created by the dissolution of the Soviet Union. For a historical nineteenth-century tsarist Russian milieu, see Boris Akunin's **Erast Fandorin** series.

Dave Robicheaux

Profession:	Police detective
Living situation:	Divorced, then twice widowed; remarried
Geographic locale:	Cajun country, Louisiana
Time period:	1987–present
Associate:	Cletus Purcel
Nemeses:	Alcohol; "the beast within"; "upper class" exploitation of the land and its poor; in *Crusader's Cross*, Valentine Chalons
Significant relationships:	Annie Ballard; Bootsie
Concerns:	The past, especially the Vietnam War; justice; Roman Catholicism; morality; environmentalism; state-supported terrorism

James Lee Burke's "passionate and unforgettable" stories featuring Cajun detective Dave "Streak" Robicheaux "are amongst the darkest, most intense novels in the genre, spiking the traditional hard-boiled novel with gothic noir" (Ashley 73). Burke pulls no punches about the "dark Southern fascination with man's iniquity"; Robicheaux's file drawer is loaded with misery, "a microcosm of an aberrant world" (*Neon Rain* 71, 11) filled with mayhem, vice, sadism, and torture. These books are not for the fainthearted—or for those of little faith.

Contradictions dominate Dave Robicheaux's life and work. In *The Neon Rain* (1987), he's a fourteen-year veteran of the New Orleans Police Department fueled with Dr. Pepper (extra cherries and lime slices) and oyster and shrimp po' boys. He's got a hard lean body, hair and moustache still black as the sins he faces, a scar from a dung-dipped *punji* stick coiling around his belly like the nightmares of 'Nam that nightly writhe inside his brain. He treats street people well and puts away bad guys, often permanently and nearly always violently, but going to Sunday Masses and frequent AA meetings can't exorcise his inner demons. Raised after his mother's death by a father who tried but left Dave and his half-brother Jimmie malnourished in body and spirit, Robicheaux now believes his "years of drinking had taught me not to trust my unconscious, because it planned things for me in a cunning fashion that was usually a disaster for me, or for the people around me, or for all of us" (*Neon Rain* 72–73). Blaming himself for the inability to control that beast within him is the guilty fallout from his conservative Roman Catholicism, exacerbating the deadly conflicts that Robicheaux seems to welcome, a chiaroscuro miniature of late-twentieth-century American culture.

In *The Neon Rain*, big-city New Orleans corruption clashes against Robicheaux's old vanishing rural Louisiana when he refuses to drop the case of a young black prostitute drowned in a bayou, echoing the nemesis he excruciatingly holds in fragile check, the redneck from 'Nam who drowns him in his nightmares. Robicheaux insists both inwardly and to Annie Ballard, who believes more in him than he can in himself, that "What happens outside of us doesn't count. It's how we react to it that's important" (*Neon Rain* 39). He hangs on despite a contract on his life, the Nicaraguan mafia, and off-the-leash government spooks, but when he discovers that his friend and partner Clete Purcel, also battling the bottle, is a bent cop, Robicheaux slips off the wagon again, framed and suspended from the police force.

Robicheaux's subsequent cases find him riding hell-for-leather on the pendulum between sobriety and alcoholism. In *Heaven's Prisoners* (1988), Annie's saved Robicheaux and married him, but their tranquil life running a bayou bait shop shatters when a nearby plane crash leaves a dead priest-activist and a live Latina child, whom Robicheaux later adopts. In the ensuing big-time drug investigation, Robicheaux's no-holds-barred style clashes with his growing sympathy for the suffering people— even the criminals—around him, a position severely tested in *Black Cherry Blues* (1989), after hit men kill Annie, who now, along with his dead father, haunts his dreams too. Debt forces Robicheaux to join New Iberia's police force in *A Morning for Flamingos* (1990), where he fights the "secret pleasure" he feels when he kills (*Neon Rain* 100) under the mission of protecting the downtrodden. Married to his old girlfriend Bootsie, Robicheaux confronts fears that constantly shake his faith as he digs into a prominent family's secrets in *Stained White Radiance* (1992) while uncovering his own mother's murder and defusing his adopted daughter Alafair's infatuation with a hoodlum in *Purple Cane Road* (2000). After losing Bootsie to lupus, Robicheaux and Clete Purcel, now straight, test the limits of their dedication to justice in *Last Car to Elysian Fields* (2003). Purcel, "the bravest and most loyal and most self-destructive man" Robicheaux says he ever knew (since he cannot know himself completely) (*Elysian Fields* 186), swings between being Robicheaux's conscience and his enforcer, because even twice widowed and middle-aged, Robicheaux is still "a magnet for trouble" (*Elysian Fields* 162). Trouble follows him through *Crusader's Cross* (2005), where he clashes with brothel owner Valentine Chalons, descended from a Norman French family going back to the crusades. When Chalons ridicules Robicheaux and his new wife, a former nun, and sends a contract killer after him, Robicheaux takes violent steps to stop Chalons, but in doing so he falls off the wagon and into a "spectacular bender" (Stasio 31).

Robicheaux does acknowledge that his wounds will never heal: "All drunks fear and desire both power and control, and sometimes even years of sobriety inside AA don't rid alcoholics of that basic contradiction in their personalities. Why should I be any different?" (*Elysian Fields* 165). Far more painful than the physical torture his antagonists inflict are the defeats this "violent and driven man" (*Elysian Fields* 301) imposes on himself, clawing himself out of the sad downward spiral of drink only to fall again and again. And yet—the "and yet" that makes Dave Robicheaux so convincing a suffering hero—somehow enough faith that grace will come saves him in his darkest nights of the soul. When, desperate, he visited Bootsie's tomb by the bayou one evening in *Elysian Fields*, her voice rises as a gift from Dave Robicheaux's tormented unconscious, overriding all the guilt and rage with which he scourges himself, like the rebellious spirit of seventeenth-century metaphysical poet George Herbert's "The Collar":

> But as I rav'd and grew more fierce and wilde
>> At every word,
> Me thought I heard one calling, *"Child!"*
>> And I reply'd *"My Lord."*

Novels: *The Neon Rain* (1987); *Heaven's Prisoners* (1988); *Black Cherry Blues* (1989); *A Morning for Flamingos* (1990); *A Stained White Radiance* (1992); *In the Electric Mist with Confederate Dead* (1993); *Dixie City Jam* (1994); *Burning Angel* (1995); *Cadillac Jukebox* (1996); *Sunset Limited* (1998); *Purple Cane Road* (2000); *Jolie Blon's Bounce* (2002); *Last Car to Elysian Fields* (2003); *Crusader's Cross* (2005).

Other series (Texas lawyer Billy Bob Holland): *Cimarron Rose* (1997); *Heartwood* (1999); *Bitterroot* (2001); *In the Moon of Red Ponies* (2004).

Stand-alone novels: Burke's stand-alone novels include *The Lost Get-Back Boogie*, now considered one of his best, published in 1986 after ten years and ninety-three rejection slips. In his literary footsteps, his daughter Alafair Burke is also writing mysteries.

Short fiction: *The Convict and Other Stories* (1985).

Selected sources: Mendelsohn, Daniel. "Quien es mas macho?" *Esquire*, October 2000: 100; Ott, Bill. Rev. of *Sunset Limited*. *Booklist*, April 15, 1998: 1376; *Publishers Weekly*. Rev. of *Cadillac Jukebox*, June 9, 1997: 35; Signor, Randy Michael. Rev. of *The Purple Cane Road*. *Book*, September 2000: 73; Stasio, Marilyn. "Swamp Thing." *New York Times Book Review*, July 10, 2005: 31; Yardley, Jonathan. "A Fun, Foul Romp Through the Bayou." *Washington Post*, June 10, 1998: D2.

Major awards: Pulitzer Prize nomination, 1987; Edgar Award, Mystery Writers of America, 1989; Guggenheim Fellow, 1989; Crime Writers' Association Gold Dagger, 1998; Edgar nomination and Hammett Prize nominee, International Association of Crime Writers, 2003.

See also: James Ellroy's noir explorations of U.S. social history prior to Watergate: the Lloyd Hopkins trilogy released in 1998 as *L.A. Noir*; the *L.A. Quartet*; and Hopkins's Underworld U.S.A. series; for the New Orleans setting, Ace Atkins; "roots music field researcher" Nick Turner series; David Fulmer's series featuring Creole Valentine St. Cyr; Carolyn Haines's Mississippi Delta series featuring New Orleans private investigator Sarah Booth Delaney; Walter Mosley's **Easy Rawlins** series; James Sallis's Lew Griffin series; Julie Smith's Louisiana series featuring female PI Talba Wallis.

Horace Rumpole

Profession:	Barrister
Living situation:	Married
Geographic locale:	London
Time period:	1978–present
Nemeses:	Judge Bullingham; "Soapy Sam" ("Bonzo") Ballard
Significant relationship:	"She Who Must Be Obeyed" (Hilda Rumpole)
Concern:	Rights of the underdog

John Mortimer, a barrister and Queen's Counsel himself, modeled his popular character Horace Rumpole on his own father, "a distinguished if eccentric barrister" specializing in divorce cases, who recited Sherlock Holmes stories to his only child on long walks in the Chiltern Hills (Herbert 136). Reversing the usual mystery progress from print to film or television, Mortimer introduced Rumpole in a 1975 television play, *Rumpole of the Bailey*, that grew into a 1978–1992 series starring Leo McKern. Mortimer then adapted the individual television episodes into short stories that he continued to write after the series closed.

Jon L. Breen of *Armchair Detective* has called Rumpole "one of the great characters of English literature" (quoted in *CA:NR* 109: 273). Horace Rumpole's career as a "shambling knight-errant" (Ashley 348) began during the Thatcher Era, which British socialists in the idealistic George Bernard Shaw mold like Mortimer himself held responsible for perpetuating "conservatives, class distinctions, unemployment." In Rumpole, Mortimer incarnated his conviction that "compassion for the less fortunate" should "be your dominant political feeling," and, as Mortimer said about idealism, apropos of his novel *Paradise Postponed*, "whether [paradise] fails or not, it's better to have believed in it than taken the other view" (quoted in *CA:NR* 109: 272). In *Rumpole and the Penge Bungalow Murders* (2004), Horace Rumpole looks back to his novice days at the Old Bailey and a case of war heroes apparently shot dead after a reunion dinner by Simon Jerrold, the son of one of them. Even though he was young then and relatively inexperienced, Rumpole tenaciously tackled the job of saving Jerrold, in the process answering numerous questions about himself, especially how he came to be the object of She Who Must Be Obeyed's desire and how he made the reputation that still echoes around London's Old Bailey today.

Rumpole's adventures all conform to the same formula: "A mystery is presented that contains the possibility of a subject to ponder—the workman's right to withhold his labor, say, or the citizen's right to remain silent when charged with an offense" (Donald E. Westlake, quoted in *CA:NR* 109: 273). Rumpole's creed "included a simple faith in trial by jury and the presumption of innocence" and his Eleventh Commandment is "Thou Shalt Not Plead Guilty" (*Rests His Case* 32), so he treats victims and perpetrators alike with good humor, uncanny discernment, and invariable concern for the underdog. According to Mortimer, "a writer of comedy…cannot afford to aim at the [defenceless], nor can he, like the more serious writer, treat any character with contempt" (quoted in *CA:NR* 109: 273), so Rumpole never fails to direct his keenest barbs at himself and what he perceives to be his own shortcomings.

Throughout his many stories, Rumpole himself remains in his late sixties. Like Samuel Johnson, he's portrayed "warts and all," usually disheveled, overweight, "soup-stained, smoking the smallest cigars and drinking the cheapest claret" (Sarah Caudwell in Herbert 170), like "Chateau Thames Embankment" (*Rests His Case* 35), and he describes himself as an "Old Bailey hack," "an old black cab plying for hire" (*Rests His Case* 32). According to Rumpole, "Q.C." stands for "Queer Customer" (*Rests His Case* 42), so he never "takes silk" in the footsteps of his formidable wife Hilda's equally formidable "Daddy" by becoming a Head of Chambers or Queen's Counsel as She Who Must Be Obeyed always hoped. Rumpole never takes on the big lucrative corporation law cases, either. He restricts himself to defending criminals when he believes there are mitigating circumstances to their cases, an occasional homicide but far more often such petty crimes as shoplifting, burglary, or fraud. He usually wins his cases.

Rumpole makes it easy for others to underestimate him, because he conceals an effective arsenal under his unprepossessing appearance. That disreputable exterior hides a sharp mind given often to quoting the "greats" of English literature, and like his literary ancestors Sherlock Holmes and Hercule Poirot, he quickly pounces on the smallest clue that can turn a case upside down and reveal the truth (Sarah Caudwell in Herbert 170). Rumpole likes to lull bumptious colleagues, opposing barristers, and hostile witnesses into dismissing him as a bumbling superannuated fool, whereupon he cannily spots their vulnerabilities and tidily skewers their mis-representations. "There is a tide in the affairs of men," Rumpole believes, "when you have to be completely ruthless" (*Rests His Case* 53). To keep his study comfortably smoke-filled, for instance, he presents his overbearing Head of Chambers "Soapy Sam" Ballard with an incriminating 1960s photo of himself as "Bonzo" Ballard playing with the Pithead Stompers and holding a guitar "in a horribly suggestive fashion" (*Rests His Case* 52). Most of the people around Rumpole, though, consider him a failure, and besides dealing with the constant sniping of She Who Must Be Obeyed, Rumpole also must contend with his Chambers colleagues who are scheming to pasture him out into retirement.

According to Sarah Caudwell, Rumpole's "virtues, rather than his shortcomings, preclude success." In the 1980s, when great universities hurled *Beowulf*, Chaucer, Dante, and the rest of the traditional literary canon wholesale out of their curricula, Rumpole as a lover of the language of Shakespeare and Wordsworth "cannot become fluent in the latest fashionable jargon." In a time of burgeoning corruption, Rumpole always puts his duty to his client first, so "he cannot be expediently polite to prej-udiced or overbearing judges." Since he compassionately understands the horrors of today's prison life, too, "he cannot summon up the ambition to appear for the prosecution, still less to pass sentence." Like many scapegoat heroes, aging Horace Rumpole "attains heroic stature not despite failure, but because of it" (Sarah Caudwell, quoted in Herbert 170). Even better, according to Alexander McCall Smith, who himself charmingly meshes a judicial mind with a playful grasp of life's humorous iniquities, Rumpole's tales are "a potent tonic against all the miserable monochrome features of our days" (Smith 35).

Novel: *Rumpole and the Penge Bungalow Murders* (2004).

Short stories: *Rumpole of the Bailey* (1978); *The Trials of Rumpole* (1979); *Rumpole's Return* (1980); *Regina v. Rumpole* (1981); *Rumpole and the Golden Thread* (1983); *Rumpole's Last Case* (1987); *Rumpole and the Age of Miracles* (1988); *Rumpole à la Carte* (1990); *Rumpole on Trial* (1992); *Rumpole and the Angel of Death* (1995); *Rumpole Rests His Case* (2002); *Rumpole and the Primrose Path* (2003).

Other series: The Maggie Perowne television series, set in an auction house: *Under the Hammer* (1994).

Other works: Mortimer also published *Three Plays* (1958) and *The Judge* (1967). He has served as editor for *Great Law and Order Stories* (1990); *Famous Trials* (1984); *The Oxford Book of Villains* (1992).

Autobiographies: *Clinging to the Wreckage* (1982); *Murderers and Other Friends* (1994); *The Summer of a Dormouse* (2000); *Where There's a Will* (2005); *Quite Honestly* (2006).

Selected sources: Coleman, Peter. "Sir John Mortimer: My Best Teacher." *Times Literary Supplement*, October 10, 2004: 4–6; O'Conner, Patricia T. "Wigged Out?" *New York Times Book Review*, December 8, 2002: 8; Scott, Whitney. Rev. of *Rumpole and the Penge Bungalow Murders. Booklist*, April 15, 2005: 144; Smith, Alexander McCall. "Closing Arguments." *The New York Times Book Review*, June 5, 2005: 35; Stasio, Marilyn. Rev. of *Rumpole Rests His Case. New York Times Book Review*, June 1, 2003: 20; Stasio, Marilyn. "The Jewel Case." *New York Times Book Review*, November 28, 2004: 17.

Major awards: Italia Prize, 1958; Screenwriters Guild Award, 1970: British Academy Award, 1980; Mortimer received the CBE in 1986 and was knighted in 1998.

See also: The J.P. Hailey (pseudonym of Parnell Hall) Steve Winslow series, modeled on Perry Mason's American courtroom dramas; Paul Levine's series featuring humorous courtroom scenes involving American former linebacker, now attorney, Jake Lassiter; Sarah Caudwell's series featuring Cambridge law professor **Hilary Tamar** and tax lawyer Julia Larwood and her colleagues. British solicitor Michael Gilbert also incorporates legal knowledge and characters into his Inspector Hazelrigg procedural series.

Mary Russell

Profession:	Assistant to Sherlock Holmes
Living situation:	American father, English mother; Jewish; orphaned; married after first novel
Geographic locale:	Home: Sussex, England; cases: worldwide, often exotic venues
Time Period:	Early twentieth century
Associate:	Sherlock Holmes

330 ■ Mary Russell

Significant relationship: Initially apprentice, then wife to Sherlock Holmes

Concerns: Theology; crime-solving; feminism

Laurie R. King claims that since Conan Doyle's Sherlock Holmes retired in 1914 and King's creation Mary Russell met him the following year, "After 1914, Holmes is mine" (*Talking Murder* 150). She creates Russell-Holmes "romance[s] in the old style, dressing up in costumes and going off to Wales or Palestine . . . great fun, but the whole basis of the thing is fantasy" (*Talking Murder* 145). King's seven Sherlock Holmes pastiches are also considered "character-driven explorations of life" (Ashley 173), and what characters her Sherlock Holmes and Mary Russell are—Holmes in his vigorous fifties the epitome of the intellectual, rigorously deductive late Victorian amateur detective, Mary Russell a brilliant, uncompromising, independently wealthy modern and liberated young woman.

In *The Beekeeper's Apprentice*, containing short stories set in 1915 (begun 1987; King's second published novel, 1994), Mary is fifteen and the orphaned daughter of an American father and an English mother, living in Sussex as the unwilling ward of her insufferable maternal aunt, when one day rebelliously wandering the Downs she encounters Holmes, recently retired and living in a nearby cottage with his motherly housekeeper Mrs. Hudson. Over the next two years, a lively series of comedy-of-manners cases ensues, with Mary's need for companionship increasingly drawing her to Holmes, who recognizes and stimulates her intellect and her capacity for keen observation. After she assists him in solving several local cases with Dr. Watson and Holmes's high-ranking spook-director brother Mycroft hovering nearby, Holmes in heavy disguise plucks Mary from her second year at Oxford and they embark for the Middle East, where under deep cover they successfully conclude politically sensitive investigations before returning to England.

Shortly before Mary comes of age and inherits her parents' considerable fortune, she escapes a houseful of dismaying relatives for London, the scene of Nero Wolfe Award–winning *A Monstrous Regiment of Women* (1995), where Mary's former Oxford classmate Lady Veronica Beaconsfield introduces her to the charismatic putative mystic Margery Childe, leader of a quasi-religious group of do-gooding women. In this novel, Mary confronts early-twentieth-century feminism, problems of the English class system, and social issues like poverty and workers' rights, while she seeks her own identity. Torn between her emotional side, which finds a women's community and a personal religion attractive, and the complicated appeal of intellectual stimulation and emotional affection that Holmes represents for her, Mary eventually discovers who she really is: Holmes's partner for life.

Mary's profound interest in theology, which she studied at Oxford and which is constantly being interrupted by the demands of their joint detecting avocation, plays a significant role in *A Monstrous Regiment of Women*. As a scholar, Mary can coolly explore the ramifications of religious belief, and as a Jew, Mary can convincingly view Christianity from the outside; her detachment and competence prove an intriguing challenge for Holmes's ambivalence about religion. In *A Letter of Mary* (1996), which finds Holmes and Mary as unconventional but convincing newlyweds, the sexual tension between them has been appropriately resolved. After a woman archaeologist brings them an ancient papyrus purportedly written by Mary of Magdala referring to herself as one of Christ's apostles, the archaeologist is murdered, and Holmes as religious skeptic and Mary as Jewish scholar pursue diverging directions to find the killer and grapple with a potential disruption of traditional religious and sexual norms: does the concept of a woman apostle threaten Christianity or enlighten it?

The Moor (1998) returns Holmes and Mary in 1923 to the murky scene of *The Hound of the Baskervilles*. *O Jerusalem* (1999) takes place in 1919 British-occupied Palestine during their unconventional courtship, and *Justice Hall* (2002), opens just hours after their return from two back-to-back cases, chronologically following their 1923 adventure of *The Moor* but linked with the characters from *O Jerusalem* (preface to *Justice Hall*). *The Game* (2004) draws on King's experience of India through her travels with her Anglo-Indian husband, tracing the intricate search Holmes and Mary Russell undertake at Mycroft's request to find a British operative missing near the border with Imperial Russia–none other than the legendary Kimball O'Hara, model for Rudyard Kipling's famous Kim. *Locked Rooms* (2005) brings Mary Russell to San Francisco in 1922, supposedly to settle her father's estate, but in actuality to come to terms with her unsettling childhood memories. Holmes enlists Pinkerton agent Dashiell Hammett to investigate an attempt on Mary's life, while Mary, until now a paragon of self-possession, confronts her own inner demons while attempting to unravel the secrets of her past, particularly the alleged "accident" that left her orphaned.

In each of these splendidly realized novels, Mary Russell proves herself a worthy partner to Sherlock Holmes in every way, matter-of-factly steeling herself to adapt to primitive plumbing, disgusting native cookery, brash and bumptious American society travelers (though she does have qualms of conscience about deceiving a trusting teenager), and the necessity of frequently leaving Holmes to unspeakable dangers while herself facing down fates worse than death in the form of murderous ruffians, amorous predatory maharajahs, and inexperienced "pig-sticking" expeditions hunting fearsome wild boar. By creating Mary Russell as an eminently suitable match for her re-created and humanized Sherlock Holmes in these romantic but satisfyingly realistic adventures, Laurie King effectively justifies the popularity of crime writing, which she herself defines as "traditional story-telling in a nontraditional age" (*Talking Murder* 153).

Novels: *The Beekeeper's Apprentice* (1993); *A Monstrous Regiment of Women* (1995); *A Letter of Mary* (1996); *The Moor* (1998); *O Jerusalem* (1999); *Justice Hall* (2002); *Locked Rooms* (2005).

Other series: **Kate Martinelli** series, featuring contemporary lesbian California police detective Martinelli: *A Grave Talent* (1993); *To Play the Fool* (1995); *With Child* (1996); *Night Work* (1999).

Stand-alone novels: *A Darker Place* (1999); *Folly* (2001); *Keeping Watch* (2003).

Selected sources (see also Kate Martinelli entry): Corrigan, Maureen. Rev. of *O Jerusalem*. *Washington Post Book World*, July 18, 1999: 5; Dowell, Pat. "Sherlock Rusticates." *Washington Post Book World*, February 20, 1994: 8; Hahn, Robert. "*PW* Talks with Laurie

King." *Publishers Weekly*, February 18, 2002: 78–79; includes review of *Justice Hall*; Melton, Emily. Rev. of *The Beekeeper's Apprentice*. *Booklist*, February 1, 1994: 997; *Mystery Guide.com*. Rev. of *The Beekeeper's Apprentice*, www.mysteryguide.com; Woodcock, Susan. Rev. of *A Letter of Mary*. *School Library Journal*, June 1997: 151.

Major awards: Edgar (Best First Novel), 1994; Agatha Award nomination, 1994, and American Library Association best book citation, 1996, all for *The Beekeeper's Apprentice*; Nero Wolfe Award, 1996, for *The Monstrous Regiment of Women*; honorary doctorate from Church Divinity School of the Pacific; also see entry for Kate Martinelli.

See also: For the real thing, Leslie S. Klinger's *The New Annotated Sherlock Holmes* (2004). For a few recent Sherlock Holmes–related novels, see such recent efforts as Carole Nelson Douglas's **Irene Adler** series; Caleb Carr's *The Italian Secretary* (2005); Brian Fremantle's series featuring detective Sebastian Holmes, the Great Detective's son; Mitch Cullin's *A Slight Trick of the Mind*, featuring an extremely aged Holmes; John Lescroart's stand-alone novel *Son of Holmes* (2003), set during World War I and featuring Auguste Lupa, rumored to be Holmes's son, conceived during one of the Great Detective's European lacunae; Barry Roberts's Holmes and Watson novels; Alan Vanneman's Holmes and Watson novels. For historical novels of the late Victorian period, see Rhys Bowen's Molly Murphy series, set in 1900s New York; Richard Crabbe's New York City detective Tom Braddock series; Oakley Hall's series featuring real-life journalist Ambrose Bierce in 1890s San Francisco; Victoria Thompson's Detective Sergeant Frank Malloy, set in New York City in the 1900s; and somewhat further back in time, Michael Killian's Civil War series featuring spy Harrison Raines and Harold Schlechter's series featuring Edgar Allan Poe in the 1840s.

Debut novel: Will Thomas's *Some Danger Involved*, modeled after Sherlock Holmes's mysteries and featuring Thomas Llewelyn and his Great Detective mentor Cyrus Barker, who explore London's Jewish quarter in the Victorian period.

Ian Rutledge

Profession:	Inspector, Scotland Yard
Living situation:	Single
Geographic locale:	England
Time period:	1919–
Associate:	The imagined voice of Corporal Hamish MacLeod
Nemesis:	Chief Superintendent Bowles
Concerns:	Post-traumatic Stress Disorder (shell shock); loss of innocence; the inescapability of the past

By November, 1918, British patriotism—"It is sweet and fitting to die for one's country"—had become what Wilfred Owen called "the old lie." In World War I Britain lost 750,000 men, a tenth of those it had mobilized, and two million returned blinded, gassed, and shell-shocked, bankrupting the nation of its future leaders. Most of Britain's young officers came from its educated class, and their battlefield life expectancy was a matter of weeks; two out of three of them died in

Europe or were forever incapacitated. Charles Todd's Scotland Yard Inspector turned Army lieutenant Ian Rutledge "covered himself with mud and glory" in France (*Test of Wills* 3), but was invalided home to spend months in hospital, wounded, severely claustrophobic, emotionally broken and silent: in the bloodbath of the Somme he had had to order his friend Hamish MacLeod executed for refusing a direct order to advance into certain death.

Ghosts long thought buried rise to haunt all of Rutledge's murder cases after he returns to Scotland Yard in 1919, ever struggling to maintain his sanity because he constantly hears Hamish's ghostly Scots voice in his mind's ear, mocking and tormenting him. He also endures the burning animosity of Chief Superintendent Bowles, a North Country miner's son who hates Rutledge for his intellect, his brilliant prewar record with the Yard, his upper-class breeding, his very survival: "If there'd been any justice," Bowles tells himself, peering into Rutledge's "thin, pale face" and "tired eyes," "a German bayonet would have finished this soldier along with the rest of them!" (*Test of Wills* 5). Bowles seeks to destroy Rutledge by sending him as an expendable scapegoat to investigate nasty cases throughout Britain where "discretion, background, and experience were essential . . . [and] someone's head was bound to roll" (*Test of Wills* 3).

A Test of Wills (1996) deals with the cold-blooded murder of popular Warwickshire Colonel Harris, a political minefield since the prime suspect is a decorated war hero and close friend of the Prince of Wales. Rutledge's most crucial witness is shell shocked, too, a constant reminder of how precarious Rutledge's own grip on reality is. Having learned to face dying in France, Rutledge now has to face living, "ten thousand memories waiting like enemies to ambush him" (*Test of Wills* 7), like those of his fiancée Jean who'd abandoned him in the hospital to his nightmares. Rutledge must probe long-buried emotions in others while his own ragged ones keep torturing him. His eventual success is tainted, for Hamish declares, "Ye'll no' triumph over me! I'm a scar on your bluidy soul" (*Test of Wills* 328).

In *Wings of Fire* (1998) Bowles's "amber goat's eyes" gleam at sending Rutledge far away to satisfy an obscure and querulous—and influential—dowager's suspicions of foul play in three family deaths, while Bowles himself pursues a series of publicity-rich Ripper-style murders in London (15). Once in Cornwall, Rutledge beats down Hamish's cynicism and probes the childhood secrets of one of the dead, Olivia Marlowe, a reclusive writer whose war poetry had helped sustain Rutledge in the trenches. Sent to identify a woman's remains on a bleak Scottish mountainside in *Legacy of the Dead* (2000)—"Failure," Chief Superintendent Bowles tells him, "is unacceptable" (18), Rutledge relives his last hours with Hamish: to save a thousand lives, Rutledge had to sacrifice one, ordering the firing squad when Hamish refused to fight. Rutledge himself delivered the coup de grâce to the severely wounded Highlander, survived a German shell only because MacLeod's body had protected him, and came home two years later bringing the dead man with him (*Legacy of the Dead* 25). This agonizing case exorcises Rutledge's thoughts of suicide, for when a shot takes him in the chest, Rutledge hurls a dirk as his Scots soldiers had taught him, killing his assailant, while Hamish insists, "I willna' let you die!" (*Legacy* 350).

The eerie relationship Rutledge shares with his dead friend Hamish gradually modulates into a less corrosive coexistence. In *Watchers of Time* (2001), Rutledge, tormented by the memories of the dead Scots he had had to order into No Man's Land, returns to work early. Wishing Rutledge "might die of septicemia" Chief Superintendent Bowles rushes him out of London again, this time on a courtesy visit to a Norfolk parish whose priest has been murdered (23, 25). Hamish's voice is quieter, often offering dour information, sober insights, and laconic warnings: "Hamish was all that had kept him awake…and even Hamish had lost his edge" (*Watchers* 143). Rutledge is learning to live with the guilt he will never completely lose. He is also coming to terms with an England forever changed, "a generation growing up wild" (*Watchers* 251), a loss of an innocence that, like his own, can never be regained. Not Bowles but Rutledge's own conscience forces him into *A Fearsome Doubt* (2002) on the eve of the Armistice's anniversary, with his faith in his professional judgment, one of the few threads holding him together, harshly shaken when the widow of a man Rutledge had sent to the gallows twelve years earlier produces evidence to clear her husband's name. Forced to confront even more of his own inadequacies and fears, Rutledge solves the crime at another harrowing personal cost, just as in his next case, *A Cold Treachery* (2005), he again approaches his private abyss, haunted by Hamish's inexorable ghost, as he probes the gruesome massacre of a rural Lake District family.

Acknowledging the past and its terrible secrets, inescapable as Hamish's scathing voice at the back of his mind, makes both Rutledge's work and his slow healing possible. Despite all his pain, Ian Rutledge repeatedly earns the right to stand with his doomed comrade Rupert Brooke, "for sense, / Invincible, inviolable, eternal…I stand for Sanity."

Novels: *A Test of Wills* (1996); *Wings of Fire* (1998); *Search the Dark* (1999); *Watchers of Time* (2000); *Legacy of the Dead* (2001); *A Fearsome Doubt* (2002); *A Cold Treachery* (2005); *A Long Shadow* (2006).

Stand-alone novel: *The Murder Stone* (2003).

Selected sources: Bliss, Laurel. Rev. of *A Cold Treachery*. *Library Journal*, January 2005: 85; Connors, Theresa. Rev. of *Legacy of the Dead*. *Library Journal*, May 1, 2003: 169; Picker, Leonard. "Anguish and Redemption: *PW* Talks with Charles Todd." *Publishers Weekly*, December 6, 2004: 47; *Publishers Weekly*. Rev. of *A Fearsome Doubt*, September 2, 2002: 57; Stasio, Marilyn. "Dead and Bloated." *New York Times Book Review*, February 6, 2005: 25.

Major awards: Barry Award, best first novel, 1997; Herodotus Award, best short story, 2001. *Wings of Fire* was shortlisted for the Ellis Peters Historical Dagger Award, Crime Writers' Association.

Web site: www.charlestodd.com.

See also: Rennie Airth's post–World War I series featuring Scotland Yard Inspector John Madden; Kerry Greenwood's **Phryne Fisher** series, set in Australia with flashbacks to World War I; Anne Perry's series featuring Chaplain Joseph Reavley, set before and during World War I: *Shoulder the Sky* (2004); *No Graves as Yet* (2005); Jacqueline Winspear's **Maisie Dobbs** series, set in England.

Father "Blackie" Ryan

Profession:	Roman Catholic priest, eventually Auxiliary Bishop
Living situation:	Single
Geographic locale:	Chicago
Time period:	1985–present
Associate:	"Mike the Cop" Casey
Concerns:	Ultra-progressive post–Vatican II Roman Catholic and ultra-liberal political and sociological positions

As an heir to G.K. Chesterton's sleuth Father Brown, enormously prolific Andrew Greeley's Father John Blackwood "Blackie" Ryan is "caring, endearing, shrewd but not wholly worldly" (Herbert 35), but as the offspring of Father Greeley's maverick sociological and theological views, Ryan can also seem inflammatory and upsetting, since Greeley has been occasionally derided by his own church as "the renegade priest who wrote 'steamy novels' to make money" (*Contemporary Authors Autobiography Series*).

Greeley describes himself as a priest first, and he has given most of his book profits away, though when he tried to pledge a million dollars for Chicago's inner-city Catholic schools, then-Cardinal Bernardin turned it down, according to Greeley "arguably the first time in history the Catholic Church has turned down money from anyone" (*CAAS*). "Arguably" is one of Blackie Ryan's favorite words, too. Blackie ironically refers to himself often as "arguably the most unimpressive of humans" (*L Train* 67), fictional Sean Cardinal Cronin's "grey eminence," recalling Cardinal Richelieu, who schemed his way to control of France's entire government in the 1500s, suppressing dissent, fostering the arts, and taxing his people into submission.

Captivated as a young man by Catholic writers like G.K. Chesterton and Evelyn Waugh, Greeley came to consider fiction "a brilliant way of passing on religion" (*CAAS*), but Blackie Ryan's religious views, like his creator's, are highly unorthodox. Greeley told the *New York Times Magazine* in 1984 that he tries in his fiction to address the religious issues closest to him, among them the position of women in the Church, the responsibilities of the Catholic hierarchy, and the issue of human sexuality. Greeley, officially refused a Chicago parish and treated as a "non-person" by the Catholic Church, advocates the ordination of women; Ryan habitually refers to God as "She." Greeley describes the present leadership of the church as "morally, intellectually, and religiously bankrupt" and its hierarchy as "mitred pinheads"; Ryan goes a step farther, only half in jest declaring that to be rid of an embarrassing subordinate (referred to as "Idiot"), "in the best traditions of the Sacred College [of Cardinals] we would have dispatched Idiot with poison" (*L Train* 13). Greeley has also promoted "sexier" sexual relationships between spouses, suggesting that a wife greet her husband "wearing only panties and a martini pitcher—or maybe only the martini pitcher" (Greeley's "How to Be Sexy" chapter in his *Sexual Intimacy*, 1973); Ryan is hypersensitive to sexual allurements between others, though resolutely celibate himself.

Like Greeley, too, Blackie Ryan finds the old Baltimore Catechism "hopelessly inadequate," insisting that in marriage, "the union between man and woman . . . discloses that God loves us with a passion that exceeds, but is not totally unlike, the passion between man and woman," a justification for Ryan's—and Greeley's—solution to the thorny pastoral problem of divorced and remarried Catholics, one at the root of many of the criminal acts Cronin sends Blackie to "see to." Both Greeley and Blackie think the whole Catholic Church annulment process should be closed down, on the grounds that "God wants everyone around the banquet table," a position that had German bishops who recently advocated it slapped down by the Vatican but followed quietly by many American Catholic pastors.

In discreetly solving cases potentially damaging to Cronin and the Archdiocese of Chicago, Blackie customarily takes just such a sub rosa approach, appealing "to the emotions and the whole personality" as "the best way to talk about religion" (*New York Times Magazine* 36). Blackie is constantly supported by his extended South Side Irish Catholic family, especially his sister Eileen, a Federal judge, and his cousin "Mike the Cop" Casey, head of a private security firm and Watson to Blackie's pudgy anti-Holmesian Coke-bottle-bespectacled investigatory persona (*L Train* 260).

Though Greeley has never been considered a great novelist, Blackie Ryan has become a highly popular fictional detective. Having gotten beyond most fleshly temptations except cookies and Bushmill's, Blackie Ryan consistently loves the sinner but hates the sin, rising in his diocese in support of his elegant "Milord" Cronin. In the process, Blackie ferrets out failings in "the private lives of powerful, celibate men." Blackie's tongue-in-cheek tales help satisfy the laity's curiosity about such men with what Abigail McCarthy has called a combination of "an apparently inside view of Catholic Church politics" and "a judicious mixture of money and clinically detailed sex" (13). Blackie's prevailing Irish cradle-Catholic mindset, too, offers insight into what Greeley called in *The Catholic Imagination* "a unique way of seeing the world . . . filled with enchantment and an expectation of the miraculous." As "grey eminence," intuitive sleuth, story-telling Irish priest, and spokesman for Andrew Greeley's vision of a more forgiving Church, Blackie Ryan makes an appealing clerical detective. Arguably.

Novels: *Virgin and Martyr* (1985); *Happy Are the Meek* (1985); *Happy Are Those Who Thirst for Justice* (1987); *Rite of Spring* (1987); *Happy Are the Clean of Heart* (1988); *St. Valentine's Night* (1989); *Happy Are the Merciful* (1992); *Happy Are the Peacemakers* (1993); *Happy Are the Poor in Spirit* (1994); *Happy Are Those Who Mourn* (1995); *White Smoke* (1996); *The Bishop and the Missing L Train* (2000); *The Bishop and the Beggar Girl of St. Germain* (2001); *The Bishop Goes to University* (2003); *The Bishop in the Neighborhood* (2005).

Other series: Greeley's mystery-romances involving Irish-American folksinger Nuala McGrail: *Irish Gold* (1994); *Irish Mist* (1999); *Irish Eyes* (2000); *Irish Love* (2001); *Irish Cream* (2005). Of similar interest: Greeley's Passover Trilogy: *Thy Brother's Wife* (1982); *Ascent into Hell* (1984); and *Lord of the Dance* (1987).

Nonfiction: Greeley has also written and edited many religious and/or sociological texts, some widely considered controversial. Collected newspaper columns: *A Piece of My Mind . . . on Just about Everything* (1983).

Autobiography: *Confessions of a Parish Priest: An Autobiography* (1986); *Andrew Greeley* (1990); *Furthermore: Memories of a Parish Priest* (1999).

Other works: Greeley has written many stand-alone novels, including *The Priestly Sin* (2004) and four science fiction novels published between 1986 and 1988.

Selected sources: Flanagan, Margaret. Rev. of *The Bishop and the Missing L Train. Booklist*, July 2000: 2002; Harrison, Elizabeth. *Andrew M. Greeley: An Annotated Bibliography*. Metuchen, NJ: Scarecrow Press, 1994; McCarthy, Abigail. Rev. of *The Cardinal Sin. Chicago Tribune*, May 24, 1981: 13; *New York Times Magazine*. Rev. of *How to Save the Catholic Church*, May 6, 1984: 36; *Publishers Weekly*. Rev. of *The Bishop and the Beggar Girl of St. Germain*, July 9, 2001: 47; Shafer, Ingrid. *The Womanliness of God: Andrew Greeley's Romances of Renewal*. Chicago: Loyola University Press, 1986; Shafer, Ingrid. *Andrew Greeley's World: A Collection of Critical Essays, 1986–1988*. New York: Warner Books, 1989.

Major awards: Popular Culture Award, 1986; Freedom to Read Award, 1987; five honorary doctorates of literature and humanities.

Web site: www.agreeley.com.

See also: For other contemporary Roman Catholic priest-sleuths: Leonard Holton's Father Joseph Breddar series; Ralph McInerny's Father Dowling series; William X. Kienzle's Father Bob Koesler series; and Mystery Writers of America Grand Master Dorothy Salisbury Davis's Father McMahon, sorely tested in her stand-alone *Where the Dark Streets Go* (1969).

S

Charlie Salter

Profession:	Inspector, Toronto Police Department
Living situation:	Married
Geographic locale:	Canada, chiefly Ontario
Time period:	1983–present
Significant relationship:	His wife, Annie Montagu Salter
Concerns:	Family; friends; justice; retirement

Englishman Eric Wright emigrated to Canada in 1951, earned degrees at the Universities of Manitoba and Toronto, became a Professor of English at Ryerson University, and at fifty-four won Canada's Crime Writers' John Creasey and Arthur Ellis awards for his first crime novel, *The Night the Gods Smiled* (1983), introducing Toronto's engaging middle-aged soft-boiled Inspector Charles "Charlie" Salter. After ten well-received Salter novels, Wright used Mel Pickett, a retired police colleague of Salter's and a minor character in *A Sensitive Case* (1990), as his new protagonist in *Buried in Stone* (1996) and *Death of a Hired Man* (2001), solving cases as a hobby from his cabin in northern Ontario. For other series, Wright also developed Lucy Trimble Brenner, a librarian who, like P.D. James's **Cordelia Gray**, takes over a detective agency as the starring sleuth in *Death of a Sunday Writer* (1996) and *Death on the Rocks* (1999), as well as Joe Barley, a lecturer in English literature who moonlights by seeking a missing exotic dancer in *The Kidnapping of Rosie Dawn* (2000). Wright then rounded off Charlie Salter's police career in *The Last Hand* (2002), a wryly humorous conclusion to one of Canada's best-loved detective series.

Queried by *Contemporary Authors* about Salter's origins, Wright indicated that he'd wanted "an absolutely typical Canadian. . . . He isn't American, he isn't English, but what is he?" Wright came up with "the essence of decency and the essence of Canadianism, too," recalling a plumbing foreman who'd been his greatly admired mentor on a construction job some thirty years previously. "He looked after me," Wright reminisced, "and that's really the sense I have of Charlie Salter—he's a man who looks after people" (*CA Online*).

According to Bernard Drew in the *St. James Guide to Crime and Mystery Writers*, Salter, not being a homicide detective, works unusual low-tech middle-class cases involving professionals—professors, local historians, doctors, and would-be actors—whose crimes Charlie always solves and whose achievements Charlie invariably takes with a grain or more of—well, salt.

From the start of *The Night the Gods Smiled*, Charlie's easy to like, an everyman most people would acknowledge as a good Joe and cherish as a friend. He loved police work until he backed the wrong superior for Deputy Chief. Now he marks time in a dead-end administrative position a long way from his early estimates of his own potential and wakes up uncomfortably from nightmares about failures, seeing fifteen boring years ahead until he's put out to pasture (*Gods* 7). Called to investigate the murder at a Montreal conference of an English professor whose career parallels his own, Salter patiently unravels the grouchy eccentricities of academia and some of his own, caring about victims and witnesses and even criminals with the "fine sense of life's small absurdities" (*Gods* 181) that continues through all his cases. In *The Man Who Changed His Name* (1986), Salter gives in to the prodding of his leftover flower child and activist ex-wife Gerry to solve a woman's murder. Charlie can't resist solving homicides even when he's on vacation, as in *Death in the Old Country* (1985), where a recently-slain body turns up at the English inn where he and his wife Annie are staying, and in *A Body Surrounded by Water* (1987), where a local historian is done in on Prince Edward Island, Annie's home territory. There Salter grumblingly spends summer holidays with Annie, their irrepressible sons Angus and Seth, and his numerous wealthy Montagu in-laws, who are hell-bent on making Salter feel "at home" but worlds apart from his cantankerous working-class father who, but for the grace of God and unconventional Annie, Salter would grow into replicating grouch for grouch.

Despite his proclivity for wryly humorous crime-solving, Salter's family remains his and his readers' chief interest. Early on, he and Annie manage to work through her "constant low-burning jealousy" over his one unfortunate extramarital slip (with Annie's friend, no less) because he cares so deeply for her. They reestablish a solid in-law–defying, great-married-sex relationship (*Gods* 71, 147) and later roll with various contemporary domestic punches like Tatty, Seth's French Canadian live-in, and the baby that Angus, abandoned by his significant other, leaves figuratively on their grandparental doorstep.

In Salter's *Last Hand* (2002), nearing mandatory retirement at sixty as the sole member of Toronto's Special Affairs Unit (actually a glorified office boy position), Charlie Salter wants badly to stay in the police job he loves. On one of the hunches that have made his reputation as more an odd duck than a lone wolf (*Hand* 55) and a threat to the high-tech homicide squad down the hall, he takes on one last case, surreptitiously interviewing suspects and lying low just as he does at poker until he calls a climactic bluff and rakes in the chips, trouncing three weaselly lawyers and a pair of crooked stockbrokers. When Annie is returning from Prince Edward Island with Angus's baby, Angus is headed to Vancouver, and Seth and Tatty are converting the basement into their very own love nest, Charlie Salter happily makes the most daring and caring move of his career, happily deciding to chuck the job and babysit— after a retirement party featuring silver-plated handcuffs and his dour Glasgow assistant playing the bagpipes (*Hand* 228). O Canada.

Novels: *The Night the Gods Smiled* (1983); *Smoke Detector* (1985); *Death in the Old Country* (1985); *The Man Who Changed His Name* (1986); *A Body Surrounded by Water* (1987); *A Question of Murder* (1988); *A Sensitive Case* (1990); *Final Cut* (1991); *A Fine Italian Hand* (1992); *Death by Degrees* (1993); *The Last Hand* (2002).

Other series: Mel Pickett, the protagonist of *Buried in Stone* (1996) and *Death of a Hired Man* (2001), appeared with Charlie Salter in *A Sensitive Case*. The Lucy Trimble series features a small-town librarian who inherits her cousin's detective agency and decides to operate it; the Joe Barley series, featuring an English lecturer who in tracing an exotic dancer clashes with his college's ideas about political correctness.

Short fiction: *A Killing Climate: The Collected Mystery Stories* (2003), containing a Charlie Salter novella written especially for this volume, "The Lady of Shalott."

Nonfiction: *Always Give a Penny to the Blind Man* (1999).

Other works: Wright also coedited *Criminal Shorts* (1992) with Howard Engel.

Selected sources: Fletcher, C. Rev. of *A Killing Climate*. *Booklist*, October 15, 2003: 394; Klett, Rex E. Rev. of *The Last Hand*. *Library Journal*, February 1, 2002: 136; *Publishers Weekly*. Rev. of *Death on the Rocks*, May 17, 1999: 60; Stasio, Marilyn. Rev. of *Death of a Hired Man*. *New York Times Book Review*, March 18, 2001: 18; Wright, Jean MacFarlane. Rev. of *A Question of Murder*. *New York Times Book Review*, October 9, 1988.

Major awards: Crime Writers' Association John Creasey Award, 1983; Arthur Ellis Awards, 1984, 1986, and best short story, 1988, 1992; Crime Writers of Canada Derrick Murdoch Award, 1998; Barry Award, 2001.

See also: For Canadian settings, Giles Blunt's homicide detective John Cardinal series, set in Canada's Algonquin Bay area; Laurence Gough's noir humor mystery series featuring Vancouver police detectives Claire Parker and Jack Willows; Peter Robinson's **Alan Banks** series for its soft-boiled approach, and Ted Wood's series featuring Vietnam veteran Reid Bennett, who resigns from the Toronto police to become a small-town one-man police force, accompanied by his German Shepherd Sam. Robinson and Wood, like Eric Wright, are Englishmen who became naturalized Canadians.

Joe Sandilands

Profession:	Commander, Metropolitan Police (Scotland Yard)
Living situation:	Single
Geographic locale:	India
Time period:	1920s
Associates:	Sir George Jardine, Lieutenant Governor of Bengal; Charles Carter (in *Ragtime in Simla*); James Lindsay (in *The Damascened Blade*)
Significant relationships:	Various
Concerns:	Morality; social responsibility

India, "the Land of Regrets," in the declining days of the British Raj, provides a stunning backdrop for Barbara Cleverly's Scotland Yard Commander Joseph Sandilands, seconded to India's Bengal Police in 1922 after four harrowing years with the Scots Fusiliers and British Army Intelligence in France and a meteoric four-year rise with London's Metropolitan Police. Sandilands, a son of the English-Scottish Borders, came out of the Western Front with three war medals, a DSO, and a scarred soul made visible in a tanned face once handsome, then battered by war and "held together with a clothes-peg," "a face with two sides, one serene, the other scarred, distorted—hard to read" (*Ragtime* 88, 31).

According to that "devious old bastard" Sir George Jardine, Lieutenant Governor of Bengal, "There's no fooling Sandilands, as they say at Scotland Yard!" (*Ragtime* 42–43). As a Yard specialist in serial killings, thirty-year-old Joe Sandilands has implemented then-new forensics methods like fingerprinting, blood-typing, door-to-door enquiries, and strings of informants as well as pioneering the application of Freudian and Jungian psychological theories to police investigations. At the start of *The Last Kashmiri Rose* (2001), after six months bringing the Bengal Police up to scratch, "He'd had enough India. He'd had enough heat. He'd had enough smells" (*Kashmiri Rose* 8). Then Jardine draws Sandilands into a case he can't resist: every March since 1910, a wife of one of the officers of the crack Bateman's Horse Regiment (the Bengal Greys) has been murdered at their headquarters in Panikhar, fifty miles south of Calcutta.

This case involves a woman Joe can't resist, either, Jardine's beautiful niece Nancy Drummond, a former Western Front army nurse married to the much older Collector of Panikhar, "a peaceful sort of chap," according to Jardine, with "Not much go about him" (*Kashmiri Rose* 11). The mutual attraction between Nancy, who's determined to stop the Panikhar murders, and Joe, who's bought a bottle or two of expensive perfume for a lady in his time, smoulders, then flames into a delicious interlude with startling repercussions. Joe "had assumed that Nancy had found him irresistible and...had felt herself free to enjoy an affair with an attractive and vigorous man passing through her life"—but Nancy had really gotten herself the baby her husband couldn't give her. Joe realizes he'd been "duped. Used." His anger, however, was "swiftly followed by shame and embarrassment," and soon cools. Saying goodbye to Nancy, he tells her he was "touched and perhaps even flattered," but he doesn't want to know the outcome: "I'm not made of marble, you know!" (*Kashmiri Rose* 225, 308).

Joe's professional methods are equally complex. At the start of each case, he takes in as many facts as he can, formulating no theories, and trusting his instincts in judging witnesses, suspects, and colleagues. He's an experienced lecturer well used to leading committees, forming opinions, "getting his own way, and above all, moving things forward" because "People of all ranks listened to him, liked him, and generally did what he was telling them" (*Kashmiri Rose* 118). In his second case, *Ragtime in Simla* (2003), he accepts Sir George's offer of a month's leave at the governor's guest house in Simla, the Himalayan foothills town and British summer capital. On his way there Joe meets Feodor Korsovsky, a flamboyant Russian operatic baritone engaged to give concerts in Simla. In Jardine's elegant open-top Packard, they pause to savor the unforgettable sight of Simla spilling "higgledy-piggledy, down from the wooded summit of a precipitous hill." Korsovsky stands, bursts into glorious song, "Pale hands I loved, beside the Shalimar"—and then is shot dead by an unseen gunman (*Ragtime* 28).

In the exhilarating mountain air where people "feel twenty years younger" (*Ragtime* 96), Joe learns that Korsovsky's is only the latest in a string of sniper killings at the Devil's Elbow on the road to Simla, a case with "an elegant, cooperative and even talkative woman. Eager to tell me all . . . with a faithful if mysterious gentleman friend in the background" (*Ragtime* 117) everywhere Joe looks. He doesn't spurn help to sort it all out. Earlier he's faced professional suspicion and jealousy from his English colleagues at the Yard and then from Panikhar's resentful police chief, but Simla's Police Superintendent Charles Carter genially takes Joe for what he is, an honest fellow policeman. Together Carter and Joe untangle both exotic and garden-variety motives, just as in *The Damascened Blade* (2004), Joe works comfortably with his old army friend James Lindsay, commander of the British army's front line fort on the wild Indian-Afghan border. There, after a Pathan prince is killed, his relatives take a traveling American heiress as hostage, giving Joe and Lindsay seven days to find and execute the murderer before the whole frontier erupts in war.

Created in the traditional Golden Age mode, Joe Sandilands and the colorful characters that surround him have "more complexity and sophistication than [Agatha] Christie typically provided" (*Publishers Weekly* 57). Resourceful and insightful as Kipling's Kim, a fictional character who had accompanied Joe "through four years in the hell of France, [heartening] him in the depths of despair," Joe Sandilands uses both sides of his personality—his detached, objective reason and the empathetic compassion the war taught him—to emerge from these perilous cases only touched, never tainted, by regrets.

Novels: *The Last Kashmiri Rose* (2001); *Ragtime in Simla* (2003); *The Damascened Blade* (2004); *The Palace Tiger* (2005).

Selected sources: Bibel, Barbara. Rev. of *The Damascened Blade*. *Booklist*, July 1, 2004: 1823; Hix, Charles. "Making the Historical Fictional." *Publishers Weekly*, November 22, 2004: 23;

Klett, Rex E. Rev. of *The Palace Tiger. Library Journal*, June 1, 2005: 107; Klett, Rex E. Rev. of *Ragtime in Simla. Library Journal*, October 1, 2003: 120; Melton, Emily. Rev. of *The Last Kashmiri Rose. Booklist*, August 1, 2002: 1929; *Publishers Weekly*. Rev. of *Ragtime in Simla*, August 4, 2003: 57.

See also: H.R.F. Keating's **Inspector Ghote** series; Paul Mann's **George Sansi** series, both set in contemporary India.

Sano Ichiro

Profession:	Most Honorable Investigator to the Shogun
Living situation:	Single; later married
Geographic locale:	Edo (old name for Tokyo), Japan
Time period:	Seventeenth century
Associate:	Hirata, Sano's chief retainer
Nemesis:	Lord Yanagisawa, Chamberlain
Significant relationship:	Lady Reiko, eventually Sano's wife and detective partner
Concern:	*Bushido*, the Way of the Warrior: Duty, Loyalty, Courage

Bushido, the samurai code or the Way of the Warrior, dominated Japan's feudal medieval period until Takugawa Ieyasu seized power as Shogun (supreme military dictator) after a brutal civil war and unified the country in 1600. Demanding unquestioning duty, loyalty, and courage in the service of a lord, *Bushido* and its values gradually gave way to machiavellian scheming and intrigue among rival aristocratic clans during the increasingly decadent Takugawa dynasty's two-hundred-year rule, when Japan was largely cut off from the outside world. As a samurai dedicated to the old *Bushido* tradition and recently-installed *sosokan* (Most Honorable Investigator) to weak-willed and paranoid Shogun Takugawa Tsunayoshi, Sano Ichiro constantly walks a dicey tightrope over a pool of power-hungry saurian courtiers, especially his wily enemy Lord Chamberlain Yanagisawa, maneuvering for Sano's fall. The exotic atmosphere of class-conscious seventeenth-century Edo (the ancient name for Tokyo), redolent with strange and titillating sexual practices, provides a dramatic backdrop for Sano's cases, which require him to exercise his own cunning while attempting to maintain the samurai's *Bushido* as well as his personal pursuit of truth and justice—stern values that give Sano's life its meaning.

In his first case, *Shinju* (1994), before he becomes the Shogun's *sosokan*, Laura Joh Rowland's Sano, son of an honorable *ronin* (a samurai without a lord) and an investigator for the Edo police, disagrees with his superiors' instructions to file the deaths of a peasant and the daughter of a prominent citizen as a *shinju*, or "double love suicide," and because of his principles, Sano undertakes a private investigation that uncovers corruption in the highest ranks of Edo society. Well schooled in the martial arts that he practices assiduously, Sano unearths the reasons behind gruesome crimes in his next case, *Bundori* (1996), where decapitated heads of descendants of warriors involved in the previous century's murder of a prominent warlord appear throughout the city. Sano again maintains his passion for the truth over political advantage in *The Way of the Traitor* (1997), a case with international ramifications that takes him and his twenty-year-old chief retainer Hirata to Nagasaki, where the murder of a Dutch trade officer has caused an international crisis and where Hirata proves his own samurai loyalty by saving Sano's life.

In the two unsettling years in which these cases take place, Sano's beloved father has died, and Sano's own quick wits and his *Bushido* fidelity to his lord the Shogun make him the Shogun's *sosokan*. Takagawa Tsunayoshi abruptly places Sano in charge of a hundred-plus professional detectives working out of Edo Palace, a dizzying and dangerous position that earns him the jealous enmity of Lord Chamberlain Yanagisawa, formerly the Shogun's homosexual lover, who just before the beginning of *The Concubine's Tattoo* (1998) plots an attempt on Sano's life. During his arranged wedding to beautiful twenty-year-old Lady Ueka Reiko, only child of Edo's most powerful magistrate, Sano reflects on his marriage as his chance to establish his own home, the only place a samurai has under his complete control, with a calm bride as his "oasis of serenity" (*Tattoo* 66, 53).

Sano soon learns that Lady Reiko, bright and willful and educated like a boy by her doting father, is anything but the compliant ideal of Sano's samurai dreams. The suspicious death of the Shogun's latest concubine just after the wedding ceremony causes Sano and Hirata to plunge into police action, leaving Sano's marriage unconsummated and Lady Reiko determined to solve the murder herself. Three days of professional and personal frustration later, Sano begins to learn husbandly patience and a whole new awareness of the plight of women in Japan's arch-patriarchal society. On their real wedding night, he finally abandons his samurai sternness and offers Reiko marriage on her own terms, so that maiden and warrior both glimpse worlds beyond any they have ever known.

Sano and Reiko combine their detective skills as well as their conjugal raptures in *The Samurai's Wife* (2000), probing the death of an imperial minister involved in a plot against the shogun that might ignite another civil war, but in *Black Lotus* (2001), Sano feels that a teenaged girl is guilty of arson and murder while Reiko insists the girl is innocent, a disagreement threatening the fabric of their marriage. In *The Pillow Book of Lady Wisteria* (2002), the ancient Japanese sexual practices connected to the death of the Shogun's heir apparent in an opulent brothel either "spice or undercut Sano's struggle to remain honorable in a dishonorable world" (*Kirkus Reviews* 226) according to the individual reader's sensibilities, a matter of taste also apparent in *The Dragon King's Palace* (2003). There Sano has to work with his enemy Lord Yanagisawa to save the Shogun's mother, Hirata's pregnant wife Midori, and Sano's own Reiko, all kidnapped by a vengeful psychopath. Reiko's efforts to engineer their escape traumatizes her severely, while Hirata violates his loyalty to his lord Sano to save Midori and their baby. Sano's moral dilemmas escalate in *The Perfumed Sleeve* (2004), *Bushido* values clashing against his obligation to protect his family as Edo reels on the brink of civil war and Reiko withdraws from him both as his lover and as his coinvestigator. *The Assassin's Touch* (2005) finds Sano now the Shogun's chamberlain and second-in-command as well as acting as a criminal investigator in a string of deaths of high government officials. Sano and Hirata pursue a martial arts master using *dim-mak*, the "touch of death," but their investigation uncovers political ramifications that profoundly affect the Shogun's regime and threaten the lives of Sano and his family.

Unable in all his cases to back away from danger in his pursuit of truth, Sano Ichiro personifies his country's peculiarly Oriental spiritual dilemma: how to temper *Bushido* with compassion, how to save face without losing soul.

Novels: *Shinju* (1994); *Bundori* (1996); *The Way of the Traitor* (1997); *The Concubine's Tattoo* (1998); *The Samurai's Wife* (2000); *Black Lotus* (2001); *The Pillow Book of Lady Wisteria* (2002); *The Dragon King's Palace* (2003); *The Perfumed Sleeve* (2004); *The Assassin's Touch* (2005).

Selected sources: *AB Bookman's Weekly*. Rev. of *The Concubine's Tattoo*, September 20, 1999: 380; Hubbard, Michelle. Rev. of *The Samurai's Wife*. *Bookreporter*, www.bookreporter.com (May 1, 2002); *Kirkus Reviews*. Rev. of *The Pillow Book of Lady Wisteria*, February 15, 2002: 226; Klett, Rex E. Rev. of *The Pillow Book of Lady Wisteria*. *Library Journal*, April 1, 2002: 146; Mathews, Laura. "Smart Women, Stylish Mysteries." *Glamour*, October 1994: 176; Notehelfer, F.G. "An Old Japanese Custom." *New York Times Book Review*, October 9, 1994: 11; Pitt, David. Rev. of *The Dragon King's Palace*. *Booklist*, February 15, 2003: 1055; *Publishers Weekly*. Rev. of *The Assassin's Touch*, June 6, 2005: 43.

See also: I.J. Parker's series featuring Gugawara Akitada, a clerk in the Ministry of Justice of eleventh-century Japan; Dale Furutani's samurai trilogy set in seventeenth-century Japan and featuring Matsuyama Kaze, an unaffiliated samurai searching for his lord's missing daughter: *Death at the Crossroads* (1998); *Jade Palace Vendetta* (1999); *Kill the Shogun* (2000); Seicho Matsumoto's contemporary novels featuring Inspector Torugay and Inspector Imanishi; Miyuki Miyabe's Sergeant Yakegami series set in contemporary Japan; S. Shizuko Natsuki's stand-alone novels; Masako Togawa's stand-alone novels; James Melville's contemporary Superintendent Tetsuo Otani series, set in the city of Kobe.

George Sansi

Profession:	Detective, Bombay Crime Branch; later private attorney
Living situation:	Single
Geographic locale:	Bombay, India
Time period:	1990s
Associates:	Sergeant Chowdhary; Annie Ginnaro
Nemesis:	Narendra Jamal, Joint Commissioner of Crime Branch
Significant relationship:	Annie Ginnaro
Concerns:	Corruption; industrial pollution; strangling tradition/ religious beliefs

Journalist Paul Mann's three searing George Sansi mysteries ruthlessly reveal the spiritual filth befouling modern India as well as occasional glimpses of the beauty lying beneath it as they depict the country's 1980s transformation from a "stunted socialist economy" to "a booming free-enterprise economy far more in tune with the entrepreneurial spirit of the Indian people" (*Ghats* xi). Mann targets specific examples of contemporary Indian corruption: the Indian movie industry, which produces three times as many films per year as Hollywood, in *Season of the Monsoon* (1992); the virtually unlimited Indian drug traffic in *Ganja Coast* (1995); and industrial environmental rape in *The Burning Ghats* (1996). Mann also notes that India, the world's oldest continuous civilization, is a land of enormous contradictions that baffle and eventually conquer its would-be Western conquerors, from Alexander the Great to "dark-suited mercenaries of Citibank, Union Carbide, and IBM" (*Ghats* xii), because their smug belief in Western technological infallibility blinds them to India's ability to guide outsiders and its own idealists into elephant traps of age-old Indian design.

East and West tragically combine in handsome, blue-eyed detective and lawyer George Louis Sansi, in *Season of the Monsoon* "an absurdly romantic figure...flesh and blood legacy of a love affair" in the dying days of the British Raj. Sansi's mother Pramila, a celebrated Bombay feminist author and university lecturer, refused to marry British General Spooner because doing so would force her to leave India. The General, whom she remembers as "the kindest man in the whole world" (*Ghats* 13), paid for George's Oxford education, but George's legitimate half-brother Eric, like most British whites, dismisses George as "some little wog salesman with a suitcase full of silk scarves" (*Monsoon* 258). Most of the Indians in Bombay's Crime Branch, modeled after Scotland Yard, are just as prejudiced. They consider Sansi "a half-caste bastard who thought he was too good to take *hafta* (bribes) like everybody else"; most of his on-the-take superiors think he is "the wrong kind of Indian with the wrong kind of degree," preventing Indian law firms from hiring him; and criminals call him "the *only* honest cop in Bombay" (*Monsoon* 23, 47, 143; italics in original).

In *Season of the Monsoon* bureaucratic corruption parallels a sadistic murder of a homosexual Film City extra, tortured, mutilated, and slain at a cinema mockup of the Temple of Kali, the Hindu goddess of destruction. While patiently unraveling the forensic evidence by hand (Bombay police did not have computers in the 1990s) with his equally honest Sergeant Chowdhary, Sansi uncovers a old pattern of serial killings involving politics at the highest Indian and British levels, the civilized haunts of wealthy and powerful Indians, the squalid slums where human life means less than nothing, the perfidy of Bombay gang lords, and the memories of an aged maharani, the perpetual chaos of "a country that can break your heart" (*Monsoon* 265).

Sansi's own heart yields to California journalist Annie Ginnaro, in India to get over a bad marriage and "to force changes upon herself, to confront the cozy California values that no longer worked for her" (*Ghats* 13). While interviewing Pramila for the *Times of India*, Annie falls in love with Pramila's complicated son, finding him "the most moral man I've ever met" (*Monsoon* 250). George falls in love with Annie, too, though he also sees and uses her as a channel of misinformation to trap a killer.

After leaving the Bombay police in disgust at its corruption, Sansi opens a private law practice in *Ganja Coast*. Sansi's former boss, power-hungry Joint Commissioner of Crime Branch Narendra Jamal, inveigles Sansi into a ploy to bring down a corrupt Goanese politician. Under cover of a luxury vacation Annie accompanies Sansi to the coastal state of Goa, where a child's strangled body has washed up on a beach frequented by stoned hippies. "There is no law here," a former police pathologist warns him, just as Annie cautions against political involvement, but Sansi, playing the game against all the odds, idealistically refuses to let anarchy win.

In *The Burning Ghats*, though, ego and the lure of power trap Sansi. His old schoolmate and former lover Rupe Seshan, now a powerful cabinet minister, offers him a commissioner's rank to probe the horrifying chemical spill that killed eleven hundred at Varanasi, where ashes of the dead are spread on the sacred Ganges. Against Annie's warnings, George takes the bait. He also spends a night, later regretted, with Rupe. With Savitri Chowdhary, "the finest policeman George has ever known" (*Ghats* 143) again at his side, Sansi brings an unscrupulous industrialist to justice, but his assignation with Rupe, splashed across the newspapers by their enemies, loses him his self-respect and marks him as a corrupt investigator, "the kind of person," Annie bitterly tells him, "you used to hate" (*Ghats* 293). His reputation and Annie both gone, Sansi returns to Crime Branch, his ideals abandoned, middle-aged and besmirched, embittered by having proved to himself his father's words: "Whatever you were inside…good or bad, India brought it out in you. To the extreme" (*Monsoon* 265).

Novels: *Season of the Monsoon* (1992); *Ganja Coast* (1995); *The Burning Ghats* (1996).

Other works: Mann has also written a series of international thrillers, notably *Traitor's Contract* (1991) and *Britannia Contract* (1993).

Selected sources: Klett, Rex E. Rev. of *The Burning Ghats*. *Library Journal*, November 1, 1996: 110; Seaman, Donna. Rev. of *The Ganja Coast*. *Booklist*, January 15, 1995: 899; Stasio, Marilyn. Rev. of *The Burning Ghats*. *New York Times Book Review*, December 22, 1996: 21; Stasio, Marilyn. Rev. of *The Ganja Coast*. *New York Times Book Review*, February 19, 1995: 25.

See also for Indian settings: H.R.F. Keating's **Inspector Ghote** series; Barbara Cleverly's **Joe Sandilands** series, set in the 1920s.

Kay Scarpetta

Profession:	Chief Medical Examiner; forensic pathologist and lawyer
Living situation:	Divorced
Geographic locale:	Richmond, Virginia
Time period:	1990–present
Associates:	Homicide detective Pete Marino; niece Lucy Farinelli
Nemeses:	Temple Gault; Carrie Grethen
Significant relationship:	Benton Wesley
Concerns:	Serial murder; rape; gay rights

Since *Postmortem* (1990), Patricia Cornwell's grisly Dr. Kay Scarpetta series has gripped crime readers' horrified attention. Rerunning "the same scenarios over and over," the series offers "gore galore for fans of the Cloaca-and-Dagger school of mystery writing" (Murphy 440). As Chief Medical Examiner for the Richmond, Virginia, Police Department, Scarpetta, an ash-blonde divorced forensic pathologist and lawyer, also consults with the FBI. In her official capacity, she must encounter and interpret all evidence left behind by serial killers, so Scarpetta's work begins at the crime scene, moves to the autopsy room and the high-tech crime lab, and often ends with court testimony (*Silk Stalkings* 2: 114). Often, too, the serial killers she pursues target her before they are apprehended and brought to justice (Herbert 172). Much of the series' tension devolves from the conflict between Scarpetta's dedication to her job and her personal needs, especially her need to keep her home life, secure and warm and redolent of fine Italian cooking, as separate from her work as possible.

Multi-award-winning *Postmortem* (1990) set the pattern for all Scarpetta's cases. An unexpected phone call hurls Scarpetta from her comfortable Richmond home into the latest in a sequence of bizarre stranglings. In the two years since becoming Chief Medical Examiner, Scarpetta has learned the hard way that "A violent death is a public event," the facet of her profession that most rubs her raw. She does what she can to preserve each victim's dignity, but the person becomes "a piece of evidence passed from hand to hand.... Privacy is destroyed as completely as life" (*Postmortem* 7–8). Scarpetta's own "special distaste" for seeing herself on the evening news bitterly counterpoints her minute examination of the crime scene's horrors, the brutalized young female victim's body, and the inescapable media-circus invasion of her own privacy.

In the merciless light of her autopsy room, the shriek of a bone saw or the ooze of bodily fluids never unnerves Scarpetta, a consummate professional so able to detach herself from her gruesome job's demands that her gloved hands "seem . . . to belong to somebody else" (*Postmortem* 22). When she forgets to remove her lab coat, the tangible symbol of her single-mindedness, on leaving work, she feels as though she's in her pyjamas (*Postmortem* 311). Outside of her morgue, however, Scarpetta's emotions are never far from the surface. She shares the pain of the bereaved, and knowing that she has no comfort for them adds both impetus to her professional crime-solving and empathetic stress to her cherished private life. That private life shatters more each time a killer stalks Scarpetta, threatening not only her life but the lives of those she loves.

Scarpetta allows few people into her private world. In *Postmortem* her young niece Lucy, her only real link with her family, is a troubled ten-year-old cybergenius, "an impossible little holy terror of enigmatic Latin descent whose father died when she was small" and whose mother, Scarpetta's sister, is too wrapped up in writing children's books to give Lucy much attention (*Postmortem* 33). Lucy adores her Auntie Kay and as the only character who ages through the series, becomes Scarpetta's trusted computer expert, graduates from the FBI Academy, takes a lesbian lover, and eventually joins the Bureau of Alcohol, Tobacco, and Firearms. Scarpetta, both profoundly fond of Lucy and emotionally drained by her ceaseless energy, cannot bring herself to send Lucy back to Miami, even though Lucy's presence makes Kay Scarpetta feel especially vulnerable.

At first, Scarpetta isn't sure whether career cop Sergeant Pete Marino, hard-nosed, vulgar, hypertensive, doesn't like women in general or herself in particular. Soon he begins to surprise her with unexpected kindness, becoming her closest friend as well as her most dependable working partner, and saving her life when she's too upset, too distracted, to defend herself—a frequent symptom of Scarpetta's Achilles' heel, her tendency to fall to pieces when what she holds most dear, including Marino, is threatened.

Benton Wesley, Scarpetta's married lover through several books, was an FBI profiler, "the creator of a better way of understanding humans who were truly psychotic, or remorseless and evil" (*Point of Origin* 394). He and Scarpetta share only a little happy time together before Wesley is lured to a dreadful death in *Point of Origin* (1998). Scarpetta blames her desire for independence for her refusal to marry him, a guilt that torments her ever afterward.

The ultimate sacrifice of her privacy is Scarpetta's eerie link with each of the serial killers she pursues: "He would want to get inside my mind as much as I wanted to get inside his" (*Postmortem* 264). This is particularly true of Scarpetta's nemeses Temple Gault and Carrie Grethen, recurrent figures in several novels. Scarpetta's recent cases have stagnated despite their increase in minutiae and emotional turbulence (Ashley 114), but overall the series' dark intensity proves as horridly magnetic as Scarpetta's compulsion to dissect the very bowels of human evil.

Novels: *Postmortem* (1990); *Body of Evidence* (1991); *All That Remains* (1992); *Cruel and Unusual* (1993); *The Body Farm* (1994); *From Potter's Field* (1995); *Cause of Death* (1996); *Unnatural Exposure* (1997); *Point of Origin* (1998); *Black Notice* (1999); *The Last Precinct* (2000); *Blow Fly* (2003); *Trace* (2004); *Predator* (2005).

Other series: Police Chief Judy Hammer series: *Hornet's Nest* (1997); *Southern Cross* (1999); *Isle of Dogs* (2001).

Nonfiction: *A Time for Remembering: The Story of Ruth Bell Graham* (1983); *Portrait of a Killer: Jack the Ripper* (2002).

Children's book: *Life's Little Fable* (1999).

Cookbooks: *Scarpetta's Winter Table* (1998); *Food to Die For: Secrets from Kay Scarpetta's Kitchen* (with Marlene Brown; 2001).

Selected sources: Guinn, Jeff. "Dissecting Patricia Cornwell." *Knight Ridder/Tribune News Service*, November 1, 2000: K1359; Hays, Charlotte, and Ivy McClure Stewart. "Politically Correct Private Eyes." *Women's Quarterly*, Summer 2001: 18; Lawson, Mark. "A Novelist at the Scene of the Crime." *Guardian*, December 8, 2001: 20; Stasio, Marilyn. Rev. of *Trace*. *New York Times Book Review*, September 19, 2004: 15; *Tangled Web UK Web site*, www.twbooks.co.uk; Wark, Penny. "I'm Over Sex and Fame." *Times* (London), November 27, 2001: 84.

Major awards: All 1990: John Creasey Award, British Crime Writers' Association; Edgar Award, Mystery Writers of America; Anthony Award, World Mystery Convention; Macavity Award, Mystery Readers International; *Prix du Roman d'Aventure*, 1991; Gold Dagger, 1993.

Web site: www.patriciacornwell.com.

See also: Colin Cotterill's series featuring Dr. Siri Paiboun, a seventy-two-year-old Laotian coroner; Jeffery Deaver's series featuring a quadriplegic NYPD forensic scientist; Susan Dunlop's series featuring Kiernan O'Shaughnessey, a former medical examiner; Aaron Elkins's series featuring globetrotting forensic anthropologist **Dr. Gideon Oliver**; Tess Gerritson's series featuring Medical Examiner Dr. Maura Isles; Archer Mayor's series featuring Vermont assistant medical examiner Dr. Joe Gunther; Kathy Reichs's series featuring forensic anthropologist Temperance Brennan, who operates in North Carolina and Quebec; Karen Slaughter's series featuring coroner Dr. Sara Hinton, set in Georgia. For a British analogue, see Keith McCarthy's series featuring London forensic pathologist Dr. John Eisenmenger.

Matthew Scudder

Profession:	Unlicensed private investigator
Living situation:	Divorced; remarried
Geographic locale:	New York City
Time period:	1976–present
Associate:	Mick Ballou
Nemeses:	Alcohol; depression
Significant relationship:	Elaine Scudder
Concerns:	Staying sober; stubborn desire for justice

"The most highly honored series in all crime fiction," the Matthew Scudder novels are the creation of Lawrence Block, "one of the most prolific and best-selling of all crime-fiction writers" (Ashley 60). Scudder himself is one of the most tormented of private-eye heroes, "an alcoholic ex-cop—a subtle reinterpretation and updating of the classic tough guy" (Murphy 47).

Scudder ages in real time through his long series. Semi-retired, looking back and confronting his mortality in *All the Flowers Are Dying* (2005), he laconically recaps his former life as though he's speaking at one of the AA meetings he's been attending faithfully for a long time. Some thirty years ago he retired from the New York City police force and moved from living in "a comfortable suburban house" and being a husband to Anita and a father to his sons Michael and Andrew, now grown up and distanced from Scudder, to living in "a monastic little room" and drinking "day in and day out, because that's what I did back then" (*Flowers* 3). In Scudder's tragic back story, he'd accidentally killed a little Hispanic girl while halting a robbery in the line of duty. It was the last straw for Scudder as a policeman, and he left the force consumed with guilt that drove him into the maelstrom of alcoholism. Dragged out of it one painful day at a time by his AA mentor Jim Faber and his own self-disgust, Scudder sobered up and found Elaine again, a expensive call girl he'd first met when he was a married cop with two kids. He loved her, was generally faithful to her, she retired and became an art and antiques dealer, they married, and it worked. "If I lost you," he tells her now after happy years together, "I really wouldn't want to go on" (*Flowers* 224).

Scudder's been through a lot. His life just after leaving the police force is un-mercifully laid out in *When the Sacred Ginmill Closes* (1986), set in 1975 and involving Scudder in the holdup of a bar that launders money for the IRA, the murder of one of his drinking buddies, and the theft of the actual (not the faked) accounts of a bar-owning friend. *Eight Million Ways to Die* (1983) depicts Scudder's descent into alcoholism, and in the novels that immediately follow, he's drinking heavily while doing "favors" for friends as an unlicensed private investigator. He's also giving about a tenth of what he makes to various churches. Even though he isn't conventionally religious, Scudder accompanies his Irish friend Mick Ballou to early Mass in New York's meat district, the brutal backdrop for his work, usually involving excruciating physical violence, like the ice-pick murder in *A Stab in the Dark* (1981), and the Edgar-winning *A Dance in the Slaughterhouse* (1991).

Later during his soul-wrenching efforts to rehabilitate, Scudder still lives by himself in the Hotel Northwestern and uses Jimmy Armstrong's saloon as a combination living room and office, but he now has a lifeline: he's going to AA meetings, looking "for something to put in the empty places alcohol used to fill" (*Flowers* 3) and living by his detective credo, "Knock on People's Doors." Scudder finally acquires a PI license in *Everybody Dies* (1991), and his first client is his longtime friend Mick Ballou.

Scudder mellows as his series proceeds, but coping with aging is one of the toughest jobs this tough guy has had to face. "You reach a certain age and it can get pretty grim, you spend all your time going to other people's funerals and waiting around for your own. Your body and your mind both start giving up ground, and the best you can hope for is that they both quit on you at the same time" (*Flowers* 224). Scudder doesn't adapt to changes easily; he avoided a cell phone as long as he could, until finally the realization that he was being ridiculous overcame "the stubbornness that seems to be an irreducible part of me" (*Flowers* 33), but he forgets to carry the phone about half the time and often forgets to turn it on when he does. He's never driven a flashy car or worn expensive clothes, he doesn't read much or take in lofty entertainment, and he's always afraid he'll break Elaine's computer; but he's sure about what really matters—his loyalty to his wife and friends and his stubborn passion for justice. Matt Scudder does the things he can manage, avoids the things he can't, and cherishes the wisdom to know the difference.

Novels: *Sins of the Fathers* (1976; rpt. 1992); *In the Midst of Death* (1976; rpt. 1995); *Time to Murder and Create* (1977; rpt. 1993); *A Stab in the Dark* (1981); *Eight Million Ways to Die* (1982); *When the Sacred Ginmill Closes* (1986); *Out on the Cutting Edge* (1989); *A Ticket to the Boneyard* (1990); *A Dance at the Slaughterhouse* (1991); *A Walk among the Tombstones* (1992); *The Devil Knows You're Dead* (1993); *A Long Line of Dead Men* (1994); *Even the Wicked* (1997); *Everybody Dies* (1999); *Hope to Die* (2001); *All the Flowers Are Dying* (2005).

Other series: The Evan Tanner series (Block's earliest), featuring an insomniac Korean war veteran academic and spy; the Bernie Rhodenbarr series, featuring a Raffles-type gentleman burglar; the Chip Harrison series, published under "Chip Harrison," its first two novels "sex-romps," then settling into the detective mode as Harrison becomes a "slightly wilder Archie Goodwin" to private detective Leo Haig's Nero Wolfe (Ashley 61).

Stand-alone novels, written as "Paul Kavanaugh": *Such Men Are Dangerous* (1969); *The Triumph of Evil* (1971); *Not Comin' Home to You* (1974); all republished under "Lawrence Block," 1985, 1986, 1986 respectively. Block has also written numerous other novels under his own name and other pseudonyms and completed an unfinished novel by Cornell Woolrich.

Nonfiction: Block has produced numerous nonfiction works, notably instruction books on writing, such as *Writing the Novel: From Plot to Print* (1979); *Write for Your Life* (1985); and *Spider, Spin Me a Web* (1988).

Autobiography: *After Hours: Conversations with Lawrence Block* (with Ernie Bulow; 1995).

Other works: Block has written several volumes of short fiction, notably *Like a Lamb to the Slaughter* (1984); *Some Days You Get the Bear* (1993), *Hit Man* (1998). He has also edited five collections of mystery short fiction by other authors.

Selected sources: *BookReporter*, www.bookreporter.com/authors (June 13, 2001), interview with Block; Burns, Landon C. "Matthew Scudder's Moral Ambiguity." *Clues*, Fall–Winter 1996: 19–32; Casella, Donna. "The Matt Scudder Series: The Saga of an Alcoholic Hardboiled Detective." *Clues*, Fall–Winter 1993: 31–50; Charyn, Jerome. *The New Mystery*. New York: Dutton, 1993; Fretts, Bruce. "N.Y. Crimes: Lawrence Block's Popular PI, Matt Scudder, Returns for Another Manhattan Murder Mystery in *Hope to Die*." *Entertainment Weekly*, November 2, 2001: 68; Stasio, Marilyn. "The Aging Action Hero." *New York Times Book Review*, March 13, 2005: 28; White, Claire E. "Talking Mystery with Lawrence Block." *Writers Write*, www.writerswrite.com (November 7, 2000).

Major awards: Nero Wolfe Award, 1979; Shamus Awards, Private Eye Writers of America, 1983, 1985, 1994; Edgar Allan Poe Awards, Mystery Writers of America, 1985, 1992, 1994, 1998 and Grand Master designation, 1994; Maltese Falcon Awards (Japan), 1986, 1990; *Grand Maître du Roman Noir* (France), 1994; Marlowe Award (Germany), 1995; Anthony Award, Private Eye Writers of America, 2001 and Lifetime Achievement Award, 2002.

Web site: www.lawrenceblock.com.

See also: Robert B. Parker's **Spenser** series; James Lee Burke's **Dave Robicheaux** series; Donald E. Westlake's Parker series (as "Richard Stark").

Sara Selkirk

Profession:	Cellist
Living situation:	Single
Geographic locale:	Bath, England
Time period:	1998–present
Associate:	Detective Chief Inspector Andrew Poole
Significant relationship:	Andrew Poole
Concerns:	Musicianship and its demands

Very few mystery series feature classical musicians as detectives—perhaps because they're too busy practicing and concertizing to sleuth. Morag Joss, however, has created a beguiling protagonist, renowned Scottish cellist Sara Selkirk, dark-haired with greeny-blue eyes and an elegant shape maintained by inveterate jogging; placed her in Bath, one of England's most enchanting spa cities; and fashioned deliciously absorbing mysteries around her unquenchable curiosity and her undeniable magnetism, both of which she struggles to balance against the demands of her art. Sara's detecting excursions are counterpointed by her developing attachment to Bath's dishy Detective Chief Inspector Andrew Poole, an amateur cellist at first her student and soon her lover, whom she finds "designed for rugby and sex and what a good thing he didn't bother with the rugby" (*Fruitful Bodies* 53).

Funeral Music (1998) opens in a minor key: After the death of her lover, a famous conductor with whom she had shared exquisite Medlar Cottage overlooking Bath, Sara suffered a breakdown and since has not performed in public. In 1974 at a Tanglewood master class, the immortal Piatigorsky confirmed seventeen-year-old Sara as "promising," and now her playing is technically superb—but after Matteo died she realizes that her intangible, unforceable spark of artistry has vanished. Her agent insists that she can't maintain her luxurious lifestyle forever from her royalties alone, sizable though they are, so Sara reluctantly agrees to play a charity concert at Bath's historic Pump Room, accompanied by her long-time friend, gay pianist James Ballantyne, himself mourning the death of a close friend. During the evening, Sara glimpses the officious Matthew Sawyer, Bath's Director of Museums and Civic Leisure Resources, and the next morning she discovers his body, grotesquely immersed in the spring supplying the ancient Roman baths. The crime becomes a turning point in Sara's life.

Words spoken long ago by master cellist Gregor Piatigorsky have been haunting her: "'What really matters is how you will use your art as a human being in a productive life. Everything hangs together; you cannot be a mentally unhealthy person and produce something of value in our difficult profession'" (*Funeral Music* 51). In her thirties and immersed in her despond over Matteo, Sara's already fearing that she might be turning into a "barking, lugubrious spinster who stares at people in public" (*Funeral Music* 33). Now, as her old friend James and Sawyer's assistant Olivia, a professional woman Sara admires, fall under suspicion of murdering Sawyer, Sara finds herself enmeshed in a complicated and frequently unnerving case full of tangled motives and human frailties. She also is increasingly attracted to Andrew Poole, an unhappily married homicide detective chief inspector whom she whimsically took on as a cello student. With Andrew conducting the official murder investigation, Sara finally realizes, "Where have I got to? Nowhere. Just been running round and round and round, story of my life" (*Funeral Music* 79).

Funeral Music resolves in a tidy solution to Sawyer's murder and a major key when she acknowledges her "harmless but slightly pathetic habit of fantasising [*sic*] about unavailable men" (*Funeral Music* 279), takes her priceless cello to her moonlit garden and for the first time in months truly plays again, her art finally returning to her hands and soul. Andrew decides to leave Valerie, and in the next installment of their relationship, *Fearful Symmetry* (1999) sweeps him and Sara into a turbulent scherzo of thwarted sexuality. Sara has returned to Medlar Cottage from a two-month concert series, looking forward to quiet candlelit evenings with Andrew, but her home is soon invaded by an incredibly sexy Hungarian composer engaged to score an opera for a local company. Andrew had tried moving out of his disastrous marriage, but he soon discovers he cannot leave "his three carelessly beautiful, maddening children" (*Symmetry* 14), so he is miserably coexisting again with Valerie, who is ruthlessly making him suffer for an affair he and Sara had to Andrew's regret only nearly, but never quite, had.

In *Fruitful Bodies* (2001), Andrew and Valerie have divorced and he and Sara have become lovers, but he can't seem to manage the decisive step of moving from his beastly little flat into Medlar Cottage, the tangible image of Sara's devotion to the dead Matteo. Andrew's post-divorce upheavals and his children's unhappiness cloud their relationship—Andrew's son even makes a pathetic stab at poisoning Sara while on an ill-fated picnic—and yet another convoluted set of homicides occurs, connected to the New Age treatment center where Sara's friend James is a reluctant patient, the prescribed health-food diet going through his distressed colon "like a bottle-brush" (*Fruitful Bodies* 103). Sara's emotional conflicts again threaten her musicianship, producing a serious emotional block as she prepares the Dvorak Cello Concerto for an important performance in Salzburg.

The mutual distress between Sara and Andrew crescendos to a cymbal-crashing climax at the very point when Sara toys with ending their three-year affair. Suddenly she realizes how appalling Andrew's police work really is, and she wonders "shamefully how she could have been so self-obsessed that she had refused even to try to understand this" (*Fruitful Bodies* 98). Abruptly, though, in one of those horrid ironies that Joss delineates so skillfully, when Sara reaches out to Andrew, full of tenderness and an overwhelming desire for early bedtime, he has to tell her what he's saved until the last possible moment: that tonight he has to babysit because "Valerie, once again at deliberately short notice, had decided she needed an evening out" (*Fruitful Bodies* 100).

It takes her fellow musician James, immune to Sara's sexual influence, to sum up the dilemma of a gifted musician who's at the mercy of her hormones: "Pure, unreconstructed diva that she could sometimes be, you had to love her because she was born to play the cello . . . sensitive also in friendship, as well as fierce, selfless, loyal and bloody funny. But . . . she was also born to conduct her love affairs in a manner that was clumsy, distracted, impetuous and extreme. And up to a point she understood this about herself . . . so you had to love her, and in any case she somehow made you, anyway" (*Fruitful Bodies* 115).

Novels: *Funeral Music* (U.K. 1998; U.S. 2005); *Fearful Symmetry* (U.K. 1999; U.S. 2005); *Fruitful Bodies* (U.K. 2001); *Puccini's Ghosts* (forthcoming).

Stand-alone novel: *Half-Broken Things* (2002).

Selected sources: MysteryReader.com/joss-funeral.html; *Publishers Weekly*. Rev. of *Fruitful Bodies*, June 6, 2005: 46; *Publishers Weekly*. Rev. of *Funeral Music*, March 14, 2005: 51; "Walters Gets a Second Stab." *Bookseller*, November 21, 2003: 27.

Award: Silver Dagger, 2003 (for *Half-Broken Things*).

See also: Harrison Gradwell Slater's *Night Music*, featuring Matthew Pierce on the trail of a lost Mozart diary.

Debut novel: Beverle Graves Myers's historical *Interrupted Aria* (2004) featuring castrato Tito Amato and set in nineteenth-century Italy.

Peter Shandy

Profession:	Professor of Agrology [*sic*]
Living situation:	Married
Geographic locale:	Environs of Balaclava Agricultural College, Massachusetts
Time period:	1978–1998
Associate:	Helen Marsh Shandy, librarian
Nemesis:	Human pretension and greed
Significant relationship:	Helen Marsh Shandy
Concerns:	Justice; horticulture; birdwatching

Breeder of the Balaclava Buster, the world's greatest rutabaga, fiftyish Professor of Agrology Peter Shandy solves a ten-volume "pure tinseltown" series (Ashley 322) beginning with *Rest You Merry* (1978) and running through *Exit the Milkman* (1996). With these murder mysteries Charlotte MacLeod revived the "cozy" mystery full of nice characters and folksy small-town or rural settings (Murphy 320). The intricately plotted and bizarrely accomplished crimes that Shandy faces increasingly overshadow his professorial activities, taking him farther and farther afield from fictional Balaclava (Massachusetts) Agricultural College into unrealistic but charming adventures, while his wife Helen, increasingly bound up with the genealogy of the Buggins family, whose ancestor founded Balaclava, develops into the real brains behind the scenes of Shandy's success.

Shandy's crime-solving career begins by accident in *Rest You Merry* when he stumbles onto the body of campus busybody Jemima Ames behind his living room sofa. Like most of the victims in this series, Jemima seems to have at least partly brought her fate on herself, and suspects abound. Shandy, at the outset a gentle middle-aged bachelor beleaguered by his neighbors' competing vulgar displays of Christmas decorations, plays the role of absent-minded professor effectively, treating colleagues, spouses, and bumptious college administrators alike with a gentle courtesy that masks a plant breeder's penchant for inductive reasoning.

Librarian Helen Marsh, who soon arrives at Balaclava to housesit for widowed Professor Ames, also has an outwardly innocuous appearance that cloaks a stiletto-keen mind inclined to weed out inconsistencies of behavior and inexorably sort motivations as if according to the Dewey Decimal system. Forced "to skip town" from her previous job in California because she pointed out that her university president's latest manuscript was "pompous nonsense, abominably written" and that he himself was "an illiterate windbag" (*Rest You Merry* 73), Helen quickly wins Shandy's heart while helping him solve a murder plot as badly tangled as twelve skeins of Christmas lights dumped higgledy-piggledy into a plastic bag last January.

As the series and its murders burgeon, Balaclava's neo-Viking President Thorkjeld Svenson appoints Shandy clandestinely to protect the college from harmful publicity by assisting Police Chief Fred Ottermole in bringing the perpetrators to justice. This unrealistically leaves Shandy, informally deputized by Ottermole, less and less time for rutabaga breeding and even teaching, which he performs in an increasingly perfunctory fashion, allowing his lab assistant to carry on virtually unsupervised.

Wrack and Rune (1982) finds Shandy and Helen, now blissfully married, called to Miss Hilda Horsefall's farm to investigate the death of hired man Spurge Lumpkin, found "suddenly, horribly, gruesomely dead" (*Wrack* 11) in a pit of quicklime. The "something" of 1983's *Something the Cat Dragged In* turns out to be the bedraggled toupee of an elderly man slain with his own cane. *The Corpse in Oozak's Pond* (1987), nominated for an Edgar, has Shandy, by now acknowledged as "Balaclava's expert on bodies found in unexpected places" (*Corpse* 13) gamely hauling the half-frozen remains of a man costumed as Balaclava's founder from the chilly pond that must be kept flowing so that the college's power plant—fueled by methane, its constantly renewable cow-manure resource—will keep running. Out owl-counting in *An Owl Too Many* (1991), Shandy is on the spot when mysterious stranger Emory Emmerick is first netted, then stabbed through the neck with an ice pick, and in *Exit the Milkman* (1996), Dairy Management professor Feldster, Peter's good friend, disappears and returns an amnesiac under ominous circumstances.

Unlikely as all the fodder for these plots may seem and as highly complicated as their solutions prove to be, Shandy soldiers stoutly through them, but he needs Helen for inspiration and balance. When bemused by modern vicissitudes like the universal undergraduate reading problem, Shandy tends to moan, "Would you believe at least three quarters of my freshman agronomy class don't know how to spell fungicide?" Helen crisply straightens him out: "Certainly I would. Furthermore, they can't look it up in the dictionary because nobody ever made them learn the alphabet" (*Something* 17). With all of MacLeod's pleasantly dotty characters swirling around him, Shandy makes a fair-minded, sensitive, kind, and only occasionally bumbling hero because Helen is the center of his life, the down-to-earth fulcrum on which all these novels rest. She asks playfully, "Why should I care for tall, handsome blond males of Nordic descent when I already have a genuine honest-to-gosh mongrel Yankee with a bald spot on top for the brains to bulge out of?" (*Milkman* 232)—why, indeed, except that it makes for pleasant cozy reading.

Novels: *Rest You Merry* (1978); *The Luck Runs Out* (1979); *Wrack and Rune* (1982); *Something the Cat Dragged In* (1983); *The Curse of the Giant Hogweed* (1985); *The Corpse in Oozak's Pond* (1986); *Vane Pursuit* (1989); *An Owl Too Many* (1991); *Something in the Water* (1994); *Exit the Milkman* (1996).

Other series: Sarah Kelling and Max Bittersohn series; as Alisa Craig; the Royal Canadian Mounted Police Inspector Madoc Rhys series; the Grub-and-Stakers Gardening and Roving Club series of Lobelia Falls, Ontario.

Short fiction: *Grab Bag* (1987); *It Was an Awful Shame and Other Stories* (1992).

Biography: *Had She But Known: A Biography of Mary Roberts Rinehart* (1994). MacLeod also edited two anthologies: *Mistletoe Mysteries* (1980) and *Christmas Stalkings* (1991).

Other works: MacLeod authored numerous books for children, two under the pen name "Matilda Hughes."

Selected sources: *Publishers Weekly*. Rev. of *Exit the Milkman*, July 1, 1996: 45; *Publishers Weekly*. Rev. of *Something in the Water*, January 31, 1994: 78; *Wilson Library Bulletin*. Rev. of *Rest You Merry*, May 1994: 86.

Awards: Nero Wolfe Award, 1987; Bouchercon Lifetime Achievement Award, 1992; Malice Domestic Lifetime Achievement Award, 1998; and five American Mystery Awards.

See also: Carolyn G. Hart's Death on Demand series featuring bookstore owner **Annie Laurance Darling** and Max Darling, set in South Carolina; Joan Hess's bookstore owner Claire Malloy series, set in Arkansas; and for far-out humor, Hess's **Arly Hanks** series, also set in Arkansas; for New England settings, Jane Langton's **Homer Kelly** series, set in New England; Nancy Pickard's **Jenny Cain** series, set in Massachusetts.

Shan Tao Yun

Profession:	Former Beijing Inspector General, then political prisoner, now unofficially released
Living situation:	Single
Geographic locale:	Tibet
Time period:	1999–present
Associate:	Lokesh, a Tibetan Buddhist lama
Nemesis:	The communist regime of the People's Republic of China
Significant spiritual relationships:	Lokesh, Gendun, Tibetan Buddhist lamas
Concerns:	Morality; genocide; Lamaist (Tibetan Buddhist) enlightenment

Since 1950 Tibet and its people have been systematically brutalized by Communist China. Eliot Pattison's conversations with Tibetans and Chinese who risked much by speaking with him anchor this heartbreaking series, a tribute to the spiritual strength and courage of the Tibetans who try to maintain their religion and cultural identity and the few outsiders who try to help them.

Deep ethnic, cultural, and religious differences divide the ethnic Mongolian Tibetans, mainly pastoral yak herders, and their Han Chinese Communist overlords. Shan Tao Yun's father, a Chinese professor, perished in Mao Tse Tung's first round of persecutions of China's intellectuals. Shan's success as a Beijing police Inspector General earned him an invitation to join and rise in the Chinese Communist Party; his personal integrity in rejecting the Party and attempting to prosecute a corrupt Party official earned him arrest, torture, and five years in China's gulag, the prison labor system where life expectancy is measured in agonizing months. In Colonel Tan's 404th People's Construction Brigade high in the Tibetan plateau near Lladrung, building roads in the service of socialism, gentle old Tibetan lamas ("superior ones") imprisoned for years saved Shan's soul.

In the 1960s, the Red Army annihilated thousands of *gompas*, monasteries that nurtured Tibet's spiritual life, dispersing, destroying, or simply hollowing out the

Tibetans who futilely tried to defend them (*Ghosts* 4), proud and independent but helpless and sadly confused at what outsiders were doing to their world (*Skull Mantra* 412). In *The Skull Mantra* (1999), Shan, resigned to his fate, is secretly meditating with the lamas, who defend themselves by taking virtuous positions against impossible odds (*Ghosts* 17), when suddenly he is plucked out to investigate a corpse dressed in American denim, a murder too important for the Communists to bury and too inflammatory for their own detectives to handle.

In the labor camp, Shan's physical joys are small, like Ivan Denisovich's: an apple, a hot cup of tea, a little extra barley gruel; his spiritual joys are alien to Western eyes. Thinking he will be returned to hard labor after solving the murder, he offers savage Colonel Tan his only cherished possession, his great-grandfather's *Tao Te Ching* divination sticks, for safekeeping. He thereby touches Tan's heart and wins a tenuous freedom: no papers and a $100 price on his head that would keep a herder's family fed for months.

Having lost most of his prior beliefs, Shan then casts his lot with his mentors—the old lama Lokesh, once trained as a healer, and Gendun, a monk who came from Yerpa, a secret *gompa* hidden deep in the mountains where Shan sheltered for a time—to try to rebuild the old religion. Lokesh sees Shan as a bridge, "just there, because we needed him" (*Ghosts* 15). To Gendun, "the shadow of Shan's prior incarnation as a senior Beijing investigator encourag[ed] him to become involved in unimportant events, drawn to the workings of logic and cause and effect that Gendun considered traps for the spiritually aware," but "for Shan, protecting the old lamas would always be more important" (*Ghosts* 43). His devotion to the lamas and the spiritual path they represent for him clashes with the "unimportant events" he must unravel to save them.

In *Water Touching Stone* (2001), Shan's defense of the endangered lamas takes him along the Old Silk Road, searching among embittered Turkic tribesmen, smugglers, corrupt Red Army soldiers, and hidden Buddhists for the killer of a revered native schoolteacher. When he succeeds, he could escape to Alaska and freedom, but Shan stays, agreeing with his lamas that Tibet is Shan's first step toward his new incarnation, the tiny crack that allows water to conquer stone.

Buddhists believe that the path leading to Nirvana, the end of suffering, requires compassion. Tibetans create beauty as a spiritual practice, to translate compassion into action, representing Buddha's myriad aspects in slim, elegant, gilt and jeweled statuettes and *thangkas*, temple banners painted brilliantly on cotton or silk with centuries-old texts, proportions, and highly complex symbolism. Practicing compassion in *Bone Mountain* (2002), Shan agrees to return the stolen eye of an idol to its distant valley, fulfilling an ancient prophecy but trapping him between the Red Army and a Western oil company. In *Beautiful Ghosts* (2004) Shan delays a month-long retreat to help Lokesh and Gendun illegally celebrate the exiled Dalai Lama's birthday at Zhoka, a ruined *gompa* once famous for its religious art. Government officials demand Shan's help to find stolen sacred art treasures, and while he struggles to protect the lamas, he receives unexpected help from the FBI and undreamed-for reunion with his son Ko, brought out of a prison coal mine to blackmail Shan.

As Shan insists to FBI Agent Corbett, Tibetans "live by truths, not facts" (*Ghosts* 117): being a prisoner is what someone else does to you; being a thief or a liar, you do to yourself (*Ghosts* 300); and so Tibet endures. Time after time, serving the truth forces Shan to abandon what he holds dearest, like his precious *Tao Te Ching* sticks, only to have them miraculously restored. Even though the Communists are moving literal and figurative mountains to obliterate the suffering soul of Tibet and its people, "This land," sighs Colonel Tan, "it makes life so difficult" (*Skull Mantra* 308).

Novels: *The Skull Mantra* (1999); *Water Touching Stone* (2001); *Bone Mountain* (2002); *Beautiful Ghosts* (2004).

Selected sources: "Book Sense's Top Mysteries." *USA Today*, July 10, 2002; Conaty, Barbara. Rev. of *Water Touching Stone*. May 1, 2001: 128; *Kirkus Reviews*. Rev. of *Beautiful Ghosts*, March 1, 2004: 203; *Publishers Weekly*. Rev. of *Beautiful Ghosts*, March 22, 2004: 66; *Publishers Weekly*. Rev. of *Water Touching Stone*, May 4, 2001: 56.

See also: For modern Chinese settings: Nicole Mones's *A Cup of Light*, set in Beijing; John Lanchester's *Fragrant Harbor*, set in Hong Kong; Lisa See's *Dragon Bones*, set along the Yangtse River; Qiu Xiaolong's Inspector Chen series, set in various modern Communist Chinese venues.

Rei Shimura

Profession:	Dealer in Japanese antiques
Living situation:	Single
Geographic locales:	Tokyo; San Francisco
Time period:	1997–present
Significant relationship:	Hugh Glendinning
Concerns:	Japanese tradition and culture; cultural identity

Sujata Massey's Indian-German parentage, her personal experience with Japanese culture, and her writing, "like silk drawn over razor blades, serene yet deadly" (Ashley 335), combine to make her heroine, antiques dealer Japanese American Rei Shimura, a complex and intriguing amateur detective in a series awarded both the Agatha and Macavity mystery awards. Rei's personal crises nearly always arise from confusion over cultural identity just as Massey confesses her own do, but Massey also pays exquisite attention to Japanese tradition and culture, admitting that after her annual month in Japan she returns to her home in Baltimore "lugging a suitcase jammed with antique textiles, photographs of my travels and notes for the next book."

In her mid-twenties in *The Salaryman's Wife* (1997), raw ambition and a lifelong thirst for things Japanese had driven Rei to leave her parents, a Japanese American psychiatrist and his Baltimore-bred American wife, antiwar sympathizers, and their San Francisco home for a tiny Tokyo apartment. Rei briefly teaches English and struggles to establish her own Japanese antiques business, since no Japanese would hire her. Able to pass as Japanese in appearance when it suits her, Rei continually finds life in Tokyo challenging. Though she speaks Japanese almost natively, she embarrassingly cannot read *kangi*, Japan's intricate written language, and her brash California-smart personality's all wrong for Japan. She'll always be a foreigner there, able to "see insecurity and tensions that nobody else did" and equipped with etiquette that by Japanese standards seems to have been learned "on a different planet." Rei almost daily "walks an uneasy line between pleasure and pain—and understanding and confusion" (*Floating Girl* 140, 3).

In *The Salaryman's Wife* Rei unofficially investigates the murder of a beautiful woman found dead in a picturesque country inn, a case that combines a conventional mystery format with both modern and traditional elements of life in Japan. Rei also falls for Scottish lawyer Hugh Glendinning, with Golden Retriever looks and "a smile like the sun" (*Samurai's Daughter* 9), creating the main conflict of the series because Rei loves him but refuses to be dependent on him. She mourns for a year after he leaves Japan at the close of *The Salaryman's Wife*.

Though she can't get Hugh out of her mind, Rei tries a brief fling with Takeo Kayama, whom she meets in *The Flower Master* (1999), where Rei's aunt, a master of *ikebana*, traditional Japanese flower arranging, suggests that Rei might achieve tranquility by enrolling in an *ikebana* school. Tranquility soon evaporates when aesthetic rivalries explode at the school and Rei has to clear her aunt, suspected of killing another master with garden shears. Rei and Takeo, a sensitive *ikebana* artist at severe odds with his wealthy family, enjoy some breezily sexy interludes, but Rei forgets about him completely during her next case, *The Floating Girl* (2000), as she explores the peculiarly Japanese *manga* world of comic book publishing that often overtly depicts violence against women—an underlying series theme. Here Rei becomes embroiled in a murder traceable to the unsettling social atmosphere of pre–World War II Japan.

Further romantic entanglements spice *The Bride's Kimono* (2001), where Rei transports a virtually priceless kimono to a Washington, D.C., museum exhibit. The body of a random acquaintance murdered at a shopping mall is initially identified as Rei, who when found alive is accused of operating a prostitution ring. Rei's familial tensions surface and receive fuller exploration in *The Samurai's Daughter* (2003), when Rei, back in San Francisco to trace her Japanese family's history, unearths disturbing truths about their prewar militaristic political orientation.

Rei's on-again, off-again beau Hugh Glendenning is now also in San Francisco working on a class action suit on behalf of victims of Japanese atrocities during the Second World War. Rei now feels more at home in Tokyo's Yanaka Shinto Shrine, worshipping not God but ancestral spirits and nature, than she does in her mother's Episcopalian Grace Cathedral, so when she accepts Hugh's latest proposal, Rei, too Japanese to turn her back on her ancestors and too American to accept the Japanese truism that "water washes everything away," finds herself trapped between her father's disapproval of the marriage and the love for Hugh that she can't deny. Caught up as well in Hugh's pursuit of justice for a murdered "comfort woman" forced into prostitution at thirteen by the Japanese Army and for a gentle acupuncturist blinded by slave labor in Japanese-run mines, Rei struggles her way toward compromise when she's ejected from Japan for choosing moral right over pragmatic reality, even abandoning her vegetarianism for a scrumptious chicken *yakitori* and her brash tendency to see human action as black or white. "So much has changed" for Rei Shimura, who recently "embraced a man who'd been part of the Nanking massacre" and discovered she herself was a descendent of an evil man "who'd led Emperor Hirohito to make very bad choices" (*Samurai's Daughter* 293). In Washington with Hugh, not as yet married and possibly a little bit pregnant at the start of *The Pearl Diver* (2004), Rei remains a *hafu*, a half-Japanese, half-American whose life has gone from frenetic to *zurekin*, "half-peak commuting." With her heart still in the Japan that rejected her, Rei's not sure she likes that.

Novels: *The Salaryman's Wife* (1997); *Zen Attitude* (1998); *The Flower Master* (1999); *The Floating Girl* (2000); *The Bride's Kimono* (2001); *The Samurai's Daughter* (2003); *The Pearl Diver* (2004); *The Typhoon Lover* (2005).

Selected sources: Klett, Rex E. Rev. of *The Pearl Diver*. *Library Journal*, August 15, 2004: 59; Leber, Michele. Rev. of *The Samurai's Daughter*. *Library Journal*, February 15, 2003: 173; Reed, J.R. Rev. of *The Salaryman's Wife*. *People*, November 17, 1997: 43; Rosen, Judith. "Fresh Blood—All Under 40." *Publishers Weekly*, April 21, 2003: 32; Tennenhouse, Mary Ann. "A Pearl of a Girl: *PW* Talks with Sujata Massey." *Publishers Weekly*, July 19, 2004: 147.

Award: Agatha Award for best first novel, 1997.

Web site: www.interbridge.com/sujata.

See also: Seichō Matsumoto's *Inspector Imanishi Investigates*; Shizuko Natsuki's *Murder at Mt. Fuji* and other non-series novels; and Masako Togawa's non-series psychological mysteries, reminiscent of Minette Walters's work. Novels set in modern Japan but written by Western authors include Isaac Adamson's series featuring Japanese-American journalist Billy Chaka; Howard Fast's series featuring Japanese-American Detective Matsuto of the Beverly Hills Police Department; James Melville's thirteen-novel Tetsuo Otani series and Janwillem van de Wetering's short story collection *Inspector Saito's Small Satori*. Series by authors with Oriental backgrounds include Leonard Chang's series featuring Allen Choice, A Korean-American San Francisco PI; Naomi Hirahara's series featuring Mas Arai, a Japanese-American gardener in a Los Angeles suburb.

Jemima Shore

Profession:	Television personality
Living situation:	Single
Geographic locale:	England
Time period:	1977–1994
Significant relationships:	Various

| *Associate*: | Cherry Bronson |
| *Concern*: | Feminism |

Sandwiched between Lady Antonia Fraser's award-winning historical biographies, her Jemima Shore series presents an independent, feisty, thoroughly modern feminist who runs her own television show, a showcase for British investigative reporting, and her personal life, a tribute to women's lib, with panache and minimal niggling regrets for her chosen single life. Drawn at least in part from Fraser's own upbringing in a wealthy aristocratic family noted for literary talent, Jemima Shore has and uses connections with people in all walks of life as she investigates hot-button social issues like abortion rights, euthanasia, birth control, and political scandal. Jemima's private secretary Cherry "Flowering Cherry" Bronson becomes her business partner when Jemima branches out from Cy Frederick's Megalith Television to her own company, JS Productions. The elegant Jemima also frequently consults with Detective Chief Inspector John Portsmouth of the Royal and Diplomatic Protection Unit, New Scotland Yard ("Pompey of the Yard"), but Jemima prefers working as a single operative, with a feline sense of mischief, a gift for stealth in little dark places, and an instinct that Frederick describes as "expensive" and Pompey refers to as an ailment. "The single word 'instinct,' drawing the fire of such quizzical males as Cy Frederick and Pompey, was in fact not quite accurate. It was more that Jemima possessed a very strong instinct for order. This would not let her rest so long as the smallest detail was out of place in the well-regulated pattern of her mind" (*Cool Repentance* 163).

Jemima narrates her first case, *Quiet as a Nun* (1977), set in the upscale boarding school of the Convent of Blessed Eleanor when Vatican II had not yet completely upended the traditional lives of its nuns and decimated their numbers. Though nominally Protestant and actually a rationalist with "no beliefs and no fears" (*Quiet* 86), Jemima's always been "morbidly intrigued by the Jesuits" and their reputation for dangerous intellectual acuity (*Quiet* 3), so she takes on Reverend Mother Ancilla's plea to investigate a classic Golden Age–type locked-room mystery, the puzzling death of Sister Miriam, formerly Jemima's old school buddy Rosabelle Powerstock, who apparently perished of starvation in the convent's medieval tower.

Now forty, Jemima's been on her own since eighteen. Solitariness is a condition of her life, and she conducts her love affairs mostly on her own terms, like her involvement with Tom Amyas, a married MP devoted to the liberal causes she loves him for. Jemima's experience makes her well aware of the sexual tensions that can plague a woman of a certain age, and she also feels regret and guilt that she never answered Rosabelle's letter asking Jemima's advice about becoming a nun, so she carefully assembles the pieces of this puzzling case, connecting her own situation to the nuns' dilemma, making a completely new picture of convent life—and her own.

In the rest of her investigations, told mainly in the omniscient third person, Jemima Shore seems to illustrate "Dorothy L. Sayers' advice about keeping romantic subplots under strict control" (Murphy 187) while she cheekily solves crimes among the British upper class. *A Splash of Red* (1981) deals with the artsy crowd and the throat-slashing of Jemima's friend Chloe, a romance novelist, but Lord Valentine

Brighton, "a bisexual gadfly," and radical politics complicate the proceedings. *Oxford Blood* (1985) finds Jemima probing irreverently among the dreaming spires and nightmarish eccentrics of "a wild, degenerate, and aristocratic circle" (Murphy 187) while in *Your Royal Heritage* (1987) Jemima, covering a Royal Wedding for American television, solves the kidnapping of a Royal Princess by an animal rights group and the murder of an obnoxious journalist. *The Cavalier Case* (1990) takes Jemima into a mélange of sex, professional tennis, and ghostly carryings-on at Lackland Court, haunted by dashing seventeenth-century Cavalier poet Decimus Meredith, first Viscount Lackland. As a lagniappe, Jemima meets "loquacious and high-spirited radical lawyer Ned Silver...and one way or another they had scarcely been apart, except during the hours of work, ever since (*Cavalier* 241)—until Ned's business trip to Singapore opening *Political Death* (1994) leaves her prone to a dramatic one-night fling with irresistible Shakespearean star Randall Birley while she investigates three suspicious demises linked to his production of *Twelfth Night*.

"He wasn't worth it," Jemima then admits ruefully to another of Birley's lovers. Jemima, "freed of her fantasies because they had in a sense been fulfilled," discovered that beneath Birley's Byronic shell lay "weakness there, or if not weakness, vulnerability" (*Political Death* 207). In *Quiet as a Nun* a younger Jemima had scoffed at Byron's insistence that love is "woman's whole existence," but after all her professional investigations and personal experimentations, New Woman Jemima Shore reaches an old, old conclusion. In *Political Death*, her "wonderful, passionate semi-detached relationship" with Ned dissolves into a "sense of desolation" when Ned isn't there to comfort her, and when he returns, "Love Conquers All."

Novels: *Quiet as a Nun* (1977); *The Wild Island* (1978); *A Splash of Red* (1981); *Cool Repentance* (1982); *Oxford Blood* (1985); *Your Royal Heritage* (1987); *The Cavalier Case* (1990); *Political Death* (1994).

Short fiction: *Jemima Shore's First Case* (1986); *Jemima Shore at the Sunny Grave* (1991). Note: *Jemima Shore Investigates* (1983) contains stories adapted from the television series by John Burke and Frances Heasman from authors other than Fraser (Ashley 168).

Other works: Frazer is best known for her historical nonfiction, including *Mary, Queen of Scots* (1969, new ed. 1994); *Faith and Treason: The Story of the Gunpowder Plot* (1996); *Marie Antoinette: The Journey* (2001).

Selected sources: Cannon, Margaret. Rev. of *Cool Repentance*. *Toronto Globe and Mail*, August 25, 1984; Clark, Beverly Lyon. Rev. of *Oxford Blood*. *New York Times Book Review*, October 13, 1985: 24; Gussow, Mel. "Antonia Fraser: The Lady Is a Writer." *New York Times Magazine*, September 9, 1984; Hooper, Brad. Rev. of *Jemima Shore at the Sunny Grave*. *Booklist*, November 15, 1992: 563; Snowman, Daniel. "Antonia Fraser." *History Today*, October 2000: 26–29.

Major awards: Fraser has won numerous awards for her historical studies and biographies. Her mystery awards include the Gold Dagger for nonfiction (1996). She was named a Commander of the British Empire in 1999.

See also: For humor and glamour: Ruth Dudley Edwards's series featuring aspiring British mystery novelist Robert Amiss; Robert Eversz's series featuring LA paparazza Nina Zero;

Lesley Grant-Adamson's detective-suspense series featuring British gossip columnist Rain Morgan; Lawrence Klavan's series featuring Roy Milano, Hollywood movie newsletter editor; Daniel Klein's series featuring Elvis Presley in Las Vegas.

Debut novel: Jim Kelly's *The Water Clock*, featuring Cambridgeshire reporter Philip Dryden.

Kate Shugak

Profession:	Former D.A.'s office investigator, now crime consultant
Living situation:	Single
Geographic locale:	"The Park" (fictional twenty-million-acre national park), Alaska
Time period:	1992–present
Associates:	Mutt, Shugak's half-wolf canine companion; Jack Morgan; later Jim Chopin; Johnny Morgan
Significant relationships:	Jack Morgan; later Jim Chopin
Concerns:	Environmental protection; child abuse; women in the wilderness

In Aleut detective consultant Kate Shugak's cases, author Dana Stabenow makes "thrills, danger, humor, pathos, fact, and fable" accompany a passion for the Alaskan wilderness and its intensely individual way of life. Kate herself, a stunning black-haired five-foot woman with a tall personality, typifies Alaska's population, part native Aleut, part Athabaskan Native American, part Anglo ancestry—including a Russian commissar, a Jewish tailor, Uncle Dieter who was probably a Nazi, "something Mediterranean" and maybe some heavy-duty work-ethic'd WASP (*Grave Denied* 180, 65). In Alaska, where "maintaining one's privacy came somewhere between a vocation and a religion" and sticking one's nose into another's business can result in a savage lopping-off, Kate and Mutt, her 140-pound half-Husky, half-wolf "alter ego, her sister, her friend, her savior" (*Grave Denied* 82) reluctantly supplement their homesteading self-sufficiency with crime consulting among "Park rats," most of whom are Kate's relatives, friends, or acquaintances.

Kate's five years of sex-crime investigating for the Anchorage D.A.'s office still give her chills. The last one, the near-fatal thread connecting her stories, scarred her body and soul and made her seclude herself on the remote homestead her father built in the Park, five miles from the nearest neighbor and twelve miles from Niniltna, the nearest town. Fourteen months later in Edgar Award winner *A Cold Day for Murder* (1992), Kate's former boss D.A. Jack Morgan persuades her—for a price—to take Mutt tracking Morgan's investigator and a ranger missing in the vast national park—the investigator being Kate's current lover.

Besides loving the wilderness, Kate can fix her own machinery, hunt and fish for her own food, build her own shelter, defend herself, and survive in the wilderness. She needs all those skills to nab killers who often threaten her and her nearest and dearest, like her elderly aunties in *Killing Grounds* (1998), accused of slaying an abusive salmon fisherman. Jack Morgan, her first great love, dies in Kate's arms, murdered at the close of *Hunter's Moon* (1999) and Kate again exiles herself in a remote fishing village until state trooper "Chopper Jim" Chopin seeks her out in *Midnight Come Again* (2000) to help solve an apparent international banking scandal.

In *The Singing of the Dead* (2001), Kate unearths a related century-old family scandal during Alaska's Gold Rush, uncovering the harsh lot of women in a primitive unforgiving land while she investigates a brutal murder comitted during a vicious election campaign. Still bereaved, she restarts her life in *A Fine and Bitter Snow* (2002). She organizes support for her friend Park Ranger Dan O'Brian, who's being hassled into early retirement by superiors who think he's too environmentally "green," and she also takes on another homicide for Chopin, smitten by Kate with Mutt's cheek-licking approval. Morgan's teenage son Johnny also moves into Kate's small cabin to escape his neglectful mother, Kate's sworn enemy. *A Grave Denied* (2003) heats up the simmering mutual attraction between Kate and lady-killer Chopin, 6′10″, 240 pounds. Kate observes that he's "Blonde. Smart. Built. With blue eyes. And a deep voice. And a great grin. And a charm of manner Casanova would have envied" (*Grave Denied* 128).

The depth of Kate's character, both her strengths and her flaws, emerges from her own past, too, especially her ambivalent relationship with her grandmother Ekaterina Moonin Shugak ("Emaa"), Aleut traditionalist and "the respected matriarch" of all area native tribes from whom "all officials—Native American tribal and United States governmental—must seek counsel" (*Silk Stalkings* 1: 82). For a long time, Kate feels "suffocated by Emaa's expectations. The bloodlines that tied her to the Park were tenacious to the point of strangulation" (*Grave Denied* 231–32). Long after Emaa succumbs to a heart attack alone, deliberately leaving Kate to take her place at an important tribal meeting, Kate realizes the important lesson Emaa taught her: By trying to escape the past, she's really holding on to it, smothering herself, just as Bobby Clark, Kate's black Vietnam vet amputee buddy, has been doing by refusing to deal with his own family back in Tennessee.

When a killer burns Kate's ancestral cabin to the ground, destroying nearly all of her possessions, the ties that seemed to bind Kate actually free her. When the Park rats build her a new home, Kate squirms at owing them, especially those she thinks helped her because she's Emaa's granddaughter. Old Sam Dementieff sets her straight in Park rat fashion: "You don't owe us squat.... Stop trying to run everyone's life and start taking care of your own" (*Taint* 7–8).

Kate swears to Emaa's memory that she's going home for good, but a new case in Anchorage again opens up secrets that some of Alaska's powerful citizens would rather leave buried in *A Taint in the Blood* (2004). She also mounts an aggressive sexual bedevilment of Trooper Jim Chopin, to her satisfaction and his dazed exhaustion. Emaa is dead, Kate tells herself, "Jack was dead....Mutt was right.... Much better to focus on today" (*Taint* 305).

Novels: *A Cold Day for Murder* (1992); *A Fatal Thaw* (1993); *Dead in the Water* (1993); *A Cold-Blooded Business* (1994); *Play with Fire* (1995); *Blood Will Tell* (1996); *Breakup* (1997); *Killing*

Grounds (1998); *Hunter's Moon* (1999); *Midnight Come Again* (2000); *The Singing and the Dead* (2001); *A Fine and Bitter Snow* (2002); *A Grave Denied* (2003); *A Taint in the Blood* (2004); *The Blindfold Game* (2006).

Other series: The Liam Campbell and Wyanet Chouinard mystery series; the Star Svensdotter science fiction series.

Selected sources: Melton, Emily. Rev. of *A Cold-Blooded Business*. *Booklist*, June 1, 1991: 1862; *Publishers Weekly*. Rev. of *A Taint in the Blood*, August 30, 2004: 35; Rowan, John. Rev. of *Killing Grounds*. *Booklist*, February 15, 1998: 989; Shepard, Jill. "Growing Up Alaskan." *Alaska*, September 1996: 18; Stasio, Marilyn. Rev. of *Hunter's Moon*. *New York Times Book Review*, May 23, 1999: 33; *Washington Post Book World*. Rev. of *Breakup*, July 27, 1997: 10.

Major award: Edgar Award, 1992.

Web site: www.stabenow.com.

See also: Canadian author Lawrence Gough's series featuring Vancouver police detectives Jack Willows and Clare Parker; American Sue Henry's Alaska series featuring state trooper Alex Jensen and dog-team racer Jessie Arnold, and Henry's cozy Alaska series featuring widow Maxine "Maxie" McNabb.

Bill Slider

Profession:	Detective Inspector, London C.I.D.
Living situation:	Estranged, then divorced
Geographic locale:	London
Time period:	1994–present
Associate:	Detective Sergeant James Atherton
Nemesis:	Detective Chief Superintendent Palfreyman
Significant relationship:	Joanna Marshall
Concerns:	The Job; domestic relationships; his children; fair play

Bill Slider's lover, violinist Joanna Marshall, calls this Shepherd's Bush Detective Inspector "Pooh Bear with a touch of Eeyore" (*Killing Time* 190), because Slider's creator Cynthia Harrod-Eagles, best known for her "history without tears" (*CA Online*) "Dynasty" and "Kirov Saga" series, makes Slider's procedurals police work plus personal pain. For Slider, solving homicides on his patch of West London is The Job, even if the odds for justice are shortening all the time. Villains are getting off lightly and "Coppers are getting shot and knifed, bashed on the head and dumped, and for what?" (*Killing Time* 3). Slider's always soul-sick at the "stupidity and waste of crime," and "the very, very bottom line" that made him take The Job in the first place is his "inability to do nothing": "he couldn't stop caring whether he cared or not" (*Killing Time* 63), and he's satisfied with his modest rank.

On The Job and off, Slider cares about almost everyone, even his estranged wife Irene. He'd spent most of his adult life with Irene, knowing she was an unhappy neglected copper's wife, but Irene, who always stuck to orange juice, hadn't been any fun in a pub, either. After Slider met Joanna Marshall, a witness in *Orchestrated Death* (1991), Joanna became everything good in Slider's personal life, though Slider's fourteen years of faithful marriage were followed by two of "bowel-churning deception" (*Killing Time* 31) before Irene ran off with flashy Ernie Newman, who could give Irene and Slider's children Matthew and Kate things Slider won't ever be able to swing on his police salary. In *Killing Time* (1998), the estranged Irene, chicly dressed, equipped with trendy vocabulary and drinking gin and tonic at lunchtime, hints she might want to come home, but Slider's now a catbox-cleaning New Man contentedly living with Joanna. He bungles the situation badly out of pity and guilt, and it suddenly dawns on Irene that his affair with Joanna preceded hers with Ernie. The resulting explosion confirms the opinion Slider's close friend and partner suave lady-killer Jim Atherton wryly states—that Bill's "a plonker when it comes to women" (*Killing Time* 271).

With colleagues, witnesses, suspects, and even villains, though, Slider's compassion makes him likeable, empathetic, and highly effective as a policeman. Protective of his homicide squad and plagued by guilt that Atherton had nearly been killed in *Blood Lines* (1996), Slider trains Atherton's temporary replacement, young black female detective Tony Hart, but he lets Tony's "dotty charm" go only so far because Slider is, after all, her boss. Slider's right, too, in thinking he's free of prejudice, considering the women on his team, "Norma" Swilley and now Tony Hart no differently than his men. For Slider, women's femininity is just a trait they have, like McLaren's fried-egg sandwich habit "or Mackay's football fanaticism or Atherton's finickitiness" (*Killing Time* 155). Slider also views his superiors' peculiarities tolerantly, even admitting to himself that his temporary Detective Superintendent boss "Little Eric" Honeyman had turned out to be not a bad old boy "for an impossible bastard" (*Killing Time* 206).

When boyish gay erotic dancer Jay Paloma, looking "like Princess Di at bay," asks Slider for help and shortly thereafter is found bludgeoned to death, Slider's overcome with what Detective Nicholls calls Slider's "Global Mommy Syndrome," his compulsion to be responsible for everyone's troubles (*Killing Time* 18, 39). That empathy allays people's fear of him as a policeman so he can quickly get at the truth they're often afraid to tell. Slider treats prostitutes like Paloma's friend Busty Parnell especially gently because their hopelessness touches his heart. Even when he's questioning a major suspect like Paloma's lover, cabinet minister Sir Nigel Grisham, Slider keeps his metaphorical gloves on, pitying Grisham though relieved that the investigation is on the right track and hoping Grisham will speedily come across with the goods.

Slider and Hart get their man in *Killing Time*, but Slider knows he's going to have to pay for his extramarital sins; should he try to placate Irene, about to descend on Slider to rant if not to bash, or wait for her solicitor's letter? He and Atherton are getting a new boss, too, Fred "The Syrup" Porson, "The Rug from Hell," full of beans after three years in the Traffic Planning Unit. Porson chivvies Slider and his team through *Shallow Grave* (1999), the touchy case of a woman found dead in a trench near the terrace of a famous historian's elegant London home, and *Blood Sinister* (2001), an even dicier outing because the strangled victim is Phoebe Agnew, a police-baiting radical left-wing journalist, leaving Slider with perpetually clenched teeth and Atherton close to a nervous breakdown. In *Gone Tomorrow* (2002), Porson's badly depressed over his wife's death and Atherton's having girlfriend problems, while Slider's personal troubles multiply; he can't provide the electronic toys and pricey fencing lessons for his children that Ernie Newman can, and worse, police and orchestra obligations are straining his relationship with Joanna. Then out of all this Eyore-like gloom, Joanna comes up pregnant and both Slider and man-about-town Atherton become engaged. Kind, modest, bumbling-with-women Bill Slider gets just the honeypot he deserves.

Novels: *Orchestrated Death* (1991); *Death Watch* (1992); *Necrochip* (1993); *Dead End* (1994); *Grave Music* (1995); *Blood Lines* (1996); *Killing Time* (1998); *Shallow Grave* (1999); *Blood Sinister* (2001); *Gone Tomorrow* (2002); *Dear Departed* (2005).

Other series: The "Dynasty" series (romance novels).

Other works: Harrod-Eagles has written numerous romances under the pen names "Emma Woodhouse" and "Elizabeth Bennett."

Selected sources: *Armchair Detective*. Rev. of *Dead End*, Summer 1994: 371; Ott, Bill. "A Hard-Boiled Gazetteer to the British Isles." *Booklist*, April 4, 1999: 1456; Stasio, Marilyn. Rev. of *Bloodlines*. *New York Times Book Review*, December 8, 1996: 50; Stasio, Marilyn. Rev. of *Gone Tomorrow*. *New York Times Book Review*, December 1, 2002: 21; *Washington Post Book World*. Rev. of *Death Watch*, February 16, 1992: 8.

Major award: Romantic Novelists Association award, 1993.

See also: Gay Longworth's Detective Inspector Jessie Driver series; Barry Maitland's Detective Sergeant Kathy Kolla series, set in London; Peter Robinson's **Alan Banks** series, set in Yorkshire.

C.D. "Seedy" Sloan

Profession:	Detective Inspector, F Division, Calleshire C.I.D.
Living situation:	Married
Geographic location:	Southeastern England
Time period:	1966–present
Associate:	Detective Constable William Crosby
Nemesis:	Superintendent Leeyes
Significant relationship:	Sloan's wife Margaret
Concern:	Growing roses

With remarkable consistency, Catherine Aird's Inspector "Seedy" Sloan has plied his investigative craft over four decades, accompanied by brash young DC "Defective" Crosby, the target of bumptious Superintendent Leeyes's wholesale disparagement of The Younger Generation. Sloan and his colleagues do not age in their setting, fictional Berebury in equally invented Calleshire, southeastern England, updated with gadgetry but eternal in human foibles. Sloan's murder cases look superficially "cozy," but underneath the warm and fuzzy surface, critics agree, Aird and Sloan address "dark truths about human character" (Herbert 6).

After years as an invalid, Aird dispensed medicine for her physician father in the small Kent town where she still lives, acquiring pharmacological expertise and insight into British village life. She also delights in puzzles and word play, and Sloan's first case, *The Religious Body* (1966), contains ample helpings of all four mystery ingredients in the classic British mystery mold.

Well-read, courteous, fiftyish Sloan, however, faces contemporary horrors undreamt of by the likes of Poirot, Wimsey, and Alleyn. Summoned to investigate the death of Sister Anne, found—head bashed in—at the foot of the cellar steps of the Convent of St. Anselm, Sloan, the hardened and "perfect policeman" (*Religious Body* 4), finds working in a pre-Vatican II convent bad enough (all the blandly polite nuns look alike) without a priest tagging along; a dragon (Sister Polycarp) at the gate; next door an Agricultural Institute full of young pub-loving men with simmering hormones (and Sloan knows just what young men are up to); a superintendent addicted to Adult Education who doesn't like Sloan's understated wit; and "Defective" Crosby, who doesn't get it—or much of anything. Fresh from his course on "Mathematics for the Average Adult," Superintendent Leeyes insists that "Money is a factor in the crime equation," shooting from the hip at the convent's suave Mother Superior with statements like "this lot may have taken vows of perpetual poverty or something idiotic like that" (*Religious Body* 63). Sloan knows, however, that murder doesn't always make sense, especially at the start of a case. He also knows that questions, especially the ones that don't get asked, reveal as much as answers. Abetted by his unflappable pathologist, Dr. Hector Smithson Dabbe, not only does Sloan stylishly identify the murderer despite Leeyes's wild hairs, but he compassionately tries to help an unfortunate innocent bystander before he returns to his roses and his beloved wife Margaret, whose gently satirized nightly face-cream ritual provides Sloan one of the major clues to crack the case.

After a run of multifarious murders involving more religion (*A Most Contagious Game*, 1967), disguised identity (*Henrietta Who?* 1968), an archaeological dig (*A Late Phoenix*, 1971), a victim crushed by a falling statue inside a locked Saxon church tower (*His Burial Too*, 1973), *The Stately Home Murder* (1970), the effects of the anthrax virus in *Little Knell* (2000) and others, all demanding ingenious solutions patiently unraveled by Sloan in the face of Leeyes's ill temper and worse theories, Sloan fetches up against ultramodern technology combined with old paraphernalia, like the labyrinth on the estate of Miss Daphne Pedlinge, an elderly wheelchair-bound World War II FANY veteran in *Amendment of Life* (2002).

A Calleshire man born and bred, Inspector Sloan "has had his full meed of the dotty and the delusional.... Every beat officer got quite good at it early on in his career" (*Amendment* 11), but this case forces him to deal with dottiness and delusions in both his constable and his superintendent. The combination of a woman's body in Miss Daphne's yew maze and a crew of eccentric suspects, pentangles chalked on the Bishop's doorstep, and a kidnapped goat taxes Sloan's most inventive investigative powers. Impeded by Superintendent Leeyes's recent gleanings from "Mathematics for the Barely Numerate," Sloan has to allay Leeyes's fears that the animal rights activists may soon appear while recovering from "Defective" Crosby's speed-demonic driving (the Constable entertains hopes of a transfer to the Calleshire Traffic Division) and tempering Crosby's infatuation with a major suspect's shapely legs. Sloan beats down the temptation to send Crosby into the maze forever.

For all his impeccable courtesy, Sloan takes nothing for granted and refuses to let anyone pull the wool over his eyes, even the local Bishop, a morally unimpeachable witness but one whose "much advertised commitment to non-aggressive behaviour" vanishes when his wife feeds his favorite dressing gown to the famished goat (*Amendment* 113). Sloan manages a grain of sympathy for Leeyes, whose own wife reputedly "noticed everything. And forgave nothing" (*Amendment* 126), but Sloan's heard too many artificial arguments—"some staged entirely for his benefit"—to be taken in (*Amendment* 153). When he sets his sights on likely suspects, Sloan readily takes off his figurative gloves because "Sporting rules...didn't apply to police questioning.... You caught your subject when he—or she—was at his most vulnerable." For all his charm, the pun-loving, rose-growing Inspector Seedy Sloan is "A policeman first, last, and all the time" (*Amendment* 89, 120).

Novels: *The Religious Body* (1966); *Henrietta Who?* (1968); *The Stately Home Murder* (1970); *A Late Phoenix* (1971); *His Burial Too* (1973); *Slight Mourning* (1975); *Parting Breath* (1977); *Some Die Eloquent* (1979); *Passing Strange* (1980); *Last Respects* (1982); *Harm's Way* (1984); *A Dead Liberty* (1986); *The Body Politic* (1990); *A Going Concern* (1993); *After Effects* (1996); *Stiff News* (1998); *Little Knell* (2000); *Amendment of Life* (2002); *Hole in One* (2005).

Short fiction: *Injury Time* (1995); *Chapter and Hearse* (2004).

Selected sources: *Armchair Detective*. Rev. of *The Body Politic*, Spring 1992: 236; Callendar, Newgate. Rev. of *The Religious Body*. *New York Times Book Review*, January 1, 1967: 19; DeCandido, GraceAnne A. Rev. of *Amendment of Life*. *Booklist*, January 15, 2004: 854; Klett, Rex E. Rev. of *Little Knell*. *Library Journal*, April 1, 2001: 137; *New Yorker*. Rev. of *The Stately Home Murder*, April 4, 1970: 46.

Major awards: Honorary M.A., University of Kent, 1985; made Member of the British Empire, 1988.

See also: Cozies humorously highlighting British eccentricities and involving intricate puzzle-plots: Clare Curzon's series featuring Detective Superintendent Mike Yeadings of the Thames Valley C.I.D.; Marjorie Eccles's Midlands Superintendent Gil Mayo series and her Detective Inspector Dave Crouch series, set in the Chilterns; E.X. Ferrars's 1940s Toby Dyke novels; Caroline Graham's Detective Chief Inspector Tom Barnaby series, set in provincial England; Ann Granger's series featuring Chief Inspector Alan Markby and Foreign Service officer Meredith Mitchell, set in the Cotswolds; Martha Grimes's Inspector **Richard Jury** series, with rich casts of quirky characters; Jill McGown's DCI Lloyd series, set in the East Midlands; Roger Ormerod's Detective Inspector Richard Patton series; Susannah Stacey's Superintendent Robert Bone series; Rebecca Tope's Detective Sergeant Den Cooper series, set in Devon; R.D. Wingfield's Inspector Jack Frost series, set in "Denton."

Rabbi David Small

Profession:	Rabbi and Talmudist
Living situation:	Married
Geographic locale:	Barnard's Crossing, Massachusetts (fictional), between Lynn and Salem, on Boston's North Shore.
Time period:	1964–1996
Associate:	Barnard's Crossing Police Chief Hugh Lanigan
Nemesis:	Anti-Semitism
Significant relationship:	The Rebbitzin (Rabbi's wife) Miriam, a rabbi's daughter
Concerns:	Judaic Law and secular law

Upon moving to a small New England town with a much smaller Conservative Jewish congregation, Rabbi David Small's creator Harry Kemelman became so fascinated "by the disaccord [*sic*] between the thinking of the rabbi and that of the congregation, and the problems it gave rise to" that when Kemelman's editor suggested he add "exciting elements" of his previous detective fiction to a book Kemelman was writing about the rabbi and his congregation, Kemelman experienced a revelation: since the basic duty of a rabbi, learned in the Law, is to judge cases brought before him, "Thus was born Rabbi David Small," the first Jewish clerical sleuth ("The Creation of Rabbi Small," special foreword to *A Weekend with the Rabbi* 4).

In *Friday the Rabbi Slept Late* (1964), the small but growing congregation of affluent Jews in Barnard's Landing, Kemelman's fictional New England town on Boston's North Shore, has just built itself a synagogue and hired its first rabbi, David Small, who proves a disappointment to most of the congregation's upwardly mobile businessmen and their country-club wives. Under thirty, thin, pale, already scholarly-stooped, and despite his wife Miriam's best efforts usually disheveled in hair and clothing, Small is anything but shaped in the image of Charlton Heston's monumental Moses. Small is a Talmudist, a scholar specializing in *pilpul*, the "tracing of fine distinctions" through the study of the Talmud, the compilation of Jewish Oral Law with rabbinical commentaries, as opposed to Jewish Scriptural Law, contained in the Torah, the Books of Moses. Small also becomes a suspect in a scandalous murder case when a corn-fed and pregnant young nanny is strangled and dumped in the synagogue's parking lot and her purse is discovered in the back seat of the rabbi's car. Even under considerable pressure, Rabbi Small refuses to cater to the whims of either Jew or Gentile. Most of his congregation fails to understand the essential principle of his rabbinical duty, to study and teach the Law and to judge moral questions by it, while well-meaning Gentiles are taken aback by his refusal to pursue cheap popularity by blessing the town's annual regatta as other clergy have done for years.

As Rabbi Small explains to his new friend, broad-minded Catholic Police Chief Hugh Lanigan, a rabbi's duties make him no better or worse than any man in his congregation. Firmly anchored in traditional Judaism, Small wants to live the life of a scholar as part of the congregation, but he's getting fed up with their inability to grasp the unpopular principles by which he functions. A Talmudist begins his study by asking questions and never stops, using logic, tact, common sense—and in Small's case, gentle, mostly self-effacing humor—to arrive at the truth. By detecting the identity of the nanny's murderer, thus proving his own innocence in *Friday the Rabbi Slept Late*, Rabbi Small wins enough support to have his temple contract renewed, but his position in Barnard's Landing remains controversial.

Not a priest in the sense of the sons of Aaron or of Lanigan's Roman Catholic Monseignor O'Brien, nor a pastor in the prophet-like sense of Yankee Protestant Dr. Skinner, the rabbi applies his Talmudic intellectual training to arrive, "rather like a male Jewish Miss Marple" (Ashley 267) at the solutions of successive homicides, simultaneously resolving one conflict after another with his temple members and their wives. After facing a series of contemporary social issues, like the drug trade, international terrorism, and fanatical religious cults, Rabbi Small leaves Barnard's Landing in *The Day the Rabbi Left Town* (1996) and takes a professorship of Judaic studies at Boston's Windermere College, where he immediately falls foul of a murdered English professor.

Rabbi Small's detective abilities derive from Judaism's intellectual openness—its willingness to question anything and everything, even himself. Chief Lanigan and Rabbi Small make an effective crime-solving team, too. While Lanigan generally draws the rabbi into their various cases, the rabbi usually either clears the name of a member of his congregation or resolves some congregational problem, combining firm judgment "with a restraint and tolerance that are promoted as 'worldly Judaism'" (T.R. Steiner, in Herbert 183). All of Rabbi Small's novels also contain passages explaining Judaic history and theology to non-Jews and modern Jews unfamiliar with their faith, while *Conversations with Rabbi Small* (1981) provides Kemelman's lengthier reflections on his religion. Following the pattern for clerical sleuthing set down by G.K. Chesterton's Father Brown, Rabbi David Small understands and empathizes with human frailty while retaining his solid theological and moral principles, basing his judgments on evidence logically gathered and interpreted fairly and leavening them with Tevye's self-deprecating "If I Were a Rich Man" humor. Rabbi Small points out, too, that while the Christian prays, "Give us this day our daily bread," the Jew gives thanks: "Blessed art Thou, O Lord, who bringest forth bread from the earth" (*Friday the Rabbi Slept Late* 146). As a teacher of comparative religions, Rabbi Small makes a big impact indeed.

Novels: *Friday the Rabbi Slept Late* (1964); *Saturday the Rabbi Went Hungry* (1966); *Sunday the Rabbi Stayed Home* (1969); *Monday the Rabbi Took Off* (1972); *Tuesday the Rabbi Saw Red* (1973); *Wednesday the Rabbi Got Wet* (1976); *Thursday the Rabbi Walked Out* (1978); *Someday the Rabbi Will Leave* (1985); *One Fine Day the Rabbi Bought a Cross* (1987); *The Day the Rabbi Resigned* (1992); *The Day the Rabbi Left Town* (1996).

Short fiction (not connected with Rabbi Small): *The Nine Mile Walk* (1967).

Nonfiction: *Conversations with Rabbi Small* (1981), reflections on the Jewish faith. Kemelman also wrote *Common Sense in Education* (1970).

Selected sources: *Booklist.* Rev. of *The Day the Rabbi Left Town,* March 15, 1996: 1243; Freese, Peter. *The Ethnic Detective.* Essen: Verlag Die Blaue Eule, 1992; Raphael, Lawrence W. "Assimilated, acculturated, or affirming: The Jewish Detective in America." *Judaism,* Winter 1997: 122–27; Rogers, Michael. Rev. of *Friday the Rabbi Slept Late. Library Journal,* September 1, 2002: 220; Stasio, Marilyn. Rev. of *The Day the Rabbi Resigned. New York Times Book Review,* February 16, 1992: 27.

Awards: Edgar Award, best first novel, 1965; Faith and Freedom Communications Award, 1967.

See also: Howard Engel's series featuring Jewish Canadian detective Benny Cooperman, working in fictional Grantham, Ontario; Sharon Kahn's humorous series featuring Ruby, the Rabbi's widow; Stuart Kaminsky's series featuring Abe Lieberman, a Jewish Chicago police detective partnered with Bill Hanrahan, a Catholic; Rochelle Krich's Molly Blume series, featuring an orthodox Jewish true crime reporter in Los Angeles.

Spenser

Profession:	Private investigator
Living situation:	Single but committed
Time period:	1973–present
Associates:	Hawk; Susan Silverman; Marty Quirk
Nemesis:	Organized crime
Significant relationship:	Susan Silverman
Concerns:	Neo-chivalric code of conduct; enduring love; family relationships

After earning his Ph.D. from Boston University in 1971 with a dissertation on the works of classic hard-boiled detective authors Raymond Chandler, Dashiell Hammett, and Ross Macdonald, Robert B. Parker says he "just sat down and wrote" *The Godwulf Manuscript* (1973), launching his perennially popular four-decade Spenser series. Parker thinks he initially "was trying to be Raymond Chandler and make another Philip Marlowe," but soon he began to "just write,"—at five pages a day, a novel takes him about four months (*Talking Murder* 208–210)—fleshing out his single-named improper Bostonian knight errant into a mortality-defying "fertility god who lowers himself into the ground each winter and comes roaring back to life each spring" (Stasio 24).

Critics agree that Spenser fulfills the accepted definition of the hard-boiled private eye raised to the level of art by Parker's literary predecessors: the man who Chandler said must go down mean streets, but is himself anything but mean, a serious professional that Macdonald, for one, patterned after real-life detectives he had known. Robert Mitchum in his prime would have been Parker's choice to play tall, tough, charming Spenser, who, like Lew Archer, covers his innate compassion with a cynical wise-cracking veneer, "some of the snappiest and sauciest dialogue in the business" (White). A Korean War vet, a former policeman canned from the Suffolk County force for being an insubordinate "hot dog" (*Bad Business* 49), and a former pro boxer with a nose broken eight times, Spenser more than holds his own in rough-and-tumble brawls.

Spenser departs, however, from the hard-boiled genre by quoting Thoreau and British poets, waxing as philosophical as Travis McGee, and whipping up culinary delicacies (he's big on butter, lamb cutlets, and his mother's salad dressing recipe) at the drop of a spatula. Parker notes, "Spenser has a love life, has a context, and has friends. He's not unhappy and he's not isolated" (*Talking Murder* 214). He maintains his ongoing monogamous relationship with counselor Susan Silverman, who earns her Harvard Ph.D. in psychology during the series. Neither Susan nor Spenser nor the lethal Hawk, initially Spenser's respected adversary and soon his trusted black "pet shark," ages much in the series. Like Lancelot, Spenser once lapsed into mad passionate lust. Its target was the luscious Brenda Loring in *Mortal Stakes*—Parker's favorite Spenser novel—who shares her surname with Philip Marlowe's lover in *The Long Goodbye*. Later, wielding a sunny smile capable of melting polar ice caps, Spenser enjoys slow dancing, looking at girls, and talking about sex with ladies, but he never strays. His heart is true to Susan and hers to him, though they maintain the single lives both need to have. In the Edgar-winning *Promised Land* (1976), probably the most impressive Spenser novel, Susan describes him as "the ultimate man, the ultimate adult" and "the biggest... kid I ever saw" (176) with an unquenchable aim to help, a sure-fire lady-killing combination. By *Big Business* (2004), Susan's suburban home has become Spenser's frequent refuge from the "mean streets," a tidy bower complete with Pearl, the beer-drinking German Shorthaired Pointer whose company they share.

All of Spenser's cases illustrate "that Parker extra, a clearly defined and beautifully executed moral code." Spenser jousts against his prevailing adversary, corruption, in a wide variety of manifestations: terrorism in *The Judas Goat* (1978), real estate speculation in *Promised Land* (1976), basketball chicanery in *Playmates* (1989), ghetto landlords in *Double Deuce* (1992), organized crime in *Small Vices* (1997), and even academic conniving in *Hush Money* (1999); but lately he's increasingly been mending wounded marriages and children's lives shattered by fear and greed, "the heart of corporate America" (*Big Business* 124).

Spenser changes and grows by developing the rules he lives by. Recuperating from being nearly murdered in *Small Vices* (1997), he meditates on the relation between mortality and morality. In *Big Business*, he's quit smoking and changed his chosen drink from esoteric wines to Budweiser and designer water. He's gathered a round table of colorful merry men—police Lieutenant Marty Quirk and "state police person Healy"; Chollo from L.A., Tedi Sapp from Georgia, Bobby Horse who's a Kiowa, Bernard J. Fortunato from Las Vegas—each encountered on one of Spenser's cases and drawn into his eccentric orbit (*Big Business* 245). Although Spenser still acquires information the old-fashioned bare-knuckled way, he now depends more often on Hawk as a strong-arm enforcer and himself relies more on wily ploys: "If you let a guy weasel on the small stuff, he thinks he's winning, and it's easier to get the big stuff out of him" (*Big Business* 221). He also has realized the value of reticence: "I had never gotten into serious trouble keeping my yap shut" (*Big Business* 51). In

Spenser's 2005 outing, *Cold Service*, Hawk has been shot and with Susan this time mostly in the background, Spenser first helps him recover, then takes a dramatic revenge on Boots Podolak and his Ukrainian henchmen, who dominate a satellite city near Boston.

As Hawk observes, "There ain't all that many of us left, guys like old Spenser and me" (*Promised Land* 182), guys, as Spenser insists, who feel "machismo isn't another word for rape and murder. Machismo is really about honorable behavior.... You can't be honorable when it's easy.... Only when it's hard.... Watch what I do, and you'll know what I am" (*Promised Land* 94, 96). Watching Spenser and Hawk over the years shows that they live by the moral code they chose. There never have been many knights in shining armor, and in a world that's largely bereft of beacons of principle, modern paladins like Spenser and his friends still give a lovely light.

Novels: *The Godwulf Manuscript* (1973); *God Save the Child* (1974); *Mortal Stakes* (1975); *Promised Land* (1976); *The Judas Goat* (1978); *Looking for Rachel Wallace* (1980); *A Savage Place* (1981); *Early Autumn* (1981); *Ceremony* (1982); *The Widening Gyre* (1983); *Valediction* (1984); *A Catskill Eagle* (1985); *Taming a Sea-Horse* (1986); *Pale Kings and Princes* (1987); *Crimson Joy* (1988); *Playmates* (1989); *Stardust* (1990); *Pastime* (1991); *Double Deuce* (1992); *Paper Doll* (1993); *Walking Shadow* (1994); *Thin Air* (1995); *Chance* (1996); *Small Vices* (1997); *Sudden Mischief* (1998); *Hush Money* (1999); *Hugger Mugger* (2000); *Potshot* (2001); *Widow's Walk* (2002); *Back Story* (2003); *Bad Business* (2004); *Cold Service* (2005).

Short Stories: *Surrogate* (single Spenser story; 1983).

Philip Marlowe series: *Poodle Springs* (1989, completed for Raymond Chandler); *Perchance to Dream* (1991).

Jesse Stone series: *Night Passage* (1997); *Trouble in Paradise* (1998); *Death in Paradise* (2001); *Sea Change* (2006).

Sunny Randall series: *Family Honor* (1999); *Perish Twice* (2000). Parker has also written stand-alone novels.

Nonfiction: Parker has written numerous nonfiction works, including *The Private Eye in Hammett and Chandler* (1984); *Parker on Writing* (1985); *Spenser's Boston* (with photographs by Kasho Kumagai; 1994); *Boston: History in the Making* (1999).

Selected sources: Cruz, Clarissa. "Mad About Spenser." *Entertainment Weekly*, September 10, 1999: 146; Fletcher, Connie. Rev. of *Back Story*. *Booklist*, January 1, 2003: 807; Geherin, David. *Sons of Sam Spade: The Private-Eye Novel in the 70s*. New York: Ungar, 1980; *Publishers Weekly*. Rev. of *Cold Service*, February 7, 2005: 27; Silet, Charles L.P. "Five Pages a Day: An Interview with Robert B. Parker." *Talking Murder*. Princeton, NJ: Ontario Review Press, 1999; Stasio, Marilyn. Rev. of *Small Vices*. *New York Times Book Review*, April 13, 1997: 24; Tallett, Dennis. *The Spenser Companion: "The Godwulf Manuscript" to "Small Vices": A Reader's Guide*. California [*sic*]: Companion Books, 1997; White, Jean. Rev. of *Pale Kings and Princes*. *Washington Post Book World*, June 21, 1987: 6.

Major awards: Edgar Allan Poe Award, 1976; and Grand Master Award, 2002, Mystery Writers of America.

See also: Reed Coleman's series featuring New York PI and wine merchant Moe Prager; Robert Crais's series featuring LA supersleuth **Elvis Cole**; David Daniel's series featuring PI Alex Rasmussen in Lowell, Massachusetts; Bill Eidson's series featuring ex-DEA agent Jack Merchant in Rhode Island; Loren Estleman's series featuring Detroit PI Amos Walker; Jeremiah Healy's series set in Boston featuring John Francis Cuddy, a Vietnam-era former military policeman who takes on PI jobs to help the unfortunate.

T

Hilary Tamar

Profession:	Oxford don; legal historian
Living situation:	Single
Geographic locale:	England, various foreign climes
Time period:	1981–2000
Associates:	Julia Larwood; Selena Jardine; Timothy Shepherd; Michael Cantrip; Desmond Ragwort
Nemesis:	The Inland Revenue
Significant relationships:	None
Concern:	Scholarship as the pursuit of Truth

Possibly the most enigmatic sleuth in mystery fiction is Professor Hilary Tamar, Tutor in Legal History and Fellow of St. George's College, Oxford. Tamar is the brainchild of long-time British barrister Sarah Caudwell, who studied classics and read law at St. Anne's College, Oxford, and later worked for Lloyd's Bank as an expert in international tax law, all areas crucial to her plots and characterizations. Caudwell also drew upon several hoary fictional conventions: mistaken identity, a stock device in Roman and Shakespearean comedy; the epistolary technique of character revelation through letters, as old as Richardson's eighteenth-century *Pamela*; Monsignor Ronald Knox's Golden Age "decalogue," ten rules of Fair Play in Detective Fiction, including specifying the location of clues (*Adonis* 276); and the ambiguous name, leaving

Professor Tamar's gender indefinite, perhaps a reflection of Coleridge's declaration that "The truth is, a great mind must be androgynous" (*Silk Stalkings* 2: 166).

Besides the great mind that modesty prevents Professor Tamar from openly acknowledging but that clearly reveals itself in Tamar's climactic solutions to intricate crimes, everything else about Tamar must be inferred from self-reflective dialogue verging on the precious and actions trembling upon the scandalous, both revealed through Tamar's own speech and actions and those of Tamar's mostly Oxonian "Bright Young Things," characters updated from the Golden Age of Mystery (Murphy 89). These include Tamar's former student Timothy Shepherd; languid blonde Selena Jardine and righteous Desmond Ragwort, moneyed self-confident young barristers of the Chancery Bar. They share quarters in "the Nursery," 62 New Square, Lincoln's Inn, with breezy Michael Cantrip, an alumnus of "the other place" (Cambridge) possessed of a "savour of iniquity" (*Adonis* 5). They are all friendly with Julia Larwood, whose propensity for getting drunk, pursuing delectably willowy young men, and skirmishing with the Inland Revenue inspires Caudwell's plots.

All the Hilary Tamar cases—Tamar calls them "experiences"—follow the same pattern: one of the Nursery tots, usually Julia, hares off to an exotic foreign locale, falls foul of some dastardly plot usually hatched by a minion of the Inland Revenue, and sends home witty and sexy pleas for help couched in the Queen's most mellifluous English. The rest muddle along ineffectually until Tamar, from the Olympian height of Oxford donship, pontificates a mathematically elegant and historically precise solution.

Hilary Tamar, whose scholar's salary scarcely approaches a successful lawyer's, periodically escapes from Oxford and the college's Bursar and resides gratis in borrowed London digs, joining the Nursery set for fine dining and protracted wining in luxe London establishments—at their expense. Tamar never buys so much as a bottle of Nierstein but minutely observes, questions, and, using the formidable weapon of logic, formulates complex hypotheses that invariably prove correct.

At the start, Tamar emphasizes scholarly objectivity by warning susceptible readers that "detective fiction is a pastime sometimes conducive to over-fanciful speculation," instead insisting on Scholarship's detached pursuit of Truth. The professor reserves venomous scorn for hypocrisy, categorizing antique dealers and the Chancery Bar as "vultures" and denouncing the Inland Revenue as a "soul-destroying occupation" (*Adonis* 74–75, 87). Tamar also abandons hope that even intimate friends will greet legitimate scholarly efforts with "discerning congratulation.... Which is very fortunate, because they don't" (*Adonis* 1).

Tamar finds having a former student explain a complicated issue as intolerable as most of the young barristers find it impossible to sit through Tamar's zealously detailed closing diatribes, which Tamar describes as "the careful process of reasoning by which the Scholar advances from established premise to ineluctable conclusion." (Selena sacrilegiously calls these flights of intellect "guesswork" [*Adonis* 254]). Tamar's attention to such detail as a tiny blob of sticking-plaster on a Palladian jaw, natural to a historical scholar of medieval English law, forces the Nursery to sidle off one by one as at the end of the first case, *Thus Was Adonis Murdered* (1981), leaving only a naïve American to applaud Hilary Tamar's erudite pronouncements.

Tamar's last case, *The Sibyl in Her Grave* (2000), treats Julia's Aunt Regina bucking the Inland Revenue's disapproval of insider trading. Tamar cleverly insists that since the historian's place is in the shadows at stage side, observing and explaining the actions of the protagonists, no time and attention can be placed on any description or account of Tamar—not, however, preventing the professor, supposedly the only character here who sees the truth clearly, from taking center stage in another classic confrontation scene.

Hilary Tamar and associates throw back often to earlier popular mystery fiction, especially in their plot pattern, reminiscent of Sheridan LeFanu's *Wylder's Hand* (1864). Their witty repartee larded with tax statutes and legalities also echoes John Mortimer's popular Rumpole series. Prolix Hilary Tamar's quintessentially Oxonian verbosity, though, elevates grim realities like sex and murder and the Inland Revenue to giddy new heights of verbal rapture.

Novels: *Thus Was Adonis Murdered* (1981); *The Shortest Way to Hades* (1985); *The Sirens Sang of Murder* (1989); *The Sibyl in Her Grave* (2000).

Short story: "An Acquaintance with Mr. Collins," *Suit of Diamonds* (1990).

Selected sources: Blockley, Mary. "Is Hilary a Woman?" *New York Times Book Review*, October 21, 1990: 42; Canfield, Rosemary M. Rev. of *The Sibyl in Her Grave*. *Magill Book Reviews*, May 1, 2001; Clark, Susan L. Rev. of *The Sirens Sang of Murder*. *Armchair Detective*, Spring 1991: 222–23; Hoffert, Barbara. "The Perfect Murder." *Library Journal*, March 1, 1991: 78; Lachman, Marvin. Rev. of *Thus Was Adonis Murdered*. *Armchair Detective*, Fall 1996: 436; Stasio, Marilyn. "Sarah Caudwell: Lawyer and Author of Mystery Novels." *New York Times Book Review*, February 6, 2000: 38.

Major award: Anthony Award for best novel, 1989.

See also: Natasha Cooper's series featuring barrister Trish McGuire; John Mortimer's **Horace Rumpole** series; M.R.D. Meek's series featuring Lennox Kemp, a disbarred and reinstated solicitor; Martin Edwards's series featuring Harry Devlin, a Liverpool solicitor-detective; Roy Lewis's series featuring Eric Ward, who does both criminal and corporate work; Keith McCarthy's series featuring British lawyer Helena Fleming; Michael Underwood's series featuring Rosa Epton, the first female British lawyer sleuth; Frances Fyfield's series featuring Helen West, like Fyfield a prosecutor for London's Metropolitan Police and Crime Prosecution Service.

Jack Taylor

Profession:	Private investigator; former Garda (member of the Garda Síochána, Ireland's national police)
Living situation:	Single; then married and divorced
Geographic locale:	Galway, Ireland
Time period:	2001–present
Associate:	Catherine Bellingham ("Cathy B")

Nemeses:	Alcohol and drugs
Significant relationships:	All failed
Concerns:	The Guards and books, mainly fiction, biography, and poetry

Irish poet and patriot William Butler Yeats thought that the Ireland of romance was with Irish martyr O'Leary in the grave, but in the depths of his guilt-ridden black Irish heart, Ken Bruen's anguished hero Jack Taylor can't quite believe it. Bruen has called Taylor "a tribute to the American private eye," but like Bruen himself, Taylor is also an old Galwegian, a species endangered by Ireland's new soul-eating Americanized prosperity. Since Taylor "feels pain to an inordinate degree," he tries unsuccessfully to shield himself from a macho world with the old Garda overcoat he won't surrender after he was booted from the force, as well as with booze and drugs (Millikin 36).

In *The Guards* (2001), Taylor recalled the pain and loves of his Galway boyhood. For his tenth birthday, his domineering Irish mother gave him a "hurley," the same sports stick he said she used "to wallop the bejaysus outa me." His father, a gentle railway man whose wife constantly belittled both him and their son, gave him a library card. To use it in the library on the second floor of Galway's old Court House, Jack had to pass the big *gardaí* on the floor below, in as much awe of them as he was of the books: "The two threads of my life had been intertwined" (*Guards* 105). Like Bruen, too, Jack Taylor became infatuated with tough metaphysical poetry like Rilke's, the interior struggles of American Trappist monk Thomas Merton, and obscure American crime fiction, inserting trenchant scraps of his reading into his lean, mean noir chronicles of the outcasts isolated from Irish society.

Slung out of the corruption-riddled Garda Síochána for boozy public disgrace and thus deprived of "the one chance of meaning" he could have given his life (*Magdalen Martyrs* 8) well before *The Guards* begins, big Jack Taylor is six-two, 180 tough pounds, and forty-five, fixated on death since his father's funeral, and scratching out a meager living "finding things," for people who think his previous career makes him able to help them. For the nervy, suspicious Irish with centuries of bloody betrayals behind them, a private investigator is uncomfortably close to an informing black-guard, but troubled souls like Ann Henderson, who believes her daughter Sarah was murdered, come to Taylor as a last resort. She tells him, "They say you're good because you've nothing else in your life" (*Guards* 13). He knows it's true.

Almost everyone in Taylor's life betrays him. Those he cherishes, like his father, the old bartender Sean, and Padraig, a forlorn wino as well-read as Taylor himself, die and leave him. The woman he'd loved back in his Garda days abandoned him, and so does Ann Henderson, the love of his life, unable to cope with Taylor's relapses to the bottle. Clancy, once his colleague in the Guards and now a Superintendent, revels in tormenting Taylor, who but for the booze might have easily surpassed Clancy in the Guards, and when Taylor's closest friend, the artist Sutton, who'd steered him down the drunkard's path, proves a Judas, Taylor takes a vengeance sure to haunt him the rest of his days.

Taylor's worst betrayals, though, are those he makes for himself, abusing people who'd wanted to be kind to him, "A reckless disregard for the feelings of others.... Add a dash of remorse and gallons of self-pity, you had the classic alcoholic in all his tarnished glory.... Numb the pain [with booze and] each fresh numbness trailed fresh damage in its wake" (*Guards* 109).

After *The Guards*, detoxed and sober, Taylor goes to London, but a year later returns to Galway with a failed marriage behind him. Drinking heavily again in *The Killing of the Tinkers* (2002), Taylor agrees to help Sweeper, an Irish Gypsy, who wants Taylor to find the killer responsible for the deaths of young men of his despised tinker clan, another case that nearly kills Taylor. Later, in *The Magdalen Martyrs* (2003), Taylor, trembling on the cusp of a fragile sobriety his doctors have warned him he must maintain or die, becomes involved with the remnants of another reviled Irish group, the "Maggies," or Magdalens, "fallen women" condemned to slave in concentration camp-like laundries run by sadistic Irish nuns. Fighting drugs now as well as the booze, Taylor again alienates all the people who try to help him: "Cathy B," a former English rock singer he'd saved earlier from drugs and worse; Brendan Flood, a former Garda who's gotten religion, and Brendan's niece Brid Nic an Iomaire ("Ridge"), a *ban* (female) Garda whose indictment seared Taylor into self-loathing: "All the grief I'd caused and endured came storming upon my soul" (*Magdalen Martyrs* 252).

Clinging to his reading, his old Garda overcoat as his tangible lifeline to the Guards, and the Irish Hail Marys he learned as a child, Taylor treads his downward-spiraling alcoholic odyssey through the smug greedy New Ireland (*Magdalen Martyrs* 150), pining for the old days now gone forever. He pauses at his father's grave in Rahoon Cemetery where Nora Barnacle, James Joyce's first love, lies; regularly visits the Poor Clare convent where the Latin mass offers him one "comfort beyond articulation" (*Guards* 45), and he sporadically dries out at a hospital—but he's never far from pushing his internal "self-destruct button" (*Guards* 82). What Yeats called Ireland's "terrible beauty" brings Jack Taylor often to the brink of despair, but it also provides him a special empathy for the suffering souls around him. As another poet claimed, "Mad Ireland" hurt Yeats into poetry; in Ken Bruen's savagely glowing pages "Mad Ireland" comes very close to doing the same for demon-wracked Jack Taylor.

Novels: *The Guards* (2001); *The Killing of the Tinkers* (2002); *The Magdalen Murders* (2003); *The Dramatist* (2006).

Other series: *The White Trilogy* (2003), containing *A White Arrest* (1998), *Taming the Alien* (1999), and *The McDead* (2000); and *Blitz* (2002) and *Vixen* (2005), all featuring Detective Sergeant Tom Brand, Chief Inspector James Roberts, and their close-to-burned-out colleagues of the South East London Police Squad.

Other novels: Bruen's hard-boiled British mysteries include *Rilke on Black* (1996); *The Hackman Blues* (1997); *Her Last Call to Louis MacNeice* (1998); *London Boulevard* (2001).

Selected sources: Ferrie, Pauline. Rev. of *The Guards* and *The Killing of the Tinkers*. *Bookview Ireland*, www.bookviewireland.ie; Graff, Keir. Rev. of *The Guards*. *Booklist*, December 15, 2002: 736; *Kirkus Reviews*. Rev. of *The Magdalen Martyrs*, February 15, 2005: 198; Macleod,

Calum. Rev. of *The Guards* and *The Killing of the Tinkers*. *Shots Magazine*, www.shotsmag.co.uk; Millikin, Patrick. "Hibernian Noir: *PW* Talks with Ken Bruen." *Publishers Weekly*, December 22, 2003: 36; Stasio, Marilyn. Rev. of *The Guards*. *New York Times Book Review*, January 26, 2003: 20.

Awards: Edgar Award nomination, 1998; Bruen has also been a finalist for the Barry and Macavity Awards.

See also: John Brady's series featuring Inspector Monogue of the Dublin C.I.D. and highlighting Trinity College; Bartholomew Gill's Chief Superintendent **Peter McGarr** series, also headquartered in Dublin.

Telemon the Physician

Profession:	Physician to Alexander the Great
Living situation:	Widowed
Geographic locale:	Greece and Persia
Time period:	330s B.C.
Associate:	Cassandra, a Theban former slave
Concern:	Alexander's destiny

Ultra-prolific historical mystery author Paul C. Doherty began his Alexander of Macedon novels with *Murder in Macedon* (1997) and *A Murder in Thebes* (1998) under the pseudonym "Anna Apostolou," first addressing the 336 B.C. slaying of Alexander's father King Philip of Macedon and then Alexander's efforts to trace his own origins with the help of two young Hebrew friends, Miriam and Simeon. Doherty used his own name for *The House of Death* (2001) and a new sleuth, Telemon the Physician, brought in 334 B.C. by Alexander to his military camp near Sestos, where Alexander, the twenty-two-year-old Captain-General of Greece, is waiting to launch his campaign to conquer the mighty Persian Empire.

Threatening omens cloud Alexander's purpose; the bulls he sacrifices prove tainted, and one by one the guides he hired to lead him into Persia fall dead, slain by a mysterious assailant who leaves cryptic warnings against the expedition. Alexander summons Telemon, a Macedonian physician who had trained with Alexander in their youth at Mieza under the swordmaster Black Cleitus, to investigate the murders, identify the Persian spy in their midst, and free Alexander to defeat Emperor Darius of Persia.

Based on Alexander's historical physician Philip the Doctor mentioned by the Roman historian Arrian, Telemon possesses sharp eyes and penetrating curiosity. He is consistently objective and even distant, but humane and kindly to the unfortunate. Telemon has always known that he lacks the warrior's killing instinct, yet he fights bravely at Alexander's side when ambushed and in the great battle of the Granicus, Alexander's first victory in Asia, which climaxes *House of Death*. In Alexander's camp, rife with murders, summary executions, treachery, and incessant plotting among Alexander's generals, all dreaming of seizing their commander's conquests for themselves, Telemon steadfastly maintains his integrity, refusing to sink to informing or deceit. To Aristander, Alexander's cross-dressing "keeper of secrets" and the tool of Alexander's witch-like mother Olympias, Telemon is especially dangerous because he thinks for himself, he always tells the truth, and he fears neither Alexander nor even the gods.

Telemon had been expected to follow in the footsteps of his father Margolis, Philip of Macedon's close friend and a ferocious brigade commander in Philip's elite Foot Companions, but soon Telemon realized that he was best fitted for scholarship at the feet of Alexander's tutor Aristotle, who quickly acknowledged and fostered Telemon's "masterful eye for symptoms" (*House* 131). Telemon never was Alexander's lover—that was Hephaistion, who strangely resembled Philip of Macedon—but Alexander protected Telemon on the parade-ground and Telemon helped Alexander with his studies, reading Homer's *Iliad* together many nights under the stars until Margolis, soul-sickened by needless slaughter, abandoned war for farming and took Telemon away from Mieza and Alexander.

Their early bond brings Telemon back to Alexander after years of studying medicine at the great ancient schools of Athens, Corinth, the island of Cos, and Thebes in Egypt, where Telemon loved and lost his wife Anula, a beautiful *heset* (temple maiden), murdered by a Persian officer Telemon then slew with his own hands. Without Anula, Telemon felt that he had nowhere else to go but to Alexander, and he steadfastly carries out his complex investigations of the espionage and murder that accompany Alexander's great Persian campaign.

In *The Gates of Hell* (2003), Telemon, who had not been quite a dominant figure in *The House of Death* and *The Godless Man* (2002), "comes to full literary life" amid the horrifying battle for Halicarnassus, seeking the murderer of the scribe Pamenes, found on the pavement below his locked room, a so-called ghost chamber where Pamenes has been struggling to decipher the Pythian Manuscript said to contain the secret chink in Halicarnassus's defenses. Assisted by Cassandra, a former Theban whom Telemon rescued from Alexander's slave pens, and daily submerged in atrocities—the crucifixions of captured spies, coups de grace administered to Alexander's wounded, brutal swordplay, and vicious espionage—Telemon says he "cannot explain the deaths of thousands. I can only concentrate on the task in hand. It keeps me sane" (*Gates of Hell* 186). More than ever, Telemon realizes that Alexander is a "man of masks," but Telemon, as Alexander's "surveyor of cause and effect" (*House* 271), faithfully serves the great commander with his logic, reflection, and evidence while remaining his own man. Doherty plans to follow Telemon in this historical recreation to Alexander's own death, focusing on the clear-eyed physician as the one man indispensable to Alexander's dreams of glory.

Novels: *The House of Death* (2001); *The Godless Man* (2002); *The Gates of Hell* (2003).

See also: Doherty's *Murder in Macedon* (1997) and *A Murder in Thebes* (1998), focusing on King Philip of Macedon and Alexander the Great, under pseudonym Anna Apostolou.

Other series: Under "Paul C. Doherty," the Hugh Corbett series, set in the reign of Edward I; the Canterbury Tales/Nicholas Chirke series, set in Chaucer's late fourteenth century; and the Egyptian series featuring Amerotke the Judge, around 1470 B.C.; under "Paul Harding," the Brother Athelstan series, set in London during the 1370s–1380s; under "C.L. Grace," the Katherine Swinbrook (a physician) novels, set in Canterbury during the time of Edward IV; under "Michael Clynes," the Sir Roger Shallot novels, featuring an agent of Cardinal Wolsey in the era of Henry VIII; under "Ann Dukthas," the Nicholas Segalla novels, which feature a time traveler investigating crimes in the times of Mary, Queen of Scots, "Bloody Mary" Tudor, Napoleon, and the Hapsburgs.

Nonseries novels: *The Death of a King* (1985); *The Masked Man* (1991); *King Arthur* (Young Adult biography); *The Whyte Harte* (1988); *The Fate of Princes* (1991); *The Serpent Among the Lilies* (1990); *The Rose Demon* (1997); *The Haunting* (1998); *The Soul Slayer* (1998); *The Great Crown Jewels Robbery of 1303* (2005).

Nonfiction: *Isabella and Edward* (2002); *The Mysterious Death of Tutankhamun* (2002).

Selected sources: Herron, Don. "Lots of History, with Mystery: *PW* Talks with Paul Doherty." *Publishers Weekly*, July 18, 2003: 82; Klett, Rex E. Rev. of *The House of Death*. *Library Journal*, June 1, 2001: 224; *Publishers Weekly*. Rev. of *The Gates of Hell*, July 28, 2003: 81; Staines, Daniel M. "The Novels of P.C. Doherty." *Scenes of Crime*, www.fortunecity.co.uk; *Stop, You're Killing Me* Web site, www.stopyourekillingme.com.

Major award: The Herodotus Award, Historical Appreciation Society, for lifetime achievement, 1999.

See also: For the Classical World of Greece and Rome: Lindsey Davis's Roman informer **Marcus Didius Falco** series, set in the A.D. 70s; John Maddox Roberts's SPQR series, featuring former aedile Decius Caecilius Metellus and set in first-century B.C. Rome; Steven Saylor's Roma Sub Rosa series featuring **Gordianus the Finder**, set in the mid-first century.

Debut novels: Michael B. Edwards's *Murder at the Panionic Games*, set in 650 B.C.; Tom Harper's *The Mosaic of Shadows*, set in eleventh-century Byzantium and featuring former bounty hunter and bodyguard Demetrios the Apokalyptor; José Carlos Somoza's *The Athenian Murder*, featuring "decipherer of Enigmas" Heracles Pontor, who solves the murders of young men at Plato's Academy of Philosophy in classical Athens.

Luke Thanet

Profession:	Detective Inspector
Living situation:	Married
Geographic locale:	Kent, England
Time period:	1981–present
Associate:	Detective Sergeant Mike Lineham
Significant relationship:	Joan Thanet
Concerns:	Fatherhood; marriage; conscience

Dorothy Simpson, a long-time teacher and marriage counselor, began to write in her forties after a lengthy illness, with "plenty of time for reflection and reassessment" (*CA Online*). The result was her long Luke Thanet series, "as much whydunits as whodunits" (Ashley 438). In a profession where he constantly encounters human viciousness, Thanet is unequivocally, refreshingly average, a good steady British policeman doing a rotten job, solving crimes with patience, throughgoing attention to detail, and as Jean M. White has remarked, "a compassionate curiosity about human beings."

Simpson likes to "double-plot" her books, interweaving past and present so that at the same time he is untangling new puzzles, Thanet must often piece together old ones in and around Sturrenden, the fictional Kentish village where he was born and raised and married to his boyhood sweetheart Joan. While the village setting appears cozy, the crimes Thanet investigates are anything but, recalling Golden Age murder fiction written by Agatha Christie and Margery Allingham, where deadly secrets lurk under placid country exteriors. Most of the victims are women whose deaths reveal largely unsuspected dark sides: the murdered wife in *The Night She Died* (1981), the prototypical dull spinster who led a quite different life in *Six Feet Under* (1982), the missing daughter of a straitlaced religious family in *Close Her Eyes* (1984), the un-wanted woman in *Last Seen Alive* (1985), the estranged wife in *Doomed to Die* (1991), and the drowned barrister's wife in *Dead and Gone* (2000), all illustrating Thanet's capacity for handling sensitive issues with tact and good sense.

Thanet adheres strictly to accepted procedure. He demands scrupulous accuracy both in the reports he himself painstakingly composes and in the work of his sub-ordinates, like Sergeant Mike Lineham, who remains at Thanet's side throughout the series. They make an effective team because their skills are complementary. Thanet easily files away reams of detail, some of which Lineham at the time pragmatically considers irrelevant, but when the minutiae start to fall into place and Lineham asks Thanet how he arrived at his conclusions, their conversations usually produce the solution to the crime (*Silk Stalkings* 1: 59–60).

The key to Luke Thanet's effectiveness as a detective is his sound grasp of what makes human beings tick, but he's no superman. He doesn't spare himself. Rather than waiting at his desk for inspiration to strike, he's constantly out interviewing, inspecting, probing. He patiently reads the silences of witnesses and suspects as well as he does their words, and even though he has to steel himself, he never shrinks from the most unpleasant aspects of his work. When viewing a murder scene for the first time, "Even after all these years he still could not face the prospect of that first sight of a corpse with equanimity." Thanet also struggles constantly to understand the incomprehensible: "Somehow he always managed to conceal the complicated jumble of emotions which invariably assailed him—pity, anger, horror, sadness, but he never managed to come to terms with the way this particular experience affected him, or to understand why he felt the way he did" (*Doomed To Die* 4).

Besides the psychological demands of his work, Thanet suffers from a bad back, worries over his children, who grow from toddlers to perplexing adolescents and eventually leave home in the series, and copes with the challenge of maintaining a good marriage with his wife Joan. Though some commentators object to Simpson's heavy emphasis on the Thanets' home life as mere "padding" (Murphy 455), it is integral to her portrayal of Luke Thanet as a convincing human being. At first con-tent to be a stay-at-home mother and a supportive wife to a homicide detective—no easy task—Joan Thanet decides she needs another outlet for her talents. Simpson told *Contemporary Authors*, "I decided to give Luke Thanet a good marriage but with the sort of problems that readers of the books would be able to identify with . . . problems that afflict everybody . . . [especially] something which I think is one of the big changes in marriage in this century, the fact that so many more women work and how this affects their relationships with their husbands" (quoted in *CA Online*).

Joan Thanet's desire for a career proves difficult for Luke to accept, because like most husbands "he is reluctant to lose any of the comforts she provides and worries that the children will suffer if she takes an outside job" (*Silk Stalkings* 1: 60). The problem comes to a head in *Element of Doubt* (1988), but Thanet undertakes an honest soul-searching, Joan goes off to college, and her mother comes to take care of the children and the house.

Having a working wife means frequent husbandly adjustments. In *Doomed to Die* (1991), Joan is happily pursuing her career, their eighteen-year-old daughter Bridget has headed off to the London cookery school she's always wanted (giving Thanet a few fatherly qualms), and son Ben is looking forward to the university four years down the road. Then Joan's mother suffers a heart attack and the Thanets abruptly find themselves in the "sandwich" generation: Mrs. Bolton can't live alone. Do they relinquish their privacy? Do they buy a house with a granny annex? Joan doesn't want to give up her job and Thanet won't let her: "A lot of men would have been horrified at the prospect [of sharing their home with their mother-in-law]," Joan tells him gratefully. "And a lot wouldn't," he replies. " 'The reasonable ones, anyway.' He grinned. 'And I, of course, am a reasonable man' " (*Doomed to Die* 154). Reasonable, compassionate—and angry enough at the thought of one human being taking the life of another to keep doing his dangerous and often thankless job—Luke Thanet personifies the best that a police force can offer the public that it serves.

Novels: *The Night She Died* (1981); *Six Feet Under* (1982); *Puppet for a Corpse* (1983); *Close Her Eyes* (1984); *Last Seen Alive* (1985); *Dead on Arrival* (1987); *Element of Doubt* (1988); *Suspicious Death* (1988); *Dead by Morning* (1989); *Doomed to Die* (1991); *Wake the Dead* (1992); *No Laughing Matter* (1993); *A Day for Dying* (1996); *Once Too Often* (1998); *Dead and Gone* (2000).

Stand-alone novel: *Harbingers of Fear* (suspense; 1977).

Selected sources: Champlin, Charles. Rev. of *Dead by Morning. Los Angeles Times Book Review*, January 1, 1989; Harris, Karen. Rev. of *Dead and Gone. Booklist*, May 1, 2000: 1677; Melton, Emily. Rev. of *No Laughing Matter. Booklist*, November 15, 1993: 1606; *Publishers Weekly*. Rev. of *Once Too Often*, January 26, 1998: 73; White, Jean M. Rev. of *Last Seen Alive. Washington Post Book World*, November 17, 1985.

Major award: Silver Dagger, 1985.

See also: Catherine Aird's **Inspector C.D. Sloan** series; W.J. Burley's series featuring Superintendent Charles Wycliffe of the Cornish C.I.D.; Jill McGown's Chief Inspector Lloyd and Sergeant Judy Hill series; Roger Ormerod's Detective Inspector Richard Patton series; Ruth Rendell's **Detective Chief Inspector Reginald Wexford** series, set in Sussex.

Melanie Travis

Profession:	Poodle trainer, later breeder; special education teacher
Living situation:	Divorced, later remarried
Geographic locale:	Stamford, Connecticut
Time period:	1995–present
Associate and mentor:	Margaret Turnbull (Aunt Peg)
Significant relationship:	Sam Driver
Concerns:	Son Davey; Poodledom; canine welfare

Laurien Berenson's authorial pedigree goes back through several well-received romances to *Double Dare* (1986), involving friends competing for a spot on the Olympic equestrian team. Later, she took the mystery bit in her teeth and shifted to the rarefied world of dog shows with divorced special education teacher Melanie Travis's first case, *A Pedigree to Die For* (1995). Berenson literally grew up in the dog show world, because her mother bred and showed Norwich Terriers and her grandmother, the model for Melanie's formidable Aunt Peg, showed Wire Fox Terriers and Scotties in the 1930s and 1940s before she became a conformation judge. Berenson herself has bred, trained, and exhibited both Standard and Miniature Poodles, having bred or finished fifteen champions in the last twenty years, so she knows the sport and its aficionados down to the last whisker.

A Pedigree to Die For (1995) emerged from a news story Berenson covered as a freelancer: Rocky, a stolen champion Toy Poodle stud valued at over twenty thousand dollars, was never recovered, despite his owner's offer of a $10,000 reward. In Berenson's novel, Melanie, four-year-old Davey's divorced single mother, struggles to make ends meet because she'd been too proud to accept alimony. Bob, her flighty ex, had unexpectedly walked out one day in search of a blonde post–teeny bopper trophy, taking the car and stereo but abandoning his son and leaving thirtyish Melanie skittish to the bone about further romantic involvements. Just when Melanie's summer job evaporates because of budget cutbacks, her Uncle Max dies of a heart attack in the kennel he and Aunt Peg maintain for their prize black Standard Poodles. Aunt Peg, a typically fearless Turnbull woman, inveigles Melanie into an elaborate scheme to find Beau, Peg's top stud, missing since Max's death.

Posing as a neophyte Poodle breeder seeking a stud for her mythical bitch, Melanie plunges into show-level Poodledom, learning its complicated idiom and its Machiavellian politics and finding the Poodles far more sensible, honest, and lovable than their backbiting professional handlers and their generally wannabe–top dog owners. She also meets Sam Driver, a Mel Gibsonesque hunk who had recently moved his Poodles to Connecticut and offered Peg a blank check for Beau. Peg finds Sam "a genuinely nice man" as well as an incredibly handsome one and pushes Sam's stock for all she's worth, but Melanie "put [her] dreams away when [her] marriage ended" and has no intention of resurrecting them now (*Pedigree* 100).

However, by the time Melanie unmasks the villain who shocked Max into heart failure and abducted Beau, Sam's ravishingly bejeaned rear and those bluer-than-blue eyes have done some resurrecting of their own. Sam's pursuit of Melanie parallels her growing involvement with Poodle grooming, training, and exhibiting through *Underdog* (1996), where Melanie enrolls Faith, the black Standard Poodle Aunt Peg gives her, in a handling class and solves the arsenic poisoning of her friend Jenny Maguire. In *Dog Eat Dog* (1996), Melanie's ex Bob reappears, wanting to take Davey back to Texas to live with Bob and his twenty-year-old fiancée just as Melanie becomes embroiled in the murder of Belle Haven Kennel Club secretary Monica Freedman, who had been threatening to expose fellow members for fraud and animal abuse. Melanie continues to hold Sam at leash length in *Hair of the Dog* (1997) while probing the murder of handler Barry Turk, as well as in *Watchdog* (1998), where Melanie shows Faith in her first adult show and saves her brother Frank from being suspected of murdering his business partner Marcus Rattigan. Melanie becomes more susceptible to Sam's charms in *Unleashed* (2000), where they're closing in on a wedding date until Sam's ex-wife Sheila is murdered, while in *Once Bitten* (2001), Sam leaves Melanie and her unreliable ex-husband Bob, seemingly older and wiser, appears to want her back.

By *Best in Show* (2003), Melanie has bred Faith and produced Eve, a luscious show quality Poodle puppy just beginning her own ring career. Bob, apparently reformed, is turning out to be a pretty fair dad to Davey, and Aunt Peg, semiretired from breeding but an active and respected Poodle judge, needs Melanie's help at the prestigious Poodle Club of America National Specialty Show when the co-owner of Bubba, a silver Miniature Poodle favored to go Best in Show, is murdered, and the victim's sister wants to scatter her ashes in center ring. Sam is back, Melanie, his engagement diamond on a chain around her neck, is yielding, and between some tender under-the-bleachers moments and laborious hours of Poodle grooming, they bring the perpetrators to justice. Melanie, Aunt Peg, and various talented Poodles carry on in *Raining Cats & Dogs* (2005), joining the visiting program of the Greenwich, Connecticut, Winston Pumpernill Nursing Home and sniffing out the killer of the bedridden aunt of a fellow dog trainer.

Although some dog-tired reviewers have found this series's audience limited to "those obsessed with show dogs" (*Kirkus Reviews* 1485), others applaud Berenson's writing as "warm and fuzzy as the dogs." Melanie's an appealingly forthright young single mom and an amateur sleuth who never takes herself too seriously, balancing her qualms about romantic involvement with her eye for a good-looking man, her devotion to Davey with her parental travails, and her growing passion for the arcane dog show world with her satiric, even caustic, views of human nature. As romantic cozy mystery heroines go, Melanie Travis often makes the cut and sometimes even takes the blue.

Novels: *A Pedigree to Die For* (1995); *Underdog* (1996); *Dog Eat Dog* (1996); *Hair of the Dog* (1997); *Watchdog* (1998); *Hush Puppy* (1999); *Unleashed* (2000); *Once Bitten* (2001); *Hot Dog* (2002); *Best in Show* (2003); *Jingle Bell Bark* (2004); *Raining Cats & Dogs* (2005).

Other works: Berenson has also written several stand-alone novels.

Selected sources: *Kirkus Reviews*. Rev. of *Hair of the Dog*, October 1, 1997: 1485; Klett, Rex E. Rev. of *Once Bitten*. *Library Journal*, September 1, 2001: 238; McLarin, Jenny. Rev. of *Best in Show*. *Booklist*, September 1, 2003: 67; *Publishers Weekly*. Rev. of *Hot Dog*, August 12, 2002: 280; *Publishers Weekly*. Rev. of *Jingle Bell Bark*, August 9, 2004: 235; Rowen, John. Rev. of *Watchdog*. *Booklist*, August 1998: 1971.

Web site: www.members.aol.com/LTBerenson.

See also: Cynthia Baxter's cozy series featuring veterinarian Jessica Popper; Susan Conant's **Holly Winter** series featuring malamutes; Carol Lea Benjamin's **Rachel Alexander** and Dashiell (a bull terrier) series; Michael Bond's **Monsieur Pamplemousse** series with the incomparable bloodhound Pommes Frites; Gerald Hammond's series featuring Scottish kennel owner John Cunningham.

Perry Trethowan

Profession:	Detective Inspector, Scotland Yard
Living situation:	Married
Geographic locale:	England
Time period:	1982–1987
Associates:	Constable Charlie Peace (beginning with *Bodies*); Superintendent Mike Oddie (beginning with *A City of Strangers*). These characters then spin off as central detectives themselves.
Significant relationship:	Janet Trethowan
Concern:	Social issues

As befits the work of a master crossword compiler called "the Jane Austen of mystery writers" (quoted in Ashley 44), Robert Barnard's Trethowan-Peace-Oddie novels are intricately plotted and impeccably characterized commentaries on British social issues: the class system, homelessness, disintegration of family life, pretentiousness, and hypocrisy. Barnard's Perry Trethowan series spawned novels featuring Trethowan's black Constable Charlie Peace, introduced in *Bodies* (1986), and Peace's Leeds Superintendent Mike Oddie, who first appears in *A City of Strangers* (1990).

Barnard thinks of himself primarily as an entertainer (Martin Edwards in Herbert 16). "Dickens is the writer in English" Barnard loves most: "he makes one weigh up one's words and see that they have a vitality of their own" (quoted in *CA Online*). *Death by Sheer Torture* (1982), Scotland Yard Detective Inspector Perry Trethowan's debut, is an over-the-top comic mystery that displays a torrential verbal vitality many adore and others deplore as bizarre: Trethowan has to investigate his own father's gauzy tights-clad death in a "do-it-yourself strappado," a sado-masochistic torture machine (*Torture* 31).

Perry (short for Peregrine) Trethowan, a happily married six-foot four-inch, seventeen-stone amateur weightlifter and shot putter, is everything his horrific minor-aristocratic watered-down artistic relatives at Harpenden House, the family estate in Northumberland, are not. Training "to be a drop-out" or going to the States to "graduate in dope-peddling" might have earned "Big Perry" at eighteen "the family blessing and a couple of thou." Instead, he wanted to join the army. His kinky father Leo found this "pathetically conformist," his aspiring stage designer Aunt Sybilla attributed it to "a dreadfully coarse nature," and his Aunt Kate, a "besotted admirer of Adolf Hitler," said he'd be "on the wrong side." Perry riposted by calling his father "a dirty-minded sadistic mediocrity" (to Leo, "mediocrity" was the unkindest cut of all), and wound up years later a Scotland Yard Detective In-spector contented to be totally estranged from his family and cut off without a penny (*Torture* 9–11).

Ordered by Superintendent Joe Grierly to Harpenden House on a "watching brief" following Leo's death, Trethowan becomes mired in "all the rest of the little oddities and secrets of one of the grand old families that make this country what it is today." Perry's genuine grief for his long-dead mother and his compassion for his sister, pregnant by their all-too-married "bastard cousin" who's been "pinching the family pictures" (*Torture* 186) changes Perry from a bemused observer of ruling-class corruption into the role a tragicomic participant in his next cases.

Barnard says, "All my characters [excluding protagonists] are pretty awful in one way or another" (quoted in *CA Online*). Promoted to Detective Superintendent in *Death and the Princess* (1982), Perry Trethowan's narrative asides nail all levels of Britain's still-kicking class structure: small-time criminals and foul-mouthed foot-ballers, pathetic aspirants to gentility, grocery-store backgrounded politicians; per-petually whining out-of-pocket younger sons of the peerage, vampiric Continental petty royalty and lusciously cunning twenty-something Princess Helena, a royal British Hedda Gabler Trethowan has to protect from the scandal she so passionately is trying to engineer. Trethowan disavows his own upper class's degraded ethics in favor of his word "as a policeman" (*Princess* 181).

Trethowan's cases address sundry awful facets of human frailty. *The Case of the Missing Brontë* (1983) brings Trethowan bang up against religious hypocrisy. The Reverend Amos Macklehose addresses "his congregation, his milch cows" "with the suggestion of American accent": "Give to proclaim the Word, brothers! Give to spread the great joy, sisters!...Come to me and ye shall find rest!" Trethowan muses, "Unpleasant, and how very dangerous too, with a shepherd of sheep who was mainly interested in their fleeces" (*Missing Brontë* 106–8). In *The Cherry Blossom Corpse* (1987; titled in Britain *Death in Purple Prose*), Perry escorts his sister Christobel to a conference for romance novelists in Bergen, Norway, integrating sympathy for lives so empty they have to be filled with bodice-busting fantasy with excruciating contempt for the publishing apparatus that exploits them. Shaping his solution of the case around the diuretic effects of expensive Norwegian firewater, Trethowan calls on Charlie Peace to round off his theory. Charlie's being black "obviously helped," because the arrogantly racist prime suspect would—and did—treat him "as lower than dirt, hardly worth consideration as part of the human race" (*Blossom* 241).

Presented like a Jane Austen heroine with abominable human frailties, Perry Trethowan must ask himself "Are they all horrid?" His originally sunnier nature sours somewhat, but he holds on to what counts—his family, his friends, and his "policeman's instinct that tells him that crime, especially murder, must not go unpunished" (*Torture* 158).

Novels:* *Death by Sheer Torture* (T; 1982); *Death and the Princess* (T; 1982); *The Case of the Missing Brontë* (T; 1983); *Bodies* (T, P; 1986); *The Cherry Blossom Corpse* (T, P; 1987); *Death and the Chaste Apprentice* (P; 1989); *A City of Strangers* (O; 1990); *A Fatal Attachment* (P, O; 1992); *A Hovering of Vultures* (P, O; 1993); *The Bad Samaritan* (P, O; 1995); *No Place of Safety* (P, O; 1998); *The Corpse at the Haworth Tandoori* (P, O; 1999); *Unholy Dying* (P, O; 2001); *The Bones in the Attic* (P; 2002).

Short fiction: *Death of a Salesperson, and Other Untimely Exits* (1989); *The Habit of Widowhood, and Other Murderous Proclivities* (1996).

Nonfiction: *A Talent to Deceive: An Appreciation of Agatha Christie* (1980); *A Short History of English Literature* (1984).

Other works: Barnard has written numerous stand-alone mystery novels, notably *Death of an Old Goat* (1974, set in Australia); *A Scandal in Belgravia* (1991); *The Graveyard Position* (2005). He also writes mysteries under the name "Bernard Bastable."

Selected sources: McDaniel, Maude. Rev. of *The Case of the Missing Brontë. Washington Post*, August 5, 1983; Prescott, Peter. Rev. of *Bodies. Newsweek*, February 24, 1986; *Publishers Weekly*. Rev. of *The Cherry Blossom Corpse*, June 12, 1987: 75; Rubins, Josh. Rev. of *A City of Strangers. New York Times Book Review*, January 7, 1990: 27; White, Jean. Rev. of *Bodies. Washington Post Book World*, January 19, 1986.

Major awards: Agatha Award, 1989; Anthony Award, 1988; Macavity Award, 1988; Nero Wolfe Award, 1991: Crime Writers' Association Golden Handcuffs Award, 1994.

Web site: www.poisonedpenpress.com/robertbarnard.

See also: Martha Grimes's **Richard Jury** series; P.D. James's **Adam Dalgliesh** series; Ruth Rendell's **Inspector Wexford** series.

Anna Turnipseed

Profession:	Special Agent, FBI
Living situation:	Single
Geographic locale:	"Indian Country," Native American reservations, United States
Time period:	1999–present
Associate:	Emmett Quanah Parker
Significant relationship:	Emmett Quanah Parker

*"T" = Trethowan; "P" = Peace; "O" = Oddie.

Concerns:	Native American emotional and sociological problems; spiritual dimensions of crime

Experiences as a sheriff's deputy and SWAT team officer patrolling Native American reservations in California gave Kirk Mitchell "a thousand vignettes to reshape into novels of any genre," because, he says, "The patrol cop who turns writer...has seen everything humanity has to offer" (quoted in *CA Online*). Mitchell's detectives are young Anna Turnipseed, a part-Asian reservation-born Modoc, Berkeley educated in sociology and a recently-graduated FBI Special Agent, and Emmett Quanah Parker, a big forty-year-old half-breed Comanche investigator for the Bureau of Indian Affairs with a criminology degree and three failed marriages to Indian women behind him. The Attorney General's office teams them up to probe criminal activity in "Indian Country," law enforcement's name for a diverse cultural entity far more expansive than the Native American reservations in all fifty United States.

Anna and Parker both realize their work can kill them. For Anna, it's "a lottery in which you routinely gamble your health, your sanity, your life itself." For Parker, "Even the smartest cop in the world is powerless...but you go on" (*Sky Woman* 66, 204). In each case, they fight fatigue and lethal combinations of white and Native American corruption laced with legal and ritualistic entanglements. Despite the peril of romantic involvement between police partners, a powerful mutual attraction draws them together, but personal problems drive them apart. For Emmett, a recovering alcoholic, "She has baggage. I have baggage. Too much baggage to journey through life together" (*Sky Woman* 38). Anna's baggage includes childhood memories of sexual abuse by her alcoholic father that prevent her from consummating her love for Emmett.

In *Spirit Sickness* (2000), Anna and Parker meet in the huge remote Navajo reservation to investigate the murders of a tribal patrolman and his wife, found in a fire-gutted police cruiser. Like all of their cases, these deaths are "wrapped in myth" (*Sky Woman* 67), requiring Anna to draw on her Modoc heritage of introspection and circuitousness, qualities that both complement and contradict Parker's blunt Comanche straightforwardness and insistence on saving face, just as her tribal history of stubborn resistance to white encroachment and consequent forced exile and isolation clashes with the Comanches' rapid adoption of white commercialism.

Solving the eerie serial killings Anna and Parker uncover together in *Spirit Sickness* allows them each to recognize and value the other's talents and culture, but grappling with the conflict between his desire and her inability to respond proves impossible. The joint therapy sessions they attempted in *Ancient Ones* (2001) fail because the clinical process makes Parker feet like a POW under interrogation. Whenever Parker tries to open up, Anna waffles and he backs away. They hide their feelings for one another in the demands of their jobs, while Anna blames the victims for triggering the nightmares that prevent her relationship with Parker from evolving naturally and slowly: "she needed those two qualities to overcome the past and have a normal relationship with a man" (*Sickness* 273).

Dream and nightmare, central to Modoc spirituality, increasingly affect Anna's life and work. Her relationship with Emmett takes a heavy blow in *Ancient Ones* (2001), set in Oregon and involving the discovery of a 14,000-year-old skeleton and a harrowing missing persons case, when Parker's intense frustration erupts into a one-night stand with a white woman in North Carolina. Plagued by nightmares from her past, Anna nevertheless rescues Parker, badly wounded, and turns down a post at the FBI's Washington Indian Desk, but she still can't commit to a relationship, telling Emmett he'll have to catch her this time.

In *Sky Woman Falling* (2003), Anna's recurring and uncannily prophetic Modoc dreams intensify. In them, death tugs at her spirit, seeming to foretell disaster for Parker, who has taught her nearly everything else she knows about police work in the field. Though she knows she loves him, Anna feels he's wrecked her trust. Her sense of betrayal has moved them beyond desire, though "they remained united by a thin strand of affection that refused to snap" (*Sky Woman* 68). This peculiar murder case among the Oneida of upstate New York spawns her dreams of falling, apparently echoing the Oneidas' creation myth of a woman flung down from heaven because of incest. Anna's dreams grotesquely parallel her situation, torn by feelings for Parker she can neither abandon nor consummate. While Emmett resents her for being untouchable, Anna resents him for touching someone else while he was waiting for her, and only their job fills the gulf widening between them. Anna's Modoc dreams become a horrible investigative tool that she can never admit to her white superiors or coworkers, "one that might make her dread sleep in the coming years" (*Sky Woman* 247).

Anna's learning the bitter lessons of maturity. She'd always thought time would heal their love wounds, but as Emmett lies near death from an axe wound one of Anna's unspeakable dreams had foretold, she realizes that if he dies, a sense of failure will always dog her. In the hospital, too, when Emmett's devout Comanche mother introduces Anna as his "significant other," Anna suddenly sees that the word "*Other* suggested other half, each of them a half of the whole, even if that whole was largely indefinable" (*Sky Woman* 290). Although Anna and Emmett Parker remain estranged during *Dance of the Thunder Dogs* (2004), with herself at that Washington job and Emmett back home in Oklahoma and sharing a romantic interlude with a former lover, Anna Turnipseed had left her Modoc fetish, a hummingbird, and her heart, by Parker's pillow in New York.

Novels: *Cry Dance* (1999); *Spirit Sickness* (2000); *Ancient Ones* (2001); *Sky Woman Falling* (2003); *Dance of the Thunder Dogs* (2004).

Other series: the "Germanicus" science fiction series.

Other works: Mitchell has also written numerous stand-alone novels and fictionalized screenplays under the name "Joel Norst."

Selected sources: Klett, Rex E. Rev. of *Dance of the Thunder Dogs*. *Library Journal*, November 1, 2004: 60; Ott, Bill. Rev. of *Spirit Sickness*. *Booklist*, May 1, 2000: 1622; *Publishers Weekly*. Rev. of *Ancient Ones*, March 5, 2001: 64; *Publishers Weekly*. Rev. of *Sky Woman Falling*, October 13, 2003: 60; Zappia, Susan. Rev. of *Cry Dance*. *Library Journal*, March 1, 1999: 110.

See also: Brian Garfield's *Relentless* (1972) and *The Three Person Hunt* (1974) starring Navajo State Trooper Sam Watchman; Richard Martin Stern's series featuring part-Apache, part

Spanish Santa Cristo police officer Johnny Ortiz, involving the Pueblo culture; Tony Hillerman's **Joe Leaphorn and Jim Chee** novels featuring the Navajo and Zuni cultures; Thomas Perry's Jane Whitefield series about a half-Irish, half Senecan "guardian" who helps endangered people assume new identities; Alanna Knight's *Angel Eyes* (1997), involving a Navajo PI and Celtic and Anasazi legends; J.A. Jance's Joanna Brady series, exploring the Apache culture of Cochise County, Arizona; Joan Hager's two interconnected series, one led by Oklahoma Cherokee police chief Mitch Bushyhead and the other by young police officer Molly Bearpaw; and Jake Page's *The Knotted Strings* (1995) and *The Lethal Partner* (1996), with blind Santa Fe sculptor Mo Bowdre and his Anglo-Hopi girlfriend Connie Barnes, novels that treat Hopi culture and ritual; Aimee Thurlo's series on Pueblo Indians features half-Navajo botanist Belara Fuller, beginning with *Second Shadow* (1993); Aimee and David Thurlo's popular Navajo Special Investigator **Ella Clah** series, as well as their *Second Sunrise* (2002) and *Blood Retribution* (2004), with half-vampire Navajo lawman Lee Nez and FBI agent Diane Lopez; and the Thurlos' *Bad Faith* (2002) and *Thief in Retreat* (2004), starring Sister Agatha of New Mexico's Our Lady of Hope Monastery, with local Native American culture as background.

Harriet Vane

Profession:	Mystery author
Living situation:	Married
Geographic locale:	England
Time period:	1936–1940
Associate:	Lord Peter Wimsey
Significant relationship:	Lord Peter Wimsey
Concerns:	World War II; loss of personal identity through marriage; female independence

In the early 1930s, Golden Age mystery novelist Dorothy L. Sayers, tempted to finish off her popular aristocratic sleuth Lord Peter Wimsey and get on to the religious works she really wanted to write, decided to marry him off as just as effective a demise. She modeled the love of his life, Harriet Vane, on herself, strong-willed, occasionally abrasive, not conventionally pretty, and unconventionally frank for her time in sexual matters. Wimsey first encountered Harriet when she was in the dock, on trial for murdering her lover, like one of Sayers's own an artist with a capital A. What happens when such a woman marries? Sayers had outlined one last Wimsey-Vane novel that she called "Thrones, Dominations," and Booker Prize finalist Jill Paton Walsh completed it from Sayers's notes, publishing it in 1998 to mixed reviews from Sayers devotees. Walsh went on to publish *A Presumption of Death* (2003), working with the blessing of the Dorothy L. Sayers Society from "The Wimsey Papers," a series of letters about the home front supposedly written by various members of the Wimsey family. Sayers published them in the *Spectator* during 1939–1940 to buck up British morale on the eve of a threatened Nazi invasion.

The posthumous collaboration between Sayers and Walsh, *Thrones, Dominations* (1998) takes place in 1936, four months after Lord Peter Wimsey's marriage to mystery writer Harriet Vane. On the national level, Britain is mourning King George V and the death of an era; and uncrowned Edward VIII is courting the notorious divorcée Mrs. Simpson and fraternizing with the Nazis. The British government recruits Lord Peter for one of his diciest secret missions, to talk sense into the new monarch (eventually to no avail). While the newlywed Wimseys are living in Lord Peter's elegant London town house attended by the impeccable Bunter, a murder investigation looms when their acquaintance, theatre producer Laurence Harwell, finds his beloved wife Rosamund strangled in her bed.

With Lord Peter off to attempt defusing His Majesty's clandestine business, Harriet becomes the focus of *Thrones, Dominations*. Even though Peter has tried to convince her that her detective writing is "a dream of justice, an ideal that had to be kept alive in a very unjust and dangerous world" (*Thrones* 46), she has begun to question its moral worth. Badgered as well by Peter's horrid sister-in-law, the domineering Duchess of Denver, to hurry up and bear Peter an heir, Harriet insists on a woman's right to make an independent living for herself, which she maintains throughout this tale of two murders and two nasty cases of blackmail, though Peter does return in time to help set matters straight. Harriet also engineers at least a partial happy ending by finding a way for the devoted Bunter to take a wife himself.

A Presumption of Death (2003), set during the early part of the war, finds Peter gone again, this time on a risky military mission, and Harriet is at their country estate coping not only with their own two children but also the rambunctious brood of Peter's sister Mary, who married Peter's close friend Inspector Charles Parker. Under such domestic circumstances, writing, not to mention independence, becomes difficult if not impossible for Harriet, somewhat limply depicted here as obsessively conjecturing what Peter must be doing and saying to her. Having managed to accept her new role as Lady Peter and learned how to direct servants, Harriet is now struggling with griping wartime necessities like food rationing (Sayers herself raised pigs for the war effort, calling all the females Fatima and the males Sir Francis Bacon). Harriet is also drawn into investigating the murder of a local Land Girl (temporary and generally unskilled wartime female farm help) in the nearby quiet village of Paggleham.

Despite such niggles about *Thrones, Dominations* as Elizabeth Bartelme's diagnosis of "slightly sentimental" and I. Pour-El's discovery of "anachronisms, inconsistencies, and tedious flashbacks" in *A Presumption of Death*, reception for Walsh's twenty-first-century Harriet Vane has ranged from middling to positive. Each time Lord Peter returns to cooperate with Harriet's sleuthing, however, these books do take on a juicier zest, evidence, perhaps, that Dorothy L. Sayers couldn't bear to do him in by marriage after all.

Novels: By Dorothy L. Sayers, featuring Lord Peter Wimsey alone: *Whose Body* (1923); *Clouds of Witness* (1926); *Unnatural Death* (1927); *The Unpleasantness at the Bellona Club* (1928); *The Five*

Red Herrings (1931); *Murder Must Advertise* (1933); *The Nine Tailors* (1934); featuring Lord Peter Wimsey and Harriet Vane: *Strong Poison* (1930); *Have His Carcase* (1932); *Gaudy Night* (1935); *Busman's Honeymoon* (1937). Short fiction: *Lord Peter Views the Body* (1928); *Hangman's Holiday* (1933); *In the Teeth of the Evidence and Other Stories* (1939); *Lord Peter: A Collection of All the Lord Peter Stories* (1972); *Striding Folly* (1972); *The Abominable History of the Man with Copper Fingers* (1982). Posthumous Lord Peter Wimsey and Harriet Vane novels completed from Sayers's materials by Jill Paton Walsh: *Thrones, Dominations* (1998); *A Presumption of Death* (2003).

Other fiction: the Montague Egg short stories, appearing in *Hangman's Holiday* (1933) and *In the Teeth of the Evidence and Other Stories* (1939).

Autobiography: Dorothy L. Sayers began two autobiographical works, "Cat o'Mary" and "My Edwardian Childhood." Neither were completed or published, but excerpts appear in various Sayers biographies.

Other works: Dorothy L. Sayers also wrote several religious plays, several volumes of essays, religious and philosophical treatises, and a translation of Dante's *Divine Comedy* (*Paradise* completed after Sayers's death by Barbara Reynolds).

Other works by Walsh: Stand-alone adult and children's novels; the Imogen Quy detective series, including *The Wyndham Case* (1995); *An Ounce of Justice* (1995); and *Debts of Dishonor* (2006).

Selected sources for *Thrones, Dominations* and *A Presumption of Death*: Bartelme, Elizabeth. "Lord Peter Loves Harriet." *Commonweal*, May 8, 1998: 26; Picker, Leonard. "Lord Peter Wimsey and Harriet Vane Redux." *Publishers Weekly*, January 20, 2003: 60; Pour-El, I. Rev. of *A Presumption of Death* (audio version, read by Edward Petherbridge). *Library Journal*, February 1, 2003: 120; *Publishers Weekly*. Rev. of *A Presumption of Death*, January 20, 2003: 59; Wilson, A.N. "The Wimsey-Vane Cocktail." *Times Literary Supplement*, January 30, 1998: 22.

Major awards: Jill Paton Walsh was a 1994 Booker Prize finalist for *Knowledge of Angels*.

See also: Golden Age mystery series with upper-class sleuths: Ngaio Marsh's Roderick Alleyn series; Josephine Tey's Inspector **Alan Grant** series. Also see contemporary authors' historical series, including Conrad Allen's George Peter Dillman series, set on pre–World War I luxury liners; James Anderson's humorous Detective C.J. Wilkins series set in English country houses of the 1930s; Marion Chesney's Edwardian period series featuring Lady Rose Summers; David Dickinson's Lord Francis Powerscourt series, set in the 1900s; Carola Dunn's Daisy Dalrymple series, set in 1920s England; Gillian Linscorr's series featuring 1900s suffragette Nell Bray; David Roberts's **Lord Edward Corinth** series, set in the late 1930s; Jacqueline Winspear's series featuring psychological investigator **Maisie Dobbs**, set in the 1930s. For contemporary authors featuring upper-class British sleuths, see Elizabeth George's **Thomas Lynley** series; Martha Grimes's **Inspector Richard Jury** series, which also features Bertie Woosterish Melrose Plant as Jury's aristocratic sidekick.

Emma Victor

Profession:	Women's rights advocate; private investigator
Living situation:	Single; lesbian
Geographic locale:	Boston; later San Francisco

Time period:	1986–present
Significant relationship:	Never-quite-ex Dr. Frances Cohen
Concerns:	Gay rights; women's rights; activism

Emma Victor, lesbian Chandleresque protagonist of Mary Wings's hard-boiled noir detective series, arrived like Wings, "just in time to successfully chronicle lesbian cultural history in the late 20th century" (Lynne Maxwell, *Gay and Lesbian Literature*). Wings produced her first two Emma Victor novels while living in Amsterdam, where as Wings commented to the *St. James Guide to Crime and Mystery Writers*, "writing about the sunny skies and crazy people who inhabit the U.S. brought me comfort, brought me home." The same wistful longing for home—where, as Robert Frost put it, when you have to go there, they have to take you in—constantly underlies Victor's tough-gay exterior, making her at once more sympathetically complex and less stereotypical a character than many of her Mike Hammerish literary ancestors of the 1940s and 1950s.

Emma Victor has already forcefully outed herself before her first detective outing, *She Came Too Late* (1986). Wings had to move the setting of this novel from San Francisco to Boston because she needed to disguise the identity of the real person she had based the murderer upon (Ashley 504), but she used her own experience as a rape and abuse telephone counselor for Victor's job and the precipitating incident introducing the murder of Victor's acquaintance and fellow lesbian Julie Arbeder. As Emma probes Arbeder's death, she is irresistibly drawn to medical researcher Dr. Frances Cohen, and they initiate a passionate affair that continues on-again, off-again for seven years through the series until Frances dumps Emma, as Emma ruefully admits in *She Came in Drag* (1999). The Emma Victor of *She Came Too Late* wryly addresses not only serious societal problems confronting women in the late 1980s, especially the often demeaning battles women's support groups wage for private and governmental support, but also wider issues like the yuppie phenomenon and the New Age movement.

In the "sinking ship" that Emma sees Boston (and by extension, other American cities) as being, she lives a streamlined, lonely life with Flossie her cat in a house that looks "in transition" (*Too Late* 49), pursuing the overheated promise of "dyke reality": "heaven between the sheets and struggle on the streets" (*Too Late* 39). Neither venue satisfies Emma for long because she's constantly worrying about her love affairs, her ego, and her intuitions, and she can't seem to help allowing nagging maternal urges to complicate her life—as when she takes home an adorable Golden Retriever puppy and names it "Safety," despite having no notion of how she can fit it into her less-than-structured existence.

Emma Victor's world is full of male strangers that she has to assume carry guns, and she often gets knocked on the head or worse for trying to stop them from using those weapons. In *She Came in a Flash* (1989), Emma's affair with Frances has cooled sufficiently for Emma to relocate to the San Francisco Bay area, publicizing a benefit concert for women's organizations. In the course of her undercover investigation of the death of her friend Jonell's sister, who had gotten involved with a weird

California religious cult, Emma is both locked up and shot as well as employed by lawyer Willie Rossini (spelled "Rosini" in Wings's later novels) to clear the name of Willie's former punk-rock-star client Nevada Storm. Emma's loyalty to her lesbian friends often reverberates to an "us against the world" drumbeat, but she constantly demonstrates its sincerity, usually by enduring brutal male-inflicted physical violence. The emotional hurts Emma suffers from what Lynne Maxwell calls the difficulties of initiating and continuing lesbian romantic relationships" (*Gay and Lesbian Literature*), however, are much more painful and long-lasting.

Painfully, too, Emma watches the sisterhood itself changing. "What has happened to us? . . . Lesbian sex used to be a revolutionary act. Now the sisterhood returns to the bookstore to watch television; famous people coming out on *television*" (*In Drag* 33–34 italics in original). The Emma Victor that Mary Wings brought back nearly a decade after her first two novels underwent psychic surgery considerably beyond the cosmetic tucks of slightly graying hair and the diamond stud piercing one nostril. She now describes herself as "a free lance people finder" (*In Drag* 32). She buys out her San Francisco housemates so she can own an attractive house on the edge of the Mission, acquires "Romea," a small, yellow, slightly dented Alfa Romeo convertible (*In Drag* 73), uncovers fraud for insurance companies, is licensed to carry (though she avoids doing so), can stay awake twenty hours (though she doesn't like to), and as she puts it pointedly to a reluctant prospective client, she's "paper-trained, too" (*In Drag* 57).

In *She Came by the Book* (1996), Frances has moved to San Francisco, too, and she and Emma are living together while Emma, as a legal investigator, takes on a case that requires her to search her own history of twenty years earlier and eventually results in a dramatic poisoning at the inaugural gala for the city's Lesbian and Gay Archive. In *She Came to the Castro* (1997) she tackles political blackmail and a global conspiracy while her relationship with Frances becomes increasingly problematic. These experiences take her novels beyond mere lesbian polemics, because they allow Emma to take some deadly potshots at the whole spectrum of today's ominous inanities represented by "the glass and plastic monolith that dominates the living room," (*In Drag* 336) as well as exploring the inner landscapes of emotionally charged relationships that almost always turn out wrong.

After Frances has left her, Emma's "gaydar" lands her new romantic possibilities, but despite the occasional passing crush, Emma realizes she's not gotten over Frances and probably won't. Her new resolution to avoid one-night stands with strangers gives way to her long-established "thing for science nerds," getting her into flaming bedroom scenes with another zaftig medical researcher, Dr. Rita Huelga, in *She Came in Drag* (1999), but after a near-fatal concussion Emma yanks herself up by the bootstraps, preserving her integrity by admitting that her life's been a balancing act between good manners and bad behavior (*In Drag* 101). Lonely as she frequently is, she's going to tough it out the same way, dismantling that hated television set once and for all. In Wings's atmospheric fiction, characterization often walks a chancy tightrope between the funny (General Gertrude of the Lesbian Revengers) and the bathetic, but despite what a *Publishers Weekly* reviewer called "the occasional turns toward comicbook [*sic*] hysteria," Emma Victor rings true as a "slayer of skeletons in closets" on the up and up even if she hangs with the down and outs (*In Drag* 264, 295).

Novels: *She Came Too Late* (1986); *She Came in a Flash* (1989); *She Came by the Book* (1996); *She Came to the Castro* (1997); *She Came in Drag* (1999).

Stand-alone novel: *Divine Victim* (1993).

Comic books: *Come Out Comix* (1974); *Dyke Shorts* (1980); *Are Your Highs Getting You Down?* (1981).

Selected sources: "In the Beginning." *Entertainment Weekly*, March 29, 1996: 56; Lambert, Pam. "She Came By the Book." *People*, April 29, 1996: 36; Maxwell, Lynne. "Once More to the Castro." *Lambda Book Report*, July–August 1999: 35; "Out Again." *Lambda Book Report*, September 2000: 31; *Publishers Weekly*. Rev. of *She Came in Drag*, May 10, 1999: 64.

Major Awards: Raymond Chandler Fulbright Award nomination for detective spy fiction, 1993; Lambda Book Award for best lesbian mystery novel, 1994.

See also: Ellen Hart's series featuring Minneapolis lesbian restaurant owner Jane Lawless; Laurie King's lesbian detective **Kate Martinelli** series; Randye Lordon's series featuring lesbian PI and ex-New York cop Sydney Sloane; Val McDermid's series featuring Scottish lesbian journalist Lindsay Gordon; Sandra Scoppettone's series featuring Greenwich Village lesbian PI Lauren Laurano; Eve Zaremba's series featuring lesbian PI Helen Karembos, operating out of Canada.

W

Kurt Wallander

Profession:	Detective Inspector, Ystad Police Department
Living situation:	Divorced
Geographic locale:	Principally Ystad, southern Sweden
Time period:	1990–present
Associates:	Police colleagues Rydberg (later deceased) and Martinsson
Nemesis:	Depression
Significant relationships:	Almost none
Concerns:	Deterioration of law and order; technology's effects on society

Like other contemporary European detectives, Henning Mankell's fatigued Detective Inspector Kurt Wallander is an "Old World [cop] on the edge of being overwhelmed by the unremitting brutality of New World crime" (Ott, *Booklist*, February 15, 1997: 1008). The abyss Wallander skirts with booze and opera and pointless affairs is neither geographic nor chronological, but sociological, an enormous societal shift that harried policemen like Wallander, middle-aged and agonizing over his ruined marriage, his aging father, and his rebellious daughter, have been too overworked to see coming. From the start of this series Wallander believes this new mindlessly violent "age of the noose" (*Faceless Killers* 280) demands a new kind of policemen who aren't "distressed when they're forced to go into a human slaughterhouse... [or don't] suffer from my uncertainty and anguish" (*Faceless Killers* 18), but even so he stubbornly continues to lead the most complicated investigations Ystad's police department faces (*Firewall* 399).

The award-winning *Faceless Killers* (1991; tr. 1996) poses Wallander and his colleagues a terrible challenge. After a neighbor finds retired farmer Johannes Lövgren brutally beaten and stabbed to death and his wife Maria hanging nearly dead from a noose, Wallander's major clue is Maria's last word, "foreigner," suggesting involvement with the enormous refugee problem caused by Sweden's policy of unregulated immigration that Wallander detests: "You can spend a lifetime in Sweden without anyone checking up on you" (*Faceless Killers* 272). As Wallander slogs through this case's draining leg- and paperwork, one promising lead petering out after another, his personal responsibilities almost always give way to his professional ones. Something had cracked in Wallander when his divorce papers arrived just before the previous Christmas, and three months after his wife Mona left him for "another life," his brown hair badly needs cutting, he's gained seven kilos from junk food, his old friends have dwindled away, and he reluctantly concludes that he has to accept life as it comes, doing the little his job allows him for his tyrannical artist father and helplessly worrying over his daughter Linda, who'd tried suicide at fourteen and now at nineteen is living with her Somalian lover.

At work, none of Wallander's colleagues is his close friend, but he has molded them into effective team. He relies heavily on Detective Inspector Rydberg, the old hand who'd made Wallander into a policeman, teaching him to patiently regard every crime scene and every home he enters as the front cover of a new book he has to read and as a voice telling the story of its occupants. Rydberg, suffering from terminal cancer through *Faceless Killers*, also taught Wallander to trust his hunches and always return to his first impressions. Wallander learned that lesson so well that he usually carries out his intuitive investigations alone, engendering dangerous jealousies among colleagues he must rely on.

As Bill Ott has also remarked (*Booklist*, April 15, 1999: 1482), Wallander tries to insulate himself from senseless horrors with logical though tedious routine police procedure through a succession of grisly cases with far-reaching sociological implications. In *The White Lioness* (1993; tr. 1998), Wallander confronts racial tensions when a murdered Swedish housewife is found in a well and the killer turns out to be a former KGB agent employed by right-wing Africaaners to train an assassin to kill anti-apartheid leader Nelson Mandela. *Sidetracked* (1995; tr. 1999), focusing on the modern phenomenon of broken families and juvenile murderers, and *The Fifth Woman* (1996; tr. 2000), dealing with the killings of four nuns and a Swedish female tourist, both show Wallander increasingly debilitated by the disintegration of contemporary society.

By *Firewall* (1998; tr. 2002), Wallander is fifty and diabetic, struggling out of a deep depression, finding concentration difficult and feeling ancient and weak, his father gone and the last friend from his youth leaving Sweden. Wallander, who even in the midst of an atrocious homicide case can't resist reaching out to a nasty tomcat or a lonely child, simply cannot understand the total lack of respect for human life he sees around him. As he probes a sickening, apparently senseless murder confessed to by two remorseless teenaged girls in a case that leads him into a cybernetic world he will never comprehend, Wallander also experiences a sordid betrayal by an attractive woman and a sleazy backstabbing by a younger member of his team whom he'd trusted. Both acts force Wallander toward briefly contemplating retirement, a thought that makes him shudder as much as being accused unjustly makes him furious.

Reluctantly accepting growing old, Wallander has managed to rebuild his relationship with Linda, who has returned to studies and respectability. Wallander rejoices when she decides to enter the police academy, because it justifies his own decision to do so years before and helps him get past the psychological firewall that cost him so many relationships, and in *Before the Frost* (2002; tr. 2005), the first Linda Wallander mystery, Wallander and Linda learn to work as colleagues, even though they drive each other near-crazy as flatmates. Joined by Stefan Lindman, a character who's haunted Wallander since *The Return of the Dancing Master* (1998; tr. 2003), in an ugly new case involving abductions and animal killings, Wallander and Linda, father and daughter, old police dog and enthusiastic newbie, break down their personal firewalls, pursuing faceless killers in a new technological society that impersonally marginalizes some and increasingly connects others—at the fearsome price of society's geometrically soaring vulnerability to sabotage and terror.

Novels: *Faceless Killers* (1996; orig. *Moerdare utan ansikte*, 1991); *The Dogs of Riga* (1997; orig. *Hundarna I Riga*, 1991); *The White Lioness* (1998; orig. *Den vita lejoninnan*, 1993); *Sidetracked* (1999; orig. *Villospaar*, 1995); *The Fifth Woman* (2000; orig. *Den femte kvinnan*, 1996); *One Step Behind* (1997; orig. *Steget efterm* 1997); *Firewall* (2002; orig. *Brandvaegg*, 1998); *The Return of the Dancing Master* (2003; orig. *Beraettelse paa tidens strand*, 1998); *Before the Frost: A Linda Wallander Mystery* (2005; orig. *Innan frosten*, 2002). Mankell has also written as-yet-untranslated stand-alone novels, two plays, and several children's books.

Selected sources: Fraser, Antonia. "Swedish Excursions in Crime." *Spectator*, April 3, 2004: 45; Grossman, Lev. "Murder Most Exotic." *Time*, June 7, 2004: 121; Ott, Bill. Rev. of *The Dogs of Riga*. *Booklist*, February 15, 1997: 1008; Ott, Bill. Rev. of *The White Lioness*. *Booklist*, August 1998: 1976; Ott, Bill. Rev. of *Sidetracked*. *Booklist*, April 15, 1999: 1482; *Publishers Weekly*. Rev. of *Before the Frost*, January 31, 2005: 34; Stasio, Marilyn. "Cult Status." *New York Times Book Review*, January 23, 2005: 21.

Major awards: Swedish Academy of Detective Stories Award and Scandinavian Criminal Society Award, both 1991; Swedish Academy of Detective Stories Award, 1995; Golden Paperback Award, 1999; Crime Writers' Association Gold Dagger Award; German Book Prize.

See also: Karin Fossum's Inspector Sejer series, set in rural Norway northwest of Oslo; for world-weary northern European detectives, Jacob Arjouni's series featuring Turkish private investigator Kemal Kayankaya, set in Frankfurt; John Harvey's Charlie Resnick series; Donna Leon's **Guido Brunetti** series; Roger Simon's PI Moses Ward series, set in Prague; Maj Sjöwall and Per Wahlöö's **Martin Beck** series.

Debut novels: Jörg Fauser's *Snowman*, a best-selling German noir mystery featuring a German porn merchant named Blum; Michelle Wan's *Deadly Slipper*, a botanical French-flavored mystery set in the Dordogne region of southwestern France.

V.I. Warshawski

Profession:	Private investigator
Living situation:	Single
Geographic locale:	Chicago
Time period:	1982–present
Associates:	None
Significant relationship:	Morrell
Concerns:	Corruption in big business and social/religious/governmental institutions; feminist issues: abortion rights and affirmative action.

In 1982, Sara Paretsky's V.I. Warshawski attacked corrupt insurance companies and labor unions in *Indemnity Only* as "one of the hardest of the hard-boiled investigators" in fiction (*Silk Stalkings* 2: 222)—and a female one, too. Professionally and personally tough as nails, she operates alone, as do her male predecessors like Lew Archer, Philip Marlowe, Sam Spade, and Mike Hammer, but Victoria Iphegenia Warshawski (maybe "Vic" but never "Vicky") broke new ground for the genre in both respects. Professionally, male PIs like Archer usually take on the "stinkers" raised by such evils as war and inflation and infiltrating otherwise "good" institutions like Hollywood, whereas Warshawski's out after "the culturally privileged social institutions" themselves, who use power and authority to protect the guilty (Kathleen Klein, in Herbert 206) and abuse the downtrodden. Personally, Warshawski's male counterparts usually bring on themselves problems, losses, or failures in significant relationships through addictions like alcoholism. Some, like Spillane's Mike Hammer, whose secret, according to Warshawski, is that "he doesn't try to think," descend into gratuitous violence and/or sex, but Bruce Murphy observes that in her occasional "matter-of-fact affairs" the intelligent feminist Warshawski "is able to have sex with someone without finding it necessary to kill them later" (514).

As narrator, Warshawski seems casually open, but she never tells more than she wants known. Growing up poor on Chicago's South Side, she learned about police work from her Polish cop father and his best friend Bobby Mallory as she learned music from her Jewish-Italian opera singer mother who let her dress up "in her [one] concert gown ... as Signora Vittoria della Cielo e Terra" (*Blacklist* 103). Warshawski studied law on a scholarship to the University of Chicago, briefly practiced as a public defender, protested in civil rights demonstrations, and divorced after a short marriage before becoming a private investigator specializing, like Lew Archer, in corporate crime. After her parents died, Warshawski also built her own "family," including Lieutenant Bobby Mallory, who is constantly urging her to settle down and have babies; her neighbor Mr. Contreras, who thinks of her as sixteen and himself as both of her parents. He shares Warshawski with her running partners Peppy, an enthusiastic Golden Retriever, and later Peppy's pup; her sometime lover newspaperman Murray Ryerson; and her longtime friend Dr. Charlotte "Lotty" Herschel.

Beginning with *Deadlock* (1984), each of Warshawski's cases begins with a problem a friend or acquaintance or current client brings her, so that her private and professional lives intertwine.

Starting with a seemingly simple request to help an individual in trouble, each of Warshawski's cases spirals into large-scale assaults on corrupt power-abusing institutions. *Deadlock* targets the shipping industry after Vic's cousin, former hockey player Boom Boom Warshawski, is shredded by a propeller on a Great Lakes freighter. *Killing Orders* (1985) blasts the hypocrisy of the Roman Catholic Church, and Warshawski stuffs *Bitter Medicine* (1987) down the throats of the smug medical community; then she tackles Chicago politics in Silver Dagger winner *Blood Shot* (1988), the Chicago police force in *Burn Marks* (1989), and both the entertainment industry and private industry in *Hard Time* (1999), where she spends a harrowing two months in jail. Through Lotty Herschel, *Total Recall* (2001) pits Warshawski against international insurance fraud that perpetuates the horrors of the Holocaust, and in the wake of 9/11, in *Blacklist* (2004) she confronts the Federal Government and McCarthyism, terrorism, and the Patriot Act.

Running at first five miles a day with the dogs and then ten a day to try to shake the post-9/11 malaise keeps Warshawski in the fighting trim she needs, since in nearly every case she proves that she can be chased, bashed, half-drowned, strung out by colds or flu, or wasted by bureaucracy-instilled "utter fatigue of soul" (*Blood Shot* 342) and still nail her target dead to rights, leaving beatings, madness, and even suicide in her wake (*Silk Stalkings* 2: 215). She likes classy classic clothes, cherishes her mother's recordings and her Venetian wineglasses, and punctures bureaucrats where it hurts most with outrageous one-liners. Although she espouses feminist issues like abortion rights and affirmative action and battles sexual discrimination as fervently as she does racial discrimination, Warshawski does it her way, refusing to cater to "the polemics of the separatist feminist" (Klein in Herbert 206). In *Blacklist* (2004) Warshawski's deep in love with journalist Morrell, who's researching a book somewhere in the Middle East, too close for Warshawski's comfort to a former lover of his own. Often angry, frustrated, and lonely, Warshawski compares herself to Penelope, who'd waited twenty years while Ulysses fiddled with Circe and outfoxed the Cyclops, until her mother's brisk advice takes over and saves her from depression: "'Don't weep over yourself. Do something'" (*Blacklist* 103). "I'm the only person I take orders from," declares V.I. Warshawski (*Indemnity Only* 163), but sometimes Mother knows best.

Novels: *Indemnity Only* (1982); *Deadlock* (1984); *Killing Orders* (1985); *Bitter Medicine* (1987); *Blood Shot* (1988); *Burn Marks* (1990); *Guardian Angel* (1992); *Tunnel Vision* (1994); *Hard Time* (1999); *Total Recall* (2001); *Blacklist* (2004); *Fire Sale* (2005).

Short fiction: *A Taste of Life* (1995); *Windy City Blues* (1995).

Stand-alone novel: *Ghost Country* (1998).

Other works: Paretsky has edited *Beastly Tales: The Mystery Writers of America Anthology* (1989); *A Woman's Eye* (mystery story collection; 1991); *Women on the Case: Twenty-six Original Stories by the Best Women Crime Writers of Our Time* (1996).

Selected sources: Glazebrook, Olivia. "Predictable Plots, Familiar Faces." *Spectator*, November 22, 2003: 58; Koch, John. Interview with Sara Paretsky. *Boston Globe*, February 5, 1992: 35; Madden, Leslie. Rev. of *Fire Sale*. *Library Journal*, June 15, 2005: 64; *Publishers Weekly*. Rev. of *Hard Time*, October 25, 1999: 44; Sharoff, Robert. "Sara Paretsky." *Crain's Chicago Business*, June 7, 2004: W72.

Major awards: Crime Writers' Association, Silver Dagger, 1998; Anthony Award, 1992; German Marlowe Award, 1993; Crime Writers' Association Diamond Dagger (2002).

Web site: www.saraparetsky.com.

See also: Linda Barnes's series featuring Boston ex–police detective, now taxi driver and blues guitarist Carlotta Carlyle series; Michael A. Black's kickboxer and PI Ron Shade series, set in Chicago; Sue Grafton's "Alphabet" **Kinsey Millhone** series, set in California; Kris Nelscott's series featuring black Chicago PI Smokey Dalton; Marcia Muller's **Sharon McCone** series, set in California; Jan Burke's series featuring southern California investigative reporter **Irene Kelly**.

Reginald Wexford

Profession:	Chief Inspector of Police
Living situation:	Married
Geographic locale:	Mainly in and around fictional Kingsmarkham, Sussex, U.K.
Time period:	1964–present
Associate:	Inspector Mike Burden
Significant relationships:	Dora Wexford, his wife; daughters Sheila and Sylvia
Concerns:	Well-being of his family; psychology; antinuclear lobbying; child abuse; media hypocrisy

Beginning with *From Doom to Death* (1964), Chief Inspector Reginald Wexford's cases parallel his stressful middle age. A genial fifty-two-year-old given to literary quotations, Ruth Rendell's Wexford passes fairly gracefully, usually wittily, through periods of self-doubt and illnesses as a sensitive husband, a bemused father, and a tolerant grandfather. He can look into the darkest human behavior and still believe in the goodness of mankind. "Corpulent and heavy, he had always been stout and always would be. His was an ugly face, the face of a Silenus with a snub nose and wide mouth.... Silenus was the companion of Bacchus, but the nearest Wexford ever got to Bacchus was an occasional pint with Inspector Burden at the Olive and Dove" (*Wolf to the Slaughter* 15).

Despite Wexford's profession, the nineteen novels of Ruth Rendell's acclaimed series emphasize psychology and character development over police procedure, as Wexford and Inspector Burden confront the upheavals in British economics and morality that produce widespread social ills. They work out of Kingsmarkham,

Sussex, an ordinary English town with ordinary people, a few rich, many working-class, some very poor. A split second's last straw of social pressure can hurl anyone "into the maw of murder" (*Silk Stalkings* 1: 64).

Like many Golden Age sleuths, Wexford relies heavily on painstaking examination of witnesses and discussing the cases in detail with Burden, but he never shows off the arcane knowledge of a Lord Peter Wimsey or the pedantry of a Sherlock Holmes. Wexford's values are also very different from theirs. Where Wimsey's offhand anti-Semitism and Holmes's intellectual superiority today seem discomfiting, Wexford's shock at prejudice and bigotry "seems normal rather than superimposed political correctness" (Murphy 422).

Rendell has maintained that the time for black and white characters has vanished. The wives and families of Wexford and Burden supply subplots crucial to complexity of character. The stiff, emotionally repressed Burden, who struggles to soothe a jittery husband in *From Doon with Death* is emotionally devastated by his own wife's death from cancer in *No More Dying* (1971). Wexford pulls Burden through while they solve a complicated kidnapping and murder, revealing new dimensions to both men. Those roles reverse in *Road Rage* (1997), when New Age ecoterrorists start to kill abductees—of whom Wexford's homemaker wife Dora is one.

In Wexford's most recent cases, he grapples with cases involving Rendell's major themes—internecine strife, child abuse, and sexual frustration as well as his daughters' marital difficulties, since they "[tell] their father everything" (*Harm Done* 344). Paul, the husband of Sheila, a successful actress with the Royal Shakespeare Company, worries Wexford: " 'He's so handsome and charming.... It's not natural to look like him and be neither gay nor unfaithful to your wife or partner or whatever' " (*Babes in the Wood* 47). In *Harm Done* (1999), Wexford has to protect a released pedophile when kidnappings rock the Muriel Campden Estate, near the battered women's refuge where his daughter Sylvia works, her own marriage badly strained. Though Neil never raises his hand to her, they divorce, which causes Dora and Wexford great grief, since they are genuinely fond of him. In *The Babes in the Wood* (2002), another missing-children case, Sylvia rebounds to Cal, who "makes her morning tea," though Dora and Wexford find him horrid: " 'That won't last,' said Wexford. 'That New Man stuff never does.... I don't understand why my daughters take up with these sorts of men. Ghastly men' " (*Babes in the Wood* 47).

Wit also pulls Wexford through his own traumas, like the aftermath of his stroke: "two circular biscuits apparently composed of sawdust and glue, a pat of unsaturated fat, half a sugarless grapefruit, black coffee and, crowning horror, a glass dish of wobbly pallid substance he took to be yoghourt" (*Murder Being Once Done* 1). On a tour to China in *Speaker of Mandarin* (1983), Wexford pays a subtle tribute to Agatha Christie in a succession of mini-puzzles that give him hallucinations. Wexford's house is blown up in *The Veiled One* (1988), but he manages to grin at workers starting to rebuild it. With his refreshingly balanced view of human nature, his uncompromising moral stance, and his ability to smile wryly when Dora, Sylvia, Sheila, and Burden have to admit as he himself often does, "we live and learn," Inspector Reg Wexford is altogether a decent man in an indecent world.

Novels: *From Doon With Death* (1964); *A New Lease of Death* (1967; U.S. *Sins of the Fathers*, 1970); *Wolf to the Slaughter* (1967); *The Best Man to Die* (1969); *A Guilty Thing Surprised* (1970); *No More Dying Then* (1971); *Murder Being Once Done* (1972); *Some Lie and Some Die* (1973); *Shake Hands for Ever* (1975); *A Sleeping Life* (1978); *Put on by Cunning* (1981; U.S. *Death Notes*, 1981); *The Speaker of Mandarin* (1983); *An Unkindness of Ravens* (1985); *The Veiled One* (1988); *Kissing the Gunner's Daughter* (1992); *Simisola* (1994); *Road Rage* (1997); *Harm Done* (1999); *The Babes in the Wood* (2002).

Short fiction (Wexford series): *Means of Evil* (1979).

Nonfiction: *Ruth Rendell's Suffolk* (1992).

Other works: Rendell has written numerous stand-alone novels and short stories like *The Rottweilor* (2004) and *Thirteen Steps Down* (2005) under both her name and under the name "Barbara Vine." Rendell has edited *A Warning to the Curious: The Ghost Stories of M.R. James* (1986); *The Reason Why: An Anthology of the Murderous Mind* (1996).

Selected sources: Adams, Michael. Rev. of *Babes in the Wood*. *Library Journal*, May 1, 2004: 153; Jakeman, Jane. "Where does Ruth Rendell End and 'Barbara Vine' Begin?" *Independent* (London), June 15, 2002: 30; Melton, Emily. Rev. of *Kissing the Gunner's Daughter*. *Booklist*, April 15, 1999: 1458; "On the Launchpad." *Booklist*, June 10, 2005; *Publishers Weekly*. Interview with Ruth Rendell. January 28, 2002: 275; Scott, Whitney. "Series Mysteries." *Booklist*, January 1, 2004: 892.

Major awards: Gold Dagger, 1976, 1986, 1987, 1991; Silver Dagger, 1984; Diamond Dagger, 1991; Edgar Award, 1975, 1984, 1987; Swedish Academy of Detection, 1980; Grand Master, 1996; MWA Grand Master, 1997.

Web site: www.twbooks.co.uk?authors/rendell.html.

See also: Catherine Aird's Inspector **C.D. Sloan** series; Robert Barnard's **Trethowen**, Peace, and Odden series; P.D. James's **Adam Dalgliesh** series. Minette Walters's stand-alone novels have been compared to the dark psychological murder mysteries Rendell writes as "Barbara Vine."

Holly Winter

Profession:	Dog trainer and magazine columnist
Living situation:	Single
Geographic locale:	Massachusetts
Time period:	1990–present
Associates:	Alaskan Malamutes Rowdy and Kimi
Significant relationship:	Steve Delaney, D.V.M.
Concerns:	Dog training; animal welfare issues

Dog book writer Darlene Arden claims that Susan Conant created the "entire genre" of canine cozy mysteries: "The characters are so incredibly rich; they come to life. But what really appeals are the details. You can tell Susan is a real dog person" (*Dog*

World, May 2005: 24). Conant's "vocational epiphany" for writing fiction occurred during a training class she attended with her first Alaskan Malamute, Natasha. Dogs were placed on a "Down/Stay," the owners left the room, and when they returned a few minutes later, one owner was missing. Conant wondered, "What if that dog owner had been murdered?" (*Dog World* 24) and her initial Holly Winter mystery, packed with dog lore and featuring her co-sleuth Rowdy, a handsome Malamute who looks like a wolf adapted to pull a sled, was born.

In all of Conant's Dog Lover's Mysteries Holly Winter, amateur dog trainer and columnist for the fictional *Dog's Life* magazine, solves murders by applying her lifelong knowledge of canine behavior and training methods to human actions and their motivations. Holly's parents Buck and Marissa Winter raised numerous pedigreed Golden Retrievers and one daughter, born at Christmastime. Holly Winter shares many of her endearing qualities with her four-legged kennel mates: intelligence, patience, loyalty, inquisitiveness, and eagerness to please. Living so closely with her own show Golden Vinnie that she sometimes inadvertently bathed and groomed herself with Hill's Flea Soap and used Ring 5 Coat Gloss on her own dark golden-colored hair, Holly is left desolate at thirty when Vinnie dies of cancer. She adopts Rowdy, a huge Malamute whose owner during a Down/Stay in an Open obedience class went on the longest Down of all, strangled with Rowdy's leash. To compete in American Kennel Club obedience trials, a dog must be registered with the AKC, but Rowdy's papers are missing, so Holly and Rowdy track down both papers and murderer, revealing intricate minutiae of the conformation (beauty contest) and obedience aspects of the sport of purebred dogs.

Holly's lover Siberian-blue-eyed Steve Delaney, the vet who held Holly's hand for half an hour after he ended Vinnie's suffering, and his German Shepherd India provide Holly moral support in all her cases. Holly's world also contains plenty of colorful humans and canines, like her tenant Rita, a "shrink," who owns Groucho, a Dachshund, and a Scottie named Willie; her neighbor Kevin Dennehy, a Cambridge cop; and Leah, Holly's bouncy young cousin and a fellow dog-trainer. As a former vice president of the Alaskan Malamute Assistance League and founder of the Alaskan Malamute Rescue of New England, Conant annually auctions off a character to be incorporated in a forthcoming novel; 2004's went for $5,700 (*Dog World* 25).

Each of Holly's cases, too, involves a different aspect of the dog sport, which Conant uses to comment on human behavior and frailty. Several are outright good-humored "cozies," like *A New Leash on Death* (1990), fictionalized Thursday night obedience training sessions in the real Cambridge Armory, but they also carry a strong message: Holly wants to establish a Nuremberg-style trial for dog-abusers. In *A Bite of Death* (1991), she adopts Kimi, an orphaned Malamute who badly needs to learn some manners, after Kimi's owner dies suspiciously. While training Kimi and solving this crime, Holly voices her "canine feminism": "If you want a lesson in power and control, take up dog training . . . you learn . . . to make things happen the way you want, even if the other guy is bigger and stronger than you are, whether the other guy is a dog or a person" (*Bite of Death* 13). For a long time Holly claimed she'd never marry, because she and Steve Delaney are each the alpha dog in their respective packs, and "If we merged packs, one of us would lose because a wolf pack never has two alphas. That's what's wrong with marriage" (*Bite of Death* 178). Delaney's divorce becomes final in *Bride and Groom* (2004), however, and Holly, now successful author of a dog-treat cookbook, *101 Ways to Cook Liver*, finally agrees to marry him.

Holly's investigations usually have tail-wagging endings. *Dead and Doggone* (1990) treats relatively benign issues of dog grooming; *Stud Rites* (1996), according to a *Publishers Weekly* critic, is "a frisky look at mayhem unleashed"; and *The Barker Street Regulars* (1998) involves Rowdy's therapy dog training for work in a local nursing home, while Holly noses around a shady psychic claiming to put elderly patients in touch with their deceased four-legged loved ones. In the hilarious parody *The Dogfather* (2003), Holly becomes dog trainer for canophile Mafia don Enzo Guarini and his elkhound puppy, and in *Animal Appetite* (2005), Holly, Rowdy, and Kimi become entangled with murders new and old as she researches the life of Hannah Duston, captured by Indians in seventeenth-century New England.

Some of Holly's cases are heart-rending. *Gone to the Dogs* (1992) and *Bloodlines* (1993), however, address the disgraceful puppy-mill business. In filthy dog concentration camps, exhausted bitches are bred as often as possible to supply pitifully weak and undersocialized irresponsibly produced puppies to pet shops whose motto is "Buy on impulse, neglect at leisure" (*Bloodlines* 4). Holly Winter, hot on the trail of this scourge of dogdom, lays siege to Puppy Luv, an outlet for such mistreated animals, forged AKC papers, and broken promises, but when Puppy Luv's owner Diane Sweet turns up murdered, Holly herself becomes a prime suspect. Holly raids a puppy mill on her own and comes close to shooting its operators in her dog-loving wrath. For all her snappy dialogue, her bottomless fund of dog-training lore, and her upbeat evangelism of the gospel of responsible pet ownership, Holly Winter's crusade is dead serious. Profiteering animal abusers are alive and well in this world, and she's going to stop them: "We can close the puppy mills, you know.... The AKC won't do it, and the USDA won't do it. We will ... before long, none of us will buy so much as a single morsel of premium kibble from a pet shop that sells dogs. Peace will come. Let it begin with us" (*Bloodlines* 256).

Novels: *A New Leash on Death* (1990); *Dead and Doggone* (1990); *A Bite of Death* (1991); *Paws Before Dying* (1991); *Gone to the Dogs* (1992); *Bloodlines* (1993); *Ruffly Speaking* (1994); *Black Ribbon* (1995); *Stud Rites* (1996); *Animal Appetite* (1997); *The Barker Street Regulars* (1998); *Evil Breeding* (1998); *Creature Discomforts* (2000); *The Wicked Flea* (2002); *The Dogfather* (2003); *Bride and Groom* (2004); *Animal Appetite* (2004). In what may seem a betrayal of dog lovers, Conant has launched a new series featuring cat person and fictional cat mystery author Felicity Pride, beginning with *Scratch the Surface* (2005). Conant and her daughter Jessica Conant-Park are also cooking up a culinary mystery series, starting with *Burned* (2005).

Selected sources: *Boston Magazine*. Rev. of *Animal Appetite*, May 1997: 58; Dale, Steve. "Cover to Cover with Susan Conant." *Dog World*, May 2005: 24; *Kirkus Reviews*. Rev. of *The Dogfather*, January 2003: 28; *Publishers Weekly*. Rev. of *Stud Rites*, May 27, 1996: 69; *Publishers Weekly*. Rev. of *Bride and Groom*, January 12, 2004: 41; *Publishers Weekly*. Rev. of *The Wicked Flea*, February 25, 2002: 46.

Award: Maxwell Award, Dog Writers Association of America, 1991.

See also: Carole Lea Benjamin's **Rachel Alexander** and Dashiell the pit bull series; Laurien Berenson's **Melanie Travis** and poodles series; a little further afield in the animal kingdom, Caroline Burnes's (Carolyn Haines) Ann Tate equine-related series and Burnes's Dawn Markey equine series.

The Women's Murder Club

Professions:	Lindsay Boxer: homicide inspector; Claire Washburn: medical examiner; Jill Bernhardt: assistant district attorney; Cindy Thomas: journalist
Living situations:	Single
Geographic locale:	San Francisco
Time period:	2001–present

For sheer relish in their crime-fighting and wrong-righting, Robin Hood and his merry men have nothing on James Patterson's Women's Murder Club, bringing together four talented San Francisco women infuriated by serial homicides that male detectives can't seem to stop. Lindsay Boxer, Claire Washburn, Jill Bernhardt, and Cindy Thomas pool their resources in an unofficial and unorthodox detection collective that defies male authority and bonds them together through their turbulent subsequent investigations. Patterson's collective protagonist has considerable potential, but as the series progresses, it focuses more and more on homicide detective Lindsay Boxer, losing some of the impact of its innovative narrative technique.

That four-woman collective seems to have sprung from Patterson's fascination with the female point of view. In an interview with *BookPage* critic Steven Womak, Patterson commented on his adopting the narrative voices of two different women for his stand-alone novel *Cradle and All*, a "reimagined" 2000 version of his 1980 novel *Virgin*, where he fictionalized the "Third Secret of Fatima," a 1917 revelation kept secret by the Catholic Church, predicting that one pregnant virgin may bear the Son of God while another pregnant virgin will bear the Son of the Devil. Patterson noted that he "grew up in a house full of women—grandmother, mother, three sisters, two female cats. I cooked for my grandmother's restaurant. . . . I like the way [women] talk, the fact that a lot of subjects weave in and out of conversations. Sometimes men are a little more of a straight line" (quoted in *CA Online*). Interweaving four female points of view in *1st to Die* (2001) allows Patterson to have each woman strike some unusual sparks from the others, enhances suspense, and piles the surprises up until the very end of the novel.

At the start of *1st to Die*, Lindsay Boxer, a San Francisco homicide inspector, is agonizing in a tough double-edged life-threatening situation. She's battling a potentially fatal autoimmune disease (not AIDS) at the same time she's tracking the serial killer responsible for murdering Bay Area honeymooners. Outraged by the brutality of the crimes, Boxer enlists black medical examiner Claire Washburn and Assistant D.A. Jill Bernhardt, who each provide a different perspective on the murders, and then—somewhat reluctantly—they allow *San Francisco Chronicle* reporter

Cindy Thomas, young and hungry for a big story, to join their little sisterhood. At Patterson's trademark sound-bite speed, a suspect is nabbed and jailed about halfway through the novel, then proved innocent and released, while Boxer's professional and physical problems multiply.

Boxer assumes more of the spotlight in each novel that follows, and the sphere of her activities concurrently swells. As a San Francisco G8 summit approaches in *3rd Degree* (2003), she even takes on the "August Spies," a worldwide terrorist organization. To gain attention for their demands that wealthy nations make hefty restitution for their supposed crimes against the underdeveloped countries the Spies claim to represent, the terrorists explode a deadly bomb and assassinate a noted economist with the deadly poison ricin. Boxer marshals her Women's Murder Club colleagues to work with FBI agents and the Deputy Director of Department of Homeland Security, again drawing on her own intuition and the talents of each woman to help her decipher the underlying motives for the crimes.

A more personal threat emerges for Boxer in *4th of July* (2004), when she is charged with police brutality while pursuing a crime family of murderers. Police mess up the arrest of two juveniles carrying illegal weapons, and what should have been a pro forma preliminary hearing for Boxer mushrooms into the specter of a sensational jury trial. Boxer tries to escape the bloodthirsty journalists hot on her heels by hiding out at her sister Cat's house on Half Moon Bay, but there she finds yet another batch of killers and alienates the Half Moon Bay police chief. Her friends of the Women's Murder Club evidently can't help her much as she hunts those murderers down, pauses to fight her way gamely through a messy acquittal, then returns to nab the Half Moon Bay killers. While Patterson's narrative pace never flags, the interwoven female conversations he found attractive and initially produced effectively in *1st to Die* seem to have gradually evaporated in subsequent installments, possibly because of collaborating, first with Andrew Gross for *2nd Chance* and *3rd Degree*, then with Maxine Paetro for *4th of July*. While the collective protagonist of the Women's Murder Club was a good and innovative idea, their law-enforcing camaraderie and literary impact apparently are declining.

Novels: *1st to Die* (2001); *2nd Chance* (with Andrew Gross; 2002); *3rd Degree* (with Andrew Gross; 2003); *4th of July* (with Maxine Paetro; 2004).

Other series: The **Alex Cross** series, featuring a black homicide detective and psychologist who leaves the Washington, D.C., police force for the FBI.

Other works: Patterson has written numerous stand-alone novels; see **Alex Cross** entry.

Selected sources: Burkhardt, Joanna M. Rev. of *3rd Degree. Library Journal*, August 15, 2004: 129; Hammond, Joanne K. Rev. of *1st to Die. Magill Book Reviews*, May 1, 2001; "James Patterson on the Spot." *Advertising Week*, November 29, 2004; *Publishers Weekly*, Rev. of *2nd Chance*, February 18, 2002: 75; *Publishers Weekly*. Rev. of *4th of July*, April 25, 2005: 39; "2005 To Be Year of James Patterson for Little, Brown." *Book Publishing Report*, March 7, 2005: 4; Womak, Steven. "Stretching the Boundaries of the Thriller." www.bookpage.com.

Major award: Edgar Award, best first novel, 1977.

Web site: www.twbookmark.com/features/Jamespatterson/index.html.

See also: While female amateur detectives, private eyes, and homicide cops have frequently appeared in the genre since the 1980s, no other series like the Women's Murder Club exists as yet. For a police procedural with a collective protagonist, see Ed McBain's 87th Precinct series, featuring detective **Steve Carella**; for an amateur detective male collective, see Isaac Asimov's Black Widowers Club mysteries, featuring a group of men who often discuss problematic crimes. This group, with one addition, also appears in Asimov's *The Union Club Mysteries* (1983). Best known as a science fiction author, Asimov also wrote the science fiction mysteries *Caves of Steel* and *The Robots of Dawn*, featuring detective Lije Bailey and his robot associate (Murphy 19).

Z

Aurelio Zen

Profession:	Police detective, Italian Ministry of the Interior
Living situation:	Single
Geographic locale:	Italy
Time period:	1988–present
Associate:	Giorgio De Angelis
Nemeses:	Corrupt government officials; the Carabinieri; the Mafia
Significant relationship:	Gemma Santini
Concerns:	Personal moral code; art; Italian history

Michael Dibdin spent several years teaching English in Perugia, Italy, acquiring a background for his crime fiction as authentic and elegant as his major figure, police detective Aurelio Zen. Descended from the lords of Venice and working, often sub rosa, for the Italian Ministry of the Interior, Zen's investigations often impinge on those of their chief antagonists, the Carabinieri, Italy's National Police. One of the most complex and convincing of literary detectives, Zen is intelligent, self-effacing, living a strict morality entirely his own, and practicing both clinical cruelty in the service of justice and devotion to the order and beauty he finds lacking in the present-day Italy he serves. In this internationally acclaimed cosmopolitan series, Zen never fails to surprise and intrigue readers with his multifaceted crime-solving prowess, highlighted against a chiaroscuro background of interwoven contemporary and historical Italian life.

Each of Zen's cases plays out in a different Italian milieu, but all illustrate the political corruption, individual venality, and suffocating bureaucracy universally discernible and lamentable today. *Ratking* (1988), Zen's first case and Dibdin's third novel, introduced Commissario Zen, whose only game is patience, dealing with the kidnapping of a wealthy industrialist in Perugia. Since Dibdin intends to show that high-level police officials are human, Zen sometimes makes errors that cause pain and grief to others, and some readers even find him an "incredible egoist who is not as smart as he thinks he is" (Murphy 542), though most concur with Frederick Busch, who called Zen simply "wonderful" in his *Ratking* debut (14). There, his character seems to function mostly as a "facilitator" (Ashley 138) because Dibdin had not originally intended to make Zen a series character.

Ratking's success, however, sent the aristocratic Zen on a grand tour of Italian crime scenes, all involving high-maintenance wealthy and influential victims. Dispatched to Sardinia in *Vendetta* (1992), Zen investigates the videotaped murder of a prominent security-conscious architect in another procedural spiked with occasional explosions of Zen's calculated application of physical violence. *Cabal* (1992), containing a wicked satire on Milan's fashion industry, opens with another death of a prominent personage, this time Prince Lodovico Ruspanti, who plummets from the cupola of St. Peter's Church during Mass. Undercover in *The Dead Lagoon* (1994), Zen, now a Vice Questore with Criminalpol, the most powerful branch of the Interior Ministry police force, returns to his native Venice, privately commissioned by his former American lover Ellen to find a kidnapped American businessman, only to be stonewalled by local corrupt officialdom. *Cosi Fan Tutti* (1996), whose comedic atmosphere may have been influenced by Dibdin's marriage to K.K. Beck, a mystery author specializing in fluffy parodies of Golden Age mysteries, sees Zen transferred in disgrace to Naples as commander of the harbor police. His blunders and his manipulation of two gangsters into being unfaithful to their girlfriends—his landlady's daughters—get Zen reprimanded for total incompetence.

Starting with *Dark Specter* (1995), Dibdin's non-series novels had turned to darker psychological themes, and he also turned Aurelio Zen aside from headlong satire and began to rehabilitate him, world-wearier and more prone to contemplate the empty recesses of his life in *A Long Finish* (1998) and *Blood Rain* (2000). *A Long Finish*, set in the lovely Italian Piedmont region, takes Zen into a tightly knit community whose members seem bent on killing one another. In *Blood Rain*, Zen's "most dangerous assignment yet," where he infiltrates the Carabinieri's anti-Mafia squad in Sicily for the Interior Ministry, the comic-opera tone of *Cosi Fan Tutti* vanishes completely in a confusing mixture of criminals and everyday sinners. *And Then You Die* (2002) features an Aurelio Zen grown still more complex, even cynical, as though contact with the black hand of the Mafia—an explosive assassination attempt in *Blood Rain*—would shadow him forever.

Ordered in *And Then You Die* to stay out of sight while convalescing at a beach resort in Tuscany, Zen meets Gemma Santini, who becomes the new woman in his life, "tough as an ox," he declares admiringly (*You Die* 162) and the only woman who has ever accepted him unquestioningly. Before he settles down with Gemma in the sleepy town of Lucca, a "White" city in the midst of largely Communist Tuscany, though, Zen battles lurking killers and the possibility of enforced retirement, a chilling prospect that haunts him through *Medusa* (2004), a case that unveils psychological deviance so terrifying that, like, the mythological Gorgon, it has turned human hearts to stone. Able to manage only a few days of quiet at Lucca with Gemma before thirsting for more police work, Zen accepts the secret orders of his Interior Ministry superior, and draws again on the resources of his shady friend Giorgio De Angelis to outwit the Carabinieri while uncovering corruption among Italy's military caste and long-buried individual moral collapse.

New York Times mystery critic Marilyn Stasio has called the Aurelio Zen novels "so delicately complex they might have been spun by spiders" (2000, 28), but the incisive personality of Aurelio Zen more nearly resembles Murano art glass, tempered in glowing fires of conviction, smooth-surfaced but hard enough to inflict torture to right a wrong; translucent, swirling with vivid colors, moods, temptations—and fragile, too, fragile enough to need a woman's gentle touch.

Novels: *Ratking* (1988); *Vendetta* (1992); *Cabal* (1992); *The Dead Lagoon* (1994); *Cosi Fan Tutti* (1996); *A Long Finish* (1998); *Blood Rain* (2000); *And Then You Die* (2002); *Medusa* (2004).

Nonseries novels: *The Last Sherlock Holmes Story* (1978); *A Rich, Full Death* (1986); *The Tryst* (1989); *Dirty Tricks* (1991); *The Dying of Light* (1993); *Dark Spectre* (1995); *Thanksgiving* (2001).

Other works: Dibdin has edited *The Picador Book of Crime Writing* (1993) and *The Vintage Book of Classic Crime* (1997).

Selected sources: Busch, Frederick. Rev. of *Ratking*. *Chicago Tribune*, January 4, 1990: 14; Del Guido, Alessia. Rev. of *A Long Finish*. *Times Literary Supplement*, September 18, 1998: 28; Osgood, Charles. "A Talk with Mystery Writer Michael Dibdin." *CBS News Sunday Morning*, November 26, 2000; Ott, Bill. "Zen and the Art of Series Maintenance." *Booklist*, May 1, 2002: 1552; *Publishers Weekly*. Rev. of *Blood Rain*, March 20, 2000: 57; Saricks, Joyce. Rev. of *Vendetta*. *Booklist*, July 1, 2003: 1910; Stasio, Marilyn. Rev. of *Blood Rain*. *New York Times Book Review*, April 2, 2000: 28; Stasio, Marilyn. Rev. of *Medusa*. *New York Times Book Review*, February 22, 2004: 15.

Major awards: Gold Dagger Award, Crime Writers' Association, 1988; CWA '92 Award, 1990; *Grand Prix de Littérature Policière*, 1994.

See also: John Spencer Hill's **Carlo Arbati** series, set in Florence; Donna Leon's **Guido Brunetti** series, set in Venice; Magdalen Nabb's **Marshal Guarnaccia** series set in Florence; Timothy Williams's Commissario Trotti series.

APPENDIX A
Authors and Their Sleuths

Note: Police titles are given below only when the sleuth is known simply by his or her last name. Except for religious titles and titles of the British peerage, no other titles are used below.

Catherine Aird, British, b. 1930	C.D. "Seedy" Sloan
Rennie Airth, South African, b. 1935	John Madden
Boris Akunin, pseud. of Grigory Chkhartishvili, Georgian, b. 1956	Erast Fandorin
Susan Wittig Albert, American, b. 1940	China Bayles
Bruce Alexander, pseud. of Bruce Cook, British, 1932–2003	Sir John Fielding
Baantjer, Dutch, b. 1923	Jurrian DeKok
Jo Bannister, British, b. 1951	Liz Graham
Robert Barnard, British, b. 1936	Perry Trethowan
Nevada Barr, American, b. 1952	Anna Pigeon
Stephanie Barron, American, b. 1953	Jane Austen
George Baxt, American, 1923–2003	Pharoah Love
M.C. Beaton, pseud. of Marion Chesney, Scottish, b. 1936	Hamish Macbeth Agatha Raisin
Carol Lea Benjamin, American, b. 1937	Rachel Alexander
Laurien Berenson, American, b. ?	Melanie Travis
Michelle Blake, American, b. ?	Lily Connor
Eleanor Bland, American, b. 1944	Marti MacAlister

Lawrence Block, American, b. 1938	Matthew Scudder
Stephen Booth, British, b. 1933	Ben Cooper
Michael Bond, British, b. 1926	Monsieur Pamplemousse
C.J. Box, American, b. ?	Joe Pickett
Lillian Jackson Braun, American, b. ?	Jim Qwilleran
Simon Brett, British, b. 1945	Charles Paris
Ken Bruen, Irish, b. 1951	Jack Taylor
Edna Buchanan, American, b. 1939	Britt Montero
Fiona Buckley, pseud. of Valerie Anand, British, b. 1937	Ursula Blanchard
James Lee Burke, American, b. 1936	Dave Robicheaux
Jan Burke, American, b. 1953	Irene Kelly
Sarah Caudwell, British, 1939–2000	Hilary Tamar
Lee Child, British, b. 1954	Jack Reacher
Barbara Cleverly, British, b. ?	Joe Sandilands
Harlan Coben, American, b. 1962	Myron Bolitar
Liza Cody, pseud. of Liza Hassim, British, b. 1944	Anna Lee
Susan Conant, American, b. 1946	Holly Winter
Michael Connelly, American, b. 1956	Harry Bosch
Patricia Cornwell, American, b. 1956	Kay Scarpetta
Robert Crais, American, b. 1954	Elvis Cole
Deborah Crombie, American, b. 1952	Duncan Kincaid
Amanda Cross, pseud. of Carolyn Heilbrun, 1926–2003	Kate Fansler
Diane Mott Davidson, American, b. ?	Goldy Bear (Schulz)
Lindsey Davis, British, b. 1949	Marcus Didius Falco
Colin Dexter, British, b. 1930	Inspector Morse
Michael Dibdin, British, b. 1947	Aurelio Zen
Peter Dickinson, British, b. 1927	Jimmy Pibble
Paul C. Doherty, British, b. 1945	Telemon the Physician
Carole Nelson Douglas, American, b. 1944	Irene Adler
John Dunning, American, b. 1942	Cliff Janeway
Aaron Elkins, American, b. 1935	Gideon Oliver
Janet Evanovich, American, b. 1943	Stephanie Plum
G.M. Ford, American, b. 1945	Frank Corso
Christopher Fowler, British, b. 1953	Arthur Bryant and John May
Antonia Fraser, British, b. 1932	Jemima Shore
Margaret Frazer, joint pseud. of Gail Frazer and Mary Monica Pulver, both American, b. 1946 and 1943 respectively	Dame Frevisse
Luiz Alfredo Garcia-Roza, Brazilian, b. 1935	Inspector Espinosa

Elizabeth George, American, b. 1949	Thomas Lynley
Bartholomew Gill, American, 1943–2002	Peter McGarr
Dorothy Gilman, American, b. 1923	Mrs. Pollifax
Sue Grafton, American, b. 1940	Kinsey Millhone
Andrew Greeley, American, b. 1928	Father "Blackie" Ryan
Kerry Greenwood, Australian, b. 1954	Phryne Fisher
Martha Grimes, American, b. 1931	Richard Jury
Batya Gur, Israeli, b. 1947	Michael Ohayon
Jane Haddam, pseud. of Orania Papazoglou, American, b. 1951	Gregor Demarkian
Barbara Hambly, American, b. 1951	Benjamin January
Steve Hamilton, American, b. 1961	Alex McKnight
Joseph Hansen, American, 1923–2004	Dave Brandstetter
Cynthia Harrod-Eagles, British, b. 1948	Bill Slider
Carolyn Hart, American, b. 1936	Annie Laurance Darling
Joan Hess, American, b. 1949	Arly Hanks
David Hewson, British, b. 1953	Nic Costa
John Spencer Hill, Canadian, 1943–1998	Carlo Arbati
Reginald Hill, British, b. 1936	Peter Pascoe and Andrew Dalziel
Tony Hillerman, American, b. 1925	Joe Leaphorn and Jim Chee
Bill James, pseud. of James Tucker, Welsh, b. 1929	Colin Harpur
P.D. James, British, b. 1920	Adam Dalgliesh Cordelia Gray
Michael Jecks, British, b. 1960	Sir Baldwin Furnshill
Morag Joss, Scottish, b. ?	Sara Selkirk
H.R.F. Keating, British, b. 1926	Inspector Ghote
Harry Kemelman, American, 1908–1996	Rabbi David Small
Laurie R. King, American, b. 1952	Kate Martinelli Mary Russell
Katherine Kurtz and Deborah Turner Harris, both American, b. 1944 and 1951 respectively	The Adept (Sir Adam Sinclair)
Jane Langton, American, b. 1922	Homer Kelly
Donna Leon, American, b. 1942	Guido Brunetti
Peter Lovesey, British, b. 1936	Peter Diamond
John D. MacDonald, American, 1916–1986	Travis McGee
Marianne Macdonald, Canadian, b. 1934	Dido Hoare
Charlotte MacLeod, American, 1922–2005	Peter Shandy
Henning Mankell, Swedish, b. 1948	Kurt Wallander
Paul Mann, nat. Australian, b. ?	George Sansi

Margaret Maron, American, b. ?	Deborah Knott
Edward Marston, pseud. of Keith Miles; British, b. 1940	Nicholas Bracewell
Sujata Massey, British, b. 1964	Rei Shimura
Ed McBain, American, 1926–2005	Steve Carella
Alexander McCall Smith, Scottish, b. 1948	Isabel Dalhousie
	Mma Precious Ramotswe
James McClure, South African, b. 1939	Tromp Kramer
Sharyn McCrumb, American, b. ?	Spencer Arrowood
Val McDermid, Scottish, b. 1955	Tony Hill
Denise Mina, Scottish, b. 1966	Maureen O'Donnell
Kirk Mitchell, American, b. 1950	Anna Turnipseed
John Mortimer, British, b. 1923	Horace Rumpole
Walter Mosely, American, b. 1952	Easy Rawlins
Marcia Muller, American, b. 1944	Sharon McCone
Magdalen Nabb, British, b. 1947	Salvatore Guarnaccia
Sharan Newman, American, b. 1949	Catherine LeVendeur
Carol O'Connell, American, b. 1947	Kathleen Mallory
Sister Carol Anne O'Marie, American, b. 1933	Sister Mary Helen
Sara Paretsky, American, b. 1947	V.I. Warshawski
Robert B. Parker, American, b. 1932	Spenser
James Patterson, American, b. 1947	Alex Cross
	The Women's Murder Club
Eliot Pattison, American, b. ?	Shan Tao Yun
Michael Pearce, British, b. 1953	The Mamur Zapt (Gareth Cadwallader Owen)
Iain Pears, British, b. 1955	Jonathan Argyll
Sharon Kay Penman, American, b. ?	Justin de Quincy
Anne Perry, pseud. of Juliet Hulme, British, b. 1938	William Monk
	Thomas Pitt
Elizabeth Peters, pseud. of Barbara Meartz, American, b. 1927	Amelia Peabody
Ellis Peters, pseud. of Edith Pargeter, British, 1913–1975	Brother Cadfael
Nancy Pickard, American, b. 1945	Jenny Cain
Ian Rankin, Scottish, b. 1960	John Rebus
Ruth Rendell, British, b. 1930	Reginald Wexford
Mike (Michael David) Ripley, British, b. 1952	Roy Angel
Candace Robb, American, b. 1950	Owen Archer
David Roberts, British, b. ?	Lord Edward Corinth
Lynda Robinson, American, b. 1951	Lord Meren

Peter Robinson, nat. Canadian, b. 1950	Alan Banks
Carolyn Roe, Canadian, b. 1943	Isaac of Girona
Kate Ross, American, 1956–1998	Julian Kestrel
Laura Joh Rowland, American, b. 1954	Sano Ichiro
John Sandford, pseud. of John Camp, American, b. 1944	Lucas Davenport
Dorothy L. Sayers, and Jill Paton Walsh, both British, 1893–1957 and b. ? respectively	Harriet Vane
Steven Saylor, American, b. 1956	Gordianus the Finder
Dorothy Simpson, British, b. 1933	Luke Thanet
Joan Smith, British, b. 1953	Loretta Lawson
Martin Cruz Smith, American, b. 1942	Arkady Renko
Julia Spencer-Fleming, American, b. ?	Clare Fergusson
Dana Stabenow, American, b. 1952	Kate Shugak
Victoria Thompson, American, b. ?	Sarah Decker Brandt
Aimee and David Thurlo, American, b. ??	Ella Clah
Charles Todd, pseud. of Caroline and Charles Todd, American mother-son writing team, b. ??	Ian Rutledge
Peter Tremayne, pseud. of Peter J.P.B. Ellis, British, b. 1943	Sister Fidelma
Per Wahlöo and Maj Sjöwall, Swedish 1926–1975 and b. 1935, respectively	Martin Beck
John Morgan Wilson, American, b. 1947	Benjamin Justice
Robert Wilson, British, b. 1957	Bruce Medway
Mary Wings, American, b. 1949	Emma Victor
Jacqueline Winspear, British, b. 1955	Maisie Dobbs
Eric Wright, nat. Canadian, b. 1929	Charlie Salter

APPENDIX B
Detectives in Their
Geographical Areas

Note: Place names in quotation marks are fictional.

United States

Alaska	Kate Shugak
Arkansas	Arly Hanks
California	Dave Brandstetter
	Harry Bosch (Los Angeles)
	Benjamin Justice (Los Angeles)
	Irene Kelly
	Sharon McCone (San Francisco)
	Sister Mary Helen (San Francisco)
	Kate Martinelli (San Francisco)
	Kinsey Millhone
	Emma Victor (San Francisco)
	The Women's Murder Club (San Francisco)
Colorado	Goldy Bear
	Cliff Janeway (Denver)
Connecticut	Melanie Travis
Florida	Travis McGee
	Britt Montero (Miami)
Illinois	Marti MacAlister
	Father "Blackie" Ryan (Chicago)
	V.I. Warshawski (Chicago)

"Indian Country"	Anna Turnipseed
Louisiana	Benjamin January (New Orleans)
	Easy Rawlins (New Orleans)
	Dave Robicheaux (New Orleans)
Maryland	Kay Scarpetta (Baltimore)
Massachusetts	Jenny Cain
	Lily Connor (Boston)
	Homer Kelly
	Peter Shandy
	Rabbi David Small (North Shore)
	Spenser
	Holly Winter
Michigan	Alex McKnight
The Midwest	Jim Qwilleran
Minnesota	Lucas Davenport
National Parks	Anna Pigeon
Navajo Reservation	Ella Clah
	Joe Leaphorn and Jim Chee
New Jersey	Stephanie Plum
New York	Rachel Alexander (New York City)
	Myron Bolitar (New York City)
	Sarah Decker Brandt
	Kate Fansler (New York City)
	Clare Fergusson (upstate)
	Pharoah Love (New York City)
	Kathleen Mallory (New York City)
	Matt Scudder (New York City)
North Carolina	Deborah Knott
Pennsylvania	Gregor Demarkian (Philadelphia)
South Carolina	Annie Laurance Darling
Tennessee	Spencer Arrowood
Texas	China Bayles
United States in general	Jack Reacher
Washington	Frank Corso (Seattle)
Washington, D.C.	Alex Cross
	Mrs. Pollifax (and the world)
Wyoming	Joe Pickett
Fictional East Coast Metropolitan area	Steve Carella and the 87th Precinct

The United Kingdom

England (general)	Irene Adler
	Jonathan Argyll

Ursula Blanchard
Lord Edward Corinth
Justin de Quincy
Julian Kestrel
Charles Paris
Mary Russell
Ian Rutledge
Perry Trethowan

London   Roy Angel
Nicholas Bracewell
Arthur Bryant and John May
Adam Dalgliesh (and other English sites)
Maisie Dobbs
Sir John Fielding
Cordelia Gray
Dido Hoare
Richard Jury (and other English sites)
Duncan Kincaid
Loretta Lawson (and Oxford)
Anna Lee
Thomas Lynley (and other English sites)
William Monk
Jimmy Pibble
Thomas Pitt
Horace Rumpole
Jemima Shore
Bill Slider
Hilary Tamar

Other English sites   Owen Archer (the North)
Jane Austen (the South)
Alan Banks (Yorkshire)
Brother Cadfael (the Welsh border)
Ben Cooper (the Peak District)
Peter Diamond (Avon and Somerset)
Dame Frevisse (Oxfordshire)
Sir Baldwin Furnshill (the West Country)
Liz Graham ("Castlemere" in the Fen Country)
Colin Harpur (unnamed Midlands city)
Tony Hill (the North)
John Madden (Surrey)
Inspector Morse (Thames Valley Constabulary)
Peter Pascoe and Andrew Dalziel (Yorkshire)
Agatha Raisin (the Cotswolds)
Sara Selkirk (Bath)
C.D. Sloan ("Calleshire")
Luke Thanet (Kent)
Harriet Vane ("Talboys," a country estate)
Reginald Wexford (Sussex)

Scotland	The Adept (Sir Adam Sinclair)
	Isabel Dalhousie (Edinburgh)
	Hamish Macbeth ("Lochdubh," the Highlands)
	Maureen O'Donnell (Glasgow)
	John Rebus (Edinburgh)

Europe

France	Monsieur Pamplemousse
	Catherine LeVendeur (and other European sites)
Greece/Persia	Telemon the Physician
Ireland	Sister Fidelma
	Peter McGarr (Dublin)
	Jack Taylor (Galway)
Italy	Carlo Arbati (Florence)
	Guido Brunetti (Venice)
	Nic Costa (Rome)
	Marcus Didius Falco (ancient Roman Empire)
	Gordianus the Finder (ancient Roman Empire)
	Marshal Salvatore Guarnaccia (Florence)
	Aurelio Zen (various Italian cities)
The Netherlands	Inspector Jurrian DeKok
Russia (Imperial)	Erast Fandorin
USSR and post-Soviet Russia	Arkady Renko
Spain	Isaac of Girona
Sweden	Martin Beck (Stockholm)
	Kurt Wallander (Ystad, southern Sweden)

Non-European Countries

Australia	Phryne Fisher
Benin and Togo, West Africa	Bruce Medway
Botswana	Mma Precious Ramotswe
Brazil	Inspector Espinosa
Canada	Charlie Salter
Egypt	the Mamur Zapt
	Lord Meren
	Amelia Peabody
India	Inspector Ghote
	Joe Sandilands
	George Sansi
Israel	Michael Ohayon

Japan	Sano Ichiro
	Rei Shimura
South Africa	Tromp Kramer
Tibet	Shan Tao Yun
Worldwide crime scenes	Dr. Gideon Oliver
	Mrs. Pollifax

APPENDIX C
Historical Detectives
Listed Chronologically

Mid-fourteenth century B.C.	Lord Meren
340–330 B.C.	Telemon the Physician
80–48 B.C.	Gordianus the Finder
A.D. 70s	Marcus Didius Falco
Mid–seventh century	Sister Fidelma
1100s	Catherine LeVendeur
Mid-1100s	Brother Cadfael
Late 1100s	Justin de Quincy
Early 1300s	Sir Baldwin Furnshill
Mid-1300s	Isaac of Girona
1360s–1370s	Owen Archer
Mid-1400s	Dame Frevisse
1560s	Ursula Blanchard
Late 1500s	Nicholas Bracewell
Seventeenth century	Sano Ichiro
Late 1700s	Sir John Fielding
Early 1800s	Jane Austen
1820s	Julian Kestrel
Mid-1800s	William Monk
1850s	Benjamin January

Late 1870s	Erast Fandorin, Thomas Pitt
1870s–1880s	Sarah Brandt
1880s–1890s	Irene Adler
1900–1920s	Amelia Peabody (Emerson)
1921, 1932	John Madden
1910s	The Mamur Zapt
1920s	Maisie Dobbs
1920s	Phryne Fisher
1920s	Ian Rutledge
1920s	Mary Russell
1930s	Lord Edward Corinth
Late 1930s–1940	Harriet Vane

APPENDIX D
Detectives Listed by
Field of Employment

Contemporary U.S. Amateur Detectives (Male)

Myron Bolitar, sports agent
Frank Corso, crime writer
Gregor Demarkian, retired FBI profiler
Cliff Janeway, bookseller
Benjamin Justice, disgraced reporter
Homer Kelly, professor of American literature
Gideon Oliver, physical anthropologist
Joe Pickett, game warden
Jim Qwilleran, cat fancier and retired newspaperman
Easy Rawlins, custodian
Jack Reacher, noir unofficial investigator
"Blackie" Ryan, Roman Catholic priest, later bishop
Peter Shandy, professor of agrology and rutabaga breeder
Rabbi David Small, Jewish rabbi

Contemporary U.S. Amateur Detectives (Female)

Rachel Alexander, dog trainer
China Bayles, herbalist and retired attorney
Goldy Bear, caterer
Jenny Cain, social worker
Lily Connor, Episcopal priest
Annie Laurance Darling, bookseller
Kate Fansler, professor of English

Clare Fergusson, former Army helicopter pilot, now Episcopal priest
Irene Kelly, investigative reporter
Deborah Knott, lawyer, later judge
Sister Mary Helen, Roman Catholic nun
Britt Montero, crime reporter
Stephanie Plum, bounty hunter
Mrs. Pollifax, CIA agent
Melanie Travis, poodle breeder and trainer
The Women's Murder Club, a homicide detective, a medical examiner, a reporter, and an assistant district attorney
Holly Winter, malamute trainer and special education teacher

Contemporary British Amateur Detectives (Male)

The Adept (Sir Adam Sinclair), paranormal investigator
Jonathan Argyll, art dealer
Roy Angel, part-time unofficial private eye (humorous)
Bruce Medway, "fixer" of trade deals
Charles Paris, actor and alcoholic
Horace Rumpole, lawyer

Contemporary British Amateur Detectives (Female)

Isabel Dalhousie, philosopher
Dido Hoare, bookseller
Loretta Lawson, lecturer in literature
Maureen O'Donnell, victim of sexual abuse
Agatha Raisin, retired public relations executive
Sara Selkirk, classical cellist
Jemima Shore, television personality

Contemporary British Amateur Detective of Debatable Gender

Hilary Tamar, professor of law, Oxford

Contemporary Foreign Amateur Detectives

Phryne Fisher, Australian heiress
Monsieur Pamplemousse and Pommes Frites, French restaurant critics
Rei Shimura, Japanese-American art dealer

Contemporary Police Detectives in Procedural Series

United States (Metropolitan)

Harry Bosch (also hard-boiled)
Steve Carella and the 87th Precinct

Alex Cross, Ph.D. in psychology
Lucas Davenport
Pharoah Love, African American and gay
Kathleen Mallory, former abandoned child
Kate Martinelli, lesbian
Dave Robicheaux
Kay Scarpetta, medical examiner

United States (Nonmetropolitan)

Spencer Arrowood, sheriff, small southern town
Ella Clah, Native American detective
Arly Hanks, southern rural police chief
Joe Leaphorn and Jim Chee, Navajo tribal police
Marti MacAlister, African American homicide detective
Anna Pigeon, National Parks Ranger
Anna Turnipseed, Native American detective

Britain (Metropolitan or Scotland Yard)

Arthur Bryant and John May, Peculiar Crimes Unit, London
Adam Dalgliesh, New Scotland Yard
Richard Jury, New Scotland Yard
Duncan Kincaid, New Scotland Yard
Thomas Lynley, New Scotland Yard
Jimmy Pibble, New Scotland Yard
Bill Slider, London C.I.D.
Perry Trethowan, Scotland Yard

Britain (Nonmetropolitan)

Alan Banks, Yorkshire
Ben Cooper, Peak District
Peter Diamond, Avon and Somerset
Liz Graham, "Castlemere" C.I.D.
Colin Harpur, unnamed Midlands city
Tony Hill, psychological profiler
Hamish Macbeth, Highlands constable
Inspector Morse, Thames Valley
Peter Pascoe and Andrew Dalziel, Yorkshire
John Rebus, Edinburgh C.I.D.
Luke Thanet, Kent Constabulary
C.D. Sloan, "Calleshire" C.I.D.
Inspector Reginald Wexford, Sussex

Foreign Police Detectives (by Country)

Inspector Espinosa, Rio de Janeiro, Brazil
Charlie Salter, Toronto, Canada

Inspector Ghote, Bombay, India
George Sansi, India (later resigned and took up law career)
Peter McGarr, Dublin, Ireland
Michael Ohayon, Israel
Carlo Arbati, Florence, Italy
Guido Brunetti, Venice, Italy
Nic Costa, Rome, Italy
Marshal Guarnaccia, Florence, Italy
Aurelio Zen, various Italian cities
Inspector Jurrian DeKok, Amsterdam, the Netherlands
Arkady Renko, Moscow, Russia (formerly USSR)
Tromp Kramer, South Africa
Martin Beck, Stockholm, Sweden
Kurt Wallander, Sweden

Contemporary Private Investigators

United States (Male)

Travis McGee, Florida
Alex McKnight, Michigan
Matt Scudder, New York City
Spenser, Boston, Massachusetts

United States (Female)

Sharon McCone, California
Kinsey Millhone, California
Kate Shugak, Alaska
V.I. Warshawski, Chicago, Illinois

United States (Gay/Lesbian)

Dave Brandstetter, California
Emma Victor, Boston, Massachusetts, and San Francisco, California

Britain (Female)

Anna Lee
Cordelia Gray

Foreign

Mma Precious Ramotswe, Botswana
Jack Taylor, Galway, Ireland
Shan Tao Yun, Tibet

Historical Detectives

Irene Adler
Owen Archer
Jane Austen
Ursula Blanchard
Nicholas Bracewell
Sarah Brandt
Brother Cadfael
Lord Edward Corinth
Justin de Quincy
Marcus Didius Falco
Maisie Dobbs
Erast Fandorin
Sister Fidelma
Sir John Fielding
The Hon. Phryne Fisher
Dame Frevisse
Gordianus the Finder
Sir Baldwin Furnshill
Isaac of Girona
Sano Ichiro
Benjamin January
Julian Kestrel
John Madden
Catherine LeVendeur
The Mamur Zapt
Lord Meren
William Monk
Amelia Peabody
Thomas Pitt
Mary Russell
Ian Rutledge
Joe Sandilands
Telemon the Physician
Harriet Vane

APPENDIX E
Awards for Mystery and
Crime Fiction

Agatha Award

A teapot presented annually since 1989 by the Malice Domestic convention.

American Mystery Award

A plaque presented annually from 1988 to 1993 by *Mystery Scene* magazine.

Anthony Award

A plaque or a sculpture presented annually since 1986 at the World Mystery Convention ("Bouchercon").

Arthur Ellis Award

An award presented annually since 1984 to Canadian authors only by the Crime Writers of Canada; named for Canada's chief hangman in the 1920s.

Barry Award

An award presented annually since 1997 by *Deadly Pleasures* magazine.

Crime Writers' Association Awards

Awards presented annually since 1956 by the British Crime Writers' Association: chiefly the Macallan Gold Dagger, the Silver Dagger, the Cartier Diamond Dagger, the John Creasey

Award, the (occasional) Rumpole Award, the Last Laugh Award, the CWA/Macallan Short Story Award, the Dagger in the Library Award (formerly the Golden Handcuffs Award), and the Ellis Peters Historical Dagger Award.

Derringer Award

Awards presented annually since 1998 for short fiction by the Short Mystery Fiction Society.

Dilys Award

Awards presented annually since 1992 by the Independent Mystery Booksellers Association.

Edgar [Allan Poe] Awards

Awards analogous to the movie industry's Oscar, presented annually since 1946 by the Mystery Writers of America, who also award the Ellery Queen Award, the Robert L. Fish Award, the Raven Award, and the Mary Higgins Clark Award.

Grand Prix de Littérature Policière

Awards presented annually since 1948 a) to French novels and b) to foreign novels translated into French.

Hammett Prize

A falcon sculpture presented annually since 1992 by the North American Branch of the International Association of Crime Writers.

Herodotus Award

A bust of Herodotus presented annually since 1999 by the Historical Mystery Appreciation Society.

Lambda Literary Award

Awards presented annually by the Lambda Literary Foundation, supporting gay, lesbian, bisexual, and transgender literature in the United States.

Lefty Award

Awards presented annually by the Left Coast Crime Convention, California.

Macavity Award

Certificates named for T.S. Eliot's "mystery cat" presented annually since 1987.

Maltese Falcon Award

Awards presented annually since 1983 by the Japanese Maltese Falcon Society.

[Philip] Marlowe Award

Awards presented annually since 1991 by the Raymond Chandler Society at the University of Ulm, Germany.

Ned Kelly Award

Awards named for Australia's most famous outlaw, presented annually since 1996 (except 1998) by the Crime Writers Association of Australia.

Nero Wolfe Award

Awards presented annually since 1979 at the Black Orchid Banquet by the Wolfe Pack, fans of the work of Rex Stout.

Swedish Academy of Detection

Awards including the Martin Beck Award (formerly the Best Foreign Novel) presented annually since 1971.

Shamus Award

Plaques presented annually since 1982 at Bouchercon by Private Eye Writers of America.

Sherlock Award

Awards presented annually by *Sherlock Holmes: The Detective Magazine.*

Trophy 813 Award

Awards named for Maurice Leblanc's novel *813*, presented annually since 1981 by the French *Societé 813*.

SELECTED BIBLIOGRAPHY

Albert, Walter. *Detective and Mystery Fiction: An International Bibliography of Secondary Sources.* San Bernardino, CA: Millefleurs, 1997.

Anderson, Julie, ed. *American Hard Boiled Mystery Writers.* Farmington, MI: The Gale Group, 2000.

Ashley, Mike. *The Mammoth Encyclopedia of Modern Crime Fiction.* New York: Carroll and Graf, 2002.

Barzun, Jacques, and W.H. Taylor. *A Catalogue of Crime.* New York: HarperCollins, 1974.

Beam, Joan. *Native Americans in Long Fiction: An Annotated Bibliography.* New York: Rowman & Littlefield, 1996.

Bleiler, Richard J. *Reference and Research Guide to Mystery and Detective Fiction.* 2nd ed. Westport, CT: Libraries Unlimited, 2004.

Breen, Job L. *What about Murder? A Guide to Books about Mystery and Detective Fiction.* New York: Rowman & Littlefield, 1993.

British Mystery and Thriller Writers since 1960. Farmington Hills, MI: Gale, 2003.

Contemporary Authors. Detroit, MI: Gale. See also *Contemporary Authors Online.* Updated regularly.

Contento, W.G., and Martin H. Greenberg. *Index to Crime and Mystery Authors.* New York: Macmillan, 1990.

DeAndrea, William L. *Encyclopedia Mysteriosa.* New York: Prentice Hall, 1994.

Derie, Kate. *The Deadly Directory: A Resource Guide for Mystery, Crime, and Suspense Readers and Writers.* Berkeley, CA: Deadly Serious Press, 2004.

Glassman, Steve. *Crime Fiction and Film in the Southwest.* New York: Popular Press, 2001.

Gray, Philip. *Mean Streets and Dark Deeds.* Bozeman, MT: Badger Press of Montana, 1998.

Green, Joseph, and Jim Finch. *Sleuths, Sidekicks, and Stooges: An Annotated Bibliography.* Gower House, UK: Ashgate Publishing Ltd., 1997.

Hardy, Phil. *The BFI Companion to Crime*. London: Cassell, 1997.

Heising, Willetta L. *Detecting Men*. Dearborn, MI: Purple Moon Press, 1998.

———. *Detecting Women*. Dearborn, MI: Purple Moon Press, 1998.

———. *Willetta's Guide to Police Detective Series*. Dearborn, MI: Purple Moon Press, 2001.

———. *Willetta's Guide to Private Eye Novels*. Dearborn, MI: Purple Moon Press, 2002.

Herbert, Rosemary. *Whodunit? A Who's Who in Crime and Mystery Writing*. Oxford: Oxford University Press, 2003.

Jarvis, Mary J. *Reader's Guide to the Suspense Novel*. New York: Macmillan, 1994.

Keating, H.R.F. *Crime and Mystery: The 100 Best Books*. New York: Carroll and Graf, 1987.

Kelleghan, Fiona, ed. *100 Masters of Mystery and Detective Fiction*. Englewood Cliffs, NJ: Salem Press, 1998.

Klein, Kathleen, ed. *Great Women Mystery Writers*. Westport, CT: Greenwood, 1994.

Kramer, John E., Ron Hamm, and Von Pittman. *Academe in Mystery and Detective Fiction: An Annotated Bibliography*. New York: Rowman & Littlefield, 2000.

Lachman, Marvin. *Reader's Guide to the American Novel of Detection*. New York: Macmillan, 1993.

Landrum, Larry. *American Mystery and Detective Novels: A Reference Guide*. Westport, CT: Greenwood, 1999.

Lockhardt, Darrell. *Latin American Mystery Writers: An A to Z Guide*. Westport, CT: Greenwood, 2004.

Mann, Jessica. *Deadlier Than the Male: Why Are Respectable English Women So Good At Murder?* New York: Macmillan, 1981.

Markowitz, Judith A. *The Gay Detective Novel*. New York: McFarland, 2004.

McSherry, Frank D. *Studies in Scarlet*. San Bernardino, CA: Borgo Press, 1999.

Murphy, Bruce. *The Encyclopedia of Murder and Mystery*. New York: St. Martin's Minotaur, 1999.

Nichols, Victoria, and Susan Thompson. *Silk Stalkings: When Women Write of Murder*. Berkeley, CA: Black Lizard Books, 1988.

———. *Silk Stalkings: More Women Write of Murder*. Lanham, MD: Scarecrow Press, 1998.

Niebuhr, Gary W. *Reader's Guide to the Private Eye Novel*. New York: Macmillan, 1993.

———. *Make Mine a Mystery: A Reader's Guide to Mystery and Detective Fiction*. Westport, CT: Libraries Unlimited, 2003.

Olderr, Steven. *The Mystery Index: Subjects, Settings, and Sleuths of 10,000 Titles*. Chicago: American Library Association, 1987.

Pederson, J.P., ed. *St. James Guide to Crime and Mystery Writers*. 4th ed. Farmington Hills, MI: Gale, 1996.

Priestman, Martin, et al. *Crime Fiction from Poe to the Present*. Tavistock, UK: Northcote House Publishers, 1997.

Raphael, Lawrence W., ed. *Mystery Midrash: An Anthology of Jewish Mystery and Detective Fiction*. Woodstock, VT: Jewish Lights Publishing, 1999.

Skinner, Robert E. *New Hard Boiled Dicks: A Personal Checklist*. San Bernardino, CA: Millefleurs, 1995.

Smith, Myron J., Jr. *Cloak and Dagger Fiction*. 3rd ed. Westport, CT: Greenwood, 1995.

Stilwell, Steven A. *What Mystery Do I Read Next? A Reader's Guide to Recent Mystery Fiction*. Farmington Hills, MI: The Gale Group, 1999.

Symons, Julian. *Bloody Murder: From the Detective Story to the Crime Novel*. New York: Mysterious Press, 1992.

Vickarel, JoAnn. *Reader's Guide to the Police Procedural Novel*. New York: Macmillan, 1995.

Winks, R.W., and Maureen Corrigan, eds. *Mystery and Suspense Writers: The Literature of Crime, Detection, and Espionage*. New York: Holiday House, 1998.

HELPFUL WEB SITES

Also see web sites for individual authors, above.

BookBrowser
www.bookbrowser.com

Book Page
www.bookpage.com

ClueLass
www.cluelass.com

The Gumshoe Site
www.nsknet.or.jp/~jkimura

The January Magazine
www.januarymagazine.com

Mysterious Readers
www.mysteriousreaders.com

Mystery Vault
www.mysteryvault.net

Stop, You're Killing Me!
www.stopyourekillingme.com

Sue Feder's Magical Mystery Tour
mywebpages.comcast.net/monkshould/

Tangled Web
www.twbooks.co.uk

The Thrilling Detective
www.thrillingdetective.com

The Ultimate Mystery/Detective Web Guide
www.magicdragon.com/UltimateMystery/index.html

INDEX

Main entries for detectives appear in **bold** type.

About the Author

MITZI M. BRUNSDALE is Professor of English at Mayville State University, Mayville, North Dakota. Her six previous books include *Student Companion to George Orwell* (Greenwood, 2000).